This book is in the tradition of non-market clearing approaches to macrodynamic analysis. It builds a series of integrated disequilibrium growth models of increasing complexity, which display the economic interaction between households, firms and government across labor, goods, money, bonds, and equities markets. Chiarella and Flaschel demonstrate how macrodynamics can be developed in a hierarchical way from economically simple structures to more advanced ones. In addition they investigate complex macrodynamic feedback mechanisms.

The book is organized into seven chapters. Chapter 1 discusses traditional macrodynamic model building. Chapters 2–4 show how Keynesian disequilibrium growth can be obtained from Tobin and Keynes–Wicksell monetary growth models. Chapter 5 treats the cases of substitution in production, and chapter 6 provides the working model of the book. Chapter 7 discusses further extensions and gives an outlook on future work.

CARL CHIARELLA is Professor of Finance at the University of Technology, Sydney. He holds doctorates in applied mathematics and in economics from the University of New South Wales. His main research interests are economic dynamics and quantitative finance. His work appears in journals such as *JEDC, JEBO, Macroeconomic Dynamics, Economic Modelling, Applied Mathematical Finance* and the *Journal of Computational Finance*. He is the author of *Elements of a Nonlinear Theory of Economic Dynamics* and the co-author, with Peter Flaschel, of *Disequilibrium, Growth and Labor Market Dynamics*.

PETER FLASCHEL is Professor of Economics at the University of Bielefeld. He completed his doctoral thesis in mathematics at the University of Bonn and his habilitation thesis in economics at the Free University of Berlin. He publishes extensively on economic theory and macroeconomic dynamics in journals such as *Econometrica, JEBO, JEDC, Macroeconomic Dynamics, Economic Modelling* and *The Manchester School*. He is the author of *Macrodynamics, Dynamic Macroeconomics* and the co-author, with Carl Chiarella, of *Disequilibrium, Growth and Labor Market Dynamics*.

The Dynamics of Keynesian Monetary Growth

The Dynamics of Keynesian Monetary Growth:

Macro Foundations

CARL CHIARELLA

School of Finance and Economics
University of Technology, Sydney
Australia

PETER FLASCHEL

Department of Economics
University of Bielefeld
Germany

CAMBRIDGE
UNIVERSITY PRESS

339.5
C53d

PUBLISHED BY THE PRESS SYNDICATE OF THE UNIVERSITY OF CAMBRIDGE
The Pitt Building, Trumpington Street, Cambridge, United Kingdom

CAMBRIDGE UNIVERSITY PRESS
The Edinburgh Building, Cambridge CB2 2RU, UK   www.cup.cam.ac.uk
40 West 20th Street, New York, NY 10011-4211, USA   www.cup.org
10 Stamford Road, Oakleigh, Melbourne 3166, Australia
Ruiz de Alarcón 13, 28014 Madrid, Spain

First published 2000

Printed in the United Kingdom at the University Press, Cambridge

Typeset in 10/12pt Times New Roman [VN]

A catalogue record for this book is available from the British Library

Library of Congress Cataloguing in Publication data
Chiarella, Carl.
The dynamics of Keynesian monetary growth: macro foundations/Carl Chiarella, Peter Flaschel.
    p. cm.
Includes bibliographical references and index.
ISBN 0-521-64351-1
1. Monetary policy. 2. Keynesian economics. 3. Macroeconomics.
I. Flaschel, Peter, 1943 – II. Title.
HG230.3.C45 2000
339.5′3–dc21   99-047714

ISBN 0 521 643511

Contents

vii

Figures

Foreword

Richard H. Day

In his effort to reorient economic theory so that it might offer an explanation of severe and prolonged recessions and insights concerning the possibilities and limitations of fiscal and monetary policies for dealing with them, Keynes introduced two factually based assumptions: first, price and wage stickiness; second, independently determined savings and investment variables. In developing the implications of these two facts, Keynes exploited the concept of demand, not at the usual level of the market for a single good, but at the level of the entire economy for the aggregate of all goods. Thus, for example, instead of an Engle curve for a single good, which gives the demand for a good in terms of real income, he exploited the dependence of aggregate demand for all goods on income, that is, the consumption function. With the real money rate of interest as the only endogenously determined price – in this case the price (or opportunity cost) of using money as an idle balance – the money market is seen to play a potential role; potential, because its role depends on sensitivity to interest rates on the markets for goods and money.

Although his analytical derivations were static and focused on a new kind of persistent unemployment situation, Keynes had in mind a dynamic theory. He fully intended to illuminate the tendency of the market economy to fluctuate due to the interactions between the monetary and real goods sectors.

Keynes' ideas were obviously relevant. Within a decade they led to a new field of economics based on a reduction of the microeconomics of many goods and prices to a macroeconomics based on a measure of the aggregate of all goods and money. Extreme assumptions were necessary to reduce the theory to the graphical dimensions required by contemporary pedagogy. This yielded the standard by which the theory became widely known: Hicks' ingenious IS–LM framework.

The deficiencies of this static, simplified version were obvious. Instead of prices and wages that adjusted stickily, it assumed prices that did not adjust at all; it included investment but not capital accumulation; it treated the money supply as exogenous instead of incorporating a dependence on credit conditions and government finance. These deficiencies motivated a large body of work aimed at reducing these deficiencies, work that continues to the present as readers of this volume will come to appreciate. But, in the meantime, a quite different body of work veered off this (then) mainstream approach. Instead of building on aggregate supply and demand of heterogeneous firms and households out of equilibrium, it built on the concept of a Robinson Crusoe or a representative agent in intertemporal equilibrium. Since only a single agent is modeled, there is no problem of coordination among markets, no need to consider savings and investment out of equilibrium, and no need to consider fluctuations caused by the interaction of money markets and goods. Instead, the source of fluctuation is sought in terms of unexplained, exogenous shocks which push equilibria around.

The intellectual advantage of this approach lies in its reliance on the equilibrium assumption which is embodied in the principle of optimality. It enables the derivation of "optimal trajectories" for consumption, labor, and capital. By means of an extended duality principle, the supporting competitive equilibrium price trajectories are implied. Along such equilibrium paths involuntary unemployment and excess capacity do not occur.

This is not the occasion to address in detail the relationship between these two approaches except to emphasize that the dynamic, aggregate supply/demand approach represents the economy as one that adjusts out of perfect coordination to disequilibrium signals, in contrast to the equilibrium approach which represents the economy as a perfectly coordinated process with no need for mechanisms of adaptation to deal with discrepancies among the constituent parts.

As the American academic establishment expanded during the last half-century into a new kind of mass market for education and science, it began to exhibit a herding phenomenon not unlike fashions in consumer goods. For a time, the macroeconomic fashion leaders were centered at a Harvard/MIT/Penn nexus in the persons of Hansen, Duessenberry, Samuelson, and Klein. Out-of-equilibrium thinking ruled macroeconomic theory and econometrics until the mid 1970s. When the leading macroeconomic equilibrium pundit moved from Carnegie Mellon to Chicago, a new fashion of equilibrium macroeconomics emerged with a new center of gravity. The new fashion leaders spread in due course to Harvard and Stanford and many points in between and beyond.

In the meantime, the serious work of extending the out-of-equilibrium aspect of macroeconomics so as to remove its deficiencies, so as to improve its ability to explain real world events and so as to improve its potential for policy repercussion analysis has continued. In England and especially in Germany and Italy, as well as to a lesser extent in the USA, this stream of work has continued until a more general and more satisfactory theory has emerged. Its potential for illuminating macroeconomic phenomena has been enhanced and its potential for providing new understanding of fiscal and monetary policy improved.

This book by Chiarella and Flaschel is a contribution to this out-of-equilibrium stream of macroeconomic theory. Beginning with Tobin's monetary growth analysis, it successively introduces realistic, complicating relationships that eliminate, step by step, some of the major deficiencies in the earlier Keynesian models. It gives a meticulous analysis of each model's properties and an equally meticulous explanation of each model's relationship to the contributions of other scholars. Anyone who wants to understand the development of macroeconomic thinking as a whole and who wants to see the modern development of the out-of-equilibrium approach, will want to study this volume.

The authors dramatically demonstrate the power of the dynamic point of view, and the potential for explaining apparent anomalies by endogenous economic forces. For example, the scatter of data suggesting a relationship between the rate of price changes and unemployment has usually been explained in terms of shifting Phillips curves. However, when the scattered dots are connected in a time sequence, irregular Phillips *spirals* are revealed. To theorists of dynamics, such spirals suggest an underlying endogenous mechanism, not stationary points at the intersection of exogenously shifting curves. By chapter 4 of the present volume, somewhat similar spirals are shown to emerge from endogenous, out-of-equilibrium, real/monetary interactions, a finding of great potential importance.

The authors modestly present their findings as work in progress, and so it is, but it is, nonetheless, a work of consummate scholarship. I have been fortunate in having been able to follow the gradual accumulation of the authors' and their collaborators' studies to their present state. It is an appropriate stage to present it in this integrated form. Every serious student of macroeconomic theory will want to know what they have done, for in this work they will find a comprehensive analytical exegesis of the steps by which the theory has reached its present state at the frontier, and an excellent jumping off point for further research. It seems to me likely that it is only a matter of time before empirical studies, based on models of the kind analyzed here, will achieve a new breakthrough in understanding real economic data and a new basis for predicting policy analysis.

Preface

"Macroeconomics has never reached a consensus and probably never will. The subject is too diverse and the approaches too varied for that to become likely." (S. Turnovsky, *Methods of Macroeconomics Dynamics*)

This book provides the reader with a systematic study of macrodynamic models of monetary growth in the Tobin, the Keynes–Wicksell and the Keynesian (if it exists) tradition. Our point of departure is, therefore, the core of descriptive macrodynamic models of monetary growth of primarily traditional origin; recent contributions of neo- or post-Keynesian type as well as other schools of thought are given scant consideration in this book. Instead, we considerably extend and refine the aforementioned model types so that they give rise to a hierarchical sequence of fully integrated macrodynamic models, each providing an improvement on the shortcomings of one or more structural equations of its predecessor. In this way we arrive at the formulation of an integrated model of the Keynes–Metzler type, with both sluggish price and quantity adjustment and under- or overemployment of both labor and capital, which may be considered as the working Keynesian prototype model of IS–LM growth.

Yet, this model type also has its shortcomings, so the hierarchical structure proposed here does not end with it, but rather will be continued in future research by way of more refined treatments of asset markets, of expectations, of the role of income distribution, of international trade in goods and financial assets, of stochastic influences, and so on. In this regard we view this book as providing "macro foundations," or a systematic way to proceed from elementary studies of models of cycles and growth with a full range of markets (labor, goods, money, bonds, equities) to ever more refined and detailed ones. Partial "micro foundations" for the structures exist in the literature and, of course, must be improved as well, but this has to be done based on the knowledge of what indeed has to be micro founded, and thus put on a firmer basis.

This book is the product of a continuing collaboration between the authors which began in 1992 when the first author was on study leave at the University of Mannheim in Germany. At a number of meetings during that period we realized that we shared a strong, common desire to set up a framework within which the non-market-clearing approach to dynamic macroeconomics could be built in a systematic, consistent, and transparent manner, starting from mainstream contributions to disequilibrium growth developed in the sixties, seventies, and eighties. We have sought to construct a framework in which such mainstream contributions to the non-market-clearing paradigm could be reformulated on a common basis and extended systematically, leading successively to more and more coherent integrated models of disequilibrium growth with progressively richer interactions between markets and sectors. In this way, we sought a framework to which further refinements, in terms of more markets, more agents, more advanced behavior of agents, could be added or inserted in a natural way, far beyond even the general working model of traditional Keynesian monetary growth that is the focus of this book. Indeed, in other work we have already started the task of these further extensions in several directions, and these are alluded to in the final chapter. Of course, we must leave to the reader to judge whether we have succeeded in our aims of providing what we would call macro foundations of traditional macrodynamics on the basis of which more recent contributions to the non-market-clearing approach to economic dynamics may be reconsidered, evaluated and used as macro perspectives for the project we have begun with this book.

Acknowledgments

The work has progressed thanks to almost annual visits since 1993 of Peter Flaschel to the School of Finance and Economics at the University of Technology, Sydney and almost equally frequent visits by Carl Chiarella to the Faculty of Economics at the University of Bielefeld. We are both deeply indebted to our respective institutions for the very strong financial support we have received which made these various visits possible, as well as other infrastructure support which allowed this project to be brought to completion.

A number of professional colleagues deserve special thanks. In particular Willi Semmler, who has offered constant encouragement and support throughout this project and the other related projects of the authors which are discussed in the final chapter. Richard Day, Reiner Franke, Gangolf Groh, Christian Groth, Cars Hommes, Klaus Jaeger, Reinhard John, Ingrid Kubin, Thomas Lux, Hans-Walter Lorenz, Reinhard Neck, Matthias Raith, Hans-Jürgen Ramser, Rajiv Sethi, and Peter Skott offered valuable comments as discussants at presentations of aspects of the material of this book at various international conferences and on other occasions. Of course, none of the aforementioned is responsible for the remaining errors in this work, neither with respect to form nor with respect to substance.

We owe a particular debt of gratitude to Alexander Khomin, formerly of the School of Finance and Economics at the University of Technology, Sydney, and now at the Commonwealth Trading Bank, Australia. He designed and built the $C++$ computer package which we used to perform many of the simulations of the model reported both here and in our other published work.

We are indebted to the anonymous referees who read the original version of the manuscript and offered many suggestions for its improvement. We would also like to thank Ashwin Rattan of Cambridge University Press for all that he has done to make the publication process as painless as possible.

Finally, we would like to express our thanks to the two persons who have borne the biggest cost during the preparation of this book, our wives Lynette Siew-Hon Chiarella and Sigrid Luchtenberg.

Notation

The notation employed throughout this book is subdivided into statically or dynamically endogenous variables and parameters, a subdivision which is here presented from the perspective of chapter 7:[1]

A Statically or dynamically endogenous variables[2]

Y^p	Potential output
Y	Output ($\neq Y^p$ = potential output in general)
$Y_c^D, Y_{c,e}^D$	Disposable income (index c: of capitalists, index e: perceived)
Y^d	Aggregate demand $C + I + \delta K + G$
Y^e	Expected aggregate demand
L^w, L^d	Employed workforce, employment of the employed workforce ($L^d = L^w$ with the exception of chapter 7)
C	Consumption
I	Investment
I^p	Planned investment $I + \mathscr{I}$ ($I^a = I + \dot{N}$ actual investment)
r	Nominal rate of interest (price of bonds $p_B = 1$)
p_e	Price of equities
S_p	Private savings
S_f	Firms' savings
S_g	Government savings
$S = S_p + S_f + S_g$	Total savings
T	Real taxes (T_w, T_c of workers and capitalists)
G	Government expenditure

[1] The NAIRU-employment rate – denoted by $\bar{V}$ in the following is the Non-Accelerating-Inflation-Rate-of-Utilization (here of the labor force), i.e., the employment-complement of the NAIRU of the literature. Starting with chapter 4 we shall make use in addition of a NAIRU concept $\bar{U}$ with respect to the rate of capacity utilization U of the capital stock K.

[2] Some of these variables will be given parameters in the earlier chapters of this book.

ρ	Rate of profit (expected rate of profit ρ^e)
$V = L^w/L$	Rate of employment ($\bar{V}$ the NAIRU employment rate)
$V^w = L^d/L^w$	Utilization rate of the employed
$U = Y/Y^p$	Rate of capacity utilization ($\bar{U}$ the NAIRU rate of capacity utilization)
K	Capital stock
w	Nominal wages
p	Price level
p^*	p-star price level of the FED/German Bundesbank
$\bar{v}$	Velocity of money circulation
π	Expected rate of inflation (medium run average)
M	Money supply (index d: demand, growth rate μ_0)
L	Normal labor supply
B	Bonds (index d: demand)
E	Equities (index d: demand)
W	Real wealth
N	Stock of inventories
N^d	Desired stock of inventories
$\mathscr{I}$	Desired rate of inventory change
γ	Trend growth rate of the capital stock
$n = n_1$	Natural growth rate
n_2	Rate of Harrod neutral technical change
$v = N/K$	Inventory–capital ratio
ω	Real wage ($u = \omega/x$ the wage share)
$u = \omega/x$	Wage share (x is labor productivity, see below)
$y = Y/K$	Output–capital ratio

B   Parameters (all parameters represent positive scalars)

y^p	Potential output–capital ratio
x	Output–labor ratio (labor productivity)
δ	Depreciation plus inventory rate
i, i_1, i_2	Investment parameters
h_1, h_2	Money demand parameters
μ_0	Steady growth rate of money supply
$\beta_w, \beta_{w_1}, \beta_{w_2}$	Wage adjustment speed parameters
β_p	Price adjustment speed parameter
$\beta_{\pi_1}, \beta_{\pi_2}$	Inflationary expectations adjustment speed parameters
β_v	Rate of employment adjustment parameter
$\beta_{\bar{v}}$	NAIRU adjustment parameter
β_γ	Trend growth adjustment parameter
β_y	Demand adjustment parameter

β_n^d	Desired inventory output ratio
β_n	Inventory or natural growth rate adjustment parameter
β_y^e	Demand expectations adjustment parameter
β_k	Accumulation regime parameter
κ_w, κ_p	Weights of short- and medium-run inflation $(\kappa = (1 - \kappa_w\kappa_p)^{-1})$
α	Weight with respect to backward and forward looking expectations
τ, τ_c, τ_w	Tax rate (of capitalists and workers) = const. (or $t^n = (T - rB/p)/K = $ const., $t_c^n = (T_c - rB/p)/K = $ const.)
s_c	Savings ratio (out of profits and interest)
s_w	Savings ratio (out of wages, = 0 in this book)
μ_2	Fiscal policy parameter

C Mathematical notation

$\dot{x}$	Time derivative of a variable x
$\hat{x}$	Growth rate of x
l', l_w	Total and partial derivatives
$y_w = y'(l)l_w$	Composite derivatives
r_0, etc.	Steady state values ($\bar{r}$ a parameter which may differ from r_0)
$l = L/K$, etc.	Real variables in intensive form
$m = M/(pK)$, etc.	Nominal variables in intensive form

General introduction

In this book we shall be concerned with the foundations of integrated macromodels of monetary growth dynamics in disequilibrium as they have been laid out (to some extent) in the sixties and the seventies. These foundations are reconsidered and reformulated as well as extended into a uniform and systematic body of macrodynamic models of closed economies with five markets and three agents. The stress here lies on disequilibrium models as we believe that there is an urgent need for progress in this neglected, but nevertheless very relevant, area of macrodynamics. We do not believe that the numerous equilibrium models of monetary growth that have been developed over the last two decades[1] will realize their potential for policy analysis if they are not supplemented and confronted with disequilibrium analyses that try to portray, with more and more descriptive exactness and analytical rigor, the macroeconomy and the policy scenarios to be investigated.

On the one hand completeness of such models is necessary when one wants to provide a systematic and comparative study of them (and their pros and cons) which can then be used as a framework and as a foundation for the further systematic development of this area of macroeconomics. Such a systematic development is almost nonexistent in the literature on disequilibrium monetary growth dynamics. Partial models may of course be of great interest if, as is generally the case, more specialized questions are considered. Yet, it should in principle always be possible to trace back what type of model has been specialized in such a study and what the general model may look like.

On the other hand completeness of monetary growth models with respect to agents and sectoral behavioral descriptions including budget restrictions and with respect to markets and their type of adjustment process is nowadays a compelling prerequisite for a broader acceptance of

---

[1] See the survey by Orphanides and Solow (1990) for example.

1

so-called macro ad-hoc (or descriptive) macromodels, to be distinguished from micro ad-hoc macromodels (where ad-hoc refers to the empirical relevance of the micro assumptions that are made). The advantage of such approaches to macro theory indeed lies in the fact that these models can more easily be made complete, and thereby tested with respect to the degree of consistency that is achieved by them, than the many micro ad-hoc models that are now the fashion. These latter models are generally partial in nature because of the restrictions that are caused by the technical complexity of the dynamic intertemporal optimization framework that they employ. Furthermore, the dynamics of such models is by technical necessity generally limited to a study of linearized systems around steady states. Such approaches automatically exclude the type of complex behavior which the models in this book can display.

Complete or integrated macrodynamic models therefore may provide a macro foundation for micro perspectives and be further developed in the light of the achievements obtained from such micro perspectives. Complete disequilibrium macrodynamic models of monetary growth therefore mainly serve the purpose of providing right from the outset a full picture of the economy in states of disequilibrium by means of more or less traditional tools or modules. These modules may subsequently be updated step by step as better descriptions of their micro foundations become available.

As we shall see in this book, there exists now a hierarchically structured class of such models which build upon each other in a step-by-step improvement of the modules they contain. Yet, even though at the end of this book we will be higher up in the hierarchy of our models, there will remain some module formulations that are obviously problematic and which therefore call for significant further improvement. There is thus the need to extend much further the project begun here. Yet, it should have become obvious to the reader by this stage that such a task can be accomplished by continuing to proceed in the manner we have developed in this book. This will indeed give rise to a structured body of theories of monetary growth in disequilibrium, up to the most recent developments of disequilibrium macrodynamics, where insights of earlier achievements are preserved and where a pathway of systematic progress to more convincing and realistic model types becomes visible. This is the main advantage of a method which provides a class of monetary disequilibrium growth macromodels that all attempt to be complete and thereby clearly show the path to their further improvement and the next required step to be taken in their further development.

The resulting prototypes of such models in this book are descriptive in the sense that they generally use traditional macro tools to describe the behavior of the various sectors of their economies. These tools may nevertheless simplify the considered behavior significantly with respect to its descriptive content in order to allow us to proceed from simple building blocks to more elaborate ones in a systematic fashion, thereby filling their descriptive or ad-hoc macro assumptions with more realism step by step. Descriptive components of such macromodels can therefore at first be fairly abstract and stylized in their "descriptive" content, due in particular to the tradition that has been established in the formulation of such components of macromodels. The basic justification for the use of such (sometimes radically simplified) building blocks is that also in this area of macroeconomics one has to start from known model structures and to go from the simple (and abstract) to the more complex (and concrete) by means of a stepwise improvement in the formulation and the analysis of intentionally complete models of monetary growth.

We shall make no attempt here to base the descriptive components of our models on micro assumptions surrounding the concept of representative agents as is now the fashion in macroeconomics,[2] since our central aim is a complete presentation and analysis of the interaction of the three sectors of our economies. This interaction will be made more refined as the book proceeds, leaving a systematic improvement of the behavior of sectors to later studies of these models (where also refinements by means of modern microfounded approaches may be taken into consideration).

The intention of this book on descriptive macrodynamic models thus is to start from the traditional roots of a more or less orthodox formulation of such monetary growth dynamics (in particular Tobin and Keynes–Wicksell models of monetary growth) in order to obtain from them and their detailed presentation and discussion (from the beginning of chapter 4 of the book) a description of a general prototype model which may properly be regarded as a Keynesian one. Such a model, which allows (as should be the case in a Keynesian model) for the investigation of unemployed labor as well as underutilized capital, has rarely been considered in the literature, and certainly not in the fully specified dynamic framework which we shall employ throughout this book.

Instead, a so-called neoclassical production function, and the marginal productivity postulate for the employment of labor, have generally been included in the existing analyses of monetary growth in such a way that only labor is considered as experiencing unemployment (due to nominal wage rigidities).[3] In chapter 5 we shall also allow for neoclassical smooth

---

[2] Note, however, that most of the (traditional) behavioral relationships we employ have received some micro foundations in the course of their use in macroeconomics.

[3] The exception to this is provided by models of the so-called neo-Keynesian or non-Walrasian type which, however, are seldom as complete as our development and presentation of the working model of Keynesian monetary growth.

factor substitution and then demonstrate that this does not prevent the analysis of underutilized capital in a Keynesian setup. In general, however, we will stick to the simpler assumption of fixed proportions in production, since this makes the Keynesian analysis of underutilized resources much more transparent.

After providing some numerical investigations of the considered models of Tobin, Keynes–Wicksell and Keynes(ian) type with or without smooth factor substitution we shall finally consider two further important extensions of the Keynesian prototype introduced here: a Metzlerian extension of this prototype when IS-disequilibrium is allowed for and a "Marxian" extension of it which avoids the use of "natural" economic magnitudes as much as possible. The final chapter will also point to a variety of omissions in the modeling framework presented here which must be addressed in order to properly make the analysis a Keynesian one, particularly since the behavior of wealth owners is still much too passively modeled in the approaches to monetary growth dynamics presented in this book. Also, investment behavior is still presented far too simply to portray accurately the trade cycle vision of Keynes' *General Theory*. All of these extensions, however, must be left for future research.

We shall consider throughout this book only macroeconomic models which fit into the standard and basic framework of a closed three-sector economy (households, firms, and government), where there exist five distinct markets (for labor, goods, money, bonds [savings deposits], and equities [perfect substitutes of bonds]).[4] Money market transactions are, of course, a mirror image of transactions on the remaining four markets and are to be related to these activities by means of budget restrictions for the three sectors assumed. In table I.1 we use the index d to denote "quantities demanded" and no index in the case of "quantities supplied." Furthermore, since we will use continuous-time models throughout this book we have to distinguish between flow and stock demand and supply since we here follow the macroeconomic tradition which distinguishes between stock and flow constraints in such a setup; see Turnovsky (1977a) and Sargent (1987) for details. This said, the symbols in table I.1 should be clear as to

---

[4] We restrict ourselves to this standard, basic framework due to our intention to stay, at least initially, very close to orthodox foundations of neoclassical and Keynesian dynamics. The following modeling framework is therefore chosen, initially, as identical to the one that is employed in such a conventional textbook of macroeconomics as that of Sargent (1987); see also Turnovsky (1977a) for a related framework. In this book we shall revise only some of the assumptions (but nevertheless very important ones) that underlie the Sargent approach to complete, or integrated, macroeconomic models. In some respects the contents of this book may thus be characterized as providing simply improved and dynamic counterparts of the three model prototypes that are at the core of Sargent's (1987, part I) mainly static analysis of them.

Table I.1. *Basic structure of closed economies*

	Labor market	Goods market	Money market	Bonds market	Equities market
Households	L	C	$M^d, \dot{M}^d$	$B^d, \dot{B}^d$	$E^d, \dot{E}^d$
Firms:	L^d	$Y, I + \delta K$	—	—	$E, \dot{E}$
Government	—	G	$M, \dot{M}$	$B, \dot{B}$	—

their economic meaning (a detailed list of the notation employed is provided at the front of this book).[5]

Table I.1 shows the basic structure of the closed economies that are considered throughout this book and it is of the same type as the one in Sargent (1987, chs. 1–5) as will become apparent from its further description in chapter 1.

We will model the behavior of our three economic agents in the usual fashion by staying close to behavioral assumptions which are firmly rooted in the tradition of descriptive macroeconomics. This guarantees that the models considered in chapters 2–7 will not depart too much from the established formulations of (textbook) macrodynamic models, though they will be generalized considerably with respect to their degree of integration. As in Turnovsky (1977a), our main aim is to develop and analyze such integrated (or complete) models of monetary growth (of closed economies) in a systematic way. In this respect it is of particular importance that the budget restrictions (BR) of all three sectors, households, firms, government (to be denoted by HBR, FBR, and GBR, respectively), are always fully specified. The behavior of the agents that is assumed to take place within these budget restrictions may, due to the traditional roots of our modeling framework, still not be too convincing. Yet, improved assumptions or derivations for the assumed behavioral relationship can easily be inserted into the complete models employed in this book, thereby changing the description of one or more sectors of the model, but not the overall formulation of the interaction of these sectors. Our conjecture is that such improvements may change details in the models' behavior but not the general finding of this book that the considered models of monetary growth do exhibit a high potential for generating undamped and, if appropriate nonlinearities are assumed, also viable patterns of cyclical growth.

[5] Planned aggregate demand Y^d is, as usual, given by $C + I + \delta K + G$. Note also that table I.1 suggests (again as is customary) that money holdings of firms are considered as unimportant and thus ignored and that there is no bond supply on the side of firms, but only equity financing if necessary.

We start with the most orthodox model of monetary growth that is available in descriptive macroeconomics: the Tobin (1965) extension of the neoclassical growth model which introduces money as a further asset into this otherwise purely real framework. This model will be introduced in chapter 2 in a form that is convenient both with respect to our general assumption of fixed proportions in production as well as from the point of view of the historical development of capitalistic economies. Our particular reformulation of this basic Tobin model will be extended in various directions in chapter 2 leading eventually to a very general formulation of it that serves as a basis for our subsequent introduction of a general model of Keynes–Wicksell type (chapter 3) and later of proper Keynesian type (chapter 4).

The general Tobin model is, however, problematic in its assumption of money-market disequilibrium and the price-adjustment equation that is built upon it. Furthermore its view of the behavior of the firm sector is extremely limited, since it allows only for production decisions in this substructure of the economy. All these weaknesses are overcome (in chapter 3) by our next prototype, the Keynes–Wicksell approach to monetary growth dynamics. Here investment decisions of firms and their financing by means of equities are considered explicitly and made consistent with the other sectors of the economy. Price adjustment is also put on a firmer basis in this model type and gives rise to the famous growth cycle mechanism of Goodwin and Rose as part of this extended framework of analysis and its dynamical implications. The inclusion of these Classical growth cycle mechanisms, by way of an improved wage–price module of the model, in a relatively pure form, is the main contribution that we will obtain from this variation of the Tobin monetary growth model.

Having improved the presentation of asset markets (in particular by assuming money market equilibrium throughout), the goods market remains a problem, since the added description of the investment behavior of firms generally now gives rise to a disequilibrium situation which is not present in the Tobin approach due to its dependence on Say's Law on the market for goods. The further development of the model (in chapter 4) to a basically Keynesian one therefore now adds IS-equilibrium. Following from this latter assumption (and the assumed wage/price adjustment behavior) the degree of utilization of the capital stock becomes the variable which will always adjust appropriately in order to make possible the assumed goods market equilibrium. In contrast to the fashionable full equilibrium version of the Tobin models we thereby arrive at the basic Keynesian prototype structure that will underlie all following generalizations of models of monetary growth exhibiting IS–LM-equilibrium and disequilibrium on the labor market and within firms. These disequilibria are then used as the basis for wage and price adjustments and the investment decision of firms.

This latter Keynesian prototype will be extended in various directions in chapters 4–7 to allow for factor substitution, technological change, wage taxation, p-star expectations, delayed quantity adjustments, endogenous natural rates and insider–outsider effects in the labor market. By the end of these extensions the Keynesian prototype will have become what we label a working Keynesian model. It will also be demonstrated to the reader that this working model still represents only a starting point (though already a fairly elaborate and consistent one) to a thorough consideration of many further extensions. Indeed section 7.7 provides a survey of such, necessary, extensions.

The way in which the basic "proper" Keynesian prototype, and then the working Keynesian model of monetary growth, is established here will in addition show that this model type overcomes important weaknesses of the predecessor models of Tobin and Keynes–Wicksell type by a systematic variation of them. Nevertheless, each of these two predecessor models is also of importance in its own right, due to the specific topics that have been considered important within these earlier prototypes. The Tobin model, for example, distinguishes between actual and perceived disposable income of households and allows consideration of a number of interesting effects that flow from this distinction, including the fact that it will represent a nonlinear model (again due to this distinction) even if all of its structural equations are linear. The consequences of distinguishing between actual and perceived disposable income will only be considered in chapter 2, while later chapters will again identify perceived with actual disposable income, leaving this specificity of the Tobin approach for the later investigations of our other models.

In our presentation of the various model types we shall mostly employ linear economic behavioral relationships. Thus nonlinearities that appear in the dynamic laws will be naturally occurring in that they are brought about by product terms such as the wage bill, state variable quotients such as the rate of employment, and some formulations being in terms of rates of growth. This serves the purpose of investigating the dynamical systems that are implied at first only in a "naturally" or "intrinsic" nonlinear setup in order to see how much "dynamical complexity" is already involved on this most basic level of the study of integrated economic systems. Occasionally we introduce, however, specific nonlinear behavioral relationships, in particular in investment functions and Phillips curves, in order to maintain economic viability of the dynamics being analyzed. However, we leave for future research a systematic study of the introduction into our general modeling framework of these and other nonlinear economic behav-

ioral relationships which have been proposed in the literature on macroeconomic fluctuations.

Throughout this book we model expectations as a weighted sum of
"backward looking" and "forward looking" components. We endow our
agents with neither the information of the model structure in which they
play out their economic roles, nor the computational ability that they
would need to form expectations in a way that is currently referred to as
"rational" in a large body of literature. Our reasons for adopting this
approach are detailed in section 1.6. In essence these reasons revolve
around a critique of the so-called jump-variable technique which the
adoption of a "rational" expectations approach would necessitate as well
as a growing body of empirical evidence which suggests that our approach
to expectations modeling may be more appropriate. However here we
stress that the future research agenda to which we have already referred
will need to incorporate the effects of heterogeneity of expectations and of
learning on the part of the various economic agents of our models.

This concludes the description of the basic line of reasoning that we will
employ in the development of our model structure. Since there is a clear
progression from model to model in this book we will generally explain the
model equations only when they appear for the first time. Before we now
proceed to such a systematic step-by-step development of prototype
models of monetary growth we will briefly consider in chapter 1 certain
roots of these approaches in the literature.

The material presented in chapters 1 to 7 of this book is neither of direct
textbook type nor written in the way of a handbook on monetary growth.
There is now a variety of advanced textbooks on macroeconomics available, ranging from traditional Keynesian analysis of extended IS–LM type
to analysis that claim to go "beyond IS–LM," see in particular Blanchard
and Fischer (1989), Carlin and Soskice (1990), Karakitsos (1992), Leslie
(1993), Turnovsky (1995), and Romer (1996). On the one hand, we add to
these presentations a new hierarchically structured set of theories and
models of monetary growth that can be used for classroom teaching. On
the other hand, we seek to draw to the attention of writers of advanced
textbooks and researchers in the field of macrodynamics the fact that
traditional analyses of models of monetary growth cannot be viewed as a
set of isolated models. Rather they must be considered as a lively body of
systematic studies which, when fully integrated, are still poorly understood
and where further investigation will provide a firm foundation and a better
understanding of existing and future developments in this area.

This book is also not a handbook on aspects of monetary economics or
more precisely a survey on the theory of monetary growth, as provided, for
example, by Orphanides and Solow (1990). Instead we show that there still

exists a large evolutionary potential in traditional macrodynamics that leads us to integrated macrodynamical models with Keynesian short-run features and Keynesian and monetarist features in the medium run as well as in the long run. These integrated models not only allow us to evaluate the contributions of the two schools of economic thought from this integrated perspective, but also serve to put into perspective more recent contributions to the theory of fluctuations and growth in monetary economies. In this way our book provides a benchmark against which alternative approaches can be judged and be developed further, including the working model of this book, towards a common core of macrodynamics that "we all can believe in."

1 Traditional monetary growth dynamics

1.1 Introduction

We reconsider in this chapter the leftover ruins of traditional monetary growth dynamics[1] which, with respect to the general dynamics they can give rise to, have so far been poorly analyzed and understood in the literature.[2]

We attempt to show to the reader, in section 1.2 in overview, and in detail in chapters 2–5, that these leftover ruins can be arranged and represented in a systematic way so that they form a hierarchical structured class of monetary growth models where each subsequent model type eliminates some of the weaknesses of the preceding model type. We then indicate in section 1.2 two ways in which this methodological approach to macrodynamics can be significantly extended beyond the existing scope of traditional models of monetary growth. Firstly, this way of proceeding in fact leads to the establishment of a proper (still traditional), but much neglected Keynesian model of monetary growth where both labor and capital exhibit fluctuating degrees of utilization independently of the assumptions that are made on "technology." Secondly, our approach leads to a further improvement of this IS–LM growth type of dynamics by allowing for sluggish price, as well as quantity, adjustments (two Phillips-curve mechanisms and a Metzlerian treatment of disappointed sales expectations) and by establishing thereby what we will call the working Keynesian model of this book. Section 1.2 therefore provides a survey of what we call the macro foundations of (disequilibrium) macroeconomics, namely the indication that there is a systematic way of proceeding from less sound and

---

[1] See Turnovsky (1995, part I) with respect to another reconsideration of integrated macrodynamics of traditional type.

[2] See for example Sargent's (1987, ch. 5) analysis of "Keynesian Dynamics" of AS–AD type and its reconsideration in Flaschel (1993, ch. 6–7) and Franke (1992a), or Stein's (1982) investigation of dynamic models of Keynes–Wicksell type and its reconsideration in Flaschel, Franke, and Semmler (1997, ch. 10).

elaborate to more sound and elaborate presentations of integrated macro-dynamic models of monetary growth. In this way we demonstrate both in this survey chapter and in more detail in chapters 2–7 a systematic procedure on the macro level by which integrated or complete macrodynamical models can be made more and more elaborate and coherent in their presentation of the fundamental feedback structures that characterize interdependence on the macro level.

Our approach proceeds independently of any justified claim for better micro foundations of macroeconomics. Indeed, improved micro foundations that emerge from research in this area should be capable of integration into appropriate modules of the macro structure that we build in this book. There is no space here, however, to go into this topic in detail. A recent approach which considers the problem of the micro foundations of macroeconomics from a critical perspective and which provides alternative and interesting micro foundations of macroeconomics (not based only on budget and technological constraints) is Hahn and Solow (1995). There it is found in particular that stickiness of wages and prices may be good for economic stability. Our treatment of Keynesian monetary growth in chapters 4–6 arrives at a similar conclusion, but from a quite different perspective.

The various steps in the building of a class of hierarchical structured models of monetary growth are made on the basis of assumptions on the structure of markets and sectors of the economy as they are used in Sargent (1987, chs. 1–5) which are indeed very convenient for the first stage of the project started in this book. We extend Sargent's (1987, part I) mainly static analysis of AS–AD macroeconomics (cum growth in his ch. 5) on the one hand into a full dynamic analysis of growing monetary economies and on the other hand into the direction of proper Keynesian models of monetary growth (where also firms are no longer on their supply schedule). In this way we lay foundations for a Keynesian approach to monetary growth which has rarely been studied in the literature so far.[3] When the final stage is reached in this book, however, the need for further extensions in the structure of Keynesian monetary growth dynamics will become apparent. Possibilities for such extensions are briefly discussed at the end of chapter 7. These provide a research agenda of systematic developments along the methodological lines established in this book.[4]

In sections 3–5 of this chapter we consider for introductory purposes basic models of Tobin, Keynes–Wicksell and AS–AD type. Very general versions of these approaches are introduced and investigated in subsequent

---

[3] See for example Orphanides and Solow (1990), where models of this type are not even mentioned.
[4] See Chiarella and Flaschel (1998f) and Chiarella et al. (1998, 1999).

chapters. Since Sargent's treatment of the AS–AD growth model focuses on the role various expectations schemes play in the dynamics generated by this model type, we in addition provide an alternative view on the modeling of expectations in section 1.6 which will be used in subsequent chapters on various levels of generality. Section 7 provides a few characterizations concerning the proper Keynesian models of monetary growth that we shall introduce and analyze in chapters 4–7.

1.2   Macro foundations of macroeconomics

The purpose of this section is to indicate to the reader that there is a hierarchical structured body of disequilibrium models of monetary growth where each subsequent stage in the development of such models improves the descriptive relevance of the preceding stage in a systematic and significant way. Independently of the need for sound micro foundations of the assumed (fairly conventional) behavioral relationships, the evolution of disequilibrium macrodynamics (which is not easily micro founded) does thereby indeed exhibit systematic progress to more and more convincing formulations of the fundamental modules of the dynamics of monetary growth in disequilibrium, and thus to the description and analysis of real growth dynamics. To show this in detail and to indicate how the framework of disequilibrium macrodynamics that we develop can be extended beyond its current scope are two of the main purposes of this book.

Subsection 1.2.1 provides a brief summary of the evolution and achievements of dynamic disequilibrium models of monetary growth in the past. Subsection 1.2.2 reviews the contributions that this book will make to the current state of the theory of monetary growth with under- or overemployed factors of production. A brief outlook on what needs to be and can be done on the basis of the results achieved in this book will conclude the subsection.

1.2.1   A brief genesis of disequilibrium models of monetary growth

We discuss in this subsection forerunners to the Keynesian model of monetary growth to be introduced in chapter 4 and developed further in subsequent chapters toward our working model of disequilibrium monetary growth dynamics.

> *The starting point*
> * Neoclassical models of monetary growth of Tobin type
> * Extension of the Solow model of real growth:
>   – towards an inclusion of financial assets

- where money market (dis-)equilibrium drives inflation
- in interaction with inflationary expectations

Neoclassical models of monetary growth were introduced into the macro-economic literature through the work of Tobin (1955, 1965) which ex-tended the Solow model of real growth by introducing monetary factors. Generalized versions of this model type were developed subsequently by Johnson (1966), Sidrauski (1967a), Hadjimichalakis (1971a,b), Nagatani (1970), Hadjimichalakis and Okuguchi (1979), and Hayakawa (1979). Bur-meister and Dobell (1970), Sijben (1977), Sargent (1987), and Orphanides and Solow (1990) give further presentations and a survey of this literature. These extensions were generally characterized by the consideration of money as an asset in addition to real capital and the use of money market disequilibrium as the foundation of the theory of inflation and inflationary expectations, coupled with Say's Law on the markets for goods (thereby excluding any goods-market problems).[5] Tobin type models have led to an enormous amount of literature on equilibrium growth models with opti-mizing behavior of economic agents, which, due to its general equilibrium nature, is not a suitable topic for a book such as this, the focus of which is on disequilibrium monetary growth theory.

Typical issues addressed by the above-cited authors were the analysis of the steady state effects of the growth rate of the money supply (and of so-called Tobin effects) and the local stability analysis of the steady state where in particular the destabilizing role of inflationary expectations was investigated when the adjustment of adaptively formed inflationary expec-tations became sufficiently fast. A detailed presentation of such stability issues is provided in Hayakawa (1984), while Benhabib and Miyao (1981) investigate the possibility of the cycles generated by Hopf bifurcations for intermediate adjustment speeds of inflationary expectations. It is shown thereby that the Cagan (1967) inflationary dynamics and the disequilib-rium approaches that were built on it by Goldman (1972) and others not only give rise locally to saddlepath situations (that are now the basis of the jump-variable technique of rational expectations models), but that there will emerge limit cycles for particular ranges in the adjustment speed of expectations from the nonlinear structure of these neoclassical models of monetary growth.

In chapter 2 we will start from the most basic (general equilibrium) version of the Tobin monetary growth model and shall subsequently

---

[5] Labor market phenomena were generally treated as in Solow (1956) by assuming full employment and the macroeconomic marginal productivity theory of income distribution. But labor market disequilibrium is easily introduced into this framework as in Goodwin (1967), here combined with neoclassical smooth factor substitution as discussed in detail in chapter 5.

establish step by step a general disequilibrium version of this model type (with money and bonds as financial assets and, of course, Say's Law remaining the [trivial] representation of goods market equilibrium). As in the evolution of the literature on models of monetary growth, we thus begin this book with the stability problems of monetary models of neoclassical growth where we, however, attempt to stress the cyclical properties of the dynamics of these models which, when necessary, may be bounded and thus imply viable cyclical oscillations through appropriate nonlinearities in the assumed behavioral relationships of neoclassical monetary growth. The main ingredients of our development of a Tobin general disequilibrium monetary growth model are listed at the head of this subsection.

The Keynes–Wicksell alternative
- Independent investment behavior based on Tobin's q
- Removal of Say's Law due to savings $\neq$ investment
- Augmented Wicksellian demand-pressure price-inflation
- Money wage Phillips curve
- Full capacity growth

The next model type that we develop is based on the Keynes–Wicksell approach to monetary growth. The most important work in this area of monetary growth theory has been provided in the late sixties and early seventies by Stein (1966, 1968, 1969, 1970, 1971) and by Rose (1966, 1967, 1969). Further contributions are Fischer (1972), Fujino (1974), Sijben (1977), Nagatani (1978), Brems (1980), Iwai (1981), and Asada (1991). In particular Stein (1982) has related this type of approach to the discussion between Keynesians, monetarists, and New Classicals, while Skott (1989a,b) provides a general theory of conflict about income distribution and of effective demand with similarities to the Keynes–Wicksell theory of monetary growth. Rose (1990) pursues the same aim from a somewhat different perspective and relates his general approach to many partial models of macroeconomic dynamics. The work of these latter two authors shows that there are still emerging important developments of this Keynes-oriented area of monetary growth theory, which in particular attempts to provide a Marshallian perspective of Keynes' theory of effective demand.

   The importance of the Keynes–Wicksell approach toward an explanation of the working of a (growing) monetary economy stems from two observations. Firstly, in the recognition that savings and investment decisions are to be differentiated from each other in an essential way (thereby denying the validity of Say's Law both in its trivial and in a more elaborate form), and that the theory of price inflation must be related to the goods market and its disequilibrium and not, as in the generalized Tobin models, to money market disequilibrium. Goods market imbalance was measured in these approaches through the deviation of investment decisions from savings decisions. The theory of inflation was based on this imbalance and augmented by expected inflation in Fischer (1972) in a monetarist fashion in order to allow for steady state equilibrium. The money market, by contrast, was now described through the usual Keynesian LM-equilibrium condition as the theory of the nominal rate of interest (the deviation of which from the nominal gross rate of profit was then used to determine the level of investment).

Secondly, that this alternative to the neoclassical view on monetary growth dynamics stressed the cyclical implications of labor market disequilibrium, the conflict over income distribution and capital accumulation. The work of Rose (1967) in particular established the Goodwinian (1967) growth cycle mechanism in an independent way and from a different perspective by relating it to a locally unstable Wicksellian theory of price inflation that gave rise to persistent fluctuations by way of appropriate assumptions on wage flexibility in a setup with smooth factor substitution. Rose (1990) provides important extensions of this type of monetary growth theory, extensions which have significantly influenced the formulation of the wage–price dynamics of our general Keynes–Wicksell model in chapter 3.

Our view on the Keynes–Wicksell contribution to the analysis of monetary growth is that it represents a decisive step forward in the macroeconomic description of such growth processes. Neoclassical and Keynes–Wicksell models of monetary growth are not situated in the hierarchy of monetary growth models on the same level of abstraction, but follow each other in this order, since the latter model type takes account of the independence of investment decisions from savings conditions and tries to incorporate this fact from a Wicksellian perspective in the simplest way possible. This extension in the approach to monetary growth also leads to an inclusion of a new financial asset besides money and bonds (equities) that is explicitly introduced, and related to Tobin's q, in our general reformulation of the Keynes–Wicksell approach in chapter 3. The main ingredients in our development of the Keynes–Wicksell alternative are listed on p. 14.

The Keynes–Wicksell type of analysis exhibits a number of problems. Firstly, the labor market is treated basically from a (neo)classical perspective in the same fashion as in the Goodwin model of the classical growth cycle, except with neoclassical factor substitution. Secondly, goods market imbalances drive prices and not quantities as in the Keynesian dynamic multiplier approach. Thirdly, capital is always operated at its full capacity as described by the usual profit-maximizing marginal productivity condition for real wages. Therefore, the (neo)classical view on capital accumulation is still, at least partially, present in this type of analysis. A logically compelling next step in the Keynesian analysis of monetary growth, therefore, should be to establish a proper type of Keynesian goods market and money market analysis in the tradition of the IS–LM approach to the description of the functioning of these two markets. This is indeed the step that was taken in the literature on Keynesian dynamics in the context of monetary growth in the late seventies.

The Keynesian AS–AD growth model
- Keynesian IS–equilibrium (in addition to LM–equilibrium)
- Infinitely flexible prices based on marginal wage costs
- Expectations – augmented money wage Phillips curve
- Profit-maximizing output decisions of firms

The textbook treatment of Keynesian monetary growth dynamics (see Turnovsky 1977a and Sargent 1987 for typical examples) dispensed with the Wicksellian approach to the determination of the price level, or rather its rate of change, by simply adding wage dynamics and inflationary expectations dynamics in a monetarist fashion and Solovian capital stock growth to the usual AS–AD approach of the Keynesian short-run macroeconomic equilibrium.[6] To date this AS–AD growth model has been considered as the representation of traditional Keynesian growth dynamics (see for example Turnovsky 1995, part I). Yet the fact remains that the full dynamics of such integrated AS–AD growth models have rarely been analyzed to a satisfactory degree, which means that the dynamic behavior of these seemingly conventional models is poorly understood.[7] This represents an important gap in the theory of monetary growth, since we therefore do not have a generally accepted pool of knowledge at our disposal against which the achievements of more recent theories of monetary growth can be usefully compared. The main elements of the Keynesian AS–AD growth model are summarized above.

There are, however, inconsistencies present in the AS–AD theory of effective demand, inflationary dynamics, and real capital accumulation. Basing the theory of the price level on its determination through marginal wage costs, as Keynes (1936) did, amounts to assuming that producers are, on the one hand, constrained by the effective demand for goods, but are, on the other hand, capable of passing on this constraint to the labor supply of households, by allowing in one way or another for profit-maximizing prices so that they can stay on their supply schedule. In our view this

[6] IS–LM equilibrium coupled with the assumption that prices are always equal to marginal wage costs, the money wage level being given at each point in time.
[7] See in particular Flaschel, Franke, and Semmler (1997) for some investigations of the dynamics of these AS–AD growth models.

basically means that firms are price takers and quantity takers at one and the same time, which would give rise to a contradiction if prices are not assumed to adjust in such a way that the level of effective demand becomes consistent with the profit maximizing level of the output of firms. Our conclusion is that the Keynesian theory of goods-market constrained firms needs a theory of the price level other than that of the neoclassical approach to the theory of the firm. Such an alternative theory might be that of monopolistic competition or even more advanced theories representing more advanced stages in the evolution of capitalistic market economies. Furthermore, a Keynesian theory of the AS–AD type (even if it were consistent) would still be a theory of full-capacity growth and would thus represent only a partial description of what we observe in reality.

Barro (1994b, p. 4) has recently come to the same conclusion from a different but related perspective, stating in particular:

We have available, at this time, two types of internally consistent models that allow for cyclical interactions between monetary and real variables. The conventional IS–LM model achieves this interaction by assuming that the price level and the nominal wage rate are typically too high and adjust only gradually toward their market-clearing values. The market-clearing models with incomplete information get this interaction by assuming that people have imperfect knowledge about the general price level.

This quotation lends further weight to our viewpoint that models of IS–LM growth with gradually adjusting wages *and* prices are the correct alternative to the general equilibrium approach to monetary growth. This perspective is in fact not a new one, but has indeed been essential for the so-called neo-Keynesian or non-Walrasian disequilibrium analysis of the short-, the medium-, and sometimes also the long-run evolution of temporary fixed price equilibria. This approach can therefore be used to improve considerably the presentation of macrodynamic disequilibrium growth of AS–AD type, though most of the efforts in this area have gone into the modeling of fixed price temporary equilibria from a microeconomic point of view (which are not reviewed in the following characterization of this approach).

Neo-Keynesian monetary growth analysis
- Three regimes of the IS–LM model: the Keynesian regime, the Classical regime, and repressed inflation
- No full capacity growth in the first and the last regime
- Varying capital utilization rates and price dynamics
- Varying labor utilization rates and wage dynamics
- Sluggish wage- as well as price-level adjustments

• Extended investment functions based on profitability
  measures and the rate of capacity utilization

From the macroeconomic point of view, the work of Benassy and Malinvaud is here of special interest for the purposes of this book, see in
particular Benassy (1986b) and Malinvaud (1980), and from the viewpoint
of monetary growth theory also the collection of essays in Hénin and
Michel (1982). Benassy (1986b) provides in particular a detailed present-
tion of the three regimes that may be of particular relevance in the analysis
of macroeconomic temporary equilibrium positions and dynamic models
of inflation, the business cycle and the role of expectations based on this
three-regime analysis. Malinvaud (1980) considers investment behavior
based on profitability *and* capacity utilization besides a consumption
function that is typical for the fixed price approach to temporary equilibrium. He incorporates these behavioral relationships into a three-regime
medium-run model of Keynesian depressions, under the additional assumption that the profitability effect of real wage changes is less significant
than the consumption effect of such changes.

We will borrow from this literature two important ideas. The first one,
which also appears in the quite different macrodynamic approach of Rose
(1990), is that there should be two Phillips-type curves in a Keynesian
macrodynamic model, one for the wage level and one for the price level.
Both of these are expectations augmented (from a cost-push perspective),
and both exhibit demand pressure components that (in the first instance)
are to be represented through the utilization rates of the two factors of
production, labor and capital. The second idea is that the investment
behavior of Keynes–Wicksell and dynamic AS–AD models, which was
based on Tobin's q solely, should in addition be augmented by capacity
considerations in order to take account not only of profitability differentials, but also of the now varying utilization rate of the capital stock.

These are the main elements (summarized in the list above) of the
neo-Keynesian analysis of (the evolution of) fixed price equilibria that we
will use in our formulation of a proper Keynesian model of monetary
growth with IS-equilibrium or IS-disequilibrium. In this way we overcome
important limitations of the growth models of Keynes–Wicksell and the
AS–AD growth type by allowing also for fluctuating utilization rates of
capital as in neo-Keynesian analyses of the medium or the long run.
However, we do not make use of the regime-switching methodology of
neo-Keynesian analyses, since we believe that there are significant buffers
in the process of capital accumulation that generally prevent the occurrence of hard kinks caused by either labor demand, in the Classical regime,
or labor supply, in the regime of repressed inflation.

1.2.2   Keynesian monetary growth dynamics: new steps in the hierarchical evolution of integrated macrodynamics

In this subsection we discuss the two basic stages in our development of a proper Keynesian model of monetary growth, i.e., the basic prototype model of this kind investigated in chapter 4 and the working model we develop from it in chapter 6.

Keynesian monetary growth analysis: the basic prototype
- Only the Keynesian regime of IS–LM growth
- Based on excess capacities for labor and capital
- NAIRU-type rate of employment and of capacity utilization
- No normal capacity growth of output outside the steady state
- Varying capital utilization rates and sluggish price level dynamics
- Varying labor utilization rates and sluggish wage level dynamics
- Extended investment function based on Tobin's q and the rate of capacity utilization of firms

The new features listed above, taken from neo-Keynesian macrodynamics that we have considered on the basis of the "Neo-Keynesian" List on page 17, are employed in chapter 4 (and chapter 5) to formulate, on the basis of the IS–LM part of AS–AD models, our basic prototype model of Keynesian monetary growth both with and without smooth factor substitution. As a Keynesian model this should, and now indeed does, exhibit imbalances in the employment of labor *as well as* capital, independently of whether there are fixed proportions in production (chapter 4) or neoclassical smooth factor substitution (as in chapter 5). This new framework for our models of monetary growth overcomes the basic problems of the Keynes–Wicksell model as well as the AS–AD growth model, namely, to measure goods-market disequilibrium either by IS-disequilibrium coupled with full capacity growth, or to have IS-equilibrium at each point in time and to put the burden of insufficient effective goods demand on the labor market solely, thereby allowing for full capacity growth as in the Keynes–Wicksell approach (of which it is in fact a limit case for price adjustment speeds going to infinity).

In our framework, however, labor and capital experience varying utilization rates caused by IS–LM equilibrium in the market for goods and money which drive prices and determine the rate of inflation on the market for labor and goods in the fashion of a wage–price spiral (augmented through expectations on wage and price inflation), and which in the case of capital also influence the investment behavior of firms. We thus arrive at the first truly Keynesian model of monetary growth in this book, and on this level of generality also in the literature. This model is introduced in chapter 4 as a systematic extension and modification of the one-sided Keynes–Wicksell representation of growth in a monetary economy developed in chapter 3. In view of the earlier quotation from Barro (p. 17) we have thus arrived at a model type which may be considered as the internally consistent fixed-price IS–LM alternative to the market-clearing models of monetary growth which are in vogue today. We note in passing that this model type is, however, not the final step in the hierarchy of disequilibrium models of monetary growth that we develop and investigate in this book.

In describing the new (and also old) building blocks of our Keynesian disequilibrium model of monetary growth we have only referred to the Keynesian IS–LM regime of the three-regime scenario generally found in macroeconomic analyses of the neo-Keynesian variety. We have thus made no reference to the other two regimes of Classical unemployment and repressed inflation. In contrast to the views in this strand of neo-Keynesian literature we believe that such an approach is justified from the descriptive point of view as well as from the viewpoint of the monetarist reformulations of the AS–AD growth model, as presented for example in Sargent (1987, part I). In this respect our model of IS–LM growth with sluggish wages and prices has borrowed from the theory of AS–AD growth with perfectly flexible prices[8] in that it incorporates not only a "natural" level of the employment of labor into its money wage Phillips-curve,[9] but also proceeds in a similar way with respect to the price level Phillips curve present in it. This latter Phillips curve is, in chapter 4, no longer based on IS-disequilibrium (which is nonexistent there), but refers to deviations of the rate of capacity utilization from a normal or desired rate of capacity utilization (less than one).

At and sufficiently near to the steady state of our IS–LM growth model, therefore, only the Keynesian regime prevails. Situations of repressed inflation or Classical capital shortage may or may not come about far off the steady state depending on how the (nonlinear) dynamics of this IS–LM growth model are formulated far off the steady state of the model. We thus believe that it is not sensible to formulate a Keynesian disequilibrium model of monetary growth from the descriptive point of view in such a way that, when in steady state, it may, by the slightest conceivable disturbance, just as easily switch into a situation of capital shortage or repressed inflation as into a Keynesian effective demand regime. Capitalist economies most of the time exhibit certain excess capacities on the market for

---

[8] Based on marginal wage costs.
[9] In the form of the employment rate complement of the so-called NAIRU.

labor as well as within firms which allow for situations of the overemployment of both factors should there be sufficient effective demand on the market for goods. A very basic example for this observation, probably not intended to support our claim, is indeed provided in Benassy (1986b, ch. 11), where only the IS–LM regime is needed in the derivation of a medium-run wage dynamics (of limit cycle type) within the scope of this regime.

There are not many monetary growth models of the neo-Keynesian variety in the literature; indeed most of them are collected in the cited volume of Hénin and Michel (1982). The reason for this, in our view, is that such growth models are very difficult to formulate and to analyze, due to the various situations of rationing and the wealth of rationing schemes that are possible in their dynamics. We shall not here or in the remainder of this book go into a discussion of these dynamic models with temporarily fixed prices and wages which treat shortages by hard restrictions (strict inequalities) in the place of smooth adjustments in the neighborhood of such shortages (based on appropriate nonlinear adjustment behavior). We have argued above that there is no need to proceed along these lines. This is certainly true from a local perspective, but, in our view, also applicable to more global types of analysis, once the typical reaction patterns of capitalistic market economies that come about in situations that approach labor or capital shortage are taken into account. Neo-Keynesian models of monetary growth have neglected such smooth regime switching processes in the neighborhood of absolute full employment ceilings and have therefore analyzed situations which are not typical for the process of capital accumulation. This is the reason why we do not consider the neo-Keynesian type of monetary growth model in chapter 4 and thereafter.

Instead, chapters 4 and 5 will provide various extensions of our prototype model of Keynesian monetary growth of chapter 4. These extensions (see page 19 for a summary list) enrich the descriptive relevance of this prototype model, but they do not add much in the direction of a significant further level in the hierarchy of disequilibrium models of monetary growth. It is in chapter 6 that the next decisive step in the systematic evolution of such disequilibrium growth models is taken, in particular motivated by some strange instability scenarios of the ultra-short-run features of our IS–LM growth prototype observed in chapter 4 as well as by the implausible asymmetric treatment of prices and quantities of that chapter. As stated above, wages and prices adjust sluggishly in the IS–LM growth model of chapter 4, yet quantities, due to the assumed IS–LM equilibrium, adjust with infinite speed to always ensure goods- (and money-) market equilibrium. Furthermore it is observed in chapter 4 that this equilibrium may be unstable when viewed from a dynamic multiplier perspective. A more symmetric treatment of the adjustment speeds of prices as well as quantities may here be preferable, and may lead to more convincing results in the explanation of growth and fluctuations. In strict contrast to the market-clearing approach to monetary growth we thus assume here that price, wages, and the output of firms all adjust with finite speed in view of the imbalances that are relevant for them. Incorporating this into the approach of chapter 4 leads to the next stage in the evolution of our disequilibrium models of monetary growth.

Keynes–Metzler monetary growth theory
- Sluggish wage and price adjustments as in IS–LM growth
- Extending IS–LM growth towards IS-disequilibrium
- Inventory adjustment mechanism of Metzlerian type coupled with a sales expectations mechanism
- The working Keynesian model of monetary growth which puts the modules of traditional Keynesian macrodynamics together
- An internally consistent Keynesian model of monetary growth to be compared with more recent developments in the literature

With this stage in the hierarchy of Keynesian models of monetary growth we arrive at our working Keynesian model, whose main elements are outlined above. This model overcomes the weaknesses of the still one-sided IS–LM growth dynamics and allows for a variety of results for a Keynesian theory of fluctuations and growth, as we shall see in chapter 6, from partial perspectives as well as an integrated or total one. Assuming a Metzlerian inventory adjustment process in the place of an instantaneous clearing of the market for goods increases the dynamics by two dimensions and leads to further buffers that can prevent a switch from the Keynesian regime to one of capital or labor shortage. As chapter 6 will show, the stability analysis of the resulting model type is already fairly demanding so that many more interesting results on this (from an economic perspective still basic) integrated prototype model of monetary growth can be expected to be obtained from future research.

This highest level in the hierarchy of our models of monetary growth is therefore but the beginning of a meaningful analysis of the Keynesian approach to the theory of fluctuations and growth. The theory obtained from our integrated perspective is thus still in its infancy. In fact, one might claim at the end of this book that our prototype model of Keynes–Metzler type is but the completion of the oversimplistic Keynes–Wicksell project of describing the macroeconomics of Keynesian monetary growth, since we have arrived again at IS-disequilibrium as a theory of quantity adjustments, but now without full capacity growth, the implied varying rate of capacity utilization being in turn one of the reasons for a changing rate of inflation.

In our view there is an urgent need for a better understanding of the dynamics of this integrated Keynesian prototype model in order to put at the disposal of economists a consistent theory of fluctuations, inflation, and growth against which the (mostly partial) achievements of newer and more modern approaches of new- or post-Keynesian type can really be judged. Otherwise, the statement that traditional Keynesian approaches to money and growth (which, as we hope to have shown, have not existed so far from a truly integrated perspective) are outdated in their potential to describe the evolution of capitalistic economies, will remain fairly superficial.

We will not pursue in this book the task of overhauling the modules of our working model of chapter 6 from the perspective of the new- or post-Keynesian theory, proceeding thereby to probably still more advanced models of Keynesian monetary growth, but leave this topic for future investigations.[10] Instead we will provide in the concluding chapter 7, on the basis of a suitable simplification of the Metzlerian inventory mechanism, a modification of our working model which proposes simple endogenous determinations of the NAIRU rate of employment and of the natural rate of growth of the economy. This modification in addition improves the formulation of the money wage Phillips curve by taking account of insider–outsider effects on the labor market and the possibility of overtime and short time working within the firm. In this way we provide one final example of how to proceed further in the development of a hierarchy of disequilibrium approaches to monetary growth which bring the modeling framework closer and closer to a situation where macroeconometric applications become reasonable and also compelling.

Looking ahead
- Further module variations of the Keynes–Metzler working model
- Toward the new-Keynesians (monopolistic wage and price sectors)
- Towards the post-Keynesians (more sophisticated asset markets) or whatever else
- Further module variations: towards modern macroeconometric model building

By the end of chapter 7 the stage is set for the development of a body of more and more consistent and convincing descriptive Keynesian macro-

---

[10] See Chiarella et al. (1999) for work in this direction.

models of monetary growth, on the basis of which a systematic and new analysis of this type of macrodynamic modeling is within reach. The way that we have chosen to arrive at this stage represents, in our terminology, the macro foundations of (disequilibrium) macroeconomics, which stresses and develops sophisticated integrated macrodynamic interaction and feedback structures in the place of more or less partial microeconomic underpinnings. Of course, our approach does not deny the value of such underpinnings. Indeed, research on these needs to proceed in parallel with the development of the framework we have outlined in order that the various macrodynamic interactions and feedbacks can have a firm theoretical basis.

We therefore start in this book from known (already fairly integrated) macrodynamic presentations of monetary growth in disequilibrium. We then make these models complete models on their respective level of abstraction and arrange them in a systematic order such that each subsequent model type can be understood as an improvement of certain important weaknesses of the preceding model. We show finally that one can arrive thereby at a model type that allows for labor- as well as goods-market disequilibrium, both with components that lie inside as well as outside the firm. We believe that this approach for the first time provides a proper starting point and integrated working model for the Keynesian analysis of business fluctuations in the utilization rates of both labor and capital and of growth in a monetary framework. We also stress once again that this synthesis of earlier attempts to provide a truly Keynesian model of disequilibrium monetary growth is at the same time a very traditional one. In our view it is remarkable that this task has been, and is still, very much neglected in the literature on Keynesian macrodynamics, even though it is now more than sixty years since the appearance of Keynes' *General Theory*.

1.3   Basic Tobin models of monetary growth

This and the following two sections consider in some detail traditional macrodynamic model building of the Tobin, the Keynes–Wicksell, and the AS–AD growth type in order to lay foundations for the generalized models of this type considered in chapters 2 and 3. Further presentations of traditional models of monetary growth can be found in Turnovsky (1977a,b, 1995), Sargent (1987), Sijben (1977).

Tobin (1955, 1961, 1965) was the first to attempt, and to succeed, in integrating possible influences of the growth in money supply into the real model of growth and capital accumulation of Solow (1956). In particular, his 1965 contribution can be viewed as laying the foundations and posing the basic questions for models of monetary growth, there in a neoclassical framework where Say's Law is assumed to hold (no independent investment function) in a refined form. He added to this neoclassical model a portfolio choice mechanism[11] and thereby connected money growth and capital formation. Other early treatments of monetary growth along the same lines were provided by Johnson (1966, 1967a,b).

This first prototype model of monetary growth is usually presented in the literature in the following way.[12]

$$\dot{K} + (\dot{M}/p) = s(Y + (\dot{M}/p)), (s = \text{const.}) \tag{1.1}$$

$$M = pYh(\rho + \pi), (h' < 0) \tag{1.2}$$

$$Y = F(K, L^d), \omega = F_L, \rho = F_K \tag{1.3}$$

$$L^d = L, w = \omega p, L = nL, (n = \text{const.}) \tag{1.4}$$

$$\dot{M} = p(TR - T) = \mu M, (\mu = \text{const.}) \tag{1.5}$$

$$\pi = \hat{p}. \tag{1.6}$$

In our following brief reconsideration of this model we assume that the reader is familiar with the Solow–Swan model of real economic growth which is built on equations (1.1), (1.3), and (1.4) of the above model, but with the simplified savings function $\dot{K} = sY$ in the place of (1.1). This real model of economic growth gives rise to the following so-called fundamental equation of economic growth[13]

$$\dot{k} = sf(k) - nk, k = K/L,$$

which states that the time-rate of change of the capital intensity, $\dot{k}$, must be equal to the difference between savings per head and nk, the amount of investment needed for pure capital-widening.

In this real growth model we have no government and no depreciation of capital. Disposable income of households Y^D is therefore simply given by output Y. In the Tobin monetary growth model, disposable income of households is not so simply handled. Instead of $Y^D = Y$, equation (1.1) is used, and is usually explained by stating that real private savings are a fixed proportion of real disposable income and are spent on either capital or real balances formation: $\dot{K}$ or $(\dot{M}/p)$ (see Orphanides and Solow 1990, p. 230, for example). Such a statement is, however, a rather condensed one; what is really involved in household savings decisions can be made more transparent in the following way.

---

[11] And a particular concept of disposable income, as we shall see below.
[12] See Orphanides and Solow (1990) for details and notation and also pp. xxii–xxiv for a list of symbols (which are fairly standard in the presently considered model type). Note also that we use $(\dot{M}/p)$ to denote the time derivative of real balances M/p and $\widehat{M/p}$ for its rate of growth.   [13] By way of $\hat{k} = \hat{K} - n = sY/K - n = sf(k)/k - n(\hat{k} = \dot{k}/k)$.

Define perceived disposable income of households by

$$Y^{De} = Y - \frac{M}{p}\pi - T + TR,$$

where π is the expected (here equal to the actual) rate of inflation, T are taxes and TR are transfers. Besides capital, the Tobin extension of the Solow model has one further asset, i.e. money, here considered in the form of real balances M/p. The above concept of perceived disposable income is exactly equal to the rate at which private households can consume while leaving their real wealth, defined by $K + M/p$, intact.[14] This is a well-known definition of perceived disposable income in the macroeconomic literature and it leads to the formulation of the following consumption function (where c is equal to $1 - s$):

$$C = cY^{De} = c\left(Y - \frac{M}{p}\pi - T + TR\right).$$

Private savings S_p is then given by actual disposable income ($Y^D = Y - T + TR$) minus consumption, i.e.

$$S_p = Y - T + TR - cY^{De} = \dot{K} + \dot{M}/p, \tag{1.7}$$

and it is spent on capital formation and the increase in nominal balances as shown in the above flow budget restriction of households (1.7). By means of the government budget restriction (1.5) this budget restriction can be further reformulated as

$$Y + \dot{M}/p - c\left(Y - \frac{M}{p}\pi + \dot{M}/p\right) = \dot{K} + \dot{M}/p,$$

or

$$(1 - c)\left(Y - \frac{M}{p}\pi + \dot{M}/p\right) = \dot{K} + \dot{M}/p - \frac{M}{p}\pi.$$

Due to $\pi = \dot{p}/p$ and $(\dot{M}/p) = \dot{M}/p - M\dot{p}/p^2 = \dot{M}/p - (M/p)(\dot{p}/p)$ this last equation then gives rise to equation (1.1). We therefore see that equation (1.1) is more than just a description of private savings behavior.

Equation (1.2) adds a simple LM equation to this description of asset accumulation where the nominal rate of interest is given by the rate of profit $\rho = F_K = (Y - \omega L)/K$ plus the expected rate of inflation π. Note that here the expected rate of inflation is equal to the actual rate of inflation since the present formulation of the model is based on the assumption (1.6) of myopic perfect foresight. Equations (1.3) and (1.4) are the conventional

[14] See Sargent (1987, pp.18–19) for details.

equations of neoclassical full employment growth (based on the neoclassical theory of income distribution). Equations (1.5) and (1.6) have already been explained above.

Comparing this model of monetary growth with the Solow growth model we thus find that its new features are,

- a capital accumulation equation[15] which is based on a new concept of perceived disposable income and a simple, but consistent government budget equation;
- a description of money-market behavior;
- the assumption of myopic perfect foresight with respect to the rate of inflation, where inflation, as a new feature, is generated by the growth in money supply.

Instead of the crude version of Say's Law employed in the Solow model ($I \equiv S = sY$) we have a more refined version of this law in the present model which follows from the two relationships (see above) $S_p = Y - T + TR - C \equiv \dot{K} + \dot{M}/p$, and $S_g = T - TR \equiv -\dot{M}/p$, i.e. $S_p + S_g = S = Y - C \equiv \dot{K}$, which states that all output not consumed will in fact be invested, since any investment in real balances must be equal to the difference between actual disposable income and output if it is assumed, as is the case here, that households absorb the increase in money supply $\dot{M}$.[16]

The above model is, as is Solow's growth model, a model of full temporary equilibrium (on the markets for goods, labor, and money), which, however, is based on Say's Law and not on some sort of Walras' Law as is sometimes believed to be the case. This is of importance when considering and interpreting its conventional extensions where money market disequilibrium is considered side by side with equilibrium in the market for both goods and for labor.

In intensive form, the above model gives rise to ($k = K/L, x = Y/L = f(k), m = M/(pL)$),[17]

$$\dot{k} = sf(k) - nk - (1 - s)m(\mu - \hat{p}), \tag{1.8}$$

$$\hat{m} = \mu - \hat{p} - n, \tag{1.9}$$

where $\hat{p}$ is obtained from (see equations (1.1), (1.2), and (1.6)) $m = h(f'$

---

[15] $\dot{K} = Y - C = S = S_p + S_g$, see the following.

[16] This formulation of Say's Law implies that the goods market will always be in equilibrium, quite independently of the state of the market for money or for labor. Such a situation is not possible in models that rely on some form of Walras' Law.

[17] If $Y^{De} = Y^D = Y - T + TR$ is assumed instead of the above we would obtain here: $\dot{k} = sf(k) - nk - (1 - s)\mu m$.

$(k) + \hat{p})f(k)$, by making use of $\dot{k} = (\hat{K} - n)k = \dot{K}/L - nk$ and equation (1.1), since $(\dot{M}/p) = (\mu - \hat{p})M/p$.

The model therefore exhibits a new term in its fundamental equation, namely $- (1 - s)m(\mu - \hat{p})$, which makes capital accumulation now also dependent on real balances per head and money market phenomena. Furthermore, it now consists of two dynamical laws (for k and m) instead of the single law (for k) of the Solow model.

The steady state of the model (where $\mu = \hat{p} + n$ holds) is described by

$$0 = sf(k) - nk - (1 - s)nm$$
$$m = h(f'(k) + \mu - n)f(k).$$

Assuming that there is a unique solution to these equations[18] it follows immediately by total differentiation ($f' > 0, f'' < 0, h' < 0$) that $dk/d\mu > 0$ must hold true, which is the so-called Tobin effect. This intuitively plausible effect states that if the return of holding money as an asset is reduced (by increasing the steady state rate of inflation $\mu = \dot{M}/M$), the relative composition of assets will shift toward capital, increasing thereby capital intensity k and output per head $y = f(k)$. Instead of the superneutrality of money (where μ does not influence the real part of the economy in the steady state), we thus have a positive influence of the growth rate of money supply on capital, output, and consumption per head.

This steady-state result has been extended, turned into a negative Tobin-effect and also shown to be non-existent through a variety of modifications of the original Tobin model in descriptive as well as optimizing macroeconomic frameworks. This literature is surveyed in Orphanides and Solow (1990) and will not be considered here, since we only want to give a brief survey on the dynamic properties of the Tobin model and its extension to adaptive expectations in this section.

Nagatani (1970) has investigated the stability of the Tobin model under the assumed situation of myopic perfect foresight and found that it exhibits saddlepoint instability. As Orphanides and Solow (1990) state: "At this time this was considered to be a fatal flaw of the model, . . ." Thus it appeared at that time that the steady-state analysis of Tobin was not supported by dynamic analysis as far as the myopic perfect foresight case (1.6) was concerned.

Yet, Sidrauski (1967a) had already shown that if inflationary expectations π are formed adaptively and at a sufficiently slow rate, then the Tobin model was globally asymptotically stable. This modification, instead of (1.8), (1.9) gives rise to

---

[18] Which can easily be shown by means of simple assumptions on f and h, since the function $nk/f(k) + (1 - s)nh(f'(k) + \mu - n)$ involved in the determination of the steady state is strictly increasing.

$$\dot{k} = sf(k) - nk - (1 - s)m(\mu - \pi),$$
$$\dot{\pi} = \beta_\pi(\hat{p} - \pi) = \beta_\pi(\mu - n - \pi - \dot{m}), (\beta_\pi > 0),$$

where m is given by $m = h(f'(k) + \pi)f(k)$, which would therefore support the steady-state arguments of Tobin again.[19] To explore the stability properties of this steady-state solution further it was also often assumed, in particular by Hadjimichalakis (1971a,b),[20] that prices are not always equilibrating, but are responding sluggishly to money market disequilibrium and, due to Fischer's (1972) proposal, also dependent on the expected rate of inflation π, as for example in the following determination of the rate of inflation:

$$\hat{p} = \beta_p(m - h(f'(k) + \pi)f(k)) + \pi.$$

The dynamic system thereby becomes a three-dimensional one and of the form

$$\dot{k} = sf(k) - nk - (1 - s)m(\mu - \pi),$$
$$\dot{m} = m(\mu - \hat{p} - n) = m(\mu - n - \pi - \beta_p(m - h(f'(k) + \pi)f(k))),$$
$$\dot{\pi} = \beta_\pi(\hat{p} - \pi) = \beta_\pi\beta_p(m - h(f'(k) + \pi)f(k)).$$

The advantage of this formulation of the dynamics around Tobin's steady state is that its feedback structure is more easily understood (or more disentangled), but at the cost of increasing the dimension of the dynamics by one and by a perhaps not widely accepted adjustment rule for the price level p. Be that as it may, this generalization of the dynamics (and modifications of it) have been extensively studied in the literature. Hayakawa (1984), for example, uses a general flow disequilibrium concept in the market for money in order to systematize the local stability properties of various approaches to the determination of $\hat{p}$ by means of special cases of it. Benhabib and Miyao (1981) show that the generalized Tobin model loses stability in a cyclical fashion by way of a Hopf bifurcation if the parameter β_π of the expectations mechanism becomes sufficiently large. The general impression that arises from these treatments of the stability problems of the Tobin model is that adaptive expectations support instability if they are formed with sufficient strength (with a lag that is sufficiently short), while their limit case $\beta_\pi = \infty$ of myopic perfect foresight directly gives instability in the form of a (local) saddlepath dynamics.

In our view, the basic explanation for such a result is that there is a positive feedback mechanism in this model and its variants, of the form

$$\pi\uparrow m - h(f'(k) + \pi(f(k))\uparrow\hat{p}\uparrow\dot{\pi}\uparrow,$$

which becomes stronger the larger the adjustment speeds β_p, β_π of prices

---

[19] The steady state of this model is the same as that of the Tobin model (1.1)–(1.6).

[20] See Sijben (1977) for an early systematic treatment of the literature on the Tobin model.

and of inflationary expectations become. This mechanism is much more general than its present appearance in generalized Tobin models and will reappear in various forms throughout this book. The value of descriptive generalized Tobin models is that investigation of the above positive feedback mechanism within them has been extensive, while it has been largely neglected so far in models of the Keynesian variety. It is the Tobin model type where the role of the adjustment parameters β_π and β_p has been investigated the most thoroughly.[21]

Summarizing, we can state that the neoclassical monetary growth model of Tobin (1965) type integrates portfolio choices and their implications for the determination of perceived disposable income into the standard descriptive neoclassical approach to real growth. It is based on Say's Law (sometimes confused with some sort of Walras' Law) and full employment of the labor force (which is not a compelling assumption, as we shall see in chapter 2). It treats the role of the government in a very simple way (confined to the supply of money which is, however, related to, and thus not independent of, fiscal policy). Many later versions of the Tobin model have assumed various forms of moneymarket disequilibrium to allow for a finite adjustment speed of the price level (some sort of a crude but dynamic quantity theory of money), combined with adaptively formed expectations or myopic perfect foresight.

The validity of the Tobin effect, the denial of the superneutrality of money in particular, was also considered by means of models which put money in the utility or the production function. Following an early proof of superneutrality by Sidrauski (1967b) in an optimizing framework most of the discussions of money in a growing economy are now based on such a micro founded approach, assuming infinitely lived individuals, overlapping generations or cash-in-advance situations (see Orphanides and Solow 1990 for a detailed presentation of these approaches). The Tobin (1965) model thereby becomes a truly neoclassical one, with optimizing agents and general equilibrium as for example in Gale (1983, ch. 2).

Orphanides and Solow (1990, p. 225) state in this regard:

The main lessons were thus already implicit in the work of Tobin and Sidrauski. For those who can bring themselves to accept the single-consumer, infinite-horizon, maximization model as a reasonable approximation to economic life, superneutrality is a defensible presumption. All others have to be ready for a different outcome.

An important further development that grew out of the discussion of

---

[21] We have already cited Hayakawa (1984). See also Chiarella (1986) and Chiarella and Lorenz (1996) for a nonlinear approach which makes the locally explosive dynamics of this model type globally viable without reference to the so-called jump-variable technique.

Tobin's approach to monetary growth was given by the treatment of myopic perfect foresight that it eventually induced. After recognizing the saddlepath instability of perfect foresight solutions (and the instability of fast adaptive expectations) most authors in monetary growth theory adapted a strategy to cope with the former problem, as it was proposed by Sargent and Wallace (1973), that turned saddlepath instability into so-called saddlepath stability by the choice of a certain jump-variable technique. This redefinition in the dynamic treatment of (local) saddlepath situations (and the devaluation of the adaptive expectations mechanism) has implied that the stability problems of the Tobin model and its extensions became irrelevant in the further discussion of monetary growth. Therefore, there has never been an attempt in the orthodox literature to overcome these related local instability scenarios by an alternative reaction to them, which assumes appropriate nonlinearities far off the steady state in order to keep the observed saddlepath dynamics of the model economically meaningful for all points in the phase space from the global point of view. Chiarella (1986, 1990) and Flaschel and Sethi (1999) develop such an approach, the essence of which is outlined in section 1.6 below. Such a reaction to local instability may produce interesting cyclical growth processes, not only for the Tobin model but also for other, less neoclassical approaches to monetary growth, as we shall see on various occasions throughout this book.

1.4 Basic Keynes–Wicksell models of monetary growth

Monetary growth models of Keynes–Wicksell type were developed in the late sixties and early seventies, in part as a reaction to the Tobin neoclassical model of monetary growth. They assume the existence of an investment behavior that is formulated independently of savings behavior, and thus no longer rely on some sort of Say's Law.[22] The instability problems of the Tobin growth model can also be established for the models of Keynes–Wicksell type, but have somehow been neglected here, since fast adaptive expectations, or even myopic perfect foresight, has not been a topic in these approaches to monetary growth dynamics.[23] Models of Keynes–Wicksell type are now almost forgotten in the discussion of monetary growth. However such neglect is not justified as these models represent a useful generalization of what is now known as textbook Keynesian dynamics, as we shall see in Chapters 3 and 5. We refer the reader to Orphanides and

---

[22] Though the version of Walras' Law these models assume is often not made explicit.

[23] See Stein (1982) for example. Fischer (1972) offers such an analysis, but is not fully correct in his findings on the local stability of the model, since he uses an incorrect expression for the trace of the Jacobian of his dynamical system at the steady state.

Solow (1990) for a brief characterization of this model type. Rose (1990) presents an isolated, but very interesting, attempt to make this model type a more consistent and general one in such a way that many other approaches to economic dynamics can be treated as special cases of it.

Models of Keynes–Wicksell type have been developed by Rose (1966, 1967, 1969) and Stein (1966, 1968, 1970, 1971) in particular and as an alternative to neoclassical models of monetary growth. Instead of money market disequilibrium, they assume goods and labor market disequilibrium, while keeping the money market always in equilibrium. In our view, this is a more plausible disequilibrium scenario than that of the Tobin models with their pre-Keynesian structure. However, Keynes–Wicksell models do not add much to the steady-state properties of the Tobin models. Their value must therefore be sought in the more plausible and interesting dynamical features to which they are supposed to give rise.

In this respect, the model developed by Rose (1967) is the most interesting one. It is kept two-dimensional by simplifying the money-market and interest-rate determination appropriately, whereas Keynes–Wicksell models of monetary growth in general need at least three dynamical laws when they are set up as complete models of monetary growth (see Fischer 1972 in this regard).[24] Keeping the dynamics two-dimensional has the advantage that global stability results can be obtained more easily than in the third dimension by assuming certain basic types of nonlinearities, and this is indeed what makes Rose's (1967) approach interesting even from today's perspective, where nonlinearities in economic behavior are receiving renewed attention.

As does the Tobin model considered in the preceding section, the Rose model assumes neoclassical smooth factor substitution, which is here represented by the following intensive form production function

$$f(l^d) = y, l^d = L^d/K, y = Y/K, f' > 0, f'' < 0, \tag{1.10}$$

instead of making use of $k = K/L$ and $x = Y/L$ as in the Solow–Tobin model. Though Rose also considers monopolistic competition, here we shall make use only of the competitive limit case of this theory of price formation. Thus, in addition to (1.10), we again assume (as in the Tobin model) the validity of the marginal productivity rule,

$$\omega = w/p = f'(l^d). \tag{1.11}$$

Money-market influences are trivialized in the Rose model by assuming that the rate of interest r is an increasing function of l^d, the labor intensity[25]

---

[24] The dynamic variables then in general are $\omega = w/p$, $m = M/(pL)$ and π.

[25] In the Tobin model (see equation (1.2) of the preceding section), we instead have $r[= \rho + \pi] = h^{-1}(m/y), m = M/(pK)$, i.e., r depends on l^d and m there.

(see Rose 1967, p. 171, for a justification of this short-cut, which is based on an endogenous money supply rule in particular).

Generalizing the simple savings function $sy = sf(l^d)$ of the Solow model, Rose assumes it to be of the form

$$s(l^d) = g(l^d, r(l^d)), s'(l^d) > 0, \tag{1.12}$$

and for investment he assumes

$$i = i(l^d), i'(l^d) > 0, \tag{1.13}$$

which he rationalizes by stating that i is a strictly increasing function of the rate of profit ρ of the model which in this context is given by

$$\rho = f(l^d) - f'(l^d)l^d = \rho(l^d), \rho'(l^d) = -f''(l^d)l^d > 0.$$

Note here, that both s and i are already calculated per unit of the capital stock K, the same as l^d and y. Note also that the rate of interest and the rate of inflation play no role in determining investment behavior (the latter also does not appear in the description of savings behavior). Investment (and saving) are thus determined solely by real magnitudes.

Since we have assumed perfect competition (or $\eta = \infty$ in the notation of Rose 1967, p. 166) we get from his general model the following special determination of price inflation

$$\hat{p} = H(i(l^d) - s(l^d)), H' > 0, H(0) = 0, \tag{1.14}$$

which states that the rate of inflation is an increasing function of the demand gap $(I - S)/K$ on the market for goods, an important ingredient of models of Keynes–Wicksell type. Similarly, wage inflation is determined by the demand gap in the market for labor $(V = L^d/L, \bar{V} = 1$ the full utilization rate of the labor force),

$$\hat{w} = G(V), G' > 0, G(\bar{V}) = 0 \text{ for } \bar{V} \in (0, 1), \tag{1.15}$$

where the function G is assumed to become steeper and steeper the farther the rate of employment departs from its fundamental position $\bar{V}$.[26] In simple economic terms, Rose's model assumes that price flexibility remains limited, while wage flexibility becomes unbounded at a certain distance from its fundamental position $\bar{V}$.

The remaining assumptions of the Rose (1967) model are

$$\hat{K} = s(l^d), \tag{1.16}$$

$$\hat{L} = n, \tag{1.17}$$

i.e., they describe the growth of the productive factors in the usual way.

[26] Which need not be the steady state position in the Rose (1967) model.

This model gives rise to the following two dynamical laws ($\omega = w/p$ the real wage):

$$\hat{\omega} = G(l^d/l) - \tilde{H}(l^d), \tilde{H}(l^d) = H(i(l^d) - s(l^d)), \tag{1.18}$$

$$\hat{l} = n - s(l^d), \tag{1.19}$$

where l^d is a strictly decreasing function of ω, namely, $l^d = (f')^{-1}(\omega)$ (see equation (1.11)).[27] It can therefore be reduced to only two – nonlinear – laws of motion for the real wage ω and for the fullemployment labor intensity l. Real wage dynamics are here driven by both excess demand in the labor market (a positive dependence) and excess demand in the market for goods (a negative dependence). This is a very interesting feature of this version of a Keynes–Wicksell model, since it is often the case in the literature (even today) that only the former disequilibrium enters the equation of real wage dynamics. Accumulation in equation (1.19), on the other hand, is described in a way that is customary for models of the Solow type. We note here that prices as well as wages are predetermined at each moment in time. Causality therefore runs from a given real wage to the thereby determined level of employment $L^d = l^d(\omega)K$, which is unusual for a *Keynesian* model of monetary growth.

Rose (1967) shows that the above model has a unique steady state, which is locally unstable if $\tilde{H}'$ is positive[28] and relatively large compared to G' at the steady state, but which is globally stable if $\tilde{H}$, the measure of price flexibility, remains bounded for all values of l^d, while the slope of G, measuring wage flexibility, approaches infinity at some distance from the steady state. This gives rise to a unique limit cycle or persistent cyclical motion in real wages and full-employment labor intensity by means of a suitable application of the Poincaré–Bendixson theorem for planar dynamical systems.

This is the employment cycle result of Rose (1967), which is derived there in a very detailed way and which is explained by him in economic terms in his section 6. We shall return to this employment cycle model in chapter 5 of this book when smooth factor substitution is added to the prototype models considered in chapters 2–4.

The locally destabilizing force of the model is a high degree of price flexibility (relative to wage flexibility at the steady state), combined with a savings and investment behavior in which investment is more sensitive to real wage changes than savings. These assumptions guarantee that the stabilizing influence of the Phillips curve G on the numerator of $\omega = w/p$ is overcome by the destabilizing influence of $\tilde{H}$ on the denominator of

[27] Rose makes use of the dynamic variable l^d in place of ω which makes the necessary calculations less straightforward.   [28] $i'(l^d) > s'(l^d)$ and $H' > 0$ and large.

$\omega = w/p$. An increase in real wages decreases goods market excess demand by so much that prices will fall faster than wages, which in turn means that real wages are further increased, etc. Note that this description only holds in the neighborhood of the steady state, since wages become more and more flexible the further the economy deviates from its steady state path. Far off the steady state, nominal wages have become so flexible, that real wage increases now exercise a negative influence on the time rate of change of real wages, since money wages now fall faster than the price level. As we have indicated above, the model thereby becomes a globally stable one, which in conjunction with the local instability produces the employment cycle that is the theme of Rose's (1967) paper.

Comparing Rose (1967) with Goodwin's (1967) famous growth cycle model furthermore suggests that the Goodwin profit squeeze mechanism is also the basic driving force in the Rose employment cycle result, but it is modified there in two ways. First, adding substitution to the model in general makes the Goodwin growth cycle converge to the steady state, i.e., it makes this model a globally asymptotically stable one. Secondly, adding the destabilizing price mechanism to the model (see above) prevents convergence to the steady state, but nevertheless ensures global stability if the wage mechanism is stronger than the price mechanism far off the steady state. The limit cycle result of Rose is therefore due to the stabilizing role of smooth factor substitution (combined with money wage flexibility) and to the destabilizing inflationary Wicksell mechanism both superimposed on the Classical growth cycle model of Goodwin.[29] This questions to some extent the label "Keynes–Wicksell" given to this model type, since the structural equations and their implications in fact appear to be more Classical than Keynesian in nature. We shall see in chapter 3 of this book that this observation holds true also in the case of the inclusion of a proper LM equation into the model, due to the Wicksellian use of IS-disequilibrium that is characteristic for all models of the Keynes–Wicksell type.

We add without demonstration that the verbal description of real wage, nominal wage, and price dynamics can be fairly complicated despite the simple structural equations of the Rose model (see also the description given in Rose 1967, p. 165, and note that the one given in Ferri and Greenberg 1989, p.51, is much too simplified). This is due to the many situations of falling and rising nominal values that can be observed in the course of this employment cycle. Note, finally, that we have equality of wage and price inflation in the steady state ω_0.

The Rose model thus differs from the Goodwin model by its more general real wage dynamics, which is backed up by a separate description

---

[29] The Goodwin growth cycle is approached by the Rose cycle for low elasticities of substitution in production and a flat $H(\cdot)$ schedule.

of nominal wage and price dynamics. This extension makes it possible for the Goodwin overshooting mechanism to be now represented by (often only) one closed orbit which is attracting all other trajectories.[30]

Keynes–Wicksell models exhibit in general an investment function that is more general than that of Rose (by including in particular interest payments as a cost of financing investment) and they explain movements in the rate of interest by means of a properly specified LM equation. Such an extension may eliminate the limit cycle from the above model in the case of a very flexible interest rate (see chapter 3). The really crucial problem for Rose's approach is, however, given by another of its omissions, namely, the accelerator expression $+\pi$ (the expected rate of inflation), in its formulation of the money wage Phillips curve mechanism[31]

$$\hat{w} = G(l^d(\omega)/l) + \pi.$$

This omission of π in the money wage dynamics is motivated by Rose (1967, p. 167) by assuming that π is a function of l^d: $\pi(l^d)$, $\pi' > 0$ which does not change the qualitative features of equation (1.15) and of the whole Rose model.

Yet, assuming the above equation in place of equation (1.15) modifies the model significantly, as we now need to specify a mechanism which explains the formation of inflationary expectations π. Doing this as in the preceding section on the Tobin model by means of $\dot{\pi} = \beta_\pi(\hat{p} - \pi), (\beta_\pi \le \infty)$ then leads to either three-dimensional dynamics (if $\beta_\pi < \infty$) or to a real wage Phillips curve $\hat{\omega} = G(l^d(\omega)/l)$ (if $\beta_\pi = \infty : \hat{p} = \pi$). The latter case of myopic perfect foresight therefore removes the destabilizing goods-market component π from the model and gives rise to a Goodwin growth cycle model with smooth factor substitution, which is known to be globally asymptotically stable, see Flaschel (1993, ch. 4).

Adding to the model the above mentioned extended investment function $i(\rho(\omega) - (r - \pi)) + n, (i' > 0)$, which refers to the real rate of interest as the appropriate determination of the costs of investment (and which has a trend term n equal to natural growth to avoid problems of steady state determination), and adding a theory of interest as in the Tobin model, i.e., a Keynesian LM equation: $M = pYh(r), h' < 0$, then gives rise to the monetary Keynes–Wicksell model as it was used in the literature after the appearance of Fischer's (1972) critique of the structural equations and the steadystate properties of Keynes–Wicksell models. Such an extension of Rose's Keynes–Wicksell employment cycle model has local stability properties that are close to those of the generalized Tobin model considered in

---

[30] We shall see in chapter 3 that Rose's assumption of smooth factor substitution is not important in this respect.

[31] Rose's result would stay intact, if one uses $+\eta\pi, \eta < 1$ in the place of $+\pi$!

the preceding section. As already stated, the local stability properties of Keynes–Wicksell models have not been carefully investigated in the literature whenever their dynamical dimension becomes larger than two,[32] so that their intimate relationship to generalized models of the Tobin type is not well-documented. Furthermore, there has been no attempt to perform a global stability analysis as in Rose (1967) for a higher dimensional Keynes–Wicksell dynamics. Interesting as the nonlinear analysis of the business cycle of Rose (1967) is in itself, it has therefore never been treated on a broader basis. Such a treatment is called for by models which truly integrate *monetary growth* and the *formation of inflationary expectations* in such an environment by means of the above LM equation, the above extended investment function and the Tobin effect in the savings function.

Summarizing, we may state that monetary growth models of Keynes–Wicksell type break with Say's Law (as they should), and establish some sort of Walras' Law by which financial assets other than money are excluded from explicit consideration (see chapter 3 for more detailed and more recent formulations). They assume LM-equilibrium as in the Tobin monetary growth model, but depart from this model by assuming a profit rate/real rate of interest-differential that drives investment decisions (see also Sargent 1987, pp.11, 83, on this point), which are then separated from savings decisions. Keynes–Wicksell models have a somewhat elaborated wage–price sector where both wages and prices are driven by corresponding demand pressure and sometimes also by appropriate cost-push terms or certain expectations about them (see Flaschel 1993, Flaschel and Sethi 1996, for a general treatment of such extended approaches). We shall provide in chapter 3 an even more general treatment of the Keynes–Wicksell prototype model which integrates Rose's (1967) nonlinear treatment with newer formulations of the wage price sector of Rose (1990) which we shall briefly consider below.

Above we have criticized Rose's (1967) formulation of the wage–price sector as being too limited with respect to cost-push terms and expectations about them. In a recent book, Rose (1990) has provided an interesting extension of this wage–price sector which by and large meets this criticism without losing the innovation his 1967 model where the real wage dynamics depend on both the market for labor *and* the market for goods. This new formulation[33] of wage–price dynamics is described by the following pair of adjustment equations or Phillips curves,[34]

---

[32] See Stein (1982) for a relatively recent, and fairly general, model of Keynes–Wicksell type for which no stability analysis is provided, even from the local point of view.

[33] See also Asada (1991) for an alternative extension of the wage price sector of a model of Keynes–Wicksell type.

[34] Slightly modified to serve our purposes in the following chapters.

$$\hat{w} = G(l^d/l) + \kappa_w \hat{p} + (1 - \kappa_w)\pi,$$
$$\hat{p} = H(i(l^d) - s(l^d)) + \kappa_p \hat{w} + (1 - \kappa_p)\pi,$$

where G and H are given as before, and where $\hat{p}, \hat{w}$ denote actual price and wage inflation and π a medium-run expected rate of inflation. The parameters κ_w, κ_p are in the interval $[0, 1]$, where the case $\kappa_w = \kappa_p = 1$ is generally excluded, since it would give rise to two independent dynamical laws for real wage determination. If this case is excluded, we can reformulate the above wage–price sector in the following way and then solve for the two variables $\hat{w} - \pi, \hat{p} - \pi$:

$$\hat{w} - \pi = G(l^d/l) + \kappa_w(\hat{p} - \pi),$$
$$\hat{p} - \pi = H(i(l^d) - s(l^d)) + \kappa_p(\hat{w} - \pi),$$

implying $(\kappa \equiv (1 - \kappa_w \kappa_p)^{-1})$,

$$\hat{w} - \pi = \kappa[G(l^d/l) + \kappa_w H(i(l^d) - s(l^d))],$$
$$\hat{p} - \pi = \kappa[H(i(l^d) - s(l^d)) + \kappa_p G(l^d/l)],$$

and therefore

$$\hat{\omega} = \hat{w} - \hat{p} = \kappa[(1 - \kappa_p)G(l^d/l) - (\kappa_w - 1)H(i(l^d) - s(l^d))].$$

We therefore get a real wage dynamics of the same type as in the original Rose model, but based now on myopic perfect foresight with respect to $\hat{w}$ and $\hat{p}$, and on a variable π which represents the state of medium-term inflationary expectations. This extension of the wage–price sector will be used in our reconsiderations of the Tobin, Keynes–Wicksell, and Keynesian prototype models and represents, in our view, the really innovative contribution of models of the Keynes–Wicksell type.

Note here also that the original Rose employment cycle determined the steady-state value of the real wage ω_0 by means of $n = s(l(\omega_0))$, which implies that we get for wage and price inflation

$$\hat{w} = G(l^d(\omega_0)/l) = \tilde{H}(l^d(\omega_0)) = \hat{p},$$

a value that is in general not zero, i.e., we may, for example, have a positive rate of inflation and also $i(l^d(\omega_0)) > s(l^d(\omega_0))$ in the steady state. The fact that the steady-state concept of Keynes–Wicksell models allows for $I \neq S$ in the steady state has been criticized by Fischer (1972), and has led to the inclusion of the accelerator term $+\pi$ in the formulation of wage–price dynamics. The above reformulation of the wage–price dynamics as in Rose (1990) is a different, or more general, answer to the problem that steady-state inflation should be compatible with the $I = S$ condition, since it is easily seen from the above that $\hat{w} = \hat{p} = \pi$ will imply $G(l^d/l) = 0$ and $H(i(l^d) - s(l^d)) = 0$ if $\kappa_w \kappa_p < 1$ holds. This approach therefore also allows for a deviation of money supply growth μ from natural growth n without implying goods-market disequilibrium in such a case.

In sum, Keynes–Wicksell models have thus led to a reformulation of wage–price dynamics which favors the use of two symmetrically built Phillips curves instead of the one of the Samuelson–Solow (1960) type which has dominated the discussion of wage and price inflation (augmented by inflationary expectations) since the invention of the Phillips curve.

1.5   Basic AS–AD growth models

1.5.1   The so-called "Classical" model and its dynamics

Today's macroeconomic textbooks generally distinguish between the so-called "Classical" and the "Keynesian" model of a monetary economy (see McCallum 1989 for example). By this distinction is meant the model of the neoclassical synthesis of Keynesian economics which assumes perfectly flexible money wages in the first case and assumes (temporarily) given money wages in the second case. Perhaps the best presentation of this distinction is given in Sargent (1987, chs. 1, 2). We shall use his presentation in this and the next subsection to briefly present fully dynamic versions of his two (mainly static) analyses of the Classical and the Keynesian model of the neoclassical synthesis (see also Sargent 1987, p.xvii, in this regard). Our dynamic versions nevertheless simply analyze what is already contained in Sargent's (1987) chapters 1, 2, and 5 by putting together the dynamic elements he proposes at various occasions in his book. In this way, complete models of this Classical and Keynesian prototype are obtained which can then be judged with respect to their implications and their true generality. Our findings will be that these two model types are much too narrow in their assumptions to allow for a meaningful comparison of (neo-)Classical and Keynesian dynamics (see chapters 2, 3 and 4 in this volume), even when it is admitted that asset markets and investment remain, as in Sargent (1987, ch. 1), specified in the neoclassical sense. In particular in the asset markets money is then held solely for transaction purposes, bonds are like savings deposits, equities are identified with these bonds via the perfect-substitutability assumption, and investment is of the Wicksellian type (see the preceding section), with trend term nK, guaranteeing a full employment steady state.

The crucial lacking element, one that distinguishes Classical from Keynesian versions, but which is lacking in all presentations of this distinction, is that labor *and* capital will be underutilized (or overemployed) during certain phases of the cycle. Or, to express it in an equivalent way, not only wages but also the price level adjust with finite speed. Neglecting this twofold disequilibrium situation produces a considerable bias in the Keynesian version of the "neoclassical synthesis" toward neoclassical results, as we shall show in chapters 3 and 4 (for fixed proportions), and in chapter 5 (for smooth factor substitution).

The contrast between the Classical and the Keynesian views on macrodynamics therefore only becomes really obvious (at a very elementary stage still, as we have seen in the preceding section), when there is symmetry in the assumption on wage and price flexibility in both the Classical (both infinitely flexible) and the Keynesian models (both less than infinitely flexible). By and large, this simply amounts to accepting the existence of a second Phillips curve, besides Phillips' nominal wage inflation curve – namely, one for the price level, which is to some extent independent of money wage dynamics and possibly also differently structured. This simple and plausible statement will lead to many new aspects in neoclassical and Keynesian macrodynamics, as we shall see in the body of this book. But before this task is undertaken, we have to sketch the state of the art in formulating the Classical and Keynesian models of the neoclassical synthesis which provide the dominant view on this distinction. We do this by making them truly models of monetary growth, so that they can be indeed compared to our subsequent monetary growth models.

The (completed) Classical model of Sargent (1987, ch. 1) consists of the following set of equations (see his p.20),

$$Y = F(K, L^d), w/p = F_L(K, L^d), L^d \equiv L,$$ (1.20)

$$C = C\left(Y - T - \delta K - \frac{M + B}{p}\pi + qI, r - \pi \right),$$ (1.21)

$$I = i(q - 1)K + nK, q = (F_K - \delta - (r - \pi))/(r - \pi),$$ (1.22)

$$Y = C + I + \delta K + G,$$ (1.23)

$$M = pYh(r), \hat{M} = \mu = \text{const.},$$ (1.24)

$$\hat{L}^s = n, \hat{K} = i(\cdot) + n = I(q - 1)/K,$$ (1.25)

$$\dot{\pi} = \beta_\pi(\hat{p} - \pi), 0 < \beta_\pi \leq \infty.$$ (1.26)

Equations (1.20) represent the usual neoclassical presentation of the full employment position of the labor market, including full employment output.[35] Equations (1.21) and (1.22) describe consumption and investment behavior based on an advanced notion of disposable income Y^D and

[35] To simplify the analysis of the dynamics analysis we have assumed that L is given in each moment in time.

Tobin's q. We shall follow Sargent's (1987, ch. 5) dynamic analysis of the Keynesian model in the following and conduct such dynamic analysis under the simplifying assumption $C = c \cdot (Y - \delta K - T)$ (and $I = i \cdot (F_K - \delta - (r - \pi))K + nK)$, and thus shall exclude Tobin effects (see section 1.2) and real interest or Mundell effects in the consumption function (i.e., we take $C_\pi \equiv 0, C_r \equiv 0$). Equation (1.23) is the goods-market equilibrium condition and equation (1.24) describes (again) the money-market equilibrium. Equations (1.25) describe factor growth as determined by the exogenous labor supply growing at the rate n. Equation (1.26) finally explains inflationary expectations (either adaptive expectations when $\beta_\pi < \infty$ or myopic perfect foresight when $\beta_\pi = \infty$).

The intensive form dynamics of the above model reads ($L/K = l$),

$$y = f(l), \omega = f'(l), \rho(\omega) = f(l) - \omega l, y = Y/K \text{ etc.} \tag{1.27}$$

$$y = c(y - t - \delta) + i(\rho(\omega) - r + \pi) + \delta + n + g, \tag{1.28}$$

$$m = yh(r), m = M/(pK), \tag{1.29}$$

$$\hat{l} = -i(\cdot), \tag{1.30}$$

$$\dot{\pi} = \beta_\pi(\mu - n - \hat{m} - i(\cdot) - \pi), \tag{1.31}$$

where $t = T/K, g = G/K$ are assumed constant (just as n, δ, see Sargent 1987, ch. 5). The last two equations describe the dynamics of the model, while the second and the third determine in an IS–LM fashion the temporary equilibrium variables m and r as functions of the dynamically endogenous variables l, π (which are statically exogenous). Note that y, ω and ρ are all obviously determined by the given l (at time t), so that the supply side of the model is very simple to calculate at each moment in time.

Equation (1.28) can be easily solved for the nominal rate of interest and gives

$$r \stackrel{IS}{=} \frac{c(y - \delta - t) + i(\rho + \pi) + n + \delta + g - y}{i}, y = f(l), \rho = \rho(l),$$

which implies $r = r(l, \pi), r_\pi = 1$. The other statically endogenous variable m is then simply given by $m \stackrel{LM}{=} f(l)h(r) = m(l, \pi)$ with $m_\pi = f(l)h'(r)r_\pi = f(l)h'(r)$.

For the rate of growth of the variable m we thereby get

$$\hat{m} = \frac{m_l}{m}\hat{l} + \frac{m_\pi}{m} \cdot \dot{\pi} = \frac{m_l l}{m}\hat{l} + \frac{h'(r)}{h(r)} \cdot \dot{\pi},$$

an equation which can be used to remove the $\hat{m}$ expression from the two dynamical laws for l and π.

Let us now consider in turn the cases of adaptive expectations and myopic perfect foresight. In the first situation we get from the above dynamical system,

$$
\hat{l} = -i(\rho(l) - r(l,\pi) + \pi), \rho(l) = f(l) - f'(l)l
$$
$$
= n - (1-c)f(l) - c(t+\delta) + \delta + g, \tag{1.32}
$$

$$
\dot{\pi} = \frac{1}{1 + \beta_\pi h'(r)/h(r)} \beta_\pi \left(\mu - n - \left[\frac{m_l l}{m} - 1 \right] \hat{l} - \pi \right). \tag{1.33}
$$

The second form of equation (1.32) immediately implies a globally asymptotically stable monotonic adjustment of the variable l to its steady-state value l_0, given by

$$
l_0 = f^{-1}((n + \delta + g - c(t+\delta))/(1-c)),
$$

which is completely independent of the π dynamics. The partial derivative of $\dot{\pi}$ with respect to π at the steady state, on the other hand, is given by

$$
\dot{\pi}_\pi = \frac{-1}{1/\beta_\pi + h'(r_0)/h(r_0)}, r_0 = r(l_0, \pi_0), \pi_0 = \mu - n.
$$

It is therefore negative for all $\beta_\pi < -h(r_0)/h'(r_0)$, and positive for all $\beta_\pi > -h(r_0)/h'(r_0)$ (and ill-defined in between).

Shocks $\Delta\mu$ in the growth rate μ of the money supply M therefore leave the real part of the steady-state solution unchanged, while the expected rate of inflation converges to the new steady-state value of the rate of inflation in the first of the above cases and diverges from it towards $\pm\infty$ according to $\Delta\mu > 0, <0$. This is all that happens in this monetary growth model in response to changes in the growth rate of money supply. Of course, shocks to the monetary part of the economy are somewhat more difficult to analyze, as one then has to treat the nonautonomous system

$$
\dot{\pi} = d(l(t), \pi),
$$

where d is the function on the right hand side of equation (1.33) and where $l(t)$ is given by the solution of (1.32).

This, however, does not prevent the general result that the steady state of the dynamical system (1.32), (1.33) is a saddlepoint for all adjustment speeds of the adaptive expectations mechanism that are chosen sufficiently high. As an economic model these dynamics are therefore incompletely specified in the case of fast adaptive expectations and hence the model needs further assumptions on its behavior far off the steady state. Such assumptions are, however, not discussed by the authors who consider the Classical version of the neoclassical synthesis to be a meaningful description of economic states and dynamics. Furthermore, even when this dynamic model is made an economically meaningful (that is to say a viable) one,[36] its dichotomizing dynamics will be of a very restrictive nature, the descriptive value of which may be very much doubted.

But advocates of such Classical models usually do not favor the assumption of adaptive expectations, so they may escape from the above conclusions by assuming the much more favored situation of myopic perfect foresight in the place of this purely backward-looking expectations mechanism. Let us therefore consider also this second case of expectations formation.

In this case, one has, because of $\pi = \hat{p}$, the following new relationships which determine now the dynamics of m by describing a locus of admissible $\dot{m}$–m combinations.[37]

$$y(l) = c(y(l) - \delta - t) + i(\rho(l) - h^{-1}(m/y(l)))$$
$$+ \mu - n - \dot{m} + \hat{l}) + n + \delta + g,$$

where $\hat{l}$ is again given by

$$\hat{l} = n - (1 - c)f(l) - c(t + \delta) + \delta - g,$$

i.e., a Solovian description of the process of real growth that is independent of the development of monetary variables. The above determination of the $\dot{m} - m$ relationship implies a functional form for this relationship of the following type:

$$\dot{m} = e(m, l), e_m > 0, e_l \gtreqless 0.$$

When this last dynamical law is taken together with the l dynamics (given above), we again obtain a dichotomizing system with an independent Solovian real growth process and a saddlepath situation (which implies complete instability, as in the case of fast adaptive expectations) for the monetary sector, *if* the above dynamics are solved by means of historically given values for the monetary variable m. Since Sargent and Wallace (1973, see also Sargent 1987, I.9), it has however become the fashion to solve such a dynamical law in a purely forward-looking way by means of an appropriate terminal condition. This is known to work if the function h is a linear function and it makes m a jump-variable which jumps whenever such a jump is needed for the fulfillment of the terminal condition. In the case of a jump in M, however, no jump in m is needed, but just a jump in the price level p (and w) such that m can remain constant, implying neutrality for the considered Classical monetary growth dynamics.

Also, a jump $\Delta\mu$ in μ will only modify the dynamical law for the variable m in the following way,

$$\dot{m} = e(m, l) - i\Delta\mu.$$

---

[36] This means that the trajectories of the dynamics stay within economically meaningful bounds.   [37] $\hat{p} = \mu - n - \dot{m} + \hat{l}, \hat{l} = n - \hat{K}.$

Such a jump will thus be superneutral (since there is no effect on $\dot{k}$ as in the Tobin model) due to the restrictive concept of disposable income here used. Therefore, the nominal magnitudes p and w together with m are but a fairly arbitrary appendage to the Solovian growth model and the $\hat{l}$-dynamics surrounding its steady state. This may be a happy state of affairs from a strictly neoclassical point of view, but – in our view – it is mainly a quite extreme and restricted type of dynamical system which is devoid of any interesting proposition on economic dynamics and monetary growth. Advocates of the Classical approach to macrostatics and macrodynamics should be capable of formulating a richer dynamics than the one we have discussed above, even in the deterministic case and on the "textbook" level considered here.

Sargent (1987, ch. 3) also considers the Tobin variant of the Classical model, the purely Classical model where investment (and the money market) need not be adjusted to a given state of aggregate supply (such that Keynesian IS–LM analysis is formally present), but where we again have Say's Law $\dot{K} = I \equiv S = Y - \delta K - C - G$ in its "real" form. In this case, bonds and real capital are perfect substitutes (and equities are no longer needed), so that we then have

$$\rho(l) + \pi = r, \rho(l) = f(l) - f'(l)l.$$

In this case, the $\hat{m}$ dynamics is even simpler and determined by

$$m = f(l)h(\rho(l) + \mu - n - \hat{m} + \hat{l}),$$

where $\hat{l}$ and $l(t)$ are given as before (there is now no investment function and IS equation which must be fulfilled simultaneously). Solved for $\hat{m}$, the above equation reads,

$$\hat{m} = \mu + \rho(l) - (1 - c)f(l) + c(t + \delta) - (\delta + g) - h^{-1}(m/f(l)),$$

and it can be treated again in the Sargent and Wallace (1973) manner discussed above. This may be considered the true Classical model, and it would lead us back to Tobin's analysis if more sophisticated concepts of disposable income were inserted into it as in section 3 of this chapter.

1.5.2   The so-called "Keynesian" model and its dynamics

The Keynesian dynamical system follows from the Classical model of the preceding section in that it dispenses with the full employment assumption (for labor!) and thus allows for $l^d = L^d/K$ to be different from $l = L/K$ and for a "sluggish" money wage adjustment of the form

$$\hat{w} = H(l^d/l) + \pi, H' > 0, H(1) = 0, \tag{1.34}$$

where 1 is assumed to represent the so-called natural rate of employment (see Sargent 1987, chs. 2 and 5, for details).

The dynamical system (1.27)–(1.31) is again valid as in section 1.4 up to the modification that we now have $\hat{l} = - i(\cdot)(\neq \hat{l}^d$, which is not treated as a dynamic variable there or here). Furthermore, m is now to be defined by $M/(wK)$, so that equation (1.29) now reads $m = (f(l^d)/f'(l^d))h(r)$. Finally, the above Phillips curve (1.34) implies $\hat{m} = \mu - H(l^d/l) - \pi - i(\cdot)$, so that we end up here with a system of the temporary equilibrium variables l^d, $y = f(l^d)$, and $r(\omega = f'(l^d))$, and the dynamically endogenous variables l, m and π. Note that l^d, r are functions of these state variables by the IS–LM equations of the model and the production function $y = f(l^d)$.

This three-dimensional dynamical system, which again needs an explicit law for the dynamics of $\hat{p}$ in the case of adaptive expectations ($\dot{\pi} = \beta_\pi(\hat{p} - \pi), \beta_\pi < \infty$), has been extensively studied by Franke (1992a). Since it is implicitly defined it gives rise to a rather complicated dynamical system in the three variables l, m, and π. Just as the Classical dynamical system in section 1.3, it shares the characteristic of being ill defined at a certain value of β_π and gives rise to saddlepath dynamics as β_π approaches ∞. In between, as Franke (1992a) shows, there exists a certain value of β_π where the system undergoes a Hopf bifurcation and loses its stability in a cyclical fashion. We thus again end up with an incompletely specified economic macrodynamic model when the adjustment speed of the adaptive expectations mechanism passes a certain critical value. Sargent's (1987, ch. 5) analysis of the model bypasses all these details completely, by concentrating on the special case $\beta_\pi = 0$ in the main, where the system can be shown to be asymptotically stable (see Flaschel 1993, ch. 6).

The general conclusion that follows from this state of the art (which has not been improved since the 1979 first edition of Sargent's 1987 book) is that these Keynesian dynamics have been only poorly investigated up to Franke's (1992a) contribution. This conclusion also extends to Turnovsky's (1977a, ch. 8) analysis of such models and the literature on such descriptive Keynesian models of macrodynamics which appeared thereafter. We shall show in chapters 4 and 5 that this sort of Keynesian dynamics is indeed a bastard one, i.e., a mixture (limit case) between full capacity Keynes–Wicksell growth models and a properly specified model of Keynesian dynamics (with under- or overutilized production capacities of firms). The implication of the foregoing is that, although we still lack a clear understanding of this model type, we do not really need such an analysis in the first place. Instead, Keynes–Wicksell models as well as Keynesian ones should each first be further explored within their own consistent frameworks.

We have so far commented only on Keynesian dynamics as in Sargent

(1987, ch. 5) in the case of adaptive expectations. The alternative situation of myopic perfect foresight is considered in Flaschel (1993, ch. 7) in great detail and can, for the purposes of the following, here be characterized briefly as follows.

In the case of $\pi = \hat{p}$, it is assumed in Sargent (1987, ch. 5) that the Phillips curve $\hat{w} = H(l^d/l) + \hat{p}$ indeed defines a real-wage Phillips curve:

$$\hat{\omega} = H(l^d/l), \omega = w/p.$$

As in section 1.4 we furthermore have the dynamical equation

$$\hat{l} = n - (1 - c)f(l^d) + c(t + \delta) - \delta - g,$$

which, together with the marginal productivity rule $f'(l^d) = \omega$, then defines an autonomous real dynamics of the Solow–Goodwin growth (cycle) type. These (asymptotically stable) dynamics of the real part of the model represent only a simple extension of the purely Solovian dynamics of the Classical model of the preceding section.

As for the monetary part of the model we once again have the equation

$$y = y(l^d) = c(y(l^d) - \delta - t) + i(\rho(l^d) - h^{-1}(m/y(l^d))$$
$$+ \mu - n - \hat{m} + \hat{l}) + n + \delta + g,$$

which is subject to the same reasoning as in the preceding section, i.e., again gives rise to a further (nonautonomous) law of motion for real balances m that may (or may not) be subjected to the jump-variable technique of the "rational expectations school."

Under myopic perfect foresight, the Sargent (1987, ch. 5) version of Keynesian dynamics, where both the price level and the wage level become jump-variables as in the Classical variant of the model, thus is not really different from that of the Classical dynamics. It would therefore seem that the assumption of rational expectations blurs important distinctions between various schools of economic thought. This topic is further pursued in the following section.

1.6   The modeling of expectations

The modeling of expectations (of wage inflation, price inflation, exchange rate depreciation, etc.) plays a central role in macrodynamic modeling and certainly will play such a role in the models of this book.[38] In fact we have already seen that the dynamical behavior of the previously discussed models can be locally stable (unstable) for low (high) speeds of adjustment

---

[38] See also Chiarella and Flaschel (1998f) for further investigations of the expectational side of macrodynamic models, there extended to the treatment of open economies.

of adaptive expectations and can be of saddlepoint type when perfect foresight is assumed.

For almost a quarter of a century formal analysis and modeling in macroeconomics has been dominated by the rational expectations hypothesis. Whilst the precise meaning of the term "rational expectations" itself provokes a deal of discussion, we shall here use it in the sense defined by Turnovsky (1995). That is, that the prediction made by economic agents of a variable of interest (e.g., rate of price inflation or rate of exchange rate depreciation) be consistent with the predictions generated by the model the agents have in mind. In continuous time deterministic models the rational expectations hypothesis reduces to myopic perfect foresight. Our modeling of expectations will be at odds with this currently fashionable approach, so the purpose of this section is to explain the rationale for the expectational mechanisms we shall adopt.

Our approach stems from our view that rational expectations modeling suffers from two defects which have never been properly addressed by its proponents. One defect is of a theoretical nature, the other is of an empirical nature. In section 1.6.1 we discuss the theoretical difficulty which involves the widely used jump-variable technique. In section 1.6.2 we review the body of empirical evidence which we believe should cause economic theorists to question the blind application of traditional rational expectations modeling. In section 1.6.3 we outline in detail the rationale for our approach to expectations modeling in this book.

1.6.1   A critique of the jump-variable technique

As we have seen in previous sections, rational expectations (perfect myopic foresight) models usually display a saddlepoint instability. The jump-variable technique was introduced by Sargent and Wallace (1973) to circumvent this troublesome feature. In essence they argued that the variable on which expectations of changes are being formed (e.g., price or exchange rates) must be able to jump discontinuously at a certain point in time in order to allow the economic variables of the system to reach a stable manifold of the saddlepoint. Thereafter, the system dynamics would lead to the equilibrium point of the model.

Sargent and Wallace expounded the jump-variable technique within the context of the simple Cagan monetary model (again see Turnovsky, 1995, ch. 3). The technique was generalized by a number of authors to handle larger models, as discussed in Buiter (1984). In larger models an issue of nonuniqueness also arises since there may be more than one way to set the economic variables onto a stable manifold, depending upon the relationship between the number of stable and unstable roots and the number of available jump-variables. These issues are discussed by Blanchard and Kahn (1980) and McCallum (1983).

As a result of the rational expectations revolution the previously widely used adaptive expectations mechanism was largely abandoned as it was perceived to be a "backward-looking" mechanism. Furthermore, under adaptive expectations economic agents are allegedly making consistent forecast errors about which they do nothing. It should be pointed out that in the early stages of the development of the jump-variable techniques for solving rational expectations models some concerns were expressed about the lack of any theory to explain the jump in economic variables as well as the arbitrariness in the selection of the jump-variables in larger-scale models. Some of these issues were articulated by Burmeister (1980).[39]

In spite of any of the foregoing lingering doubts, the rational expectations viewpoint has come to dominate in macroeconomic modeling. Expectational schemes such as adaptive expectations or variants of it came to be perceived as somehow "irrational."

In our critical reappraisal of the jump-variable techniques we shall argue that, if the economic variables are allowed to follow the unstable paths that exist under both adaptive expectations and rational expectations, then economic forces will eventually come into play that stabilize the motion of the economic variables towards an attractor on which they exhibit self-sustaining endogenous fluctuations. The exact nature of the attractor depends on the dimension of the model under consideration. When one allows expectations to tend to the perfect foresight (rational expectations) limit in this framework, we see that it is the expectational variable which jumps discontinuously. However in our framework this jump is imposed by the system dynamics rather than being arbitrarily imposed by the economic model builder.

We expound the discussion of the standard approach to the jump-variable technique within the framework of the Cagan model of monetary dynamics. We choose a version which allows for lagged portfolio adjustment in the money market. We do this in order to make more explicit the saddlepoint structure of the dynamics. The classical discussion of this model (see, e.g., Turnovsky 1995) assumes instantaneous portfolio adjustment, in which case the saddlepoint structure becomes degenerate in a certain sense. We should also point out, however, that there are good theoretical and empirical reasons for assuming lagged portfolio adjustment (see, e.g., Tsiang 1982, Kearney and MacDonald 1985).

---

[39] In this connection it is also worth recalling the comment of Blanchard (1981, p.135) who, in applying the jump-variable technique to the value of the stock market, states: "Following a standard if not entirely convincing practice, I shall assume that q always adjusts so as to leave the economy on the stable path to equilibrium."

Our version of the Cagan monetary dynamics model is expressed as

$$m^d = p + f(\pi),\tag{1.35}$$

$$m^s = m,\tag{1.36}$$

$$\dot{p} = \beta_p(m^s - m^d) = \beta_p(m - p - f(\pi)),\tag{1.37}$$

$$\dot{\pi} = \beta_\pi(\dot{p} - \pi).\tag{1.38}$$

Here $m = \ln M$ ($M = $ nominal stock of money), $p = \ln P$ ($P = $ price level), $\pi = E(\dot{p}) = $ expected rate of price inflation, and β_p, β_π are speeds of adjustment of price and inflationary expectations respectively.

The money demand function f is assumed to satisfy $f' < 0$. For the moment we simply assume

$$f(\pi) = -a\pi, \ (a > 0),\tag{1.39}$$

which is the standard assumption in the traditional jump-variable literature. However, we shall have more to say about the specification of the money demand function later.

We have deliberately specified the expectations mechanism (1.38) as adaptive. However, by setting the speed of adjustment $\beta_\pi = \infty$ we can recover the perfect foresight limit

$$\pi = \dot{p}.\tag{1.40}$$

Under adaptive expectations the system (1.35)–(1.38) reduces to the two-dimensional dynamical system

$$\dot{p} = \beta_p(m - p + a\pi),\tag{1.41}$$

$$\dot{\pi} = \beta_\pi(\beta_p(m - p) + (\beta_p a - 1)\pi).\tag{1.42}$$

Under perfect foresight ($\beta_\pi = \infty$), (1.41) and (1.42) reduce to the one-dimensional system

$$\dot{p} = \frac{1}{(a - 1/\beta_p)}(p - m).\tag{1.43}$$

Note first of all the equilibrium values

$$\bar{p} = m, \bar{\pi} = 0\tag{1.44}$$

under both expectation schemes.

In the following analysis we consider only the case

$$a - 1/\beta_p > 0,\tag{1.45}$$

on the argument that the speed of price adjustment is quite high. We note in this regard that the traditional discussion (e.g. Turnovsky 1995) sets $\beta_p = \infty$.

The eigenvalue structure of the adaptive expectations system (1.41)–(1.42) is easily calculated to be

$$\lambda_1^{a.e.}, \lambda_2^{a.e.} = \frac{\beta_\pi \beta_p \varepsilon}{2}\left[1 \pm \sqrt{1 - \frac{4}{\beta_\pi \beta_p \varepsilon^2}}\right], \tag{1.46}$$

where
$$\varepsilon \equiv a - 1/\beta_p - 1/\beta_\pi.$$

Since we are interested in this section in the limit $\beta_\pi \to \infty$, we assume β_π is sufficiently large that $\varepsilon > 0$. We also assume that $\beta_\pi \beta_p$ is sufficiently large that λ_1, λ_2 are real. Thus, for β_π sufficiently large, both eigenvalues are positive and the equilibrium is an unstable focus. This behavior is also illustrated in the phase diagram figure 1.1.

Note that as $\beta_\pi \to \infty$ the eigenvalues behave like

$$\lambda_1^{a.e.}, \lambda_2^{a.e.} = \frac{1}{\varepsilon}, \left(\beta_\pi \beta_p \varepsilon - \frac{1}{\varepsilon}\right). \tag{1.47}$$

Thus, as the perfect foresight limit is approached, one eigenvalue remains positive but finite, whilst the second becomes an infinitely large positive number. This behavior is indicated in figure 1.1 by the vector field with double arrowheads. In the perfect foresight limit all trajectories move infinitely quickly in the π direction to the left or right depending on the relation of the initial value to the line $\dot\pi = 0$.

Now consider the one-dimensional perfect foresight system (1.43). Its eigenvalue is given by

$$\lambda^{p.f.} = \frac{1}{a - 1/\beta_p} > 0. \tag{1.48}$$

We note from (1.47) that

$$\lambda^{p.f.} = \lambda_1^{a.e.}(\beta_\pi = \infty),$$

consistent with the view that perfect foresight is the limiting case of adaptive expectations.

Clearly the dynamic behavior under perfect foresight is unstable. The dynamics are illustrated in figure 1.2.

We see that all trajectories except the one satisfying $p(0) = m$ are unstable. It is assumed that previously the economy was settled at the equilibrium $\bar p$ and that at $t = 0$, money supply has increased to m to create the new equilibrium $\bar p = m$. The jump-variable technique asserts that economic forces will come into play such that the price level will jump discon-

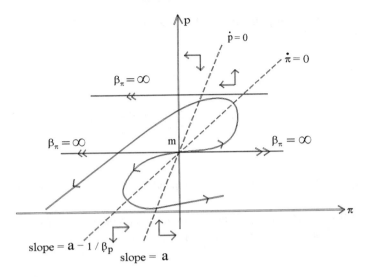

Figure 1.1 Phase diagram of the dynamics under adaptive expectations

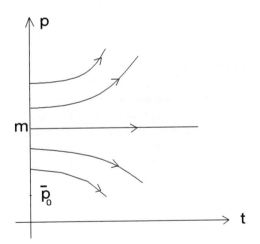

Figure 1.2 Instability in the perfect foresight limit

tinuously from $\bar{p}_0$ to m at $t = 0$ so as to place the economy on the stable manifold

$$p(t) = m, \forall t.$$

This solution to the instability problem is conceptualized (justified) by the procedure of integrating equation (1.43) forward over the interval $(t, T)(T > t)$. Thus

$$p(t) = [p(T)e^{-T/\varepsilon}]e^{t/\varepsilon} + \frac{1}{\varepsilon} \int_t^T e^{(t-s)/\varepsilon} m(s) ds$$

$$= [me^{-T/\varepsilon} + (p(0) - m)]e^{t/\varepsilon} + \frac{1}{\varepsilon} \int_t^T e^{(t-s)/\varepsilon} m(s) ds. \qquad (1.49)$$

Letting $T \to \infty$

$$p(t) = [p(0) - m]e^{t/\varepsilon} + \frac{1}{\varepsilon} \int_t^\infty e^{(t-s)/\varepsilon} m(s) ds. \qquad (1.50)$$

Sargent and Wallace (1973) argue that $p(t)$ must remain bounded as $t \to \infty$. It is clear that this can only be the case if

$$p(0) = m,$$

which again corresponds to the price jump $\bar{p}_0 \to m$ in figure 1.2. Now (1.50) reads

$$p(t) = \frac{1}{\varepsilon} \int_t^\infty e^{(t-s)/\varepsilon} m(s) ds, \qquad (1.51)$$

which is the so-called "forward looking" solution of the rational expectations approach. Through it, knowledge of future changes in m can be impounded into prices at time t. This forward-looking or anticipating behavior is claimed as one of the great advantages of the rational expectations approach. However at this point we want to stress that all of this is crucially dependent on the market/economic agents in this economy being able to compute precisely and instantaneously the required jump $\bar{p}_0 \to m$ at $t = 0$. This in turn requires economic agents to have, or behave as if they have, complete knowledge of the model of the economy that they inhabit. For this reason we would argue that the "forward-looking" solution in relation to equation (1.58) should more appropriately be termed the "full knowledge of the model" solution.

Some of the weaknesses of the jump-variable technique were well recognized by its early proponents. First of all it requires on the part of economic agents complete knowledge of the model, instantaneous and low cost access to market data, and a high degree of (low cost) computational power. These are required if the agents are to be able to compute $\pi = \dot{p}$ at each t (this assumes no information lags) and to compute precisely the jump $\bar{p}_0 \to m$. This latter calculation becomes more demanding the larger is the model. Furthermore, if the model contains some nonlinearity the

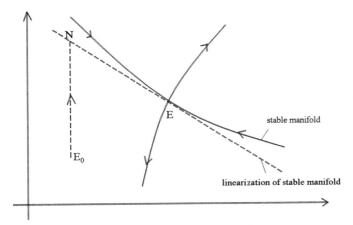

Figure 1.3 Jump to linearization of stable manifold

calculation of the stable manifold becomes a further nontrivial computational problem faced by the economic agents. It will not suffice to jump onto the linearization of the stable manifold since trajectories starting on it will be unstable as shown in figure 1.3.

Secondly, there is no theory to explain the jump $\bar{p}_0 \rightarrow m$. Somehow the market makes it happen. If the jump occurs at time t_0 then the model under discussion applies for $t < t_0$ and for $t > t_0$, but at the precise point of major economic interest, $t = t_0$, the model is "switched off" and the jump, for which we have no model, occurs.

The foregoing criticisms were acknowledged by the original proponents of the rational expectations (jump-variable) paradigm. They generally seemed (implicitly) to argue that the approach was nevertheless worth pursuing as it provided a polar case, with the implication that more realistic models reflecting the informational and computational limitations of real world economic agents would not behave very differently. However, in order for the polar case to be useful, the modeling framework must enjoy a certain "robustness" property, namely, that it must have the same qualitative properties as models which are "close" to it in some topological sense.

An important, but unfortunately ignored, criticism of the jump-variable technique has been made by George and Oxley (1985) and Oxley and George (1994). They make the point that the jump-variable technique yields a structurally unstable model. This implies that the polar case does not enjoy the robustness property referred to earlier. To some extent this is a restatement of the criticism that agents need complete knowledge of the model (and its coefficients). Thus, if (in matrix notation) the real model is

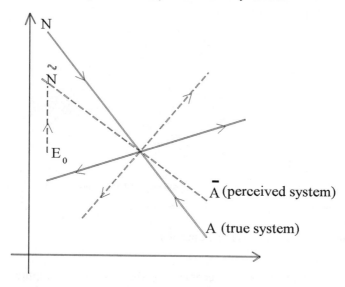

Figure 1.4   The true and the perceived system

$\dot{x} = Ax$, whereas agents due to imprecise knowledge of the coefficients perceive $\dot{x} = \tilde{A}x$, where $\| A - \tilde{A} \| < \varepsilon$ (ε some small quantity), then they will get the jump wrong and proceed on some unstable path as shown in figure 1.4; i.e., they jump from E_0 to $\tilde{N}$ instead of E_0 to N. Under the dynamics of A (the true system) the initial point $\tilde{N}$ is on an unstable trajectory.

An aspect of the jump-variable technique that has not been discussed is the very rationale for its use. This rationale seems to be that, unless it is applied, the economic variables will move off to $+\infty$ or $-\infty$ along the unstable paths of the saddlepoint. However this rationale seems to ignore totally the possibility (and indeed strong likelihood) that other economic pressures will come into play as economic quantities move further and further from their equilibrium values. Typically, the models to which the jump-variable technique is applied have in the background some story about the allocation of wealth between alternative assets. Certainly this will be the case for the models we consider in this book. Furthermore, the expectational variable usually plays a role in determining the return differential between the alternative assets. Thus, in the Cagan monetary dynamics model, the expected rate of inflation plays a role in determining the allocation of agents' wealth between money and physical capital. As the expectational variable moves far from equilibrium the allocation of wealth will move to an extreme, i.e., all in money or all in physical capital.

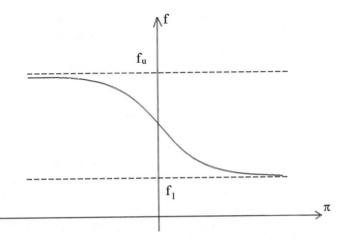

Figure 1.5   Nonlinearity in the money demand function

Thus the asset demand function must be bounded above and below as illustrated in figure 1.5 for the money demand function of the Cagan model. As $\pi \to +\infty$ money loses all value as a store of wealth and agents prefer to hold wealth in the form of physical capital. Hence money demand sinks to some minimum level f_l determined say by transactions demand. At the other extreme as $\pi \to -\infty$ the expected rate of price deflation is so great that agents want to hold a minimum amount of wealth in physical capital and the maximum amount possible in money. The upper limit f_u thus represents the largest fraction of wealth that it is possible to hold in the form of money.[40]

Thus we see that it is essential to model the asset demand functions as nonlinear functions. The linear (or linearized) asset demand functions of these models (e.g., equation (1.39) above) only hold close to equilibrium and fail completely in capturing these important portfolio adjustment effects. It is important to stress that these nonlinear effects do not result in some second-order effect to the dynamical picture obtained from the linearized model. Rather, they are crucial to the dynamical behavior of the model and result in a qualitatively different dynamical picture. It is here that the significance of the point about structural instability made by George and Oxley is appreciated.

In our review of the jump-variable technique we showed how perfect foresight can be viewed as the limiting case of adaptive expectations as the speed of adjustment of expectations, β_π, tends to ∞. The eigenvalue analysis of adaptive expectations with β_π sufficiently large indicated two positive

---

[40] It is also possible to arrive at such a nonlinear money demand function by using a two-period utility maximizing model, see Chiarella (1990, ch. 7).

eigenvalues. As $\beta_\pi \to \infty$, one eigenvalue tended to the one of the perfect foresight model whilst the second tended to ∞. We see from figure 1.1 that this infinite eigenvalue represents infinitely fast motion in the π direction, whereas motion in the p direction remains finite. This picture is in sharp contrast with that from the jump-variable technique which *imposes* an infinitely fast movement on p at $t = 0$. The infinitely fast eigenvalue is hidden from sight in any analysis which starts from the perfect foresight model (i.e., equation (1.43)). The fact that the one-dimensional system (1.43) is the limiting case of the two-dimensional system (1.41)–(1.42) has not been appreciated in the literature. There is, in fact, a mathematical theory of such dynamical systems which "lose" a dimension as the coefficient on a derivative term tends to zero (i.e., as $1/\beta_\pi \to 0$ in equation (1.42)). These are known as singularly perturbed systems, and an excellent account for our purposes is given by Andronov, Vitt, and Chaikin (1966, chapter 10). The important point that emerges from this theory is that, to obtain the true dynamic picture of the lower dimensional system (i.e. (1.43)), it is necessary to consider the higher dimensional system (i.e., (1.41)–(1.42)) and proceed to the limit (i.e., $\beta_\pi \to \infty$).

Analysis of the dynamical system (1.37)–(1.38), when the money demand function has the qualitative shape in figure 1.5, yields the phase diagram shown in figure 1.6. Chiarella (1986, see also Flaschel and Sethi 1999), has shown that, for β_π sufficiently large, trajectories are attracted to the stable limit cycle. Furthermore, in the perfect foresight limit as $\beta_\pi \to \infty$ the limit cycle tends to a limiting limit cycle or relaxation cycle as shown in figure 1.6. On this perfect foresight relaxation cycle prices move continuously, but nonsmoothly, and expectations move discontinuously, as shown in figure 1.7, which illustrates motion from the initial point. A more complete discussion of the economics behind figures 1.6 and 1.7 is given in Flaschel (1993).

1.6.2   The empirical evidence

The empirical literature on expectations formation that we review is drawn from studies of foreign exchange markets. This choice reflects the wide availability of data for such markets. However, our choice is also guided by the consideration, that if there is any market in which the rational expectations view should hold, it is the foreign exchange market. This market is highly liquid, not dominated by any one, or group of, economic agents, and information in it and about it is disseminated very rapidly indeed. We first discuss papers which study survey data of exchange rate expectations and then an econometric study based on a structural open economy macroeconomic model.

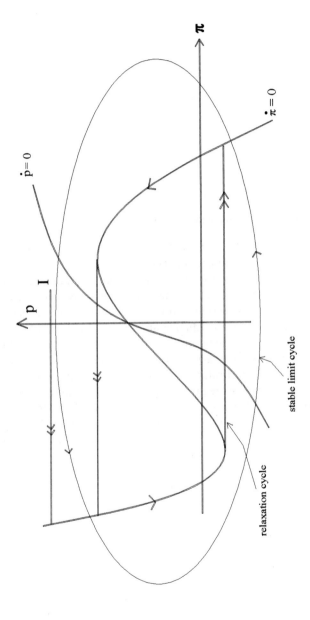

Figure 1.6 Relaxation oscillation in inflationary expectations

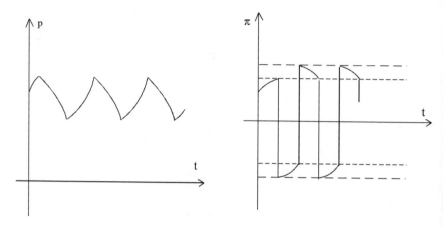

Figure 1.7   Time series presentation of the relaxation oscillation

Cagan (1991) analyses weekly data on forward mark–pound exchange rates for 1921–1923. He finds that predicted changes in the spot rate based on these forward rates are biased downward substantially and do not pass the standard tests of rationality.[41] He further finds that adaptive expectations outperform rational expectations during this period. Cagan suggests that this could be explained by a gradual adaptation of the market to the new volatile regime of German hyperinflation. Cagan's comment that, "if the coefficient[42] were to become large enough, the adaptive formula approaches the strict definition of rational expectations" is quite consistent with the modeling viewpoint we are proposing, namely, to analyze rational expectations (perfect foresight) as the limit of adaptive expectations as the speed of adjustment goes to infinity. The studies of Frankel and Froot (1987, 1990) use various survey data of exchange rate expectations and perform various tests of the rationality of expectations formation. They find evidence of systematic expectational errors and the operation of some kind of adaptive scheme. They also conclude that heterogeneous expectations play an important role in determining market dynamics. In particular, they suggest that the simultaneous existence of fundamentalist (i.e., adjusting expectations to a long-run equilibrium) and chartist (i.e., adjusting expectations to recent price trends) elements may more realistically characterize the operation of foreign exchange markets. Allen and Taylor (1990) come to a similar conclusion.

Motivated by the study of Frankel and Froot, Papell (1992) estimates a stylized version of the Dornbusch (1976) model of exchange rate dynamics.

---

[41] I.e., that under rational expectations, prediction errors are unbiased and serially uncorrelated for successive data points.   [42] I.e. coefficient of adaptive expectations.

He formulates the model under both rational expectations and adaptive expectations. The model is estimated for seven countries and he is unable to distinguish econometrically between adaptive expectations and rational expectations. This econometric evidence is also consistent with our view of casting the modeling of expectations within an adaptive expectations framework and treating rational expectations/perfect foresight as a limiting case. Papell's empirical results would be consistent with the estimated value of β_π[43] being large but less than infinite.

1.6.3 Heterogeneous expectations

In view of the empirical evidence of Frankel and Froot and Allen and Taylor discussed in the last subsection, we seek to model expectations as a weighted average of fundamentalist and chartist elements. We do so in almost the simplest manner possible, but do indicate how this approach could be elaborated upon considerably.

We develop our heterogeneous approach to expectations modeling within the context of the Cagan monetary dynamics model. However, we will apply the same general approach to other expectations schemes used in this book.

We use subscript 1 to denote the group of economic agents who form expectations using chartist (i.e., technical analysis or time series) techniques and subscript 2 to denote the second group of economic agents who form expectations using fundamentalist (i.e., theory/model based) techniques.

Considering first the chartists, the simplest type of rule they could follow is described by the adaptive expectations scheme

$$\dot{\pi} = \tilde{\beta}_{\pi_1}(\hat{p} - \pi_1).^{44} \tag{1.52}$$

On the other hand, the fundamentalists would form expectations in a forward-looking way according to

$$\dot{\pi} = \tilde{\beta}_{\pi_2}(\hat{p}^* - \pi_2), \tag{1.53}$$

where $\hat{p}^*$ is the fundamentalists' view on the long-run or equilibrium rate of inflation. This could be based on some model of the economy or the so-called p-star inflation rate theory.[45]

---

[43] A direct comparison with Papell is difficult as his expectation variable is on the level of exchange rates rather than on the change in exchange rates as in Dornbusch's and our own approaches.

[44] A far more general class of rules would be $\pi(t) = \int_{-\infty}^{t} \Omega(t - s)\hat{p}(s)ds$, where Ω is, for example, some kind of exponential weighting function.

[45] The p-star inflation rate theory as it is used by the FED or the German Bundesbank is based on the quantity theory of money and the concept of potential output, which is used to estimate the p-star price level by means of this theory (see chapter 6 for details).

We assume the proportions of chartists and fundamentalists to be fixed at α and $(1 - \alpha)$.[46] Thus the average expected rate of inflation, π, is given by

$$\pi = \alpha\pi_1 + (1 - \alpha)\pi_2, (0 \leq \alpha \leq 1). \tag{1.54}$$

From (1.52) and (1.53), and performing some manipulations, we find that

$$\dot{\pi} = \tilde{\beta}_{\pi_1}(\dot{p}^a - \pi) + (\tilde{\beta}_{\pi_2} - \tilde{\beta}_{\pi_1})(1 - \alpha)(\dot{p}^* - \pi_2), \tag{1.55}$$

where $\dot{p}^a = \alpha\dot{p} + (1 - \alpha)\dot{p}^*$.

We note that, in order to obtain an aggregated expectations mechanism that only depends on aggregate expectations, we need to set

$$\tilde{\beta}_{\pi_1} = \tilde{\beta}_{\pi_2} \equiv \tilde{\beta}_{\pi}, \tag{1.56}$$

in which case (1.55) reduces to

$$\dot{\pi} = \alpha\tilde{\beta}_{\pi}(\dot{p} - \pi) + (1 - \alpha)\tilde{\beta}_{\pi}(\dot{p}^* - \pi). \tag{1.57}$$

By setting $\alpha\tilde{\beta}_{\pi} = \beta_{\pi_1}$ and $(1 - \alpha)\tilde{\beta}_{\pi} = \beta_{\pi_2}$ we obtain the aggregate expectations mechanism

$$\dot{\pi} = \beta_{\pi_1}(\dot{p} - \pi) + \beta_{\pi_2}(\dot{p}^* - \pi). \tag{1.58}$$

This mechanism, and possible extensions of it, will be employed throughout the book. It has the analytical advantage that it allows us to ignore the laws of motion of individual expectations π_1 and π_2.

We note in passing that the proportion of chartists is given by

$$\alpha = \frac{\beta_{\pi_1}}{\beta_{\pi_1} + \beta_{\pi_2}}$$

in this particular form of our aggregate expectations mechanism. A mechanism of this type has been employed by Groth (1988) in his study of the consequences of a combined adaptive and forward looking expectations scheme.

For most of our dynamic models in this book we shall simply take $\dot{p}^*$ to be π_0, the steady state equilibrium level of π, so that (1.58) specializes to

$$\dot{\pi} = \beta_{\pi_1}(\dot{p} - \pi) + \beta_{\pi_2}(\pi_0 - \pi). \tag{1.59}$$

In chapter 4, however, we shall use the full p-star concept as used by the FED of the United States of America or the German Bundesbank in order to represent the forward-looking component in the average expectations formation.

Equation (1.59) nests many special cases which are considered in the

---

[46] A more complete and satisfactory treatment would allow their proportions to evolve according to the success of the two predictors in the recent or more distant past. We return to this point later.

literature. Thus, $\beta_{\pi_2} = 0$ (i.e., $0 < \beta_{\pi_1}, \alpha = 1$ so that chartists dominate) yields adaptive expectations. The case $\beta_{\pi_1} = 0, 0 < \beta_{\pi_2}$ (i.e., $\alpha = 0$ so that fundamentalists dominate) yields modified regressive expectations.[47] The case $\beta_{\pi_1} = \infty, \beta_{\pi_2} < \infty$ (i.e., $\tilde{\beta}_\pi = \infty, \alpha = 1$, so that chartists dominate and have infinitely fast speed of adjustment) corresponds to myopic perfect foresight. Finally the case $\beta_{\pi_2} = \infty, \beta_{\pi_1} < \infty$ (i.e., $\tilde{\beta}_\pi = \infty, \alpha = 0$, so that fundamentalists dominate and have infinitely fast speed of adjustment) corresponds to asymptotically rational expectations (see Stein 1982).

As we have mentioned earlier, a more complete treatment of expectations would allow the fraction α of chartists to evolve according to the dynamic evolution of the key economic quantities. Approaches to such a more complete treatment have been explored by both Brock and Hommes (1997) and by Sethi (1996). The task of integrating such evolutionary expectations mechanisms into the models discussed in this book remains an important topic for future research. A preliminary analysis has been undertaken by Chiarella and Khomin (1999).

1.7 A new integrated approach to Keynesian monetary growth

Now that we are near the close of this chapter, let us briefly summarize what we have claimed will be the achievements of this book on Keynesian monetary growth dynamics.

1.7.1 The basic Keynesian prototype model: IS–LM growth dynamics

Progress in our modeling of this type of growth analysis takes its point of departure from Sargent's (1987, part I) framework for macroeconomic model building with its three sectors (households, firms, and the government) and its five markets (labor, goods, money, bonds,[48] and equities[49]) and also from our generalized growth models of Tobin and Keynes–Wicksell variety. These model types are also investigated, although from a different point of view, in Sargent (1987, part I), the latter type in the limit situation of perfectly flexible prices.

The AS–AD growth model is generally considered as allowing for two important variants (here discussed in section 1.5) namely the classical variant with perfectly flexible prices and wages and the Keynesian variant with only sluggish changes in the money wage due to labor market imbalances and inflationary expectations. The proper Keynesian variant of this

---

[47] We use the term modified regressive expectations, as in the language of Dornbusch (1976) regressive expectations would read $\hat{\pi} = \beta_{\pi_2}(\pi_0 - \hat{p})$.
[48] As the instrument of finance of the government.
[49] As the instrument of finance of the firm.

approach, however, should, as we have seen, integrate capacity utilization problems of firms and exhibit sluggishness not only with respect to wages, but also with respect to prices. This model type will considered in detail in chapter 4.

A simple change and extension of the AS–AD growth model type seems therefore to be sufficient in order to arrive at a proper and internally consistent Keynesian model, now of IS–LM growth with prices responding sluggishly to imbalances in the market for goods (measured by the rate of capacity utilization within firms) and expectations on wage inflation. Yet this stage of disequilibrium growth theory demands one further change in the setup of the model, since the varying degree of capacity utilization of firms should now also be taken into account in their investment behavior.

From a formal perspective, these are small, but nevertheless unavoidable, changes in the overall structure of AS–AD growth models typically used for analyzing the growth of monetary economies from a Keynesian perspective. Yet, as chapter 4 will demonstrate, the dynamical analysis of processes of monetary growth is considerably changed thereby, particularly in comparison to the predecessor model of Keynes–Wicksell type of chapter 3. There is thus a significant qualitative change involved when going from the Keynes–Wicksell (or the limiting AS–AD) growth model to the IS–LM growth model, with its typical wage–price spiral of demand-pull and cost-push type. This gives the reason why we call this IS–LM growth model the fundamental Keynesian prototype model of monetary growth, inflation, and fluctuations in the utilization rates of both capital and labor, while its predecessor models of Keynes–Wicksell or AS–AD type are considered as still incomplete from a Keynesian perspective. We shall furthermore show in chapter 5 (and chapter 4) that it is not difficult to incorporate into this Keynesian prototype model smooth factor substitution (and technological change, more elaborate taxation schemes, more complex wage–price spirals) in order to make it at least as general as the AS–AD growth model that preceded it.

1.7.2   The Keynesian working model: Keynes–Metzler monetary growth dynamics

There are, however, some features of this basic as well as general Keynesian prototype model observed in chapter 4 which suggest that there are still some fundamental problems present in this model type. Using the dynamic multiplier process as a further justification of the temporary IS–LM equilibrium position indicates stability problems for this equilibrium position for certain sets of parameter values. Furthermore, there are three possible scenarios for these parameter values with quite different comparative static properties of the IS–LM equilibrium which (to some extent) are separated from each other through discontinuities in the model's behavior. This suggests that ways have to be found by which the partial instability of the dynamic multiplier process can be integrated and overcome without leading to particular situations where the model is ill defined.

Chapter 6, the core chapter of the book, which finally presents the fundamental working model of our Keynesian monetary growth analysis, integrates and thereby removes the observed multiplier instabilities (working in the background of the model of chapter 4) by just taking note of one simple implausibility left in the model of this chapter, namely its asymmetric treatment of the adjustment speeds of wages and prices on the one hand (which are finite), and that of quantities on the other hand (which – due to the assumed goods market equilibrium – is infinite). There is, indeed, a well-known (theoretically as well as empirically relevant) way out of this problematic asymmetry, namely, the appropriate integration of the Metzlerian inventory adjustment mechanism into the prototype model of chapter 4. Allowing in the spirit of this inventory model for disappointed sales expectations one has then to formulate how these expectations and the output decisions of firms are in fact revised (on the basis of observed sales), and this in the light of their accumulated factual inventories compared to their desired inventory level in the framework of a growing economy.

This task is solved in chapter 6 along lines proposed by Franke and Lux (1993) and Franke (1996), leading to a model that is on the one hand fairly elaborate in its price, wage, quantity, and expectations adjustment mechanisms (implying at least six laws of motion for its central state variables), but which on the other hand is still of a very traditional type as far as its basic modules (when considered in isolation) are concerned. We shall present in chapter 6 an analysis of this model of monetary growth from the perspective of appropriately isolated typical subdynamics of it, as well as from the perspective of their integrated interaction, and shall find that the isolated perspectives, often well known from the literature on Keynesian dynamics, do not properly inform us on their behavior when they are integrated and interacting with each other. This implies that there is an urgent need for a further understanding of this integrated Keynesian monetary growth dynamics, which can be satisfied in the present book only in a preliminary way.

Chapter 6 therefore supplies on the one hand an internally consistent Keynesian model of monetary growth of fairly traditional type and with a well-balanced structure, but it also shows on the other hand that we still have a very limited understanding of the working of its dynamics due to the high dimensionality involved. We have therefore arrived at a benchmark model, whose further detailed analysis is urgently needed in order to really understand the achievements of the generally low-dimensional analyses of economic dynamics of the more recent literature on (Keynesian) monetary growth.

The *Papers and Proceedings of the American Economic Review* have recently published a discussion on "Is there a core to practical macroeconomics that we should all believe?" with contributions by Blanchard (1997), Blinder (1997), Eichenbaum (1997), Solow (1997), and Taylor (1997). Our reading of this discussion is that the working model of Keynes–Metzler type we will arrive at in chapter 6 (and which we extend further on the supply side in chapter 7) provides a general prototype of an integrated (traditional type of) macrodynamics of the short, the medium, and the long run that is in many respects closely related to this discussion, also with respect to the term "practical." Our working model can at the least be used as a point of departure for the further discussion of integrated macrodynamics with demand- and supply-side features and their relationships with structural macroeconometric model building. In this regard we also refer the reader to the discussion on macroeconomic modeling in a changing world in Allen and Hall (1997).

1.7.3   The path ahead

We start the analysis of the dynamics of Keynesian monetary growth in chapter 3 with the generalized Keynes–Wicksell approach, which employs external disequilibrium concepts both on the market for labor as well as on the market for goods. Compared to this starting point, chapter 6 may be considered as the truly Keynesian completion of the project begun with these Keynes–Wicksell prototype models, since it returns to assuming disequilibrium in both external labor and external goods markets (besides allowing for endogenously determined disequilibrium within firms as measured through the rate of capacity utilization). We may therefore claim that the proper integrated model of Keynesian monetary growth, as the traditional starting and reference point for all further models of this type, has thereby been found (and is not at all easy to analyze).

Yet, the analysis of our model cannot finish at this point, though it will not be extended very much further within the scope of this book. In a final step, in chapter 7, we add to our working model with sluggish price as well as quantity adjustments an endogenous determination of natural rates of employment and growth, as well as a sluggish adjustment of the rate of employment in the light of over- or undertime work within the firm, and show that some new and interesting dynamical features will be established thereby. At least equally important, however, would have been to allow for a more elaborate structure of financial markets, or for more developed mechanisms of wage and price settings, and further important extensions or refinements of the modules of the working model listed in the final sections of chapter 7. These are, however, topics that must be left for future investigation.

1.7.4 One final methodological remark

Throughout this book we rely on models of monetary growth which are based on linear behavioral or technological relationships for as long as this is possible and meaningful.[50] This allows us to concentrate on and to investigate the existence and implications of unavoidable "natural" non-linearities first. These models generally allow an explicit calculation of temporary equilibrium positions and can often be adequately studied as to their dynamic behavior by means of eigenvalue calculations and the associated Hopf bifurcations. Specific further nonlinearities (in money demand, in investment demand, in production, etc.) should and will be introduced at a later stage and justified to some extent. They are in particular needed if globally explosive dynamics are implied through the linear version of monetary growth (with only "naturally" occurring nonlinearities), where one is of course compelled to add and to discuss the forces that may or will come about when the economy departs by too much from its steady-state position.

Despite these occurrences, the book can nevertheless be based in many of its parts on linear behavioral and technological relationships (for methodological reasons and for reasons of simplicity), and it shows in this way that there is much to do and to discuss even on this preliminary level of the analysis of the dynamics of monetary growth, where only unavoidable naturally occurring nonlinearities are taken into account.

1.8 Mathematical tools

We may say that recently, the non-market-clearing as well as the market-clearing approaches to macroeconomics apply similar technical tools in studying macrodynamics. Both borrow from recent advances in the mathematical literature on nonlinear discrete or continuous time dynamical systems. In general the dynamic analyses that exist in the literature are confined to dimensions two or three (even in continuous time) and thus

---

[50] In the case of money demand we specialize further and make use of Taylor expansions of functions with, on the one hand, output and, on the other hand, nominal interest and wealth as arguments and use in addition to that the capital stock K as a proxy for real wealth; see Chiarella et al. (1998) for a full treatment of wealth effects on the market for money as well as for goods.

much less ambitious than the continuous time dynamical systems that we are analyzing in this book as we approach the working model of Keynesian monetary growth and its extensions in chapters 6 and 7.

We want to mention the particular technical tools that are involved in our study. We use the established toolbox of local stability analysis based on linear approximations and of the global stability analysis of planar systems.

The local tools are basically given by the necessary and sufficient conditions of the Routh–Hurwitz theorem (see Gantmacher 1959, ch. 15, and Brock and Malliaris 1989, ch. 3, in particular), and they are here applied in dimensions two and three (see also the appendix to this section). As mentioned, we do, however, also investigate continuous time dynamical systems of much higher dimension. There, we can prove local asymptotic stability by approaching them from lower dimensional models where we always check at each step that the determinant has the appropriate sign for local asymptotic stability and make use of the fact that eigenvalues depend continuously on the parameters of the dynamics.

For planar systems we prove global stability (boundedness of the dynamics in appropriately chosen economic domains of the considered phase space) by making use of invariant sets to which the Poincaré–Bendixson theorem can then be applied to prove the existence of periodic motions (generally attracting limit cycles), or of (local or global) Liapunov functions which have the shape of a sink and which can also be used to characterize invariant subsets of the phase space (where often the trajectories point inwards and thus converge to the steady state). The Poincaré–Bendixson theorem is discussed in detail in Hirsch and Smale (1974, ch. 11) and Arrowsmith and Place (1990, ch. 3).[51] Both of these books also present the theory of Liapunov functions in their chapters 9 (section 3) and 5 (section 4), respectively (see also Brock and Malliaris 1989, ch. 4).

We also make use of special limit cycle configurations, so-called relaxation oscillations (or limit limit cycles), which arise when certain speeds of adjustment parameters approach infinity (see Arrowsmith and Place 1990, 4.4, Chiarella 1990, 2.6, and Strogatz 1994, 7.5).

Also, local Hopf bifurcation theory is frequently used in this book. Presentations of this material that are not too technical are provided in Guckenheimer and Holmes (1983, ch. 3), Arrowsmith and Place (1990, 5.5), Wiggins (1990, 3.1), Perko (1993), and Strogatz (1994, ch. 8).

Numerical methods and problems are discussed in Parker and Chua (1989) and by Hairer, Nørsett, and Wanner (1987), in particular in the former, with special emphasis on the treatment of chaotic systems or

---

[51] See also Wiggins (1990) and Perko (1993).

strange attractors (defined by excluding points of rest, limit cycles and quasi-periodic motion from discussion). Our calculation of bifurcation diagrams and Liapunov exponents of high dimensional dynamical systems (where nonlinearities needed to generate complex dynamics may be considerably weaker than in low dimensional systems) follows the proposals made by Parker and Chua in this respect. Strange attractors and chaotic motions are discussed in Guckenheimer and Holmes (1983), Wiggins (1990), and Strogatz (1994).

There exist meanwhile also a variety of detailed surveys on dynamical tools for economists where traditional and newer methods for analyzing nonlinear dynamics are presented and exemplified by dynamic economic models in particular. See in this regard Medio (1991, 1992), Tu (1994), Gandolfo (1997), Lorenz (1997), and Puu (1997), where the techniques discussed above are also presented and illustrated by means of examples from the economic literature.

All these sources fully cover the dynamical tools that we will use in this book and should be consulted by the reader for the details of the mathematical propositions we derive as we proceed from chapter 2 to the higher dimensional structures that we finally obtain for the working model (and its extensions) in chapters 6 and 7.

Concerning programming tools used in the numerical investigations of this book we have primarily relied on the programming language Gauss by Aptech Systems and on SND, a Windows 95 package of our own for simulating continuous and discrete time dynamical models, developed by A. Khomin (see Chiarella, Flaschel, and Khomin 1998 for further details). Occasionally we have used Locbif (see Khibnik et al. 1993) to draw bifurcation curves in two parameter spaces, and DMC by G. Gallo, (see Medio 1992), for the presentation of limit cycles and the like.

Appendix

We gather here for easy reference the details of the Routh–Hurwitz conditions for the stability of the three-dimensional dynamical system

$$\frac{d}{dt}\begin{bmatrix} x_1 \\ x_2 \\ x_3 \end{bmatrix} = J \begin{bmatrix} x_1 \\ x_2 \\ x_3 \end{bmatrix}, \tag{1.60}$$

where

$$J = \begin{bmatrix} a_{11} & a_{12} & a_{13} \\ a_{21} & a_{22} & a_{23} \\ a_{31} & a_{32} & a_{33} \end{bmatrix}. \tag{1.61}$$

We recall first that the principal minors J_i (the determinants obtained by eliminating the row and column containing a_{ii}) are given by

$$J_1 = \begin{vmatrix} a_{22} & a_{23} \\ a_{32} & a_{33} \end{vmatrix}, \quad J_2 = \begin{vmatrix} a_{11} & a_{13} \\ a_{31} & a_{33} \end{vmatrix}, \quad J_3 = \begin{vmatrix} a_{11} & a_{12} \\ a_{21} & a_{22} \end{vmatrix}.$$

The characteristic equation of the dynamical system (1.60) turns out to be

$$\lambda^3 - \text{trace } (J)\lambda^2 + (J_1 + J_2 + J_3)\lambda - \det J = 0. \tag{1.62}$$

The Routh–Hurwitz necessary and sufficient condition for the stability of the system (1.60) can be expressed as

$$\text{trace } (J) < 0,$$
$$J_1 + J_2 + J_3 > 0,$$
$$\det J < 0,$$

and

$$-\text{trace } (J)(J_1 + J_2 + J_3) + |J| > 0.$$

2 Tobinian monetary growth: the (neo)Classical point of departure

In this chapter we introduce a Classical reformulation of the Tobin (1965) model of monetary growth, with fixed proportions in production and Classical saving habits. Section 2.1 presents the standard full equilibrium version of this model type, while section 2.2 considers the money-market disequilibrium extension of it which was extensively studied in the seventies and the early eighties. By means of these reformulations of models of the literature we shall recapitulate some of the important results obtained for this monetary growth model type concerning non-superneutrality of the steady state and the pure Tobin effect, instability of the steady state due to what we call the Cagan effect in the money demand function, and certain new limit cycle results which can be built on such local instability.

The chapter then proceeds, in section 2.3, by providing some new extensions to these Tobin type models. First, since the Tobin models rely on an elaborate form of Say's Law for the market for goods, it is very easy and natural to extend the model to labor market disequilibrium. This disequilibrium is here due solely to capital shortage or abundance and is completely decoupled from the situation on the market for goods. This extension, which basically reformulates the wage–price sector of the model, generally increases the dynamic dimension of the model by two to four, since there is now room for disequilibrium fluctuations of the real wage as well as fluctuations in the growth rate of the capital stock. An important question in this context will be how cycle mechanisms known to exist for these subdynamics (which are related to the names of Goodwin and Rose) combine with the above Cagan cycle on the nominal side of the model and generate thereby more complex dynamics in comparison to such limit cycle subcases. Due to the difficulties in analyzing such nonlinear continuous time dynamics of dimension four, only some general results and a numerical investigation of the four-dimensional case will be possible here.

Section 2.4 then presents another generalization of this approach to monetary growth by extending it to include bonds and government debt and by falling back on the situation of general equilibrium for the four markets of this extended model.[1] We here investigate the consequences of alternative concepts of disposable income that have been used in the literature in models which embrace the consequences of government debt. The dynamics of the model will then again be of dimension two, and will become identical to the initial case (section 2.2) of no government debt if Barro's concept of disposable income is employed.[2]

Finally, in section 2.5 we synthesize the previous two extensions of the Tobin type models into a general neoclassical model of monetary growth with disequilibrium on money and labor markets. The intention here is not so much to provide a really general version of this model type, but rather to formulate a complete neoclassical model of monetary disequilibrium growth which is as consistent as possible, in particular with respect to the budget constraints of the various sectors of the economy. This model demonstrates that there are two paths for future developments. Either a return to its full equilibrium version as a research paradigm, which is the general viewpoint of most of the models of monetary growth of the recent past, or to develop the general disequilibrium version further by offering in particular more convincing descriptions of the particular disequilibrium situation that is responsible for price increases in the Tobin model. It is this latter viewpoint that is taken up in the next two chapters where a systematic variation of the general Tobin model is performed that finally transforms it into a proper Keynesian monetary growth model with problems of effective demand and demand pressure inflation descriptions. As an intermediate step, we shall, in the next chapter, confront the general Tobin model with a general Keynes–Wicksell model that is obtained from the literature of the seventies by again completing the model structures of that literature in the way already indicated for the Tobin model.

It is our hope that such systematic extensions and modifications of prototype models of descriptive monetary growth theory will convince the reader that there still is a high potential, which is unexploited but valuable, for future developments in these approaches. This potential has simply been ignored during the progress that has been made in the theory of monetary growth in the recent past.

---

[1] There is not yet a market for equities in the Tobin models of monetary growth, due to the lack of an independent investment function in this type of model.

[2] See Barro (1974) and Sargent (1987, I.10).

2.1 The basic equilibrium version of Tobin's model of monetary growth: superneutrality and stability?

We now start our investigation of the consequences of introducing money as an asset in a dynamic Classical framework in a Tobinian way which is here made as complete and consistent as possible by the specification of the budget constraints of all three sectors: households, firms, and the government. Note here in particular that the flow constraint of households is often represented in this type of literature by an identity of the kind $\dot{K} + (\dot{M}/p) = s_c(Y - \delta K - \omega L^d - (\dot{M}/p))$, if the expected rate of inflation equals the actual one. As the following shows, this is, however, not a good starting point for the presentation of the model, since this identity already is an aggregate of the budget restrictions of households and the government as the following discussion should make clear.

The equations of the model are:[3]

1 *Definitions (remuneration and wealth):*

$$\omega = w/p, u = \omega/x, \rho = (Y - \delta K - \omega L^d)/K, \tag{2.1}$$

$$W = M/p + K. \tag{2.2}$$

2 *Households (workers and asset holders);*

$$W = M^d/p + K^d, M^d = h_1 p Y + h_2 p K(\bar{r} - (\rho + \pi)), \bar{r} = \text{const.}, \tag{2.3}$$

$$Y_c^{De} = \rho K - \frac{M}{p}\pi - T, \tag{2.4}$$

$$C = \omega L^d + (1 - s_c)Y_c^{De}, s_w = 0, \tag{2.5}$$

$$S_p = \omega L^d + Y_c^D - C = Y - \delta K - T - C$$
$$= s_c\left[\rho K - \frac{M}{p}\pi - T\right] + \frac{M}{p}\pi, \tag{2.6}$$

$$= \dot{M}^d/p + \dot{K}^d,$$

$$\hat{L} = n = \text{const.} \tag{2.7}$$

3 *Firms (production units solely):*

$$Y = yK(= Y^p = y^p K), L^d = Y/x, y, x = \text{const.} \tag{2.8}$$

4 *Government (monetary and fiscal authority):*

$$\dot{M} = \mu_0 M, \mu_0 = \text{const.}, \tag{2.9}$$

---

[3] See pp. xxii–xxiv for the employed notation.

$$G = \bar{g}K, \bar{g} = \text{const.,} \tag{2.10}$$

$$T = G - \dot{M}/p[S_g = T - G = -\dot{M}/p]. \tag{2.11}$$

5 *Equilibrium conditions (asset markets):*

$$M = M^d[K = K^d], \tag{2.12}$$

$$\dot{M} = \dot{M}^d[\dot{K} = \dot{K}^d]. \tag{2.13}$$

6 *Say's Law on the market for goods for "full employment":*

$$\dot{K}^d = S_p + S_g = S = Y - \delta K - C - G = \dot{K}, \tag{2.14}$$

$$L^d = L[\hat{K} = n]. \tag{2.15}$$

7 *Combined adaptive and regressive expectations:*

$$\dot{\pi} = \beta_{\pi_1}(\hat{p} - \pi) + \beta_{\pi_2}(\mu_0 - n - \pi), \beta_{\pi_i} \in [0, \infty], i = 1, 2 \tag{2.16}$$

The above model is subdivided into seven sections which will reappear in all later, more extended models. The formulations of the equations in the various sections of the model are not without repetitions, repetitions by which we intend to make the contents of and the connections between these equations more transparent. This most basic of our models of monetary growth still abstracts from an independent investment behavior of firms and can thus still ignore the market for equities. In the tradition of the Tobin models of monetary growth of the seventies it also assumes that government expenditure is financed either by money or by taxes (government debt and bonds will be introduced at a later stage of modeling in this chapter).

The equations (2.1) and (2.2) in the first section provide the definitions of important macroeconomic magnitudes, namely, of the real wage ω, the wage share u (x gross output per laborer), the actual rate of profit ρ and real wealth W, which here consists of real money balances and the capital stock solely.

We assume two groups of households in all of our models, workers and asset holders (capitalists), for whom we are assuming Classical saving habits, i.e., workers do not save (constant savings propensity $s_w = 0$) while capitalists save a constant fraction (constant savings propensity s_c) of their perceived disposable income Y_c^{De}. Since we assume in chapters 2–4 fixed proportions in production (in order to simplify the exposition), and thus shall allow for (smooth) factor substitution only later on, we need such an assumption on differentiated savings habits in order to obtain a steady-state solution for such a model, which generally does not exist for fixed proportions technologies in the frequently assumed case $s_w = s_c = s$. This latter assumption furthermore is further from reality than the one we employ. Of course, assuming Kaldorian differentiated saving habits would be even better (extended possibly also to other groups of savers such as pension funds for example). This extension is, however, completely avoided in the present book and must be left for future investigations.[4]

As already indicated, the decision of workers is a trivial one here. They just consume what they get as income in the current period (ωL^d) and thereby fulfill their budget restriction in the simplest conceivable way. The decision of asset holders, by contrast, concerns, on the one hand, the allocation of their wealth between real balances (demand, M^d/p) and real capital (demand, K^d) and, on the other hand, their savings decision (the accumulation of new wealth).

Due to the wealth constraint of asset holders (see equations (2.3)), we only need to specify their stock demand M^d for money. The stock demand for real capital is then obtained as a residual from this constraint. The money demand of capitalists is here postulated as is usual in Tobin models of monetary growth. That is, it depends on gross output Y as a proxy for the volume of transactions and on the rate of return differential $\rho + \pi$ between capital holding and money holding, i.e., the rate of profit earned in production plus the expected rate of inflation (to be defined later on). Note that we here employ a linearized function for describing this demand – which in general could be of the form $M^d/(pK) = m^d(Y/K, \rho + \pi)$.

In this book, we rely on models of monetary growth which are based on linear behavioral or technological relationships for as long as this is possible and meaningful in order first to investigate the existence and implications of "natural" nonlinearities. These models generally allow an explicit calculation of temporary equilibrium positions and can often be adequately studied as to their dynamic behavior from a local perspective by means of eigenvalue calculations and the like. Specific nonlinearities (in money demand, in factor relationships, etc.) should and will be introduced and justified at later stages to some extent. Nevertheless, the book is based in many of its parts on linear behavioral and technological relationships and it shows in this way that there is much to do and to discuss even on this preliminary level of the analysis of monetary growth dynamics where only unavoidable naturally occurring nonlinearities are taken into account.

Equation (2.5) describes aggregate planned consumption C as the sum of the two components we have already described above by referring to ωL^d and Y_c^{De} as the perceived disposable income of workers and asset owners. The latter perceived income is defined in a Hicksian way, i.e., it is based on deductions that guarantee that real wealth, as defined in (2.2), stays intact should all perceived income actually be consumed. In the present simple

---

[4] See Chiarella et al. (1998) for the details of such an approach.

case this means that purchasing power losses of money balances must be replaced through deductions[5] from actual disposable income $Y_c^D = \rho K - T$ of capitalists, i.e., from profit income after taxes T. For reasons of simplicity with respect to workers' behavior, we have assumed here that all taxes are paid out of profits (just as all money is held solely by capitalists).[6]

Total private savings S_p (see equation (2.6)) is defined by total disposable income of households minus consumption: $\omega L^d + Y_c^D - C = Y - \delta K - T - C$ and, of course, here is equal to the savings of capitalists out of their perceived disposable income. The intended allocation of their savings is described by the flow magnitudes $\dot{M}^d/p$, $\dot{K}^d$ which in equilibrium, as shown below, give rise to subsequent changes in real balances $m = M/p$ ($\dot{m} = \dot{M}/p - \hat{p}(M/p)$) and real capital formation $\dot{K}(d = \text{demand})$.[7]

Finally, it is assumed in (2.7) that normal labor supply L grows with a given rate n which is also equal to the growth rate of the total population. Later in this chapter and in other chapters we shall allow for overtime work which means that the number L should not be interpreted as the maximum supply of labor hours available in the economy in the models that follow.

Section 3 of the model, (2.8), describes the behavior of firms in the most elementary way available in a two-factor world. Firms produce output with a fixed proportions (linear) technology using capital and labor inputs, the former at full capacity. That is, they face no demand constraint on the market for goods and no supply constraint on the market for labor, due to the prevalence of Say's Law on the market for goods (see (2.14)) and since there is full employment on the market for labor by assumption (as expressed in (2.15)). Note here that labor demand L^d is determined by the level of the capital stock in each period in the following simple way $L^d = yK/x$.[8]

Section 4 of the model considers the government sector. We here assume, as a slight generalization of the original Tobin approach, that money supply M grows at a constant rate μ_0 and that government expenditure is a fixed proportion of the capital stock K (and thus also of GNP Y). Taxes are then residually determined through the government budget restraint, the GBR (2.11), since the model abstracts from bond financing of government expenditures. Government savings S_g is therefore equal to the negative of the new supply of money $\dot{M}$ and is thus negative if this flow supply is positive (which will generally be the case for growing economies). In the steady state we get for the ratio $t = T/K$ the expression $\bar{g} - \mu_0 m_0$, where

---

[5] Just as in the standard treatment of the depreciation δK of the capital stock K.

[6] See appendix 2 of chapter 4 for an extension of the models of chapters 2–4, where, in particular, wage income taxation is taken into account.

[7] Note that later on m will denote $M/(pK)$ due to our general choice of notation.

[8] Note that we assume that neither firms nor workers hold money in this formulation of the model.

$m_0 = (M/(pK))_0$ which must then be constant. Taxes[9] (lump-sum and on profit income solely) thus grow just as all other real magnitudes with the natural rate of growth n in the steady state. They are (under suitable initial conditions) positive if money supply grows at a slower pace than labor supply and negative under the reversed inequality sign, in which case the extra money flow into the economy is given as a transfer to asset holders.

In section 5 of the model it is assumed that the money market (2.12) is always cleared with respect to stock demand and supply, which by the wealth constraint (2.2) implies that the stock capital market will be in equilibrium as well. This can be thought to be achieved by instantaneous price level changes, in the spirit of the quantity theory of money, for any given value of the rate of profit ρ. The value of the rate of profit ρ in turn is determined for any value of the price level p by the "full employment" assumption (2.15) on the market for labor, which basically demands the fulfillment of the condition $\hat{K} = n$ through an appropriate choice of the rate of profit ρ brought about by an adjustment of money wages (again for any given price level p).[10]

It is obvious that these two conditions interact with each other and thus jointly determine the equilibrium values of both p and ρ (and w via $\rho(\omega) = y(1 - \omega/x) - \delta$).

In addition to these asset market clearing conditions, equation (2.13) states that new supply of money will always be absorbed by (asset-holding) households. First, government can of course always issue newly printed money by purchasing commodities with it (thereby reducing the tax payments of the household sector in the present model). Secondly, it is assumed as background of the equation $\dot{M} = \dot{M}^d$ that households leave the decision to reallocate their thereby increased money holdings in their portfolio to the "next period,"[11] just accepting this additional money for the time being.[12] The government thus can here predetermine part of the nominal flows in household savings decisions, while the remainder of it is used for real capital accumulation and is determined in its real size by the above adjustments of the price level and the rate of profit. This clearly shows that

---

[9] Or, if negative, transfers.

[10] Note here that this full employment steady-state condition does not determine the level of employment which, depending on initial conditions, could in principle take on any value here.

[11] Note that there are no determining variables in the asset flow demand expressions provided here.

[12] This simplifying assumption follows from the usual procedure of continuous-time macro-dynamics to distinguish between a Walras' Law of Stocks and a Walras' Law of Flows, and is here made obvious through the use of the two symbols, e.g. $\hat{K}, \hat{K}^d$ instead of only $\hat{K}$, as is customary in the literature (see Sargent 1987, II.7, for example). In our view, a more integrated treatment of asset markets is necessary – at least in a second step – to give the investment decision $\hat{K}$ a more independent role. Since we, however, start from orthodox formulations of models of monetary growth, we will not deal with such an extension in the present book.

the decision to invest in real capital formation is here limited in its freedom by the actions of the government.

If equation (2.13) is guaranteed, it follows immediately that Say's Law for the market for goods must be true. But this latter consequence depends (as just stated) on the condition that households always accept the newly supplied money and formulate no flow demand for money that is independent of it. The consequence of this assumption is Say's Law as formulated in equation (2.14). That is, that the aggregated value of private and government savings must then be equal, on the one hand, to the intended rate of change of the capital stock $\dot{K}^d$ (i.e., the investment goods demand of asset holders) and, on the other hand, to the demand gap in the market for goods as it is described by the right hand side in (2.14) (i.e., to the supply of new capital goods). In the present model there is thus always (at any level of production) just sufficient demand to buy this production: (extra) supply always creates the (extra) demand for it. There are consequently no goods-market problems to be observed in this model type.

The final equation of the model (2.16) describes the formation of inflationary expectations π used in the definition of the rate of return differential $\rho + \pi$ as well as in the definition of disposable income Y_c^{De} of capitalists. Inflationary expectations can here be either purely backward looking (adaptive expectations) if $\beta_{\pi_2} = 0$ holds true or purely forward looking (towards the new steady state value $\mu_0 - n$ of the rate of inflation) if $\beta_{\pi_1} = 0$ holds (regressive expectations); or they may be a combination of both. Groth (1988) discusses the consequences of such a mechanism of combined adaptive forward looking expectations in the framework of IS–LM dynamics, which will enter the stage in this book when we turn to Keynesian versions of monetary growth dynamics. Groth's particular formulation of this mechanism is $\dot{\pi} = \beta_\pi(\alpha\hat{p} + (1 - \alpha)(\mu_0 - n) - \pi)$, which, however, is easily shown to be equivalent to our formulation (2.16) by setting $\beta_\pi = \beta_{\pi_1} + \beta_{\pi_2}$ and $\alpha = \beta_{\pi_1}/\beta_\pi$. Our approach may therefore also be interpreted as saying that inflationary expectations are revised in the light of their difference from a weighted average of actual short-run and actual long-run (steady-state) inflation. Of course, it may be questioned whether such an expected rate of inflation should be used in the formation of rate of return and disposable income expectations. Other proposals of closing the model with respect to expectations formation should therefore be taken into account when they appear as more appropriate for the present dynamic setup of the model. The advantage of our formulation, however, is that it is of considerable generality since it contains many cases of the literature as special cases ($\beta_{\pi_i} \in [0, \infty], i = 1, 2$).

This closes our discussion of the building blocks of our most basic model of monetary growth. We stress again that the equations which describe the behavior of households, firms and the government have been chosen in as simple a form as possible in order to allow for a most transparent treatment of the basic insights of the Tobin model of monetary growth and its discussion in the literature. However, this collection of traditionally used descriptive macrobehavioral assumptions may not yet represent the best choice in view of the budget restraints they are assumed to fulfill. From the viewpoint of consistency and also from the perspective of a micro-founded partial equilibrium analysis there may thus still exist improvements in this stylized presentation of the assumed behavior of households in particular, which are not provided in this book. Improvements in the generality of the employed framework will, however, be provided step by step throughout the book, as the discussion of the Tobin model and later of Keynes–Wicksell, Keynesian, Keynes–Metzler models, etc. proceeds. Narrow or problematic features of the overall picture of the working of the economy will thereby be overcome to a considerable degree by the close of this book, while sectoral behavioral assumptions are kept as similar as possible in order to allow for a proper comparison of the results obtained for the different model extensions and modifications considered. Their further improvement incorporating, for example, the earlier mentioned extension to differential saving habits, more elaborate expectations mechanisms, and a more integrated treatment of asset markets will, however, here be left for future research.[13]

Having constructed a monetary growth model with Tobinian as well as Classical features we have now to proceed to the analysis of this model. This task involves the consideration of its temporary equilibrium position (the short-run analysis[14] as determined by full employment and money-market equilibrium), the investigation of its evolution through time (medium-run analysis),[15] and steady-state analyses (long-run positions and their changes).[16]

From a consideration of (2.2), (2.6), (2.10), (2.11), and (2.14) we find that there are two equations in the model which determine its temporary equilibrium positions in relative form, namely[17] (setting $\bar{r} = r_0$, i.e., equal to its steady-state value, see below),

---

[13] See Chiarella et al. (1998) for the details of such an approach.

[14] Of the variables ρ, m.

[15] By studying the π-dynamics in its interaction with the variable m.

[16] In particular, the dependence of income distribution on the growth rate μ_0 of the money supply.

[17] From (2.13), (2.14)

$$\dot{K} = S_p + S_g = s_c\left[\rho K - \frac{M}{p}\pi - T\right] + \frac{M}{p}\pi - \frac{\dot{M}}{p} \text{ (by (2.6) and (2.11))}$$

$$= s_c\left[\rho K - \frac{M}{p}\pi - G + \frac{\dot{M}}{p}\right] + \frac{M}{p}\pi - \frac{\dot{M}}{p} \text{ (by (2.11))}.$$

Hence (2.17) follows by use of (2.9), (2.10) and the definition of m.

$$n = \hat{K} = s_c(\rho - \bar{g}) - (1 - s_c)(\mu_0 - \pi)m, m = \frac{M}{pK}, \qquad (2.17)$$

and, from (2.3) and (2.12),

$$m = h_1 y + h_2(r_0 - \rho - \pi), \qquad (2.18)$$

which can be solved for the equilibrating variables ρ and m, representing equilibrating money wage and price level adjustments via the labor and the money markets. Note with respect to this argument that there is a one-to-one map between these latter nominal magnitudes and ρ, m to be derived from

$$\rho = y - \delta - \omega l^d, \omega = w/p, m = M/(pK),$$

with $y, \delta, l^d = y/x$ and M, K being given magnitudes.

Inserting (2.18) into (2.17) gives

$$n = s_c(\rho - \bar{g}) - (1 - s_c)(\mu_0 - \pi)[h_1 y + h_2(r_0 - \rho - \pi)], \qquad (2.19)$$

from which

$$\rho = \frac{s_c \bar{g} + (1 - s_c)(\mu_0 - \pi)(h_1 y + h_2(r_0 - \pi)) + n}{s_c + (1 - s_c)(\mu_0 - \pi)h_2}, \qquad (2.20)$$

which gives a well-defined function $\rho(\pi)$ on the open interval $(-\infty, \mu_0 + s_c/(1 - s_c)h_2)$.[18] This function passes through the point

$$(\pi_0, \rho_0) = (\mu_0 - n, n(1 + (1 - s_c)h_1 y)/s_c + \bar{g})$$

(due to the definition of $r_0 = \rho_0 + \pi_0$), and its slope is given by

$$\rho'(\pi) = -\frac{(1 - s_c)}{s_c}[h_1 y + h_2(r_0 - \rho - \pi) + h_2(\mu_0 - \pi)],$$

as can be easily obtained from applying the implicit function theorem to equation (2.20). The slope of $\rho(\pi)$ at $\pi_0 = \mu_0 - n$ is therefore negative and equal to

$$\rho'(\pi_0) = -\frac{(1 - s_c)}{s_c}(h_1 y + h_2 n).$$

It should be larger than -1 when empirical magnitudes are taken into account. Assuming this to be true the function m defined by (2.18),

$$m(\pi) = h_1 y + h_2(r_0 - \rho(\pi) - \pi) \qquad (2.21)$$

[18] $\rho = \bar{g} + n$ in the case $s_c = 1$.

possesses the property

$$m'(\pi_0) = -h_2(\rho'(\pi_0) + 1) < 0.^{19}$$

The temporary equilibrium values of the rate of profit ρ and real balances per unit of capital m thus both depend negatively on the unique state variable of this dynamic model, i.e., the expected rate of inflation π. This concludes the short-run analysis of the model.

Turning now to the medium-run dynamics of the model, one has to start from the inflationary expectations mechanism

$$\dot{\pi} = \beta_{\pi_1}(\hat{p} - \pi) + \beta_{\pi_2}(\mu_0 - n - \pi),$$

which gives rise to the dynamic law

$$\dot{\pi} = (\beta_{\pi_1} + \beta_{\pi_2})(\mu_0 - n - \pi) - \beta_{\pi_1}\hat{m},$$

this latter equation being due to $\hat{p} = \mu_0 - n - \hat{m}$ and the definition of $m = M/(pK)$. Note that since m is a function of π from (2.21) then $\hat{m} = m'(\pi)/m(\pi)\,\dot{\pi}$ must hold in addition. This finally gives the autonomous law of motion for inflationary expectations

$$\dot{\pi} = \frac{1}{1 + \beta_{\pi_1}\dfrac{m'(\pi)}{m(\pi)}}(\beta_{\pi_1} + \beta_{\pi_2})(\mu_0 - n - \pi). \tag{2.22}$$

This equation has a unique steady state $\pi_0 = \mu_0 - n$ with $\rho_0 = \rho(\pi_0) = \bar{g} + n(1 + (1 - s_c)h_1 y)/s_c$ and $m_0 = m(\pi_0) = h_1 y$.

It is of course also possible to express the dynamic law of this basic Tobin model in terms of m, via equation (2.21), which turns out to be

$$\hat{m} = \frac{1}{\pi'(m)m + \beta_{\pi_1}}(\beta_{\pi_1} + \beta_{\pi_2})(\mu_0 - n - \pi(m)). \tag{2.23}$$

The derivative of the right hand side of the differential equation (2.22) at the steady state is given by

$$\left.\frac{\partial\dot{\pi}}{\partial\pi}\right|_{\pi_0} = -\frac{1}{1 + \beta_{\pi_1}\dfrac{m'(\pi_0)}{m(\pi_0)}}(\beta_{\pi_1} + \beta_{\pi_2}),$$

with $m(\pi_0) = h_1 y > 0$. Since we have $m'(\pi_0) < 0$ by our above assumptions, it thus immediately follows that there is a unique value $\beta_{\pi_1}^0$ of the parameter

---

[19] $m'(\pi_0) = -h_2$ in the special case $s_c = 1$.

β_{π_1} below which the dynamics are stable and above which they are unstable.[20] As is well known from various formulations of Tobin's monetary growth model, the steady state is thus unstable if backward looking inflationary expectations are sufficiently fast.

Finally, concerning long-run comparisons, one has to note first that a proper comparison demands that the reference value of the money demand function $r_0 = \rho_0 + \pi_0$ has to be kept fixed. Otherwise, the accompanying shift in money demand (via the switch of r_0 from the old to the new steady state) would suggest superneutrality of money, since the steady-state expression

$$\rho_0 = \frac{n(1 + (1 - s_c)h_1 y)}{s_c} + \bar{g}$$

does not then depend on the rate of growth of the money supply. For a true steady-state comparison, one has to consider the expression (2.20), however, for a fixed value of r_0 and $\pi = \pi_0 = \mu_0 - n$. From this expression there follows

$$\rho'(\pi_0) = -\frac{(1 - s_c)nh_2}{s_c + (1 - s_c)nh_2} \leq 0,$$

which in the presence of smooth factor substitution would imply an increase in capital intensity, i.e., the Tobin effect as it is normally presented (see, for example, the discussion in chapter 1, section 1.3).[21] Money is therefore not superneutral in the present model, so that both questions in the title of this section have found a negative answer.

There exist two important special cases with respect to the above dynamics, namely, the cases of asymptotically rational expectations $\beta_{\pi_2} = \infty(\beta_{\pi_1} < \infty)$ and myopic perfect foresight $\beta_{\pi_1} = \infty(\beta_{\pi_2} < \infty)$. In the first case the law of motion (2.22) reduces to $\pi = \mu_0 - n$, which gives stationarity for the expected rate of inflation. This case shows the above-discussed Tobin effect in its most basic or pure setup, i.e., as a pure comparison of steady-state situations without any need to consider the troublesome question of the stability of models of monetary growth.

The second case implies via the second equation preceding (2.22) $\pi = \hat{p} = \mu_0 - n - \hat{m}$ which, together with the equilibrium relationship $m(\pi)$ derived above, then gives

$$\dot{p} = \dot{\pi} = \frac{m(\pi)}{m'(\pi)}(\mu_0 - n - \pi) = \frac{m(\hat{p})}{m'(\hat{p})}(\mu_0 - n - \hat{p}), \qquad (2.24)$$

[20] The system is ill defined in the borderline case.   [21] See also chapter 5.

due to $\dot{m}(\pi) = m'(\pi)\dot{\pi}/m(\pi)$. Given that $m'(\pi_0) < 0, m(\pi_0) = h_1 y > 0$, we obtain in this case of myopic perfect foresight a negative Jacobian at the steady state, and thus always have local instability as in the case of fast adaptive expectations.

Sargent and Wallace (1973) consider a partial model of equation (2.20) and its background which exhibits the same qualitative features as this complete model of monetary growth. Observing there, in a linear framework, global instability of their steady-state solution, they conclude that people would react in such a situation by always choosing stability from among the possible dynamic scenarios. In the present situation, this would mean that an unanticipated change in the growth rate μ_0 of money supply $\Delta\mu_0$, just induces a corresponding jump in inflationary expectations $\Delta\pi_0(=\Delta\mu_0)$, which would leave the system in a steady state had it been there. The centrifugal forces of the dynamics (2.24) are thereby prevented from coming into operation. The motivation for this jump-variable technique is that people and the public sector would not tolerate or support purely explosive dynamics and thus implement somehow this jump-variable behavior. Yet, the present model is nonlinear, so the local stability analysis is not sufficient to support such a procedure. Global stability aspects therefore have to be taken into account before definite conclusions can be reached. Furthermore, the price level (and the level of money wages) have been assumed to perform jumps whenever this is needed for the assumed situation of general equilibrium. This makes the temporary equilibrium part highly interdependent (even in the simple model considered here), and it also makes the derivation of the one law of motion that is here allowed very cumbersome. Introducing into the framework a delayed adjustment of the price level[22] (and later of money wages), via further differential equations, has the twofold advantage (as we shall see) of being (more) realistic with respect to the actual behavior of inflation rates as well as making the temporary equilibrium part in its interaction with the assumed laws of motion much more transparent. The cost of this added realism and transparency is that the number of the laws of motion to be considered is increased thereby, necessitating the use of more sophisticated tools of dynamic analysis or even numerical simulation.

A step in this direction is provided in the section immediately following. It will in particular show that the Sargent and Wallace (1973) jump-variable methodology is by no means compelling if global aspects of such nonlinear monetary growth dynamics are taken into account. This conclusion is independent of the particular price dynamics employed in the next section which will be subject to change (in what we believe is a

---

[22] See also Turnovsky (1995, p.76) in this matter.

direction of more empirical meaningfulness) from chapter to chapter in this book.

We stress finally that the steady-state results of this section remain true throughout this chapter.

2.2   The money-market disequilibrium extension: further stability analysis

There has been a tendency to make the assumption of a sluggish adjustment of the price level in the face of money-market disequilibrium in the development of the literature on descriptive monetary growth models of the Tobin type. Such an extension of the general equilibrium version has the advantage of making the dynamics of the model less intertwined (by adding a second dimension to it via the assumed time lag in the adjustment of prices to money market disequilibrium) so that the dynamic processes can be studied in a richer environment. The consequences of certain nonlinearities in the money demand function can here be studied in particular by means of a new approach to the well known instability problem of such models of monetary growth.

The equations of the model are:

1 Definitions (remuneration and wealth):

$$\omega = w/p, u = \omega/x, \rho = (Y - \delta K - \omega L^d)/K, \tag{2.25}$$

$$W = M/p + K. \tag{2.26}$$

2 Households (workers and asset-holders):

$$W = M^d/p + K^d, M^d = h_1 p Y + h_2 p K(\bar{r} - (\rho + \pi)), \bar{r} = \text{const.} \tag{2.27}$$

$$Y_c^{De} = \rho K - \frac{M}{p}\pi - T, \tag{2.28}$$

$$C = \omega L^d + (1 - s_c) Y_c^{De}, s_w = 0, \tag{2.29}$$

$$S_p = \omega L^d + Y_c^D - C = Y - \delta K - T - C = s_c \left[\rho K - \frac{M}{p}\pi - T \right]$$
$$+ \frac{M}{p}\pi$$
$$= \dot{M}^d/p + \dot{K}^d, \tag{2.30}$$

$$\hat{L} = n = \text{const.} \tag{2.31}$$

3 *Firms (production units solely):*

$$Y = yK(= Y^p = y^p K), L^d = Y/x, y, x = \text{const.} \tag{2.32}$$

4 *Government (monetary and fiscal authority):*

$$\dot{M} = \mu_0 M, \mu_0 = \text{const.}, \tag{2.33}$$

$$G = \bar{g}K, \bar{g} = \text{const.}, \tag{2.34}$$

$$T = G - \dot{M}/p[S_g = T - G = -\dot{M}/p]. \tag{2.35}$$

5 *Equilibrium and disequilibrium conditions (asset markets):*

$$M \neq M^d[K \neq K^d], \tag{2.36}$$

$$\dot{M} = \dot{M}^d[\dot{K} = \dot{K}^d, \text{ see } 6]. \tag{2.37}$$

6 *Say's Law on the market for goods and "full employment":*

$$\dot{K}^d = S_p + S_g = S = Y - \delta K - C - G = \dot{K}, \tag{2.38}$$

$$L^d = L[\hat{K} = n]. \tag{2.39}$$

7 *Inflation and inflationary expectations:*

$$\hat{p} = \beta_p((M - M^d)/(pK)) + \eta\pi + (1 - \eta)(\mu_0 - n), \eta \in [0, 1], \tag{2.40}$$

$$\dot{\pi} = \beta_{\pi_1}(\hat{p} - \pi) + \beta_{\pi_2}(\mu_0 - n - \pi), \beta_{\pi i} \in [0, \infty], i = 1, 2. \tag{2.41}$$

This modification of the model of section 2.2 and similar variants of the Tobin model have played a prominent role in the discussion of Tobin type models of monetary growth and their (in)stability in the literature; see in particular the papers by Hadjimichalakis (1971a,b, 1973, 1981a,b), Hadjimichalakis and Okuguchi (1979), Hayakawa (1979, 1983, 1984), and Benhabib and Miyao (1981).

It is, however, obvious that the disequilibrium approach to a theory of the rate of inflation chosen here is at the same time very simple and problematic. It is simple since it only adds to the model of the preceding section the hypothesis that there will be in general a stock disequilibrium (2.36) between desired and actual money balances. This disequilibrium is then used to determine the rate of inflation as being proportional to the excess supply in the money market[23] augmented by an "acceleration" term which reflects, in its first component, current inflationary expectations and, in its second component, the future steady state rate of inflation. On the one hand, this approach to inertia in the price level dynamics allows in the steady state simultaneously for inflation and money-market equilibrium. On the other hand, it assumes (in line with certain empirical observations)

[23] Or equivalently, proportional to the excess demand in the market for the capital stock.

that the inertia effect of current inflationary expectations on the rate of inflation is only partial in nature ($\eta < 1$). The advantage of this formulation of price level dynamics (2.40) in comparison to the preceding section is that it makes the determination of the rate of inflation an explicit one, while the model of the preceding section (which assumes with respect to (2.40) an infinite adjustment speed $\beta_p = \infty$) must be subjected to considerable mathematical reformulation before its determination of the rate of inflation is fully transparent. The difference here is that the price level can now only adjust through time while it is capable of performing jumps in the preceding model whenever an exogenous shock occurs in the data of the model. The simultaneous determination of the price level and the rate of profit in the preceding model has now given way to a simple determination of the rate of profit by means of the full employment condition and a delayed adjustment of the price level corresponding to the disequilibrium in the market for money holdings.

The problematic feature of this extension is that all of its assets markets are now in (stock) disequilibrium. The theory of inflation introduced by this extension can therefore be regarded only as a preliminary step towards a more convincing approach to the determination of the rate of inflation (as it will be introduced in chapter 3 and more particularly in chapter 4). Note that the new flow of money $\dot{M}$ is still simply accepted by asset holders for the time being so that Say's Law on the market for goods remains valid in the same way as in the preceding model.

Our main interest in the following analysis of this extended model is that it allows the instability problems observed in the last section for adaptively formed expectations as well as for myopic perfect foresight to be treated in more depth (and in a quite different light, by way of assuming an appropriate nonlinearity in the money demand function), since we have now an explicit, though not too convincing, formulation of the dynamics of the price level at our disposal.[24]

In the present model, prices p are given at each moment in time and the money wage rate adjusts instantaneously to establish the equilibrium condition $\hat{K} = n$. As in the case considered in the preceding section we have (see equation (2.17))

$$\hat{K} = s_c(\rho - \bar{g}) - (1 - s_c)(\mu_0 - \pi)m, \tag{2.42}$$

where $m = M/(pK)$ and π are subject to the laws of motion determined below. This last equation gives

$$\rho = \bar{g} + \frac{n + (1 - s_c)(\mu_0 - \pi)m}{s_c} \tag{2.43}$$

[24] To be investigated now from a global and nonlinear point of view.

as equilibrium value of the rate of profit $\rho = y - \delta - (w/p)y/x$, which determines the unique level of money (and thus real) wages where capital and the labor force grow at the same pace. We note that ρ is now a nonlinear function of the two state variables m and π.

To derive the laws of motion for the aforementioned two state variables, we first express the state of the money market by means of the excess demand function $X^p = m - (h_1 y + h_2(r_0 - (\rho + \pi)))$, where we now assume $r_0 (= \bar{r})$ to be given by $\rho_0 + n$ and ρ_0 by $\bar{g} + n + (1 - s_c)nh_1 y/s_c$ (recall the steady-state relationships which followed from equation (2.22)), as definitions of the reference rates we employ in the money demand function. Inserting the functional expression for ρ obtained above into this equation we obtain

$$X^p(m, \pi) = \left[1 + h_2 \frac{1 - s_c}{s_c}(\mu_0 - \pi)\right] m + h_2\pi + \text{const.},$$

where const. is given by $-h_1 y + h_2(\bar{g} + n/s_c - r_0)$ and is <0 if $\pi_0 \geq 0$ holds true.

Due to $\dot{m} = \mu_0 - n - \hat{p}$, the dynamic law for $\hat{p}$ gives rise to our first differential equation

$$\dot{m} = [\mu_0 - n - \beta_p X^p - \eta\pi - (1 - \eta)(\mu_0 - n)]m,$$
$$= [\eta(\mu_0 - n - \pi) - \beta_p X^p]m, \qquad (2.44)$$

and for the second state variable we get from equation (2.41)

$$\dot{\pi} = \beta_{\pi_1}(\beta_p X^p - (1 - \eta)(\pi - (\mu_0 - n))) + \beta_{\pi_2}(\mu_0 - n - \pi),$$
$$= ((1 - \eta)\beta_{\pi_1} + \beta_{\pi_2})(\mu - n - \pi) + \beta_{\pi_1}\beta_p X^p. \qquad (2.45)$$

The two differential equations (2.44) and (2.45) represent an autonomous nonlinear differential equation system in the variables m and π.

Proposition 2.1: Under the assumption $1 + h_2(1 - s_c)n/s_c \neq 0$ the steady state of the dynamical system (2.44)–(2.45) with $m_0 \neq 0$ is unique and given by

$$m_0 = h_1 y, \pi_0 = \mu_0 - n.$$

The steady state values of r and ρ are therefore exactly the ones we have used as reference in the money demand function m^d.

Proof: Setting equations (2.44) and (2.45) equal to zero gives the following linear equation system for $\mu_0 - n - \pi, X^p$.

$$\begin{pmatrix} \eta m & -\beta_p m \\ (1 - \eta)\beta_{\pi_1} + \beta_{\pi_2} & \beta_{\pi_1}\beta_p \end{pmatrix} \begin{pmatrix} \mu_0 - n - \pi \\ X^p \end{pmatrix} = \begin{pmatrix} 0 \\ 0 \end{pmatrix}.$$

The determinant of the matrix on the left hand side is positive ($m_0 \neq 0!$), implying only a zero solution of this equation system. Thus $\pi_0 = \mu_0 - n$ and $m = h_1 y + h_2(r_0 - \rho - \pi_0)$, where r_0 is given as defined above – based on the expression

$$\rho_0 = \bar{g} + \frac{n + (1 - s_c)nh_1 y}{s_c}$$

for the rate of profit. On the other hand proceeding directly from (2.43) we have

$$\rho = \bar{g} + \frac{n + (1 - s_c)nm}{s_c}.$$

Due to our choice of the reference rate $\bar{r}$ in the money demand function we therefore know that $m_0 = h_1 y$ can fulfill these equations simultaneously, and thus provides a steady-state solution for the dynamics. Furthermore, the above functional expression for $X^p(m, \pi)$ can be uniquely solved for m_0, (due to $\pi_0 = \mu_0 - n$), implying that there can be no further steady state solution of the dynamics (apart from the one that corresponds to $m_0 = 0$). ∎

Proposition 2.2: Assume $s_c \geq 1/2, h_1 y < 1$ and $\beta_p > (1 - \eta)/X_\pi^p(> 0)$. There then exists exactly one value $\beta_{\pi_1}^H$ of the parameter β_{π_1} where the system (2.44)–(2.45) undergoes a Hopf-bifurcation by switching from local asymptotic stability to local instability as β_{π_1} passes through $\beta_{\pi_1}^H$ from below. Generally, this loss of stability is accompanied by either the death of an unstable limit cycle or the birth of a stable limit cycle (periodic motion) as the bifurcation parameter $\beta_{\pi_1}^H$ is crossed from the left.

Proof: The Jacobian of the dynamical system (2.44)–(2.45) at the steady state reads

$$J = \begin{pmatrix} -\beta_p X_m^p m_0 & -\beta_p X_\pi^p m_0 - \eta m_0 \\ \beta_{\pi_1}\beta_p X_m^p & \beta_{\pi_1}\beta_p X_\pi^p - (1 - \eta)\beta_{\pi_1} - \beta_{\pi_2} \end{pmatrix}.$$

This gives for the determinant of J the expression

$$\det J = \beta_p(\beta_{\pi_1} + \beta_{\pi_2})X_m^p m_0,$$

which is always positive, since the steady-state value of $X_m^p = 1 + h_2(1 - s_c)/s_c n$ is positive for all $n \geq 0$.

On the other hand for the trace of J we obtain

$$\text{trace } J = -(1 - \eta)\beta_{\pi_1} - \beta_{\pi_2} - \beta_p X_m^p m_0 + \beta_{\pi_1}\beta_p X_\pi^p,$$

with

$$X_\pi^p = h_2 \left(1 - m_0 \frac{1 - s_c}{s_c} \right) > 0,$$

if the (empirically plausible) restrictions $m_0 < 1, s_c \geq 1/2$ are assumed.[25] Furthermore $\beta_p X_\pi^p > 1 - \eta$ by the assumption on the parameter β_p. For any given parameter values β_p, β_{π_2} (with $\beta_p X_\pi^p > 1 - \eta$) we therefore get a positive number

$$\beta_{\pi_1}^H = \frac{\beta_p X_m^p m_0 + \beta_{\pi_2}}{\beta_p X_\pi^p - (1 - \eta)},$$

at which trace J becomes zero (it is negative for $\beta_{\pi_1} < \beta_{\pi_1}^H$ and positive for $\beta_{\pi_1} > \beta_{\pi_1}^H$). In view of this simple situation with respect to trace J and det J, the proof of the Hopf bifurcation is now a routine exercise; see, e.g., Benhabib and Miyao (1981) for the details in a related, but three-dimensional situation (the third dimension arising due to their use of smooth factor substitution). ∎

In respect of this bifurcation result we note that for $\eta = 1, \beta_{\pi_2} = 0$, the above bifurcation value reduces to $\beta_{\pi_1}^H = X_m^p m_0 / X_\pi^p$ which is formally closely related to the so-called Cagan (1967) stability condition and the Tobin (1975) stability condition on $\beta_{\pi_1}(< \beta_{\pi_1}^H)$, see Groth (1992, 1993) for details. Similar conditions for local asymptotic stability will reappear in later chapters of this book. Furthermore, lower parameter values of η and higher values for β_{π_2} increase the stability domain, while the influence of β_p is ambiguous. Whether the Hopf bifurcation that has been shown to occur is supercritical, subcritical or degenerate[26] has to be determined by numerical simulations of the model, due to the analytical difficulties involved in the calculation of the Liapunov coefficient (see Kuznetsov 1995) which distinguishes between these three cases. Though the loss of stability at $\beta_{\pi_1}^H$ is necessarily accompanied by a cyclical reaction pattern, such cycles will disappear (giving rise locally to monotonic explosiveness) when the parameter β_{π_1} is further increased. This is due to the fact that it enters both trace J and det J in a linear fashion, so that $\Delta = (\text{trace } J)^2/4 - \det J$ must become positive for sufficiently large β_{π_1}, implying real eigenvalues for the Jacobian of the dynamics at the steady state.

The genesis of instability is the autofeedback chain

$$\pi \uparrow X^p \uparrow \hat{p} - \pi \uparrow \hat{\pi} \uparrow$$

[25] As the expression for the trace shows, the partial derivative $X_m^p(X_\pi^p)$ plays a similar role as the Keynes effect (Mundell effect) in IS–LM models, but now in a Tobin (1965) type model.

[26] Giving rise to stable or unstable limit cycles or center type dynamics, respectively.

and is based on the positive reaction of the excess supply of real balances on expected inflation. As shown, this reaction pattern becomes the dominant one, if β_p is larger than $(1 - \eta)/X_\pi^p$ and β_{π_1} is chosen sufficiently large.

Let us next calculate the isoclines of the above two-dimensional system. These turn out to be

$$\eta(\mu_0 - n - \pi) = \beta_p X^p, \text{ (from } \dot{m} = 0),$$
$$[(1 - \eta)\beta_{\pi_1} + \beta_{\pi_2}](\pi + n - \mu_0) = \beta_{\pi_1}\beta_p X^p, \text{ (from } \dot{\pi} = 0).$$

Inserting the expression for X^p we have derived above then gives respectively[27]

$$m = \frac{(\eta(\mu_0 - n - \pi))/\beta_p - h_2\pi - \text{const.}}{1 + h_2(1 - s_c)(\mu_0 - \pi)/s_c}, \text{ (from } \dot{m} = 0),$$

and

$$m = \frac{[(1 - \eta)\beta_{\pi_1} + \beta_{\pi_2}](\pi + n - \mu_0)/(\beta_{\pi_1}\beta_p) - h_2\pi - \text{const.}}{1 + h_2(1 - s_c)(\mu_0 - \pi)/s_c},$$

(from $\dot{\pi} = 0$).

These two curves intersect at the steady state (m_0, π_0). The first isocline is below the second to the right of this steady state $(\pi < \pi_0)$ and above it to its left $(\pi > \pi_0)$.

For the remainder of this section we assume for simplicity $s_c = 1$. This gives for $\dot{m} = 0$

$$m = \eta(\mu_0 - n - \pi)/\beta_p - h_2\pi - \text{const.,}$$

indicating that m is a decreasing function of π. For $\dot{\pi} = 0$ we get

$$m = [(1 - \eta)/\beta_p + \beta_{\pi_2}/(\beta_{\pi_1}\beta_p)](\pi + n - \mu_0) - h_2\pi - \text{const.,}$$

which is again a linear function of π and decreasing (increasing) according to

$$(1 - \eta)/\beta_p + \beta_{\pi_2}/(\beta_{\pi_1}\beta_p) - h_2 < 0(> 0).$$

Assuming values of β_p such that $(1 - \eta)/\beta_p - h_2 < 0$ holds again gives that sufficiently large β_{π_1} will imply a decreasing $\dot{\pi} = 0$ isocline and a locally unstable steady state of the dynamics (2.44), (2.45).

Let us assume that this situation prevails at and around the steady state. Due to the wealth constraint (2.3), it is obvious that $W \geq M^d/p \geq 0$ should be fulfilled by the demand function for real balances. The postulated linear shape for M^d/p can therefore be true only for a certain neighborhood of the steady state. Far away from the steady state, nonlinearities in this demand

---

[27] const. $= h_2(\bar{g} - n/s_c - r_0) - h_1 y < 0$ [if $\pi_0 \geq 0$].

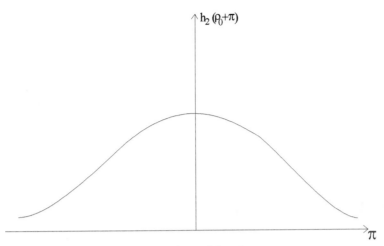

Figure 2.1   Simple nonlinear money demand function

function must necessarily arise. A simple and still preliminary formulation in the case $s_c = 1$ ($\rho = \rho_0$) is given by the assumption of the dependence of the money demand function parameter h_2 on π displayed in figure 2.1.

The shape of the $h_2(\cdot)$ schedule implies that h_2 must approach zero for large positive as well as negative values of inflationary expectations. The sensitivity with respect to the rate of return differential is therefore decreasing the further away this differential is from its steady state value 0. We stress that this nonlinearity is chosen for expositional reasons solely. Asset markets are not the central theme of the present book (due to its method of model progression), but in future research they will have to be reformulated in a way that we sketch in the last chapter of this book.[28]

The phase diagram in figure 2.2 indicates how the dynamics change when monetary disequilibrium growth takes account of the money demand nonlinearity in figure 2.1.[29] The arrows in this figure indicate the direction of motion off the isoclines. In view of these adjustment directions we have drawn a rectangle (beginning with point A) that is obviously an invariant set of these dynamics, since the horizontal line cannot be crossed by any trajectory. This figure therefore suggests as a routine application of the Poincaré–Bendixson theorem the following proposition.

---

[28] Then, in particular the pK component of money demand must be replaced by pW, leading to a greater interdependence between the real and the financial sectors of the economy.

[29] See Chiarella (1990, ch. 7) for another approach of this kind in the case $\eta = 0, \pi_0 = \mu_0 - n = 0$.

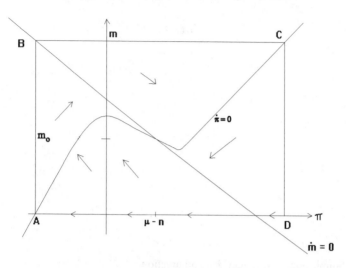

Figure 2.2   Bounded fluctuations for disequilibrium monetary growth

      Proposition 2.3: For the dynamical system (2.44)–(2.45) incorporating the money demand nonlinearity of figure 2.1 there exists at least one (attracting) periodic motion in the domain $ABCD$.

We note that this periodic motion is implied by global aspects and not by local ones as was the case in proposition 2.2.

      Proposition 2.4: Assume $\beta_{\pi_2} = 0$. Then, the isoclines of the dynamical system of proposition 2.3 are independent of the size of β_{π_2} and the system tends to relaxation oscillations as the parameter β_{π_1} goes to infinity.

If β_{π_1} is increased towards infinity the dynamics therefore approach the situation of a relaxation cycle as depicted in figure 2.3. Therefore, despite the fact that we get a monotonically explosive situation around the steady state as $\beta_{\pi_1} \to \infty$ (as shown above), we will always have a unique and attracting monetary growth cycle in this model when viewed from a global perspective. This situation will also hold true if $\beta_{\pi_2} > 0$ is assumed, given that the $\dot{\pi} = 0$ isocline converges to the isocline shown in figure 2.3.

    We thus arrive at the conclusion that Tobin type (local) monetary growth instability will in fact generally give rise to viable limit cycle dynamics if global aspects are taken into account. Note, however, that this may not be the case if the forward-looking elements in the price dynamics, $(1 - \eta)(\mu_0 - n)$, and the expectations mechanism, $\beta_{\pi_2}(\mu_0 - n - \pi)$, are suppressed (as is often done) by assuming $\eta = 1$ and at the same time $\beta_{\pi_2} = 0$.

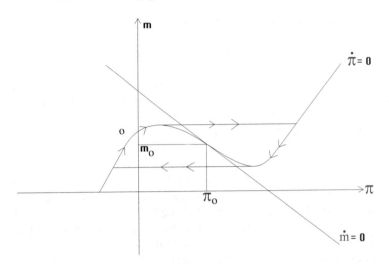

Figure 2.3 The case of relaxation oscillations or *limit limit* cycles (for $\eta < 1$, $\beta_{\pi 1} = \infty$

In this case, the $\dot{\pi} = 0$ isocline is given by $m = -h_2(\pi)\pi -$ const. and does not give rise automatically to the upward sloping parts we have used above to show the existence of a stable limit cycle and the viability of the considered dynamics.

Apart from this latter case, however, we have that the unstable steady state is surrounded by persistent fluctuations in real balances per unit of capital m and inflationary expectations π, where m (and p) is moving in a *continuous* fashion, while inflationary expectations *jump* at certain points in time in order to establish a new perfect foresight equilibrium $\hat{p} = \pi$, with either a high rate of inflation which will start declining after this jump occurred or a low, but then rising, rate of inflation. Both of these continuous movements are terminated after a certain amount of time when another jump to the opposite situation again occurs. The limit case $\beta_{\pi 1} = \infty (\pi = \hat{p})$ of perfect foresight thus here is of quite a different nature in comparison to the jump-variable technique (for p) commonly used in macroeconomic theory since Sargent and Wallace's (1973) basic formulation of it. This is due to the fact that the global point of view adopted here automatically limits the explosive situation to regions around the steady state. It was the assumption that this explosive behavior was global that was used by Sargent and Wallace to justify their argument that unforeseen shocks in the money supply could only lead to jumps in the price level p, so that the endogenous variables (m, π) just remain in the steady state at such a case.

Sargent and Wallace not only assume $\beta_{\pi_1} = \infty (\hat{p} = \pi)$, but also $\beta_p = \infty (m = h_1 y + h_2(r_0 - \rho - \pi)$ with ρ fixed at a given value). In this case, the above two isoclines become identical (equal to $m = -h_2 \pi -$ const.). The dynamics then again become of the type considered in the preceding section if one considers this limit case without paying attention to its neighboring case of a very high, but finite adjustment speed of prices. If compared with these neighboring cases, however, we see that the limit cycle considered in figure 2.3 simply grows in amplitude (in the π-direction) towards infinity as $\beta_p \to \infty$. This means, on the one hand, that the model is not yet well defined (that is to say viable) for $\beta_p \to \infty$ and, on the other hand, that the resulting limit limit limit cycle ($\pi = -\infty \to \pi = +\infty \to \pi = -\infty$, etc.) again suggests a difference to the Sargent and Wallace jump-variable technique. We conclude that such models of monetary growth (as well as the ones of subsequent chapters) should be further extended and be analyzed taking account of their intrinsic nonlinearities as well as further extrinsic ones. Such analysis will further support the conclusion that their dynamical behavior is more likely to exhibit persistent fluctuations around the steady state rather than to be of the stable saddlepath type converging toward it that is generally employed in the literature.

This latter stable saddlepath dynamics is of a purely forward looking behavior where agents do not take into account any experience obtained from the past up to the present date. Our approach, by contrast, combines backward and forward looking elements ($\eta < 1, \beta_{\pi_2} > 0$) in a still simple way in order to obtain quite different conclusions from those of the monetary growth dynamics of the neoclassical variety. Now, myopic perfect foresight is made compatible with persistent fluctuations if the adjustment speed of the price level is finite, so that only inflationary expectations π can (and quite sensibly will) perform jumps at certain points in time.[30]

2.3   Labor-market disequilibrium and cyclical monetary growth

We now extend the model to include labor-market disequilibrium and a (somewhat) sluggish adjustment of nominal wages in the light of such disequilibrium. This immediately adds two new laws of motion to the dynamics we have discussed so far, namely, the resulting real wage dynamics and the now generally fluctuating growth rate of the capital stock. The interaction of these two dynamic variables has been extensively studied in models of cyclical growth of the Goodwin and Rose type. The question which then arises is in what way will the overshooting cyclical features of

---

[30] See Flaschel and Sethi (1999) for a more elaborate treatment of this topic.

these real growth models reappear in such a higher dimensional model of monetary growth?
The equations of the model are:

1 Definitions (remuneration and wealth):

$$\omega = w/p, u = \omega/x, \rho = (Y - \delta K - \omega L^d)/K, \tag{2.46}$$

$$W = M/p + K. \tag{2.47}$$

2 Households (workers and asset holders):

$$W = M^d/p + K^d, M^d = h_1 pY + h_2 pK(\bar{r} - (\rho + \pi)),$$
$$\bar{r} = \text{const.}, \tag{2.48}$$

$$Y_c^{De} = \rho K - \frac{M}{p}\pi - T, \tag{2.49}$$

$$C = \omega L^d + (1 - s_c)Y_c^{De}, s_w = 0, \tag{2.50}$$

$$S_p = \omega L^d + Y_c^D - C = Y - \delta K - T - C = s_c\left[\rho K - \frac{M}{p}\pi - T\right]$$
$$+ \frac{M}{p}\pi,$$

$$= \dot{M}^d/p + \dot{K}^d, \tag{2.51}$$

$$\hat{L} = n = \text{const.} \tag{2.52}$$

3 Firms (production units solely):

$$Y = yK(= Y^p = y^p K), L^d = Y/x, y, x = \text{const.} \tag{2.53}$$

4 Government (monetary and fiscal authority):

$$\hat{M} = \mu_0, \tag{2.54}$$

$$G = \bar{g}K, \bar{g} = \text{const.} \tag{2.55}$$

$$T = G - \dot{M}/p[S_g = T - G = -\dot{M}/p]. \tag{2.56}$$

5 Equilibrium and disequilibrium conditions (asset markets):

$$M \neq M^d[K \neq K^d], \tag{2.57}$$

$$\dot{M} = \dot{M}^d[\dot{K} = \dot{K}^d, \text{ see } 6]. \tag{2.58}$$

6 Say's Law on the market for goods and labor-market disequilibrium:

$$\dot{K}^d = S_p + S_g = S = Y - \delta K - C - G = \dot{K}, \tag{2.59}$$

$$L^d \neq L[V = L^d/L \neq \text{const.}].\qquad(2.60)$$

7 Wage–price inflation and inflationary expectations:

$$\hat{w} = \beta_w(V - \bar{V}) + \kappa_w \hat{p} + (1 - \kappa_w)\pi,\qquad(2.61)$$

$$\hat{p} = \beta_p((M - M^d)/(pK)) + \kappa_p \hat{w} + (1 - \kappa_p)\pi,\qquad(2.62)$$

$$\dot{\pi} = \beta_{\pi_1}(\hat{p} - \pi) + \beta_{\pi_2}(\mu_0 - n - \pi), \beta_{\pi^i} \in [0, \infty], i = 1, 2.\qquad(2.63)$$

The model of the preceding section 2.2 is here extended to allow for the treatment of labor-market disequilibrium (2.60), where it is assumed that the rate of employment V is now varying around its so-called natural level $\bar{V}(< 1)$, which, as in most macroeconomic treatments of the so-called NAIRU rate of employment, is given exogenously (see however chapter 7 for an exception). We assume here, as well as in all other models that follow, that the maximum value of the rate of employment V (which includes overtime work[31]) is considerably larger than 1 and that this absolute ceiling to the employment of the labor forces is never reached by the medium-run dynamics investigated in this book. This is an assumption or restriction which helps to avoid regimes of so-called repressed inflation, an assumption which may be justified by a very high degree of wage flexibility near absolute full employment such that this flexibility induces the dynamics to stay away from absolute full employment. Note that our formulation of Say's Law (2.59) does not depend on the fact that there is now labor-market disequilibrium present in our Tobin type model.[32]

Here, however, we shall remain with linear economic mechanisms and thus defer the consideration of the aforementioned nonlinearity close to absolute full employment to later investigations. Our wage adjustment equation (2.61) therefore does not yet allow for the treatment of such conjectured stabilizing mechanisms. Wage inflation $\hat{w}$ is here strictly proportional to deviations of the rate of employment V from its NAIRU level $\bar{V}$ (which need not be determined by the so-called NAR, the natural rate of unemployment). Wage inflation is furthermore assumed to be influenced by the observed actual rate of price inflation $\hat{p}$ as well as the expected medium-run rate of inflation π, which is assumed to follow some average of the short and the steady rate of inflation, $\hat{p}$ and $\mu_0 - n$. A similar assumption is made for the determination of price inflation (2.62), which modifies the formula used in the preceding section. Note that the use of (2.62) (and of $(1 - \kappa_p)\pi$) in the place of (2.40) (and there of $\eta\pi$) explains from another perspective why empirical observations on the value of η generally report a

[31] See the model of chapter 7 for a more detailed treatment of this aspect.
[32] It is easy to establish that $Y - \delta K - C - G = \dot{K}$ must hold true in this model type at all moments in time independently of the state of the labor market.

value of less than 1. Note, furthermore, that the term $\kappa_p \hat{w}$ incorporates the usual procedure of static markup pricing (a cost-push term) into the determination of price inflation. Note, finally, that we have already stressed that the term $(M - M^d)/(pK)$ may not represent a convincing expression for all remaining influences on the rate of inflation (the demand pressure factors).

The formal structure of our wage and price adjustment equations is the same as that used in Rose (1990), to whom we owe this idea of representing the wage–price module of the model, though its interpretation and application differ considerably from that of Rose.[33] Note that these wage and price adjustment equations can also be represented in the following form:

$$\hat{w} = \pi + \beta_w(V - \bar{V}) + \kappa_w(\hat{p} - \pi),$$
$$\hat{p} = \pi + \beta_p((M - M^d)/(pK)) + \kappa_p(\hat{w} - \pi).$$

Represented in this format they can be interpreted as follows. Deviations of price and wage inflation from the expected medium-run evolution of inflation π as such are caused on the one hand by disequilibria in the money market or in the labor market (representing the demand-pressure factors) and deviations of actual wage or price inflation from the expected rate π (representing cost-push factors). These equations can therefore be conceived as a considerable generalization of many other formulations of wage and price inflation (though of course the formulation of one of the demand pressure terms needs further improvement as discussed earlier).

The above two equations are linear equations in the unknowns $\hat{w} - \pi, \hat{p} - \pi$, which are easily solved (on the basis of the assumption $1 - \kappa_w\kappa_p \neq 0$ which is made throughout this book). They give rise to the following expressions for these two unknowns ($\kappa = (1 - \kappa_w\kappa_p)^{-1}$):

$$\hat{w} - \pi = \kappa[\beta_w(V - \bar{V}) + \kappa_w\beta_p((M - M^d)/(pK))], \tag{2.64}$$

$$\hat{p} - \pi = \kappa[\kappa_p\beta_w(V - \bar{V}) + \beta_p((M - M^d)/(pK))], \tag{2.65}$$

which in turn imply for the dynamics of the real wage $\omega = w/p$,

$$\hat{\omega} = \hat{w} - \hat{p}$$
$$= \kappa[(1 - \kappa_p)\beta_w(V - \bar{V}) - (1 - \kappa_w)\beta_p((M - M^d)/(pK))]. \tag{2.66}$$

These representations of the dynamic laws that govern the nominal and the real magnitudes of the wage–price module will be often used throughout this book and its various model types.[34] This completes the description of

---

[33] See also Solow and Stiglitz (1968) for a similar approach to the wage–price level interaction.

[34] Since the magnitudes of $\dot{M}/p$ and of w, ρ are predetermined at each moment of time, it is here demanded that S_p always fulfills the side condition $S_p - \dot{M}/p \geq -\delta K$.

the innovations in the present variant of the Tobin model type (see sections 2.1 and 2.2 for the description of its other, unchanged components).

There are now four state variables of the model and four corresponding laws of motion which form an autonomous system of differential equations of dimension four. These laws read

$$\hat{\omega} = \kappa[(1 - \kappa_p)\beta_w X^w - (1 - \kappa_w)\beta_p X^p], \tag{2.67}$$

$$\hat{l} = n - s_c(\rho - \bar{g}) + (1 - s_c)(\mu_0 - \pi)m, \tag{2.68}$$

$$\hat{m} = \mu_0 - n - \pi - \kappa[\kappa_p\beta_w X^w + \beta_p X^p] + \hat{l}, \tag{2.69}$$

$$\dot{\pi} = \beta_{\pi_1}\kappa[\kappa_p\beta_w X^w + \beta_p X^p] + \beta_{\pi_2}(\mu_0 - n - \pi), \tag{2.70}$$

where we have made use of the abbreviations,

$$X^w = V - \bar{V}, V = l^d/l, l^d = y/x,$$
$$X^p = (M - M^d)/(pK) = m - m^d,$$
$$m^d = h_1 y + h_2(r_0 - \rho - \pi),$$
$$\rho = y(1 - \omega/x) - \delta.$$

Note for future reference that

$$X^w = \frac{y}{lx} - \bar{V},$$

$$X^p = m - \frac{h_2 y}{x}\omega + h_2\pi - h_1 y - h_2(r_0 - y + \delta).$$

Equation (2.67) follows directly from (2.66) and the definitions of X^w and X^p above. Equation (2.68) follows from $\hat{l} = n - \hat{K}$ and the expression for $\hat{K}$ which is obtained from manipulations similar to those that lead to equation (2.17). Equation (2.69) is obtained from $\hat{m} = \mu_0 - \hat{p} - \hat{K} = \mu_0 - n - \pi + (\hat{p} - \pi) + (n - \hat{K})$ by making use of (2.65) and (2.68). Equation (2.70) follows from (2.63) and (2.65).

The unique interior steady state of the dynamical system (2.67–2.70) is the same as the one obtained in section 2.2, but in addition now includes the equilibrium conditions $V = \bar{V}, m = m^d$.[35] Thus we can write the steady-state values as

$$\omega_0 = (y - \delta - \rho_0)/l^d, l^d = y/x \tag{2.71}$$

$$\rho = \frac{n(1 + (1 - s_c)m_0)}{s_c} + \bar{g}, \tag{2.72}$$

[35] In the proof of this assertion, one has to make use of the two equations $\hat{p} - \pi = 0$ and $\hat{\omega} = 0$ as simultaneous linear equations for X^w and X^p, which imply $X^w = 0, X^p = 0$ as their only solution.

$$m_0 = h_1 y, \tag{2.73}$$

$$\pi_0 = \mu_0 - n, \tag{2.74}$$

$$r_0 = \rho_0 + \pi_0, \tag{2.75}$$

$$l_0 = y/(x\bar{V}). \tag{2.76}$$

Note that we have again made use of r_0 in the place of $\bar{r}$ in the money demand function m^d, which simplifies the calculation of the steady state. Taking this into account the non-superneutrality of money follows again, as in section 2.2.

Let us consider two polar subcases of the full dynamics first. One subcase (the real cycle) is determined by $\kappa_w = 1$ and $s_c = 1$, which gives the autonomous subdynamics for ω and l,

$$\hat{\omega} = \beta_w X^w, \tag{2.77}$$

$$\hat{l} = n - (\rho - \bar{g}), \tag{2.78}$$

where $X^w = y/(xl) - \bar{V}, \rho = y(1 - \omega/x) - \delta$. The real cycle implied by (2.77)–(2.78) is a standard formulation of the Goodwin (1967) growth cycle model. It therefore gives rise to closed trajectories solely.

The other subcase (the monetary cycle) is given by $\kappa_w = 1$, $\beta_w = 0$, $\omega = \omega_0$, and $l = l_0(\hat{l} = 0)$, and results in the two autonomous dynamic laws for m and π,

$$\hat{m} = \mu_0 - n - \pi - \kappa\beta_p X^p, \tag{2.79}$$

$$\dot{\pi} = \kappa\beta_{\pi_1}\beta_p X^p + \beta_{\pi_2}(\mu_0 - n - \pi), \tag{2.80}$$

where X^p is given by $m - h_1 y - h_2(r_0 - \rho_0 - \pi)$. This model is but a special case of the two-dimensional model of section 2.2 (with $\rho \equiv \rho_0$ and $\eta = 1$ basically). The propositions of section 2.2 also apply here (though with less stringent assumptions), which justifies the designation "monetary cycle" of this submodel. Note here that local instability is again due to $X_\pi^p > 0$ (i.e., a positive feedback of expected on actual inflation), while X_m^p is a stabilizing influence.[36] These two arguments both apply to the trace of the Jacobian J of the system (2.79), (2.80), since det $J > 0$ is always true.

Having obtained two independent cycle generating mechanisms as subsystems of the full four-dimensional dynamics (one new, one known from section 2.2), we now proceed to a preliminary investigation of their interaction. It is known from the literature, (cf chapters 1 and 3 of this book), that the center-type stability of the Goodwin model can be made explosive if an appropriate price-dynamics mechanism is added to it, as, for example, in

---

[36] A negative feedback of the price level on the rate of inflation.

Rose (1967). Global stability is then obtained via smooth factor substitution and ever increasing wage flexibility when the system departs further and further from its steady state. This Rose mechanism is also present in the current framework, but due to the more general structure it is not now possible to disentangle the real and monetary mechanisms as in Rose (1967) and related approaches. The issue of analyzing separately the real and monetary sectors in such a framework is taken up in chapter 3.

To see the above point in a basic format, assume again $s_c = 1$, but now set $\kappa_w < 1$ so as to switch on the interaction of the price dynamics with the real cycle. Furthermore, $\beta_{\pi_1} = 0(\beta_{\pi_2} < \infty)$ is assumed so as to allow us to ignore the π dynamics for the time being. We then get the following fully interdependent three-dimensional dynamical system

$$\hat{\omega} = \kappa[(1 - \kappa_p)\beta_w X^w - (1 - \kappa_w)\beta_p X^p], \tag{2.81}$$

$$\hat{l} = n - (\rho(\omega) - \bar{g}), \tag{2.82}$$

$$\hat{m} = -\kappa[\kappa_p \beta_w X^w + \beta_p X^p] + \hat{l}, \tag{2.83}$$

with $X^w = yl/x - \bar{V}, X^p = m - (h_1 y + h_2(r_0 - \rho(\omega) - \mu_0 + n)), \rho(\omega) = y(1 - \omega/x) - \delta$.

The Jacobian of the dynamical system (2.81)–(2.83) at its steady state is given by

$$J = \begin{bmatrix} \kappa(1 - \kappa_w)\beta_p \omega_0 h_2 y/x & -\kappa(1 - \kappa_p)\beta_w \omega_0 y/(xl_0^2) & -\kappa(1 - \kappa_w)\beta_p \omega_0 \\ l_0 y/x & 0 & 0 \\ (\kappa\beta_p h_2 + 1)m_0 y/x & \kappa\kappa_p \beta_w m_0 y/(xl_0^2) & -\kappa\beta_p m_0 \end{bmatrix}, \tag{2.84}$$

which has the sign structure

$$J = \begin{pmatrix} + & - & - \\ + & 0 & 0 \\ + & + & - \end{pmatrix}, \tag{2.85}$$

since $X_\omega^p (= -h_2 y/x) < 0, X_m^p (= 1) > 0$ hold. Therefore $\det J < 0$ and the principal minors J_3, J_1 satisfy $J_3 > 0, J_1 = 0$. Furthermore $J_2 (= \kappa(1 - \kappa_w)\beta_p \omega_0 m_0 y/x) > 0$ by a simple explicit calculation of this principal minor of J. For trace J we have

$$\text{trace } J = -\kappa(1 - \kappa_w)\beta_p X_\omega^p \omega - \kappa\beta_p X_m^p m.$$

The first term in this trace represents the destabilizing Rose effect, stating that a declining real wage (due to a rising price level) will induce a further rise in the price level and thus further declining real wages and so on. The second term in the trace is the stabilizing effect that price level increases exercise on the rate of price inflation via a reduction of the real money supply. The above partial derivatives read explicitly

$$X_\omega^p = -h_2 y/x, X_m^p = 1.$$

The Rose effect will therefore dominate the trace of J if h_2 is large and thus interest rate flexibility low. This indeed resembles the assumptions made by Rose (1967) in the Keynes–Wicksell framework in order to obtain local instability for the steady state. The Rose mechanism therefore operates in similar fashion in the framework of neoclassical *monetary* growth.

Proposition 2.5: The monetary growth model (2.81)–(2.83) is locally asymptotically stable if β_w and h_2 are chosen sufficiently small.

Proof: The role of h_2 in trace J has already been considered above. It remains to be shown that the coefficients a_1, a_2, a_3 of the characteristic polynomial of J (which are already all positive) fulfill the Routh–Hurwitz condition[37] $b = a_1 a_2 - a_3 > 0$, where $a_1 = -\text{trace } J, a_2 = J_2 + J_3, a_3 = -\det J$.

To show this last condition for local asymptotic stability, we note that $\beta_w = 0$ implies $a_3 = 0$ (since $|J| = 0$), while a_1 (for h_2 sufficiently small) and a_2 stay positive. Therefore, $b > 0$ for β_w sufficiently small. ∎

Proposition 2.6: The monetary growth model (2.81)–(2.83) undergoes a Hopf bifurcation as the parameter h_2 is increased, starting from a position of local asymptotic stability as described in the preceding proposition.

Proof: The result is easily established by considering the effect of an increasing h_2 on trace J, see Benhabib and Miyao (1981) for the details of the proof strategy. ∎

Loss of stability therefore comes about in a cyclical fashion, accompanied by birth or death of certain periodic motions. Note that the role of β_p and β_w with respect to such a loss of instability is not as obvious, as these parameters have no influence on the sign of trace J, but have to be considered via their influence on the b term of the Routh–Hurwitz condition in proposition 2.5. We here can only state that large values of β_p will

---

[37] See pp.67–68 for a summary of details of the Routh–Hurwitz condition for three-dimensional dynamical systems.

imply stability, when trace $J < 0$ is fulfilled, since $a_1 a_2 \sim \beta_p^2$ and $a_3 \sim \beta_p$ hold. Note finally that the model is always locally asymptotically stable if $k_w = 1$ is again assumed (the Goodwin subcase).

We have so far assumed $s_c = 1$. The case $s_c < 1$ implies extending the dynamics with the differential equations for l,

$$\hat{l} = n - s_c(\rho(\omega) - \bar{g}) + (1 - s_c)nm, \tag{2.86}$$

generated via the concept of disposable income of households that is employed in the present type of monetary growth model. The Jacobian of the resulting dynamical system is obtained by adding to the Jacobian (2.84) the matrix

$$\begin{pmatrix} 0 & 0 & 0 \\ 0 & 0 & (1 - s_c)nl_0 \\ 0 & 0 & (1 - s_c)nm_0 \end{pmatrix}.$$

These are, however, minor additions to the structure so far analyzed that will not alter the qualitative dynamic behavior already obtained. We therefore conclude that the concept of disposable income of these Tobin type models does not influence its stability properties in a significant way. The same is, of course, true with respect to the model of section 2.2.

Let us now consider the general four-dimensional case (2.67)–(2.70). With respect to the Jacobian J of this system at the steady state[38] we can state:

Proposition 2.7: The Jacobian J (at the steady state) of the full four-dimensional dynamical system (2.67)–(2.70) satisfies $|J| > 0$.

Proof: Note first that the Jacobian in question is given by

$$J = \begin{bmatrix} \kappa(1 - \kappa_w)\beta_p\dfrac{h_2 y}{x}\omega_0 & -\kappa(1 - \kappa_p)\beta_w\dfrac{\bar{V}}{l_0}\omega_0 & -\kappa(1 - \kappa_w)\beta_p\omega_0 & -\kappa(1 - \kappa_w)\beta_p h_2\omega_0 \\ s_c\bar{V} & 0 & l_0(1 - s_c)(1 + \beta_m)n & -l_0(1 - s_c)(1 + \beta_m)m_0 \\ m_0\left\{\kappa\beta_p\dfrac{h_2 y}{x} + \dfrac{s_c\bar{V}}{l_0}\right\} & m_0\kappa\kappa_p\beta_w\dfrac{\bar{V}}{l_0} & m_0\{-\kappa\beta_p + (1 - s_c)(1 + \beta_m)n\} & -m_0\{(1 + \beta_m)(1 + (1 - s_c)m_0) + \kappa\beta_p h_2\} \\ -\beta_{\pi_1}\beta_p\kappa\dfrac{h_2 y}{x} & -\beta_{\pi_1}\beta_w\kappa\kappa_p\dfrac{\bar{V}}{l_0} & \beta_{\pi_1}\beta_p\kappa & \beta_{\pi_1}\beta_p\kappa h_2 - \beta_{\pi_2} \end{bmatrix}.$$

To prove the proposition one has to note first that there are many linear dependencies present in this Jacobian which, when removed by elementary

---

[38] We note the following derivatives at the steady state:
$$X_\omega^w = X_m^w = X_\pi^w = 0, X_l^w = -y/(xl_0)^2,$$
$$X_\omega^p = -h_2 y/x, X_m^p = 1, X_\pi^p = h_2, X_l^w = 0.$$

row and column operations, make this proposition obvious. Thus det J can be reduced to[39]

$$
\begin{vmatrix}
0 & -\kappa(1-\kappa_p)\beta_w\dfrac{\bar{V}}{l_0}\omega_0 & \dfrac{-\beta_p\omega_0}{\kappa_p} & 0 \\[2ex]
s_c\bar{V}+l_0(1-s_c)(1+\beta_m)\dfrac{nh_2y}{x} & 0 & l_0(1-s_c)(1+\beta_m)n & -l_0(1-s_c)(1+\beta_m)(m_0+h_2n) \\[2ex]
0 & 0 & 0 & -m_0(1+\beta_m)-\dfrac{m_0\beta_{\pi_2}}{\beta_{\pi_1}} \\[2ex]
0 & -\beta_{\pi_1}\beta_w\kappa\kappa_p\dfrac{\bar{V}}{l_0} & 0 & -\beta_{\pi_2}
\end{vmatrix}
$$

from which the assertion

$$
\det J = m_0\omega_0\kappa\beta_{\pi_1}\beta_w\beta_p\left(1+\beta_m+\frac{\beta_{\pi_2}}{\beta_{\pi_1}}\right)\frac{\bar{V}}{l_0}
$$
$$
\left[s_c\bar{V}+l_0(1-s_c)(1+\beta_m)\frac{nh_2y}{x}\right] > 0
$$

follows. ■

Proposition 2.8: The steady state of the four-dimensional system (2.67)–(2.70) is locally asymptotically stable if $\beta_w, h_2, \beta_{\pi_1}$ are chosen sufficiently small.

Proof: The case with $\beta_{\pi_1}=0$ [β_{π_2} arbitrary] has already been proven above to be locally asymptotically stable when h_2 and β_w are chosen sufficiently small, since the system then separates into independent locally stable three-dimensional dynamics (with three eigenvalues having negative real parts), and an appended one-dimensional differential equation with a negative (zero) eigenvalue if $\beta_{\pi_2} > (=)0$. Since the eigenvalues depend continuously on the parameters of the model, the eigenvalues of the related four-dimensional case with $\beta_{\pi_1} > 0$ and sufficiently small must also have negative real parts throughout. ■

The trace of the Jacobian of the four-dimensional case at the steady state is now given by

$$
\text{trace } J = -\kappa(1-\kappa_w)\beta_pX_\omega^p\omega - \kappa\beta_pX_m^pm + \beta_{\pi_1}\kappa\beta_pX_\pi^p - \beta_{\pi_2},
$$
$$
= \kappa\beta_ph_2[(1-\kappa_w)\omega y/x + \beta_{\pi_1}] +
$$

---

[39] This simplification has been achieved by the following set of elementary row and column operations

$$
\text{col. } 1 + \frac{h_2y}{x}\text{col. 3}, \quad \text{col. } 4 - h_2\text{col. 3}, \quad \text{row } 3 + \frac{m_0}{\beta_{\pi_1}}\text{row 4},
$$

$$
\text{col. } 3 + \frac{\beta_pl_0}{\beta_w\kappa_p\bar{V}}\text{col. 2}, \quad \text{row } 3 - \frac{m_0}{l_0}\text{row 2}.
$$

$$m(1 - s_c) (1 + \beta_m)n - (\kappa\beta_p m + \beta_{\pi_2}).$$

Continuing the arguments on the trace in the three-dimensional subcase considered above we can therefore state ($X_\pi^p > 0$) trace $J > 0$ iff h_2 and β_p (or β_{π_1}) are sufficiently large for given values of the components of the trace. Price flexibility (for sufficiently large h_2) and fast adaptive expectations thus work against local asymptotic stability, due again to the Rose effect together with the Cagan effect, on the one hand, and the Cagan effect alone, on the other hand (in the real and the monetary part of the model, respectively).

Note here that β_w does not play a role in the size of the trace. This will not be so in subsequent chapters. Note again, that the Tobin effect enters the Jacobian in such a way as to avoid its amplification by appropriate parameter choices. Instability caused by inflationary expectations is therefore primarily due to the Cagan effect (based on the asset demand substitution process) rather than to the Tobin (disposable income) effect (in the case $s_c < 1$), since $X_\pi^p = h_2 > 0$ and $X_m^p = 1 > 0$.

Summarizing, the four-dimensional case represents a synthesis of Goodwin's growth cycle model with a two-dimensional cycle of Cagan type in the monetary part of the model, augmented by a Rose effect in the first component of the trace ($X_\omega^p < 0$). These are cycle generating mechanisms which are coupled through the dependence of X^p on m and π (the Cagan and the Tobin effect), on the one hand, and the influence of X^w and X^p on the rate of inflation (and on $\hat{l}$ on $\hat{m}$), on the other hand. Due to the above propositions, cycles in the four-dimensional case will arise via Hopf bifurcations if β_p, h_2, and β_{π_1} are chosen appropriately, i.e., in particular the system can lose stability only in a cyclical fashion. Note here that economic four-dimensional examples of Hopf bifurcations are rare in the literature and that alternative methods, in particular global ones, of proving cyclical phenomena in this dimension will in general demand very special situations.

Let us, finally, compare briefly the above Goodwin–Rose extension with the basic format of the Tobin model of the literature. To obtain this latter model type, one has to assume $s_w = s_c = s[G = 0, \delta = 0]$, and $\beta_w = \beta_p = \beta_{\pi_1} = \infty$, and add smooth factor substitution. There is thus already a considerable difference to be noted between these two versions of neoclassical monetary growth theory.

2.4   General equilibrium with a bond market: concepts of disposable income and Ricardian equivalence

In this section we extend the general equilibrium version of the Tobin model by including government debt and bonds. This has the advantage that monetary policy can now be separated in a clearer way from fiscal policy and it puts the question of the (non)superneutrality of money into a more adequate environment, since additional money supply (through a higher rate of growth) can, in principle, now be exercised through open market policies and thus no longer implies changes in either taxes or government expenditures (i.e., changes in fiscal policy). Furthermore, the presence of bonds implies that there now exist competing formulations for disposable income, depending in particular on the answer that is given to the question: Are government bonds net wealth?

The equations of the model are:[40]

1 Definitions (remuneration and wealth):

$$\omega = w/p, u = \omega/x, \rho = (Y - \delta K - \omega L^d)/K, \tag{2.87}$$

$$W = (M + B)/p + K, p_b = 1. \tag{2.88}$$

2 Households (workers and asset holders):

$$W = (M^d + B^d)/p + K^d, M^d = h_1 p Y + h_2 p K(1 - \tau)(\bar{r} - r), \tag{2.89}$$

$$Y_c^{De} = \rho K + rB/p - \frac{M + B}{p}\pi - T, \tag{2.90}$$

$$C = \omega L^d + (1 - s_c)Y_c^{De}, s_w = 0, \tag{2.91}$$

$$S_p = Y^D - C = Y - \delta K + rB/p - T - C = s_c Y_c^{De} + \frac{M + B}{p}\pi,$$

$$= (\dot{M}^d + \dot{B}^d)/p + \dot{K}^d, \tag{2.92}$$

$$\hat{L} = n = \text{const.} \tag{2.93}$$

3 Firms (production units solely):

$$Y = yK(= Y^p = y^p K), L^d = Y/x, y, x = \text{const.} \tag{2.94}$$

4 Government (monetary and fiscal authority):

$$G = T - rB/p + \mu_2 M/p, \text{ or}$$
$$G = T - (r - \pi)B/p + \mu_2 M/p \text{ [see (2.96)]}, \tag{2.95}$$

---

[40] This model as it is formulated below, at first makes use of the conventional Hicksian definition of perceived disposable income (here of asset holders solely) $Y_c^{De} = \rho K + rB/p - \frac{M + B}{p}\pi - T$, which is to be distinguished from actual disposable income $Y^D = \rho K + rB/p - T$ (see Sargent 1987, p.18). A prominent alternative definition for Y_c^{De} is the Barrovian one, which in the present context is given by $Y_c^{De} = \rho K + rB/p - \frac{M}{p}\pi - \frac{\dot{B}}{p} - T$. This definition will give rise to Ricardian equivalence also in the present model as we shall see below. See also Sargent (1987, ch. I.10).

$$T = \tau(\rho K + rB/p), \tag{2.96}$$

$$S_g = T - rB/p - G[= - (\dot{M} + \dot{B})/p, \text{ see below}], \tag{2.97}$$

$$\hat{M} = \mu_0, \tag{2.98}$$

$$\dot{B} = pG + rB - pT - \dot{M}[= (\mu_2 - \mu_0)M]. \tag{2.99}$$

5 *Equilibrium conditions (asset markets):*

$$M = M^d = h_1 pY + h_2 pK(1 - \tau)(\bar{r} - r), \tag{2.100}$$

$$B = B^d[K = K^d]:(1 - \tau)r - \pi = (1 - \tau)\rho, \tag{2.101}$$

$$\dot{M} = \dot{M}^d, \dot{B} = \dot{B}^d[\dot{K} = \dot{K}^d, \text{ see } 6]. \tag{2.102}$$

6 *Say's Law on the market for goods and "full employment":*

$$\dot{K}^d = S_p + S_g = S = Y - \delta K - C - G = \dot{K}, \tag{2.103}$$

$$L^d = \text{const.} \cdot L[\hat{K} = n]. \tag{2.104}$$

7 *Adaptive, regressive, or perfect expectations:*

$$\dot{\pi} = \beta_{\pi_1}(\hat{p} - \pi) + \beta_{\pi_2}(\mu_0 - n - \pi), \beta_{\pi_i} \in [0, \infty], i = 1, 2. \tag{2.105}$$

The model presented above returns to the general equilibrium formulation of our most basic Tobin model in section 2.1, but extends this model by introducing bonds and interest rate phenomena.

In section 1 of this formulation we have therefore added, in comparison to the gross real rate of return on capital ρ, the gross real rate of interest $r - \pi$ and a definition of real wealth W which now includes bonds issued by the government. These bonds are of the fixed-price variety (with price $p_b = 1$) and varying nominal interest payments r per bond ($r =$ the nominal rate of interest). In assuming this type of bond we follow Sargent (1987, p.12), who states that this asset can be viewed essentially as a savings deposit. This is done solely for reasons of comparison and analytical simplicity, and will surely demand change once the stage is reached where problems of the financial sector are analyzed more thoroughly. Yet, in this book, we will make use of this type of government asset solely and will add equities (as perfect substitutes for such bonds when the stage of an independent investment behavior and the financing of it is reached; see chapter 3). Throughout the book, the asset structure will therefore remain a very simple one, in fact one that should not give rise to severe economic problems of the type discussed under the heading "financial fragility," and the like. The financial side of all of our models thus only prepares the ground for future research on more problematic asset structures, imperfect substitutability, etc., whose results will allow a useful comparison with those obtained in this book for this simplest setting of the financing of government expenditures (and later on also of firms' investment expenditure).

Section 2 of the model integrates bond holdings and bond demand into household behavior. Looking at the wealth constraint we have now three components of asset demand where the demand for money is essentially the same as in our former models, but now based on the nominal rate of interest in place of the former rate of return differential between money and real capital. Note also that we now allow for a rule of tax collection by means of a given tax rate τ, which means that we have to employ the net rate of interest (after taxes) in the money demand function.

In accordance with our definition of real wealth we have to revise the concept of disposable income as perceived by asset holders employed thus far. It must now also include a term $(B/p)\pi$ that refers to the purchasing power losses of real bond holdings. Furthermore, asset owners now receive interest payments besides profits, which have to be added to their (perceived) disposable income. These are the necessary changes in equations (2.91) and (2.92) with respect to income accounts. The intended allocation of savings in (2.92) must, of course, now also include bonds as the alternative for asset holders.

There is at present no change necessary in the description of firms. The government sector, however, is to be reformulated in a significant way to include a consistent description of its debt financing. Taxes (2.96) are now based on profits and interest payments and assumed to be a constant fraction of them.[41] Note that the government expenditure equation (2.95) is different from the rule we have employed so far. It is based on taxes, augmented by a term $\mu_2 M/p$ which takes account of the fact that government should continuously supply extra money in a growing economy and spend it on extra government purchases of goods, here to the extent described by the parameter μ_2. Note also that the most appropriate parameter value for μ_2 is given by n, the natural rate of growth, implying that government debt will then be zero in the steady state, as we shall see later on.[42]

Government savings (2.97) are in the present model additionally reduced by the interest payments on outstanding debt (if B is positive), and they can now be financed (if they are negative) by additional money as well as bond supply $\dot{M}, \dot{B}$. Since the magnitudes of G, T, and $\dot{M}$ are all determined by policy rules, the amount of new debt financing is determined passively in

[41] Taxes on wage income are here excluded solely for reasons of simplicity, not because this is more appropriate; see appendix 2 of chapter 4 for the general case.

[42] It will be positive and growing in the case $\mu_2 < n$ and negative (describing a creditor position) in the opposite case.

this model and has to be calculated from the government budget restraint (GBR), as given in equation (2.99). There is one new equilibrium condition now present, i.e., equation (2.101). This equation states that real capital and bonds are assumed to be perfect substitutes (with equal net rates of return). Money market clearance (2.100) then implies that both the bond market and the market for real capital are also cleared. This is so since excess demand for these two assets together must be zero by the wealth constraint, and since capitalists are willing to accept any composition of bonds and real capital in their portfolios.

So much for stock equilibrium. Flow equilibrium for these three assets now demands two conditions (see (2.102)). As already explained for the non-bond situation, the government can always "sell" newly printed money and asset holders have been assumed to accept this inflow of money until they reallocate their portfolios in the "next period." But can government also sell any desired amount of new bonds $\dot{B}$? This is, in fact, assumed in (2.102), and can be rationalized by the perfect substitution assumption, whereby any arbitrarily small decrease in the return of bonds would induce asset holders to accept the new supply of bonds completely. Money and bond inflows are in this way assumed to be accepted by wealth owners (and are only subject to portfolio choices in the "next" instant). This now predetermines two nominal magnitudes in the savings decisions of wealth owners, and it assumes that the establishment of overall stock-market equilibrium and of the full employment condition $\hat{K} = n$ is brought about by the three equilibrating variables p, ρ and r – the price level, the rate of profit and the nominal rate of interest, respectively.

The remainder of the model, including the implied kind of Say's Law, is then of the same type as in section 2.1 of this chapter and needs no further explanation. This concludes the description of our bond-market extension of the Tobin model.

In order to derive again a system of autonomous differential equations for this general equilibrium macrodynamic model (now with the additional state variable b), we have to consider its temporary equilibrium positions first.

In the present model, the (temporary) full employment condition reads

$$
\begin{aligned}
n = \hat{K} &= (S_p - \dot{M}/p - \dot{B}/p)/K \text{ (using (2.97))} \\
&= s_c(\rho + rb - (m + b)\pi - t) + (m + b)\pi - \mu_0 m - \beta b \\
&\quad \text{(using (2.90), (2.92), and (2.102)),}
\end{aligned}
$$

where t is given by $\tau(\rho + rb)$ and $\beta = \hat{B} = \dot{B}/B$. This gives as first equation for the temporary equilibrium variables $\rho, m,$ and r.

$$
n = s_c(1 - \tau)(\rho + rb) + (1 - s_c)\pi(m + b) - \mu_2 m, \tag{2.106}
$$

since $\beta b = \dot{B}/(pK) = (\mu_2 - \mu_0)m$ by (2.99). The second equation is, as in section 2.1, given by (using (2.100) and (2.101))

$$m = h_1 y + h_2(r_0 - r)(1 - \tau), \tag{2.107}$$

with

$$r = \rho + \pi/(1 - \tau). \tag{2.108}$$

We simply state here in advance that the unique steady state of this model is given by

$$\pi_0 = \mu_0 - n, \tag{2.109}$$

$$m_0 = h_1 y, \tag{2.110}$$

$$\rho_0 = \frac{\mu_0 m_0 + n}{s_c(1 - \tau)}, \tag{2.111}$$

$$r_0 = \rho_0 + \pi_0, \tag{2.112}$$

$$b_0 = \frac{\mu_2 - \mu_0}{\mu_0} m_0, \tag{2.113}$$

which also provides us with the value of r_0 used in the above equilibrium conditions. Of course, one has to check this assertion on the interior steady state when the final dynamic equations have been determined.

Inserting equations (2.107)–(2.108) into (2.106) gives

$$\rho = \frac{n - \pi b + (\mu_2 - (1 - s_c)\pi)(h_1 y + h_2(r_0 - \pi/(1 - \tau)))}{s_c(1 - \tau)(1 + b) + (\mu_2 - (1 - s_c)\pi)h_2}, \tag{2.114}$$

which shows the profit rate ρ as a function of π and b. Inserting this into the equation (2.107) implies dependence on π and b for this second equilibrium variable. The temporary equilibrium part of the model therefore rests on quite lengthy expressions. This will change radically in the model of the next section, where more stress is laid on lagged instead of instantaneous adjustment processes.

In the following we will concentrate on the case $s_c = 1$, which gives us the functions $\rho(\pi, b), m(\pi, b)$ in the form

$$\rho = \frac{n - \pi b + \mu_2(h_1 y + h_2(r_0 - \pi/(1 - \tau)))}{(1 - \tau)(1 + b) + \mu_2 h_2} \equiv \rho(\pi, b), \tag{2.115}$$

$$m = h_1 y + h_2(r_0 - \rho - \pi)(1 - \tau) \equiv m(\pi, b). \tag{2.116}$$

Equation (2.115) implies $\rho_b < 0$ near the steady state and also

$$\rho_\pi = -(b + \mu_2 h_2/(1 - \tau))/((1 - \tau)(1 + b) + \mu_2 h_2),$$

$$= -\frac{1}{(1-\tau)}\frac{(1-\tau)b + \mu_2 h_2}{(1-\tau)(b+1) + \mu_2 h_2} < 0.$$

For m_π and m_b we obtain from (2.116) that near the steady state $m_b > 0$ and

$$m_\pi = h_2(-\rho_\pi - 1)(1-\tau),$$

$$= h_2\left[\frac{(1-\tau)b + \mu_2 h_2}{(1-\tau)(b+1) + \mu_2 h_2} - 1\right],$$

$$= -\frac{h_2}{(1-\tau)(b+1) + \mu_2 h_2} < 0.$$

The dynamical equations for π and b, the state variables of the present model, are given by

$$\dot{\pi} = (\beta_{\pi_1}(1 + \beta_m) + \beta_{\pi_2})(\mu_0 - n - \pi) - \beta_{\pi_1}\hat{m},$$
$$\dot{b} = (\mu_2 - \mu_0)m - \mu_0 b + b\hat{m}.$$

These equations are obtained from (2.98) and (2.105) by noting that $\hat{p} = \mu_0 - n - \hat{m}$ holds by definition, i.e. $\hat{p} - \pi = \mu_0 - n - \pi - \hat{m}$, and because (again by definition) of $\hat{b} = \hat{B} - \hat{p} - n = (\mu_2 - \mu_0)m/b - (\mu_0 - \hat{m})$ by use of (2.99). For $\hat{m}$ we have to insert into the above two laws of motion $\hat{m} = (m_\pi/m)\dot{\pi} + (m_b/m)\dot{b}$, which gives:

$$\dot{\pi}(1 + \beta_{\pi_1}m_\pi/m) + \beta_{\pi_1}m_b/m\dot{b} = (\beta_{\pi_1} + \beta_{\pi_2})(\mu_0 - n - \pi),$$
$$\dot{\pi}(-m_\pi b/m) + (1 - m_b b/m)\dot{b} = (\mu_2 - \mu_0)m - \mu_0 b.$$

In matrix notation the last two equations may be expressed as[43]

$$
\begin{pmatrix} \dot{\pi} \\ \dot{b} \end{pmatrix} = \begin{pmatrix} 1 + \beta_{\pi_1}m_\pi/m & \beta_{\pi_1}m_b/m \\ -m_\pi b/m & 1 - m_b b/m \end{pmatrix}^{-1} \begin{pmatrix} (\beta_{\pi_1} + \beta_{\pi_2})(\mu_0 - n - \pi) \\ (\mu_2 - \mu_0)m(\pi, b) - \mu_0 b \end{pmatrix},
$$

$$
= \frac{1}{\Omega}\begin{pmatrix} 1 - m_b b/m & -\beta_{\pi_1}m_b/m \\ m_\pi b/m & 1 + \beta_{\pi_1}m_\pi/m \end{pmatrix} \begin{pmatrix} (\beta_{\pi_1} + \beta_{\pi_2})(\mu_0 - n - \pi) \\ (\mu_2 - \mu_0)m(\pi, b) - \mu_0 b \end{pmatrix}, \quad (2.117)
$$

where

$$\Omega = (1 + \beta_{\pi_1}m_\pi/m)(1 - m_b b/m) + \beta_{\pi_1}(m_b/m) \cdot (m_\pi b/m)$$
$$= 1 + \beta_{\pi_1}m_\pi/m - m_b b/m.$$

This latter expression is zero for

$$\beta_{\pi_1}^0 = \frac{m_b b/m - 1}{(m_\pi/m)},$$

[43] It is now easy to check that the interior steady state is as described by equations (2.109)–(2.113).

which may be a negative or a positive number (or by chance 0). For all $\beta_{\pi_1} > \beta_{\pi_1}^0$ we know however that $\Omega < 0$ must hold true ($m_\pi < 0, m_b > 0$).

The Jacobian of the dynamical system (2.117) at its steady state is given by

$$J = \frac{1}{\Omega} \begin{pmatrix} 1 - m_b b_0/m_0 & -\beta_{\pi_1} m_b/m_0 \\ m_\pi b_0/m_0 & 1 + \beta_{\pi_1} m_\pi/m_0 \end{pmatrix} \begin{pmatrix} -(\beta_{\pi_1} + \beta_{\pi_2}) & 0 \\ (\mu_2 - \mu_0)m_\pi & (\mu_2 - \mu_0)m_b - \mu_0 \end{pmatrix}.$$

For $\beta_{\pi_1} > \beta_{\pi_1}^0$ we therefore get

$$\det J = -\frac{1}{\Omega}(\beta_{\pi_1} + \beta_{\pi_2})((\mu_2 - \mu_0)m_b - \mu_0).$$

The expression for the det J is negative if

$$\mu_0(1 + m_b) > \mu_2, (m_b > 0),$$

holds true, which is in particular so if $\mu_2 = \mu_0(b_0 = 0)$ is assumed as a basic reference case. We thus get for the general equilibrium Tobin model with bonds:

Proposition 2.9: Assume $s_c = 1, \mu_2 = \mu_0$. The dynamic system (2.117) for π, b is of saddlepoint type near the steady state.

In such a situation (and related cases) we thus have that the instability result of section 2.1 for fast adaptive expectations carries over to the case where bond dynamics are included. This general equilibrium case is therefore characterized, on the one hand, by low dimensional dynamics and on the other hand, by a fairly contorted instantaneous feedback chain. We shall see for the general Tobin model of the next section that the opposite will hold for a system that favors disequilibrium adjustment processes in the place of equilibrium conditions. The characterization given for the equilibrium model holds a fortiori when myopic perfect foresight $\beta_{\pi_1} = \infty(\pi = \hat{p})$ is assumed in the place of fast adaptive expectations. The resulting dynamic system is then given by (for $s_c = 1$),

$$\hat{m} = \mu_0 - n + (1 - \tau)\left[\rho(m, b) - r_0 + \frac{m - h_1 y}{h_2}\right],$$

$$\dot{b} = (\mu_2 - \mu_0)m + (\hat{m} - \mu_0)b,$$

since the *LM* equation

$$m = h_1 y + h_2(r_0 - \rho(m, b) - \hat{p}/(1 - \tau)), \hat{p} = \mu_0 - n - \hat{m},$$

then gives rise to a differential equations for the variable m. The function $\rho(m, b)$ is obtained from the labor market condition (see (2.106) with $s_c = 1$)

$$n = (1 - \tau)(\rho + (\rho + \hat{p}/(1 - \tau))b) - \mu_2 m,$$

where $\hat{p}$ has to be replaced by $\hat{m}$ and then by the above expression for $\hat{m}$.

There is a way by which the present general equilibrium version can be completely reduced to the basic prototype considered in section 2.1 of this chapter. This possibility arises when *the Barro definition of perceived disposable income* of households is used in place of the concept so far employed (see Sargent 1987, pp.47ff., for details). This concept of perceived disposable income assumes that government bonds do not constitute net wealth when the intertemporal government budget constraint is taken into account by households. In the context of the present macrodynamic framework this leads to the following definition of Y_c^{De} (see again Sargent 1987):

$$Y_c^{De} = \rho K + rB/p - (M/p)\pi - \dot{B}/p - T.$$

Together with the GBR $G = T - rB/p + \dot{M}/p + \dot{B}/p$, this gives

$$Y_c^{De} = \rho K + \dot{M}/p - (M/p)\pi - G$$
$$= \rho K + (\mu_0 - \pi)M/p - G.$$

We assume now that $\bar{g} = G/K$ is a constant (and $\mu_2 = \mu_0$), i.e., a fixed (tax-independent) rule for government expenditures, but leave completely open, how much of the deficit $G + rB/p - \mu_0 M/p(\equiv T + \dot{B}/p)$ is paid through taxes and how much through the issuing of new debt. The growth rate of the capital stock is in this case determined by ($S_p = Y_c^D - (1 - s_c)Y_c^{De}$)

$$\hat{K} = \left(S_p - \left(\frac{\dot{M}}{p} + \frac{\dot{B}}{p}\right)\right)/K, \text{ (using the fourth equality in (2.92)).}$$

Recall that $S_p = Y^D - C = Y^D - \omega L^d - (1 - s_c)Y_c^{De}$ (using (2.91) and the first equality in (2.92)). From the second equality in (2.92) and (2.87) we then have

$$S_p = \rho K + \omega L^d + \frac{rB}{p} - T - C$$

$$= \rho K + \frac{rB}{p} - T - (1 - s_c)Y_c^{De}.$$

Equating the two expressions for S_p we obtain

$$Y^D = \rho K + \frac{rB}{p} - T + \omega L^d.$$

The definition of disposable income under consideration is

$$Y_c^{De} = \rho K + \frac{rB}{p} - \frac{M}{p}\pi - \frac{\dot{B}}{p} - T,$$

hence

$$Y^D - Y_c^{De} - \omega L^d = \frac{M}{p}\pi + \frac{\dot{B}}{p}.$$

Substituting into the first expression for S_p we obtain

$$S_p = \frac{M}{p}\pi + \frac{\dot{B}}{p} + s_c Y_c^{De}.$$

Hence

$$\hat{K} = \left[\frac{M}{p}\pi - \frac{\dot{M}}{p} + s_c Y_c^{De}\right]/K = \left[\frac{M}{p}(\pi - \hat{M}) + s_c Y_c^{De}\right]/K$$

$$= \left[\frac{M}{p}(\pi - \mu_0) + s_c Y_c^{De}\right]/K = m(\pi - \mu_0) + s_c\frac{Y_c^{De}}{K}$$

$$= m(\pi - \mu_0) + s_c[\rho + (\mu_0 - \pi)m - \bar{g}].$$

This is the growth equation (2.17) of section 2.1 for the capital stock in an economy without bonds. Coupled with the equilibrium conditions $n = \hat{K}, m = h_1 y + h_2(r_0 - \rho - \pi)(1 - \tau)$, it therefore gives rise to the same equilibrium relationships and the same dynamic equation for the state variable π as in the basic version of the Tobin monetary growth model of section 2.1.

We thus get that the real dynamics are independent of the bond dynamics (not shown here), and also independent of how the "government deficit" $\bar{g} + rb - \mu_0 m$ is divided between taxes and new bonds. Ricardian equivalence makes the real economy independent of this composition of the government financing structure. Of course, the volume of government expenditure $\bar{g}$ relative to the capital stock and the growth rate of the money supply will influence the real dynamics and its steady state.

Despite its simplicity (only one law of motion), the model of section 2.1 therefore represents an important special case of general equilibrium growth dynamics with three assets and factor and product markets. With this extension of the equilibrium approach to monetary growth we leave the realm of such models and will consider in the remainder of this book the alternative disequilibrium approach to monetary growth, structured in a specific hierarchical way, solely. For the development of the equilibrium approach, which has dominated the literature until now, the reader is referred to the survey article of Orphanides and Solow (1990) in particular.

2.5   A general disequilibrium version of the neoclassical model of monetary growth

We now are in a position to formulate a very general monetary growth model of the Tobin type by appropriately integrating the two preceding versions. This general version will mainly serve the purpose of representing the proper point of departure for our subsequent formulations of integrated models of monetary growth of Keynes–Wicksell and of Keynesian type, which both are models of labor-market as well as goods-market disequilibrium. Of course, one may always choose, if one prefers to do so, to return to general equilibrium supply-side versions of monetary growth dynamics as exemplified by the model of the preceding section.[44] This is the model type that, due to its formal elegance and its logical consistency, but not necessarily due to its relevance, has attracted the attention of most macroeconomists in the past two decades, as exemplified by the survey article by Orphanides and Solow (1990). However our alternative approach in the next chapter will be to dispense with the asset-market disequilibrium of this section, to acknowledge an independent investment behavior of firms and its financing by means of equities, and to shift the problematic money-market disequilibrium description and its inflationary consequences to the market for goods, where price adjustment rules are much more plausibly established.

The equations of the model[45] are:[46]

1 Definitions (remuneration and wealth):

$$\omega = w/p, u = \omega/x, \rho = (Y - \delta K - \omega L^d)/K, \tag{2.118}$$

$$W = (M + B)/p + K, p_b = 1. \tag{2.119}$$

2 Households (workers and asset holders):

---

[44] Given by the double limit case $\beta_p = \infty, \beta_w = \infty$ of the following version of Tobin's monetary growth model.

[45] The alternative tax policy rule which holds $(T - rB/p)/K$ constant (as in our later models of Keynes–Wicksell and Keynesian type) in the place of the present formulation $(T - (r - \pi)B/p)/K = $ const. is not appropriate as a simplifying tool in the present Tobin model, where government bonds represent net wealth and are considered in the formation of perceived disposable income.

[46] The parameter τ has to be removed from all equations of the following model if the second alternative in equation (2.126) is chosen as the tax collection rule.

$$W = (M^d + B^d)/p + K^d, M^d = h_1 pY + h_2 pK(1 - \tau)(\bar{r} - r), \quad (2.120)$$

$$Y_c^{De} = \rho K + rB/p - \frac{M + B}{p}\pi - T, \quad (2.121)$$

$$C = \omega L^d + (1 - s_c)Y_c^{De}, s_w = 0, \quad (2.122)$$

$$S_p = Y^D - C = Y - \delta K + rB/p - T - C = s_c Y_c^{De} + \frac{M + B}{p}\pi,$$

$$= (\dot{M}^d + \dot{B}^d)/p + \dot{K}^d, \quad (2.123)$$

$$\hat{L} = n = \text{const.} \quad (2.124)$$

3 Firms (production units solely):

$$Y = yK(= Y^P = y^P K), L^d = Y/x[y, x = \text{const.}, V = L^d/L]. \quad (2.125)$$

4 Government (fiscal and monetary authority):

$$T = \tau(\rho K + rB/p) \text{ [or } t_r^n = (T - (r - \pi)B/p)/K = \text{const.]}, \quad (2.126)$$

$$G = T - rB/p + \mu_2 M/p \text{ [or} \quad (2.127)$$
$$= t_r^n K + \mu_2 M/p], \quad (2.128)$$

$$S_g = T - rB/p - G[= -(\dot{M} + \dot{B})/p, \text{ see below]}, \quad (2.129)$$

$$\hat{M} = \mu_0, \quad (2.130)$$

$$\dot{B} = pG + rB - pT - \dot{M}[= (\mu_2 - \mu_0)M]. \quad (2.131)$$

5 Equilibrium conditions (asset markets):

$$B = B^d : (1 - \tau)r - \pi = (1 - \tau)\rho, \quad (2.132)$$

$$\dot{M} = \dot{M}^d, \dot{B} = \dot{B}^d[\dot{K} = \dot{K}^d, \text{ see 6]}. \quad (2.133)$$

6 Equilibrium result (Say's Law on the market for goods):

$$\dot{K}^d = S_p + S_g = S = Y - \delta K - C - G = \dot{K}. \quad (2.134)$$

7 Wage–price sector (adjustment equations):

$$\hat{w} = \beta_w(V - \bar{V}) + \kappa_w \hat{p} + (1 - \kappa_w)\pi, \quad (2.135)$$

$$\hat{p} = \beta_p((M - M^d)/(pK)) + \kappa_p \hat{w} + (1 - \kappa_p)\pi, \quad (2.136)$$

$$\dot{\pi} = \beta_{\pi_1}(\hat{p} - \pi) + \beta_{\pi_2}(\mu_0 - n - \pi). \quad (2.137)$$

This model merely represents the synthesis of the models of sections 2.3 and 2.4 and thus introduces no new relationships into our discussion of the

Tobin model of monetary growth.[47] Of course, it also inherits the weaknesses stated for its predecessors, which in our view can only be overcome by extending this framework in the way we shall describe in chapters 3 and 4.[48] Nevertheless, we have reached at this point a very general presentation of the Tobin approach to monetary growth which provides an important starting point for our future analysis of disequilibrium monetary growth dynamics. This very general Tobin model is indeed a very useful point of departure for the further improvement of such general prototype models of disequilibrium growth toward the completeness, plausibility, and consistency of their building blocks and their assumed interactions.[49] We stress here with respect to the government sector (2.126)–(2.131) that its most basic aspect is the formulation of its budget restraint. The above formulation of three simple policy rules by which this restriction can be filled represents only one of many examples of how to describe conceivable government behavior within its budget restraint.

As far as the mathematical investigation of this general Tobin model is concerned, we will confine ourselves here to a presentation of its dynamics in intensive form as well as an important special case, together with a determination of its steady-state values and some general properties of its Jacobian. This general version of the Tobin model serves primarily the purpose of preparing the groundwork for the Keynes–Wicksell model of the following chapter, which is there derived as a systematic modification and improvement of this *general disequilibrium version* of a Tobin model. We shall close this section with some numerical simulations of this general model of monetary growth.

Let us first rewrite **the general dynamical model** (2.118)–(2.137) as a five-dimensional autonomous dynamical system in the five variables $\omega = w/p, l = L/K, m = M/(pK), \pi, b = B/(pK)$. By calculations of the same

---

[47] Note here that the following chapters will make use of the simple concept of actual disposable income $\rho K + rB/p - T$ in the place of the Hicksian one $\rho K + rB/p - (M + B)\hat{\pi}/p - T$. This means that the π-term in the formulation of the above tax collection rule (and the government expenditure rule) will become superfluous and will subsequently be removed from the model's presentation.

[48] Note that the real wage and thus also the rate of profit is predetermined at each moment of time – just as in our Tobin model with labor-market disequilibrium. This means that the rate of interest is adjusted towards the rate of profit here, either because of the perfect substitutability assumption with respect to bonds and real capital holdings or simply by the voluntary choice of the government. See Flaschel (1993) and Wolfstetter (1982) for a similar treatment of the government sector in a Goodwin growth cycle model without money. Prices and wages finally are driven by money-market and labor-market disequilibrium. This (problematic) scenario will be reformulated in the next chapter from the perspective of Keynes–Wicksell models.

[49] Since the magnitudes of $\dot{M}/p, \dot{B}/p$ and w, ρ are now predetermined in each moment of time, we here impose that S_p always fulfills the side condition $S_p - \dot{M}/p - \dot{B}/p \geq -\delta K$.

type as in the preceding sections we obtain from (2.118)–(2.137) the intensive form equations:

$$\hat{\omega} = \kappa[(1 - \kappa_p)\beta_w X^w + (\kappa_w - 1)\beta_p X^p], \tag{2.138}$$

$$\hat{l} = n - s(\cdot), \tag{2.139}$$

$$\hat{m} = \mu_0 - n - \pi - \kappa[\beta_p X^p + \kappa_p \beta_w X^w] + \hat{l}, \tag{2.140}$$

$$\dot{\pi} = \beta_{\pi_1}\kappa[\beta_p X^p + \kappa_p \beta_w X^w] + \beta_{\pi_2}(\mu_0 - n - \pi), \tag{2.141}$$

$$\dot{b} = (\mu_2 - \mu_0)m - (\pi + n)b - (\kappa(\beta_p X^p + \kappa_p \beta_w X^w) - \hat{l})b, \tag{2.142}$$

where we employ the abbreviations:[50]

$$\rho = y - \delta - \omega l^d, l^d = y/x = \text{const.},$$
$$X^w = l^d/l - \bar{V},$$
$$X^p = m - (h_1 y + h_2(1 - \tau)(\bar{r} - r)),$$
$$r = \rho + \pi/(1 - \tau),$$
$$t = \tau(\rho + rb),$$
$$g = t - rb + \mu_2 m,$$
$$s(\cdot) = s_c(1 - \tau)(\rho + rb) + (1 - s_c)\pi(m + b) - (g - (t - rb)).$$

Note here that the above presentation of the dynamics again makes use of the relationship

$$\hat{p} - \pi = \kappa[\beta_p X^p + \kappa_p \beta_w X^w], \kappa = (1 - \kappa_w \kappa_p)^{-1} \tag{2.143}$$

for the deviation of the actual rate of inflation from the expected one (see section 2.3) and that the $s(\cdot)$ equation can be easily obtained from

$$s(\cdot) = \hat{K} = S_p/K + S_g/K = y - \delta - C/K - G/K,$$

by use of the consumption function of the private sector and the government expenditure rule.

We disregard the boundary steady state solutions $\omega, l, m = 0$ (caused by the growth rate formulation of the corresponding laws of motion) in the following determination of steady-state solutions of the above dynamics. These values of the variables $\omega, l,$ and m are economically meaningless and will not appear as relevant attractors in the stability investigations to be performed. A general and global analysis of the system should of course take the stability properties of such steady-state boundary points of the

---

[50] Note with respect to the $s(\cdot)$ equation that the term $(1 - s_c)\pi(m + b)$ is solely due to the distinction drawn between the actual and the perceived disposable income of asset owners. This expression, and with it the Tobin effect, will disappear from the growth equation of the capital stock if perceived disposable income is set equal to actual disposable income, as will be done in all following chapters of the book. Combined with the assumption $t^n = t - rb = \text{const.}$, this provides one way in these later chapters of making the GBR irrelevant for the dynamics of the rest of the model.

dynamics (2.138)–(2.142) into account. For simplicity, we also assume here that the parameter $\bar{r}$ in the above model is always equal to the steady-state value r_0. This assumption simplifies the calculation of the steady-state values without loss in generality, but it should be kept in mind or dispensed with if steady state comparisons are being made.

Proposition 2.10: There is *a unique steady-state solution* or point of rest of the dynamics (2.138)–(2.142) fulfilling $\omega_0, l_0, m_0 \neq 0$. This steady state is determined by

$$l_0 = y/(x\bar{V})[l_0^d = l_0\bar{V} = y/x = \text{const.}], \tag{2.144}$$

$$m_0 = h_1 y, \tag{2.145}$$

$$\pi_0 = \mu_0 - n, \tag{2.146}$$

$$b_0 = (\mu_2 - \mu_0)m_0/\mu_0, \tag{2.147}$$

$$\rho_0 = \frac{n + \mu_2 m_0 - s_c\pi_0 b_0 - (1 - s_c)\pi_0(m_0 + b_0)}{s_c(1 - \tau)(1 + b_0)},$$

$$r_0 = \rho_0 + \pi_0/(1 - \tau),$$

$$\omega_0 = (y - \delta - \rho_0)/l_0^d. \tag{2.148}$$

Proof: Setting the right hand side of the equations (2.139) and (2.149) equal to zero implies that $\mu_0 - n - \pi = \kappa[\beta_p X^p + \kappa_p\beta_w X^w]$ must hold in the steady state. Inserting this relationship into the right hand side of (2.141) then gives that $\pi_0 = \mu_0 - n$ must hold in the steady state. This in turn implies by (2.143) the equality of $\hat{p}$ and π_0. From equations (2.138) and (2.140) we then get the following system of equations for the variables X^p, X^w

$$0 = (1 - \kappa_p)\beta_w X^w + (\kappa_w - 1)\beta_p X^p,$$
$$0 = \beta_p X^p + \kappa_p\beta_w X^w.$$

It is easily shown for $\kappa_w\kappa_p < 1$ that this linear equation system can be uniquely solved for X^w and X^p, and that these two terms in turn must both be zero. This implies the first two of our steady-state equations (2.144), (2.145). Equation (2.145) immediately follows from our assumption $\bar{r} = r_0$ and (2.146) has already been shown above. Next, (2.147) is obtained by solving the $\dot{b} = 0$ equation for the steady-state value of b (recall $X^w, X^p = 0$). The equation for ρ_0 is then obtained from (2.139), i.e., $n = s(\cdot)$, by solving this equation for ρ_0, since we have $\rho_0 - t_0^n = (1 - \tau)(1 + b_0)\rho_0 + \pi_0 b_0$ and $g_0 - t_0^n = \mu_2 m_0$ in the steady state. The calculation of ω_0, r_0 is then straightforward. This concludes the proof of existence and uniqueness of the interior steady state solution. ∎

We assume with respect to this steady-state solution first of all that the parameters of the model are chosen such that $\rho_0 > 0$ holds true. This is obviously the case if the growth rate of the money supply μ_0 and the parameter μ_2 are set equal to the natural rate of growth n, since the tax parameter τ must satisfy $\tau \in (0, 1)$. The case just described can be regarded as the basic steady-state configuration of the general model, since the government then just supplies the correct amount of money for the growth path of the real part of the model and it injects this necessary amount of new money by buying goods (in addition to the ones that are financed by taxes), i.e., there is no need for government debt or credit in this situation ($b_0 = 0$!). The steady-state rate of profit is in this case simply given by $(n + \mu_0 m_0)/(s_c(1 - \tau)) > 0, m_0 = h_1 y$. Secondly, we must here also assume that this expression for the rate of profit is less than $y - \delta$, so that there is a positive steady-state level of the real wage ω_0 that is associated with it. This should always be fulfilled since the magnitudes of n, h_1, and μ_0 are all small from an empirical point of view. On the basis of these assumptions we thus have a unique and meaningful interior solution to the steady-state equations. It is assumed that the parameters of the model in general do not depart by so much from those of this basic steady state configuration that the conditions $\rho_0, \omega_0 > 0$ will be violated. Note, finally, that $\pi_0 = \mu_0 - n$ should not be chosen so negative that $r_0 > 0$ will not hold true. All following investigations will be confined to stability considerations of or around this steady-state solution of our models.

Let us next consider the case of a tax collection rule of the form $t_r^n = t - (r - \pi)b = $ const. supplemented by $g = t_r^n + \mu_2 m$ as the specification of the government expenditure rule and show that these two assumption allow a reduction by one in the dimension of the dynamical system under consideration.[51] We here, in addition, simplify the notation of the resulting four-dimensional dynamics by setting the value of $\bar{V}$ equal to 1, allowing thereby for values of V larger than one.

The variable b only enters the equations (2.138)–(2.141) via the $s(\cdot)$

---

[51] Note that we have to make use of $t^n = (T - rB/p)/K$ in the place of t_r^n in the following chapters, due to the different concept of perceived disposable income used in those chapters, to allow for the same reduction in the dimension of the dynamical system under consideration. The equation (2.150) is then to be replaced by

$$\hat{l} = n - (s_c(\rho - t^n) - \mu_2 m),$$

and the excess demand situation X^p that governs the movements of prices will then be redefined, as will be the nominal rate of interest r. These, however, are all changes that will become necessary in the following chapters on the Keynes–Wicksell and the Keynesian prototype model.

equation. In view of the above two respecifications of tax and expenditure policy, we get for $s(\cdot)$ the expressions

$$
\begin{aligned}
s(\cdot) &= s_c(\rho - (t - rb)) + (1 - s_c)\pi(m + b) - (g - (t - rb)) \\
&= s_c(\rho - t_r^n + \pi b) + (1 - s_c)\pi(m + b) - (g - t_r^n + \pi b) \\
&= s_c(\rho - t_r^n) + (1 - s_c)\pi m - (g - t_r^n) \\
&= s_c(\rho - t_r^n) + (1 - s_c)\pi m - \mu_2 m,
\end{aligned}
$$

the last of which shows that the growth rate of the capital stock no longer depends on the path of the stock of bonds, but only on the dynamic variables $\rho(\omega)$, m, and π. Furthermore, the entry J_{55} in the Jacobian J of the dynamical system (2.138)–(2.142) is in this case simply given by $-(\pi_0 + n)$ at the steady state of this system. The eigenvalue structure of the dynamics at the steady state is therefore given by the eigenvalues $(\lambda_{1,\ldots,4})$ of the four-dimensional system (2.149)–(2.152) below plus the eigenvalue $\lambda_5 = -(\pi_0 + n)$. Stability assertions on the subsystem (2.149)–(2.152) therefore immediately hold for the complete model (2.138)–(2.142), at least from a local point of view.

Thus, we consider the four-dimensional subsystem

$$\hat{\omega} = \kappa[(1 - \kappa_p)\beta_w X^w + (\kappa_w - 1)\beta_p X^p], \tag{2.149}$$

$$\hat{l} = n - (s_c(\rho - t_r^n) + (1 - s_c)\pi m - \mu_2 m), \tag{2.150}$$

$$\hat{m} = \mu_0 - n - \pi - \kappa[\beta_p X^p + \kappa_p \beta_w X^w] + \hat{l}, \tag{2.151}$$

$$\dot{\pi} = \beta_{\pi_1}\kappa[\beta_p X^p + \kappa_p \beta_w X^w] + \beta_{\pi_2}(\mu_0 - n - \pi), \tag{2.152}$$

where $X^w = l^d/l - 1$, $X^p = m - (h_1 y + h_2(r_0 - r))$, $\rho = y - \delta - \omega l^d$ and $r = \rho + \pi$.

Note again that $y, x = $ const. and that $y/x = l^d$ holds. Note furthermore that the steady-state solution of the five-dimensional system is now to be based on the expression

$$\rho_0 = t_r^n + \frac{n + \mu_2 m_0 - (1 - s_c)\pi_0 m_0}{s_c}.$$

All other expressions for the steady state remain unchanged under the above simplification of the dynamics.

We note, finally, that the assumption $t^n = t - rb = $ const. will not be sufficient here to suppress all influences of the dynamic variable b on the rest of the system. This is due to the Tobin effect in the growth equation for the capital stock. The dynamics of b, and thus the GBR, will, however, exercise no feedback on the remaining dynamical equations if, instead of the above, $s_c = 1$ is assumed (no Tobin effect). A third way of making the GBR irrelevant is provided when Barro's definition of perceived disposable income and $t^n = \text{const.}, g = t^n + \mu_2 m$ is used (see the preceding section), which transforms the $\hat{K}$ equation to the form $\hat{K} = s_c(\rho - g) - (1 - s_c)(\mu_0 - \pi)m$, thereby again allowing a reduction by one in the dimension of the dynamical system to be studied.

A further reduction in the dimension of the independent dynamical system can then be obtained, as we know from the preceding sections, from the assumptions $\beta_{\pi_1} = 0, \beta_{\pi_2} = \infty$. These assumptions imply $\pi \equiv \mu_0 - n$, which suppresses the Mundell effect, given by the positive dependence of the inflation rate on the expected rate of inflation,[52] by keeping inflationary expectations constant along all trajectories of the model. These reduced dynamical systems (with an appended b equation) represent basic disequilibrium versions of neoclassical models of monetary growth to be compared with the corresponding models of the next two chapters.

Let us finally once again consider the original Tobin scenario of government policy in the framework of the extended model. This scenario rests on the assumptions $B, G \equiv 0, \mu_2 = \mu_0$, which implies $t = - \mu_0 m$. We then get for $\hat{K}$ the differential equation $\hat{K} = y - \delta - c$, which, by use of (see equation (2.122)) $c = \omega l^d + (1 - s_c)[\rho - \pi m - t]$, becomes $\hat{K} = s_c \rho - (1 - s_c)(\mu_0 - \pi)m$, also in the case of disequilibrium in the market for money and for labor.

We do not derive here any stability results for the system (2.138)–(2.142), but turn immediately to the dichotomizing model (2.149)–(2.152).

Lemma 2.1: Assume $\mu_0 = n$, i.e. $\pi_0 = 0$. Then, the determinant of the Jacobian of the dynamical system (2.149)–(2.152) at the steady state is always positive. Furthermore, the determinant of this system enlarged by (2.142), the bond dynamics, is always negative.

Proof: As above; see proposition 2.7. ∎

Proposition 2.11: Assume $\mu_2 = \mu_0 = n$ and μ_0 sufficiently small. Assume furthermore $\beta_{\pi_2} = \infty(\beta_{\pi_1} < \infty)$, i.e., $\pi \equiv \pi_0 = \mu_0 - n$. Then, the steady state of the three-dimensional dynamics (2.149)–(2.151) is locally asymptotically stable for all β_w, h_2 sufficiently small.

Proof: Analogous to the one in section 2.3 (also for $s_c \leq 1$, as is here allowed). ∎

Proposition 2.12: Assume the situation considered in the preceding proposition with $\beta_{\pi_2} < \infty$. Then, the steady state of the four-dimensional

---

[52] Here via the equation that determines the nominal rate of interest.

dynamical system (2.149)–(2.152) is locally asymptotically stable for all β_{π_1} chosen sufficiently small.

Proof: As above, see proposition 2.8. ∎

Proposition 2.13: Assume $\mu_2 = \mu_0 = n$ and μ_0 sufficiently small, h_2 sufficiently large. Then there exists a minimal parameter value $\beta_p^H > 0 (\beta_1^{H\pi} > 0)$ where the dynamical system (2.149)–(2.152) switches from local asymptotic stability (up to this point) to local instability via a Hopf bifurcation as this value is passed through from below.

Proof: Calculating the trace of J at the steady state gives for the terms that involve either β_p or β_{π_1}

$$\kappa\beta_p[(1 - \kappa_w)h_2 l^d \omega_0 - m_0 + \beta_{\pi_1}h_2].$$

This term shows that $\beta_p \uparrow$ will make the trace positive if the term in brackets is positive, while $\beta_{\pi_1} \uparrow$ will accomplish this in all situations. Note that the remainder of the trace is given by $+\mu_2 m_0 - \beta_{\pi_2}$, and is assumed to be negative. The application of the Hopf bifurcation theorem is then a routine exercise; see Benhabib and Miyao (1981) for a comparable analysis of a system with a similar structure. ∎

The above are statements about the possible local behavior of the dynamical system (2.149)–(2.152). In order to go beyond these local results we have to turn to numerical analysis, because the dimension of the dynamical system and the interconnectedness of the equations make analytical approaches very difficult, if not impossible.

An example of such an investigation is presented below, but first, let us briefly compare the components of the dynamical system (2.149)–(2.152) with those of the model of section 2.3 which, as we have just seen, provided propositions of a very similar type. The basic difference in these two models (without and with a bond market) is the difference in the government expenditure rule and the GBR. Thus we have $t = \bar{g} - \mu_0 m$ in section 2.3, and $g = t_r^n + \mu_2 m$ in section 2.4.

Though the second model (of this section) has a bond market, its influence on the remainder of the dynamics was suppressed, however, by the assumption on t_r^n. In this way, we can see that there is a close relationship between the models of these two sections.

By contrast, there is a huge difference between the models of this and the preceding section. In the present section, instantaneous (static) relationships are trivial and do not create any problems for the calculation of the five-dimensional dynamics based on them. In section 2.4, equilibrium conditions are lengthy and the two-dimensional dynamical system based on them is at first only implicitly given. Therefore, a variety of transformations were needed before a single instability result could be derived. In this section, significantly more dynamic laws are employed instead. Nevertheless, due to the repetitive expression in the structure of these laws, analytical propositions on these dynamics are possible and can surely be extended beyond those provided here.

Chapters 3 and 4 will build on the general framework provided in these last two sections by trying to remove certain obvious weaknesses step by step. We shall therefore now always start from a five-dimensional dynamical system in general and only subsequently provide an analysis of some of its important substructures. Furthermore, actual disposable income and perceived disposable income will be identical in our subsequent investigations. Thus, in this book discussion of different concepts of disposable income has been restricted to the framework of Tobin type models. Of course incorporation of alternative definitions of disposable income in the model types developed in later chapters remains an important future research agenda.

We close this section on the general Tobin model by some numerical simulations of this model for the four-dimensional case just considered. The general parameter set for the following phase plots and time series presentations is shown in table 2.1. Parameter values will be taken from this set unless they are specified differently for specific simulation runs.

The real (= Goodwin) growth cycle is obtained from the four-dimensional model by setting $\kappa_w = 1$, $\mu_2 = 0$ and $\pi = \pi_0 = 0(\beta_{\pi_1} = \beta_{\pi_2} = 0)$. The dynamic interaction between real wages ω and the factor ratio l is at the heart of this cycle, which exhibits the closed orbit structure of the Goodwin model, as can be seen from figure 2.4. Note that the dynamical behavior of real balances m does not feed back into the real part of this special economy and that inflationary expectations indeed remain stationary.

Next, the pure monetary cycle is obtained from the four-dimensional case by setting β_w and κ_w equal to zero and by assuming $l = l_0(\hat{l} = 0)$. The phase plots and time series displayed in figure 2.5 show that this monetary cycle is asymptotically stable and thus shrinking in amplitude, i.e., the Cagan stability condition holds true for the chosen parameter set.

One may now expect on the basis of the situations depicted in figures 2.4 and 2.5 that the interaction of these two cycle-generating mechanisms produces again a convergent cyclical process. Yet, assuming $\kappa_w = 0.5$ as in the general parameter set to allow for such an interaction adds the Rose mechanism to the real cycle (making the first entry in the Jacobian of this dynamics positive, see section 2.3). Of course, in such a four-dimensional dynamical system there may also exist other reasons that falsify the above

Table 2.1.

$y^p = 1, x = 2, l^d = 5.$
$s_c = 0.8, \delta = 0.1, n = \mu_0 = 0.05; \mu_2 = 0.1, t_r^n = 0.08.$
$h_1 = 0.1, h_2 = 0.06, i = 1, \beta_k = 1.$
$\beta_w = 0.05, \beta_p = 10, \beta_{\pi_1} = 1.3, \beta_{\pi_2} = 0, \kappa_w = \kappa_p = 0.5.$

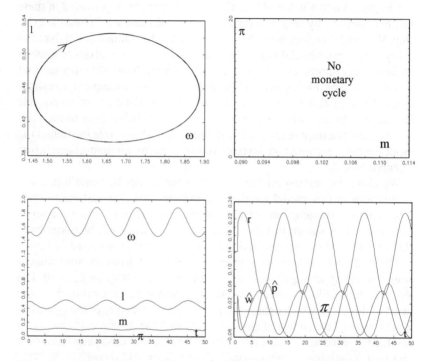

Figure 2.4   Disentangled real cycle in the Tobin model

expectation, but surely the Rose type instability is the easiest to understand in this context. Be that as it may, the result of this coupling of two cycles is the explosive real and monetary cycle shown in figure 2.6.

In the present case, it can be shown that price flexibility works in favor of economic stability and that wage flexibility does not. Therefore, assuming the following nonlinear price adjustment function

$$\beta_p \tan(c_1 X^p)/c_1 (\beta_p = 10, c_1 = 50)$$

in the place of our former choice $\beta_p X^p, \beta_p = 10$ should make the dynamical behavior shown in figure 2.6 more viable. Note that this new adjustment

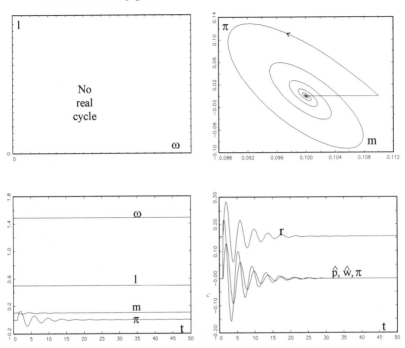

Figure 2.5 Disentangled monetary cycle in the Tobin model

function for the price level just states that price level flexibility will increase the further the economy departs from goods-market equilibrium.[53] The simulation shown in figure 2.7 indicates that the working of this type of nonlinearity leads to limit cycle behavior when the equilibrium is locally unstable.

Note that inflation rates are still very large in this last simulation of the model and are thus not yet to be taken too seriously. Nevertheless, even under such extreme circumstances, the viability or boundedness of the dynamics is now guaranteed through the simple extrinsic nonlinearity in the price level adjustment equation.

2.6 Outlook: independent investment behavior and Wicksellian price dynamics

In this chapter on neoclassical monetary growth, we have assumed that net investment and the rate of capital accumulation are always fully deter-

[53] Where the extent of this disequilibrium must here fall in the range $[-pi/100, pi/100]$, 0 standing for goods market equilibrium and pi the real number π.

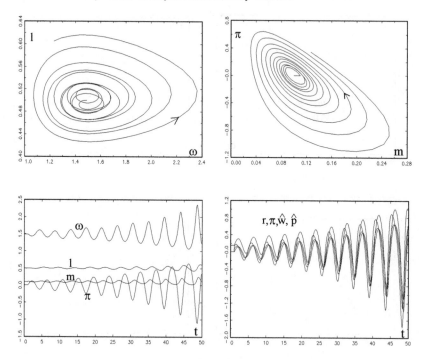

Figure 2.6   Combined real and monetary cycle of the Tobin model

mined by (i.e. identical to) the flow of savings and that the rate of change of the price level is determined by disequilibrium (or equilibrium) in the market for money. These are surely questionable features of the Tobin type models of monetary growth.

There are, in fact, many more drawbacks in this approach to monetary growth, as will become apparent as our analysis proceeds, but one may nevertheless claim that these two features of the neoclassical approach are its most questionable ones. Goods-price dynamics is determined on the market for goods (and not on the market for money) through equilibrium or disequilibrium conditions on this market. But in the present chapter there exists no equilibrium condition (algebraic equation) or disequilibrium condition (differential equation) with respect to the market for goods from which the price level or its rate of change can be derived. Furthermore, direct investment of savings is not the relevant characteristic of (at least modern) market economies, which means that the basic forces that drive investment plans have to be determined and added to the general model of monetary growth we have developed in this chapter.

These fundamental weaknesses of the present macrodynamic model are

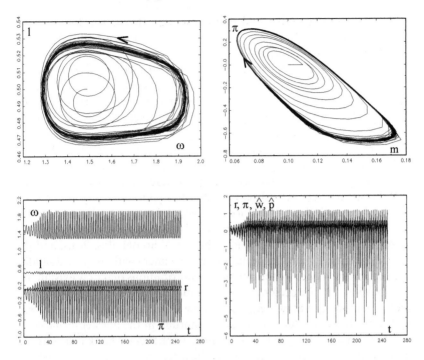

Figure 2.7 Combined real and monetary cycle of the Tobin model with additional nonlinearity in the price reaction function

overcome in the next chapter by (1) taking note of the fact that the investment decisions of firms are not identical to the savings decisions of households, but are determined by variables that differ in an essential way from the ones that determine the flow of savings, and (2) allowing for disequilibrium on the market for goods, in the place of disequilibrium in the market for money, in a very basic way through deviations between the rate of investment and the rate of savings by making the rate of change of the price level now dependent on this discrepancy between the supply and the demand for goods rather than for money.

This modification of the Tobin or neoclassical type of approach gives rise to the Keynes–Wicksell approach to monetary growth, the dynamics of which was investigated with respect to some basic features from the late sixties up to the early eighties (see chapter 1).

The following chapter extends and improves this type of dynamic analysis considerably. Its main objective, however, is to show that there is a systematic improvement of the neoclassical approach to monetary growth that makes this monetary growth model more convincing from a descriptive economic perspective, and that allows an extension to the dynamic results obtained in the present chapter to a model with both labor- and goods-market disequilibrium.

There is thus some improvement and overhaul in certain modules of the neoclassical model of monetary growth as we proceed to the next chapter. This puts this model on a firmer basis from a macroeconomic perspective, but is still far from representing the final improvement that has to be made in order to obtain a model of monetary growth that can be considered as the working model for an analysis of Keynesian monetary growth.

The alternative way of proceeding is, in view of the analysis presented in this chapter, to return to the general equilibrium model of section 2.4 and to elaborate this type of analysis further. This is indeed the way mainstream monetary growth theory has chosen to go, and that in particular into the direction of micro founding the behavioral relationships that are employed through intertemporal optimizing behavior of households, firms, and the government in a rational expectations environment with its typical saddle-path structure. In view of the numerous contributions that now exist in this area of research, the present book attempts to show that progress in the theory of monetary growth may also come about in a complementary way by laying stress on situations of disequilibrium in the market for labor as well as the market for goods. This is done in the present book in a coherent framework which respects the budget restrictions of the various sectors, but which is not so decided with respect to the type of optimizing strategies (and their aggregation) that really take place within these budget restraints and that may (or may not) lead to the aggregate behavior assumed in these types of macromodels.

3 Keynes–Wicksell models of monetary growth: synthesizing Keynes into the Classics

In their book, Ferri and Greenberg (1989, ch. 4) present some nonlinear deterministic labor-market theories of business cycles which are based on three variants of what they call the missing equation, i.e., the Phillips curve mechanism. The three approaches they consider are Rose (1967), Goodwin (1967) and Ito (1980), which make use of a special nonlinear money-wage Phillips curve, a linear real-wage Phillips curve, and a piecewise linear (regime switching) real-wage Phillips curve, respectively. In addition, an equation describing capital accumulation is derived in each of the three cases, and also a price adjustment equation in the case of Rose's model.

In the present chapter, we shall make use of a general model of Keynes–Wicksell type[1] to show that these and other well-known models of cycles and growth can all be considered as *special cases* of this prototype model, so that they all belong to one particular theory, which despite its "Keynes–Wicksell" origin is fairly (neo)Classical or supply-side oriented in nature. Such a statement does not, in our view, devalue this model type from a Keynesian perspective, but it leads us instead to a general and unifying framework of Keynes–Wicksell models[2] with which models that attempt to be of a (more) Keynesian type[3] can be usefully compared.

Since our general Keynes–Wicksell prototype model synthesizes Goodwin's Classical growth cycle and Rose's "Keynesian employment cycle" (based on sluggish wages and prices and smooth factor substitution), it must inherit the dynamic features of these real models to some extent. This

---

[1] See also Chiarella and Flaschel (1996a) for a discussion of this model type, where more stress is laid on a consideration of the government budget restraint and the occurrence of complex dynamics.   [2] Which may also be called models of "supply side Keynesianism."

[3] I.e., attempt to represent models of "demand side Keynesianism," despite the presence of an elaborate wage–price module (representing "aggregate supply" as this is often called in the literature).

result will, in fact, be shown in the following sections on the basis of a fixed proportions technology. Smooth factor substitution can be easily added to our model (see chapter 5), but we will not investigate here its (often obvious) implications.[4] We here stress that such an extension does not introduce a new theory of real wages into the model, since the marginal productivity postulate does not represent a theory of real wages in this context, as it is often incorrectly believed. Real wages changes are instead determined by demand pressures on the market for labor *and* for goods, and they determine employment in a Classical fashion if smooth factor substitution is allowed for.

The Classical nature of the model on this basis primarily arises from the fact that output is determined through supply side conditions, i.e., we will have full capacity growth throughout. The Keynesian IS–LM (dis)equilibrium block here only serves to determine the rate of inflation, and it is fed back into the real part of the model via the real wage dynamics, expectations, and the real rate of interest as one determinant of investment behavior. This is the Keynes–Wicksell portion of this predominantly (neo)Classical approach to monetary growth and cycles.

In the next section, we present the general model. In section 3.2 we present in intensive form the five laws of motion to which it gives rise. We then focus on the central four-dimensional subcase obtained when lump sum taxes net of interest payments are held constant per unit of capital, which allows us to ignore the government budget constraint (GBR). This four-dimensional subcase is the standard general reference for all of our investigations of the considered prototype models. The remaining fifth dynamic law, the dynamics of the government budget constraint, is seldom explicitly treated either in this chapter or in the subsequent chapters of the book.

It is our intention in this book to build the analysis of the most general model on a systematic and detailed investigation of its important two-, three-, and four-dimensional subcases representing the private sector of the economy. This will already be very difficult in the four-dimensional case of this chapter, which therefore represents at present the final step in our investigations of properties of the fundamental prototype models of monetary growth. From the viewpoint of completeness of such models, the GBR is nevertheless necessarily involved in their complete formulation and will thus always be included in the initial presentation and explanation of the general case (here of the fifth dimension). In later work we intend to

---

[4] Such an extension simply adds two further equations ($\omega = f'(l^d)$, $y = f(l^d)$) to the model and two further unknowns (l^d, y), which in general leads to an increase in the stability of the model.

study the role of the GBR and also various feedback policy rules that can be built upon it in a systematic fashion.[5]

Two-dimensional subcases of Goodwin and Rose growth cycle type based on a number of simplifying assumptions are investigated in sections 3.3 and 3.4 by means of Liapunov functions and the Poincaré–Bendixson theorem, respectively. One-dimensional discrete-time versions of these models which can give rise to chaotic dynamics are also briefly considered, as well as Ito's regime switching model which (in our reinterpretation of it) adds boundary conditions (ceilings) to the Goodwin growth cycle. In section 3.5, interest rate flexibility is added to the Rose employment limit cycle via a less extreme formulation of money-market equilibrium, and is found to imply that the limit cycle of the two-dimensional case disappears if the flexibility of the interest rate becomes sufficiently large. This section, however, still makes use of an extreme type of "asymptotically rational expectations" in its treatment of inflationary expectations, in order that the implied dynamical system of dimension 3 remains. This allows for typical applications of the Routh–Hurwitz and the Hopf bifurcation theorems in the characterization of the stability features and the cyclical properties of the system near the steady state.

Sections 3.6 and 3.7, finally, consider various types of inflationary expectations, the pure monetary cycle to which they can give rise and the general four-dimensional dynamics when this cycle is integrated with the real cycle considered previously. This four-dimensional case is investigated by means of computer simulations and from the perspective of the various submodels we have treated analytically in the preceding sections. Section 3.6 also briefly introduces the limit case model where product prices adjust with an infinite speed, a case which has been very central in the literature on Keynesian dynamics and which will be taken up again at the end of chapter 4 on the Keynesian prototype model.

3.1   The general prototype model

The following model type is derived by way of a systematic variation of the general Tobin prototype model discussed at the end of chapter 2. These variations concern the assumed investment behavior of firms and its financing, asset-market equilibrium conditions, and the description of goods-market disequilibrium on which the theory of price inflation is now based. On the other hand, we now disregard for reasons of simplicity the fundamental distinction made in the Tobin models between actual and perceived disposable income of the household sector.

---

[5] See, for example, Chiarella et al. (1998) in this respect.

The equations of the model are:[6]

1 Definitions (remuneration and wealth):

$$\omega = w/p, u = \omega/x, \rho = (Y - \delta K - \omega L^d)/K, \tag{3.1}$$

$$W = (M + B + p_e E)/p, p_b = 1. \tag{3.2}$$

2 Households (workers and asset holders):

$$W = (M^d + B^d + p_e E^d)/p, M^d = h_1 p Y + h_2 p K (1 - \tau)(\bar{r} - r), \tag{3.3}$$

$$C = \omega L^d + (1 - s_c)[\rho K + rB/p - T], s_w = 0, \tag{3.4}$$

$$S_p = \omega L^d + Y_c^D - C = Y - \delta K + rB/p - T - C \\ = s_c[\rho K + rB/p - T] = s_c Y_c^D = (\dot{M}^d + \dot{B}^d + p_e \dot{E}^d)/p, \tag{3.5}$$

$$\hat{L} = n = \text{const.} \tag{3.6}$$

3 Firms (production units and investors):

$$Y = yK(= Y^p = y^p K), L^d = Y/x[y, x = \text{const.}, V = L^d/L], \tag{3.7}$$

$$I = i(\rho - (r - \pi))K + \gamma K[\gamma = n], \tag{3.8}$$

$$p_e \dot{E}/p = I + (S - I) = S = S_p + S_g = Y - \delta K - C - G. \tag{3.9}$$

$$\hat{K} = \beta_k I/K + (1 - \beta_k)S/K \\ = I/K + (1 - \beta_k)(S/K - I/K), \beta_k \in [0,1], \tag{3.10}$$

$$\dot{N} = \delta_2 K + \beta_k(S - I). \tag{3.11}$$

4 Government (fiscal and monetary authority):

$$T = \tau(\rho K + rB/p) \text{ [or } t^n = (T - rB/p)/K = \text{const.]}, \tag{3.12}$$

$$G = T - rB/p + \mu_2 M/p, \tag{3.13}$$

$$S_g = T - rB/p - G[= -(\dot{M} + \dot{B})/p, \text{ see below}], \tag{3.14}$$

$$\hat{M} = \mu_0, \tag{3.15}$$

$$\dot{B} = pG + rB - pT - \dot{M}[= (\mu_2 - \mu_0)M]. \tag{3.16}$$

---

[6] The parameter τ has to be removed from all equations of the following model if the second alternative in equation (3.12) is chosen as the tax collection rule (in which case $\tau = (t^n + rb)/(\rho + rb)$. Note here also that the money demand function which we employ in (all of) the following represents an appropriate linearization of its following general form $M^d = M^d(pY, -\pi, (1 - \tau)r - \pi, pK)$, where the term pK is used for the time being as a proxy – for reasons of mathematical simplification – of the influence of nominal wealth pW on money demand (see Chiarella et al. 1998 for the inclusion of more general representations of such wealth effects). Note, finally, that the magnitude $\dot{E} = \dot{E}^d$ in the following model can also be negative – in the case in which the supply of new money and new bonds exceeds private savings. In this extreme case, firms sell so much from their inventories that they can finance investment from these "windfall profits."

5 *Equilibrium conditions (asset markets):*

$$M = M^d = h_1 p Y + h_2 p K (1 - \tau)(\bar{r} - r)[B = B^d, E = E^d], \quad (3.17)$$

$$p_e E = (1 - \tau)\rho p K / ((1 - \tau)r - \pi), \quad (3.18)$$

$$\dot{M} = \dot{M}^d, \dot{B} = \dot{B}^d [\dot{E} = \dot{E}^d]. \quad (3.19)$$

6 *Disequilibrium situation (goods market):*

$$S = S_p + S_g = Y - \delta K - C - G, \quad (3.20)$$

$$I = i(\rho - r + \pi)K + nK, \quad (3.21)$$

$$S \neq I.$$

7 *Wage–price sector (adjustment equations):*

$$\hat{w} = \beta_w (V - \bar{V}) + \kappa_w \hat{p} + (1 - \kappa_w)\pi, \quad (3.22)$$

$$\hat{p} = \beta_p ((I - S)/K) + \kappa_p \hat{w} + (1 - \kappa_p)\pi, \quad (3.23)$$

$$\dot{\pi} = \beta_{\pi_1}(\hat{p} - \pi) + \beta_{\pi_2}(\mu_0 - n - \pi). \quad (3.24)$$

The important innovation of this general Keynes–Wicksell prototype model is the assumption that investment plans (now of firms) are done independently of the savings decisions of asset owners, up to the fact that they will be confronted and in some way or another be coordinated with these saving plans through market interactions. This new fact, in conjunction with the assumed LM-equation (3.17), can be viewed as being responsible for the label "Keynes" in the name of this model type. The particular form of the investment function (3.8) and the particular determination of the inflation rate (3.23) is responsible for the name "Wicksell" in this type of literature.

The foregoing are the obvious and generally documented characteristics of models of Keynes–Wicksell type, while further necessary consequences of these changes in comparison to the model of the preceding chapter have been by and large ignored in the literature. This is in particular due to the fact there did not exist a general model of the Tobin type from which this new model could be obtained through systematic variations of its structural equations, and with which the Keynes–Wicksell model could be compared in detail. Our following discussion of the new equations of this Keynes–Wicksell model (in comparison to those of the model of section 2.5) will indeed show that it represents a very systematic variation of this former model which improves it considerably with respect to plausibility, completeness, and consistency.

The newly added investment function (3.8) assumes that investment per unit of capital is determined in a natural, and here linear, way by the differential that is now allowed to exist between the rate of return ρ on capital and the real rate of return $r - \pi$ on government bonds.[7] This differential was zero in the Tobin models of monetary growth in which capital (held by households) and bonds were perfect substitutes. There is a further trend term γ in this investment function which is here for simplicity set equal to n (see chapter 7 for an endogenization of this term).

Investment is assumed in this model to be entirely financed by equities issued by firms. The asset structure that is available to capitalists (or pure asset holders) therefore now consists of outside money, government bonds, and equities (see Sargent 1987, p.12, for the same starting point). Equities and bonds are assumed to be perfect substitutes in the eyes of asset holders, which represents the most basic assumption that can be made in this context. We assume in this model that there are no planned retained earnings of firms, which means that all expected profits $\rho p K$ are paid out to equity owners in each period. The after-tax return per unit of equity to equity owners is therefore $(1 - \tau)\rho p K / E$. The price of equities (determined by the above perfect substitute assumption) is denoted by p_e ($p_b = 1$ the price of bonds). Thus the actual rate of return on equities per unit of money is given by $(1 - \tau)\rho p K / (p_e E)$. Under the perfect substitute assumption this must be equal to $(1 - \tau)r - \pi$, the real rate of interest after taxes, which is the context of the equation (3.18).[8]

Wealth owners now hold equities in place of real capital, which is under the command of firms with regard to its use for production as well as with regard to its intended rate of change in time. Thus we have to replace the real wealth component K in asset owners' portfolios by $p_e E / p$, with respect to actual holdings as well as with respect to stock demand (giving rise to a

---

[7] Note here that the expected inflation rate π used in the calculation of the real rate of interest represents an average over the medium run in our interpretation of the wage–price dynamics of module 7 of the model (see also section 2.5). In principle, this also requires that the expected rate of return and the nominal rate of interest are to be considered as representing such averages. This is easily done by assuming certain dynamic feedback rules for these average concepts in view of their short-run equivalents (see Flaschel, Gong, and Semmler 1998 and Chiarella et al. 1998). Due to the hierarchical order of the models developed and investigated in this book, such extensions are here left for the future in order to proceed in a systematic way from low to high dimensional macrodynamic model building. Furthermore, one might also argue on empirical grounds that investment depends negatively on expected inflation π, as faster inflation may create an uncertain environment for investors. The role that inflationary expectations will play in the following is thereby reversed. We do not go into this topic here any further, but will adhere to the traditional way in which the investment function has been formulated in models of Keynes–Wicksell type. The topics indicated in this footnote must therefore be left for future research.

[8] Note that we here follow Sargent (1987, p.18) and assume that the expected change in the price of equities is zero.

new form of Walras' Law of Stocks). Furthermore, the savings decision of capitalist households now, of course, includes, besides money and bonds, the term $p_e \dot{E}^d / p$, i.e., that part of private savings that is intended to go into equities. These aspects are reflected in equations (3.2)–(3.6).

Note here that we stick to the assumption that all taxes are paid by capitalists. Note, furthermore, that we no longer distinguish between the actual and the perceived disposable income of capitalist households. This distinction has been extensively treated in the preceding chapter, so that it may be admissible to use the simple income concept $Y - \delta K - T$ as perceived disposable income for the private sector as a whole from now on. Note here finally that this income is based on production plans and not on actual sales, just as in the models of Tobin type. Of course, the discussion of more elaborate concepts of perceived disposable income needs to be pursued in future investigations of the models proposed in this book.

Firms issue equities in order to finance investment, and they have by assumption no retained earnings with respect to their planned production and planned proceeds. Investment may and will differ from total savings in models of Keynes–Wicksell type in general which means that planned production and proceeds $\rho p K$ and actual sales and proceeds will be different from each other. The amount of production that is not sold is given by $S - I = Y - \delta K - C - I - G$.[9] Yet, this additional production has already (by assumption) been paid out to equity holders, which means that firms have to issue new equities as described in (3.9), not only in order to finance their investment, but also to finance any difference between expected and actual proceeds. Newly issued equities are therefore equal in amount to total savings, which implies that private savers will be just content with the supply of new equities by firms.

Since we have independent investment behavior with $I \neq S$ in general, there is now the choice between investment goods supplied or demanded in the determination of actual capital accumulation $\dot{K}$. These two polar cases are described in (3.10) by means of the parameter $\beta_k (= 0, 1)$, and are to be discussed briefly with respect to their consistency in the light of the other equations of the model.

Let us first consider the case $\beta_k = 0$, which is identical with the $\dot{K}$ assumption of the Tobin type models. In this case, we assume that firms involuntarily invest their extra supply of goods in new machinery and finance this extra investment as described above by issuing further equities, if supply Y exceeds aggregate demand $C + I + \delta K + G$. In the opposite case, where $I - S > 0$ holds, they are forced to cancel this amount of their investment plans and orders by assumption. In the present model the only

---

[9] The expression δK represents that part of production that is kept by firms for capital replacement purposes and for voluntary inventory changes.

consequence of these actions of firms is therefore given by the price adjustment equation (3.23), which says that any discrepancy between demand and supply $C + I + \delta K + G - Y = I - S$ gives rise to corresponding price movements according to the so-called law of demand. The immediate consequences of goods-market disequilibrium are thus purely nominal in the present model. In comparison to the model of section 2.5 this nevertheless represents a significant improvement, since the price level is here no longer driven by an imbalance in the market for the stock of money (an imbalance which does not exist in the present model, see (3.17)), but in a Wicksellian fashion by relative imbalances in the market for goods. The picture that emerges from this discussion of the case $\beta_k = 0$ is that of a supply driven economy, as in section 2.5, but now one with a Keynes–Wicksell goods and money market demand block which determines the rate of inflation $\hat{p}$ and the nominal rate of interest r. Since all goods produced are used for consumption or investment purposes in the present case there is no need to consider inventory changes $\dot{N}$ explicitly. This is obtained from equation (3.11) by setting $\delta_2 = 0$ in addition to the assumption $\beta_k = 0$, i.e., equation (3.11) can be ignored in this case.

The latter remark is not true for the alternative case $\beta_k = 1$, where capital accumulation is assumed to be driven by investment plans and not by intended savings. In this case there must be corresponding movements in inventories N which are determined by the imbalance in the market for goods as described in equation (3.11). Inventories increase when output exceeds aggregate demand ($S > I$) and they decrease in the opposite case ($S < I$). Note here also that we are considering a growing economy, which means that there is a further reason for ongoing inventory changes, namely, that inventories have to grow in order to stay in line with the permanent growth in production and the capital stock. For simplicity, we assume here that a certain portion of output (and thus of the capital stock) is retained by firms for this purpose so that these inventory changes can be treated simply as capital depreciation and simply be aggregated with it ($\delta = \delta_1 + \delta_2$), just representing a portion of actual production that (generally) does not leave the sphere of production. The case $\beta_k = 1$ thus can be characterized as being more demand oriented than the case $\beta_k = 0$ and thereby perhaps somewhat more in line with Keynesian concepts of monetary growth. Note that equation (3.9) is also valid in this case, meaning again that firms have to finance new investment *and* dividends that are not yet backed up by sales, but represented only by an increase in inventories (if $S > I$ holds; in the opposite case we instead have that part of the new investment is financed by unexpected sales from inventories). Again the immediate effects of goods-market disequilibrium are purely nominal ones.

The description of these two polar cases shows that intermediate cases are also conceivable ($\beta_k \in (0, 1)$) where any unsold production goes partly into unplanned inventory changes and partly into unintended real capital formation,[10] with obvious changes in this description if investment demand exceeds currents savings.[11] We shall, however, pay no attention to this intermediate case in the following, but simply state here that its stability properties will in fact be intermediate with respect to the ones we shall establish for the two polar cases.

We thus end up here with a significantly revised description of the behavior of firms (which induces only minor changes in the description of household behavior as we have seen above). By contrast there is no change necessary in the formulation of the government sector when going from the general Tobin model to this general version of a model of Keynes–Wicksell type.

As already stated, we are no longer dependent here on money-market disequilibrium in the formulation of an explicit (demand-pull) theory of the rate of inflation $\hat{p}$ (see again (3.23), and note its use of a relative expression for the state of goods-market disequilibrium). Otherwise, the description of the wage–price module is the same as in the general Tobin model of section 2.5. We thus have in this model the usual LM-equilibrium of Keynesian models which, by the wealth constraint of asset holders and the perfect substitute assumption for bonds and equities, implies that the other asset markets must be cleared as well (see (3.17)). The perfect substitute assumption (3.18) has already been explained above, while (3.19) again states that asset holders will voluntarily accept the additional supply of money and bonds and adjust their resulting changed portfolios only in the "subsequent period". Due to the implied equality $S = S_p + S_g = p_e \dot{E}^d / p$ (see (3.5) and (3.14)), we obtain from (3.9) the equation $\dot{E} = \dot{E}^d$ (see (3.19)), i.e., general consistency with respect to flows[12] (besides the general consistency for stocks (3.17)).

This concludes our description of the general Keynes–Wicksell model of this section (which, besides labor market disequilibrium, now also exhibits

---

[10] Both being financed by issuing new equities, since firms have no earnings from current production.

[11] Note that this also covers the case of an excessive new bond and money supply ($\dot{M} + \dot{B} > p S_p$) by the government, in which case we can have negative aggregate savings S and a reduction in the stock of equities financed by excessive sales of firms from inventories. A constraint of the type $pS = p_e \dot{E} > 0$ is therefore not really necessary in the present formulation of the model. Note also that in such a case it is not only investment demand, but also other demand (here implicitly assumed to be satisfied before investment demand is considered), that is (completely) met by appropriate inventory changes. Also in such a situation it is therefore only investment demand that can be rationed in the present model.

[12] Note here again that this "simple" assumption bears strong consequences with respect to the ability of the government to influence the pace of capital accumulation. Nevertheless, we shall not dispense with this standard assumption of continuous-time macrodynamic theory in this book, but shall leave its detailed reconsideration for future investigations.

goods-market disequilibrium as the explanation of price inflation). We stress once again that it is mainly the firms sector which has received an extensive reformulation here accompanied by a new arrangement of equilibrium and disequilibrium conditions and their implication for the formulation of the wage–price module. In our view this model type is much more convincing than the general Tobin model of the preceding chapter. Nevertheless, in discussing this model we shall find that it is still fairly neoclassical in its structure and its implications due to some definite weaknesses it contains. These weaknesses concern the description of goods-market disequilibrium and the treatment of unplanned inventory changes. In most treatments these weaknesses are generally simply removed from view by the assumption of an infinite adjustment speed of prices, as we discuss in a later section of this chapter. Better ways to overcome these weaknesses (and the differences that this implies for the working of such a model) will be the theme of the next chapter.

As far as the mathematical investigation of this general Keynes–Wicksell model is concerned, we will confine ourselves here mainly to the case $t^n = t - rb = $ const., where lump sum taxes are varied in such a way that the ratio of taxes net of interest to the value of the capital stock remains constant over time. This assumption will allow us to disregard the GBR and the evolution of government debt in the following, at least from a local point of view. In making use of this simplifying device we here follow a similar assumption of Sargent's (1987, ch. 5) "dynamic analysis of a Keynesian model," which is the basic reference with respect to the models we shall investigate in this chapter and in chapters 4 and 5.

3.2   The intensive form of the model

Before we now start with the step-by-step investigation of the four-dimensional case with $t^n = t - rb = $ const., let us first rewrite **the general dynamical model** (3.1)–(3.24), without any simplifying assumptions, as an autonomous dynamical system in the five variables $\omega = w/p$, $l = L/K$, $m = M/(pK)$, π, and $b = B/(pK)$.[13]

---

[13] Note that the system in fact exhibits two further laws of motion for the variables $v = N/K$ and $e = E/K$ which, however, do not feed back to the other laws of motion of the model. These two laws read:

$$\dot{v} = \delta_2 + \beta_k(s(\cdot) - i(\cdot) - n) - nv + \hat{l}v \; [v_0 = \delta_2/n],$$

$$\hat{e} = \frac{(1-\tau)r - \pi}{(1-\tau)\rho} s(\cdot) - n + \hat{l} \; [e_0 \text{ indeterminate}].$$

It is, of course, necessary to check that both v and e remain nonnegative and finite in the course of the dynamic evolution of the above dynamics. Note that the second law implies that the number of equities grows with the rate n in the steady state, while bonds B and money M both grow with the rate μ.

By calculations of the same type as in the preceding chapter (see in particular section 2.3) we obtain from (3.1)–(3.24) the intensive form equations:

$$\dot{\omega} = \kappa[(1 - \kappa_p)\beta_w X^w + (\kappa_w - 1)\beta_p X^p], \tag{3.25}$$

$$\hat{l} = n - s(\cdot) \text{ or } -i(\cdot)(\beta_k = 0 \text{ or } 1), \tag{3.26}$$

$$\hat{m} = \mu_0 - n - \pi - \kappa[\beta_p X^p + \kappa_p\beta_w X^w] + \hat{l}, \tag{3.27}$$

$$\dot{\pi} = \beta_{\pi_1}\kappa[\beta_p X^p + \kappa_p\beta_w X^w] + \beta_{\pi_2}(\mu_0 - n - \pi), \tag{3.28}$$

$$\dot{b} = (\mu_2 - \mu_0)m - (\pi + n)b - (\kappa(\beta_p X^p + \kappa_p\beta_w X^w) - \hat{l})b, \tag{3.29}$$

where we employ the abbreviations:

$$\rho = y - \delta - \omega^d, l^d = L^d/K = y/x = \text{const.},$$
$$X^w = l^d/l - \bar{V} = y/(xl) - \bar{V},$$
$$X^p = i(\cdot) + n - s(\cdot),$$
$$r = \bar{r} + (h_1 y - m)/(h_2(1 - \tau))[h(y,r) = h_1 y + h_2(1 - \tau)(\bar{r} - r),$$

see (3.3)],

$$t = T/K = \tau(\rho + rb), t^n = t - rb,$$
$$g = t^n + \mu_2 m,$$
$$s(\cdot) = s_c(\rho - t^n) - (g - t^n),$$
$$i(\cdot) = i(\rho - r + \pi).$$

Note here that in the above presentation of the dynamics we have made use of the formula $\hat{p} - \pi = \kappa[\beta_p X^p + \kappa_p\beta_w X^w]$ for the deviation of the actual rate of inflation from the expected one, and that the $s(\cdot)$ equation can be easily obtained from $s(\cdot) = \hat{K} = y - \delta - C/K - G/K$ by inserting into it the consumption function and the government expenditure rule.

In the following determination of steady-state solutions of the above dynamics we again disregard the boundary solutions $\omega, l, m = 0$ which arise from the growth rate formulation of certain laws of motion. These values of the variables ω, l, and m are economically meaningless and will not appear as relevant attractors in the stability investigations to be performed. A general and global analysis of the system should, of course, take into account the stability properties of such boundary points of rest of the dynamics (3.25)–(3.29). For simplicity, we also assume here that the parameter $\bar{r}$ in the above model is equal to the steady-state value r_0. This assumption simplifies the calculation of the steady-state values without loss in generality, but it should be kept in mind or dispensed with if steady state comparisons are being made.

Proposition 3.1: There is a *unique steady-state solution* or point of rest of the dynamics (3.25)–(3.29) fulfilling $\omega_0, l_0, m_0 \neq 0$.[14] This steady state is determined by:[15]

$$y_0 = y^p, \tag{3.30}$$

$$l_0 = y_0/(x\bar{V}), l_0^d = y_0/x, \tag{3.31}$$

$$m_0 = h_1 y_0, \tag{3.32}$$

$$\pi_0 = \mu_0 - n, \tag{3.33}$$

$$b_0 = (\mu_2 - \mu_0)m_0/\mu_0, \tag{3.34}$$

$$\rho_0 = \frac{n + \mu_2 m_0 - s_c \pi_0 b_0}{s_c(1 - \tau)(1 + b_0)},$$

$$r_0 = \rho_0 + \pi_0,$$

$$\omega_0 = (y_0 - \delta - \rho_0)/l_0^d. \tag{3.35}$$

Proof: The equations (3.26) and (3.27) (set equal to zero) imply that $\mu_0 - n - \pi = \kappa[\beta_p X^p + \kappa_p \beta_w X^w]$ must hold in the steady state. Inserting this into (3.28) then gives that $\pi_0 = \mu_0 - n$ must hold. This in turn implies by (3.27) the equality of $\hat{p}$ and π_0. From the equations (3.25) and (3.27) we then obtain the following simultaneous equation system for the variables X^p and X^w:

$$0 = (1 - \kappa_p)\beta_w X^w + (\kappa_w - 1)\beta_p X^p,$$
$$0 = \beta_p X^p + \kappa_p \beta_w X^w.$$

It is easily shown for $\kappa_w \kappa_p < 1$ that this linear equation system can be uniquely solved for X^w and X^p, which must then both be zero. This implies the first two of our steady-state equations (3.30) and (3.32). Equation (3.32) then immediately follows from our assumption $\bar{r} = r_0$ and (3.33) has already been shown above. Next, (3.34) is obtained by solving the $\dot{b} = 0$ equation for the steady-state value of $b(X^w, X^p = 0)$. The equation for ρ_0 is then obtained from (3.26), i.e., $n = s(\cdot)$, by solving this equation for ρ_0, since we have $\rho_0 - t_0^n = (1 - \tau)(1 + b_0)\rho_0 + \pi_0 b_0$ and $g_0 - t_0^n = \mu_2 m_0$ in the steady state. The calculation of ω_0, r_0 is then straightforward ($i(\cdot) = 0!$). This concludes the proof of existence and uniqueness for the interior steady state solution. ∎

---

[14] The following presentation of this steady state of the dynamics immediately implies that money is not superneutral in this model, i.e., the rate of growth of the money supply exercises an influence on the real side of the steady state of the model.

[15] It is easy to calculate for the additional dynamic variables $N/K, p_e E/(pK)$ the steady-state values: δ_2/n and $(1 - \tau)\rho_0/((1 - \tau)r_0 - \pi_0)$, respectively.

We assume with respect to this steady-state solution first of all that the parameters of the model are chosen such that $\rho_0 > 0$ holds true. This is obviously the case if the growth rate of the money supply μ_0 and the parameter μ_2 are set equal to the natural rate of growth n, since the tax parameter τ must satisfy $\tau \in (0, 1)$. The case just described can be regarded as the basic steady-state configuration of the general model, since the government then just supplies the correct monetary frame for the growth path of the real part of the model and it injects this necessary amount of new money by buying goods (in addition to the ones that are financed by taxes), i.e. there is no need for government debt or credit in this situation $(b_0 = 0!)$. The steady-state rate of profit is in this case simply given by $(n + \mu_0 m_0)/(s_c(1 - \tau)) > 0, m_0 = h_1 y$. Secondly, we must here also assume that this expression for the rate of profit is less than $y - \delta$ so that there is associated with it a positive steady-state level of the real wage ω_0. This condition should always be fulfilled since the magnitudes of n, h_1, and μ_0 are all small from an empirical point of view. On the basis of these assumptions we thus have a unique and meaningful interior solution to the steady-state equations. It is assumed that the parameters of the model in general do not depart by so much from those of this basic steady-state configuration that the conditions $\rho_0, \omega_0 > 0$ will be violated. Note, finally, that $\pi_0 = \mu_0 - n$ should not be chosen so negative that $r_0 > 0$ will not hold true.

Let us now start with the investigation of **the case $t'' = t - rb = $ const.** We here in addition simplify the notation of the four-dimensional dynamics that results in this case by setting the value of $\bar{V}$ equal to 1. Since the variable b only enters the equations (3.25)–(3.28) via the $s(\cdot)$ equation (which only depends on t''), we immediately see that the first four dynamical laws and their components do not depend on the variable b. Furthermore, the entry J_{55} in the Jacobian J of the dynamics (3.25)–(3.29) is in this case simply given by $-(\pi_0 + n)$ at the steady state of this system. The eigenvalue structure $(\lambda_{1,...,4})$ of the dynamics at the steady state is therefore given by that of the system shown below plus the eigenvalue $\lambda_5 = -(\pi_0 + n)$. Stability assertions on the subsystem (3.25)–(3.28) therefore immediately also hold for the complete model (3.25)–(3.29), at least from a local point of view.

In light of the foregoing discussion we are led to consider the four-dimensional system:

$$\hat{\omega} = \kappa[(1 - \kappa_p)\beta_w(y/(xl) - 1) + (\kappa_w - 1)\beta_p(i(\cdot)) + n - s(\cdot))], \tag{3.36}$$

$$\hat{l} = n - s(\cdot) \text{ or } -i(\cdot)), (\beta_k = 0 \text{ or } 1), \tag{3.37}$$

$$\hat{m} = \mu_0 - \pi - n - \kappa[\beta_p(i(\cdot)$$
$$+ n - s(\cdot)) + \kappa_p\beta_w(y/(xl) - 1)] + \hat{l}, \tag{3.38}$$

$$\dot{\pi} = \beta_{\pi_1}\kappa[\beta_p(i(\cdot) + n - s(\cdot)) + \kappa_p\beta_w(y/(xl) - 1)]$$
$$+ \beta_{\pi_2}(\mu_0 - n - \pi), \tag{3.39}$$

where

$$s(\cdot) = s_c(y - \delta - \omega y/x - t^n) - \mu_2 m,$$
$$i(\cdot) = i(y - \delta - \omega y/x - (r_0 + (h_1 y - m)/h_2) + \pi).$$

Note here again that $y, x = $ const. still holds (as in the last chapter) in the context of the Keynes–Wicksell model of this chapter and that the parameter τ is now no longer present in this model variant. Note, furthermore, that the steady-state solution of the four-dimensional system is now based on the expression $\rho_0 = (n + \mu_2 m_0)/s_c + t^n$. All other expressions for the steady state remain unchanged under the above modification.[16] The above dynamic system will now be investigated by starting from an appropriate two-dimensional subcase of it.

3.3   The Goodwin growth cycle case

This section starts from a set of simplifying assumptions which imply that the real part of the Keynes–Wicksell model of this chapter gives rise to dynamics of the Goodwin (1967) growth cycle type. The overshooting profit squeeze mechanism of that model is thus an integral part of our general Keynes–Wicksell model.[17]

In order to obtain the simple two-dimensional center type dynamics of this growth cycle model from the above four-dimensional model one has to make the following four assumptions:

$\kappa_w = 1$: The real wage dynamics is independent of the goods market.

$r = r_0$: Infinite interest elasticity of money demand at the steady state $(h_2 = \infty.)$

$\pi = \mu_0 - n$: Extreme asymptotically rational expectations $(\beta_{\pi_2} = \infty, \beta_{\pi_1} < \infty)$.

[16] I.e., we have $(\bar{U}, \bar{V} = 1)$:

$$y_0 = y^p, l_0^d = y_0/x, l_0 = l_0^d,$$
$$\pi_0 = \mu_0 - n, m_0 = h_1 y_0,$$
$$\omega_0 = (y_0 - \delta - \rho_0)/l_0^d, r_0 = \rho_0 + \mu_0 - n.$$

Note here that Sargent (1987, ch. 5) obtains the superneutrality of this steady state by assuming $g = $ const. and $\mu_2 = 0$ in addition to the above assumption $t^n = $ const.

[17] See Flaschel (1984, 1993), Flaschel and Sethi (1996), and Flaschel, Franke, and Semmler (1997) for various representations and investigations of the Goodwin growth cycle model and its extensions, and Flaschel and Groh (1995) for some empirical observations on this model type that extend Solow's (1990) reappraisal of this very fundamental model of cyclical growth.

$\mu_2 = :$ Government is a creditor in the steady state: $b_0 = - m_0$.

In the **case** $\hat{K} = i(\cdot) + n$ (i.e. $\beta_k = 1$), the first three of the above assumptions are in fact already sufficient to imply the cross-dual growth cycle dynamics of the Goodwin model for *the real part of the model* (3.1)–(3.24), since we then get from equations (3.36) and (3.37) the following special dynamic equations ($y, x = $ const., $l^d = y/x$):

$$\hat{\omega} = \beta_w(l^d/l - 1), \tag{3.40}$$

$$\hat{l} = - i(y - \delta - \omega l^d - r_0 + \mu_0 - n). \tag{3.41}$$

It is obvious from these equations that $r = r_0$ removes the influence of the money market on the real part of the model ($r_0 = \rho_0 + \mu_0 - n$), that $\pi = \mu_0 - n$ removes the dynamics of expectations formation, and that $\kappa_w = 1$ suppresses the impact of the goods-market disequilibrium on the dynamics of the real-wage.

Since l^d and y are given magnitudes in the model (3.1)–(3.24), the above two equations are easily reformulated in terms of Goodwin's original dynamic variables $u = \omega l^d/y = \omega/x$ (the share of wages) and $V = l^d/l$ (the rate of employment):

$$\hat{u} = \beta_w(V - 1) \equiv h^1(V), \tag{3.42}$$

$$\hat{V} = i(y - \delta - uy - r_0 + \mu_0 - n) \equiv h^2(u). \tag{3.43}$$

Proposition 3.2: The trajectories of the dynamical system (3.42)–(3.43) stay positive if they start in the positive domain of $\mathbb{R}^2$ and are all closed orbits.

Proof: It is easily shown that all orbits which start in the positive orthant must stay in it, since the boundary of this domain is an invariant subset of the above dynamics. The proof that all trajectories of this dynamical system are closed orbits is also straightforward if one makes use of the following function

$$H(u, V) = - \int_{u_0}^{u} (h^2(\tilde{u})/\tilde{u})d\tilde{u} + \int_{V_0}^{V} (h^1(\tilde{V})/(\tilde{V})d\tilde{V}.$$

This function is zero at the steady-state values u_0, V_0 and positive elsewhere. Furthermore, one easily gets $\dot{H} = H_u \cdot \dot{u} + H_V \cdot \dot{V} = (- h^2(u))\hat{u} + h^1(V)\hat{V} \equiv 0$, i.e., the function H is a Liapunov function.[18] Due to the shape of this function, it follows that all orbits must be closed (see Flaschel 1993, ch. 4, for the details of such reasoning). The resulting phase portrait of this dynamical system is well-known (see again Flaschel 1993, ch. 4, for the graphical details). ∎

---

[18] See Hirsch and Smale (1974, pp.192ff.), and Brock and Malliaris (1989, pp.94 ff.).

All observations in the preceding proof can be reformulated in a straight-forward way for the original presentation of the dynamical system (3.40)–(3.41) in the variables ω and l, and they also hold for all nonlinear labor market reaction functions $\beta_w(l^d/l)$ with $\beta_w(0) = 1, \beta'_w > 0$ (see the next section for the introduction of such nonlinear Phillips curves).

The remaining dynamical equations of this growth cycle case are

$$\dot{m} = -\kappa(\beta_p(i(\cdot) + n - s(\cdot)) + \kappa_p\beta_w(V-1)) - i(\cdot) = f^1(u, V),$$
$$\dot{b} = -\mu_0 m - (\hat{p}(\cdot) + \hat{K}(\cdot))b = f^2(u, V, m, b).$$

Since we only want to show here that Goodwin's growth cycle is part of the fully interdependent dynamics of the general model, we do not discuss this appended dynamical system in the special case we are considering in the present section. Of course, Goodwin's type of dynamics will also be present and tend to dominate if $r \approx r_0$ (high interest elasticity of money demand) and $\kappa_w \approx 1, \beta_{\pi_2} \approx \infty$ holds, but may be modified significantly in its over-shooting feature when less extreme parameter values are given.

The Goodwin model is even more closely mirrored if **the alternative case** $\hat{K} = s(\cdot)$ (i.e., $\beta_k = 0$) is considered. In this case, the further above assumption $\mu_2 = 0$ on government behavior is needed, if one wants the dynamics of ω, l (i.e., u, V) to be fully independent of the rest of the system. This is due here to the form of the savings per unit of capital function

$$s(\cdot) = s_c(y - \delta - \omega l^d - t^n) - \mu_2 m.$$

The belief that (real) wage flexibility will give rise to full employment steady growth, at least in the long-run, is supported most when Kuh's (1967) version of the Phillips curve is used in the Goodwin context, see Akerlof and Stiglitz (1969, pp.272–274) for such an application. This version of the Phillips curve can be formulated as follows (see Ferri and Greenberg 1989, p.75). Set

$$\omega = \beta_w(V)y/l^d, \text{ i.e., } u = \beta_w(V).[19]$$

With respect to the model (3.42)–(3.43), this latter equation replaces (3.42) and gives, in conjunction with (3.43):

$$\hat{V} = i(y - \delta - \beta_w(V)y - r_0 + \mu_0 - n) \text{ or}$$
$$\dot{V} = iy(\beta_w(V_0) - \beta_w(V))V = H(V),$$

where V_0 is defined by $\beta_w(V_0) = 1 - (\rho_0 + \delta)/y, \rho_0 = r_0 - (\mu_0 - n) (u_0 = \beta_w(V_0))$. These values characterize the steady state of the model and we assume here that an economically meaningful solution $V_0 > 0$ exists. This steady state is obviously globally asymptotically stable, since we have

[19] $\beta_w(\cdot)$ may be nonlinear and is assumed to fulfill $\beta_w(V) \in (0,1), \beta'_w > 0$. Note that the expression $x = y/l^d$ in this new Phillips curve represents labor productivity Y/L^d.

$\dot{V} > 0$ to the left of V_0 and $\dot{V} < 0$ to its right. Employment decreases to the right of V_0 and with it the real wage until income redistribution induces a growth rate of the capital stock that is equal to the growth rate of the labor force n (the opposite occurs to the left of V_0). It has become common usage to call $1 - V_0$ the natural rate of unemployment and to consider V_0 as the "full" employment rate (see Akerlof and Stiglitz 1969, p.271, for an early example of this). The model therefore gives the most straightforward demonstration of the long-run stability of the full-employment situation.

Note, however, that the present explanation of "natural" employment $V_0 = \beta_w^{-1}((y - \delta - r_0 + \mu_0 - n)/y)$ (assumed to lie between 0 and 1) is far from being "natural," as its dependence in particular on β_w and μ_0 shows.

Furthermore, even this simple model of growth and (un)employment can give rise to complex dynamics if it is reformulated in discrete time, even if $\beta_w(V)$ is assumed to be a linear function of V. In this latter case it gives rise to the following well-known difference equation that allows for "chaos" at appropriate parameter values for i, y and β_w, namely, $V_{t+1} = V_t(1 + iy\beta_w(V_0 - V_t))$ (see Pohjola 1981 and Ferri and Greenberg 1989 for its treatment in this context). We thus can associate even chaotic behavior with this most basic form of a full-employment "adjustment" mechanism if the parameter β_w becomes sufficiently large (V_0 sufficiently small) (see again Pohjola 1981 for details).

Ferri and Greenberg (1989) consider in chapter 4.8 another approach to labor market dynamics which they call a **neoclassical disequilibrium approach**. This approach, which is based on neo-Keynesian regime switching methods, takes account of the fact that the employment rate V cannot increase beyond 1 if 1 stands for the ceiling of absolute full employment.[20] The Goodwin model (3.40)–(3.41), for example, has then to be modified as follows (l^d a given magnitude):

$$\hat{\omega} = \beta_w(l^d/l - 1), \tag{3.44}$$

$$\hat{l} = \begin{cases} -i(xl^d - \delta - \omega l^d - r_0 + \mu_0 - n), & \text{if } l \ge l^d \\ -i(xl - \delta - \omega l - r_0 + \mu_0 - n), & \text{if } l \le l^d, \end{cases} \tag{3.45}$$

to take account of the fact that employment and production cannot increase beyond the full employment level: $l^d \le l, y \le xl$. This model is considered in Ito (1980) in full detail and with regard to the mathematical complexities to which such a regime switching approach can give rise.

There is, however, one fundamental shortcoming of such regime switching approaches which lies in the fact that they usually identify the steady-

---

[20] Note here that we have used "1" in the four-dimensional dynamics (3.36)–(3.39) to denote that level of employment where there is no money wage drift from the side of the labor market, which is assumed to be a magnitude significantly below full employment.

state rate of employment with the maximum rate of employment. Such a view is not shared by many macroeconomists, quite independently of the particular justification they may give for the assumption (or derivation) of a positive magnitude V_0 or $1 - V_0$, often called the natural rate of (un)employment (or the NAIRU if a broader definition is given to this positive steady state concept of (un)employment). We here use the value 1 for V_0 for simplicity to denote the "natural" level of the employment rate and thus have to use $V_{max} > 1$ if we want to refer to some sort of absolute full employment ceiling.

Introducing such a full employment ceiling into the equations (3.40)–(3.41) gives, instead of (3.44)–(3.45), the equations ($l^d = y/x =$ const.):

$$\hat{\omega} = \beta_w(l^d/l - 1), \tag{3.46}$$

$$\hat{l} = \begin{cases} -i(xl^d - \delta - \omega l^d - r_0 + \mu_0 - n), & \text{if } l \geq l^d/V_{max}, \\ -i(xlV_{max} - \delta - \omega lV_{max} - r_0 + \mu_0 - n), & \text{if } l \leq l^d/V_{max}. \end{cases} \tag{3.47}$$

This implies that the dynamics are of the same type as those of (3.40)–(3.41) as long as l stays within $(l^d/V_{max}, +\infty)$, i.e., within a certain neighborhood of the steady-state value $l_0 = l^d \in (l^d/V_{max}, +\infty)$. Only if l falls below l^d/V_{max} is there such a shortage of the labor supply that output must fall below the potential output $Y^p = yK$ and will thus modify the path of capital accumulation (and that of l). Of course, the Phillips curve may have kinks in addition, as in Ferri and Greenberg (1989, p.62), at various levels of the employment rate. This, however, only modifies the shape of the closed orbits of the Goodwin model, not its qualitative features.

The phase portrait shown in figure 3.1 summarizes the above findings on labor supply bottlenecks in the Goodwin model. Leaving aside such bottlenecks from the side of labor supply and (by the use of equations (3.11) and (3.23)), and also certain bottlenecks from the side of capacity output including inventories, therefore simply means that the dynamics of system (3.1)–(3.24) is restricted to such a domain of economically meaningful values where neither productive capacity plus inventories nor natural capacity ($L_{max} = L \cdot V_{max}$) becomes a binding constraint for the growth path $\hat{K} = i(\cdot)$ of the economy.[21] Important as such switches in economic regimes may be from a global point of view, they can at first be safely neglected in the study of the fundamental properties of the dynamic system (3.1)–(3.24) and its special cases. Ceilings to economic activity (caused by the existing supply of goods including inventories)[22] and the present

---

[21] Which would lead to regimes of absolute goods supply shortages or absolute labor supply shortages.

[22] Note here however that equations (3.11) and (3.23) are not without problems, problems

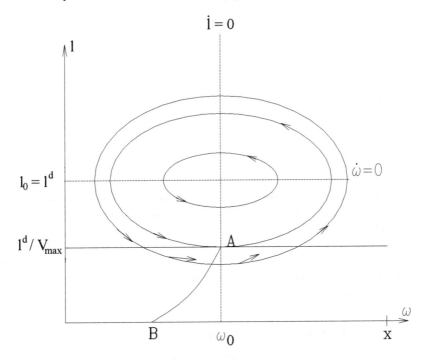

Figure 3.1 Ceilings to the validity of the Goodwin growth cycle approach

volume of maximum labor supply are of no importance for the economic evolution near the steady state.

Of course, they have to be added eventually to any global treatment of the Keynes–Wicksell model, but will then not give rise to a *new theory* of labor market dynamics. Instead, there is only a switch in the determination of the isocline $\dot{l} = 0$ below $l^d/V_{\max}$ as shown in figure 3.1 by the curve AB,[23] given by

$$\omega = (x - (\delta + r_0 - (\mu_0 - n)))/(lV_{\max}),$$

which should lead to it having a positive slope with respect to empirically plausible values of the parameters δ, r_0, n and μ_0. This is, of course, no significant modification of the dynamics of the Goodwin model.

This last statement can be further substantiated by means of the Liapunov function

$$H(\omega, l) = \int_{\omega_0}^{\omega} \frac{h^2(\tilde{\omega})}{\tilde{\omega}} d\tilde{\omega} - \int_{l_0}^{l} \frac{h^1(\tilde{l})}{\tilde{l}} d\tilde{l},$$

for the dynamical system (3.46)–(3.47) where $h^1(l)$ is given by $\beta_w(l^d/l - 1)$ and $h^2(\omega)$ by $-i(xl^d - \delta - \omega l^d - r_0 + \mu_0 - n)$. This function is of the same type as the Liapunov function we used before and it gives rise to[24]

$$\dot{H} = \begin{cases} 0 & \text{if } l \ge l^d/V_{max} \\ h_1(l)[h^2(\omega) + i(xlV_{max} - \delta - \omega lV_{max} - r_0 + \mu_0 - n)] & \text{if } l \le l^d/V_{max} \end{cases}$$

$$\le h^1(l)[h^2(\omega) - h^2(\omega)] = 0.$$

This implies that the original closed orbits of the Goodwin model are crossed inwards by the trajectories of this new dynamical system in the region below l^d/V_{max} (see figure 3.1), so that the closed orbit of figure 3.1 that runs through A becomes a limit cycle for all trajectories that start at points outside of it. The closed orbits of the Goodwin model thus characterize this dynamical system in the long run also in the cases where regime switching takes place.

3.4   The Rose employment cycle extension

In this section we remove one of the simplifying assumptions of the preceding section. We show that the limit cycle result of Rose (1967) can then be obtained through the interaction of the Goodwin profit squeeze mechanism (of the preceding section) and locally destabilizing and globally stabilizing relative adjustment speeds of wages and prices. These latter forces were the basic ingredients of Rose's nonlinear theory of the employment cycle.[25]

We have considered in the preceding section four variants of Goodwin's growth cycle model and have argued in particular that it is far from obvious that the real wage mechanism $\hat{\omega} = \beta_w(l^d/l - 1)$, or even a simplification of it, will guarantee full employment equilibrium in the long run. Smooth factor substitution with a sufficiently high elasticity of factor substitution may alter this conclusion to some extent, but only insofar as it thereby becomes an empirical question of whether Goodwin or Solow provides the more convincing approach to the supply-side determined path of capital accumulation.

In the present section we shall now demonstrate that the Solovian

---

[24] If $\omega < x = Y/L^d$, i.e. as long as profits remain positive.

[25] See Flaschel (1993), Flaschel and Sethi (1996), and Flaschel, Franke, and Semmler (1997) for various representations and investigations of the Rose employment cycle model and its extensions.

outcome (of a monotonic convergence to the full-employment growth path) becomes even more unlikely if it is realized, as in Rose's (1967) model of the employment cycle, that even in a supply-side driven economy the evolution of real wages is driven not only by the disequilibrium in the labor market but also by disequilibrium in the market for goods. This proposition also extends to the case of smooth factor substitution as Rose (1967) has already shown with a similar real growth model. The essential ideas behind his employment limit cycle are, however, also more easily grasped in the context of a fixed proportions technology as we shall show in this section.

In order to obtain a Rose type model as a special case of our general framework (3.1)–(3.24) we have only to assume $\kappa_w < 1$[26] as modification of the assumptions of section 3.3 (all other assumptions of that section remain intact). The Goodwinian dynamical system (3.40)–(3.41) is thereby extended to the dynamical system (see also equations (3.22) and (3.23)):

$$\hat{\omega} = \kappa[(1 - \kappa_p)\beta_w(l^d/l - 1) + (\kappa_w - 1)\beta_p(i(\cdot) + n - s(\cdot))], \quad (3.48)$$

$$\hat{l} = -i(\cdot), \text{ (or } n - s(\cdot)), \quad (3.49)$$

where $i(\cdot) = i(y - \delta - \omega l^d - r_0 + \mu_0 - n)$ and $s(\cdot) = s_c(y - \delta - \omega l^d - t^n)$, as in section 3.3.

In order to study the dynamics of this extended model, let us again consider the case $\dot{K} = I$ (i.e. $\beta_k = 1$) first. Making use again of the Liapunov function

$$H(\omega, l) = \int_{\omega_0}^{\omega} \frac{h^2(\tilde{\omega})}{\tilde{\omega}} d\tilde{\omega} - \int_{l_0}^{l} \frac{h^1(\tilde{l})}{\tilde{l}} d\tilde{l},$$

where $h^1(l) = \kappa(1 - \kappa_p)\beta_w(l^d/l - 1)$, $h^2 = -i(\omega)$. This Liapunov function is of the type we have considered for the system (3.40)–(3.41) in the preceding section. Here we obtain the following proposition.

Proposition 3.3: The steady state of the dynamical system (3.48)–(3.49) is globally asymptotically stable (totally unstable) if $i < s_c(i > s_c)$.[27]

Proof: Calculating the time derivative of H along the trajectories of (3.48) and (3.49) yields:

$$\dot{H} = -h^1(l)\hat{l} + h^2(\omega)\hat{\omega}$$
$$= h^2(\omega)\kappa(\kappa_w - 1)\beta_p(i(\cdot) + n - s(\cdot)).$$

If $i < s_c$ holds, we get that the slope of $i(\cdot) + n - s(\cdot)$ is positive

---

[26] Together with $\kappa_p < 1$, of course.
[27] The dynamics are of Goodwinian type if $i = s_c$ holds.

$(= (- i + s_c)l^d)$. Furthermore $i(\cdot) + n - s(\cdot) = 0$ at $\omega = \omega_0$, i.e., this expression is negative to the left of ω_0 and positive to its right. The same holds true for the function $h^2(\omega) = - i(\cdot)$ which, taken together with the previous result, implies $\dot{H} < 0$ for $\omega \neq \omega_0$. The assertion then follows from the usual theorems on Liapunov functions, for which we refer the reader to Hirsch and Smale (1974, pp.196ff.), and Brock and Malliaris (1989; pp.89ff.). In the same way one can show $\dot{H} > 0$ if $i > s_c$. ∎

Up to now we have made use of linear relationships in the market for labor as well as for goods to investigate Rose's (1967) broader view on real wage dynamics. We have obtained a result similar to his, namely, that the steady state will be locally unstable if investment reacts more sensitively to real wage changes than total savings. In this case a drop in real wages will create extra goods demand pressure and thus extra inflation, which will induce a further fall in real wages and thus destabilize the neutral closed orbit structure of the Goodwin model. This locally explosive dynamical behavior is turned into global stability in Rose (1967) by means of an appropriate nonlinearity in the excess demand function of the labor market and by making use of neoclassical smooth factor substitution. In Flaschel and Sethi (1996), it is shown how this strategy can be applied to the present context. Here, however, we want to stick to fixed proportions in production and thus will have to introduce at least one further nonlinearity in order to obtain Rose's limit cycle result for a system of type (3.48)–(3.49).

The nonlinearity that Rose uses in the labor market is a very natural one if one takes into account the Classical nature of our general model and its special cases. It is of the form[28] displayed in figure 3.2.[29]

According to this form the money wage will become very flexible farther off the steady state (by way of a rising adjustment speed for larger deviations of the employment rate from its "natural" level 1). The proof of proposition 3.3 immediately shows that this nonlinearity alone is insufficient in successfully overcoming the total instability of the case where $i > s_c$ holds. In fact, $\dot{H} > 0$ holds quite independently of the form of the Phillips curve, as long as $\kappa_w < 1$ is true (while the case $\kappa_w = 1$ brings us back to the closed orbit structure of the Goodwin model). The phase portrait of (3.48)–(3.49) for $i > s_c$ is then easily shown to be of the type[30] displayed in

---

[28] See also Akerlof and Stiglitz (1969, p.278) on this sort of Phillips curve.

[29] This law (see figure 3.2) replaces the linear function $\beta_w(V - 1)$.

[30] The $\dot{\omega}$–isocline is given by:

$$l^d/b < 1 = \cfrac{l^d}{\beta_w^{-1}\left[\dfrac{1 - \kappa_w}{1 - \kappa_p}\beta_p(i(\cdot) + n - s(\cdot))\right]} = \cfrac{l^d}{\beta_w^{-1}\left[\dfrac{1 - \kappa_w}{1 - \kappa_p}\beta_p(s_c - i)l^d\omega + \text{const.}\right]} < l^d/a,$$

and is thus a strictly increasing function of ω for $i < s_c$.

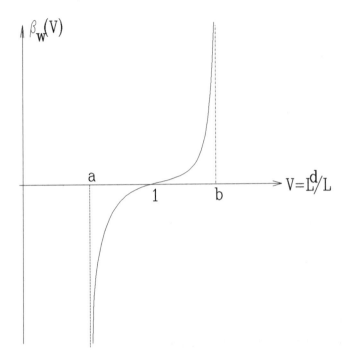

Figure 3.2 A nonlinear law of demand in the labor market

figure 3.3.[31]

In the case $\kappa_w = 1$, the restricted phase diagram of figure 3.3 is again filled with closed orbits as in the Goodwin model, while $\kappa_w < 1$ yields trajectories which point inwards with respect to these closed orbits for $s_c > i$ and outwards in the case $s_c < i$. Though the dynamical motion is thus now restricted to a corridor around the steady-state value $l_0 = l^d(V = 1)$, it is not viable as we have just seen.

In view of the shape of the $\dot{\omega} = 0$ isocline,[32] and the mathematical equation underlying it, it is natural to introduce a further nonlinearity, now in the market for goods, in order to obtain global viability for the considered dynamics, namely by means of investment behavior. Here we assume the type of nonlinearity[33] displayed in figure 3.4a.

Thus, though investment is more sensitive than savings with respect to real wage changes around the steady state, the opposite is the case for

---

[31] Note here that the true upper bound on the variable ω is given by $((y - \delta - t^n)/y)\,x$ and not by x as in figure 3.3.

[32] $\dot{\omega} = 0$ is horizontal if $\kappa_w = 1$ holds.

[33] Note the formal similarity to the Kaldor (1940) trade cycle model.

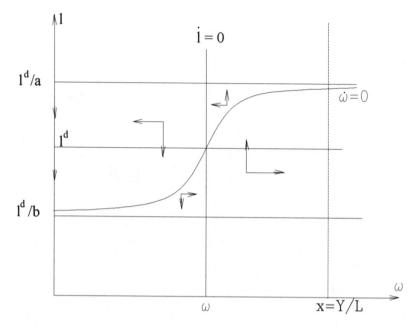

Figure 3.3 Implications of nonlinearity in the labor market

larger deviations of the real wage from its steady-state level ω_0. The phase portrait in figure 3.3 is changed by these assumptions as shown in figure 3.4b.[34]

We have added to this phase portrait one cycle of the closed orbit structure of the Goodwin subcase ($\kappa_w = 1$) of this two-dimensional dynamical system, and will now show that the trajectories in the case $\kappa_w < 1$ point inwards with respect to each of these Goodwin cycles in the regions to the left of $\underline{\omega}$ and to the right of $\bar{\omega}$. By contrast, they point outwards within these two values of ω.

Proposition 3.4: We consider the Liapunov function of proposition 3.3,

$$H(\omega, l) = \int_{\omega_0}^{\omega} \frac{h^2(\tilde{\omega})}{\tilde{\omega}} d\tilde{\omega} - \int_{l_0}^{l} \frac{h^1(\tilde{l})}{\tilde{l}} d\tilde{l},$$

$$h^1(l) = \kappa(1 - \kappa_p)\beta_w(l^d/l - 1), h^2 = -i(\omega),$$

[34] Note that the cycle is clockwise – and between the limits a, b – when the variables u, V are used in the place of ω, l.

(a)

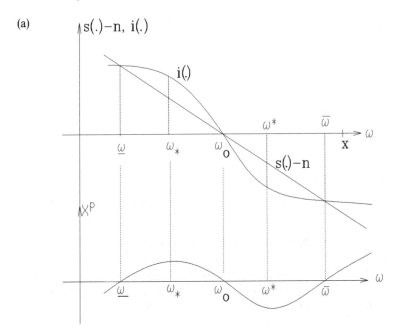

(b)

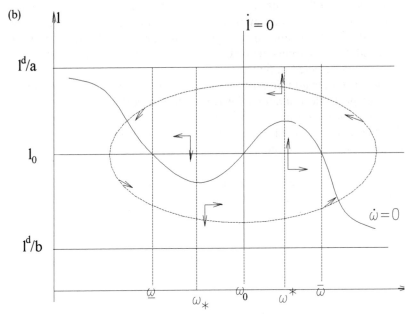

Figure 3.4 (a) A nonlinear investment-savings relationship; (b) a Rose limit cycle in the fixed proportions case

but now augmented by the two nonlinearities just considered. We have in the present case:

$$\dot{H} < 0 \text{ for all } \omega < \underline{\omega} \text{ or } \omega > \bar{\omega},$$

and

$$\dot{H} > 0 \text{ for } \underline{\omega} < \omega < \bar{\omega}.$$

Proof: For $\omega < \underline{\omega}$ we have $0 < i(\cdot) < s(\cdot) - n$ and $-i(\cdot) < 0$, whilst for $\omega > \bar{\omega}$ we have $s(\cdot) - n < i(\cdot) < 0$ and $-i(\cdot) > 0$ by assumption. The function H therefore fulfills

$$\dot{H} = \kappa(1 - \kappa_w)\beta_p(i(\cdot) + n - s(\cdot))i(\cdot) < 0 \text{ for all } \omega < \underline{\omega} \text{ and all}$$
$\omega > \bar{\omega}$

(and it is positive in between these bounds on ω). Since we know that $\dot{H} = 0$ along the closed orbits of the Goodwin case $\kappa_w = 1$, we thus get that the trajectories of the dynamical system (3.48)–(3.49), modified by the above two nonlinearities, must point inwards along those segments of the Goodwin cycle that lie outside of the interval $(\underline{\omega}, \bar{\omega})$. ■

Any trajectory off the steady state consequently must cycle around it (since it has to stay inside of an appropriate Goodwin cycle when it leaves the above depicted domain on its right hand side). It is, however, not yet excluded that this occurs in an explosive fashion towards the boundaries of the domain depicted in figure 3.3.

Assume now in addition that $\kappa_p \to 1$ if $\omega/x \to (y - \delta - t^n)/y$, i.e., there is a full cost-push effect of nominal wages with respect to the formation of the price rate of inflation if real wages tend to eliminate profit income. The $\dot{\omega} = 0$ isocline then tends to the horizontal line l^d/b as ω tends to this limit. In this case we furthermore can state the following.

Proposition 3.5: The ω-limit sets[35] of trajectories starting to the left of $(y - \delta - t^n)x/y$ are all compact, nonempty and do not contain the steady state (ω_0, l_0), i.e., by the Poincaré–Bendixson theorem[36] they must be closed orbits.

All trajectories which start to the left of $(y - \delta - t^n)x/y$ are thus attracted by some limit cycle within this set or are closed orbits themselves. This is illustrated by the simulation of the real cycle model displayed in figure 3.5, which is based on nonlinearities in the investment function and the Phillips

[35] The sets of all limit points of the considered trajectories.
[36] See Hirsch/Smale (1974, p.248).

Table 3.1.

$s_c = 0.8, \delta = 0.1, y = 1, x = 2, l^d = 0.5, n = 0.05.$
$h_1 = 0.1, h_2 = \infty, i = 1, \beta_k = 1.$
$\beta_w = 1, \beta_p = 1, \kappa_w = \kappa_p = 0.5, \beta_{\pi_1} = 0, \beta_{\pi_2} = 0.$
$\mu_0 = 0.05, \mu_2 = 0, t^n = 0.35.$

---

curve mechanism of the type

$$i(\cdot) = \text{atan}(10*pi*(\rho - r + \pi))/(10*pi),$$
$$X^w = \tan(1.25*pi*(V - 1))/(1.25*pi) \text{ for } V \geq 1,$$
$$X^w = \tan(2.5*pi*(V - 1))/(2.5*pi) \text{ for } V \leq 1,$$

and on the set of parameters displayed in table 3.1.

The steady state of this real cycle model is disturbed at time $t = 1$ by a supply-side shock. Note here that the depicted limit cycle is based on the variables u and V of the Goodwin growth cycle model and that the range covered by the variation of goods market excess demand allows for four different states. Note, furthermore that the loop showing up in the Phillips curve in the lower right hand portion of figure 3.5 is clockwise and not counterclockwise, as empirical observations have suggested.

Note that in the above we have not provided a complete proof of proposition 3.5, since we have only conjectured in the present situation that all trajectories of this dynamical system can be continued without bound (and that they and their limit sets stay in the interior of the economically motivated rectangle depicted in figure 3.3). The application of the Poincaré–Bendixson theorem is therefore not straightforward in the present situation. Such ambiguities can be avoided when the l^d/a-curve can be shown to be (slightly) negatively sloped, as will be the case in the next chapter and also in chapter 5 when we allow smooth factor substitution.

The limit cycle approach of Rose's (1967) employment cycle model thus also applies to the present context and could be further investigated as in Rose (1967). An important property of the above assumptions is that the dynamical behavior is thereby restricted to economically meaningful values of ω. Observe also that the problem encountered in section 3.3 with respect to labor supply bottlenecks can now be completely avoided just by choosing the parameter b in the Phillips curve of figure 3.2 such that $l^d/V_{\text{max}} \leq l^d/b$ holds true.

We have treated so far only the case $\dot{K} = I$ (or $\hat{I} = -i(\cdot)$). The alternative case $\dot{K} = S$ (or $\hat{I} = n - s(\cdot)$) is similar and will give rise to the same results as $\hat{I} = -i(\cdot)$ (since $n - s(\omega) = n - s_c(y - \delta - \omega l - t^n)$ is then of the same qualitative form as the function $-i(\omega)$). Of course, an appropriately

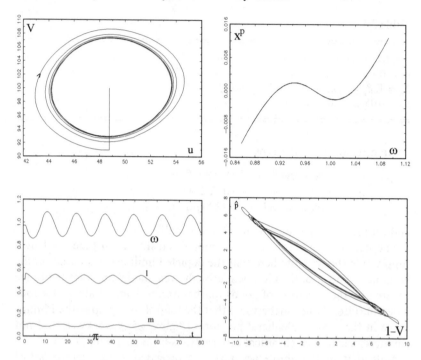

Figure 3.5   The real cycle of the Keynes–Wicksell model

chosen nonlinear $s(\cdot)$ function can also be used to investigate the dynamical behavior of (3.48)–(3.49) under such a modification.

In sum, we may conclude that the Rose extension introduces local instability into the Goodwin labor-market dynamics, but also provides the means of establishing global stability, giving rise to a limit cycle result instead of the structurally unstable closed orbit structure of the Goodwin model. This is definitely an improvement over Goodwin's growth cycle result. The robustness of Rose's employment cycle will be further investigated in the following section.

3.5   Monetary growth cycles: the basic case

Removing one further assumption, namely, that concerning interest rate inflexibility in the real Goodwin/Rose growth cycle dynamics, we show in this section that the now integrated real and monetary dynamics will suppress the Rose employment (limit) cycle result with its instability of the steady state, if the flexibility of nominal interest rates becomes sufficiently high. This is mainly due to the Keynes effect which, as has often been emphasized by static analysis, also fulfills its supposed stabilizing role in a three-dimensional dynamic growth context. The resulting asymptotic stability of the steady state will, however, often rest nevertheless on cyclical adjustment patterns.

So far, we have only studied the cyclical properties of the real part of the model by making it independent of money-market phenomena and expectations through appropriate assumptions on the interest rate elasticity of money demand, on the adjustment of expectations, and on one further secondary assumption which, taken together, removed the influence of money and bonds (expressed per unit of capital value), i.e., of the variables m and b from real-wage dynamics and capital accumulation. In this section, we will now integrate the impact of the evolution of m on the real dynamics by allowing the interest rate r to fluctuate and by allowing to be positive the parameter μ_2, which describes the extent by which government expenditures are money financed.

The assumptions $\beta_{\pi_2} = \infty (\beta_{\pi_1} < \infty)$ and $t^n = (T - rB)/K = \text{const.}$ will, however, still be made in order to allow inflationary expectations to hold static at the steady state value $\pi = \mu_0 - n$ and, as always, for a treatment of the model where bonds can remain implicit. Medium-run adjustments in expectations will be considered in the next section.

The model to be investigated in this section is thus given by the three-dimensional dynamical system[37]

$$\hat{\omega} = \kappa[(1 - \kappa_p)\beta_w(V - 1) + (\kappa_w - 1)\beta_p(i(\cdot) + n - s(\cdot))], \qquad (3.50)$$

$$\hat{V} = \hat{K}(\cdot) - n, \qquad (3.51)$$

$$\hat{m} = \mu_0 - \hat{p}(\cdot) - \hat{K}(\cdot), \qquad (3.52)$$

where

$\hat{K}(\cdot) = i(\cdot) + n \text{ (or } s(\cdot)),$
$i(\cdot) = i(y - \delta - \omega l^d - r + \mu_0 - n),$
$s(\cdot) = s_c(y - \delta - \omega l^d - t^n) - (g - t^n),$
$g = t^n + \mu_2 m, t^n = \text{const.}$
$r = r(m) = r_0 + (h_1 y - m)/h_2, r' < 0 \text{ and}$
$\hat{p}(\cdot) = \mu_0 - n + \kappa[\beta_p(i(\cdot) + n - s(\cdot)) + \kappa_p \beta_w(V - 1)].$

With respect to this model we are able to prove the following proposition which asserts that flexibility of the nominal rate of interest of a sufficiently

[37] Rose (1967) assumes for the following monetary extension of his model of the employment cycle the relationship $r = r(y)$ (with a variable ratio y due to the existence of neoclassical factor substitution), which allows – as in his paper – a reduction of the dynamics again to dimension two in the two real variables ω and l. In the context of the present dynamical model this does not represent, however, a convincing simplification.

high degree will remove the Rose-type local instability from the real part of the model and thus also the possibility of it generating an employment limit cycle.

Proposition 3.6: The steady state of the dynamical system (3.50)–(3.52) is locally asymptotically stable if $-r'(m_0) = 1/h_2$ is set sufficiently large.

Proof: (for the case $\hat{K} = i(\cdot) + n$): For the Jacobian J of the dynamical system (3.50)–(3.52) at the steady state we obtain

$$
J = \begin{pmatrix}
\kappa(\kappa_w - 1)\beta_p l^d(s_c - i)\omega_0 & \kappa(1 - \kappa_p)\beta_w\omega_0 & \kappa(\kappa_w - 1)\beta_p(-ir' + \mu_2)\omega_0 \\
-il^d V_0 & 0 & -ir' V_0 \\
il^d V_0 - \kappa\beta_p(s_c - i)l^d m_0 & -\kappa\kappa_p\beta_w m_0 & ir' V_0 - \kappa\beta_p(-ir' + \mu_2)m_0
\end{pmatrix}.
$$

By means of the standard rules for the calculation of determinants, the determinant of J is easily shown to be equal to

$$
|J| = \begin{vmatrix}
\kappa(\kappa_w - 1)\beta_p(s_c - i)l^d\omega_0 & \kappa(1 - \kappa_p)\beta_w\omega_0 & \kappa(\kappa_w - 1)\beta_p(-ir' + \mu_2)\omega_0 \\
-il^d V_0 & 0 & -ir' V_0 \\
0 & -\kappa\kappa_p\beta_w m_0 - \dfrac{1 - \kappa_p}{1 - \kappa_w}\beta_w m_0 & 0
\end{vmatrix}
$$

$$
= \left(\kappa\kappa_p\beta_w m_0 + \kappa\frac{1 - \kappa_p}{1 - \kappa_w}\beta_w m_0\right)\begin{vmatrix} \kappa(\kappa_w - 1)\beta_p(s_c - i)l^d\omega_0 & \kappa(\kappa_w - 1)\beta_p(-ir' + \mu_2)\omega_0 \\ -il^d V_0 & -ir' V_0 \end{vmatrix}
$$

$$
= + \begin{vmatrix} - & - \\ - & + \end{vmatrix} < 0
$$

This result also holds for $\mu_2 = 0$ and it is independent of the size of r'. This is the first of the four Routh–Hurwitz conditions (see Brock and Malliaris 1989, pp.75ff., and the appendix to section 1.8), which are necessary and sufficient for the local asymptotic stability of the steady state.

The next condition demands that the sum of the leading principal minors: $J_1 + J_2 + J_3$ of the above Jacobian must be positive. Due to the "0" in the middle of the Jacobian J, this positivity is obviously true for J_1 and J_3. For $J_2 = \begin{vmatrix} J_{11} & J_{13} \\ J_{31} & J_{33} \end{vmatrix}$ we obtain

$$
J_2 = \begin{vmatrix} \kappa(\kappa_w - 1)\beta_p l^d(s_c - i)\omega_0 & \kappa(\kappa_w - 1)\beta_p(-ir' + \mu_2)\omega_0 \\ il^d V_0 & ir' V_0 \end{vmatrix}
$$

$$
= \begin{vmatrix} \kappa(\kappa_w - 1)\beta_p l^d\omega_0 & \kappa(\kappa_w - 1)\beta_p\mu_2\omega_0 \\ il^d V_0 & ir' V_0 \end{vmatrix}
$$

$$= \begin{vmatrix} - & - \\ + & - \end{vmatrix} > 0$$

This result also holds for $\mu_2 = 0$ and it is independent of the size of r'.
The third condition is trace $J < 0$. We calculate

$$\text{trace } J = \kappa(\kappa_w - 1)\beta_p l^d (s_c - i)\omega_0 + ir' V_0 - \kappa\beta_p(-ir' + \mu_2)m_0.$$

The condition trace $J < 0$ is obviously fulfilled when Rose's model is locally asymptotically stable $(i < s_c)$, and it can always be fulfilled in the opposite case $(i > s_c)$ if r' is chosen sufficiently large.

The final Routh–Hurwitz condition is $(-\text{trace } J)(J_1 + J_2 + J_3) + \det J > 0$. To see that this condition can be fulfilled for derivatives $r'(m_0)$ which are chosen sufficiently large in absolute value it suffices to note that $(-\text{trace } J)(J_1 + J_2 + J_3)$ is a quadratic function of r', whereas $\det J$ depends only linearly on it. The sign structure of trace J and J_1, J_2, J_3 we have discussed above then implies that b must become positive for sufficiently large values of $|r'|$. ∎

In the following proposition we establish that a limit cycle is born as $r'(m_0)$ decreases in value.

Proposition 3.7: There exists exactly one value of $r'(m_0)$ (denoted $r'(m_0)^H$) such that the steady state is unstable for r' in $(r'(m_0)^H, 0)$ and stable in $(-\infty, r'(m_0)^H)$. At the value $r'(m_0)^H$ a Hopf bifurcation occurs, i.e., in particular, the stability proven for large $|r'(m_0)|$ is lost in a cyclical fashion as $r'(m_0)$ increases across this bifurcation value.

Proof: The proof of proposition 3.6 has shown that we have for the quantities $a_1 = -\text{trace } J, a_2 = J_1 + J_2 + J_3$ and $a_3 = -\det J$ the relationships

$$a_1 = \alpha_1 |r'(m_0)| + \beta_1, (\alpha_1 > 0),$$
$$a_2 = \alpha_2 |r'(m_0)| + \beta_2, (\alpha_2 > 0),$$
$$a_3 = \alpha_3 |r'(m_0)|, \quad (\alpha_3 > 0).$$

The polynomial $b(|r'(m_0)|) = a_1(|r'(m_0)|)a_2(|r'(m_0)|) - a_3(|r'(m_0)|)$ must be quadratic and bear to the linear function $a_1(|r'(m_0)|)$ the relationship shown in figure 3.6.

We know that there exists a unique $|r'(m_0)|$ where $a_1 = -\text{trace } J$ will be zero. It follows that b must be negative at this value of $|r'(m_0)|$, since $a_3 = -\det J$ is positive throughout. We thus get that a_1, a_2, a_3, and b must all be positive to the right of $|r'(m_0)^H|$ in the figure 3.6. This proves the first

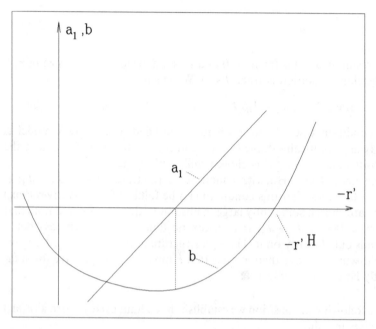

Figure 3.6   The two Routh–Hurwitz coefficients a_1, b

part of the proposition, since b cannot become positive again for lower $|r'(m_0)|$ before a_1 has turned negative.

The second part of this proposition can be proved as in the proof of a Hopf bifurcation for the general Tobin model considered in Benhabib and Miyao (1981). ■

This last proposition tells us that, at least in a certain neighborhood of $r'(m_0)^H$, the dynamical behavior of (3.50)–(3.52) must therefore be of a cyclical nature. We know, furthermore, from the preceding section that it is of this same kind also for values of $r'(m_0)$ sufficiently close to "0." It can therefore be expected that the model gives rise to monotonic adjustment paths to its steady state, if at all, only if $r'(m_0)$ is sufficiently close to $-\infty$.

The proof of propositions 3.6 and 3.7 for the case $\dot{K} = S$ is similar. The Hopf-bifurcation theorem can furthermore also be applied to the parameters β_p and β_w, and will give rise to similar propositions depending upon the influence of the real wage on excess demand in the market for goods. This issue is discussed further in the next chapter.

In sum, we have so far found that money wage flexibility and interest rate flexibility work in favor of economic stability, while price flexibility generally works against economic stability.

3.6   Expectations and the pure monetary cycle

Due to our formulation of inflationary expectations (3.24), we have the choice between adaptive, regressive,[38] and myopic perfect foresight expectations (or a combination of these). As we shall see, regressive expectations preserve the stability properties of the model of the preceding section, while adaptively formed expectations can, when sufficiently fast, destabilize the dynamics through the working of the Mundell effect. Myopic perfect foresight expectations can be treated as the limit case of adaptive expectations and thus face the same instability problems as fast adaptive expectations. Furthermore, there are economic reasons why this situation of myopic perfect foresight should be excluded from our models in their present formulation and analysis should be restricted to situations where both forward and backward looking behavior prevail.

After having considered (in the following discussion) various special cases of expectations formation, we shall then apply the forward and backward looking expectations mechanism to an investigation of the medium run. In this medium run factor growth is ignored on the side of production and real wage changes are suppressed by means of the two assumptions $\beta_w = 0, \kappa_w = 1$, i.e., nominal wages are of an extremely sluggish type with respect to demand pressure on the labor market and the actual rate of inflation has a full impact effect on nominal wage formation. These assumptions result in a monetary dynamics subsector of the Cagan type, i.e. the isolated dynamic interaction between the two variables m and π. Such a system of monetary dynamics has been often studied in the framework of pure money-market adjustments under adaptive expectations as well as under perfect foresight.[39] Here, however, we shall consider the product market and its adjustments instead and the influence of an additional variable, the nominal rate of interest, which is determined by money-market equilibrium. This situation will give rise to a pure monetary limit cycle in the above two variables if the nonlinear investment function of section 3.4 is again assumed to apply.

Because of the applicability of the assumption for the generation of real limit cycles, (see figure 3.4) also to the generation of monetary cycles it is obvious that these two cycle models can be coupled with each other if the above two assumptions on β_w and κ_w are relaxed. This coupling of the real with monetary cycles will be briefly investigated in section 3.7 by means of computer simulations.

Our analysis in this section proceeds by analyzing various limiting cases

---

[38] See appendix 2 of chapter 4 for an extension and alternative explanation of this forward-looking component of inflationary expectations.

[39] See Chiarella (1990, ch. 7) and Turnovsky (1995, ch. 3).

of the expectations mechanism and the limiting case of infinite speed of price adjustment.

We first consider regressive expectations by setting $\beta_{\pi_1} = 0, \beta_{\pi_2} < \infty$. In the case of purely regressive expectations, the 3×3 matrix J in the proof of proposition 3.6 is augmented by a fourth column and a fourth row, the latter being represented by

$$(0 \quad 0 \quad 0 \quad -\beta_{\pi_2})$$

since the new fourth dynamical law is here simply given by $\dot{\pi} = \beta_{\pi_2}(\mu_0 - n - \pi)$. We thus can state the following.

Proposition 3.8: The local stability properties of the four-dimensional dynamical system under regressive expectations are the same as those of the dynamical system (3.50)–(3.52) considered in section 3.5.

Assuming purely regressive expectations thus does not add very much to the analysis of section 3.5, the main difference being that inflationary expectations now slowly adjust to any new steady state value of $\mu_0 - n$, while they immediately jump to it in the cases we investigated previously.

We consider next adaptive expectations by setting $\beta_{\pi_2} = 0, \beta_{\pi_1} < \infty$. In the case of adaptive expectations the resulting four-dimensional dynamical system becomes fully interdependent, since at least the evolution of ω and m depends on π and that of π on the evolution of all three other dynamic variables. The evolution of inflationary expectations π is now determined by $\dot{\pi} = \beta_{\pi_1}(\hat{p} - \pi)$, where $\hat{p} = \pi + \kappa[\beta_p i(\cdot) + n - s(\cdot)) + \kappa_p \beta_w(V - 1)]$. This gives for the dependence of π on itself the expression $\partial \dot{\pi}/\partial \pi = \beta_{\pi_1} \kappa \beta_p i'$ > 0, since $i(\cdot)$ (but not $s(\cdot)$) depends positively on inflationary expectations π. This expression ($=J_{44}$ of the Jacobian of this extended dynamical system) shows that the model of section 3.5 can always be made locally unstable by choosing the parameter β_{π_1} sufficiently high. As is known from other models, we here recover the result that adaptive expectations create, at least locally, explosive behavior if they become sufficiently fast. On the basis of the foregoing observations we state the following.

Proposition 3.9: The trace of the Jacobian matrix J can be made as positive as desired by choosing the adjustment parameter β_{π_1} sufficiently large.

We conjecture that the loss of stability that comes about by increasing β_{π_1} from "0" to "$+\infty$" will occur again in a cyclical fashion by means of a Hopf bifurcation, as was the case in the previous section.[40]

---

[40] See Flaschel (1993, ch. 6) for investigations of a related situation.

Next we consider myopic perfect foresight by setting $\beta_{\pi_2} = 0, \beta_{\pi_1} = \infty$. The fact that the trace of J approaches $+\infty$ for $\beta_{\pi_1} \to \infty$ in the just-considered case of adaptive expectations indicates that the limit case $\beta_{\pi_1} = \infty$, i.e. $\pi = \hat{p}$, may be of a problematic nature. In this case, the two Phillips-type adjustment mechanisms (3.22) and (3.23) of our general framework reduce to

$$\hat{\omega} = \beta_w(V - 1), \tag{3.53}$$

$$\kappa_p\hat{\omega} = - \beta_p((I - S)/K), \tag{3.54}$$

and thus give rise to two different and seemingly contradictory real wage dynamics if $\kappa_p > 0$ and $\beta_p < \infty$ holds true, unless labor-market disequilibrium $V - 1$ and goods market disequilibrium are always proportional to each other by means of the factor $-\beta_p/(\beta_w\kappa_p)$. Under this side condition the model is of the form (in the case $\dot{K} = I$)

$$\hat{\omega} = \beta_w(V - 1), \tag{3.55}$$

$$\hat{V} = i(\rho(\omega) - r(m) + \hat{p}), \tag{3.56}$$

$$\hat{m} = \mu_0 - \hat{p} - i(\rho(\omega) - r(m) + \hat{p}) - n, \tag{3.57}$$

where $\hat{p}$ has to be calculated from

$$\kappa_p\beta_w(V - 1) = - \beta_p(i(\rho(\omega) - r(m) + \hat{p}) + n - s_c(y - \delta - \omega l^d - t^n)$$

$$+ \mu_2 m).$$

This gives for $\hat{p}$ the expression

$$\hat{p} = [- \kappa_p(\beta_w/\beta_p)(V - 1) + s_c(y - \delta - \omega l^d - t^n)$$
$$- \mu_2 m - n]/i - \rho(\omega) + r(m). \tag{3.58}$$

In the special case $\kappa_p = 0$[41] (and $\mu_2 = 0$), which implies $I = S$ or $i(\cdot) + n = s(\cdot)$, this determination of the rate of inflation $\hat{p}$ reduces to[42]

$$\hat{p} = (s_c(y - \delta - \omega l^d - t^n) - n)/i - \rho(\omega) + r(m). \tag{3.59}$$

We then get for the second of the above three laws of motion

$$\hat{V} = s_c(y - \delta - \omega l^d - t^n) - n, \tag{3.60}$$

and thus again the simple growth cycle model (which we have investigated in section 3.3) as far as the real dynamics (ω, V) is concerned. For the third

---

[41] Or $\beta_p = \infty$, see the following.
[42] Such a situation is investigated in Sargent (1987, ch. 5) for the case of a constant value of g and $\mu_2 = 0$ by means of the saddlepath methodology introduced in Sargent and Wallace (1973). See the following for further discussion of this methodology.

law of motion, which does not feed back into the real part of the model under the assumed circumstances, we furthermore obtain

$$\dot{m} = \dot{m}(\omega, V, m) \text{ with } \dot{m}_m > 0, \tag{3.61}$$

which gives rise to the saddlepoint instability situation to which the Sargent and Wallace (1973) jump-variable methodology is then generally applied in the literature.

Yet, the question remains, whether the adaptive expectations case should not be reformulated first in such a way that it gives rise to a viable dynamics also in the case of a fast adjustment of adaptive expectations. Otherwise, there is the danger that the perfect foresight limit just formally inherits economically implausible reaction patterns of the adaptive expectations case which are, in the case of myopic perfect foresight, then hidden in the algebraic conditions to which the equation $\pi = \hat{p}$ gives rise. In this regard, a plausible alternative to the conventional saddlepath procedure can be obtained by nonlinear modifications of the adaptive case and the consequent limit cycle and limit limit cycle results in the simple Cagan framework of Sargent and Wallace (1973) as expounded by Chiarella (1986, 1990, ch. 7) and Flaschel and Sethi (1999).

We finally consider forward and backward looking expectations by choosing $\beta_{\pi_1} \in (0, \infty), \beta_{\pi_2} \in (0, \infty)$. This case formally represents the summation of the case of adaptive and regressive expectations and it thus inherits the stability and instability features of its two borderline cases we have just discussed. Note here that this combined situation can also be expressed as

$$\dot{\pi} = (\beta_{\pi_1} + \beta_{\pi_2})[\alpha \hat{p} + (1 - \alpha)(\mu_0 - n) - \pi], \alpha = \frac{\beta_{\pi_1}}{\beta_{\pi_1} + \beta_{\pi_2}}. \tag{3.62}$$

This form states that a certain weighted average of the currently observed rate of inflation and of the future steady-state rate is the measure according to which the expected medium-run rate of inflation is changed in an adaptive fashion.[43]

Note also that the actual rate $\hat{p}$ can be interpreted as myopically forward as well as backward looking as long as the adjustment speed β_p of prices p stays finite, i.e. as long as prices are a differentiable function of time. This means that the above formula can also be interpreted as being forward looking in both of its measures of the short and the long run. Again, it then means that expected medium-run inflation is changed in the direction of an average of these two measures of inflation.

Stressing the present mixed case of expectation formation as the truly

---

[43] See Groth (1988) for further details on the discussion and analysis of such a combined mechanism and appendix 2 of chapter 4 for the introduction of a more elaborate definition of the forward looking component of this mechanism.

general one thus means that we insist on a proper combination of short-run and long-run information in the determination of the evolution of the expected rate of inflation that is used in our expressions for the formation of planned investment, wages as well as prices. We recall that these are given by

$$i(\cdot) = i(\rho(\omega) - (r - \pi)),$$
$$\hat{\omega} = \beta_w(\cdot) + \kappa_w\hat{p} + (1 - \kappa_w)\pi = \pi + \beta_w(\cdot) + \kappa_w(\hat{p} - \pi),$$
$$\hat{p} = \beta_p(\cdot) + \kappa_p\hat{w} + (1 - \kappa_p)\pi = \pi + \beta_p(\cdot) + \kappa_p(\hat{w} - \pi).$$

Myopic perfect foresight may be considered to be included as a limiting case in the last two equations, but should not be identified with the rate π as in the above considered one-sided myopic perfect foresight case, since this eliminates an important economic distinction in the present model (between the rates $\hat{p}$ and π) and also introduces strange implications as we have seen above (see equations (3.53) and (3.54)). Corresponding to the medium-run character of the rate π, one has to interpret the measure M of the money supply in a broader sense in order to relate the determination of the nominal rate of interest also to the medium run.

We do not consider in this book the extension just discussed in order to ensure that the dynamical system brought about by the wage–price sector not be of too high a dimension. Improvements in the formulation of this sector would therefore still be helpful in showing that the situation where only myopic perfect foresight prevails (and nothing else) should be considered as too exceptional for a representation of the wage–price dynamics of complete models of monetary growth.

Keynes–Wicksell models have not really been considered in the literature on descriptive monetary macrodynamics, even on the textbook level. Their limit case $\beta_p = \infty(I = S)$, which is usually based on a neoclassical production function (see chapter 5, section 3), is, however, generally taken to represent the Keynesian variant of the neoclassical synthesis and thus viewed as underlying the widely accepted Keynesian AS–AD formulation of monetary growth dynamics as discussed by Sargent (1987, ch. 5), for example. We here show that the resulting model is nevertheless a purely supply side model of monetary growth and thus demonstrate that the label "Keynesian" for this type of growth dynamics is totally misleading.[44] There, in fact, does not yet exist a proper formulation of "Keynesian" monetary growth dynamics in all those model variants that start from Patinkin's (1965) neoclassical synthesis in their formulation of monetary growth. Such models are generally developed by simply adding nominal wage rigidity to the Patinkin formulation of the full employment case.

---

[44] See chapter 5 for more details on this assertion.

As just stated, our general framework (3.1)–(3.24) of Keynes–Wicksell type has remained alive mostly through textbook presentations of the special case $\beta_p = \infty$ of AS–AD growth, i.e. by the case where goods-market equilibrium prevails at all moments of time. This model is usually characterized as representing "Keynesian dynamics," see Turnovsky (1977, ch. 8, 1995, ch. 2) or Sargent (1987, ch. 5), for example. By assuming goods-market equilibrium throughout, the Wicksellian theory of inflation is only present in the background of the model and, if at all, only considered explicitly as an ultra short-run adjustment mechanism, as in Sargent (1987, ch. 2).

It is obvious from our above discussion of the case of myopic perfect foresight that the model is then (for $\mu_2 = 0$) of a purely Classical Goodwin growth cycle type in the case of market clearing prices $p(\beta_p = \infty)$, since we then simply get as the dynamics for the real sector the two differential equations,

$$\hat{\omega} = \beta_w(V - 1),$$
$$\hat{V} = s_c(y - \delta - \omega l^d - t^n), l^d = y/x,$$

whereas for the monetary part of the model we obtain by way of the IS–LM equilibrium conditions the single nonautonomous differential equation

$$\hat{m}(t) = -r(m(t)) + f(t),$$

where $f(t)$ collects the dynamics of the predetermined real variables involved in the IS–LM equations.

An infinite adjustment speed of the price level with respect to (potential) goods-market disequilibrium combined with myopic perfect foresight thus gives rise to the same situation as we obtained above for the case where the goods market was forced into equilibrium by assuming $\kappa_p = 0$ and myopic perfect foresight. In both cases we have goods-market equilibrium on the basis of a full utilization of the capital stock at each moment in time, so that here nothing is left from the Keynes part of this model type. This issue is discussed further in chapter 5.

This degeneracy of the model for an infinite adjustment speed of the price level p is less obvious in the model with adaptively formed expectations, which in the case $\kappa_w = 0$[45] is described by the differential equations

$$\hat{\omega} = \beta_w(V - 1) - (\hat{p} - \pi),$$
$$\hat{V} = i(\rho(\omega) - r + \pi),$$
$$\dot{\pi} = \beta_\pi(\hat{p} - \pi),$$

where r and $\hat{p}$ have to be determined from the equations for IS–LM-

---

[45] This is generally assumed in such "Keynesian" IS–LM growth models.

equilibrium. The Classical nature of this particular IS–LM-equilibrium version of the Keynes–Wicksell model also becomes obvious, however, when it is realized that such models always assume that the capital stock is fully utilized. In the present case this then gives rise to the equations (we continue to assume $\mu_2 = 0$)

$$i(\rho(\omega) - r + \pi) + n = s_c(y - \delta - \omega l^d - t^n), y, l^d = \text{const.}$$
$$m = h_1 y + h_2(r_0 - r), y = \text{const.},$$

the first of which gives the rate of interest r as a function of the real wage ω and expected inflation $\pi (r = r(\omega, \pi))$, while the second one then determines on this basis real balances per unit of capital m (and thus implicitly the price level p and its rate of change $\hat{p}$).

The foregoing analysis is, however, a very Friedmanian usage of the IS–LM block of such a monetary growth model. It makes the above dynamical system a three-dimensional one, since both r and $\hat{p}$ can be expressed solely as functions of ω, V, and π.

The general conclusion here is that the IS–LM-equilibrium subcases of our general Keynes–Wicksell model do not become strictly Keynesian models simply by assuming $I = S$ in the place of $I \neq S$, but instead owe their characteristic features still to the Classical nature of this Keynes–Wicksell approach to economic dynamics. This topic is reconsidered in section 3 of chapter 5.

For the remainder of this section we assume, on the basis of the above discussion, that the parameter values β_p, β_{π_1}, and β_{π_2} are all positive and finite. We thus exclude the one-sided cases we have considered above from the following discussion of the interaction of expectations first with the price dynamics and then with the real cycle of the model. We here also assume $\mu_2 = \mu_0 = n$ for reasons of simplicity.

In order to derive the pure form of the monetary cycle in this case we shall make the following two sets of assumptions:

(i) $\beta_w = 0, \kappa_w = 1$, so that the real wage is made a constant and in addition is set equal to its steady state value,

(ii) $\dot{K} = n(\dot{L} = n)$, in which case the additional capacity effects of investment that are caused by profitability differentials (but not its trend component) are suppressed on the supply side of the model (and only there). The labor intensity $l = L/K$ thus is a constant in the following and is set equal to its steady state value l^d in addition.

Both sets of assumptions can be justified in the usual way by stating that the intent of the present investigation is confined to some sort of pure medium-run analysis. They here simply serve to reduce the dimension of the above-considered dynamical system by two to a two-dimensional one in the variables m and π. The resulting dynamical system reads[46]

$$\dot{m} = \mu_0 - n - \pi - \kappa\beta_p(i(\cdot) + n - s(\cdot)), \tag{3.63}$$

$$\dot{\pi} = \beta_{\pi_1}\kappa\beta_p(i(\cdot) + n - s(\cdot)) + \beta_{\pi_2}(\mu_0 - n - \pi), \tag{3.64}$$

where

$$i(\cdot) + n - s(\cdot) = i(\bar{\rho} - r(m) + \pi) + n - s_c(\bar{\rho} - t^n) + nm = g(m, \pi),$$

with $g_m > 0, g_\pi > 0$.[47]

The isoclines $\dot{m} = 0, \dot{\pi} = 0$ of the above two-dimensional dynamical system are implicitly defined by

$$0 = \mu_0 - n - \pi - \kappa\beta_p g(m, \pi), \tag{3.65}$$

$$0 = \beta_{\pi_1}\kappa\beta_p g(m, \pi) + \beta_{\pi_2}(\mu_0 - n - \pi). \tag{3.66}$$

Equations (3.65) and (3.66) are globally well defined functions m of π. The function defined by (3.65) has slope

$$m'(\pi) = -\frac{\kappa\beta_p g_\pi + 1}{\kappa\beta_p g_m}.$$

On the other hand the function defined by (3.66) has slope

$$m'(\pi) = \frac{\beta_{\pi_2} - \beta_{\pi_1}\kappa\beta_p g_\pi}{\beta_{\pi_1}\kappa\beta_p g_m}.$$

These two expressions immediately show that the slope of the first isocline is always negative and smaller than the slope of the second isocline. The latter slope is positive far off the steady state (for positive values of the parameter β_{π_2}), but may become negative in a certain neighborhood of the steady state if a nonlinear shape for the investment function is assumed as in section 3.4 (see figure 3.4) and if the sizes of the various adjustment speeds are chosen appropriately. This follows immediately from the relationship $g_\pi = i'(\cdot)$ and the fact that the slope of the investment function becomes zero far off the steady state by assumption.

The phase portrait of the above dynamics of dimension two may therefore appear as in figure 3.7. Such a phase portrait can be easily tailored for an application of the Poincaré–Bendixson theorem such that the non-

---

[46] Note that the rate of profit is constant in the present context.

[47] It is easy to show in the case of the above two-dimensional dynamical system that the conditions for the Hopf-bifurcation theorem will apply with respect to the parameter β_{π_1}. The following demonstration of the conditions that imply the validity of the Poincaré–Bendixson theorem, however, gives rise to a situation that is much more general than that of a Hopf limit cycle (or that of a Hopf closed orbit structure).

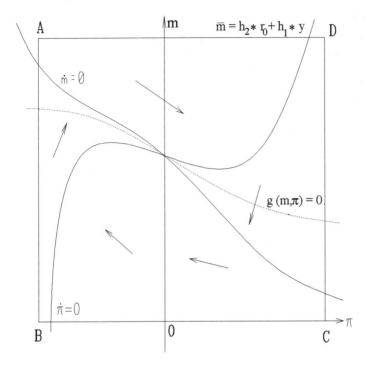

Figure 3.7 Phase diagram of the pure monetary cycle

negativity of the nominal rate of interest is assured.[48] To this end, one only has to choose the parameter β_{π_2} sufficiently large so that the isocline $\dot{\pi} = 0$ cuts the horizontal parts of the box depicted in figure 3.7 (the position of the other isocline is independent of this parameter).

The derivation of limit cycle results is therefore in the present purely monetary situation much easier than in the case of the real cycle considered in section 3.4, but it obeys the same principles as were used there to obtain such a result. Figure 3.8 shows a simulation of this application of the Poincaré–Bendixson theorem. Note that the excess demand contour shown in figure 3.8 (top right) is now strictly decreasing, since the savings component in the excess demand function is constant here. The data for this simulation are displayed in table 3.2.

---

[48] As long as m lies below the value $\bar{m}$ at which $r = r(m)$ is zero.

Table 3.2.

$s_c = 0.8, \delta = 0.1, y = 1, x = 2, l^d = 0.5, n = 0.05.$
$h_1 = 0.1, h_2 = 0.2, i = 1, \beta_k = 1.$
$\beta_w = 0, \beta_p = 1, \kappa_w = 1, \kappa_p = 0.5.$
$\beta_{\pi_1} = 0.6, \beta_{\pi_2} = 0.15.$
$\mu_0 = \mu_2 = 0.05, \beta_m = \beta_g = 0, t^n = 0.35.$

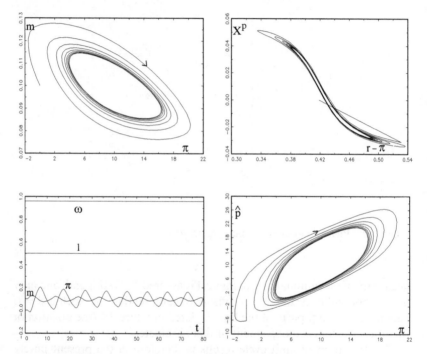

Figure 3.8   Simulation of the pure monetary limit cycle

3.7   The real and the monetary cycle in interaction

We have considered in section 3.5 the local Rose-type instability that is caused by a negative dependence of goods-market disequilibrium on the real wage $(i > s_c)$ which, when coupled with a sufficient strength of speed of adjustment of prices, gives rise to a positive dependence of the time rate of change of real wages on their level. Let us call this situation, in which $\hat{p}'(\omega) > 0$, a positive Rose effect for simplicity. In addition, we have investigated in section 3.6 the local instability of the pure monetary mechanism that is caused by the positive Mundell effect in the investment function $(\hat{p}'(\pi) > 0)$. These two destabilizing mechanisms, and the ways in which we limited their instability potential, will be integrated in this section by allowing for their full dynamic interaction in four dimensions.

Before we turn to this topic, let us briefly explain why proposition 3.6 (where we had $\beta_{\pi_1} < \infty$ and $\beta_{\pi_2} = \infty$) must also hold for all $\beta_{\pi_1} > 0$ chosen sufficiently small and $\beta_{\pi_2} < \infty$. This result follows from the following three observations; (i) the four-dimensional situation with $\beta_{\pi_1} = 0$ and $\beta_{\pi_2} \neq 0$ applied to this proposition exhibits three eigenvalues with negative real parts and one further eigenvalue which is zero; (ii) the determinant of the Jacobian at the steady state of the dynamics (the product of the eigenvalues) is positive for all $\beta_{\pi_1} > 0$; and (iii) eigenvalues depend continuously on the parameters on the dynamics. The case $\beta_{\pi_1} > 0$, sufficiently small, is therefore characterized by at most two complex eigenvalues with negative real parts and one negative eigenvalue, as in the situation described in proposition 3.6, and one further negative eigenvalue which is close to zero.

It is easy to show in addition that the stability just demonstrated must be lost if the parameter β_{π_1} is made sufficiently large (since $J_{44} > 0$ is thereby made the dominant expression in the trace of the matrix J). Since the determinant of the Jacobian at the steady state is always positive, we in addition know that this loss of stability will occur by way of a Hopf bifurcation, i.e., by way of the "death" of an unstable limit cycle or by way of the "birth" of a stable limit cycle. From the local perspective we therefore know that the four-dimensional dynamics exhibits cyclical behavior at least for a certain range of values of the parameter β_{π_1}.

In figures 3.5 and 3.8 we have furthermore considered the real cycle and the monetary cycle (each in two dimensions) from a global perspective by adding a typical nonlinearity to the investment function of the model. This allowed us to apply the Poincaré–Bendixson theorem to these two situations and to conclude that there will be persistent fluctuations in the real and the monetary parts of the model whenever its steady state is locally unstable, and that the two submodels are viable ones in a certain domain of their state variables.

Since these two cycle mechanisms have been based on the same nonlinearity (in the investment function), we are interested in studying how they interact on the basis of this viability generating nonlinearity. For the moment, however, this can only be answered by means of numerical investigations, an example of which is presented in what follows.[49]

The following simulation displayed in figure 3.9 makes use of a nonlinear

---

[49] This coupled growth cycle model can be usefully compared with Hicks' (1974) analysis of the real and monetary factors in economic fluctuations.

Table 3.3.

$s_c = 0.8, \delta = 0.1, y = 1, x = 2, l^d = 0.5, n = 0.05.$
$h_1 = 0.1, h_2 = 0.2, i = 1, \beta_k = 1.$
$\beta_w = 0.1, \beta_p = 2, \kappa_w = 0.95, \kappa_p = 0.5, \beta_{\pi_1} = 0.9, \beta_{\pi_2} = 0.4.$
$\mu_0 = \mu_2 = 0.05, \beta_m = \beta_g = 0, t^n = 0.35.$

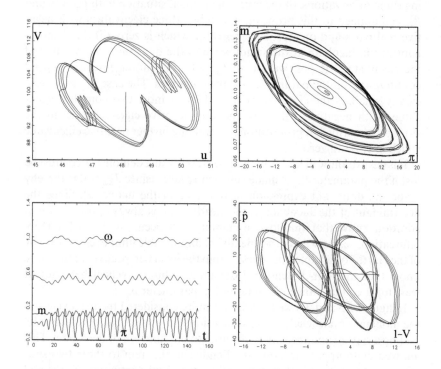

Figure 3.9   Coupled real and monetary oscillators

investment function given by

$$i(\cdot) = \operatorname{atan}(10*pi*(\rho - r + \pi))/(10*pi),$$

which has the shape discussed in section 3.5. For the Phillips curve we take
the asymmetric shape given by

$$X^w = \tan(1.25*pi*(V - 1))/(1.25*pi) \text{ for } V \geq 1,$$
$$X^w = \tan(2.5*pi*(V - 1))/(2.5*pi) \text{ for } V \leq 1.$$

The parameter values for the simulation are set out in table 3.3.

The steady state of this economy is disturbed at time $t = 1$ by a labor-supply shock. As can be seen from figure 3.9, the real cycle and the monetary one are here interacting with each other and are generating superimposed fluctuations of a limit cycle type, with the monetary cycle being faster than the real one.

Chiarella and Flaschel (1996a) show that more complex interactions between the real and the monetary cycle of this chapter are possible. Their simulations indicate that the interaction of the two cycle generating mechanisms may produce interesting phenomena, though not yet complex dynamics.

3.8   Outlook: less than full capacity growth

Some fundamental shortcomings of the neoclassical approach to monetary growth of chapter 2 led us to develop the Keynes–Wicksell model of this chapter. Similarly, there is also a fundamental drawback of the present type of monetary growth model that makes it absolutely necessary to revise and extend it further in order to get more descriptive accuracy for the modules that form the basic structure of a growing monetary economy. This basic drawback relates to the feature (displayed by all monetary growth models of Keynes–Wicksell type) that firms always produce at full capacity, independently of the actual state of aggregate demand. Goods-market or IS-disequilibrium is thus always based on deviations of aggregate demand from potential output, and then used only to provide the measure for the demand-pressure component of price dynamics or of the theory of inflation, and also to some extent in the equation describing capital accumulation.

Yet, in the real world, labor and capital are often simultaneously underutilized or overemployed, and in any case both generally not used on a "normal" or "potential" level. Under- or overemployment is thus not only a characteristic of labor supply but also of capital supply, and must therefore be taken into account by any model of monetary growth that attempts to be a generally applicable one.

But how can a varying rate of utilization be introduced into the present framework of a Keynes–Wicksell model of monetary growth? In the following chapter this is done by assuming goods-market equilibrium in the usual way of an IS–LM approach to the determination of output and employment, and thus of the rate of capacity utilization of both capital and labor. Keynesian goods-market equilibrium is therefore now used, in the place of IS-disequilibrium without the multiplier process, in order to derive and explain the level of capacity utilization within the firm. This measure of disequilibrium is not accompanied in chapter 4 by disequilibrium outside the firm (on the market for goods).[50]

Nothing unusual (in the sense of being novel) is therefore needed in order to make the Keynes–Wicksell prototype model really a Keynesian model of monetary growth with both labor and capital under- or overutilized. In view of this obvious and natural modification of the Keynes–Wicksell approach to monetary growth it is, however, very astonishing not to find in the literature a well-established body of such Keynesian IS–LM growth theory. Orphanides and Solow (1990), for example, in their survey of the literature on money, inflation, and growth, provide a brief survey on models of Keynes–Wicksell type, but do not mention any attempt to construct a growth model of the IS–LM variety.

Going from Keynes–Wicksell to Keynesian monetary growth dynamics therefore represents a crucial and compelling step in the further development of descriptive models of monetary growth. This step, which takes into account that there is in general also disequilibrium within the firm, will now be undertaken and considered in its implications. It will lead us in particular to the result that the dynamics becomes much more differentiated through the new characteristic of the model that it is only the rate of output, and not the price level and its dynamics, that is directly determined through goods market (equilibrium) conditions. The dynamics of the price level will now be derived indirectly and, in a second step, through the disequilibrium level of capacity utilization as it is implied by goods-market equilibrium (as the proper representation of the demand pressure component in the explanation of price inflation).

Proceeding in this way the next chapter will therefore fill an important and crucial gap in the literature on monetary growth, though it will not yet lead us, to a (final) basic working model of Keynesian monetary growth dynamics. This goal will be attained in chapter 6. Despite this intermediate character of chapter 4 it will, however, clearly demonstrate that there is something essential missing in the literature on Keynesian monetary growth. This missing element is not so much one with respect to specific and novel module formulations, but basically one with respect to an integrated treatment and detailed analysis of module interactions of a properly defined model of IS–LM growth.

---

[50] The effects of such outside disequilibrium for the dynamics of the model will be added to the model and be studied in chapter 6.

4 Keynesian monetary growth: the missing prototype

In this chapter, we shall further improve the general disequilibrium version of the Tobin type models of chapter 2. We recall that this version was already considerably extended and improved in chapter 3 in the direction of more descriptive relevance and greater consistency as far as the treatment of basic disequilibrium situations in the real part of the economy was concerned. Of course, much still remains to be done in the pursuit of such aims, and this will still be the case by the end of this book.[1] Nevertheless, the model prototype of this chapter represents for the first time a version that can be the basis of all future developments of the structure of such monetary growth models. It not only integrates problems of effective demand on the market for goods in a basically coherent way, but also portrays the fundamental consequences of such an integration in an integrated model of monetary growth.

The prototype model we arrive at in this chapter can also be considered to provide the minimal extension of monetary growth models of a more orthodox type (as we have considered them in the preceding chapters) to a proper and basically complete Keynesian model of such an economy. Yet, due to this heritage, the model still exhibits many features which may appear as questionable from a post-Keynesian and other perspectives. It is, however, our intention in this book to lay the foundations of a descriptive Keynesian theory of monetary growth through a systematic increase in the complexity of such a model type by starting from conventional approaches to Keynesianism, to some extent even from the standard macroeconomic textbook level. Therefore, model substructures which may seem indispensable from a more developed Keynesian perspective, for example approaches which give asset markets a much more dominant role than we have done so far, cannot be included until the scene is properly set for such further developments. One of the main aims of this book is to achieve the

---

[1] See the survey of open problems in section 7.7.

proper setting of the scene. Hence a considerable number of typically Keynesian questions must here be left for future research.

We are also convinced that a systematic treatment of Keynesian models of monetary growth which starts from orthodox foundations is of value in its own right and will also help in the understanding of models which at first sight seem to be quite different in their structure. From this perspective it may be claimed that the present chapter is a core chapter for the intentions of this book.

Section 4.1 will present the general, but still basic, Keynesian prototype model and explain its structure.[2] We also derive in this section the intensive form of this model and determine its unique interior steady-state solution. The simplified version of the model, where we neglect the GBR, will close this section. In section 4.2 we provide some basic considerations of the temporary equilibrium part of the model in general as well as of the important special case in which there is a given rate of interest. This special case is employed in section 4.3 from the perspective of (and as part of) the real growth/real wage dynamics of the Goodwin model, now with Keynesian demand problems. We shall find that the Goodwin type dynamics of the preceding chapter (see section 3.3) are considerably changed by the introduction of such demand problems. Section 4.4 then integrates the Rose type influence of the market for goods on the formation of the real wage and considers from a local as well as from a global point of view how much of the stabilizing potential of flexible money wages (considered in section 3.4 for the Keynes–Wicksell prototype) will remain in the Keynesian analog to this earlier section.

The next section 4.5 then integrates monetary phenomena into these real growth cycle models by way of money market dependent interest rate flexibility and its impact on investment behavior. As in the corresponding section of the preceding chapter we demonstrate here a variety of local (in)stability results including the loss of asymptotic stability at certain parameter values of the model via the occurrence of Hopf bifurcations. Section 4.6 briefly expands the dynamic dimension of the model to four by allowing for adjustments in the expectations of medium-run inflation, and it considers the destabilizing potential of the Mundell effect in particular. Yet, such a higher dimensional analysis has to remain very preliminary here, though its integration of various cycle generating mechanisms appears to be very interesting. Finally, section 4.7 briefly considers a limiting case which is very important with respect to the existing literature on Keynesian dynamics, namely the case of Keynesian AS–AD growth where it acquires the features of a supply side model and becomes closely related to results found for the Keynes–Wicksell prototype.

---

[2] See also Chiarella and Flaschel (1995) for another detailed discussion of this model type.

4.1   A general Keynesian model of monetary growth

4.1.1   Description of the model

We are now in the position to provide a prototype model of Keynesian type on the same level of generality as the general Keynes–Wicksell model of the preceding chapter. This model shows the minimum modifications that have to be made to this earlier model in order to transform it to one that can really be considered Keynesian. That is, a model where output is determined by effective demand (here IS-equilibrium), which allows, for underutilized capital as the new representation of goods-market disequilibrium, and which allows for underutilized labor. The utilization rate of the capital stock is here considered as the variable which adjusts immediately to clear the market for goods "on the surface," while the price level will respond to changes in capacity utilization only with a time delay (given by the reciprocal value of the adjustment speed β_p of prices p). Our modeling procedure thus assumes that supplies (output) respond faster than prices (the price level), in the strict sense that the former variable is assumed as a statically endogenous one, i.e., capable of performing jumps to restore temporary equilibrium, while the latter is assumed as dynamically endogenous, i.e., changes continuously in time according to its law of motion.

Textbook and other presentations of the Keynesian model often also treat the price level as a statically endogenous variable (determined by the marginal wage cost rule). We shall demonstrate in chapter 5 that the Keynesian model becomes a supply determined model when prices as well as quantities adjust with infinite speed. Such a modification of the model should therefore be considered as one which leads us back to a (neo)Classical scenario and should consequently be excluded from the set of proper (i.e., demand determined) Keynesian models. One may nevertheless insist that prices and quantities should be treated in a more symmetrical way, since prices and quantities may not differ by so much in their adjustment behavior from wages as the very strict hierarchy assumed above entails. This may indeed be a relevant proposal and it will be taken up in chapter 7, where we will assume that the adjustments of both output and prices occur with a finite speed, just as wages, but may be very different in size, nevertheless.[3]

Most of the following equations (and symbols) are the same as in the

---

[3] Note here however that "output" Y is in fact "the rate of output" or "output speed" in a continuous time model, and therefore has quite a different dimension as compared to the price level p. Such a speed variable may change instantaneously (jump) without leading to jumps in the level of output (and the level of prices). Nevertheless, a Keynesian model should also be capable of allowing for finite adjustments in output speed (see chapter 7).

Keynes–Wicksell model of the preceding chapter and will not be explained here once more. As already stated, the output Y of firms is now determined by effective demand as in IS–LM models of textbook (or more elaborate) type. This means that we now have to distinguish between this output Y and potential output Y^p as in equation (4.7). The resulting rate of capacity utilization, denoted by U, will exercise influence on investment behavior as well as on price formation. These are the essential changes in going from the general Keynes–Wicksell model to the Keynesian one of this chapter. The extent of these changes may seem small, in particular when compared with the ones necessary to go from the Tobin case to the Keynes–Wicksell case. But they definitely improve the consistency of the Keynes–Wicksell approach significantly. One central question that arises is how much will in fact be changed in the quantitative responses of the system over time through the adoption of the indirect mechanism with respect to the consequences of goods-market disequilibrium (via the capacity utilization rate U) rather than the direct price mechanism of the Keynes–Wicksell model, which was based on direct goods-market disequilibrium at full capacity utilization. In particular we are interested in the effects of such changes on inflation as well as on investment.

Note that we still have fixed proportions in production (y^p and x are given parameters), though output per unit of capital y is now a variable of the model. The case of smooth factor substitution will be treated in chapter 5 for all three prototype models, where we will demonstrate in particular that such an addition does not modify our prototype models, and in particular the Keynesian one, in any essential way.

As in the case of the labor market and the associated widely accepted concept of a natural (or nonaccelerating rate of inflation) rate of employment $\bar{V} < 1$, we now also assume as given a natural rate of capacity utilization $\bar{U} < 1$, which describes the benchmark between expansionary and contractionary effects on prices and investment. We assume, furthermore, that the distance of the maximum rate of capacity utilization $U_{\max} = 1$ from the natural rate of capacity utilization $\bar{U}$ as well as the distance of the actual rate of employment V from the maximum rate of employment (of the employed) $V_{\max} > 1$ will both always stay positive so that the maximum rates can be neglected as limits in all following investigations. Of course, supply bottlenecks, as they are generated by absolute limits on the employment of the labor force L and by the capital supply K, must be added eventually for a really complete analysis of the model by considering modifications of the assumed economic behavior when the economy comes close to or is at $V_{\max}, U_{\max}$. Neo-Keynesian regime switching approaches identify $\bar{U}$ with $U_{\max}$ and $\bar{V}$ with $V_{\max} = 1$, and thus claim that the steady state path of a capitalistic economy is always right at the border to such absolute supply bottlenecks.[4] In our view, such assumptions, however, do not represent a good description of the working of a capitalist economy.[5]

The equations of the model are:[6]

1 Definitions (remuneration and wealth):

$$\omega = w/p, u = \omega/x, \rho = (Y - \delta K - \omega L^d)/K, \tag{4.1}$$

$$W = (M + B + p_e E)/p, p_b = 1. \tag{4.2}$$

2 Households (workers and asset holders):

$$W = (M^d + B^d + p_e E^d)/p, M^d = h_1 pY + h_2 pK(1 - \tau)(\bar{r} - r), \tag{4.3}$$

$$C = \omega L^d + (1 - s_c)[\rho K + rB/p - T], s_w = 0, \tag{4.4}$$

$$S_p = \omega L^d + Y_c^D - C = Y - \delta K + rB/p - T - C$$
$$= s_c[\rho K + rB/p - T] = s_c Y_c^D$$
$$= (\dot{M}^d + \dot{B}^d + p_e \dot{E}^d)/p, \tag{4.5}$$

$$\hat{L} = n = \text{const.} \tag{4.6}$$

3 Firms (production units and investors):

$$Y^p = y^p K, y^p = \text{const.}, U = Y/Y^p = y/y^p, (y = Y/K), \tag{4.7}$$

$$L^d = Y/x, x = \text{const.}, V = L^d/L = Y/(xL), \tag{4.8}$$

$$I = i_1(\rho - (r - \pi))K + i_2(U - \bar{U})K + \gamma K, (\gamma = n), \tag{4.9}$$

$$p_e \dot{E}/p = I, \tag{4.10}$$

$$\hat{K} = I/K. \tag{4.11}$$

4 Government (fiscal and monetary authority):

$$T = \tau(\rho K + rB/p), [\text{or } t^n = (T - rB/p)/K = \text{const.}], \tag{4.12}$$

$$G = T - rB/p + \mu_2 M/p, \tag{4.13}$$

$$S_g = T - rB/p - G[= -(\dot{M} + \dot{B})/p, \text{ see below}], \tag{4.14}$$

$$\dot{M} = \mu_0, \tag{4.15}$$

$$\dot{B} = pG + rB - pT - \dot{M}[= (\mu_2 - \mu_0)M]. \tag{4.16}$$

---

[4] We here instead use nonrepressed inflation and buffers provided by the behavior of firms in order to avoid switches away from the Keynesian regime to so-called Classical regimes or regimes of repressed inflation, at least for a normal functioning of the economy around its steady-state path; see Chiarella et al. (1999, ch. 3) for a further discussion of this topic.

[5] See chapter 7 for a further buffer that is created by capitalist firms in order to circumvent the capital stock constraint.

[6] The parameter τ has to be removed from all equations of the following model if the second alternative in equation (4.12) is chosen as the tax collection rule.

5 *Equilibrium conditions (asset markets):*

$$M = M^d = h_1 pY + h_2 pK(1 - \tau)(\bar{r} - r) [B = B^d, E = E^d], \quad (4.17)$$

$$p_e E = (1 - \tau)\rho\rho K / ((1 - \tau)r - \pi), \quad (4.18)$$

$$\dot{M} = \dot{M}^d, \dot{B} = \dot{B}^d [\dot{E} = \dot{E}^d]. \quad (4.19)$$

6 *Equilibrium condition (goods market):*

$$S = p_e \dot{E}^d = S_p + S_g = Y - \delta K - C - G = I = p_e \dot{E}. \quad (4.20)$$

7 *Wage–price Sector (adjustment equations):*

$$\hat{w} = \beta_w(V - \bar{V}) + \kappa_w \hat{p} + (1 - \kappa_w)\pi, \quad (4.21)$$

$$\hat{p} = \beta_p(U - \bar{U}) + \kappa_p \hat{w} + (1 - \kappa_p)\pi, \quad (4.22)$$

$$\bar{\pi} = \beta_{\pi_1}(\hat{p} - \pi) + \beta_{\pi_2}(\mu_0 - n - \pi). \quad (4.23)$$

There is one central weakness and problematic feature in the formulation of the general Keynes–Wicksell prototype model of the preceding chapter which indeed disqualifies it as a candidate for a truly Keynesian dynamic model as (at least) its limiting case $\beta_p = \infty$ (augmented by a neoclassical production function) is generally viewed and classified (see for example Sargent 1987 and McCallum 1989). This weakness stems from the fact that the firms of this model always operate at full capacity $Y \equiv Y^p$ (which is also true for the case of smooth factor substitution we shall consider in chapter 5), as if Say's Law would hold true. Of course, there may be deficient or excess demand in this model on the market for goods, but its effect solely is on the rate of inflation of this economy (if $\hat{K} = S/K$ holds), while there are in addition unplanned inventory fluctuations with no further consequences (!) in the case where $\hat{K} = I/K$ holds (see section 3.1 in chapter 3 for details). It is furthermore simply assumed in this Keynes–Wicksell prototype that these inventory fluctuations stay within such bounds that their influence on the evolution of quantities can be neglected in this model.

In the limit case $\beta_p = \infty$ of the Keynes–Wicksell model, this un-Keynesian feature of the model becomes even more pronounced. It then gives rise to a model with full capacity utilization (but unemployed labor, due to nominal wage rigidities), where the Keynesian IS–LM equilibrium part is solved through price and nominal interest rate adjustments and thereby adjusted to the predetermined supply of commodities in each period. The model is then definitely following proposals made by Friedman in the early seventies with respect to a monetarist reformulation of IS–LM analysis, and may therefore be characterized as being of Wicksell–Friedman rather than of Keynes–Wicksell type.

Be that as it may, the inevitable conclusion is that this model must be reformulated in order to arrive at a Keynesian demand oriented model with its implications for both the utilization of capital as well as of labor. A further hint on the need for such a reformulation is given by the empirical fact that severe disequilibrium on the side of capitalistic firms does not so much show up in demand and (full capacity) supply imbalances for their products as in the Keynes–Wicksell model, but rather in a severely underutilized capital stock, since production is relatively easily adjusted to deficient aggregate demand. The disequilibrium measure used in the Keynes–Wicksell model of the preceding chapter (in the price adjustment equation (3.23)) is therefore only appropriate when firms always operate at full capacity (as was the case in that model type), but it is very implausible in a model that allows for underutilized capital as a Keynesian model should do.[7]

The Keynesian model of this chapter therefore starts again from IS-equilibrium, which makes the measure of goods-market disequilibrium of the preceding chapter completely irrelevant for the discussion of the determinants of the rate of inflation. However IS-disequilibrium will eventually be integrated into our "proper" (though still very simple) prototype of Keynesian dynamics in chapter 6, where we shall further demonstrate that the Keynes–Wicksell treatment of it is indeed very misleading as far as the "Keynes" label in denoting this model type is concerned.

Starting from the general Keynes–Wicksell model type of section 3.1, the derivation of a proper model of Keynesian monetary growth dynamics is in fact not very difficult and demanding, so one may wonder why the prototype model developed here is not yet a standard model of the macroeconomic literature of Keynesian dynamics. An explanation for this fact is provided in chapter 5, where it is in particular shown that the widespread (and unreflected) use of a neoclassical production function in combination with the Classical postulate on the equality between the actual marginal product of labor and the real wage in the conventional macroeconomic literature may be responsible for the bastard model of Keynesian dynamics so widely used in the literature. The exception to this characterization of Keynesian dynamics is given by so-called fixed-price approaches where,

---

[7] One essential difference of these dynamics to the dynamics of the general Keynes–Wicksell model is that the $\hat{p}$ dynamics are now more roundabout, since the IS part of the model now no longer determines the rate of inflation directly, but instead determines the equilibrium output ratio y which then via the rate of capacity utilization determines the rate of inflation. Note here that low degrees of capacity utilization are much more plausible than large $I < S$ discrepancies as a general description of goods-market disequilibrium. Note also that goods-market disequilibria now have, and indeed must have, an impact on investment behavior. This is the other essential modification when going from the Keynes–Wicksell to the Keynesian model.

however, the dominance of the so-called Keynesian regime, as described by our prototype model, is not clearly established and where there is no far-reaching and generally accepted prototype of monetary growth available.

The range of modifications leading from the Keynes–Wicksell prototype to the above Keynesian one is in fact small, in particular when compared with the modifications that were necessary to go from the general Tobin model in section 2.5 to its Keynes–Wicksell extension in section 3.1. Equation (4.7) describes the basic new fact of the model in definitional terms, namely, that this model now allows for varying degrees of utilization U of the productive capacity of firms. This extension immediately gives rise to an extended formulation of investment behavior (again in a linear form for the time being), which is now not only dependent on rate of return differentials, but also on the actual degree of capacity utilization. The extent to which productive capacity is used depends here, as in standard textbook presentations of Keynesian type, on the state of effective demand as it is determined by goods and asset market equilibrium (4.17)–(4.20).

The final important modification of the model is given by equation (4.22), which formulates a second type of Phillips curve, in addition to the proper Phillips curve (equation (4.21). This second Phillips curve relates price inflation with deviations of actual capacity utilization U from the desired one, $\bar{U}$.[8] This desired rate of capacity utilization is exogenously given and it plays the same role as the NAIRU rate of employment $\bar{V}$ in the many models of inflation theory that are based on such a concept (or even on the so-called natural rate of (un)employment). The above symmetric formulation of wage and price Phillips curves has been fairly neglected in the macroeconomic literature on inflation, due, on the one hand, to the identity that is normally assumed between the rate of wage and of price inflation (based on the original Samuelson and Solow 1960 assumption of a simple static markup theory of the price level) and, on the other hand, to the assumed validity of Okun's Law, according to which the utilization of labor and capital are assumed to be positively related. This, however, need not be the case in the current model, which demands that we have to distinguish between the above two Phillips curves (and their NAIRUs) from now on.[9] It would be interesting to have empirical observations on this second type of curve in comparison to the many observations that exist

[8] Note that the present approach measures the actual rate of capacity utilization indirectly by means of the expression $y = Y/K$, implying that this second type of Phillips curve can easily be estimated.

[9] Fair (1997a,b) has recently investigated such combinations of two Phillips curves, in a simplified as well as in an extended form (that integrates technical progress in the way we will discuss it at the end of this chapter) from the empirical point of view for the USA and twenty-seven other countries. These works thus provide empirical support for the wage–price dynamics as it is formulated in this chapter.

for its money-wage counterpart. We here stress once again that the above type of markup pricing behavior is also (at least partly) present in this goods-market reaction curve through the term $\kappa_p \hat{w}$.

This concludes the description of the innovations of the present Keynesian prototype model in comparison to its Keynes–Wicksell predecessor. Note here that we assume for the time being that firms have perfect knowledge of the current aggregate demand schedule[10] $Y^d(Y,\ldots)$, which depends on their output and employment decision and on which they base their market-clearing production decision $Y = Y^d(Y,\ldots)$, as well as their delayed price adjustment $\hat{p} = \ldots$ as described by the price Phillips curve (4.22) with its demand-pressure and cost-push components (see Fair 1997a,b for empirical tests of this Phillips curve for twenty eight countries). Based on such an empirically motivated price Phillips curve we are thus assuming that firms do their best with respect to the output decision they are facing. We will allow for a simple error-correction model of sales expectations in chapter 6 (section 3), where we describe the updating of such point expectations in a way based on Metzler (1941), Franke and Lux (1993), and Franke (1996), and where we shall see that this makes the integrated dynamics more complex, but also more robust.[11] The goods-market equilibrium situation of this chapter can then be reestablished as a limit of this Metzlerian inventory adjustment mechanism, a limit case with some peculiar properties, as we shall see in the course of this chapter. Note therefore also that an explicit treatment of inventories is not necessary in the present chapter since the level of production is always equal to the level of aggregate demand. Note, finally, that we make use of the Keynesian regime of the regimes considered by non-Walrasian theory (see Malinvaud 1980, for example, as far as the determination of the short-run level of output is concerned). This can be and is justified by the buffers and adjustment processes that surround the steady state of our models of chapters 4 to 7. The relevance of regime switches (towards the regimes of classical unemployment or repressed inflation, see again Malinvaud 1980), is investigated in Chiarella et al. (1999, ch. 3) for a general model of the type of the working model of chapter 6 of this book and found to be of secondary importance compared to the Keynesian regime of demand constrained output of firms.

4.1.2 Intensive form of the model and steady-state behavior

As far as the mathematical analysis of the model is concerned, we again concentrate on the version which assumes that taxes net of interest payments per value unit of capital are a given magnitude. The tax rate τ can

---

[10] Given by $Y^d/K = \omega(L^d/K) + (1 - s_c)(\rho - t^n) + i_1(\rho - (r - \pi)) + i_2(Y/Y^p - \bar{U}) + n + \delta + t^n + \mu_2(M/pK)$. [11] See also Hahn and Solow (1995, p.7) in this respect.

then again be suppressed, in particular in the investment equation and in the perfect-substitute assumption.

Before we start the analysis of this special case $t^n = (T - rB/p)/K = \text{const.}$, let us briefly present **the general case** of an endogenous determination of this ratio and thus the existence of a feedback mechanism (still a simple one!) of government debt accumulation $\dot{B}$ on the rest of the dynamics. From calculations similar to those in the preceding chapter, we obtain from (4.1)–(4.21) the following autonomous five-dimensional dynamical system in the variables $\omega = w/p$, $l = L/K$, $m = M/(pK)$, π, and $b = B/(pK)$:

$$\hat{\omega} = \kappa[(1 - \kappa_p)\beta_w X^w + (\kappa_w - 1)\beta_p X^p], \tag{4.24}$$

$$\hat{l} = n - s(\cdot) = -i_1(\cdot) - i_2(\cdot), \tag{4.25}$$

$$\hat{m} = \mu_0 - \pi - n - \kappa[\beta_p X^p + \kappa_p \beta_w X^w] + \hat{l}, \tag{4.26}$$

$$\dot{\pi} = \beta_{\pi_1}\kappa[\beta_p X^p + \kappa_p \beta_w X^w] + \beta_{\pi_2}(\mu_0 - n - \pi), \tag{4.27}$$

$$\dot{b} = (\mu_2 - \mu_0)m - (\pi + n)b - (\kappa(\beta_p X^p + \kappa_p \beta_w X^w) - \hat{l})b, \tag{4.28}$$

where we employ again the abbreviations ($\bar{r} = r_0$ again):

$\rho = y - \delta - \omega l^d, l^d = L^d/K = y/x$ (y not const.!),
$X^w = V - \bar{V} = l^d/l - \bar{V} = y/(xl) - \bar{V}$,
$X^p = U - \bar{U} = y/y^p - \bar{U}$,
$r = r_0 + (h_1 y - m)/(h_2(1 - \tau))[m^d(y, r) = h_1 y + h_2(1 - \tau)(r_0 - r)$,
see (4.3)],
$t = T/K = \tau(\rho + rb), t^n = t - rb$,
$g = t^n + \mu_2 m$,
$s(\cdot) = \hat{K} = s_c(\rho - t^n) - (g - t^n) = I/K$,
$i_1(\cdot) = i_1(\rho - r + \pi)$,
$\kappa = (1 - \kappa_w \kappa_p)^{-1}$.

As new relationships, we now have in addition $i_2(\cdot) = i_2 X^p$, and the following IS–LM determination of actual output per capital $y = Y/K (\neq y^p = Y^p/K)$:

$$s(\cdot) = s_c(1 - \tau)(\rho + rb) - \mu_2 m =$$
$$i(\cdot) = i_1(y(1 - u) - \delta - r + \pi) + i_2(U - \bar{U}) + n. \tag{4.29}$$

We note that this equation can be solved explicitly for output per unit of capital y (see the next sections for some details on this determination of y). The steady state of this model is the same as that of the Keynes–Wicksell model described in section 2 of the preceding chapter, up to the obvious influence of the steady-state rate of capacity utilization $\bar{U}$ which is now less than 1.

Let us now again assume $t'' = t - rb =$ **const.** and remove the parameter τ from the equations of the model (since taxes are now lump sum).[12] Furthermore, we set $\bar{U} = \bar{V} = 1$ for notational simplicity.[13] This gives again a four-dimensional dynamical system in ω, l, m, π with an appended equation for the dynamics of b, since the influence of rb on $s(\cdot)$ and g (and thus on y) is thereby suppressed. These dynamics will be investigated in the remainder of this chapter with respect to local as well as global stability properties for a variety of subcases, following a sequence of generalizations similar to those of the treatment of the Keynes–Wicksell model in chapter 3.

We assume in this analysis that the implied evolution for b will remain a bounded one. This can be expected to hold at least for the case of an asymptotically stable steady state of the four-dimensional subsystem (4.24)–(4.27) for $\omega, l, m,$ and π, since X^p, X^w, and $\hat{l}$ all tend to zero in this case. The dynamical behavior of b will then be dominated by $\dot{b} = (\mu_2 - \mu_0)m - (\pi + n)b$, with the steady-state value of b being given by $b_0 = (\mu_2/\mu_0 - 1)m_0$. Note here also that the coefficient $-(\pi + n)$ of b on the right hand side of this differential equation characterizes the entry J_{55} of the Jacobian of the full dynamics (4.24)–(4.28), and thus gives the fifth eigenvalue of this Jacobian in the uncoupled situation. The local stability properties of the four-dimensional subsystem (4.30)–(4.33) below are therefore augmented by the additional b equation and its eigenvalue in a straightforward way.

There is again *a unique steady-state* configuration for the dynamical system (4.24)–(4.28) with $\omega_0, l_0, m \neq 0$. In the present, case with $t'' =$ const. $(\bar{r} = r_0, \bar{U} = \bar{V} = 1)$ this steady state is given by

$$y_0 = y^p, l_0^d = y_0/x, l_0 = l_0^d,$$
$$\pi_0 = \mu_0 - n,$$
$$m_0 = h_1 y_0,$$
$$\rho_0 = t'' + \frac{n + \mu_2 m_0}{s_c},$$
$$\omega_0 = (y_0 - \delta - \rho_0)/l_0^d,$$
$$r_0 = \rho_0 + \mu_0 - n.$$

As in the preceding chapter, we assume that the parameters of the model are chosen such that the last three steady-state values are all positive. All following analysis will be confined to stability investigations of or around this steady state of the given model.

[12] This is seen by noting from the above that $\rho + rb = y - \delta - \omega y/x + rb$ and that $\tau(\rho + rb) = t = t'' + rb$, hence $(1 - \tau)(\rho + rb) = y(1 - u) - \delta - t''$, where $u = \omega/x$, the share of wages in gross national product.

[13] This may be achieved through an appropriate redefinition of the sizes of the parameters x, β_w and y^p, β_p.

Summarizing, the system (with $t^n = $ const.) that we shall investigate in this chapter reads:

$$\hat{\omega} = \kappa[(1 - \kappa_p)\beta_w(y/(xl) - 1) + (\kappa_w - 1)\beta_p(y/y^p - 1)], \tag{4.30}$$

$$\hat{l} = n - s_c(y(1 - \omega/x) - \delta - t^n) + \beta_g(y/(xl) - 1) + \mu_2 m, \tag{4.31}$$

$$\hat{m} = \mu_0 - \pi - n - \kappa[\beta_p(y/y^p - 1) + \kappa_p\beta_w(y/(xl) - 1)] + \hat{l}, \tag{4.32}$$

$$\dot{\pi} = \beta_{\pi_1}\kappa[\beta_p(y/y^p - 1) + \kappa_p\beta_w(y/(xl) - 1)]$$
$$+ \beta_{\pi_2}(\mu_0 - n - \pi), \tag{4.33}$$

where y is given by the solution of[14] ($u = \omega/x, x = $ const.)

$$s(\cdot) = s_c(y(1 - u) - \delta - t^n) - \mu_2 m =$$
$$i(\cdot) = i_1(y(1 - u) - \delta - (r_0 + (h_1y - m)/h_2) + \pi)$$
$$+ i_2(y/y^p - 1) + n. \tag{4.34}$$

In section 4.2 we shall briefly investigate the IS–LM subsector of the model, in particular in the case where the nominal rate of interest and the expected rate of inflation are given magnitudes. There exist then three typical situations for the dependence of effective demand y on income distribution. These three cases give rise to three different phase diagrams when we consider the simple Goodwinian interaction between real wage formation and capital accumulation in section 4.3, phase plots which no longer need be very close to the original structurally unstable center type dynamics of the Goodwin model. The Rose extension of the real wage dynamics is considered next, in section 4.4, particularly in their potential to generate limit cycles from the Goodwin overshooting mechanism still present in two of the three cases. Section 4.5 extends to three the dimension of the dynamical system by again including the money market and interest rate phenomena. We shall see there that the Keynes effect will play a prominent role in the return to asymptotic stability that turns out to be observed in this case. This increase in the potential for stability is, however, again reduced or overthrown when adaptively formed expectations are added to the model (in section 4.6) due to the destabilizing potential of the Mundell effect.

4.2   Comparative statics: the IS–LM subsector

As already noted, the temporary equilibrium part of the model (in the case $t^n = $ const.) determines actual output per unit of capital y, and the rate of interest r, at each moment in time by means of equation (4.34) and $r = r_0 + (h_1y - m)/h_2$. The implied equation for the determination of IS–LM output thus reads:

[14] See equation (4.29) and footnote 12.

$$s_c(y(1-u) - \delta - t^n) = n + \mu_2 m + i_1(y(1-u) - \delta - (r_0 +$$
$$(h_1 y - m)/h_2) + \pi) + i_2(y/y^p - 1). \quad (4.35)$$

Proposition 4.1: Equation (4.35) defines a function $y(u, m, \pi)$ which is locally well defined whenever the denominator in the following expressions for its partial derivatives is nonzero:

$$y_u = \frac{\partial y}{\partial u} = \frac{(s_c - i_1)y}{(s_c - i_1)(1-u) + i_1 h_1/h_2 - i_2/y^p},$$

$$y_m = \frac{\partial y}{\partial m} = \frac{\mu_2 + i_1/h_2}{(s_c - i_1)(1-u) + i_1 h_1/h_2 - i_2/y^p},$$

$$y_\pi = \frac{\partial y}{\partial \pi} = \frac{i_1}{(s_c - i_1)(1-u) + i_1 h_1/h_2 - i_2/y^p}.$$

Proof: A routine exercise in comparative statics. Note that the above equation (4.35) can also be solved explicitly with respect to the variable y. ∎

The common denominator of the expressions proposition 4.1 shows the three different forces that act on output per unit of capital y via investment and savings behavior, i.e., the real-wage effect $(s_c - i_1)(1-u)$, the capacity effect $-i_2/y^p < 0$, and the interest-rate effect $+i_1 h_1/h_2 > 0$. The sign of the real-wage effect depends on the relative sensitivity of savings and investment with regard to changes in the real wage. The sign of the denominator can be positive or negative, depending on the choice of s_c, i_1, i_2 and h_1, h_2 in particular.

Two cases will be of particular importance in the following, namely $h_2 \approx \infty$ and $h_2 \approx 0$. In the second case, the interest-rate effect dominates the denominator and makes it unambiguously positive, if $i_1 > 0$ holds. We then get:

Corollary 4.1: Assume that $y > 0, u \in (0, 1)$ is guaranteed and that h_2 is chosen sufficiently small. Then: $y_u \gtrless 0$ iff $s_c \gtrless i_1, y_m > 0, y_\pi > 0$.

The effect $y_m > 0$ is called the Keynes effect in the literature, while $y_\pi > 0$ is the so-called Mundell effect. Increasing money supply and inflationary expectations thus both increase economic activity in this case.

The first case $h_2 \approx \infty$ is the (hypothetical) case of the liquidity trap we have already made use of in the exploration of the most basic type of dynamical behavior of the Keynes–Wicksell model. This case will be investigated again below as the starting case of our analysis of the dynamical system (4.30)–(4.33).

Note that the Keynes effect and the Mundell effect are reversed in sign if the denominator expression becomes negative, i.e., if $s_c < i_1$ and h_1/h_2 sufficiently small. Note that y_u will then generally be positive.

Note finally, that $\rho_u = y_u(1 - u) - y$ can be negative (for $1 - u > 0$), even if $y_u > 0$ holds.[15] Most of the ensuing investigations will rely on the prevalence of the conditions $\rho_u < 0$, $y_m > 0$ and $y_\pi > 0$, i.e., on a normal functioning of the profitability effect of real wage increases, the Keynes effect and the Mundell effect (but with $y_u \gtrless 0$).

Let us now consider **the case** $r = r_0(h_2 = \infty)$, $\pi = \mu_0 - n(\beta_{\pi_2} = \infty)$, which we have used in section 3.3 to show that Goodwin's growth cycle model can be considered a special case of the Keynes–Wicksell prototype model. We also assume again $\mu_2 = 0$, in order to obtain a two-dimensional dynamical system (in ω, l) for this special case, which is independent of the rest of the model. In this case we can easily solve (4.35) for the level of y and get from this equation:

$$
\begin{aligned}
y &= \frac{s_c(\delta + t^n) - i_1(r_0 + \delta - \pi_0) - i_2 + n}{(s_c - i_1)(1 - u) - i_2/y^p} \\[2mm]
&= \frac{(s_c - i_1)(1 - u_0) - i_2/y^p}{(s_c - i_1)(1 - u) - i_2/y^p} \\[2mm]
&= \frac{(s_c - i_1)(1 - u_0)y^p - i_2}{(s_c - i_1)(1 - u)y^p - i_2} y^p = \frac{N}{D} \cdot y^p.
\end{aligned}
\tag{4.36}
$$

For the denominator D of this expression we can have one of the situations depicted in figure 4.1 (cases 1, 2a, and 2b: $(s_c > i_1)$, case 3: $(s_c < i_1)$) if $u_0 \in (0, 1)$ holds. Due to the last expression in (4.36), we always have $D = -i_2$ at $u = 1$. The denominator D is thus positive in a neighborhood of the steady state value u_0 only in case 1 where we have $s_c - i_1 > 0$ and sufficiently large relative to the size of i_2. The benchmark case between cases 2 and 3, finally, is given by a horizontal line ($s_c - i_1 = 0$) that passes through $-i_2$. Figure 4.1[16] implies for the shape of the function $y(u)$ the two (four) possibilities[17] displayed in figures 4.2a[18] and 4.2b.[19]

Furthermore, the rate of profit $\rho(u) = y(u)(1 - u) - \delta$ is a decreasing

[15] ρ_u will indeed be negative as long as $y_m, y_\pi > 0$ and $i_2/y^p < h_1/h_2$ holds, i.e., for all i_2 that are sufficiently small.

[16] Note in figure 4.1 that the numerator (and the denominator) is negative at (around) the steady state value of u in the cases 2a, 2b, and 3.

[17] Note that, in the cases 3 and 2b, the delimiting vertical line at A_1, A_{2a} must run instead through the points A_3, A_{2b}, respectively. This enlarges the relevant phase space in an obvious way.

[18] The sign of the derivative ρ' only becomes important when the dynamic law for relative factor proportions l is considered, see the next section.

[19] $y(u) \to 0$ as $u \to \infty$ in figure 4.2b.

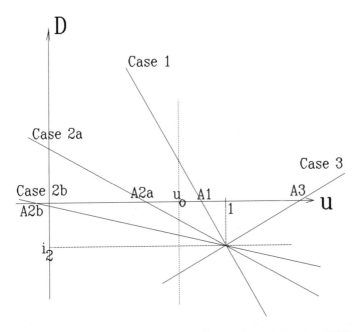

Figure 4.1   The denominator in the effective demand function (4.36)

function of the wage share u, and thus of an expected type, in cases 2 and 3. This is obvious for cases 2a and 2b and follows for case 3 from

$$y(u)(1-u) - \delta = \frac{i_2 + (i_1 - s_c)(1 - u_0)y^p}{i_2/(1-u) + (i_1 - s_c)y^p} y^p - \delta,$$

since the numerator of this expression is positive in case 3.

Summarizing, we thus have, in the present context, $y_m = 0$, $y_\pi = 0$, and $\rho'(u) < 0$ in these two cases, while case 1 behaves perversely insofar as we then have a positive impact of the share of wages u on output y as well as on the rate of profit ρ (by a similar reasoning as in case 3 just considered). It is to be expected that we will get a strange type of dynamical behavior in this latter case.

Finally, we make three further points. Firstly, we note that $\rho(u)$ will be constant in the case $i_2 = 0$, which should be considered a problematic situation. Secondly, we see that in the case $i_1 = 0$ we have only the capacity effect operating in the investment function, which nevertheless gives a meaningful situation (of type 1, 2a, or 2b).

Thirdly, we observe that ω_0 will be positive in the present special case if

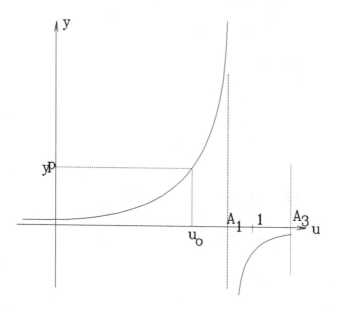

Figure 4.2a   Effective demand in case 1 ($\rho' > 0$) and case 3 ($\rho' < 0$): a too weak capacity effect (case 1) or $s_c < i_1$ (case 3)

the data of the model fulfill $s_c(y^p - \delta - t^n) - n > 0$. The steady-state value of ω_0 is then determined by $s_c(y^p - \delta - \omega_0 y^p/x - t_n) = n$, which implies that $\rho_0 = y^p - \delta - \omega_0 l_0$ must be positive as well ($n > 0$). Due to $\rho_0 = y^p(1 - u_0) - \delta$, we then get $u_0 < 1$ (and $u_0 = \omega_0/x > 0$). This justifies our assumption $u_0 \in (0, 1)$, made in figures 4.1 and 4.2. Note also that since r_0 should be positive, one has to assume that $\rho_0 + \mu_0 - n$ is positive, which is justified for μ_0 sufficiently close to n, the natural rate of growth.

Putting the comparative-static discussion of this section into perspective, one may be inclined to relate the results here presented to the discussion on profit-led and wage-led growth as defined and investigated in particular in various contributions to the volume edited by Epstein and Gintis (1995). However we believe that, before this literature may be compared and considered, the present stage of our modeling of Keynesian monetary growth must first be developed further into the direction of the working model of chapter 6 and beyond, where the comparative-static results of the present section reappear in a robust dynamic, but much less clear-cut and visible form. Several contributions in the volume by Epstein and Gintis (1995) on structural macrodynamics (see in particular the papers by Gordon) can, indeed, be usefully contrasted with the result we

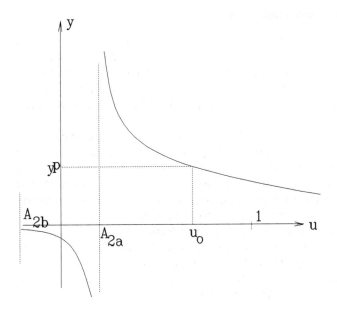

Figure 4.2b Effective demand in cases 2a and 2b ($\rho' < 0$): a strong capacity effect (relative to $s_c - i_1 > 0$)

will obtain on the basis of the present section in the dynamical analyses that follow, in particular concerning the mixed empirical results reported by various contributors to the aforementioned volume, on wage-led vs. profit-led growth, on the full employment profit squeeze, the investment/ savings relationship, and more. Structural macroeconomics, which attempts to integrate the insights of Marx, Kalecki, and Keynes for the short, the medium, and long run[20] and which stresses the medium- and long-run aspects of macroeconomic interdependence, surely represents a decisive step forward in the understanding of economic evolution and in the articulation of a new macropolicy for sustainable economic growth, with which the results obtained in this book on integrated Keynesian dynamics of traditional type must be compared and evaluated.[21]

---

[20] See here also Dutt (1984, 1990, 1992) and Taylor (1983, 1984, 1991).

[21] See Flaschel (1998a–d) and Chiarella et al. (1999), who extend the working model of this book to allow for an evaluation of such approaches to effective demand, capacity utilization, and the conflict about income distribution, and Chiarella and Flaschel (1998c–f), who pursue such topics for the case of open economies.

4.3   Growth cycle implications

This section repeats the analysis of section 3.3 of the preceding chapter, now for the Keynesian model type. It shows, in particular, that a much more varied outcome for the Goodwin (1967) profit squeeze mechanism occurs in the Keynesian version of real growth, which in one case bears no resemblance to the overshooting mechanism of the original growth cycle model.[22]

The construction of a real subsector of the model which is dynamically independent of the rest of the model is performed in the same way as in the growth cycle subcase of chapter 3. The assumptions $r = r_0$ (the "liquidity trap" at the steady-state rate of interest r_0) and $\pi = \mu_0 - n$ (infinitely fast regressive expectations) imply again that investment per unit of capital will depend on the wage share $u = \omega/x$. However, now it also depends on the rate of capacity utilization $U = y/y^p$. The further assumption $\kappa = 1$ removes the Rose effect (the influence of the theory of inflation on the dynamics of real wages) from the dynamics of the real sector.

Yet, we now have Keynesian demand problems, and therefore a Goodwin-type dynamical system of the kind

$$\hat{u} = \beta_w(y(u)/(xl) - 1), u = \omega/x, \tag{4.37}$$

$$\hat{l} = n - s_c(\rho(u) - t^n), l = L/K, \tag{4.38}$$

with $\rho(u) = y(u)(1 - u) - \delta$. Where, y is no longer a constant (equal to y^p), but determined by equation (4.36). Note that we no longer have $\hat{V} = -\hat{l}$ for the rate of employment $V = l^d/l$, since $l^d = y/x$ is no longer a given magnitude but dependent on y, which in turn is a function of u. The use of Goodwin's variables u and V is therefore no longer a straightforward matter. Since the original Goodwin growth cycle is structurally unstable, we may also expect that it will be changed into various subcases, depending on whether case 1, 2, or 3 of the preceding section is considered as determining the behavior of $y(u)$ and $\rho(u)$.

The Jacobian of the dynamical system (4.37)–(4.38) at the steady state is given by

$$J = \begin{pmatrix} \beta_w y'(u)/(xl)u & \overbrace{-\beta_w y(u)/(xl^2)u}^{1/l} \\ -s_c\rho'(u)l & 0 \end{pmatrix}. \tag{4.39}$$

For the three cases considered in the preceding section we thereby get the following for the behavior of the dynamical system (4.37)–(4.38) near the steady state.

[22] See also Franke and Asada (1993) for a synthesis of Keynes–Goodwin type.

Proposition 4.2: The dynamical system (4.37)–(4.38) is described locally by saddlepath dynamics in case 1 ($y' > 0, \rho' > 0$), by a stable node or focus in the cases 2a and 2b ($y' < 0, \rho' < 0$), and by an unstable node or focus in the case 3 ($y' > 0, \rho' < 0$).

Proof: Evaluating the above Jacobian in these three situations gives:

$$\text{case 1: } J = \begin{pmatrix} + & - \\ - & 0 \end{pmatrix}, \text{ cases 2a and 2b: } J = \begin{pmatrix} - & - \\ + & 0 \end{pmatrix},$$

$$\text{case 3: } J = \begin{pmatrix} + & - \\ + & 0 \end{pmatrix}.$$

These three representations immediately imply the three assertions of the proposition by means of the usual characterization of local phase plots via the signs of the determinant and the trace of the Jacobian.[23] ■

An appropriate application of Olech's theorem (see Flaschel 1984 for details) should here imply that the last two stability characterizations also hold in the large, i.e., in the positive orthant $\Re_+$.

The following proposition shows that cases 2 and 3 give rise to a Goodwin type dynamical behavior if the wage adjustment parameter is chosen sufficiently small.

Proposition 4.3: Cases 2 and 3 will exhibit cyclical dynamical behavior if and only if

$$\beta_w < - 4 \frac{s_c \rho'(u)u}{(y'(u)u/y)^2}(> 0).$$

Proof: A straightforward implication of the calculation of the discriminant Δ: $4\Delta = (\text{trace } J)^2 - 4 \det J$ of the Jacobian of the dynamics at the steady state, which is negative, and thus gives rise to complex roots, when the stated condition is fulfilled. ■

The phase diagrams of the three types of dynamical behavior just considered are displayed in figures 4.3a–c (see figures 4.1 and 4.2 in the preceding section with respect to the boundary values $A_i, i = 1, 2, 3$).[24]

---

[23] See Flaschel (1993, ch. 4).

[24] Note that in figure 4.3c case 2 will switch to case 3 (and vice versa) through an appropriate change in the parameter i_1 in a continuous fashion and that the dynamics will pass through the Goodwin center type dynamics in this situation.

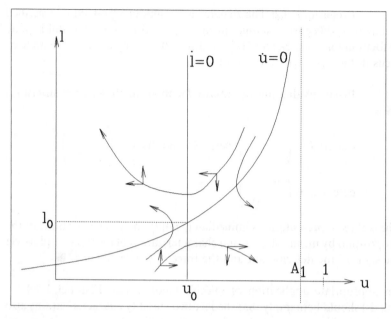

Figure 4.3a   Case 1: the "paradise" case $(y'(u), \rho'(u) < 0)$: a saddlepoint

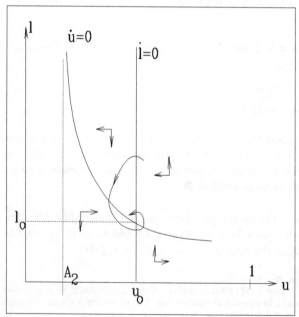

Figure 4.3b   Case 2: the "orthodox" case $(y'(u), \rho'(u) < 0)$: stable node or focus

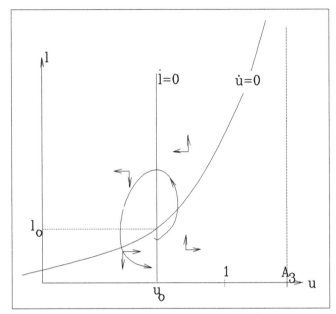

Figure 4.3c   Case 3: the "mixed" case ($y'(u) > 0$, $\rho'(u) < 0$): unstable node or focus

We note here without proof (see section 4.4 for details) that the mass purchasing power argument is valid in the cases 1, 2a, and 2b in the sense that an increase in the real wage will, ceteris paribus, increase excess demand $\Delta y^d = y^d - y = (i_1 - s_c)(1 - u)y + i_2 y/y^p + \text{const.}$, which leads to an increase in effective demand y in the first case and to a decrease of it in cases 2a and 2b. The mass purchasing power argument is therefore only supported by case 1, when the goods-market reaction is taken into account. In case 3, finally, we have that the cost effect of real wage increases outweighs the immediate mass purchasing power effect, so that there is excess supply created initially. Taking again into account the goods-market reaction to this disequilibrium situation, however, here nevertheless gives that effective demand is increased by the real wage increase.

It is possible to tailor further the dynamical system in the stable case 2 so that its trajectories stay within a certain corridor around the steady state. To this end, assume, as in section 3.4, that the adjustment speed of money wages with respect to labor market disequilibrium is of the nonlinear type displayed in figure 4.4.

The value of l which together with $y(u)$ satisfies $l^d/l = y(u)/(xl) = V_a$ or $= V_b$ is given by $l_a = y(u)/(xV_a)$ or $l_b = y(u)/(xV_b)$. Along these curves the rate of change $\hat{u}$ will be $-\infty$ or $+\infty$, respectively. We thereby get for case 2

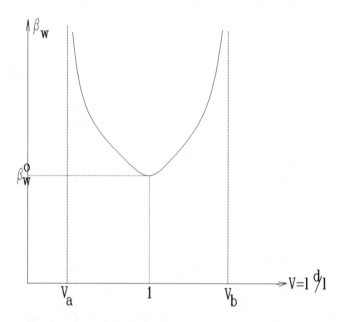

Figure 4.4   The parameter $\beta_w(V)$ of the wage adjustment function $\beta_w(V)(V-1)$

the restricted phase diagram displayed in figure 4.5 since $V_a < 1$ and $V_b > 1$, due to our normalization of the value of $\bar{V}$ guaranteeing that the employment rate will stay between $0 < V_a$ and $V_b < V_{max}$.[25]

The locally asymptotically stable situation of case 2 can thereby easily be extended to an economically meaningful domain around the level "1" of the "natural" rate of employment. A similar construction is not possible in the other two cases. However, these will be further discussed in the next section, when the Rose real-wage mechanism is added to the dynamics.

A number of other (unsatisfactory) features of the model should be pointed out. Firstly, it still lacks a mechanism which keeps the evolution of the share of wages u below 1. Secondly, we note that all three curves $\dot{u} = 0$, l_a, and l_b are increasing in case 3, i.e., the horizontal arrows of figure 4.5 are then pointing outside instead of to the inside of the compact domain

---

[25] Note that $y(u) \to \infty (\to 0)$ for $u \to A_2(\to \infty)$. The shaded area depicted in figure 4.5 therefore always exists, but it may be bounded to the right by a value of u that is larger than 1. In order to obtain a value smaller than 1 one has to assume in addition

$$y(1)/x < y(u_0)/(xV_b), \text{ i.e., } \frac{y(1)}{y(u_0)} = 1 - \frac{(s_c - i_1)(1 - u_0)y^p}{i_2} < \frac{1}{V_b},$$

i.e., V_b sufficiently close to 1.

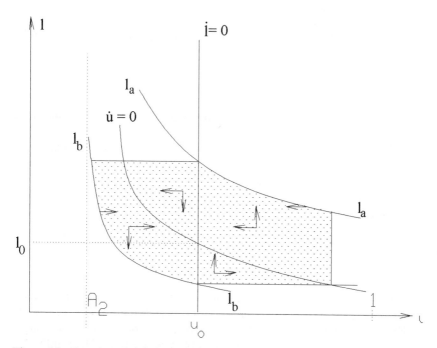

Figure 4.5 A region of global stability for case 2

depicted there. The instability of case 3 is therefore significantly increased if wages become more and more flexible the further the rate of employment departs from its steady-state value 1, leading here to a collapse of the dynamics in finite time.[26]

Let us finally consider here cases 1–3 from the perspective of ultra short-run goods-market disequilibria and possible adjustment problems resulting from them. The IS-equilibria we have considered above have been derived from the goods-market equilibrium condition $y^d = uy + (1 - s_c)(1 - u)y + i_1(1 - u)y + i_2 y/y^p + $ const. $ = y$, where const. in particular includes $t^n + \delta$. For the excess demand function we get from this expression, $\Delta y^d = y^d - y = (i_1 - s_c)(1 - u)y + i_2 y/y^p + $ const., and thus for the partial derivative of this function with respect to output per unit of capital y we have

$$\Delta y_y^d = (i_1 - s_c)(1 - u) + i_2/y^p \begin{array}{l} < 0, \text{ (case 1)}, \\ > 0, \text{ (cases 2a, 2b, 3)} \end{array}$$

---

[26] In Flaschel (1993, pp.166ff.) case 3 (with $i_1 = 0$) is made to have a viable dynamical behavior via an appropriately delayed type of markup pricing and the assumption that κ_w will be less than 1 for u close to 1.

(see figures 4.3a–c).

From the perspective of simple textbook analysis and its dynamic multiplier story, one might stipulate[27]

$$\dot{y} = \beta_y(\Delta y^d) = \beta_y(y^d(y) - y), \beta_y > 0,$$

and thus obtain stability in case 1 and instability in cases 2 and 3. The IS-equilibria of cases 2 and 3 may therefore be rejected as tool of analysis as we have used them here.

The excess demand situation described above also helps to explain in more depth why we had $y'(u) > 0$ in cases 1 and 3 and $y'(u) < 0$ in case 2.

Case 1: The aggregate demand function we have in this case is given by

$$y^d = y + [\underbrace{(i_1 - s_c)(1 - u)}_{-} + i_2/y^p]y + \text{const.},$$

which implies that a rising share of wages u will give rise to a higher level of aggregate demand for any given value of y, i.e., $u \uparrow (y \text{ given}) \Rightarrow y^d \uparrow \dots \Rightarrow y \uparrow$. Excess demand is consequently created (the mass purchasing power argument) if IS-equilibrium prevailed initially. A restoration of IS-equilibrium furthermore requires a higher level of output, since we have in this case $y_y^d < 1$. Taken together we therefore here obtain $y'(u) > 0$.

Case 2: The aggregate demand function in this case has the form

$$y^d = y + [\underbrace{(i_1 - s_c)(1 - u)}_{-} + i_2/y^p]y + \text{const.},$$

which again implies that a rising share of wages u will give rise to a higher level of aggregate demand for any given value of y, i.e., $u \uparrow (y \text{ given}) \Rightarrow y^d \uparrow \dots \Rightarrow y \downarrow$. Excess demand is consequently again created (the mass purchasing power argument) if IS-equilibrium prevailed initially. A restoration of IS-equilibrium now, however, requires a lower level of output since we have in this case $y_y^d > 1$, so that excess demand is only brought back to zero by a decrease in aggregate output ($\Delta y_y^d > 0$). Taken together we therefore here obtain $y'(u) < 0$.

Case 3: The aggregate demand function in this final case has the form

[27] K of a given magnitude here.

$$y^d = y + [\underbrace{(i_1 - s_c)}_{+}(1 - u) + i_2/y^p]y + \text{const.},$$

which now implies that a rising share of wages u will give rise to a lower level of aggregate demand (real wage cost argument) for any given value of y, i.e., $u \uparrow (y$ given$) \Rightarrow y^d \downarrow \ldots \Rightarrow y \uparrow$. Excess supply is here consequently created if IS-equilibrium prevailed initially. A restoration of IS-equilibrium then requires a higher level of output since we have in this case $y_y^d > 1$. This excess supply is brought back to zero by an increase in aggregate output $(\Delta y_y^d > 0)$. Taken together we therefore here obtain $y'(u) > 0$.

In sum, we thus have that increases in real wage $\omega(= ux)$ have an initial mass purchasing power effect in cases 1 and 2, since the extra consumption through wage-earners' additional income exceeds the reduction in capitalists' consumption and investment caused by this real wage increase (for a given y). Output y must then be increased in case 1 (and decreased in case 2) in order to eliminate again the demand gap caused by such a real-wage increase. Only in case 1 does the argument of those who favor mass consumption therefore hold, that real-wage increases will lead to more output rather than less, while there only seems to be increased (excess) demand in case 2 (as long as y is held constant), a situation which, however, must indeed lead to output shrinkage eventually when goods market equilibrium is restored.

Case 3, finally, does not support the mass consumption argument right from the start, since real-wage increases here lead to a drop in aggregate demand (y given), due to a strong reduction in investment demand. However, since the marginal propensity to spend out of income is larger than 1 (again due to investment demand), the resulting excess supply is removed by an increase in economic activity. Strong investment demand responses to increasing output therefore here eliminate again the negative demand gap caused by the dominant cost effect of real-wage increases.

But how do we cope with the situation that the dynamic multiplier, which would be expected to lead us from old to new equilibria, is unstable in the last two cases?

Following Benassy (1986a),[28] we can first of all make the situation of instability more manifest, by assuming, as does Benassy, that investment does not depend on actual demand, but rather on expected demand, which adjusts to actual demand with some lag. The resulting situation of an IS–LM equilibrium model with delayed output expectations of investors is

---

[28] See appendix 1 to this chapter for the presentation of a model of this type.

here described by the two equations (y^* = expected demand per unit of capital)

$$y^s \equiv y = uy + (1 - s_c)((1 - u)y - \delta - t^n) + \delta + t^n$$
$$+ i_1((1 - u)y^* - \delta - r_0 + \pi_0) + i_2(y^*/y^p - 1) + n \equiv y^d,$$
$$\dot{y}^* = \beta_{y^*}(y - y^*).$$

Inserting the first equation (solved for y) into the second one then gives rise to $[y = i_1(\cdot) + i_2(\cdot) + \text{const.}/(s_c(1 - u))]$

$$\dot{y}^* = \beta_{y^*} \frac{i_1(\cdot) + i_2(\cdot) + s_c(1 - u)y^* + \text{const.}}{s_c(1 - u)}$$

$$= \beta_{y^*} \frac{[(i_1 - s_c)(1 - u) + i_2/y^p]y^* + \text{const.}}{s_c(1 - u)},$$

which describes a stable adjustment process iff $(i_1 - s_c)(1 - u) + i_2/y^p < 0$ holds (iff case 1 holds). Hence, one may regard cases 2 and 3 as providing the unstable situation of the Benassy IS–LM model, which may lead to global stability when an appropriate wage adjustment mechanism is added to it as in Benassy (1986a).

The first solution to the observed multiplier instability of cases 2 and 3 may therefore exist in an extension of the dynamics of this section by means of the *third* dynamical law

$$\dot{y}^* = \beta_{y^*}(y - y^*). \tag{4.40}$$

Our conjecture on the resulting three-dimensional dynamics is that this will increase the instability of case 3, and overthrow the stability of case 2, if β_{y^*} becomes sufficiently large. This implies that these dynamics must be studied further, when more is known about constraining factors, which are capable of ensuring the global stability of this extended dynamical system. The following sections will explore some possibilities for such global (or even local) stabilizers from a two-dimensional point of view. Due to the increase in the dynamical dimension that is caused by (4.40), computer simulations may, however, be essential in order to study the global behavior of this Benassy-like extension properly.

Are there possibilities other than (4.40) which allow us to maintain the use of IS-(LM-)equilibria when treating the system (4.37)–(4.38)?

A first possibility (in fact now the orthodox position) would assume myopic perfect foresight instead of the adaptive mechanism (4.40). This approach is usually informally justified by the assumed reaction of agents to the cumulative instability inherent in the expectational process (4.40). Assuming $y = y^*$ would therefore be very natural from such a point of view, which then would apply the jump-variable technique in order to avoid cumulative instability.

Another approach, the one we shall favor here, is provided by de la Grandville (1986), who shows that stable and unstable IS-(LM-)equilibria cannot be characterized by the slopes of IS and LM curves alone: "For *one* such system and *one* inventory policy, the trajectories of output and interest rate can either be stable or unstable" (p.31). Therefore, even with a specified inventory policy (which is not considered in the case of the simple dynamic multiplier story), there is no clear-cut stability result to be expected from the situation given in cases 2 and 3. This being so, one approach is to model the inventory adjustment process in its full details and analyze its various stability outcomes completely. Alternatively, one may just stick to the use of IS-(LM-)equilibrium as a low-dimensional representation of a much more complicated, and rarely investigated, dynamical system and accept that there does not exist a stable IS-(LM-)slope configuration per se which really justifies the use of IS-equilibrium concepts. In this chapter we shall take this latter position, while the inventory adjustment process is integrated into the dynamics of the Keynesian model in chapter 6, leading to the central working model of Keynesian type of this book.

If, however, one insists that the IS-equilibrium should be stable in the straightforward way of the dynamic multiplier story, there may still exist further possibilities to improve the situation given by cases 2a, 2b, and 3, e.g., (i) by introducing a positive savings propensity of workers $s_w > 0$ and the like,[29] (ii) by allowing for interest rate flexibility (see section 4.5), or, (iii) by (as already described) using the Benassy modification of IS-*equilibrium* with a sluggish adjustment of the income concept used in investment behavior to have a stable multiplier combined with an (in general destabilizing) expectations-correcting mechanism.

We are aware at this point that future investigation has to improve *and* modify the views here adopted. This task will be undertaken in chapter 6, where there will no longer arise the necessity to distinguish between the cases 1, 2a, 2b, and 3 of this section.

4.4   Employment cycle extensions

The three outcomes of the preceding section are here further analyzed by including again the more complicated real-wage mechanism of the Rose (1967) employment cycle, in which the dynamics of the real wage also depends on the state of the market for goods. We shall find that there is a

---

[29] In such a case $\Delta y_y^d = (i_1 - s_c)(1 - u) + i_2/y^p - s_w u < 0$ becomes more likely.

trade-off between the stabilizing/destabilizing effects of wage–price flexibility depending upon the sign of $y'(u)$. Such a scenario will again allow for Rose's (1967) nonlinear limit cycle analysis where, however, the stabilizing and destabilizing factors may now interchange their roles.

We therefore extend the dynamic feedback possibilities of the model as in section 3.4 by allowing for $\kappa_w < 1$ while keeping all other assumptions as in section 4.3. The dynamical system for u, l then reads (recall $\rho(u) = y(u)(1 - u) - \delta$):

$$\hat{u} = \kappa[(1 - \kappa_p)\beta_w(y(u)/(xl) - 1) + (\kappa_w - 1)\beta_p(y(u)/y^p - 1)], \quad (4.41)$$

$$\hat{l} = n - s_c(\rho(u) - t^n), [g = t^n]. \quad (4.42)$$

From equation (4.42) we can determine the steady-state value of u (via $\hat{l} = 0$) as given by $y(u_0)(1 - u_0) = \delta + t^n + n/s_c$. With respect to this value of u we have, by assumption, $r_0 = \rho(u_0) + \mu_0 - n$, and therefore $n = s(\cdot) = i_1(\cdot) + i_2(\cdot) + n$, with $i_1(\cdot) = 0$, i.e., $i_2(\cdot) = 0$, which implies $y(u_0) = y^p$, i.e., we have full capacity utilization at the steady-state value of the share of wages u. By equation (4.41) we then get for the steady state (via $\hat{u} = 0$): $y^p/(xl_0) = 1$ or $l_0 = y^p/x$, as in the Goodwin subcase considered in the previous section.

The above extension of the Goodwin case implies for the entry J_{11} of the Jacobian J of equation (4.39) in the preceding section

$$J_{11} = u\kappa[(1 - \kappa_p)\beta_w/(xl) + (\kappa_w - 1)\beta_p/y^p]y'(u),$$

while all other elements in the matrix J remain unchanged. This immediately implies the following:

Proposition 4.4: (1) Increasing price flexibility β_p destabilizes case 2 ($y', \rho' < 0$) and stabilizes case 3 ($y' > 0, \rho' < 0$) of the preceding section as far as the local asymptotic stability of the steady state is concerned. These switches in stability will occur by way of Hopf bifurcations;[30] (2) The reverse effect holds for increases in wage flexibility β_w. These switches in stability will again occur by way of Hopf bifurcations.

In sum, we get in this Keynesian context that either increasing price flexibility or increasing wage flexibility may be stabilizing, but not both. Which one will be stabilizing depends (if i_2 is sufficiently large so that case 1 can be excluded) on the sign of $(i_1 - s_c)$, and therefore on the relative sensitivity of investment and savings to changes in the real wage. If equilib-

---

[30] Since the determinant of the Jacobian is always positive in the given situation.

rium output y falls (rises) with a rising real wage, the stabilizing role falls on $\beta_w (\beta_p)$.

In order to obtain phase portraits for cases 2 and 3[31] we calculate the $\dot{u} = 0$ and $\dot{l} = 0$ isocline of these two cases first. For the $\dot{l} = 0$ isocline we have, as in section 4.3, that $\rho(u_0) = t^n + n/s_c$, which determines a vertical curve in (u, l)-space. And for $\dot{u} = 0$, we obtain by (4.41) $l = (1/x)/((1 - q)/y(u) + q/y^p)$, where we set $q = (1 - \kappa_w)\beta_p/(1 - \kappa_p)\beta_w$.

The $\dot{u} = 0$ isocline is well defined as long as $U = y(u)/y^p > 1 - 1/q$ (note that $q > 0$) holds true, since the denominator of the above fraction is then positive (and only then). This domain includes the steady-state value $U_0 = 1$, but the interval to the left of U_0 that it includes becomes small if β_p becomes large relative to β_w. The derivative of this isocline reads l' $(u) = (1 - q)y'(u)/([(1 - q)/y(u) + q/y^p]^2 xy^2)$, i.e. $l(u)$ is strictly decreasing in case 2 ($y' < 0$) if $q < 1$ holds and strictly increasing if $q > 1$. For $q = 1$, the isocline will be strictly horizontal. Case 3 ($y' > 0$) will give rise to results that are exactly opposite to those of case 2.

For $q > 1$, we have $1 - 1/q < 0$, i.e., the $\dot{l} = 0$ isocline is well defined for all u for which $y(u)$ is well defined (see the figures in section 4.3). Furthermore, its slope is of the same type as that of the $\dot{l} = 0$ isocline in section 4.3, i.e., case 2 and case 3 have the same phase portraits as in the Goodwin case as long as β_p is so small that $q = (1 - \kappa_w)\beta_p/(1 - \kappa_p)\beta_w < 1$ holds true.

As q approaches 1 (from below) the $\dot{u} = 0$ isoclines in these figures will become flatter and flatter and are strictly horizontal lines finally for $q = 1$. This reestablishes the closed-orbit structure of the original Goodwin model, since the model then reduces to

$$\hat{u} = \kappa(1 - \kappa_p)\beta_w y(u)\left[\frac{1}{xl} - \frac{1}{y^p}\right],$$ (4.43)

$$\hat{l} = n - s_c y(u)(1 - u)) + \delta + t^n,$$ (4.44)

which can be treated in the same way as the Goodwin-like versions we have established for the Keynes–Wicksell prototype model in chapter 3. In addition to proposition 4.4, we can now state that case 2 remains of the stable type we considered in the preceding section and that case 3 remains of the unstable type as long as $q < 1$ holds, and that both cases undergo a bifurcation at $q = 1$ (passing the Goodwin closed-orbit structure at this value of q) and then become explosive for $q > 1$ in case 2 and stable for $q > 1$ in case 3.

Case 2 therefore switches from stability to instability at $q = 1$ because of

---

[31] Case 1, the paradise case, is dismissed here because it looks too unlikely from an empirical point of view.

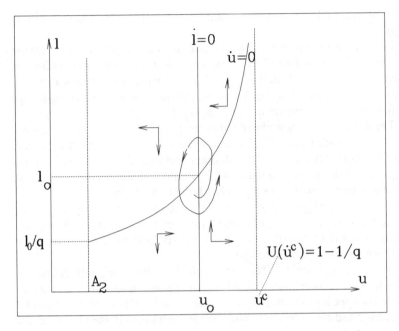

Figure 4.6   Instability for case 2 via the Rose effect ($y' < 0, q > 1, \beta_p > \frac{1-\kappa_p}{1-\kappa_w}\beta_w$)

the Rose (or β_p) effect of price formation on real wages, giving rise then to a phase portrait of the type displayed in figure 4.6.

By contrast, case 3 switches from instability to stability by passing through the Goodwin center case at $q = 1$, now giving rise to a phase portrait of the type shown in figure 4.7 when β_p is further increased.

We claim, but do not prove here, that this case should also be asymptotically stable from a global point of view, that is, each trajectory which starts between u^c and A_3 (at not a too high level of l) should converge to the steady state (u_0, l_0).

Let us now also consider the unstable cases, case 2 with $q > 1$ and case 3 with $q < 1$, from a global point of view. We want to see to what extent these cases may be stabilized far off the steady state by either a nonlinearity in wage adjustment or in price adjustment of the type we have considered in the Rose section of the Keynes–Wicksell prototype.

Case 2 ($q > 1$ at the steady state): Assume, as in the preceding section, that wage adjustment becomes infinitely fast as the rate of employment $V = y/(xl)$ approaches the level $0 < V_a < 1$ from above and $V_b > 1$ from below. This nonlinear Phillips curve mechanism is displayed in figure 4.8.[32]

---

[32] Note that we now employ a nonlinear adjustment *function* $\beta_w(V)$ in the place of the linear adjustment *function* $\beta_w \cdot (V - 1)$. Note also that $q(1) = ((1 - \kappa_w)/(1 - \kappa_p)) \beta_p/\beta_w(1) > 1$ is assumed here.

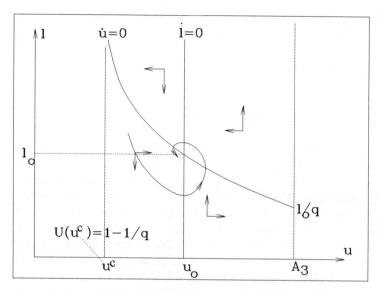

Figure 4.7   Stability for case 3 via the Rose effect ($y' > 0, q > 1$)

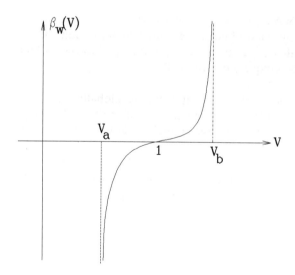

Figure 4.8   The nonlinear Phillips-curve mechanism once again

By contrast, the price adjustment speed is assumed as constant in the present situation and of such a size that $q(1) = ((1 - \kappa_w)/(1 - \kappa_p)) \beta_p/ \beta_w(1) > 1$ (i.e., $\beta_p > ((1 - \kappa_p/(1 - \kappa_w)) \beta_w(1))$ holds. In place of the above $\dot{u} = 0$ isocline we would then obtain

$$l = \frac{y(u)/x}{\beta_w^{-1}\left(\dfrac{1 - \kappa_w}{1 - \kappa_p}\beta_p\left(\dfrac{y(u)}{y^p} - 1\right)\right)},$$

which is well defined as long as $y(u)$ is (see section 4.3), since $V_a > 0$ has been assumed. Furthermore, $l_b(u) < l(u) < l_a(u)$, where $l_a(u) = y(u)/(xV_a)$, $l_b(u) = y(u)/(xV_b)$ as in the preceding section. The last phase diagram for case 2 is therefore modified by this nonlinearity in wage adjustment behavior in the way shown in figure 4.9, since the denominator of the $\dot{u} = 0$ isocline is restricted to the interval $[V_a, V_b]$, while $y(u) \to \infty$ for $u \to A_2$ (from above), and $y(u) \to 0$ for $u \to \infty$.[33] The existence of the shaded compact domain in figure 4.9 allows in principle for the application of the Poincaré–Bendixson theorem. Note that this domain can extend to the right of $u = 1$, and thus needs in this case further restrictions to guarantee that the share of wages u stays below $u = 1$. This can be done, for example, by means of an appropriate choice of V_a and l_a. The result we have obtained in this way is summarized by the following.

Proposition 4.5: All trajectories which start in the shaded domain depicted in figure 4.9 approach a limit cycle contained in this domain that contains the steady-state u_0, l_0 in its interior (or are equal to such a limit cycle which may not be uniquely determined).

Wage flexibility may therefore be the appropriate globally stabilizing factor in the case we have called the orthodox one ($y'(u) < 0$) for a fixed type of price flexibility, that was chosen large enough to destabilize the steady state locally.

Case 3 ($q < 1$ at the steady state, $y'(u) > 0, u \in (0, 1)$): In principle, price flexibility should now be stabilizing if it increases sufficiently far off the steady state (for any given degree of wage flexibility β_w), since it leads to $q > 1$ far off the steady state.

---

[33] The picture in figure 4.9 is obtained with $\bar{u} < 1$ if it is assumed that

$$y(1)/(xV_a) < y(u_0)/(xV_b), \text{ i.e., } \frac{y(1)}{y(u_0)} = 1 - \frac{(s_c - i_1)(1 - u_0)y^p}{i_2} < \frac{V_a}{V_b}(< 1)$$

holds (recall that $s_c > i_1$ in this case), i.e., if V_a and V_b are sufficiently close to 1. Note here that a construction as in figure 4.5 of the preceding section allows the use of the value 1 in the place of V_a, which is a less-restrictive assumption.

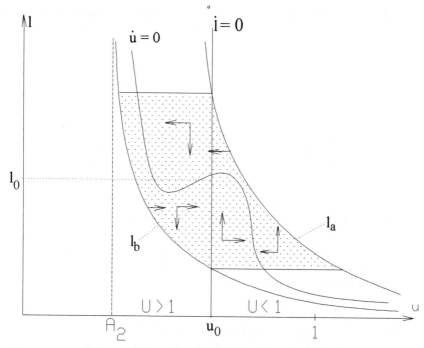

Figure 4.9 Viability in the locally unstable case 2 (the real cycle, case 1)

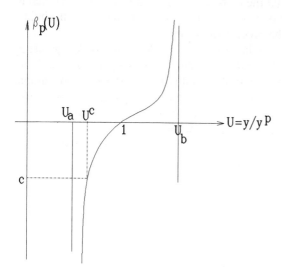

Figure 4.10 A second Phillips-curve mechanism

Let us assume in analogy to case 2 above that the situation depicted in figure 4.10 holds for the price adjustment coefficient β_p. In this case we have for the $\dot{u} = 0$ isocline

$$
l = \frac{y(u)/x}{1 + \dfrac{1 - \kappa_w}{1 - \kappa_p} \dfrac{\beta_p(y(u)/y^p)}{\beta_w}},
$$

which is only well defined as long as $c = \beta_w(1 - \kappa_p)/(1 - \kappa_w) < -\beta_p(\cdot)$ holds true (see figure 4.10[34] [note that $U > U^c, u > u_c$, since $y'(u) > 0$ holds in this case[35]]). It can be shown that the phase portrait that is implied by this new situation is as depicted in figure 4.11.

This situation will again allow for an application of the Poincaré–Bendixson theorem, now leading to the following.[36]

Proposition 4.6: All trajectories which start in an appropriately chosen compact domain of figure 4.11 approach a limit cycle that is contained in this domain.[37]

We make a number of remarks in respect of the foregoing discussion. Firstly, the assumption of only the boundary behavior of the price level at U_b is already sufficient for such a limit cycle result. Secondly, the unstable (mixed) case 3 of Goodwin type is here stabilized by some sort of anti-Rose effect. Thirdly, the fact that the U_b boundary is vertical is new and different from the l_b situation, but of course l_b and l_a refer to infinite wage flexibility, which is of no help in the present situation.

In sum, we therefore have the results that β_w flexibility works against β_p instability in case 2 ($y' < 0$), while β_p flexibility works against β_w instability in case 3 ($y' > 0$). Thus, the kind of flexibility that is needed for the global stability of the dynamical system depends on the $i_1 \gtrless s_c$ regime. Whatever this particular regime may happen to be, one flexibility is always stabilizing, while the other is then necessarily destabilizing.

We make one final remark. Consider briefly case 1, to see what happens

[34] Note that we now employ a nonlinear adjustment *function* $\beta_p(U)$ in the place of the linear adjustment *function* $\beta_p \cdot (U - 1)$.

[35] We assume that U^c and U_b are chosen such that $U^c = y(u^c)/y^p$: $U_b = y(u_b)/y^p$ determine values of u with $0 < u^c < u_b < 1$.

[36] Note here that the upward sloping line in figure 4.11 still needs to be justified with respect to its existence and that trajectories are "pointing inwards horizontally" at the right hand boundary of the depicted shaded domain. The application of the Poincaré–Bendixson theorem is therefore not straightforward in this situation.

[37] This result is now based on local instability of the steady state caused by a sufficiently high wage flexibility, turned into global stability by an ever-increasing price flexibility far off the steady state.

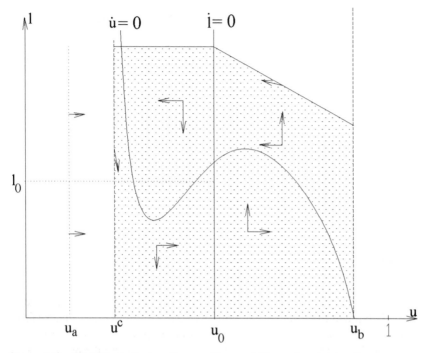

Figure 4.11   Viability in the locally unstable case 3 (the real cycle, case 2)

in this case when q passes through 1 and becomes larger than 1. Figure 4.12 depicts the relevant phase diagrams. Here we see that the dynamical behavior in this case remains of a saddlepoint type even if prices become very flexible. This case therefore cannot be made asymptotically stable by increasing wage or price flexibility.

4.5   Keynesian monetary growth: the basic case

In this section we now dispense with the assumption $h_2 = \infty (r = r_0)$ maintained in the analyses of sections 4.3 and 4.4. We show that the addition of (sufficient) interest rate flexibility may, due to the Keynes effect, generate (local) asymptotic stability in the now integrated real and monetary growth dynamics of this section, and may thus eliminate the Rose-type limit cycles. We shall, on the other hand, see that the potential for local Hopf bifurcations, for example, with respect to speeds of price adjustment, is significant in this three-dimensional extension of the two-dimensional dynamics of preceding sections. The interaction of real and monetary factors can therefore still give rise to cyclical evolutions for a given value of the parameter h_2

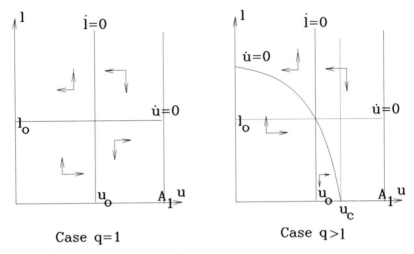

Case q=1   Case q>1

Figure 4.12   The stability switch in case 1

if speeds of price adjustment become sufficiently high, and may thus explain the joint occurrence of growth and fluctuations on the macro level. Note here that we still maintain the assumption $\beta_{\pi_2} = \infty$ (asymptotically rational expectations) in this section, so that the destabilizing role of the Mundell effect remains excluded from the investigation of the dynamical behavior of the model.

We have so far assumed with respect to money demand that it is given by

$$m^d(y,r) = h_1 y + h_2(r_0 - r), m_1^d = h_1 > 0, m_2^d = -h_2 < 0$$

(with $h_2 = \infty$ in the analysis of the last two sections). LM-equilibrium thus gives rise now to the expression:

$$r = r_0 + \frac{h_1 y - m}{h_2} (= r_0 \text{ if } h_2 = \infty)$$

as the implied determination of the nominal rate of interest. Let us now go to the opposite extreme and consider values of the parameter h_2 which are sufficiently small (to be characterized below) that the rate r may now become very sensitive to changes in the values of m or y.

The investigations of the present section will all be local in nature (concerning only a certain neighborhood of the steady state of the model). Proposition 4.1 of section 4.2 implies that, for any h_2 chosen sufficiently small, the partial derivatives of this proposition are all well defined and fulfill

$$y_u \gtreqqless 0 \text{ iff } s_c \gtreqqless i_1, y_m > 0^{38} \tag{4.45}$$

for the function $y(u, m)$ that is then implied by equation (4.35) and for a neighborhood of the steady state. We assume in this section that h_2 is chosen such that (4.45) holds true. It is also easy to show by means of equation (4.35) that the function $\rho(u, m) = y(u, m)(1 - u) - \delta$ must have a negative derivative $\rho_u(u) = y_u(u)(1 - u) - y(u)$ for all combinations of the s_c, i_1 parameters, if h_2 is sufficiently small, so that there is no longer a possibility for case 1 as in sections 4.3 and 4.4.

Since we have only added interest-rate flexibility to the analysis of the preceding section (but still maintain the assumption of π held equal to $\mu_0 - n$), we now have to consider the three-dimensional dynamical system

$$\hat{\omega} = \kappa[(1 - \kappa_p)\beta_w X^w + (\kappa_w - 1)\beta_p X^p], \tag{4.46}$$

$$\hat{l} = n - s(\cdot), \tag{4.47}$$

$$\hat{m} = - \kappa[\beta_p X^p + \kappa_p \beta_w X^w] \, \hat{l}, \tag{4.48}$$

where

$$X^w = l^d/l - 1, l^d = y/x,$$
$$X^p = y/y^p - 1,$$
$$s(\cdot) = s_c(\rho - t^n) - \mu_2 m,$$

and with $\rho = y - \delta - \omega l^d = y(1 - u) - \delta$, and $u = \omega/x$ given as discussed above.

After a little algebraic manipulation the dynamical system (4.46)–(4.48) can be represented in the form

$$\dot{u} = (\bar{\beta}_w X^w - \bar{\beta}_p X^p)u, \tag{4.49}$$

$$\hat{l} = (\text{const.} - s_c \rho + \mu_2 m)l, \tag{4.50}$$

$$\hat{m} = - [\bar{\bar{\beta}}_p X^p + \bar{\bar{\beta}}_w X^w + s_c \rho - \mu_2 m - \text{const.}]m, \tag{4.51}$$

where $\bar{\beta}_w, \bar{\bar{\beta}}_w, \bar{\beta}_p, \bar{\bar{\beta}}_p$ are all positive constants.

In order to investigate the stability of the dynamical system (4.49)–(4.51) at the steady state (as determined in section 4.1), we have to consider the eigenvalue structure of its Jacobian

$$J = \begin{pmatrix} (\bar{\beta}_w X_u^w - \bar{\beta}_p X_u^p)u & \bar{\beta}_w X_l^w u & (\bar{\beta}_w X_m^w - \bar{\beta}_p X_m^p)u \\ -s_c \rho_u l & 0 & -s_c \rho_m l + \mu_2 l \\ -(\bar{\bar{\beta}}_p X_u^p + \bar{\bar{\beta}}_w X_u^w + s_c \rho_u)m & -\bar{\bar{\beta}}_w X_l^w m & -(\bar{\bar{\beta}}_p X_m^p + \bar{\bar{\beta}}_w X_m^w + s_c \rho_m - \mu_2)m \end{pmatrix} \tag{4.52}$$

[38] Note that this differs considerably from the y_u characterizations given in sections 4.3 and 4.4. Note also that the final partial derivative y_π (> 0 here) is not yet of importance in this section. Its sign represents the Mundell effect of a rise of inflationary expectations on the level of effective demand, while $y_m > 0$ is an implication (or reformulation) of the Keynes effect of conventional IS–LM models.

evaluated at the steady state $u = u_0, l = l_0, m = m_0$. Since the parameter μ_2 can be considered as small we shall neglect it in the following calculations of stability criteria.[39]

Lemma 4.1: The determinant det J of the Jacobian J in equation (4.52) has the same sign as $-y_m$, that is to say its sign is completely determined by the sign of the Keynes effect.

Proof: Subtracting an appropriate multiple of the second row from the third row and then an appropriate multiple of the first from the third gives

$$\det J = \begin{vmatrix} \sim & \sim & \sim \\ \sim & 0 & \sim \\ -(\tilde{\beta}_p X_u^p + \tilde{\beta}_w X_u^w)m & -\tilde{\beta}_w X_l^w m & -(\tilde{\beta}_p X_m^p + \tilde{\beta}_w X_m^w)m \end{vmatrix}$$

$$= \begin{vmatrix} \sim & \sim & \sim \\ \sim & 0 & \sim \\ -\gamma X_u^p m & 0 & -\gamma X_m^p m \end{vmatrix}$$

where γ is equal to $\tilde{\beta}_p + \tilde{\beta}_w/\tilde{\beta}_w(m/u)$ and where $\sim$ denotes unchanged entries of the Jacobian J.

This latter determinant in turn can be shown in the same way to be equal to

$$\begin{vmatrix} \tilde{\beta}_w X_u^w u & \tilde{\beta}_w X_l^w u & \tilde{\beta}_w X_m^w u \\ -s_c \rho_u l & 0 & -s_c \rho_m l \\ -\gamma X_u^p m & 0 & -\gamma X_m^p m \end{vmatrix} = -\tilde{\beta}_w X_l^w u \begin{vmatrix} -s_c \rho_u l & -s_c \rho_m l \\ -\gamma X_u^p m & -\gamma X_m^p m \end{vmatrix}$$

$$= -\tilde{\beta}_w X_l^w u \begin{vmatrix} -s_c y_u(1-u)l + s_c yl & -s_c y_m(1-u)l \\ -\gamma y_u/y^p m & -\gamma y_m/y^p m \end{vmatrix}$$

$$= \tilde{\beta}_w \gamma u m s_c yl y^p X_l^w y_m = -cy_m$$

where c is positive, since $X_l^w = -y/(xl^2)$ is always negative. ∎

Lemma 4.2: The three leading principal minors of the Jacobian J in equation 4.52 read

$$J_1 = \begin{vmatrix} J_{22} & J_{23} \\ J_{32} & J_{33} \end{vmatrix} = -s_c l \tilde{\beta}_w m y_m (1-u) X_l^w$$

[39] Such an assumption is justified, for example, if $s_c \rho_m > \mu_2$ holds.

$$J_2 = \begin{vmatrix} J_{11} & J_{13} \\ J_{31} & J_{33} \end{vmatrix} = s_c y u m (\tilde{\beta}_p/y^p - \tilde{\beta}_w/(xl)) y_m$$

$$J_3 = \begin{vmatrix} J_{11} & J_{12} \\ J_{21} & J_{22} \end{vmatrix} = s_c l \tilde{\beta}_w X_l^w u \rho_u, \rho_u = y_u(1 - u) - y < 0.$$

Proof: Given that $J_{22} = 0$, the only nontrivial calculation is for J_2. Adding a multiple of the last column of J_2 to its first one gives

$$J_2 = \begin{vmatrix} 0 & \sim \\ -s_c y(-1)m & \sim \end{vmatrix} = - s_c y m (\tilde{\beta}_w X_m^w - \tilde{\beta}_p X_m^p) u. \blacksquare$$

Proposition 4.7: The steady state of the dynamical system (4.49)–(4.51) is locally asymptotically stable if $s_c > i_1$ and β_w sufficiently small.

Proof: Due to $y_m > 0, \rho_u < 0$, throughout, we have det $J < 0$ and $J_1, J_3 > 0$ (since $X_l^w < 0$). A sufficiently small β_w will then also make $J_2 > 0$. Furthermore, the trace of J is given by

$$(\tilde{\beta}_w y_u/(xl) - \tilde{\beta}_p y_u/y^p) u - (\tilde{\beta}_p y_m/y^p + \tilde{\beta}_w y_m/(xl) + s_c \rho_m) m,$$

where $\rho_m = y_m(1 - u)$. In the case $s_c > i_1$ we know that y_u will be positive while y_m and ρ_m are always positive. Therefore, trace J is negative in all of its components, apart from the first term, which will not be relevant for its sign if β_w is chosen sufficiently small. Consider, finally, $b = (-$ trace $J)(J_1 + J_2 + J_3) + $ det J. It is easy to show that $b > 0$ holds when $\beta_w = 0$ is assumed. Thus, $b > 0$ for all β_w sufficiently small. Thus the sufficient conditions for local asymptotic stability of the Routh–Hurwitz theorem (see the appendix to section 1.8) all hold true here. $\blacksquare$

Corollary 4.2: Proposition 4.7 also holds if the parameter β_p is chosen sufficiently large instead of β_w being chosen sufficiently small.

Proof: Since det J does not depend on β_p, while trace J and $J_1 + J_2 + J_3$ both depend linearly and positively on it, (recall $y_u > 0$ under the given assumption $s_c > i_i$), we can always choose a β_p sufficiently large such that $J_2 > 0$, trace $J < 0$ and $b > 0$ will be fulfilled. $\blacksquare$

The case $s_c > i_1$ can therefore always be stabilized by a sufficient degree of wage inflexibility or price flexibility. Price flexibility (wage flexibility) in this case therefore leads to local economic stability (instability). Of course, since only trace J, J_2 and b can create stability problems in a fairly simple fashion, there will also exist a variety of further cases where local asymptotic stability will hold true.

If the parameter h_2 in the money demand function is chosen sufficiently small, we not only know that (4.45) must hold, but obtain also (see the relevant expressions in proposition 4.1) that $y_m \mapsto 1, y_u \mapsto 0$ as h_2 approaches zero. Thus trace J must always be negative for parameters h_2 that are sufficiently small. This result allows us to prove the following proposition in respect of the case $s_c < i_1$.

Proposition 4.8: The assertion of proposition 4.7 will also hold true for $s_c < i_1 (y_u < 0)$ if the parameter h_2 is chosen sufficiently small.

Proof: An obvious adaptation of the proof of proposition 4.7 and the foregoing remarks of the sign of trace J for h_2 sufficiently small. ∎

We thus end up with the result that the case of a small parameter h_2 always favors β_p flexibility and β_w inflexibility as carriers of local asymptotic stability. Recall that in section 4.4 we saw that the case of a large (infinite) parameter h_2 favored wage flexibility in one case (where price flexibility was then destabilizing) and price flexibility in another case (where wage flexibility was destabilizing). The new asymmetry between wage and price flexibility of this section seems to be due to the Keynes effect $y_m > 0$ (or $y_p < 0$), which was absent in the case $h_2 = \infty (r \equiv r_0)$ of section 4.4.

We also deduce from the above propositions that assuming that both wages and prices will react to disequilibria in a sufficiently sluggish way will not always lead to local asymptotic stability. The outcome rather will depend on the relative size of β_w and β_p, though an increase in interest sensitivity increased may overcome the possibility of instability.

We now prove two propositions concerning the occurrence of Hopf bifurcations in the dynamical system (4.49)–(4.51).

Proposition 4.9: Assume $s_c > i_1$, so that $y_u > 0$. There is exactly one value $\beta_w^H > 0$ for the parameter β_w which separates asymptotically stable steady states $(\beta_w < \beta_w^H)$ from unstable ones $(\beta_w > \beta_w^H)$. At β_w^H a Hopf bifurcation occurs.

Proof: Due to det $J < 0$, the quadratic function $b(\beta_w)$ provides the determining expression (i.e., $b(\beta_w) = 0$) for the minimum value of β_w^H, where the stability of the steady state is lost for the first time. Furthermore, there can be only one situation where $b(\beta_w)$ crosses the positive part of the horizontal axis twice, since we already know $b(0) > 0$. This situation is depicted in figure 4.13.

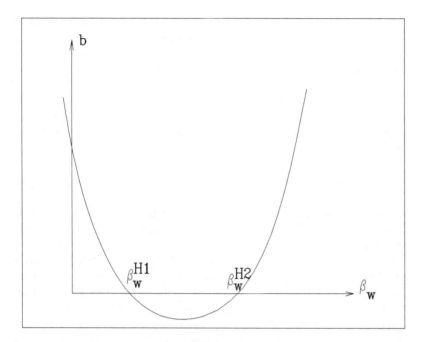

Figure 4.13   Determination of the bifurcation parameter value $\beta_w^{H_1}$

When either $-\text{trace } J$ or $J_1 + J_2 + J_3$ (which are linear functions of β_w) are strictly decreasing, they must cut the horizontal axis between the values $\beta_w^{H_1}$ and $\beta_w^{H_2}$ shown in figure 4.13, i.e., local asymptotic stability cannot be reestablished then after $\beta_w^{H_2}$ is crossed. If, however, both $-\text{trace } J$ and $J_1 + J_2 + J_3$ are strictly increasing,[40] they are given by the functional forms

$$-\text{trace } J = a_1\beta_w + a_2,$$
$$J_1 + J_2 + J_3 = b_1\beta_w + b_2,$$

where all coefficients are strictly positive. But then

$$(-\text{trace } J)(J_1 + J_2 + J_3) = a_1b_1\beta_w^2 + (a_1b_2 + b_1a_2)\beta_w + a_2b_2,$$

which gives a quadratic function that assumes its minimum at $\beta_w^{\min} = \dfrac{-(a_1b_2 + b_1a_2)}{2a_1b_1} < 0$, i.e., the situation depicted in figure 4.13 is then not possible. Therefore, no reswitching towards stability is possible once $\beta_w^{H_1}$ has been crossed.

---

[40] We neglect here the borderline case with slope 0.

The proof of a Hopf-bifurcation situation at $\beta_w^{H_1}$ is now a routine exercise (see Benhabib and Miyao 1981 for details, in particular with respect to the use of Orlando's formula for the proof that the eigenvalues cross the imaginary axis at $\beta_w^{H_1}$ with a positive speed). ∎

Proposition 4.10: Assume $s_c < i_1$, so that $y_u < 0$. There is exactly one value $\beta_w^H > 0$ for the parameter β_w which separates asymptotically stable steady states $(\beta_w < \beta_w^H)$ from unstable ones $(\beta_w > \beta_w^H)$. At β_w^H a Hopf bifurcation occurs.

Proof: Completely analogous to the proof of proposition 4.9. ∎

We should point out here that similar results with respect to the parameter β_p are not so easily obtained and may possibly work in the reverse direction.

Finally in this section, we note that the above calculations give quite a bit of information about the Jacobian J. In particular, they have shown that (i) sign det J (and sign J_1) depends solely on the sign of the Keynes effect y_m, where we always have $y_m > 0$; (ii) sign J_3 depends solely on the sign of the profitability effect, ρ_u (< 0 always); (iii) on the other hand, sign (trace J) depends on the signs of y_m and y_u as well as on the relative sizes of the parameters β_w, β_p (in their interaction with y_u);[41] (iv) sign J_2 depends on the sign of y_m in interaction with the relative sizes of the parameters β_w, β_p; and (v) the term $b = (- \text{trace } J)(J_1 + J_2 + J_3) + \det J$ is more difficult to judge and must be analyzed as in the proof of proposition 4.7. Should $-\text{trace } J$, J_1, J_2, and J_3, however, all be positive, it suffices to check $J_{12}J_{23}J_{31}$ and $J_{13}J_{21}J_{32}$ for positivity, since these are the only elements in det J which can then overturn the positivity of b.

4.6   Monetary and real factors in Keynesian cyclical growth dynamics

In sections 4.3 and 4.4 we analyzed the dynamics of the real sector of our Keynesian prototype model. In section 4.5 we added interest-rate flexibility to the dynamic analysis, thereby increasing the dimensions of the dynamical system being analyzed to three. In that section the feedback from expectations formation was switched off. Our aim in this section is to incorporate the expectations feedback mechanism and thus analyze the dynamics of the full four-dimensional model equations (4.30) to (4.33). We first discuss the expectations mechanism and various important subcases. Then we analyze the pure monetary cycle (i.e. the m, π dynamics) inherent

---

[41] This is the Rose conflict between β_w and β_p.

in the model. We then consider the real cycle when the investment function has a particular nonlinear form which we use as a mechanism to constrain the dynamics in the situation of local instability. Finally in this section, we consider the interaction of the real and monetary cycle using numerical simulations.

In this chapter we have shown that the results we obtained for the case of the Keynes–Wicksell model type in chapter 3 are not completely overthrown when this supply-side Keynesian model is modified to a demand-side version of the determination of the output of firms. On the contrary, the cyclical growth dynamics of the Keynes–Wicksell case reappears in the Keynesian case, though it is now embedded in a much more diversified structure of possible stability scenarios. This overall result is perhaps not too surprising, since our changes to the Keynes–Wicksell model, though important from the viewpoint of proper theorizing, have been few. The wage–price module therefore still seems to play a dominant role in the determination of the dynamics of the model.

4.6.1   The expectations mechanisms

In this subsection we consider the impact of expectations formation on the dynamics of the models of this chapter. We proceed as in section 3.7 of the preceding chapter by considering the main important subcases. As the analysis is analogous to that section we only give brief comments here.

Regressive expectations $(\beta_{\pi_1} = 0, \beta_{\pi_2} < \infty)$: This special case of our general expectation mechanism again does not modify the results of the three-dimensional case where expectations have been assumed to be always equal to the steady state rate of inflation.

Adaptive expectations $(\beta_{\pi_2} = 0, \beta_{\pi_1} < \infty)$: In the case of adaptive expectations, the four-dimensional dynamics becomes fully interdependent, since the evolution of π now depends on ω, l, and m and that of ω, l, and m on π. The evolution of inflationary expectations π is in this case determined by equation (4.33) with $\beta_{\pi_2} = 0$. From this we calculate for the dependence of π on itself the expression

$$\dot{\pi}_\pi = \beta_{\pi_1} \kappa [\beta_p y_\pi / y^p + \kappa_p \beta_w y_\pi / (xl)]. \tag{4.53}$$

This expression ($= J_{44}$ of the Jacobian of the extended dynamics) shows that the model of section 4.5 can also be made locally unstable via the addition of adaptive expectations by choosing the parameter β_{π_1} sufficiently high, if the Mundell effect y_π is normal ($y_\pi > 0$). As is known from other models we thus also obtain here, under the assumption just made, the result that adaptive expectations create (at least locally) explosive behavior if they become sufficiently fast. However, this situation is now no longer as universal as in the Keynes–Wicksell case.

Myopic perfect foresight $(\beta_{\pi_2} = 0, \beta_{\pi_1} = \infty)$: The fact that trace J approaches $+\infty$ for $\beta_{\pi_1} \to \infty$ in the just considered case of adaptive expectations again indicates that the limit case $\beta_{\pi_1} = \infty$, i.e. $\pi = \hat{p}$, may be of a problematic nature. In this case, the two Phillips-type adjustment mechanisms (4.21) and (4.22) of our general framework reduce to

$$\hat{\omega} = \beta_w(y/(xl) - 1), \tag{4.54}$$

$$\kappa_p \hat{\omega} = \beta_p(y/y^p - 1), \tag{4.55}$$

where y is determined by equation (4.35) of section 4.2. This case therefore gives rise to two different and seemingly contradictory real wage dynamics if $\kappa_p > 0$ and $\beta_p < \infty$ holds true unless labor-market disequilibrium $V - 1$ and goods-market "disequilibrium" are always proportional to each other with the proportionality factor $-\beta_p/(\beta_w\kappa_p)$. This implies that the utilization rates of the two factors of production are strictly inversely related to each other and therefore give rise to a "perverse" sort of Okun's Law. In the case $\kappa_p = 0$, by contrast, we always have full utilization of the capital stock and therefore another pronounced departure from the validity of Okun's Law. We conclude that the case of strict myopic perfect foresight is again problematic from an economic point of view.

Forward and backward looking expectations: From a formal point of view this case represents the summation of the case of adaptive and regressive expectations and it thus inherits the stability and instability features of its two limit cases we have just discussed. These now combined expectation mechanisms can also be represented by the relationship

$$\dot{\pi} = \beta_\pi[\alpha\hat{p} + (1 - \alpha)(\mu_0 - n) - \pi], \alpha = \frac{\beta_{\pi_1}}{\beta_{\pi_1} + \beta_{\pi_2}},$$

$$\beta_\pi = \beta_{\pi_1} + \beta_{\pi_2}. \tag{4.56}$$

This form states that a certain weighted average of the currently observed rate of inflation and of the future steady-state rate is the measure according to which the expected medium-run rate of inflation is changed in an adaptive fashion.

Our discussion of the perfect foresight case suggests that $\alpha \neq 1$ should hold at all times so that medium-run expectations of inflation are never governed by the short-run actual rate of inflation solely, but should always contain some nonmyopic forward-looking component. By contrast, it is perfectly legitimate to set the adjustment speed parameter β_π equal to ∞, giving $\pi = \alpha\hat{p} + (1 - \alpha)(\mu_0 - n)$ as the rule for inflationary expectations.

Infinite speed of price adjustment $(\beta_p = \infty)$: This case is considered in detail in section 5.3.2 of chapter 5, where it is in particular shown that, augmented by smooth factor substitution, it represents the prototype case of Keynesian dynamics of the macroeconomic literature that derives from the so-called neoclassical synthesis. We shall there also see that this case can again be characterized as supply-side Keynesianism. In fact, the Keynesian model with a perfectly flexible price level is basically identical to the same limit case for the Keynes–Wicksell model where the price level and the nominal rate of interest adjust aggregate demand to the predetermined level of aggregate supply at each moment in time.

4.6.2   The pure monetary cycle

In this subsection, we assume on the basis of the above discussion that the parameter values β_p, β_{π_1}, and β_{π_2} are all positive and finite, and thus exclude from consideration the one-sided limit cases we have just considered. We here also assume $\mu_2 = \mu_0 = n$ for reasons of simplicity.

In order to derive the pure form of the monetary cycle we shall again make use of the following two sets of assumptions:

- $\beta_w = 0, \kappa_w = 1$: The real wage is thereby made a constant of the model and it is set equal to its steady-state value in addition.
- $\hat{K} = n = \hat{L}$: The labor intensity $l = L/K$ thus is a constant in the following model and it is set equal to its steady state value l^d in addition.

Both sets of assumptions can be justified in the usual way by stating that the intent of the present investigation is confined to some pure sort of medium-run analysis. They here simply serve to reduce the dimension of the dynamical system (4.30)–(4.33) by two to two (in the variables m and π). The resulting dynamical system reads[42]

$$\hat{m} = \mu_0 - n - \pi - \kappa\beta_p(y/y^p - 1), \tag{4.57}$$

$$\dot{\pi} = \beta_{\pi_1}\kappa\beta_p(y/y^p - 1) + \beta_{\pi_2}(\mu_0 - n - \pi), \tag{4.58}$$

where the output–capital ratio y is given by[43]

$$\begin{aligned}
s_c(y(1 - u_0) - \delta - t^n) = {} & n + nm + i_1(y(1 - u_0) - \delta \\
& - (r_0 + (h_1 y - m)/h_2) + \pi) \\
& + i_2(y/y^p - 1).
\end{aligned} \tag{4.59}$$

---

[42] Note that the output–capital ratio and the rate of profit are not constant in the present context.   [43] Here we set $u_0 = \omega_0/x$ and $\mu_2 = 0$ for simplicity.

As in sections 3.4 and 3.6 of the preceding chapter, the following investigation makes use of a nonlinear i_1 component of the investment function $i(\cdot)$, here of the type

$$i_1(\rho - r + \pi) = c_1 \cdot \tanh(i_1(\rho - r + \pi)/c_1), \rho = y(1 - u_0), c_1 > 0. \tag{4.60}$$

This function has slope i_1 at the origin and its range is limited to the interval $(-c_1, c_1)$ as can be easily checked. With respect to this investment function one gets for the partial derivatives of the function $y(m, \pi)$ implicitly defined by the goods-market equilibrium condition, i.e., equation (4.59),

$$y_m = \frac{n + i'_1(\cdot)/h_2}{(s_c - i'_1(\cdot))(1 - u_0) + i'_1(\cdot)h_1/h_2 - i_2/y^p},$$

$$y_\pi = \frac{i'_1(\cdot)}{(s_c - i'_1(\cdot))(1 - u_0) + i'_1(\cdot)h_1/h_2 - i_2/y^p}.$$

These partial derivatives are well defined and nonnegative if the conditions $s_c(1 - u_0) - i_2/y^p > 0, h_1/h_2 - (1 - u_0) > 0$ hold, since the denominator in the above fractions is then always positive (and larger than $s_c(1 - u_0) - i_2/y^p$). In this case we always have a normal Keynes effect $y_m > 0$ as well as a normal Mundell effect $y_\pi > 0$ associated with the considered dynamics.

The steady state of the dynamical system (4.57)–(4.58) is as determined in section 4.1, viz. $m_0 = h_1 y^p, \pi_0 = \mu_0 - n = 0$, since we assume $\mu_0 = n$. Its Jacobian at the steady state is given by

$$J = \begin{pmatrix} -\kappa \beta_p y_m/y^p m & -(1 + \kappa \beta_p y_\pi/y^p)m \\ \beta_{\pi_1} \kappa \beta_p y_m/y^p & -\beta_{\pi_2} + \beta_{\pi_1} \kappa \beta_p y_\pi/y^p \end{pmatrix}. \tag{4.61}$$

The sign of the determinant of this Jacobian is easily shown to equal the sign of y_m and is thus positive, while the trace of J is given by $\kappa \beta_p/y^p(\beta_{\pi_1} y_\pi - y_m m) - \beta_{\pi_2}$. For $\beta_{\pi_1} = 0$ we therefore get a positive determinant and a negative trace of the matrix J and thus local asymptotic stability of the steady state. It is easily shown, furthermore, that the dynamical system undergoes a Hopf bifurcation when the parameter β_{π_1} is chosen sufficiently large, due to the dominance of the Mundell effect y_π that then comes about.

The following construction of conditions that imply the validity of the Poincaré–Bendixson theorem gives rise, however, to a situation that is much more general than that of a Hopf (limit) cycle (or that of a Hopf closed-orbit structure) at some intermediate value of the parameter β_{π_1}. To this end we have first to calculate the slopes of the isoclines for the (π, m) phase diagram of the above dynamical system. These are given by:

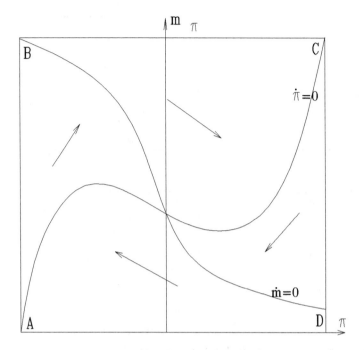

Figure 4.14   The pure monetary cycle

$$\text{for } \dot{m} = 0, m'(\pi) = -\frac{y_\pi + \dfrac{1}{\kappa\beta_p/y^p}}{y_m} < 0,$$

and

$$\text{for } \dot{\pi} = 0, m'(\pi) = -\frac{y_\pi - \dfrac{\beta_{\pi_2}}{\beta_{\pi_1}\kappa\beta_p/y^p}}{y_m} \gtreqless 0.$$

These isoclines give rise to the phase diagram of figure 4.14 for this pure monetary cycle model. The invariant box shown in this diagram can be obtained by choosing the parameter β_{π_2} appropriately large such that the $\dot{\pi} = 0$ isocline cuts the horizontal axis just once (to the left of the steady-state value $\pi_0 = 0$). If this is given, the rectangle shown can be constructed by following the sequence of points A, B, C, D. Note here that the conditions on the parameter β_{π_2} may be such that the slope of the $\dot{\pi} = 0$ isocline is positive throughout, in which case there is a stable steady state and thus

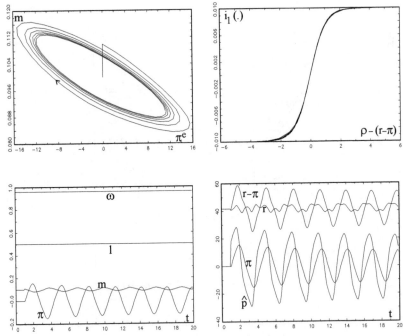

Figure 4.15   A numerical example for the pure monetary cycle

no compelling reason for the existence of a limit cycle in the above diagram. In the opposite case (where the situation depicted in figure 4.14 holds) the existence of at least one limit cycle, and the proposition that all trajectories in the above domain are attracted by one such cycle (or identical to it), are an immediate consequence of the Poincaré–Bendixson theorem. The assumptions made indicate, however, that the scope for the application of this theorem in the present context may be small.

Figure 4.15 shows a numerical simulation of this limit growth cycle which is based on the parameter restrictions we have discussed above. The parameter values of this simulation are shown in table 4.1.

This collection of plots shows a monetary (limit) cycle similar to the one we depicted in section 3.6, and also shows the nonlinearity of the investment function employed in the generation of this cycle. The lower two diagrams add some time-series plots to this numerical example of the m, π dynamics with an interesting pattern for the real and the nominal rate of interest. Note here that the amplitude of the fluctuations of the rate of inflation is fairly large in this pure monetary cycle.

Table 4.1.

$s_c = 0.8, \delta = 0.1, y^p = 1, x = 2, l^d = 0.5, n = 0.05.$
$h_1 = 0.1, h_2 = 0.1, i_1 = 1, i_2 = 0.3, c_1 = 0.01.$
$\beta_w = 0, \beta_p = 1, \kappa_w = 1, \kappa_p = 0.5, \beta_{\pi_1} = 1.1, \beta_{\pi_2} = 0.3.$
$\mu_0 = \mu_2 = 0.05, \beta_m = \beta_g = 0, t^n = 0.35.$

4.6.3   Investment nonlinearity and the real cycle

In this subsection we assume as in the previous one that the parameter values β_p and β_{π_1} are positive and finite and that $\mu_2 = 0$ holds in order to remove monetary influences from the real part of the cycle as in section 4.4 ($\mu_0 = n$ again for reasons of simplicity).

The other assumptions of section 4.4 that were used for isolating the real cycle were:

• $h_2 = \infty$, i.e., $r = r_0$, and
• $\beta_{\pi_2} = \infty$, i.e., $\pi = \mu_0 - n = 0$.

These two assumptions here simply serve to reduce the dimension of the full dynamics by two to two (now in the variables $u = \omega/x, l$), thereby again allowing a preliminary investigation here of the real part of the model (as an isolated substructure of the full dynamics). The resulting autonomous subdynamics in the variables u and l read

$$\hat{u} = \kappa[(1 - \kappa_p)\beta_w(y(u)/(xl) - 1) + (\kappa_w - 1)\beta_p(y(u)/y^p - 1)], \quad (4.62)$$

$$\hat{l} = n - s_c(y(u)(1 - u) - \delta - t^n), \quad (4.63)$$

with the output–capital ratio $y(u)$ implicitly given by

$$s_c(y(u)(1 - u) - \delta - t^n) = n + i_1(y(u)(1 - u) - \delta - r_0)$$
$$+ i_2(y(u)/y^p - 1). \quad (4.64)$$

This model has been extensively studied in section 4.4 with respect to a linear shape of the investment function in the implicitly defined $y(u)$ relationship (and linear or nonlinear market adjustment functions). It will now be briefly investigated by assuming as in the preceding subsection the nonlinear shape

$$i_1(\rho - r_0) = c_1\tanh(i_1(\rho - r_0)/c_1), \rho = y(u)(1 - u) - \delta, c_1 > 0,$$

for the profitability component in investment behavior of the employed investment schedule $i(\cdot)$ in the place of the nonlinearities we employed in section 4.4. This function of ρ is strictly increasing and zero at $\rho = r_0$, and it

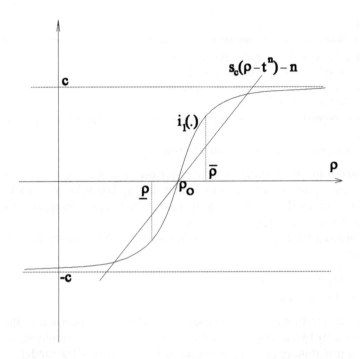

Figure 4.16   The nonlinear component of the investment function

approaches two bounds $c_1, -c_1$ as $\rho \to \pm \infty$.[44] Furthermore, there exist
exactly two values $\underline{\rho}, \bar{\rho}$ of ρ where the slope of this function is equal to s_c, if
the parameter i_1 is chosen larger than s_c. Figure 4.16 summarizes this
situation.[45]

With respect to such a reformulated investment function one gets (as in
section 4.2 of this chapter) for the derivative of the function $y(u)$ defined by
the above goods-market equilibrium condition (4.64),

$$y'(u) = \frac{(sc - i'_1(\cdot))y(u)}{(s_c - i'_1(\cdot))(1 - u) - i_2/y^p} = \frac{N}{D}. \tag{4.65}$$

This derivative, and the function $y(u)$, are locally well defined around the
steady state u_0 if $D = s_c(1 - u_0) - i_2/y^p < 0$ holds true, which is assumed in
the following.[46] Closer inspection of the denominator D of this derivative

---

[44] See figure 4.15 for a numerical plot of this function for $c_1 = 0.01$.
[45] Note that we have $y = y^p$ when the above investment curve intersects the depicted savings
line.
[46] This assumption is the opposite of an assumption we made in the subsection on the pure
monetary cycle.

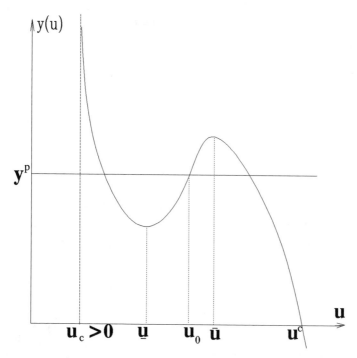

Figure 4.17 A nonlinear goods-market equilibrium curve

furthermore shows that it (and the function $y(u)$) is well-defined on the interval $(u_c, 1)$, at which the value of u_c is given by the first point to the left of u_0 where the denominator D vanishes (this will happen at a value $u_c > 0$ if $s_c > i_2/y^p + i'_1(y(0) - r_0)$ is assumed in addition). We shall work in the following with the opposite assumption, i.e., we assume that $u_c < 0$ holds. Let us provisionally here also assume for the following that the function $y(u)$ fulfills the conditions $y(1) < 0, y(0) > y^p, y(u) > 0$ for $u < u_0$.[47] Due to equation (4.65) it must then therefore have the general shape depicted in figure 4.17.

First we need to locate the values $\bar{u}, \underline{u}$ in this figure. It is easy to obtain from equation (4.64) (by substituting into it $\rho = y(1 - u) - \delta$[48]) the result that the derivative of the thereby defined function $\rho(u)$ is given by

$$\rho'(u) = \frac{i_2 y/y^p}{(s_c - i'_1(\cdot))(1 - u) - i_2/y^p}.$$

This derivative is strictly negative on the whole interval $(0, u^c), u_0 < u^c < 1$

[47] The first condition is implied by $s_c(\delta + t^n) + n \geq i(-r_0 - \delta) + i_2$.
[48] And $y = (\rho + \delta)/(1 - n)$.

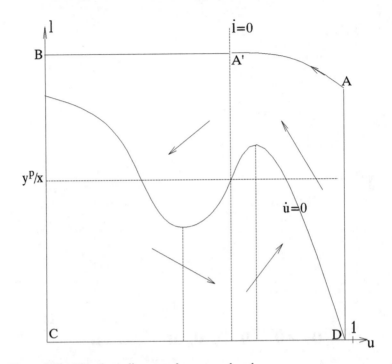

Figure 4.18   The phase diagram of a pure real cycle

where the values of the function $y(u)$ are positive (see figure 4.17). It follows that there exist uniquely determined values $\underline{u}, \bar{u}$ in $(0, u^c)$ such that $\rho(\underline{u}) = \underline{\rho}, \rho(\bar{u}) = \bar{\rho}$, since $y(u)$ passes once again through y^p to the left and to the right of u_0.

Let us now calculate the isocline $\dot{u} = 0$. As in section 4.4, it is easily shown to be of the form $l = (1/x)/((1 - q)/y(u) + q/y^p)$ where $q = (1 - \kappa_w)\beta_p/(1 - \kappa_p)\beta_w$. It follows that this expression is always well defined in the above situation $(u \in (0, u^c))$ when $q < 1$ is assumed. The derivative of this isocline reads

$$l'(u) = \frac{(1 - q)y'(u)}{[(1 - q)/y(u) + q/y^p]^2 xy(u)^2},$$

i.e., the slope of this isocline has the same sign as that of the $y(u)$ curve shown in figure 4.17. It furthermore cuts the horizontal axis at the same value of u as the $y(u)$ curve, though it will still be finite in value when the former curve is infinite (at $u = u_c < 0$).

The assumed situation thus gives rise to the phase diagram shown in

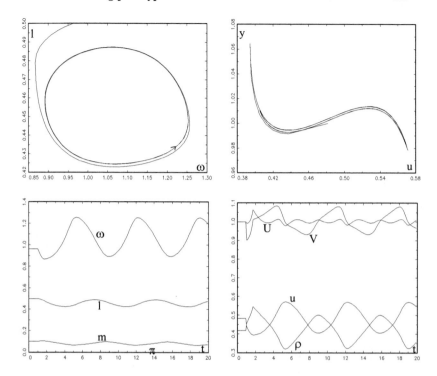

Figure 4.19   A simulation of the pure real cycle

Table 4.2.

$s_c = 0.8, \delta = 0.1, y^p = 1, x = 2, n = 0.05.$
$h_1 = 0.1, h_2 = 10000, i_1 = 0.9, i_2 = 0.3, c_1 = 0.1.$
$\beta_w = 4, \beta_p = 0.4, \kappa_w = 0.2, \kappa_p = 0.5, \beta_{\pi_1} = 0, \beta_{\pi_2} = 0.$
$\mu_0 = 0.05, \mu_2 = 0, \beta_m = \beta_g = 0, t^n = 0.35.$

figure 4.18 for the dynamical system (4.62)–(4.63). This phase diagram suggests that the conditions of the Poincaré–Bendixson theorem are fulfilled, since (i) no trajectory can leave the positive orthant, and (ii) a trajectory that connects A with A' can always be found. The set enclosed by $ABCD$ is therefore an invariant set of the considered dynamics. Hence, due to the instability of its unique steady-state, the limit set of each trajectory which starts in the domain must be a closed curve.

The diagrams of figure 4.19 provide a simulation study of this partial real limit cycle. The parameters of this simulation are shown in table 4.2. In the

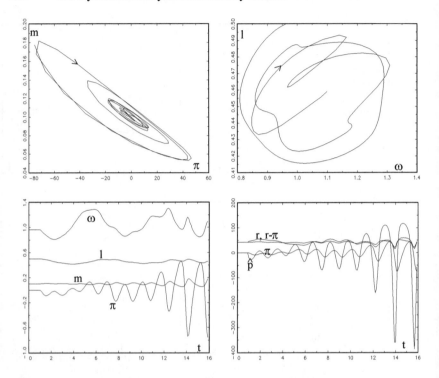

Figure 4.20a A simulation of the joint monetary and the real cycle in the intrinsically nonlinear case (with no investment nonlinearity)

top right is shown the nonlinear $y(u)$-function that is generated by the nonlinearity in the investment function for those u-values that are in fact reached through the depicted trajectory. Remarkable in these figures is also the fact that the rate of capacity utilization is not closely correlated with the rate of employment of the labor force. The rate of profit, by contrast, moves strictly inversely to the share of wages (though the function $y(u)$ is not monotonic).

4.6.4   The real and monetary cycles in interaction

Let us now consider briefly the above real and monetary cycles in interaction, i.e., the four-dimensional dynamical system (4.30)–(4.33).[49]

By exploiting the many linear dependencies of the Jacobian of the four-dimensional case $t^n = $ const. at the steady state as in lemma 4.1 (see

---

[49] More detailed investigations of these and other interactions of the given state variables follow in chapter 6 where the "working model" of the hierarchy of models of monetary growth of this book is introduced and investigated.

Table 4.3. *Parameter set for figure 4.20a*

$s_c = 0.8, \delta = 0.1, y^p = 1, x = 2, n = 0.05.$
$h_1 = 0.1, h_2 = 0.1, i_1 = 0.9, i_2 = 0.3.$
$\beta_w = 4, \beta_p = 4, \kappa_w = 0.2, \kappa_p = 0.5, \beta_{\pi_1} = 1.1, \beta_{\pi_2} = 0.3.$
$\mu_0 = \mu_2 = 0.05, \beta_m = \beta_g = 0, t^n = 0.35.$

also chapter 6 for further calculations of this type in the case of a dynamical system of an even higher dimension), it is not difficult to show that the determinant of this Jacobian is always positive. Stability can therefore only become lost in a cyclical fashion, by way of a Hopf bifurcation in general.[50] Furthermore, situations where the steady state of the dynamics is indeed locally asymptotically stable can be obtained by extending the propositions of the three-dimensional case of the preceding section to the present situation with medium-run inflationary expectations by assuming parameter values for β_{π_1} that are sufficiently small and by applying continuity arguments with respect to the real parts of the eigenvalues of the corresponding three-dimensional subcases.

When stability gets lost through an increasing parameter β_{π_1}, and there is for example not an attracting limit cycle that keeps the dynamics bounded in such a case, the question arises as to what are the further economic nonlinearities that can be meaningfully employed to make the explosive dynamics viable. Such further constraining mechanisms can arise as thresholds, as PID (proportional, integral, derivative) feedback controllers, through increasing flexibility of appropriate variables as the system moves further and further away from the steady state, etc. We will here choose the first type of nonlinearity, in the employed investment function, for a first simulation of its effects on the four-dimensional dynamics of this chapter.

We have seen that nonlinearities in the investment function are difficult to treat analytically even in the two partial and autonomous two-dimensional cases we have considered above. The present stage of the investigation of the interaction of these two-dimensional dynamics thus allows only for numerical presentations of this full dynamical system in the presence of the investment nonlinearity. Figures 4.20a and 4.20b provide, on this basis, a first brief impression of how an explosive situation in the linear case may be tamed, at least for some time, by the only nonlinearity (i.e. in the investment function) we have considered in this section.

The parameter values for figure 4.20a with only natural nonlinearities

---

[50] The role of price and inflationary expectations flexibilities is here again of decisive importance.

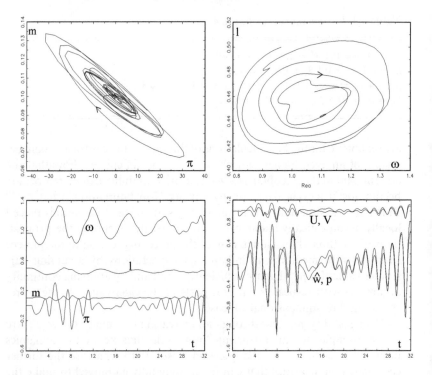

Figure 4.20b A simulation of the joint monetary and the real cycle in the extrinsically nonlinear case

Table 4.4. *Parameter set for figure 4.20b*

$s_c = 0.8, \delta = 0.1, y^p = 1, x = 2, n = 0.05.$
$h_1 = 0.1, h_2 = 0.1, i_1 = 0.9, i_2 = 0.3, c_1 = 0.1.$
$\beta_w = 4, \beta_p = 4, \kappa_w = 0.2, \kappa_p = 0.5, \beta_{\pi_1} = 1.1, \beta_{\pi_2} = 0.3.$
$\mu_0 = \mu_2 = 0.05, \beta_m = \beta_g = 0, t^n = 0.35.$

are given in table 4.3. We see from figure 4.20a that the dynamics are explosive over a fairly short time horizon.

In the simulation of figure 4.20b we introduce the nonlinear investment function by using the tanh-function of equation (4.60) with the value 0.1 for the parameter c_1, and keep all other parameter values unchanged. For easy reference the full parameter set is displayed in table 4.4. The plots in figures 4.20a and 4.20b show at the top the real and the monetary "cycle" we have studied in the preceding subsections in isolation from each other.

The plots of figure 4.20b show that the explosive cycle in figure 4.20a can indeed be "tamed" to some extent and for some time. It is however also apparent that further extrinsic nonlinearities are needed here in order to get a dynamical system with truly bounded trajectories. We shall not go into this question here any further, but shall proceed in the following chapters to further extensions of the Keynesian prototype dynamics established in this chapter where the question of the "viability" of the employed dynamics will be posed anew and considered from a more advanced and more refined perspective.

Before closing, we note finally that the plot in the lower right hand box of figure 4.20b shows the time series of two pairs of variables that are often identified and displayed solely by one magnitude in macroeconomic reasonings and presentations, namely, on the one hand, the rate of employment of the labor force V vs. the rate of capacity utilization U of firms and, on the other hand, the rate of price inflation $\hat{p}$ vs. the rate of wage inflation $\hat{w}$. We consider it important that these variables are introduced and their dynamical laws investigated independently of each other (as to the degree of independence they can really have from each other). We also believe it is important that conditions are explicitly provided (and justified with respect to their empirical contents) which allow the use, on the one hand, of only one variable to represent "capacity utilization" and, on the other hand, of only one variable to represent "inflation." Such an analysis would provide reasons for (or against) the validity of Okun's Law, on the one hand, and, on the other, for the extent to which the reliance on simple markup pricing rules is really justified in models of the interaction of unemployment and inflation.

4.7   Outlook: adding smooth factor substitution

When we motivated the basic modification of the Keynes–Wicksell model that led us to the present chapter we stated that proper Keynesian models of monetary growth have rarely been discussed in the literature on monetary growth. There is, however, a seemingly important exception to this rule, given by the Keynesian AS–AD model of monetary growth as it is for example discussed in detail in Sargent (1987, ch. 5). This model type employs IS–LM-equilibrium, and the so-called AD curve that derives from it, as well as the AS schedule representing the situation where prices equal marginal wage costs. For medium-run analysis it then adds a money wage Phillips curve and a scheme for expectations formation and for long-run analysis of the conditions for factor growth.

Yet, if one considers this model thoroughly, one can again find that this model type is not really of a Keynesian nature, since the capital stock is fully employed as in models of Keynes–Wicksell type. This is due to the fact that firms always operate at their profit maximum in this AS–AD growth model, and thus are on their supply schedule at each point in time. But, again, a Keynesian theory of fluctuating growth should allow for an under- or overutilized capital stock besides the under- or overemployment of labor, and thus for capital and labor to be off their supply schedules. Since the AD–AS growth model employs a neoclassical production function and allows on this basis for smooth factor substitution, the task now is in particular to formulate this proper Keynesian approach to fluctuating growth in the presence of a technology which allows smooth factor substitution in place of the fixed proportions we have assumed so far.

It is the purpose of the following chapter to do exactly this and to show on this basis that the AS–AD growth case represents but a bastard limit case between the general Keynes–Wicksell and the proper Keynesian model of monetary growth, where both capital and labor are generally over- or underemployed, as the economy evolves. Furthermore, and for completeness, we shall also investigate the neoclassical approach (the Tobin model type) in the next chapter for the case of smooth factor substitution which, as the Keynes–Wicksell variant, was and remains a model with full capacity growth. Yet, at the core of this chapter is the development of a prototype model with a varying degree of labor as well as capital utilization in the presence of smooth factor substitution. To do this, the AS schedule is reinterpreted as the locus of potential output with which the actual output of firms subject to a Keynesian effective demand regime has to be compared in order to define the rate of capacity utilization on the basis of a given neoclassical production function.

This is the proper interpretation of the AS schedule which makes this schedule a reference schedule with respect to which there is price adjustment in the medium run along the same lines as in the present chapter on Keynesian monetary growth.

Models of monetary growth of Tobin or Keynes–Wicksell type have generally been considered on the basis of smooth factor substitution. The next chapter, therefore, only shows in this regard how this assumption is to be formulated in our general prototype models of this type, leading to more flexibility, further adjustment processes, and more stability in these setups basically. With respect to the Keynesian approach to monetary growth of this chapter, the next chapter will, however, show that this type of additional flexibility does not add much to the proper understanding of Keynesian IS–LM growth analysis. This is in contrast to the widely held belief that smooth factor substitution will undermine basic assertions of a Keynesian analysis of growth, stability, and business fluctuations. The next chapter will therefore demonstrate that the perspective of chapter 4 is not changed in an essential way through the introduction of smooth factor substitution.

Appendix 1: The Benassy business cycle model

It is useful to compare the limit cycle results of section 4.4 with another well known cycle model of the IS–LM variety, namely Benassy's (1986a) non-Walrasian model of the business cycle. On the one hand, we can use Benassy's proof of the conditions of the Poincaré–Bendixson limit cycle theorem to fill out the details in our applications of this theorem. On the other hand, contrasting the limit cycle generating mechanism of the Benassy model with the mechanisms we have used in the previous section may help to clarify the advantages and disadvantages of these different derivations of business cycle fluctuations.

The Benassy (1986a) IS–LM cycle model[51] assumes no growth, i.e., $L = \bar{L}, K = \bar{K}(\hat{I} = 0)$, and smooth factor substitution which is governed by the marginal wage cost pricing rule in the usual way, i.e., $p = w/F_L(L, \bar{K})$. As we shall see in more detail in the next chapter (section 5.4), this result assumes that prices are adjusting with infinite speed if there is any deviation from full capacity utilization, so that such capacity mismatch is always avoided thereby.[52] For a Keynesian model it is, however, more appropriate to allow for capacity utilization problems and to check what additional features of the model may be generated thereby. We thus make use again of the simplifying assumption of fixed proportions in production in establishing also this model's basic structure. This allows for the immediate inclusion of capacity utilization problems (as we know from the rest of this chapter), which have not been considered in Benassy's (1986a) paper apart from his use of the acceleration principle.

In order to stay close to Benassy's two-dimensional approach to economic dynamics and his use of the nominal wage rate as one of the dynamic variables we add the usual markup pricing formula (in the place of the above marginal productivity rule) to the present formulation of the model, which in particular implies that there is no difference between wage and price inflation as is usually assumed in Phillips-curve approaches to the determination of the rate of inflation. In sum, we therefore have

$$L^d = Y/x, \bar{Y}^p = y^p \bar{K}, p = (1 + z)\frac{wL^d}{Y} = (1 + z)\frac{w}{x}, x, z = \text{const.}$$

[51] Compare section 5.4 for a treatment of the smooth factor substitution case.
[52] The basic problem here however is why there is an accelerator mechanism as in Benassy (1986a) in the presence of perpetual full capacity utilization.

for the description of production and pricing in place of Benassy's original assumptions.

Benassy (1986a) uses the following effective demand block for the determination of equilibrium output Y and the rate of interest r:

$$C(Y,p) + I(Y^e,r) \overset{IS}{=} Y, \tag{4.66}$$

$$pm^d(Y,r) \overset{LM}{=} \bar{M}, \tag{4.67}$$

where Y^e is the demand expected by investors when planning their current investment decision. Since growth is disregarded in the Benassy model ($Y^p = \text{const.}$), the variable Y^e is here reinterpreted and reformulated as the expected degree of capacity utilization $U^e = Y^e/\bar{Y}^p$, which takes the place of the actual degree of capacity utilization we have used in the Keynesian model of this chapter.[53]

As a further necessary ingredient we need a specification of the formation of demand and capacity utilization expectations of investors. This is done in the form of the following standard adaptive expectations mechanism

$$\dot{U}^e = \beta_{U^e}(U - U^e), U = Y/\bar{Y}^p.$$

Finally, there is a money wage Phillips curve in the Benassy model of the simple form

$$\hat{w} = \phi(L^d/\bar{L}), \phi' > 0, \phi(0) < 0, \phi(1) = \infty,$$

which here translates immediately into the usual price-inflation form by means of the above assumption of a markup pricing of firms $\hat{p}(= \hat{w}) = \phi(Y/(x\bar{L}))$. This means that either the price level or the level of nominal wages can be used in the final formulation of the dynamics of the model.

The IS–LM equations imply for output and the interest rate the functions $Y(U^e,p), r(U^e,p)$, by means of the usual assumptions on such a demand block; see Benassy (1986a, pp.134ff.). This in turn implies that we have to deal with the autonomous two-dimensional dynamical system

$$\dot{U}^e = \beta_{U^e}(Y(U^e,p)/\bar{Y}^p - U^e), Y_{U^e} > 0, Y_p < 0, \tag{4.68}$$

$$\hat{p} = \phi(Y(U^e,p)/(x\bar{L})), \phi' > 0, \phi(V_0) = 0, \tag{4.69}$$

and to explore its local and global stability properties. The steady state is determined by $Y_0 = V_0 \cdot (x\bar{L})$ and $Y(Y_0, p_0) = Y_0$ (see Benassy 1986a, pp.138 ff.) with respect to its existence and uniqueness. For the Jacobian at the steady state we have

---

[53] The influence of the rate of profit ρ and of the (expected) rate of inflation π as they are present in our Keynesian model is neglected in Benassy's formulation of investment behavior. The (destabilizing) Mundell effect ($Y_\pi > 0$) in particular is thus excluded there. Note that Benassy instead includes a (stabilizing) Pigou effect ($C_p < 0$) into his formulation of IS–LM equilibrium.

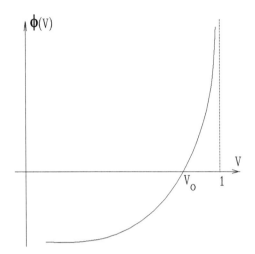

Figure 4.21 Benassy's money wage Phillips curve

$$J = \begin{pmatrix} \beta_{U^e}(Y_{U^e}/\bar{Y}^p - 1) & \beta_{U^e}Y_p \\ \phi'Y_{U^e}/(x\bar{L}) & \phi'Y_p/(x\bar{L}) \end{pmatrix}. \tag{4.70}$$

Benassy assumes that at the steady state the condition[54] $\beta_{U^e}(Y_{U^e}/\bar{Y}^p - 1) + \phi'Y_p/(x\bar{L}) > 0$ holds (which follows if $Y_{U^e}/\bar{Y}^p > 1$ and β_{U^e} is chosen sufficiently large), and thus guarantees its local instability. For the shape of the Phillips curve he moreover assumes (in order to obtain global stability for the considered dynamics) the general shape shown in figure 4.21.

Figure 4.22 shows the phase diagram that Benassy then derives from such a situation. Note that in this figure the labels $1, 1 - \varepsilon$, and V_0 denote the curves which satisfy $Y(U^e, p) = \text{const.} \cdot (x\bar{L})$, and where const. is set equal to $1, 1 - \varepsilon$, and V_0 respectively.

Benassy shows that the vector field corresponding to (4.68)–(4.69) must point inward along the $(1 - \varepsilon)$ curve if ε is chosen sufficiently small (since $\dot{p} = \infty$ along the 1 curve), and thus gets that the $(1 - \varepsilon)\&(1 - \varepsilon)\&B\&D$ domain is an invariant subset of the dynamics (if the point D is chosen such that it lies below the $\dot{p} = 0$ isocline). The properties of this domain then imply that there exists at least one limit cycle in this domain around the steady state of the model.[55]

---

[54] This amounts to the assumption of a Harrodian cumulative instability situation in the setup of a full capacity utilization model as far as the original Benassy model is concerned.

[55] Benassy's method of proof is also applicable to the Rose-type situations we have considered above and can be usefully employed in the formulation of the proofs of such limit cycle results. We have only sketched such proofs in section 4.4 and in this appendix.

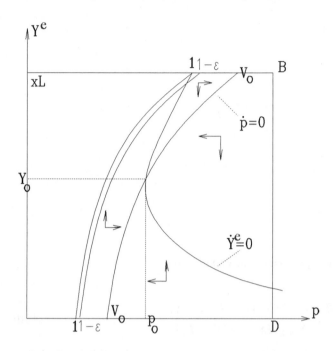

Figure 4.22   Construction a viability domain for the Benassy model

The outcome of the Benassy cycle model thus is to turn the explosive dynamics – caused by demand expectations of investors that are sufficiently strong in their impact on investment behavior (and thus on effective demand) – into a viable one if there is nearly infinite upward nominal wage flexibility near the full employment ceiling. The Keynes and the Pigou effects then induce contractionary forces near this full employment ceiling that successfully counteract the destabilizing influence of the demand expectations of firms.

The locally destabilizing role of the Mundell effect Y_π is obtained in the Benassy model by the accelerator term U^e in the investment function, which must have an impact effect on goods-market equilibrium which is larger than 1 in order to obtain the local instability result. As already stated, global stability is then achieved by the assumption of a one-sided nonlinearity in the labor market, since an increase in wages is always contractionary in the present context and thus does not stimulate effective demand as was possible in section 4.4.

What then finally distinguishes this limit cycle result from the corresponding results in section 4.4 and earlier sections of this book? We first note here that there is no real-wage mechanism (neither a Goodwin type one nor the Rose type one) necessary for the mechanics of the Benassy model. Instead, real wages may be safely assumed to be constant in time (as we have indicated above) without sacrificing an essential feature of the Benassy cycle model. The cycle of this model is instead generated by an accelerator investment mechanism (which must operate with sufficient strength), combined with the globally stabilizing role of the Keynes (and the Pigou) effect due to rapid wage increases when the full employment ceiling is approached.[56]

Benassy's model thus is basically a so-called AD–AS model (where the A(ggregate) S(upply) function may be a horizontal curve) augmented by a locally destabilizing accelerator mechanism. The basic message of the model therefore is that, whatever the reasons for local instability, the Keynes effect (cum Pigou effect if desired) is a sufficiently strong mechanism to keep the model a viable one provided there are sufficiently strong price effects near the full employment ceiling. We stress here that one such nonlinearity is already sufficient in this context to create bounded dynamical behavior. This appendix thus provides a bridge to the monetary forces added in the later sections of this chapter to the real growth dynamics on which we focused solely in the earlier sections. The resulting system (in the absence of Mundell effects on aggregate demand and inflation acceleration terms in the Phillips curve mechanism) also exhibits considerable potential for stabilizing the economy, as we saw in section 4.5 for the monetary growth dynamics model of dimension three.

Appendix 2: Technical change, wage taxation, average inflation, and p-star expectations

In this appendix we sketch how the model of section 4.1 can be extended in various directions that make it more plausible from the empirical point of view while remaining in the framework of its four laws of motion for the private sector of the economy.

The first extension is to a fixed proportions technology which exhibits Harrod-neutral technical progress at a constant rate n_2. This takes account of the fact that labor productivity x as well as labor intensity l^d exhibit, from a long-run perspective, a positive trend in capitalist market economies. They thus cannot be treated as given constants when the aim of the investigation is to reproduce some of the stylized facts of growth patterns and business fluctuations. Harrod-neutral technical progress is in the case of a fixed proportions technology defined by a given potential output–

---

[56] There is no further nonlinearity necessary here for the achievement of global stability.

capital ratio $y^p = Y^p/K$ and a growing output–employment ratio $x = Y/L^d$, with a given growth rate $\hat{x} = n_2$ which, in addition, is here assumed to be independent of the level of output that is actually produced. These assumptions imply that the actual ratios $k^d = K/L^d$, $l^d = L^d/K$ (describing actual capital and labor intensity) will change over time, not only because of fluctuations in the utilization rate of the capital stock, but also in the steady state where we will have $\hat{k}^d = n_2 = -\hat{l}^d$.[57] These assumptions and their implications are part of Kaldor's list of the stylized facts of growth theory (see Jones 1975, pp.7–8, for example).

The prototype Keynesian model is further extended by (i) allowing now for a constant wage income tax rate, (ii) letting medium-run inflationary expectations now be determined by an average of price and wage inflation (instead of only price inflation), and (iii) by basing the forward-looking component on a basic version of the so-called p-star concept of the German Bundesbank (and other central banks) in order to allow for a more refined treatment of forward-looking expectations. All these extensions will extend the final dynamical systems they imply only in a straightforward and clearly understandable way, making the dynamics richer but not less transparent.

These new assumptions on the technology of our economy imply the following changes in the model of section 4.1. Labor productivity x now follows a growth trend with constant rate n_2, i.e., the variable x is now determined by $x = x_0\exp(n_2 t)$. Trend growth in the output of the economy, with the rate of employment a fixed magnitude, will therefore now occur at the rate $n + n_2$, i.e., the growth in labor supply plus that in labor productivity. This new "natural" growth trend of the economy consequently has to be used in the money supply rule, in the trend component of the investment schedule, and in the formulation of inflationary expectations replacing the former natural growth rate n.[58] Finally, the wage–price module of our economy has also to reflect the growth in labor productivity, on the one hand, through an augmented target of workers that, besides expected current and medium-run inflation, now is also based on the constant increase in labor productivity that they observe. On the other hand, the partial markup pricing objective assumed to underlie the term $\kappa_p\hat{w}$ in our price formation rule now gives rise to the expression $\hat{w} - n_2$ as the cost-push reference for firms, which thus has to be used in the place of $\hat{w}$ in this equation for the formation of the rate of price inflation.

[57] Note in what follows that l and l^d will be used to denote labor intensity magnitudes in efficiency units.

[58] Note that this new trend growth rate is also the most natural one to be used for the parameters μ_0 and μ_2, which again implies that the steady state is then inflation free and debt free.

The most significant change in the dynamics takes place in the equation which describes the formation of inflationary expectations: $\dot{\pi} = \beta_{\pi_1}(\hat{p} - \pi) + \beta_{\pi_2}(\mu_0 - (n_1 + n_2) - \pi)$. On the one hand, we replace the adaptive term in this adjustment equation by $\beta_{\pi_1}(\alpha\hat{p} + (1 - \alpha)(\hat{w} - n_2) - \pi) = \beta_{\pi_1}(\alpha(\hat{p} - \pi) + (1 - \alpha)(\hat{w} - n_2 - \pi))$, which states that adaptive expectations are now based on an average of price and wage inflation (the latter only insofar as this inflation rate deviates from the trend in labor productivity growth). Note here that the earlier situation is reproduced when $\alpha = 1$ is assumed. The rationale for this extension is that economic agents believe to some extent that wage inflation will become price inflation in the end (if it exceeds the rate of productivity growth), and that they therefore integrate aspects of wage inflation into their views on medium-run inflation.[59]

On the other hand, we assume with respect to the forward-looking component in the formation of inflationary expectations that economic agents adopt the so-called p-star concept used by some monetary authorities in their calculation of future price changes.[60] A basic version of this concept is as follows: Economic agents assume that the price level is determined in the longer run by the quantity theory of money and by normal output, i.e., the moving attracting equilibrium of future price levels is assumed at each moment in time to be given by $p^* = \bar{v}M/(\bar{U}Y^p)$, where $\bar{v}$ is the velocity of money (estimated or assumed as a constant). Since there is no inside money in the present model, the magnitude M is fully under the control of the central bank. The only remaining problem for the bank as well as the other economic agents then is to estimate the development of normal output, which in our model is given by potential output times the desired rate of capacity utilization.

In terms of growth rates the above equation gives rise to $\hat{p}^* = \mu_0 - \hat{K}$, due to our assumption of a fixed proportions technology. The monetary authority as well as the public therefore has in this case only to obtain knowledge of the growth rate of the capital stock in order to calculate this present rate of growth of the center of gravity of the price level, rightly or wrongly assumed to exist for the actual rate of inflation. We here assume that the actual rate of growth of the capital stock is common knowledge and thus end up with the following reformulation of the forward-looking

---

[59] It is also not difficult to formulate a separate equation for expected price and wage inflation. However, the dimension of the dynamics is thereby increased by one.

[60] We owe the knowledge of this concept to D. Malliaropulos, who, however, is not responsible for the particular form given to it in the following. The quantity theoretic approach here employed can be obtained from our formulation of the money market by setting the parameter h_2 equal to zero, which gives as money-market equilibrium the equation $M = h_1 p Y = h_1 p Y^p U$. Replacing U by its steady-state value $\bar{U}$ then gives the equation shown for the estimation of p^*.

term in our standard equation for the formation of inflationary expectations: $\beta_{\pi_2}(\hat{p}^* - \pi) = \beta_{\pi_2}(\mu_0 - \hat{K} - \pi)$.

Note that this term reduces to our earlier formulation of forward looking inflationary expectations when it is assumed that both the money supply and the capital stock grow at their steady rates. Note also that this is only a second step toward a more advanced theory of future inflation. Further steps necessarily must use more elaborate models of price forecasting than have been introduced here, which take more of the present structure of the model into account than only the long run quantity theory of money to which it gives rise to ($\bar{v} = 1/h_1$!). This, however, is only a matter of sophistication (which from a numerical point of view will create no real additional difficulties), and not a matter of a completely different approach to the formulation of the theory of inflationary expectations.

A final extension contained in the following model is that it is now assumed that wage income is taxed proportionally. This extension does not change the dynamical equations of the model and mainly serves to give a closer correspondence of the model structure with actual taxation procedures.[61]

The equations of the Keynesian IS–LM growth model with the above set of extensions are:

1 Definitions (remuneration and wealth):

$$\omega = w/p, u = \omega/x, \rho = (Y - \delta K - \omega L^d)/K, \tag{4.71}$$

$$W = (M + B + p_e E)/p, p_b = 1. \tag{4.72}$$

2 Households (workers and asset holders):

$$W = (M^d + B^d + p_e E^d)/p, M^d = h_1 pY + h_2 pK(1 - \tau_c)(r_0 - r), \tag{4.73}$$

$$C = \omega L^d - T_w + (1 - s_c)[\rho K + rB/p - T_c], \tag{4.74}$$

$$T = T_w + T_c, T_w = (1 - \tau_w)\omega L^d, \tag{4.75}$$

$$S_p = Y - \delta K + rB/p - T - C = s_c[\rho K + rB/p - T_c] = s_c Y_c^D$$
$$= (\dot{M}^d + \dot{B}^d + p_e \dot{E}^d)/p, \tag{4.76}$$

$$\hat{L} = n_1 = \text{const.} \tag{4.77}$$

3 Firms (production units and investors):

$$Y^p = y^p K, y^p = \text{const.}, U = Y/Y^p = y/y^p(y = Y/K), \tag{4.78}$$

---

[61] See Flaschel, Gong, and Semmler (1998) for a much more advanced treatment of the tax and transfer policies of the government.

$$L^d = Y/x, \hat{x} = n_2(x = x_0\exp(n_2 t)), V = L^d/L = Y/(xL), \quad (4.79)$$

$$I = i_1(\rho - (r - \pi))K + i_2(U - \bar{U})K + \gamma K, \gamma = n_1 + n_2, \quad (4.80)$$

$$p_e\dot{E}/p = I, \quad (4.81)$$

$$\hat{K} = I/K. \quad (4.82)$$

4 *Government (fiscal and monetary authority):*

$$T = \tau_w\omega L^d + T_c, \quad (4.83)$$

$$T_c = \tau_c(\rho K + rB/p), \quad (4.84)$$

$$G = T - rB/p + \mu_2 M/p, \quad (4.85)$$

$$S_g = T - rB/p - G[= -(\dot{M} + \dot{B})/p, \text{ see below}], \quad (4.86)$$

$$\hat{M} = \mu_0, \quad (4.87)$$

$$\dot{B} = pG + rB - pT - \dot{M}][= (\mu_2 - \mu_0)M]. \quad (4.88)$$

5 *Equilibrium conditions (asset markets):*

$$M = M^d = h_1 pY + h_2 pK(1 - \tau_c)(r_0 - r), [B = B^d, E = E^d], \quad (4.89)$$

$$p_e E = (1 - \tau_c)\rho pK/((1 - \tau_c)r - \pi), \quad (4.90)$$

$$\dot{M} = \dot{M}^d, \dot{B} = \dot{B}^d[\dot{E} = \dot{E}^d]. \quad (4.91)$$

6 *Equilibrium condition (goods market):*

$$S = p_e\dot{E}^d = S_p + S_g = Y - \delta K - C - G = I = p_e\dot{E}. \quad (4.92)$$

7 *Wage–price sector (adjustment equations):*

$$\hat{w} = \beta_w(V - \bar{V}) + \kappa_w(\hat{p} + n_2) + (1 - \kappa_w)(\pi + n_2), \quad (4.93)$$

$$\hat{p} = \beta_p(U - \bar{U}) + \kappa_p(\hat{w} - n_2) + (1 - \kappa_p)\pi, \quad (4.94)$$

$$\dot{\pi} = \beta_{\pi_1}(\alpha(\hat{p} - \pi) + (1 - \alpha)(\hat{w} - n_2 - \pi)) + \beta_{\pi_2}(\mu_0 - I/K - \pi). \quad (4.95)$$

This Keynesian model with Harrod-neutral technical change is formally identical to the Keynesian model without technical progress as far as this modification of it is concerned. This can be seen as follows. Equations (4.93) and (4.94) can be rearranged in the usual way, now giving rise to

$$\hat{w} - \pi - n_2 = \beta_w(V - \bar{V}) + \kappa_w(\hat{p} - \pi),$$
$$\hat{p} - \pi = \beta_p(U - \bar{U}) + \kappa_p(\hat{w} - \pi - n_2).$$

Solving for the two variables $\hat{w} - \pi - n_2, \hat{p} - \pi$, these two equations imply

$$\hat{w} - \pi - n_2 = \kappa[\beta_w(V - \bar{V}) + \kappa_w\beta_p(U - \bar{U})],$$

$$\hat{p} - \pi = \kappa[\beta_p(U - \bar{U}) + \kappa_p\beta_w(V - \bar{V})],$$

where both of these equations will now be used in the formulation of the dynamic laws for π. Subtracting the second from the first equation furthermore implies for the share of wages $u = wL^d/(pY)$:

$$\hat{u} = \hat{w} - \hat{p} - n_2 = \kappa[(1 - \kappa_p)\beta_w(V - \bar{V}) + (\kappa_w - 1)\beta_p(U - \bar{U})],$$

which gives the first of the differential equations employed in the following in the same form as in the earlier models without technical change (where $\hat{\omega} = \hat{u}$ held).

We denote by L^e, L^{de} labor supply and employment measured in efficiency units, i.e., $L^e = L\exp(n_2 t)$ and by, $L^{de} = L^d\exp(n_2 t)$ denote effective labor supply and effective employment as distinct from labor supply and employment in "natural" units. From calculations as in the preceding chapters we then obtain from the model (4.71)–(4.95), **the five-dimensional dynamical system**, now expressed in terms of the variables $u = \omega/x, l = L^e/K, m = M/(pK), \pi$ and $b = B/(pK),$[62]

$$\hat{u} = \kappa[(1 - \kappa_p)\beta_w X^w + (\kappa_w - 1)\beta_p X^p], \tag{4.96}$$

$$\hat{l} = n_1 + n_2 - s(\cdot) = -i_1(\cdot) - i_2(\cdot), \tag{4.97}$$

$$\hat{m} = \mu_0 - \pi - (n_1 + n_2) - \kappa[\beta_p X^p + \kappa_p\beta_w X^w] + \hat{l}, \tag{4.98}$$

$$\dot{\pi} = \beta_{\pi_1}(\alpha(\hat{p} - \pi) + (1 - \alpha)(\hat{w} - n_2 - \pi))$$
$$+ \beta_{\pi_2}(\mu_0 - (n_1 + n_2) - \pi - \hat{l}), \tag{4.99}$$

$$\dot{b} = (\mu_2 - \mu_0)m - (\pi + n_1 + n_2)b - b(\kappa(\beta_p X^p + \kappa_p\beta_w X^w)) - \hat{l}, \tag{4.100}$$

where, besides the expressions derived above, we have to employ the abbreviations

$$\rho = y(1 - u) - \delta, u = \omega/x,$$
$$l^d = L^{de}/K = \exp(n_2 t)L^d/K = \exp(n_2 t)y/x = y/x_0 \,(y \text{ not const.!}),$$
$$X^w = V - \bar{V}, V = l^d/l,$$
$$X^p = U - \bar{U}, U = y/y^p,$$
$$r = r_0 + (h_1 y - m)/(h_2(1 - \tau_c)),$$
$$t = T/K = \tau_w\omega l^d + \tau_c(\rho + rb) \equiv t_w + t_c,$$
$$g = t_w + t_c - rb + \mu_2 m = t^n + \mu_2 m,$$
$$t_c^n \equiv \tau_c(\rho + rb) - rb \equiv t_c - rb, t^n \equiv t_w + t_c^n,$$
$$s(\cdot) = \hat{K} = s_c(1 - \tau_c)(\rho + rb) - \mu_2 m = i(\cdot)$$
$$i(\cdot) = i_1(\rho - r + \pi) + i_2(U - \bar{U}) + n_1 + n_2,$$

[62] Note that we make use of the letter l to denote L^e/K, both for simplicity and in order to keep the notation close to that of the preceeding sections.

and where again actual output per capital $y = Y/K(\neq y^p = Y^p/K)$ is obtained by solving the IS–LM relationship

$$s(\cdot) = s_c(1 - \tau_c)(y(1 - u) - \delta + rb) - \mu_2 m = i(\cdot)$$
$$= i_1(y(1 - u) - \delta - (r_0 + (h_1 y - m)/(h_2(1 - \tau_c))) + \pi)$$
$$+ i_2(y/y^p - \bar{U}) + n_1 + n_2$$

now with $u = \omega/x$, the share of wages in gross national income in the place of ω, the real wage. We note that the steady state of this dynamical system is the same as in the five-dimensional Keynesian monetary growth model of section 4.1.2 if $n_1 + n_2$ is set equal to n (and $x = x_0$), since the tax rate for wage income does not influence the interior point of rest of the dynamics and since all remaining terms reduce either to their former expressions or to zero in the steady state.

In view of these equations it is obvious that this dynamical system is of nearly the same type as the corresponding Keynesian model without technical change, wage taxation, and the other changes we have made to the model, the major innovation being the inclusion of $\hat{I}$ in the forward-looking component of inflationary expectations. The model is thus, on the one hand, closer to reality than the one of section 4.1, but nevertheless, due to its construction, has a structure of basically the same intensive form. This is in particular true with respect to the inclusion of wage taxation which, on the one hand, is necessary due to the empirical reasoning, but which, on the other hand, here only means a redistribution of income between the same marginal (= average) propensity to consume of workers and the government. Concerning technical change, the use of Harrod neutral technical progress, as is well known, needs nothing more than a reinterpretation of the magnitudes we have employed so far in this chapter, in order to include the stylized fact of positive trend in labor productivity into our models of monetary growth. We do not go into a theoretical investigation of this extended model here, but only claim that its analytical properties do not depart very much from those of the Keynesian prototype model investigated in the preceeding sections of the present chapter, as we have indicated above.

5 Smooth factor substitution: a secondary and confused issue

In this chapter we recapitulate the prototype models of chapters 2, 3, and 4 by adding to them smooth factor substitution in the place of fixed proportions in production. Our main findings will be that

- the Tobin prototype models (discussed in section 5.1) will generally[1] be increased in their dynamic dimension by one, now exhibiting the dynamics of the (full employment) labor intensity in addition;
- the Keynes–Wicksell prototype model (discussed in section 5.2) will exhibit further stabilizing mechanisms by the inclusion of a neoclassical production function;
- the Keynesian model (discussed in section 5.3) will not be changed in its general qualitative features, still exhibiting underutilized labor as well as capital, even with the addition of a neoclassical production function.

We thus find that smooth factor substitution does not essentially modify the distinctions we have drawn between the three prototype models considered in the preceding chapters. It is worth highlighting this result in view of the fact that the fixed coefficient assumption is often criticized in the literature for the narrowness of results it seems to imply. It is certainly true, however, that the addition of smooth factor substitution makes the models somewhat more complicated to handle due to the extra flexibility this substitution principle adds to them. The advantage of the assumption of fixed coefficients in production therefore is to make the fundamental economic principles of each of these theories of monetary growth more transparent and more easily understandable. We shall hence retain this assumption in the chapters that follow this digression on smooth factor substitution.

This generalization of the production technology of the considered economy has the additional effect of making the models used in chapters 2

---

[1] Up to the cases where the labor market is in disequilibrium.

and 3 easier to compare with their forerunners in the literature. Finally, we can demonstrate through this extension in section 5.3 that the standard textbook model of Keynesian dynamics (see Sargent 1987, ch. 5, for example), is but a limit case of both the Keynes–Wicksell supply-side approach as well as of our Keynesian model where, however, the features of the Keynes–Wicksell model will dominate. This bastard situation will again demonstrate that the usage of Keynesian models in the orthodox literature is strongly biased toward supply side economics, and thus not well suited to understand properly even the basics of Keynesian economics.

Including smooth factor substitution is thus not only a secondary issue with respect to the working of the models, but has also often led to considerable confusion in the presentation, interpretation, and investigation of Keynesian monetary growth dynamics.

5.1   The Tobin case: one further integrated law of motion

5.1.1   The general equilibrium case

5.1.1.1   Adaptive expectations

Let us first reconsider the basic general equilibrium subcase of the Tobin models of chapter 2 which we have investigated there in section 2.1 for the case of fixed proportions in production by means of one dynamical law. The only changes in the equations of this model concern equations (2.8) and (2.15). Under the assumption of smooth factor substitution (2.8) is to be replaced by $Y(= Y^p) = F(K, L^d)$, where the function F has the usual properties of a neoclassical production function (see, e.g. Sargent 1987, pp.7ff.). Equation (2.15) is then justified by the marginal productivity rule $F_L = \omega = w/p$ which is the motivation for the assumption that the equality $L = L^d(\not\Rightarrow \hat{K} = n!)$, i.e., full employment holds *at each point in time* (the "const." in (2.15) is generally set equal to 1 in such a context!).

By virtue of Euler's theorem on homogeneous functions, we then get from (2.1) for the rate of profit ρ the equality $\rho = K_K$. In intensive form $(Y/K = y = f(l), l = L/K$, see Sargent 1987, p.118, for details) we thereby get for the discussion of the dynamics of the revised model the new relationships

$$y = f(l), \omega = f'(l), \rho = f(l) - f'(l)l = \rho(l),$$

where $f'(l) > 0, f''(l) < 0$ and $\rho'(l) > 0$ hold true.

Since the ratio $l = L^d/K = L/K$ is no longer fixed ($\hat{K} \neq \hat{L}^d = n$ in general), its movement in time must be explained, and this is done by means of the dynamic law

$$\hat{l} = \hat{L} - \hat{K} = n - (y - \delta - c - \bar{g}) \text{ (using 2.14)}$$

$$= n - s_c(\rho(l) - \bar{g}) + (1 - s_c)(\mu_0 - \pi)m, \tag{5.1}$$

since $y = f(l), c = \omega l + (1 - s_c)[\rho(l) - m\pi - t]$, (from (2.4) and (2.5)) and (from (2.11) and (2.9)) $t = \bar{g} - \mu_0 m$ (δ and $\bar{g}$ are given magnitudes).

Furthermore, equation (2.12) for money-market equilibrium now reads $m = h_1 f(l) + h_2(r_0 - \rho(l) - \pi)$, from which

$$\pi = r_0 - \rho(l) + \frac{h_1 f(l) - m}{h_2} = \pi(l, m). \tag{5.2}$$

Finally, the expectations revision mechanism (2.16) of section 2.2 gave rise in that context to the dynamic law (see equation (2.23))

$$\hat{m} = \frac{1}{\pi'(m)m + \beta_{\pi_1}}[(\beta_{\pi_1} + \beta_{\pi_2})(\mu_0 - n - \pi(m)].$$

This equation is no longer appropriate, since π now depends on m and l and since $\hat{K} = n$ (which in turn implies $\hat{l} = 0$) no longer holds. In the present situation, this expectations formation mechanism instead gives rise to $\dot{\pi} = \pi_l \hat{l} + \pi_m \hat{m} = \beta_{\pi_1}(\mu_0 - n - \hat{l} - \hat{m} - \pi) + \beta_{\pi_2}(\mu_0 - n - \pi)$, since we have by the definition of $m = M/(pK)$ that $\hat{p} = \mu_0 - n - \hat{l} - \hat{m}$ must be true. This last equation can be rearranged to yield

$$\hat{m} = \frac{-\pi_l l + \beta_{\pi_1}}{\pi_m m + \beta_{\pi_1}}\hat{l} + \frac{\beta_{\pi_1} + \beta_{\pi_2}}{\pi_m m + \beta_{\pi_1}}(\mu_0 - n - \pi). \tag{5.3}$$

Taken together, equations (5.1)–(5.3) constitute an autonomous system of differential equations of dimension two (in the variables l and m). This system replaces the single dynamic equation (2.22) (or its equivalent in terms of m namely equation (2.23)) of the model of section 2.1. It takes account of the fact that labor intensity $l = L/K$ is now a variable of the model (the movement of which is explained by two independent laws of motion for the variables L and K), and that the substituted variable π now also depends on this labor intensity l (via y and ρ). This dynamic system has now to be investigated with respect to the implications to which it gives rise because of the added flexibility in y, l, and ρ.

Note here, first of all, that equation (5.3) is a direct generalization of equation (2.23) we have derived in the nonsubstitution case ($\hat{l} = 0, \pi = \pi(m)$). Note, furthermore, that the partial derivative $\hat{m}_m$ is given by (at the steady state)

$$\hat{m}_m = \frac{\beta_{\pi_1} - \pi_l l}{\beta_{\pi_1} + \pi_m m_0}\hat{l}_m - \frac{\beta_{\pi_1} + \beta_{\pi_2}}{\beta_{\pi_1} + \pi_m m_0} \cdot \pi_m,$$

where $\hat{l}_m = (1 - s_c)n - (1 - s_c)\pi_m m_0 > 0, (\pi_m = -1/h_2 < 0)$. The sign of π_l is, however, ambiguous, since $\pi_l = -\rho'(l) + h_1 f'(l)/h_2$ (it is negative if h_1 is chosen sufficiently small). Independently of the sign of this partial derivative we can here, however, state that $\dot{m}_m$ must become positive if the parameter β_{π_1} is chosen sufficiently large (noting that $\pi_m m_0 < 0$).

In addition, we have for $\hat{l}_l$ the expression $\hat{l}_l = -s_c \rho'(l_0) - (1 - s_c)\pi_l m_0$, which again is ambiguous in sign. This expression, however, does not depend on β_{π_1} which implies that the trace of the Jacobian J of the given dynamical system can always be made positive by choosing β_{π_1} sufficiently large. This reproduces the instability result of section 2.2 (for adaptive expectations) as far as the trace of the present two-dimensional dynamics is concerned.

Yet, in section 2.2, we had trace $J = \det J > 0$ (in dimension one), while it is a common observation that the two-dimensional monetary growth dynamics model exhibits saddlepath stability, i.e., that $\det J < 0$ holds. The question therefore remains whether this condition can be established for the dynamical system (5.1)–(5.3) as well.

To show this, we note first that

$$\det J = \begin{vmatrix} \hat{l}_l & \hat{l}_m \\ -a\pi_l & -a\pi_m \end{vmatrix}, a = (\beta_{\pi_1} + \beta_{\pi_2})/(\pi_{2m0} + \beta_{\pi_1})$$

must hold at the steady state. Some simplifications yield that

$$\det J = \begin{vmatrix} -s_c\rho' & (1 - s_c)n \\ -a\pi_l & -a\pi_m \end{vmatrix} = s_c a \rho' \pi_m + a(1 - s_c)n\pi_l.$$

Nagatani (1970, p.172) assumes $h_1 f'(l) - h_2 \rho'(l) < 0$ for the (more general) money demand function he employs. This condition is equivalent to $\pi_l < 0$ which (together with $\pi_m < 0$) then implies $\det J < 0$ (if a is made positive through an appropriate choice of β_{π_1}). Note again, that the Nagatani condition $\pi_l < 0$ can always be fulfilled by choosing the parameter h_1 sufficiently small.

Our findings in this section on adaptive expectations thus are that the results for the case of fixed proportions in production are confirmed and further qualified in the smooth factor substitution case, now also allowing for an adjustment of labor intensity l when the economy is outside the steady state. Nothing essential is, however, added to the earlier model by the integration of flexibility in the choice of factor proportions. Assuming such proportions as fixed has the advantage of making the model and its dynamics much more transparent, and thus helps to clarify the basic mechanisms that are at work in such models of monetary growth.

5.1.1.2 Perfect foresight

In the case of myopic perfect foresight ($\hat{p} = \pi$) we obtain from equations (5.1) and (5.2) of the preceding subsection the two dynamical laws

$$\hat{l} = n - s_c(\rho(l) - \bar{g}) + (1 - s_c)(\mu_0 - \hat{p})m, \tag{5.4}$$

$$\hat{p} = r_0 - \rho(l) + (h_1 f(l) - m)/h_2, \tag{5.5}$$

where we again have by definition of m the further dynamic relationship

$$\hat{m} = \mu_0 - n + \hat{l} - \hat{p} \ \text{(or} \ \hat{p} = \mu_0 - n + \hat{l} - \hat{m}).$$

Inserting this latter relationship into (5.4) and (5.5), and solving for $\hat{l}$ and $\hat{m}$, then gives rise to the dynamical system

$$\begin{bmatrix} 1 + (1 - s_c)m & -(1 - s_c)m \\ -1 & 1 \end{bmatrix} \begin{pmatrix} \hat{l} \\ \hat{m} \end{pmatrix} = \begin{pmatrix} n - s_c(\rho - \bar{g}) + (1 - s_c)nm \\ \mu_0 - n - r_0 + \rho - (h_1 f(l) - m)/h_2 \end{pmatrix}$$

or (noting that det $[\ldots] = 1$)

$$\begin{pmatrix} \hat{l} \\ \hat{m} \end{pmatrix} = \begin{pmatrix} 1 & (1 - s_c)m \\ 1 & (1 - s_c)m + 1 \end{pmatrix} \cdot \begin{pmatrix} a_1(l, m) \\ a_2(l, m) \end{pmatrix}$$

where a_1 and a_2 denote the right hand side of the preceding equation system.

Noting that a_1 and a_2 are zero at the steady state, we readily calculate the determinant of the Jacobian J of this system at the steady state to be

$$\det J = \begin{vmatrix} -s_c \rho' l_0 & (1 - s_c)n l_0 \\ m_0(\rho' - h_1 f'/h_2) & m_0/h_2 \end{vmatrix},$$

which is identical to the determinant of the preceding subsection up to the expression $a = (\beta_{\pi_1} + \beta_{\pi_2})/(\pi_2 m_0 + \beta_{\pi_1})$, which is equal to 1 for $\beta_{\pi_1} = \infty$. The Nagatani condition therefore once again implies det $J < 0$, and thus a saddlepath situation at the steady state of the above dynamics. Note here that this condition is stronger than is strictly necessary in order to obtain saddlepath dynamics.

The general conclusion of this subsection is the same as in the preceding one. Assuming smooth factor substitution extends the dimension of the dynamics to be considered by "1," but does not add new features to it. The basic mechanism that is at work here is therefore best understood when fixed proportions in production are assumed. These conclusions extend to the general equilibrium Tobin model with bonds, which, however, is not treated here anew.

As in the consideration of the literature on the Tobin model in chapter 1, all calculations can, of course, also be done by making use of $k = K/L$

instead of $l = L/K$ as the basis of the intensive form formulations. In this case, one has to make use of $x = f(k), x = Y/L, \rho = f'(k), \omega = f(k) - f'(k)k$ in the place of $y = f(l), y = Y/K, \omega = f'(l), \rho = f(l) - f'(l)l$ in the equations we considered above.

5.1.2 Disequilibrium in the money market and monetary growth cycles

So far, the rate of inflation $\hat{p}$ has been defined implicitly by money-market equilibrium and has been derived from this equilibrium condition by means of appropriate calculations. Starting now from disequilibrium in the money market serves (again) the purpose of presenting an explicit theory of the rate of inflation (whether a bad or good one has already been discussed in chapters 2–4). This explicit approach to the determination of the rate of inflation yields (see section 2.2)

$$\hat{p} = \beta_p(m - h_1 y - h_2(r_0 - \rho - \pi)) + \eta\pi + (1 - \eta)(\mu_0 - n)$$
$$= \beta_p(m - h_1 f(l) - h_2(r_0 - \rho(l) - \pi)) + \eta\pi + (1 - \eta)(\mu_0 - n).$$

Coupled with the laws of motion for l and π (see section 5.1.1.1), this now gives rise to a three-dimensional dynamical system in the variables l, m, and π ($\hat{m} = \mu_0 - n + \hat{l} - \hat{p}$ by definition), which can be expressed as

$$\hat{l} = n - s_c(\rho(l) - \bar{g}) + (1 - s_c)(\mu_0 - \pi)m, \tag{5.6}$$

$$\hat{m} = \eta(\mu_0 - n - \pi) + \hat{l} - \beta_p(m - h_1 f(l) - h_2(r_0 - \rho(l) - \pi)), \tag{5.7}$$

$$\dot{\pi} = \beta_{\pi_1}(\beta_p(m - h_1 f(l) - h_2(r_0 - \rho(l) - \pi)) \\ + (1 - \eta)(\mu_0 - n - \pi)) + \beta_{\pi_2}(\mu_0 - n - \pi). \tag{5.8}$$

In comparison to section 2.2 we have again one more dynamic law, i.e., equation (5.6), which substitutes thereby the algebraic condition $n = s_c(\rho(l) - \bar{g}) - (1 - s_c)(\mu_0 - \pi)m$ of that earlier section. The two-dimensional dynamical system of section 2.2 was shown to exhibit considerable potential for Hopf bifurcation results by means of its various adjustment speed parameters. We expect here that this also holds true for the extended dynamical system (5.6)–(5.8). We will demonstrate that this is indeed the case by taking the parameter β_{π_1} as a typical example of a bifurcation parameter. In order to do this, the coefficients of the characteristic polynomial of the dynamical system (5.6)–(5.8) have to be calculated first and then used to form the conditions of the Routh–Hurwitz theorem.

Lemma 5.1: The determinant of the Jacobian of the dynamical system (5.6)–(5.8) at the steady state is given by

$$\det J = -l_0 m_0(\beta_{\pi_1} + \beta_{\pi_2})\beta_p[s_c\rho' - a(1 - s_c)n]$$

where $a \equiv h_1 f'(l_0) - h_2 \rho'(l)$. This determinant is therefore in particular negative when the Nagatani condition $a < 0$ (h_1 sufficiently small) is fulfilled.

Proof: The determinant $\det J$ is readily calculated as:

$$\det J = m_0 l_0 \begin{vmatrix} -s_c \rho' & (1 - s_c)n & -(1 - s_c)m_0 \\ \beta_p a & -\beta_p & -\eta - \beta_p h_2 \\ 0 & 0 & -\beta_{\pi_1} - \beta_{\pi_2} \end{vmatrix}$$

which implies the above assertions. ∎

Lemma 5.2: The principal minors J_1, J_2, J_3 of J are given by ($a < 0$ again)

$$J_1 = m_0 \begin{vmatrix} (1 - s_c)n & -(1 - s_c)m_0 - (1 + \beta_{\pi_2}/\beta_{\pi_1}) \\ \beta_p \beta_{\pi_1} & -(\beta_{\pi_1} + \beta_{\pi_2}) + (\beta_p h_2 + \eta)\beta_{\pi_1} \end{vmatrix} > 0$$

if $\beta_p > (1 - s_c)n$,

$$J_2 = l_0 \beta_{\pi_1} \begin{vmatrix} -s_c \rho' & -(1 - s_c)m_0 \\ -a\beta_p & -(1 - \eta) - \beta_{\pi_2}/\beta_{\pi_1} + \beta_p h_2 \end{vmatrix},$$

$$J_3 = l_0 m_0 \begin{vmatrix} -s_c \rho' & (1 - s_c)n \\ \beta_p a & -\beta_p \end{vmatrix} > 0.$$

Proof: By straightforward calculations. ∎

Lemma 5.3: The trace of J is given by: $-s_c \rho' l_0 - (\beta_p - (1 - s_c)n)m_0 - (1 - \eta)\beta_{\pi_1} - \beta_{\pi_2} + \beta_{\pi_1}\beta_p h_2$

Proof: A straightforward calculation. ∎

Proposition 5.1: Assume $a < 0$ and $\beta_p > (1 - s_c)n$. The steady state of the dynamical system (5.6)–(5.8) is locally asymptotically stable for all $\beta_{\pi_1}, \beta_{\pi_2} > 0$ that are chosen sufficiently small.

Proof: The Routh–Hurwitz conditions for local asymptotic stability are: trace $J < 0$, $\det J < 0$, $J_1 + J_2 + J_3 > 0$, and $b = (-\text{trace } J)(J_1 + J_2 + J_3) + \det J > 0$.
It is obvious that trace $J < 0$ and $J_1 + J_2 + J_3 > 0$ for $\beta_{\pi_1} = 0$ under the given assumption $\beta_p > (1 - s_c)n$. Furthermore $\det J < 0$ for $\beta_{\pi_1} > 0$ and

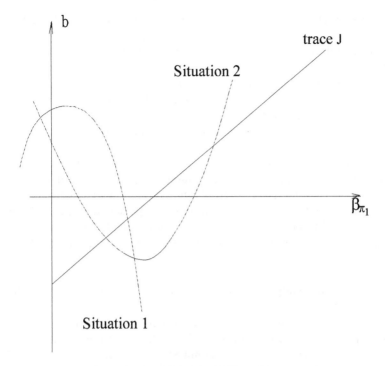

Figure 5.1   The determination of the Hopf-bifurcation parameter

$a < 0$, and det $J \leq 0$ for $\beta_{\pi_1} = 0$ and $a < 0$. In the latter case, we however have in addition that $(-\text{trace } J)(J_1 + J_2 + J_3) > -\det J > 0$ must hold. These Routh–Hurwitz conditions must therefore hold for all β_{π_1} sufficiently small, since the involved expressions are all continuous functions of β_{π_1}. ∎

Proposition 5.2: Assume $a > 0$ and $\beta_p > (1 - s_c)n$. There exists a unique parameter value $\beta_{\pi_1}^H$ such that $b(\beta_{\pi_1}^H) = 0$, and there is local asymptotic stability as in proposition 5.1 for all $\beta_{\pi_1} \in (0, \beta_{\pi_1}^H)$ and local instability for $\beta_{\pi_1} > \beta_{\pi_1}^H$. At $\beta_{\pi_1}^H$ the Jacobian J of (5.6)–(5.8) has one negative and a pair of pure imaginary roots.

Proof: It is easy to see that J_1, J_2, J_3, trace J and $-\det J$ are all linear functions of type $\alpha + \beta \beta_{\pi_1}$ of β_{π_1} with positive parameters α, β, up to J_3 (where $\beta = 0$), J_2 (where $\beta \geq 0$), trace J (where $\alpha < 0$), and det J (where $\alpha = 0$). The expression $b = (-\text{trace } J)(J_1 + J_2 + J_3) + \det J$ is therefore a quadratic function of β_{π_1} with $b(0) > 0$ and $b < 0$ at the uniquely determined values β_{π_1}, denoted $\beta_{\pi_1}^1$ and $\beta_{\pi_1}^2$, where trace J (and $J_1 + J_2 + J_3$)

become zero. This gives rise to the graphical situation shown in figure 5.1.

By virtue of the given information, there are therefore only two situations possible for the function $b(\beta_{\pi_1})$ (Sit. 1 or Sit. 2). Both of these situations imply that there is a unique parameter value $\beta_{\pi_1}^H > 0$ at which the system loses its stability, since b changes its sign (from a positive to negative) when this value is passed (from the left). Furthermore, b cannot become positive again, before β_{π_1} passes the value $\beta_{\pi_1}^1$ where the trace of J becomes positive, i.e., there is no return to local asymptotic stability. ∎

Proposition 5.3: Assume $a > 0$ and $\beta_p > (1 - s_c)n$. Then there exists exactly one value $\beta_{\pi_1}^H$ of the parameter β_{π_1} where the dynamical system (5.6)–(5.8) undergoes the Hopf bifurcation by switching from local asymptotic stability to local instability as β_{π_1} passes through $\beta_{\pi_1}^H$ from below. Generally, there is either the death of an unstable limit cycle or the birth of a stable limit cycle as the bifurcation value $\beta_{\pi_1}^H$ is crossed from below.

Proof: Analogous to the proof in Benhabib and Miyao (1981). ∎

This proposition reformulates theorem 2 in Benhabib and Miyao's (1981) treatment of the Tobin model for the Tobin model currently under consideration. It allows for the same comments as the original theorem of Benhabib and Miyao and states in particular that there exist periodic cycles either at $\beta_{\pi_1}^H$ or in a neighborhood to the left (repelling) or to the right (attracting) of this critical value.

Assuming an appropriate nonlinearity in the h_2 component of the money-demand function, we have shown in the corresponding case of fixed proportions (section 2.2) by means of the Poincaré–Bendixson theorem that there then also existed a limit cycle from the global point of view. This result is easily transferred to the present case of a three-dimensional dynamical system when the condition $s_c = 1$ holds. In this case we get, from (5.6)–(5.8), $\hat{l} = n + \bar{g} - \rho(l), \rho'(l) > 0$, and $\hat{m}, \hat{\pi}$ given as in section 2.3 with $\rho = f(l) - f'(l)l$ in the place of $\rho = n + \bar{g}$.

As the first dynamic law here shows, the steady-state value of l can only be disturbed by real shocks $(n, \bar{g}, f(\cdot))$. The results of section 2.2 (for $s_c = 1$) therefore immediately apply to the above special case as long as ρ remains at its steady-state value. The monetary sector thereby exhibits a further limit cycle generating mechanism which is due to a weakening of the Cagan (money-demand) effect far off the steady state. We expect this limit cycle result to hold also for real disturbances and resulting adjustments of the ratio l to its new steady-state value as well as for savings ratios $s_c < 1$ (at least) sufficiently close to 1, in which case the dynamical equations for l, m, and π are interdependent due to the Tobin effect then present.

5.1.3   Steady-state analysis and the enlarged Tobin effect

So far we have considered stability issues in their resemblance to those obtained for the case of fixed proportions in production, and neglected the question of the existence and uniqueness of steady-state solutions and their properties under smooth factor substitution. This gap needs to be closed, in particular since the interest in models of the Tobin type often is concentrated on the question of (non-)superneutrality of money and thus on properties of its steady state.

The steady state of the models of this section is determined by the following equations

$$\pi_0 = \mu_0 - n, \tag{5.9}$$

$$n = s_c(\rho(l_0) - \bar{g}) - (1 - s_c)nm_0, \tag{5.10}$$

$$m_0 = h_1 f(l_0) + h_2(\bar{r} - \rho(l_0) - \mu_0 + n), \tag{5.11}$$

where $\bar{r}$ is now an arbitrary positive parameter, not necessarily equal to $r_0 = \rho(l_0) + \mu_0 - n$ as we have hitherto assumed for simplicity. Equations (5.10) and (5.11) give rise to the equation

$$\begin{aligned}\text{const.} &\equiv n + s_c\bar{g} + (1 - s_c)nh_2(\bar{r} - \mu_0 + n) \\ &= s_c\rho(l_0) + (1 - s_c)n[h_2\rho(l_0) - h_1 f(l_0)] \equiv s_c\rho(l_0) + b(l_0),\end{aligned}$$

for the unknown full employment labor intensity l_0. Since $\bar{r} > \mu_0 - n$ should hold true, the constant on the left hand side of this equation can be assumed to be positive. Furthermore, we again assume that the Nagatani condition $m_l < 0$ holds true for the above money-demand function $m = h_1 f(l) + h_2(\bar{r} - \rho(l) - \mu_0 + n)$.[2] The function on the right hand side of the above equation is then strictly increasing in both of its components (and 0 for $l = 0$, also with respect to both components). The Inada conditions for the production function $y = f(l)$ then imply that there is a (uniquely determined) value of l_0 for which the above equation is fulfilled.

Figure 5.2 depicts this finding. It also shows that the steady-state value of the labor intensity ratio l_0 depends negatively on the growth rate μ_0 of the money supply, which is the central result (on non-superneutrality of the money-supply process) of models of the Tobin type.

Increasing the growth rate μ_0 increases the steady-state rate of inflation $\pi_0 = \mu_0 - n$ by the same amount, thereby decreasing the return of holding money as a financial asset. The relative composition of assets will thereby

---

[2] $h_1 = 0$, for example, implies this condition.

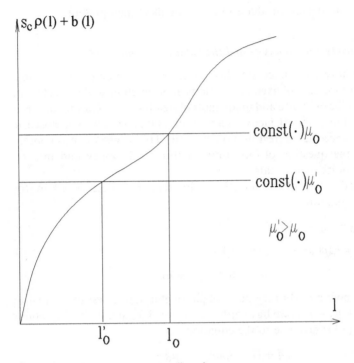

Figure 5.2   The non-superneutrality of money

be shifted towards capital, increasing capital intensity $k = K/L$ and output per worker $x = Y/L$, while decreasing at the same time labor intensity l and output per unit of capital y. This summarizes the basic quantity effects of changing money supply growth which, under smooth factor substitution, gives rise not only to distributional effects (as in section 2.1), but also, due to the neoclassical theory of income distribution, to changes in the ratio in which the two factors of production are employed.

We make two final remarks in respect of the Tobin model. Firstly, the assumption of smooth factor substitution becomes a necessary one in the case (common in the literature) where $s = s_c = s_w$ is assumed, since there will be no steady-state solution under fixed proportions with a uniform rate of savings out of profit and wages.

Secondly, on the basis of the Nagatani condition $m_l < 0$, we have that the Tobin general equilibrium model type is globally asymptotically stable as is the Solow real growth model $\hat{l} = n - s_c(\rho(l) - \bar{g}) + (1 - s_c)(\mu_0 - \pi)m$, as long as expectations π are fixed ($= \mu_0 - n$, for example). The usually observed instability of the Tobin-type dynamics therefore comes from quite another source, as can, for example, be seen by removing the Tobin effect from this monetary growth model type, by setting $s_c = 1$. In the case of adaptive expectations and a somewhat sluggish adjustment of prices we get in this case from lemma 5.3 the stability condition

$$0 > \text{trace } J = -\beta_{\pi_2} - (1 - \eta)\beta_{\pi_1} + \beta_p[\beta_{\pi_1} - 1/h_2]h_2m_0,$$

which once again shows the stabilizing potential of the parameters β_{π_2} and $\eta < 1$, while the interaction of adaptive expectations and the adjustment speed of prices is a potential source of instability. This, however, should be related to mechanisms investigated in particular by Cagan and not so much with studies of the Tobin effect[3] and the stable dynamics implied when it is working in isolation.

5.2 The Keynes–Wicksell case: increased stability through increased flexibility

The extension of the general Keynes–Wicksell model (3.1)–(3.24) and its intensive form dynamical laws (3.25)–(3.29) to smooth factor substitution is particularly simple and straightforward. In the place of the equations in (3.7) we now assume that employment L^d is determined by the marginal productivity principle $\omega = F_L(K, L^d) = F_L(1, l^d), l^d = L^d/K$,[4] and that the corresponding potential output $Y^p = Y$ is given by the production function $Y = F(K, L^d)$ underlying this marginal productivity rule ($V = L^d/L$ again). This reformulation of the employment and output relationship is all that is needed to extend the Keynes–Wicksell model to continuous substitution.

There is no change in the formal presentation of the laws of motion (3.25)–(3.29) of this model. In the accompanying algebraic equations, however, we obtain, due to the above considerations,

$$l^d = l^d(\omega) = f^{-1}(\omega), y = y(l^d)[\rho(\omega) = f(l^d(\omega)) - \omega \cdot l^d(\omega) - \delta],$$

in place of the hitherto fixed coefficients l^d and y (the parameter $x = Y/L^d$ is no longer needed).

In the equations for the steady-state values (3.30)–(3.35), we have now to replace the first condition (3.30) by

$$y_0 = f(l_0^d), l_0^d = l^d(\omega_0), l_0 = l_0^d/\bar{V}$$

which makes the calculation of the steady-state values for l^d, y, and ρ slightly more interdependent. In the case $\mu_2 = \mu_0(b_0 = 0)$, the basic equa-

---

[3] The functions $\hat{l}(m)$ and $m(\mu_0)$ are the basis of the Tobin effect (the first is increasing, the second decreasing).

[4] Note that ω is given at each moment of time in this model type, so that there is the causal static relationship $l^d = l^d(\omega)$ in this context.

tion for the determination of these values reads $\rho_0(\omega_0) = (n + \mu_0 h_1 f(l^d(\omega_0)))/s_c(1 - \tau)$, for which a unique solution $\omega_0 > 0$ has to be shown to exist. This is again easy if $h_1 = 0$ is assumed.

The general five-dimensional dynamical system governing the dynamics of this Keynes–Wicksell model is again reduced to a four-dimensional dynamical system by the assumption $t^n = \text{const.}$, and to a three-dimensional one by way of the further assumption $\pi = \mu_0 - n$ (a consequence of assuming $\beta_{\pi_2} = \infty$). The basic case of an independent real sector of the economy is finally obtained by assuming $h_2 = \infty$, i.e., $r \equiv r_0, \mu_2 = 0$. The following investigations will start from this basic case and briefly consider how the propositions of the fixed proportions situation are changed by the assumption of smooth factor substitution.

5.2.1   The Goodwin case

The two differential equations

$$\hat{u} = \beta_w(V - \bar{V}), u = \omega/x = \omega l^d/y,$$
$$\hat{V} = i(y - \delta - uy - r_0 + \mu_0 - n), V = l^d/l,$$

of the fixed proportions case of section 3.4 now demand the use of the dynamic variable ω in the place of u, since l^d and y now both depend on ω. This variable change allows again a treatment of this dynamical system by means of a suitably chosen Liapunov function H.

In order to show this, we first calculate the percentage rate of change of the variable V, making use of the functional relationship $l^d = l^d(\omega)$ (or $\omega = f'(l^d)$) to obtain

$$\hat{V} = \hat{l}^d - \hat{l} = l^{d'}(\omega)\dot{\omega}/l^d(\omega) - n + \hat{K} = \varepsilon(\omega)\dot{\omega} + g(\omega).$$

In this last expression, $\varepsilon(\omega) < 0$ stands for $l^{d'}(\omega)\omega/l^d(\omega)$ and $g(\omega), (g'(\omega) < 0)$ expresses that $\hat{K}$ depends (only) on ρ in a positive way, and thus on ω in a negative way,[5] independently of whether it is explained by I/K or S/K (or a combination of both).

The above two differential equations thus give rise to

$$\dot{\omega} = \beta_w(V - \bar{V}) = h(V), \tag{5.12}$$

$$\hat{V} = \varepsilon(\omega)\beta_w(V - \bar{V}) + g(\omega), \tag{5.13}$$

in the case of smooth factor substitution. This reformulation of the model allows again for the type of Liapunov function we have used in section 3.3 for (3.29) and (3.30), which here reads

---

[5] To see this note that $\rho(\omega) = f(l^d(\omega)) - \omega l^d(\omega) - \delta \Rightarrow \rho'(\omega) = - l^d(\omega) < 0$.

$$H(\omega, V) = - \int_{\omega_0}^{\omega} g(\tilde{\omega})/\tilde{\omega} d\tilde{\omega} + \int_{V}^{\bar{V}} h(\tilde{V})/\tilde{V} d\tilde{V}.$$

It is easy to show that this function fulfills

$$\dot{H} = \varepsilon(\omega) h(V)^2 < 0, \text{ if } V \neq \bar{V} = V_0 (= 0 \text{ otherwise}).$$

Hence we obtain the following.

Proposition 5.4: The steady state $\omega_0 [g(\omega_0) = 0]$, $V_0 = \bar{V}$ of the dynamical system (5.12)–(5.13) is globally asymptotically stable in the positive orthant of $\mathbb{R}^2$.

Proof: A standard application of the theory of Liapunov functions (see, e.g., Hirsch and Smale 1974, pp.195–6). ■

Smooth factor substitution therefore makes the center type dynamics of the original Goodwin growth cycle model a convergent one. In addition it can be shown that this convergence becomes monotonic (loses its generally cyclical properties) if the elasticity of factor substitution is chosen sufficiently high. By contrast, the originally closed orbit structure of the Goodwin model is approached again, if this substitution elasticity gets smaller and smaller (the same holds if the parameter β_w is decreased instead). These considerations indicate how the models we considered in section 3.3 will be modified in the presence of a neoclassical production function $Y = F(K, L^d)$.

5.2.2 The Rose case

We recall that the Rose case is obtained by taking all the assumptions that give rise to the Goodwin case, but replacing $\kappa_w = 1$ by $\kappa_w < 1$. Equation (5.12) is in this case thus expanded to the form

$$\dot{\omega} = \kappa[(1 - \kappa_p)\beta_w(V - \bar{V}) + (\kappa_w - 1)\beta_p(i(\cdot) + n - s(\cdot))], \quad (5.14)$$

where $i(\cdot) + n = i(\rho(\omega) - r_0 + \mu_0 - n) + n$ and $s(\cdot) = s_c(\rho(\omega) - t^n)$ are the two functions we have denoted by $g(\omega)$, $l(\omega)$ in the preceding subsection. As far as the dynamic law (5.13) is concerned, it is now more appropriate to make use of a formulation in terms of $l(= l^d(\omega)/V)$, which turns out to be

$$\hat{l} = n - g(\omega), g(\omega) = i(\cdot) + n \text{ or } g(\omega) = s(\cdot) \quad (5.15)$$

This, of course, requires that V be replaced by $l^d(\omega)/l$ in equation (5.14).

In order to derive global stability (but generally not asymptotic stability) for this extended dynamical system of the real sector, we assume again for

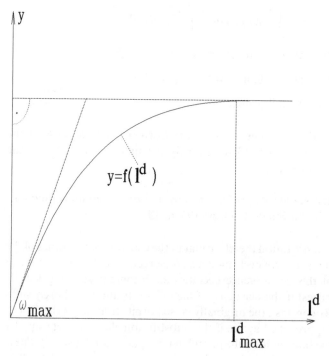

Figure 5.3   A restricted neoclassical production function

the $\beta_w(V - \bar{V})$ part of the money-wage Phillips curve of this model the nonlinear shape we have used in section 3.4 in order to make the dynamics of the Rose extension of the employment cycle viable. The nonlinear investment function that we also used in section 3.4 is now no longer necessary in order to obtain such a result, and is thus replaced here by a nonlinear smooth production technology.

Let a and $b(0 < a < b)$ again denote the limits of the assumed nonlinear Phillips curve, where wage inflation becomes $-\infty$ and $+\infty$, respectively (see page 149, figure 3.2). To ease the following presentation, we assume here for simplicity that the production function $y = f(l^d)$ is of the form displayed in figure 5.3. This form has the property that the marginal product of labor is less than infinite at $l = 0$, and becomes zero at a certain finite level of the labor intensity l^d.

In this case, the dynamical system (5.14)–(5.15) gives rise to the phase diagram shown in figure 5.4. Due to the above assumption on the range of possible marginal products of labor, we know that the decreasing function $l^d(\omega)$ must cut the axes of the positive orthant at ω_{max} and l_{max}. This fact then also holds true for the rescaled functions $l = l^d(\omega)/a$ (where $\hat{\omega} = -\infty$

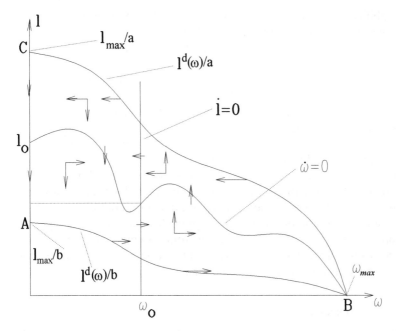

Figure 5.4 The viability domain of the Rose dynamics under smooth factor substitution

holds, since $V = l^d(\omega)/l = a$ along this curve) and $l = l^d(\omega)/b$ (where $\dot\omega = +\infty$ holds true). Note here that these two curves have the same origin B and that they enclose the open domain of (ω, l) combinations where the dynamics (5.14)–(5.15) is well-defined (the open region ABC).

The isoclines $\dot\omega = 0, \dot l = 0$ of (5.14) and (5.15) are given by

$$l = l^d(\omega)\left(\beta_w^{-1}\left[\frac{(1 - \kappa_w)\beta_p(i(\cdot) + n - s(\cdot))}{1 - \kappa_p}\right] + \bar V\right)^{-1},$$

$$\omega = \omega_0.$$

Due to the assumed shape of the β_w function (see again figure 3.2), we know that the first expression is always well defined and must always lie between $l^d(\omega)/b$ and $l^d(\omega)/a$ (see figure 5.4). The above two isoclines then divide the phase space as shown in figure 5.4.

By employing a proof similar in spirit to that in Benassy (1986a) (see also Flaschel and Sethi 1996), it is not very difficult to show that the Poincaré–Bendixson theorem can be applied to the situation depicted in figure 5.4 if wage flexibility is so low at the steady state that the β_p term implies its local instability ($i > s_c$). Sluggish wages near the steady state, and ever-increasing wage flexibility far off it, therefore imply the existence of a limit cycle as in Rose (1967), now independently of any nonlinearity in the market for goods.

The details of such an analysis are spelt out in Benassy (1986a) and Flaschel and Sethi (1996) and will not be repeated here. Here it is sufficient to have sketched the result, that in Keynes–Wicksell models (of a special type) we can get global stability solely through appropriate assumptions on wage flexibility in conjunction with smooth factor substitution. Note here that the viability domain ABC of this dynamical system can be tailored to empirically plausible magnitudes simply by making an appropriate choice of the two bounds a and b for the Phillips curve. Note also, however, that this neoclassical supply-side dynamical behavior (which can be much more complicated than is generally admitted by supply-side economists) is not yet too convincing from an empirical point of view. Indeed, this comment is generally true for the Keynes–Wicksell model type, as we have remarked in earlier chapters.

5.2.3   Monetary growth dynamics

Allowing now again for interest rate flexibility ($h_2 < \infty$) extends the dynamics (5.14)–(5.15) to a three-dimensional dynamical system by means of the extended relationships

$$i(\,\cdot\,) + n = i(\rho(\omega) - r + \mu_0 - n) + n,$$
$$s(\,\cdot\,) = s_c(\rho(\omega) - t^n) - \mu_2 m,$$
$$r = r_0 + (h_1 y(\omega) - m)/h_2,$$

and the further dynamical law for $m(= (M/pK))$

$$\hat{m} = \mu_0 - g(\,\cdot\,) - \pi - (\hat{p} - \pi), \pi = \mu_0 - n,$$

where $g(\,\cdot\,)$ is again given by either $i(\,\cdot\,) + n$ or $s(\,\cdot\,)$ and

$$\hat{p} - \pi = \kappa[\beta_p(i(\,\cdot\,) + n - s(\,\cdot\,) + \kappa_p \beta_w(V - \bar{V})],$$
$$V = l^d(\omega)/l, y(\omega) = f(l^d(\omega)).$$

Note first that the function $\rho(\omega) = y(\omega) - \delta - \omega l^d(\omega)$ is but a nonlinear extension of the formerly linear expression used in section 3.5 (see section 3.2 for the definition of ρ), namely $\rho(\omega) = y - \delta - \omega l^d, l^d = y/x, y, x = $ const. ($\rho'(\omega) = - l^d(\,\cdot\,) < 0$ in both cases). Note also that the rate of interest now also depends on ω, so that $r_\omega = h_1 f'(l^d) l^{d'}(\omega) < 0$ now holds. This negative dependence on the real wage can be aggregated with the negative dependence of ρ on ω, so that neither the $i(\,\cdot\,)$ nor the $s(\,\cdot\,)$ equation is changed qualitatively by the addition of smooth factor substitution. This fact extends to the $\hat{p} - \pi$ equation as far as its β_p component is concerned. The β_w component, however, is here (and also in the $\hat{\omega}$-equation) different from the situation of fixed proportions, where it was a function of l solely ($l^d = y/x = $ const.). Now $l^d = l^d(\omega)$ due to smooth substitution which introduces via $\beta_w(\cdot)$ a new derivative into the determination of the Jacobian of such a three-dimensional dynamical system (in the $\hat{\omega}$ — as well as in the $\hat{m}$ — part of it).

The sign structure of the Jacobian at the steady state of section 3.5 was

$$J = \begin{pmatrix} ? & + & - \\ - & 0 & + \\ ? & - & - \end{pmatrix},$$

and it is now augmented by the addition of a further matrix of the form

$$\begin{pmatrix} - & 0 & 0 \\ 0 & 0 & 0 \\ + & 0 & 0 \end{pmatrix}.$$

Such an addition does not modify the results we have stated in section 3.5 for the matrix J as far as its trace, the principal minors J_1, J_2, and J_3, and the determinant of J are concerned. This conclusion can also be extended to the final Routh–Hurwitz condition

$$b = (-\text{trace } J)(J_1 + J_2 + J_3) + \det J,$$

which then shows that the addition of smooth factor substitution increases the range for local asymptotic stability (see proposition 3.6 in section 3.5 in particular).

Despite this improvement in the stability properties caused by smooth factor substitution, the qualitative stability results of section 3.5 are not significantly modified by this flexibility in the use of factors of production. With this observation we close our reconsideration of the Keynes–Wicksell prototype and its (by and large confirmed) stability properties.

5.3   The Keynesian case with smooth factor substitution

5.3.1   The Keynesian IS–LM growth model generalized

This section presents a possible, though in its particular form not too compelling, extension of the production function used in the Keynesian model of chapter 4, namely, to neoclassical smooth factor substitution as was done for the Tobin and Keynes–Wicksell model types in sections 5.1 and 5.2. It is here included for methodological reasons and is intended to show that the standard neoclassical production function can be used in the Keynesian context as well, without leading to a loss in the substance of this unique approach to underutilized (or overutilized) labor as well as underutilized (or overutilized) capital.

The Tobin and Keynes–Wicksell type models of monetary growth have generally been associated with the assumption of a neoclassical production function and have been analyzed within such a framework. To do the same for our Keynesian type model may not appear as natural as for these earlier supply-side models, since there has been (and perhaps still is) a tradition in Keynesian growth economics which rejected (and continues to reject) the use of such a production function, having its roots in the works of Harrod, Kaldor, and Sraffa in particular. Yet, we believe (see also Marglin, 1984a, for similar arguments) that the particular type of production theory employed should not prevent the formulation of a proper Keynesian model where both labor and capital can be unemployed (or overemployed). Keynesian monetary growth dynamics should also exist as a meaningful model if technology is of the neoclassical production function type, quite independently of the question whether this function is really appropriate in this context. Assumptions about technology should consequently not be decisive for a proper understanding of various schools of thought and their way of formulating the essential aspects of the forces governing monetary growth and cycles.

Therefore, our Keynesian model of chapter 4, with its distinctive features regarding the determination and implications of underutilized capital (besides underutilized labor), should survive the introduction of a neoclassical production function in place of the fixed proportions technology so far assumed.

We shall make use of such a production function as it is described in the introductory pages of Sargent (1987, ch. 1) for the so-called "Classical" model: "In this one-good economy capital represents the accumulated stock of the one good that is available to assist in production. We assume that at any moment the stock of capital is fixed both to the economy and to each individual firm".[6]

In light of the foregoing we shall now proceed as follows. Since prices and wages are given at any moment in time in our Keynesian model type, and since output and interest are determined by the IS–LM part of the model, firms cannot adjust their rate of capacity utilization to the profit-maximizing full capacity level, since they may then experience unintended inventory changes in particular. Such changes will be treated in chapter 6, but here we insist on IS–LM (and thus goods-market) equilibrium, which

---

[6] See Sargent (1987, pp.8ff.) for further details of such a description.

means that firms just produce the level of output that equals effective demand at each moment in time. As in other fixed-price approaches to Keynesian dynamics, we consequently must assume here that firms are uniformly rationed (in proportion to their profit-maximizing capacity level) in order to guarantee that the allocation of labor in our one-good economy is still an efficient one, and that their output is therefore indeed described by the value of the macroeconomic production function at the current level of the capital stock and of employment. In Sargent's (1987, pp.7ff.) analysis of the allocation of labor among firms which differ in size (but not in technology), this is achieved by the use of the marginal productivity rule for each individual firm. As a consequence, output is always at its profit maximizing or full capacity level, which is appropriate in a Keynes–Wicksell model, but not in a Keynesian one as we have shown when comparing the model types of chapters 3 and 4. We here therefore assume (by the above rationing hypothesis) that labor is always used efficiently, but generally not at the full capacity level of firms. Of course, an inefficient use of the employed may indeed occur, and will complicate the analysis considerably, since there is then a wide variety of choices for the rationing scheme to be employed with respect to the given number of firms.

Here, however, firms are rationed in proportion to their profit-maximizing productive capacity (they thus exhibit a uniform rate of capacity utilization with respect to this level) and they increase (consciously or unconsciously, by the law of demand) this capacity by price increases (thereby making higher output levels profitable), or quantity reactions (intended and realized increases in the capital stock), whenever the usage of their profitable capacity passes a certain threshold $\bar{U} < 1$ (as in chapter 4).

It is assumed in this chapter that firms may approach their full capacity utilization level $U = 1$, but that they never[7] reach this point of (from the viewpoint of profitability) "absolute" capacity utilization where marginal wage costs have become equal to the momentarily given price of output. It is, however, easily conceivable (see Powell and Murphy 1997 for a macroeconometric approach of this type) that firms extend their production beyond their profit maximum in order to satisfy their customers, in order to defend their market shares and the like. Thus this upper economic bound is in fact not so binding as it is generally believed to be in the neo-Keynesian description of rationing equilibria of Classical type.

Smooth factor substitution, therefore, in principle allows the capital stock constraint to be ignored (at least temporarily during the business cycle). It is, therefore, in fact much easier to treat than the case of fixed proportions in technology, where $U = 1$ is an absolute limit to any further

---

[7] At least not at the present stage of the formulation of the model.

increase in the level of production. Instead of a switch into the "Classical regime" of neo-Keynesian type we may therefore simply allow for a significant increase in the adjustment speeds of prices and the rate of investment when the level of (profit maximizing) potential output is reached and crossed, which, as Chiarella et al. (1999) show, is then occurring only over short intervals of time. The present chapter can therefore also be interpreted, as in Powell and Murphy (1997), as providing a theory of adjustments of the price level and of the capital stock based on medium-run oriented first-order conditions, which act like moving targets for these two decision problems of firms, while the decision on the rate of production is based on (correct) point expectations on the sales of firms.

Let us stress that the usage that is here made of the concept of a neoclassical production function is not very close to the putty–putty interpretation in the literature on this function. Rather it is here only assumed that the various capital stocks of the firms of this economy are utilized in an overall efficient way by means of a specific allocation of labor throughout the economy. This description of actual output and efficient labor allocation in conjunction with the above concept of profit-maximizing potential output is all that is needed to go from our Keynesian model of chapter 4 to the case of "smooth factor substitution" in production, a technology concept which here thus only allows for such substitution in the medium and the long run.

The equations of the Keynesian model with smooth factor substitution are:

1 *Definitions (remuneration and wealth):*

$$\omega = w/p, u = \omega/x, \rho = (Y - \delta K - \omega L^d)/K, \tag{5.16}$$

$$W = (M + B + p_e E)/p, p_b = 1. \tag{5.17}$$

2 *Households (workers and asset holders):*

$$W = (M^d + B^d + p_e E^d)/p, M^d = h_1 p Y + h_2 p K(\bar{r} - r), \tag{5.18}$$

$$C = \omega L^d + (1 - s_c)[\rho K + rB/p - T], s_w = 0, \tag{5.19}$$

$$\begin{aligned}
S_p &= \omega L^d + Y_c^D - C = Y - \delta K + rB/p - T - C \\
&= s_c[\rho K + rB/p - T] = s_c Y_c^D \\
&= (\dot{M}^d + \dot{B}^d + p_e \dot{E}^d)/p,
\end{aligned} \tag{5.20}$$

$$\hat{L} = n = \text{const.} \tag{5.21}$$

3 *Firms (production units and investors):*

$$\omega = F_L(K, L^p), Y^p = F(K, L^p), U = Y/Y^p, \tag{5.22}$$

$$L^d \text{ det'd via } Y = F(K, L^d), V = L^d/L \tag{5.23}$$

$$I = i_1(\rho - r + \pi)K + i_2(U - \bar{U})K + \gamma K, \gamma = n, \quad (5.24)$$

$$p_e \dot{E}/p = I, \quad (5.25)$$

$$\hat{K} = I/K. \quad (5.26)$$

4 Government (fiscal and monetary authority):

$$T = t^n K + rB/p, t^n = \text{const.}, \quad (5.27)$$

$$G = T - rB/p + \mu_2 M/p, \quad (5.28)$$

$$S_g = T - rB/p - G[= -(\dot{M} + \dot{B})/p, \text{ see below}], \quad (5.29)$$

$$\hat{M} = \mu_0, \quad (5.30)$$

$$\dot{B} = pG + rB - pT - \dot{M}[= (\mu_2 - \mu_0)M]. \quad (5.31)$$

5 Equilibrium conditions (asset markets):

$$M = M^d = h_1 p Y + h_2 p K(\bar{r} - r)[B = B^d, E = E^d], \quad (5.32)$$

$$p_e E = \rho p K/(r - \pi), \quad (5.33)$$

$$\dot{M} = M^d, \dot{B} = \dot{B}^d[\dot{E} = \dot{E}^d]. \quad (5.34)$$

6 Equilibrium condition (goods market):

$$S = p_e \dot{E}^d = S_p + S_g = Y - \delta K - C - G = I = p_e \dot{E}. \quad (5.36)$$

7 Wage–price sector (adjustment equations):

$$\hat{w} = \beta_w(V - \bar{V}) + \kappa_w \hat{p} + (1 - \kappa_w)\pi, \quad (5.37)$$

$$\hat{p} = \beta_p(U - \bar{U}) + \kappa_p \hat{w} + (1 - \kappa_p)\pi, \quad (5.38)$$

$$\dot{\pi} = \beta_{\pi_1}(\hat{p} - \pi) + \beta_{\pi_2}(\mu_0 - n - \pi). \quad (5.39)$$

The range of changes in the formulation of the Keynesian monetary growth dynamics of chapter 4 is given by the equations (5.22) and (5.23). The equations in (5.22) describe the potential employment schedule (which is based on the marginal productivity rule $\omega = F_L$) and the corresponding concept of potential output Y^p. Actual employment is derived in (5.23) from actual output (governed by the principle of effective demand), and these two actual magnitudes are used in the same way as in chapter 4 to define the actual rate of capacity utilization U and of employment V. The thus defined rate U is then used as in that chapter to explain the demand pressure components $i_2(\cdot), \beta_p(\cdot)$ in investment and pricing behavior (see equations (5.24) and (5.38); the cost-push components are as before).

Summing up, the model of chapter 4 is thereby changed in a minimal way without giving up any of its essential principles of the working of a

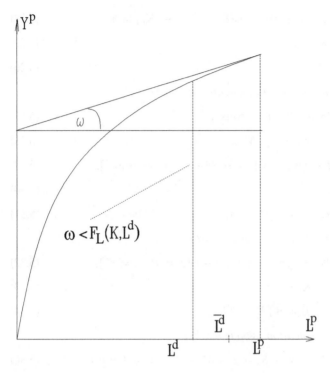

Figure 5.5   Potential and actual employment and output

capitalist economy. By contrast, the literature on Keynesian dynamics generally identifies the ratios U and $\bar{U}$ with 1 and introduces thereby a considerable element of confusion into the discussion of Keynesian dynamics, as we shall further explain in the next section. This is here avoided by the simple, and at present admittedly restrictive, procedure (and assumptions) that firms always operate to the left of the value L^p in the figure 5.5,[8] and that they speed up price increases and capacity extension beyond the threshold $\bar{L}^d$ (corresponding to the NAIRU level $\bar{U}$) well before full capacity utilization $U = 1$ is in fact reached.[9] In this way, it may be possible that the economy evolves according to these (and further) rules without hitting the ceiling L^p where a regime switch could take place. The analysis of such regime switches could be considered as an extension of the present

---

[8] Note here that an increase in the real wage ω implies an increase in the rate of capacity utilization U for any given level of employment L^d – due to a closer profitability barrier.

[9] A more general behavior of firms with respect to this "capacity limit" is motivated and modeled in Chiarella et al. (1998), based on the empirical observation that firms in fact choose to produce (from time to time) beyond the point where output price equals marginal costs in order to satisfy their customers' demand.

model.[10] This is in our view the simplest possibility for the extension of the Keynesian model of chapter 4 to variable factor proportions in technology.

The above model gives rise to the following set of intensive form differential equations[11] in the variables ω, l, m, and π:

$$\hat{\omega} = \kappa[(1 - \kappa_p)\beta_w(l^d/l - \bar{V}) + (\kappa_w - 1)\beta_p(f(l^d)/y^p(\omega) - \bar{U})], \quad (5.40)$$

$$\hat{l} = n - s_c(f(l^d) - \delta - \omega l^d - t^n) + \mu_2 m, \quad (5.41)$$

$$\hat{m} = \mu_0 - \pi - n - \kappa[\beta_p(f(l^d)/y^p(\omega) - \bar{U}) \\ + \kappa_p\beta_w(l^d/l - \bar{V})] + \hat{l}, \quad (5.42)$$

$$\dot{\pi} = \beta_{\pi_1}\kappa[\beta_p(f(l^d)/y^p(\omega) - \bar{U}) \\ + \kappa_p\beta_w(l^d/l - \bar{V})] \\ + \beta_{\pi_2}(\mu_0 - n - \pi), \quad (5.43)$$

where l^d is given by the solution of

$$i_1\left(f(l^d) - \delta - \omega l^d - t^n - r_0 - \frac{h_1 f(l^d) - m}{h_2} + \pi\right) \\ + i_2(f(l^d)/y^p(\omega) - \bar{U}) + n = s_c(f(l^d) - \delta - \omega l^d - t^n) - \mu_2 m, \quad (5.44)$$

and where $y^p(\omega) = f((f')^{-1}(\omega))$ is the full capacity output–capital ratio of firms at the prevailing level of the real wage ω. Note here that $(y^p)'(\omega) < 0$ holds because of the properties of the production function $Y = F(K, L^d)$.

Differentiating equation (5.44) with respect to the statically and dynamically endogenous variables gives the expression

$$[(s_c - i_1)(f'(l^d) - \omega) - i_2 f'(l^d)/y^p(\omega) + i_1 h_1 f'(l^d)/h_2]dl^d \\ = [(s_c - i_1)l^d - i_2 f(l^d)(y^p)'(\omega)/(y^p(\omega))^2]d\omega \\ + (\mu_2 + i_1/h_2)dm + i_1 d\pi.$$

We assume that the bracketed expression in front of dl^d is nonzero at the steady-state solution of the model (and thus in a neighborhood of it; see the following presentation of these steady-state values). There thus exists a unique function $l^d = l^d(\omega, m, \pi)$ in a neighborhood of this steady state which just solves the above equilibrium condition (5.44) and which is continuously differentiable.

Note here that the special conditions $\mu_2 = 0$, $h_2 = \infty$, and $\beta_{\pi_2} = \infty(\pi = \mu_0 - n)$ again imply that l^d is a function of only the real wage ω which can be discussed in the same way as the one we considered in section 4.2 in the case of fixed proportions. The above differential of the equilibrium condition then implies

[10] See Chiarella et al. (1999, ch. 3) for the details on treating such ceilings.
[11] Compare the corresponding equations in section 4.1.2.

$$\frac{dl^d}{d\omega} = \frac{(s_c - i_1)l^d - i_2 f(l^d)(y^p)'(\omega)/(y^p(\omega))^2}{(s_c - i_1)(f'(l^d) - \omega) - i_2 f'(l^d)/y^p(\omega)},$$

which is easily reduced to the corresponding expression in section 4.2 on the basis of the assumptions $y = f(l^d) = xl^d$, $y^p = $ const.$(u = \omega/x)$ of that section.[12] There will therefore again exist three possible situations for the implicitly defined function $l^d(\omega)$ as in section 4.2. Note here also that the range of validity of case 3 of the $l^d(\omega)$ relationship is enlarged by the inclusion of smooth factor substitution due to the additional and negative expression $-i_2 f(l^d)(y^p)'(\omega)/(y^p(\omega))^2$ that now appears in the numerator of the preceding fraction.

We do not go into the details of a treatment of the resulting two-dimensional dynamical system here, but do note that there is now just one term to be added to the Jacobian we considered in section 4.3, which is given by $(1 - \kappa_w)\beta_p f(l^d)(y^p)'(\omega)/(y^p(\omega))^2$, and which appears in its J_{11} entry. This term is negative for $\kappa_w < 1$ (due to $(y^p)'(\omega) < 0$), and it adds considerable further stability to this two-dimensional case[13] independently of the sign and strength of the term $(l^d)'(\omega)$, and thus of the particular of the three cases of section 4.4 that may be under consideration.

There is again *a unique steady-state* configuration for the dynamical system (5.40)–(5.43), with $\omega_0, l_0, m \neq 0$ when the usual assumptions on the neoclassical production function $y = f(l^d)$ are made and when the parameters μ_2 and h_1 are chosen sufficiently small (such a choice can be justified by reference to the empirical magnitudes of these parameters). In the present case $t^n = $ const. $(\bar{r} = r_0$ as always) this steady state is given by[14]

$$n = s_c(f(l_0^d) - \delta - \omega_0 l_0^d - t^n) - \mu_2 m_0,$$
$$f(l_0^d) = \bar{U} y^p(\omega_0) = \bar{U} f((f')^{-1}(\omega_0)),$$
$$m_0 = h_1 y_0,$$
$$y_0 = f(l_0^d), l_0 = l_0^d/\bar{V}$$
$$\pi_0 = \mu_0 - n,$$
$$\rho_0 = y_0 - \delta - \omega_0 l_0^d,$$
$$r_0 = \rho_0 + \mu_0 - n.$$

The existence of a unique steady state is easily proven by noting that the second of the above steady-state conditions defines a falling function $l^d(\omega)$ via the implicit function theorem, while the first one implies by the same theorem a rising function $l^d(\omega)$ when the third steady-state condition is

[12] Since we then get from the above that $\dfrac{dl^d}{d\omega} = \dfrac{(s_c - i_1)l^d}{(s_c - i_1)(x - \omega)y^p - i_2 x} y^p$.

[13] The determinant is not changed in its sign by this single additional term, since $J_{22} = 0$ still holds.

[14] Due to the same reasoning as used in section 3.2 for such a steady-state determination.

inserted into it (and when the parameters μ_2 and h_1 are chosen sufficiently small[15]). Having determined the steady-state values of ω and l^d, it is then obvious how to get the steady state values m_0, l_0, y_0, ρ_0, and r_0 (the steady-state value π_0 is determined independently of all these calculations). Note that the steady-state value of r has been used in the definition of the money demand function, by which it is in fact established that the above type of steady-state calculation is possible. As in the preceding chapter, we assume that the parameters of the model are chosen such that the three steady-state values for ω, i, and m are all positive.

The analysis in section 4.5 of the basic case of an integrated monetary growth dynamics is obviously also relevant for the present case of smooth factor substitution if we artificially assume in the formulation of the four differential equations (5.40)–(5.43), and only there, that potential output per capital y^p is a fixed magnitude (in place of its negative dependence on the real wage ω). The steady-state values and the properties of the function $l^d(\omega, m, \pi)$ that is determined by IS–LM equilibrium as shown above will generally differ from each other for the case of fixed factor proportions and smooth factor substitution. But the Jacobian in this artificial situation is then of the same form as in section 4.5, and thus gives rise to the same qualitative conclusion as we derived there. Essential differences to this earlier consideration of local stability and Hopf bifurcation situations can therefore only arise from the additional elements in this Jacobian that stem from the dependence of y^p on the real wage ω. These additional expressions give rise to the matrix

$$J_+ = \begin{pmatrix} \kappa(\kappa_w - 1)\beta_p U_\omega \omega & 0 & 0 & 0 \\ 0 & 0 & 0 & 0 \\ -\kappa\beta_p U_\omega m & 0 & 0 & 0 \\ \beta_{\pi_1}\kappa\beta_p U_\omega & 0 & 0 & 0 \end{pmatrix} = \begin{pmatrix} - & 0 & 0 & 0 \\ 0 & 0 & 0 & 0 \\ - & 0 & 0 & 0 \\ + & 0 & 0 & 0 \end{pmatrix},$$

which has to be added to the one in section 4.5 in order to give the full Jacobian matrix J of the system (5.40)–(5.43) at the steady state. Here U_ω denotes the positive dependence of the rate of capacity utilization on the real wage and is given by $-f(l^d)(y^p)'(\omega)/(y^p(\omega))^2$.

Making use of this particular qualitative structure of additional entries in the Jacobian J of the dynamics at the steady state, it is then easily shown in reference to the calculations and assumptions of section 4.5 that the trace and the determinant of this matrix J become more negative through the inclusion of these additional terms. At the same time the principal minor J_2

---

[15] We have $f'(l_0^d) > \omega_0$ by the chosen side condition $U < 1$ (motivated through the choice of a steady state utilization rate $\bar{U}$ which is less than one). The positive slope of the considered function then follows if it is assumed in addition that $f'(l_0^d)(1 - \mu_2 h_1) > \omega_0$ holds true.

becomes more positive thereby (the other principal minors are not changed through the inclusion of J_+). These results are in particular due to the property $J_{22} = 0$ of the Jacobian J. Three of the four Routh–Hurwitz conditions for local asymptotic stability are therefore improved through the inclusion of J_+. The remaining condition, $-\text{trace} \ J \cdot (J_1 + J_2 + J_3) + \det J > 0$, however, shows no clear-cut change since $\det J < 0$ has become more negative and since there is one term here added to it which is not cancelled by the additional expressions in $-\text{trace} \ J \cdot (J_1 + J_2 + J_3)$. The stabilizing potential of smooth factor substitution consequently remains somewhat limited in the Keynesian prototype model.

The general conclusion from this discussion nevertheless is that the replacement of a fixed proportions technology with a neoclassical production function is of secondary importance in the evaluation of the basic properties of proper Keynesian models of monetary growth with both under- or overutilized labor and capital. Here the case of fixed proportions (which we have treated in detail in chapter 4) has the twofold advantage of containing already all necessary elements for the study of such a monetary growth dynamics and of allowing us to probe the central features of such growth dynamics in a more transparent and less intertwined way. That such a simplification in the treatment of technology can indeed be illuminating will become particularly clear in section 5.3.2 where the (textbook) treatment of Keynesian dynamics that is currently the standard one is shown to be both misplaced and confusing as far as the Keynesian character of such standard models is concerned.

5.3.2   The bastard limit case: AD–AS growth

In textbook presentations of the so-called Keynesian static or dynamic model it is generally assumed that prices are completely flexible and that they fully adjust at each moment of time to marginal wage costs, which are in these models determined in reference to a neoclassical production function. Nominal wages, by contrast, are in these formulations of Keynesian statics or dynamics given at each moment of time, while their rate of change is made endogenous by way of a standard money-wage Phillips curve (just as in the preceding chapters of this book).

Allowing for complete price level flexibility (i.e. by setting $\beta_p = \infty$) in the Keynesian model of the preceding subsection at first sight appears to be unproblematic, since this assumption has been the standard description of aggregate supply in the Keynesian literature and since also Keynes (1936) did not refute this postulate of Classical economics (as he called this assumption). Yet, looking at the consequences of making this assumption in the context of the model of the preceding subsection shows that this model becomes a supply-side determined model thereby as far as utilization of the capital stock is concerned.

Assuming $\beta_p = \infty$ first of all gives rise to the identity $U \equiv \bar{U}$ in place of the price adjustment rule (5.38). Capacity utilization problems therefore disappear from this form of the model, which makes it admissible to set $\bar{U} = 1$ in addition, as is customary. On the basis of given money wages, we then get the conventional schedules of aggregate demand and aggregate supply from the IS–LM equations (5.32) and (5.36), and the marginal productivity principle (5.22). Keynes (1936) interpreted this principle as determination of the price level ($p = w/F_L$), supplementing his determination of firms' output and the nominal rate of interest via multiplier theory (effective demand) and liquidity preference (IS–LM). Demand-constrained producers therefore were supposed to choose this level of prices to accompany their demand-constrained output decision.

The formal consequence of assuming $\beta_p = \infty$ is, however, independent of this reinterpretation of the marginal productivity rule. Output, interest, and prices are now simultaneously determined by the intersection of the aggregate demand and supply schedule as components of the temporary equilibrium part of the model. Prices are no longer dynamically endogenous as in the preceding sections of this chapter, but have become statically endogenous. Nevertheless, their time rate of change has to be calculated (these become a complex expression of the dynamically endogenous variables as shown by Franke 1992a) in the application of the expectations formation mechanism (5.39).

Further straightforward consequences of this type of price flexibility are that the i_2 term can now be ignored in the investment function (5.24). Furthermore, it is customary in the presentation of the resulting model to set the values of κ_w and β_{π_2} equal to 0.

The resulting model is then given by the following set of equations:

1 Definitions (remuneration and wealth):

$$\omega = w/p, u = \omega/x, \rho = (Y - \delta K - \omega L^d)/K, \tag{5.45}$$

$$W = (M + B + p_e E)/p, p_b = 1. \tag{5.46}$$

2 Households (workers and asset holders):

$$W = (M^d + B^d + p_e E^d)/p, M^d = h_1 p Y + h_2 p K(\bar{r} - r), \tag{5.47}$$

$$C = \omega L^d + (1 - s_c)[\rho K + rB/p - T], s_w = 0, \tag{5.48}$$

$$S_p = \omega L^d + Y_c^D - C = Y - \delta K + rB/p - T - C$$

$$= s_c[\rho K + rB/p - T] = s_c Y_c^D$$
$$= (\dot{M}^d + \dot{B}^d + p_e \dot{E}^d)/p, \tag{5.49}$$

$$\hat{L} = n = \text{const.} \tag{5.50}$$

3 Firms (production units and investors):

$$\omega = F_L(K, L^d), Y^p = F(K, L^d), \tag{5.51}$$

$$V = L^d/L, \tag{5.52}$$

$$I = i(\rho - r + \pi)K + \gamma K + \gamma K, \gamma = n, \tag{5.53}$$

$$p_e \dot{E}/p = I, \tag{5.54}$$

$$\hat{K} = I/K. \tag{5.55}$$

4 Government (fiscal and monetary authority):

$$T = t^n K + rB/p, t^n = \text{const.}, \tag{5.56}$$

$$G = T - rB/p + \mu_2 M/p, \tag{5.57}$$

$$S_g = T - rB/p - G[= -(\dot{M} + \dot{B})/p, \text{ see below}], \tag{5.58}$$

$$\hat{M} = \mu_0, \tag{5.59}$$

$$\dot{B} = pG + rB - pT - \dot{M}[= (\mu_2 - \mu_0)M]. \tag{5.60}$$

5 Equilibrium conditions (asset markets):

$$M = M^d = h_1 pY + h_2 pK(\bar{r} - r)[B = B^d, E = E^d], \tag{5.61}$$

$$p_e E = \rho pK/(r - \pi), \tag{5.62}$$

$$\dot{M} = \dot{M}^d, \dot{B} = \dot{B}^d[\dot{E} = \dot{E}^d]. \tag{5.63}$$

6 Equilibrium condition (goods market):

$$S = p_e \dot{E}^d = S_p + S_g = Y - \delta K - C - G = I = p_e \dot{E}. \tag{5.64}$$

7 Wage–price sector (adjustment equations):

$$\hat{w} = \beta_w(V - \bar{V}) + \pi, \tag{5.65}$$

$$\dot{\pi} = \beta_\pi(\hat{p} - \pi). \tag{5.66}$$

This is the model that Sargent (1987) uses as basis for his analysis of Keynesian dynamics.[16]

The first thing that has to be noted here is that the same model is also

---

[16] Coupled with the assumption $s_c = s_w = s$ on the savings propensities of capitalists and workers, since this assumption does now, due to assumption of smooth factor substitution, allow for a steady-state solution.

obtained from the Keynes–Wicksell model (with smooth factor substitution) by setting $\beta_p = \infty$ there. This assumption also suppresses the explicit theory of inflation of this model by way of its implication that $I = S(U = \bar{U} = 1$ is assumed in this supply-side oriented Keynes–Wicksell prototype model right from the start). Assuming $\beta_p = \infty$ therefore implies in each case the missing causality of the following two equalities $I = S, U = \bar{U} = 1$ for both the Keynesian and the Keynes–Wicksell model and makes them formally indistinguishable thereby.[17]

Note here, however, that the marginal productivity principle $\omega = F_L$ was explicitly used in the Keynes–Wicksell model (in the case $\beta_p < \infty$) to determine employment through the there assumed behavior of firms as price-taking profit-maximizing units which face no demand constraint. The same principle is used in our Keynesian model of the preceding subsection ($\beta_p < \infty$) to determine the extreme (= profit-maximizing) level of output $Y^p(Y^p = F(K, L^p), F_L(K, L^p) = \omega)$. This hypothetical level is then compared with the actual level of output of demand-constrained, price-setting firms in order to formulate on this basis the effects on the rate of investment and on the rate of change of the price level in view of the discrepancy of actual output from a certain "normal" portion of this profit-maximizing output (in the framework of price-setting firms).

In the limit $\beta_p = \infty$, this difference in the setup of causal relationships of the Keynes–Wicksell and the Keynesian model type disappears and is replaced by the conventional aggregate demand and aggregate supply argument (determining the variables Y, r, and p), as we have discussed above. In this limit, it is therefore no longer obvious whether employment can be basically imagined to be determined from the side of supply or from the side of demand. In fact it is determined by the intersection of aggregate supply and aggregate demand, and thus from both sides simultaneously. Nevertheless, Keynesian theory is, or attempts to be, a theory of effective demand constraints on the market for goods with consequences for both labor and capital. One therefore has to judge to what extent it is still represented in this framework of an infinitely flexible price level (and a sluggishly evolving level of nominal wages).

The non-Keynesian character of the present limit case is most strikingly revealed when the case of fixed proportions in production is again assumed. We then get from the assumption $\beta_p = \infty$ that the IS–LM equilibrium part of the model determines the price level p and the nominal rate of interest r, again for both the Keynes–Wicksell model and the Keynesian model, in the same way. The IS–LM equations are thus solved for the

---

[17] Note here that the implied equality of investment I and total savings S allows the parameters β_k, δ_2 of the disequilibrium version of the Keynes–Wicksell model to be ignored.

variables p and r on the basis of the given potential output of firms $Y^p = y^p K$. This is a very Friedmanian solution of the conditions for goods-and money-market equilibrium (though not one with full employment of the labor force). Perfectly flexible prices and interest rates here always adjust aggregate demand to a predetermined level of aggregate supply, so that quite obviously the model is no longer one of the Keynesian variety.[18]

This strictly neoclassical structure of the fixed proportions case with perfectly flexible prices is also present in the smooth factor substitution case, the only difference being that supply is now responsive to changes in the price level and is determined in conjunction with goods and money demand on the basis of the equality of prices with marginal wage cost (in the Keynesian story).[19]

We conclude that perfect price flexibility is not compatible with a Keynesian structure in models of monetary growth, but leads to a more or less obvious supply-side theory of the temporary equilibrium position of the economy, despite the formal presence of a Keynesian IS–LM block. The bastard case $\beta_p = \infty$ therefore inherits more from supply-side Keynesianism (the Keynes–Wicksell prototype model) than from demand-side Keynesianism (our Keynesian prototype model). Though Keynes–Wicksell models of monetary growth are allegedly considered as more or less outdated now (see, for example, the survey by Orphanides and Solow 1990), they have therefore, in fact, implicitly survived in the literature in the widely accepted form of so-called models of Keynesian dynamics, by suppressing their questionable treatment of goods-market disequilibrium through infinitely flexible prices[20] and by ignoring at the same time their fundamental supply-side orientation. Simply assuming money-wage rigidity, as in the Keynesian variant of the neoclassical synthesis (as is generally done, see Sargent 1987, chs. 1–2, for example), is insufficient to arrive at a truly Keynesian prototype of monetary growth. Such a prototype is in fact missing in the literature on monetary growth dynamics (see again the survey by Orphanides and Solow 1990).

In order to solve[21] the Keynesian variant of the neoclassical synthesis

---

[18] This adjustment process is but a refinement of the Classical view on the role of the rate of interest to always equate aggregate savings with aggregate investment at the full capacity level (see Flaschel 1993, ch. 2, for details). This version of Say's Law is explicitly criticized in Keynes (1936, chs. 2 and 14) as the main fault in the Classical theory of employment and output.

[19] And through the equality of the real wage with the marginal product of labor in the Keynes–Wicksell case – which, however, does not make a difference to the Keynesian case in the formal investigation of the model.

[20] By assuming goods-market equilibrium throughout, the Wicksellian theory of inflation is only present in the background of the model and, if at all, only considered explicitly as an ultra short-run adjustment mechanism, as in Sargent (1987, ch. 2).

[21] We set $\mu_2 = 0 (g = t^n)$ as in Sargent (1987) for simplicity.

presented above, one has first of all to choose the appropriate state variables for the intensive form of the model. Here, it is to be noticed that the variable $m = M/(pK)$ can no longer serve this purpose, since it has now become statically endogenous. As state variables it is now appropriate to make use of l, π, and $v = M/(wK)$, i.e., to use now wage units in the measurement of real balances per unit of capital. The IS–LM, or better the AD–AS, equations then allow the determination of real balances m, the nominal rate of interest r, the real wage ω, the labor intensity l^d, the rate of profit ρ, and the output–capital ratio y from the temporary equilibrium part of the model as functions of the dynamically endogenous variables v and π. On the basis of these functional dependencies, one thereby gets in this case of perfectly flexible prices the autonomous dynamical system

$$\hat{l} = n - s_c(\rho - t^n),\tag{5.67}$$

$$\hat{v} = \mu_0 - n - \pi + \hat{l} - \beta_w(l^d/l - \bar{v}),\tag{5.68}$$

$$\dot{\pi} = \frac{1}{1 + m_\pi/m\beta_\pi}[\beta_\pi(\mu_0 - n - \pi + \hat{l} - m_v/m\dot{v})].\tag{5.69}$$

This, now explicit, system of differential equations can be treated as the original Sargent (1987, ch. 5) model was treated in Franke (1992a), and will give rise to the same Hopf-bifurcation situation obtained by the latter author if the parameter β_π is chosen sufficiently large.

Sargent (1987, ch. 5) also considers a further limit case of this model where $\beta_\pi = \infty$ holds (i.e. $\pi = \hat{p}$, the case of myopic perfect foresight). In this case we lose the third dynamical law of the system (5.67)–(5.69) and get from the money-wage Phillips curve of the model a real-wage Phillips curve $\hat{\omega} = \beta_w(l^d/l - \bar{V})$. This new representation of the Phillips curve provides the reason why Sargent (1987, ch. 5) now considers the real wage ω, and no longer the money wage, as a new state variable of the system. Hence we now can employ this variable ω in the place of the above v in the description of the dynamics of this limit case of the above model so that we obtain

$$\hat{l} = n - s_c(\rho(\omega) - t^n),\tag{5.70}$$

$$\hat{\omega} = \beta_w(l^d(\omega)/l - \bar{V}).\tag{5.71}$$

Note here that both the rate of profit and the employed labor intensity are decreasing functions of only the real wage now (because of the marginal productivity rule and the assumed neoclassical production function). This implies that the dynamical model (5.70)–(5.71) is self-contained. It is in fact now a simple Solovian real growth model combined with a sluggish adjustment of real wages as in the Goodwin growth cycle model. This simple dynamical model implies a globally asymptotically stable adjust-ment process towards the Solovian steady state. In this connection see Flaschel (1993, chs. 4, 6, and 8) who shows in particular that the model is now a completely supply-side determined one, since the Keynesian IS–LM sector does not appear at all in its laws of motion.[22]

Incorporating perfect price level flexibility into the Keynesian model of chapter 4 raises the question of why this is not also admissible for wage level flexibility. Indeed, wage levels and price levels should not be treated in this strictly asymmetric way. Instead, if one allows for the possibility of a perfectly flexible price level (which instantaneously adjusts and thereby removes any imbalance in the use of the capital stock or on the market for goods), one should also be prepared to allow for complete wage flexibility. Alternatively one may accept that both the wage level and the price level actually need at least some time to adjust to imbalances in the market for labor and for goods (as we have assumed in our Keynesian prototype model).

Allowing for this further limit case, now in the adjustment of wages, gives rise to the law of motion

$$\hat{l} = n - s_c(\rho(\omega(l)) - t^n),$$

as an extremely simple supply side response of the model. This is so since the real wage can now be determined from the equilibrium condition on the market for labor $l = l^d(\omega)/\bar{V}$ as a function of the full employment labor intensity l.

Instead of proceeding in this way to more and more extreme joint special cases of the Keynes–Wicksell as well as the Keynesian prototype model, we would, however, maintain that the Keynesian model is much closer to reality if the alternative direction is taken, namely, that of a price as well as a wage level that are at least somewhat sluggish in their reaction to imbalances in the utilization of the capital stock and the labor force, respectively. We therefore propose to leave the above border situations between supply-side Keynes–Wicksell and demand-side Keynesian monet-ary growth models and to return to the adjustment equations for wages and prices we have used throughout this book, namely,

$$\hat{w} = \beta_w(\cdot) + \kappa_w \hat{p} + (1 - \kappa_w)\pi_p = \pi_p + \beta_w(\cdot) + \kappa_w(\hat{p} - \pi_p),$$
$$\hat{p} = \beta_p(\cdot) + \kappa_p \hat{w} + (1 - \kappa_p)\pi_w = \pi_w + \beta_p(\cdot) + \kappa_p(\hat{w} - \pi_w).$$

[22] It is used in this model for the sole purpose of determining the rate of inflation $\hat{p}$, (and hence also the rate of change of real balances m) via IS–LM equilibrium and thus through an adjustment of aggregate demand toward predetermined aggregate supply by appropriate changes in this rate of inflation and the nominal rate of interest. The Wicksellian character of this procedure is again obvious.

Note that we have here allowed for separate expressions for expected medium-run price and wage inflation π_p and π_w. These adjustment equations yield a complete description of the wage–price module by assuming in addition and in a symmetric fashion the two mechanisms for changes in wage and price expectations given by

$$\dot{\pi}_w = \beta_\pi^w[\alpha_w\hat{w} + (1 - \alpha_w)(\mu_0 - n) - \pi_w], \alpha_w \in [0, 1],$$
$$\dot{\pi}_p = \beta_\pi^p[\alpha_p\hat{p} + (1 - \alpha_p)(\mu_0 - n) - \pi_p], \alpha_p \in [0, 1].$$

The interpretation of these four dynamical laws is the same as before, in terms of a mixture of forward- and backward-looking behavior of now both wage earners and firms. Besides the assumptions $\beta_\pi^w, \beta_\pi^p < \infty$, we have then to assume only that κ_p and κ_w are not equal to 1 at one and the same time (which excludes that both prices and wages exercise a full cost-push impact effect on each other)[23] and that α_p and α_w are not equal to one at 1 and the same time (which excludes that both wage earners and firms are purely backward looking in their behavior). We may even allow adjustment of expectations under these circumstances to be infinitely fast ($\beta_\pi^w, \beta_\pi^p = \infty$) without obtaining supply-side models as we have considered them above.

We observe in closing this section that nearly all textbook treatments of wage–price dynamics (the medium run) and growth dynamics (the long run) are not obtained as a proper extension of their short-run model, generally the Keynesian IS–LM model, but are in fact in contradiction to their theory of the short run, by removing part or all of the determination of income and nominal interest of the IS–LM approach from their theory of the medium and the long run.

5.4   Outlook: sluggish price as well as quantity dynamics

Assuming smooth factor substitution as in the present chapter has increased the descriptive contents of the Keynesian model of monetary growth, yet has not essentially modified its theoretical structure, as we have just seen. In appendix 2 of chapter 4, we have already analyzed the extensions of this prototype model which add technology change, more refined expectations mechanisms, and wage taxation in particular, but which assume the less complex case of a fixed proportions technology. We saw that these changes add descriptive realism to the Keynesian model of monetary growth, without changing its structure in an essential way.

---

[23] Otherwise, capacity utilization levels on the labor market and within firms move inversely to each other, or there would be a contradiction between the wage and the price adjustment equation.

We have considered in chapter 4 and in this chapter various extensions of the Keynesian prototype model of monetary growth that have added to its descriptive content (or its realism when used as a framework for macro-econometric model building). Each of these extensions was important in its own right, but not of decisive importance when the theoretical soundness of the chosen approach to Keynesian monetary growth is the main issue. In this respect the following chapter will, however, be of decisive importance, since it will remove one final basic defect (one problematic asymmetry) from our Keynesian prototype model that is responsible for some peculiar properties of the basic prototype which we observed in chapter 4. In particular, the three different equilibrium subcases of this approach and the instability phenomena surrounding two of them.

These subcases, in fact, cease to be of any importance (they simply do not occur) when another important descriptive element of Keynesian dynamics is taken into account. Besides a symmetric treatment of labor and capital utilization, we should also allow for a symmetric treatment of price and output adjustments, by allowing for (somewhat) sluggish output adjustment besides the sluggish price and wage adjustment so far assumed. This new element not only adds further realism to our Keynesian model of monetary growth (since we allow thereby for the fact that firms do not always have perfect sales expectations), but it also leads to a dynamic analysis of this revised model which is significantly different from that of chapter 4, and which is not subject to any subdivision into equilibrium regimes and their instability consequences discussed there.

There are two ways in which a sluggish output adjustment can be introduced into our IS–LM-equilibrium model of monetary growth. The first is along the lines of Kaldor's (1940) analysis of the trade cycle and Tobin's (1975) analysis of medium-run price dynamics, namely, by using the conventional dynamic multiplier in the place of the static one of IS–LM equilibrium. The second is a proper integration of the Metzlerian inventory adjustment mechanism into our Keynesian model of monetary growth. From a mathematical point of view, the first approach is generally preferable to the economically preferable alternative approach. However, the second approach is the only one that can be considered as internally consistent. Nevertheless, conditions can be provided where it reduces to the first approach, which is then easier to analyze due to the fact that its dynamics are of a lower dimension.

With this revision of the Keynesian prototype model of monetary growth, we therefore finally arrive at the model type which can be considered as the working model of the Keynesian analysis of monetary growth and business fluctuations. Of course, further modifications and extensions of this model type will also be needed in the future to make some or all of the modules of the model of a more modern type.[24] Yet none of these modifications will require the dismantling or recasting of what we will have established by the end of the next chapter. Namely, the basic framework for a Keynesian analysis of monetary growth of both theoretical as well as empirical relevance.

Further possibilities for extensions and refinements of the chosen framework will be discussed in the final chapter of this book. There we shall also provide further examples of how the model type of chapter 6 can be extended still further in the direction of more descriptive content without losing sight of the theoretical framework of Keynesian monetary growth dynamics that has been systematically developed in this book. Taken together, chapters 5, 6, and 7 therefore provide modifications of the basic Keynesian prototype model of monetary growth (two secondary ones and one that is essential) that add realism to it, and that should be integrated into an overall approach to Keynesian monetary growth dynamics when this model comes to be used for macroeconometric purposes. In this theoretically oriented book, such an integration (which, in fact, is easy to perform) is not, however, provided, in order to keep the presentation of the various model types on a less involved and technical level.

---

[24] For example, the simple type of cost-push and demand-pull wage and price inflation we have considered so far surely needs further discussion.

6 Keynesian monetary growth: the working model

6.1 Introduction

In this chapter we continue to build the Keynesian prototype model of chapter 4 on a firmer and more general basis. We will find that the more general model of this chapter, at one and the same time, avoids the separation into three types of comparative static analysis of the IS–LM equilibrium part of the model (section 4.2) and also avoids the ultra short-run stability problems observed in section 4.3.

We have already extended the Keynesian prototype model of chapter 4, for wage taxation, technical change, average inflation, and a more refined concept of forward-looking behavior, the so-called p^*-concept (see appendix 2 of chapter 4), and in chapter 5 by allowing for smooth factor substitution. Although these extensions are all important from an empirical point of view, we consider them as secondary as far as the conceptual issue of building a proper Keynesian model of monetary growth is concerned. This is also obvious from the fact that these extensions can be applied to all three of the general prototype models of this book (chapters 2–4) in a uniform way.

In the present chapter we now show how the simple goods-market disequilibrium approach of the Keynes–Wicksell model of chapter 3 can be integrated into the Keynesian, or IS–LM, model of monetary growth, still based on goods-market equilibrium, in chapter 4. In this way we now will arrive at a general prototype or working model of Keynesian monetary growth that is based on sluggish price/wage as well as sluggish quantity adjustment processes, and which thereby avoids the awkward ultra short-run problems (and their comparative static counterpart) of the one-sided disequilibrium adjustment processes of the Keynesian prototype model of chapter 4.

In sum, the model of this chapter can therefore be considered as the synthesis of the Keynesian models of chapters 3 and 4, which attempted to provide an alternative to the neoclassical model of monetary growth that we provided in a general format in chapter 2. This new monetary growth model is of Keynes–Metzler type and (as its name implies) in particular adds a Metzlerian inventory adjustment mechanism (based on sales expectations) to the Keynesian model of chapter 4. It treats goods-market disequilibrium as causing a set of quantity adjustment processes and this, in contrast to the Keynes–Wicksell model type, for less than full capacity growth in general. Price and wage inflation is again driven by the levels of capacity utilization on the market both for goods as well as for labor. However goods-market (IS) disequilibrium proper initially only causes inventory considerations by firms which, only in a second phase and coupled with sales expectations, are transmitted to the use of productive capacity and to the dynamics of the price level.

Of course, the extensions of chapters 4 and 5 should be added also to the present Keynes–Metzler extension of the Keynesian model. The incorporation of such extensions, however, can be achieved in an obvious way, as in chapters 4 and 5, and will not be repeated here in order not to overload the structure of our working Keynesian model. Finally, we will discuss in the next chapter a list of the shortcomings and omissions that are still contained in the working model type developed in this chapter. Thus the working Keynesian model developed in this chapter must still be considered as an intermediate stage in the development of a macrodynamic model that can be considered as satisfactory in all respects.

As will be obvious from the list of shortcomings presented in the final chapter 7 (see section 7.7), it is not possible to remove all of these from our working model in one single book. We will thus concentrate in this chapter basically on one of its crucial problematic characteristics, namely, the asymmetry that has existed so far in the treatment of the speed of adjustments of prices and quantities. We have assumed that quantities are always market clearing in the sense of the IS–LM equilibrium theory of effective demand and thus always adjust with infinite speed, while prices and wages adjust more or less sluggishly, responding to the disequilibria that exist in the employment of the services of capital and labor.

In chapter 4 we based price level changes on the imbalance *caused by goods-market (IS) equilibrium* within firms between their actual and their desired rate of capacity utilization. This was an improvement on the problematic $I \neq S$ disequilibrium approach to the theory of inflation adopted by Keynes–Wicksell models of chapter 3. We shall allow again for IS-disequilibrium as in the Keynes–Wicksell model type; now, however, by adding firstly a Kaldor (1940) quantity dynamics and, secondly, a Metzler (1941) quantity adjustment process to the model. This corrects and generalizes at one and the same time the Keynes–Wicksell and the Keynesian prototype model by an appropriate synthesis of the two model types and their theory of price inflation.

We shall show in chapter 7, finally, how, for the Kaldorian adjustment process, further important rigidities that characterize all of our model types so far can be removed. These final improvements concern the exogeneity of the full rate of employment $\bar{V}$ and the natural rate of growth of the economy which we have assumed so far as given. We shall refine the adjustment processes on the labor market and endogenize the trend component in the investment function and on the labor market in a way that allows for an endogenous determination of the steady-state rate of growth as well as the steady-state rate of (un)employment.

One consequence of our choice of the endogeneity of these rates will be that there is then hysteresis in the dynamics, i.e., these rates are no longer uniquely determined and there is then also path dependence in the long-run behavior of the trajectories of the dynamics. Also, in order to allow for an adjustment of the NAIRU rate of employment, we have to distinguish then, on the one hand, between the rate of employment that refers to the labor market and, on the other hand, the one within firms (the rate of employment of the employed labor force). This introduces further delays in the adjustment of the rate of employment on the labor market (by distinguishing inside from outside effects), and it makes the description of employment relationships also more realistic.

In sum, we will therefore in chapter 7 eliminate the use of so-called natural rates in the formulation of our Keynesian monetary growth dynamics by introducing appropriate adjustment processes for them. In addition, we will also base the model on finite adjustment speeds caused by goods-market disequilibrium (introduced in the present chapter), though we here choose a particularly simple version of it. All other markets (i.e., the asset markets) are still assumed to be in equilibrium in this final chapter of the book, in exactly the same way that they have been modeled in the previous chapters.

Before turning in the present chapter to a full description of goods-market disequilibrium and its dynamic consequences, we consider the "naive" Keynesian version of the goods-market disequilibrium adjustment, i.e., the simple dynamic multiplier story of output adjustments. This version considers goods-market disequilibrium and its consequences as in the well-known Kaldor (1940) trade cycle model or in the model of a Keynesian depression of Tobin (1975) and will be called the Kaldor–Tobin (KT) model for these reasons.[1]

---

[1] This model represents the simplest case of a monetary growth model with sluggish wage, price, as well as quantity adjustments that allows the discussion of price/output stability issues as in Tobin (1975); see also Tobin (1992, 1993) on this matter.

This version of the Keynesian model with both sluggish price and quantity adjustments is mathematically simpler to treat and, though unconvincing from the viewpoint of economic consistency, not unrelated to the mathematical structure of the monetary growth model with a full description of goods-market adjustment processes along Metzlerian lines that follows later on. Indeed, we shall see that a simple reformulation of the fuller model will give rise to a dynamic structure that is very similar to the one with the dynamic multiplier story. This latter and simpler approach, though economically unconvincing, may thus nevertheless reveal important dynamic properties in a setup that contains only a five-dimensional dynamical system rather than a six-dimensional one, as in the model with fully elaborated quantity adjustment processes.[2]

Due to the high dimensions of the dynamical systems considered in this chapter, there will only be few analytical results possible here. Of course there always remains the possibility of investigating typical two- or three-dimensional isolated subdynamics of such general approaches by disentangling them via appropriate assumptions, as we have done in earlier chapters. General results are here concentrated on the fact that such Keynesian models of monetary growth allow for a great variety of situations where the Hopf bifurcation theorem can be applied, based on the generally given fact that the determinant of the Jacobian (evaluated at the steady state) of each of the considered systems of chapters 2–7 is nonzero and of the sign demanded by the Routh–Hurwitz conditions for local asymptotic stability.[3] We will show here that the types of Hopf bifurcation that occur in the general dynamics will not have much in common with those that characterize the isolated subdynamics. From a mathematical point of view this is not very astonishing, due to the difference that exists between the full dynamics and the isolated subdynamics. But from an economic perspective this implies that the pure integration of known two- or three-dimensional prototype (real, monetary, or inventory) dynamical processes will lead to a dynamic behavior of the integrated dynamics that cannot be judged from these lower-dimensional prototypic, but partial, subdynamics. This raises the question of the meaningfulness of considering real or monetary or inventory adjustment processes in isolation.

Finally, it comes as not unexpected that the five- or six-dimensional dynamical models that we will investigate in this chapter are capable of

[2] In the same way, it may be shown that the two-dimensional Kaldorian trade cycle model may be very similar in its implications to the three-dimensional Metzlerian extension of it which considers the two state variables "sales expectations" and "inventories" in the place of only one: "output" (which again puts such disequilibrium analysis on a more convincing basis, but which also makes it dynamically more complex).

[3] In the dynamic models of chapter 7 this only holds for the subdynamics where hysteresis effects (which imply a zero overall determinant) have been removed.

producing "chaotic" dynamics, in particular since they combine cycle mechanisms in the real, the monetary, and the inventory subsectors that are fairly independent of each other. From an economic point of view, however, this seems to occur only in situations of a more or less extreme nature. For example, in a state space domain where economic viability of the considered dynamics is already violated and which seems to be at the border of mathematical viability as well. Alternatively, chaotic dynamics can occur within the domain of economic viability by making use of adjustment speeds of prices, wages, or expectations that seem very large, and by adding appropriate bounds to these price dynamics.

This latter observation needs further explanation. As in chapters 2–5, we at first consider our monetary growth dynamics with only linear behavioral relationships, i.e., we only allow for natural or unavoidable nonlinearities as they come about through growth rate formulations or products or quotients of certain state variables caused by value expressions, typical ratios of growth theory, and the like. In these only intrinsically nonlinear situations, a conclusion based on many simulation runs of these models is that limit cycles or superimposed limit cycles are the most that one can generally expect to obtain for the dynamics under consideration. Only at the edge of mathematical viability of the observed attractors does one find more complex dynamical patterns, as we shall demonstrate later on in this chapter.

The need arises to add further nonlinearities, perhaps motivated by nonlinearities in the behavior of economic agents, to the considered dynamics in order to make them viable from an economic point of view and also with respect to broader parameter ranges of the models. We have done this in chapters 2–5 from various perspectives concerning investment behavior, price and wage adjustment speeds, and nonlinearities in the specified technological relationships. In this chapter we now introduce a further and very basic nonlinearity, namely a simple kinked Phillips curve that takes account of the stylized fact that the growth rate of the level of nominal wages can easily become positive, but only rarely becomes negative. This very basic institutionally determined nonlinearity in the behavior of wage levels will allow us at one and the same time to increase dramatically the domain of viability of the considered dynamics as well as to show how chaotic attractors will come about in such situations.

Nevertheless, as will be shown, a period-doubling route to chaos will also then only come about when, for example, the adjustment speed of nominal wages (when growing) becomes very high. Therefore, sufficiently sluggish wages (and prices) generally only create a fairly "ordinary" dynamics of persistent fluctuations, despite the presence of various interacting cycle mechanisms. We conclude from this that integrated Keynesian models of monetary growth (of dimension 4 to 8) exhibit dynamic feedback chains that still interact with each other in very simple loops. Nevertheless, this integration produces dynamical features that do not mirror the dynamical features of its partial components models.

The next section introduces the Kaldor–Tobin model of monetary growth and briefly discusses its stability properties. Section 6.3 then extends this model to include Metzlerian inventory adjustments, and thus we arrive at our working model of Keynesian monetary growth. This section also provides stability considerations that relate appropriate subdynamics with the full six-dimensional dynamics of this model type. Section 6.4 finally considers a monetary growth model that represents an intermediate case between the models of sections 6.2 and 6.3, and in particular shows that this dynamic model can give rise to interesting numerical simulations when a very basic extrinsic nonlinearity is added to it. We conclude this chapter with some observations on the relationship of the models discussed to macroeconometric model building.

6.2 The Kaldor–Tobin model of monetary growth

In this section we consider a simple possibility of extending the IS–LM equilibrium framework of chapter 4 to a treatment of goods-market disequilibrium of a Keynesian type which makes use of sluggish quantity as well as price adjustment processes in the market for goods. This is in contrast to the conventional purely nominal Keynes–Wicksell treatment of the consequences of IS-disequilibrium situations that we considered in chapter 3. This section will therefore provide improvements of the general models of both chapters 3 and 4 by introducing a Keynesian dynamic multiplier treatment of goods-market adjustment processes. Moreover, it represents an important intermediate step in the derivation of an elaborate and fully consistent treatment of goods-market disequilibrium – see the Keynes–Metzler model in the next section – that helps in the understanding of the structure and implications of this core model of our book (see also its alternative formulation in the section 6.4).

Prominent examples of the dynamic multiplier approach to the treatment of goods-market disequilibrium as a component part of a larger dynamical system are the real two-dimensional trade cycle model of Kaldor (1940) and the medium-run three-dimensional dynamical model of Keynesian depressions and recessions of Tobin (1975). These two models have both been extensively discussed in the literature on Keynesian dynamics. These two approaches to macroeconomic dynamics are here at least partially embedded into a full Keynesian model of monetary growth, and thus are allowed to interact with each other to some extent. We stress, however, that the stationary Kaldorian approach to business cycle theory exhibits some problems when put into the context of a growing economy (see in particular Skott 1991 on this matter). We also stress that this model type represents only an intermediate step to a complete and consistent Keynesian model of monetary growth with sluggish price as well as quantity adjustments. Due to its origins we will refer to this model type as the Kaldor–Tobin (KT) model in the following discussion.

The equations of this model of monetary growth are:[4]

1 Definitions (remuneration and wealth):

$$\omega = w/p, u = w/x, \rho = (Y - \delta K - \omega L^d)/K, \tag{6.1}$$

$$W = (M + B + p_e E)/p, p_b = 1. \tag{6.2}$$

2 Households (workers and asset holders):

$$W = (M^d + B^d + p_e E^d)/p, M^d = h_1 p Y + h_2 p K (1 - \tau)(\bar{r} - r), \tag{6.3}$$

$$C = \omega L^d + (1 - s_c)[\rho K + rB/p - T], s_w = 0, \tag{6.4}$$

$$S_p = \omega L^d + Y_c^D - C = Y - \delta K + rB/p - T - C$$
$$= s_c[\rho K + rB/p - T] = s_c Y_c^D$$
$$= (\dot{M}^d + \dot{B}^d + p_e \dot{E}^d)/p, \tag{6.5}$$

$$\hat{L} = n = \text{const.} \tag{6.6}$$

3 Firms (production units and investors):

$$Y^p = y^p K, y^p = \text{const.}, U = Y/Y^p = y/y^p, (y = Y/K), \tag{6.7}$$

$$L^d = Y/x, x = \text{const.}, V = L^d/L = Y/(xL), \tag{6.8}$$

$$I = i_1(\rho - (r - \pi))K + i_2(U - \bar{U})K + \gamma K, \gamma = n, \tag{6.9}$$

$$p_e \dot{E}/p = I + (S - I) = Y - \delta K - C - G = Y - Y^d + I, \tag{6.10}$$

$$\hat{K} = I/K. \tag{6.11}$$

4 Government (fiscal and monetary authority):

$$T = \tau(\rho K + rB/p), [\text{or } t^n = (T - rB/p)/K = \text{const.}], \tag{6.12}$$

$$G = T - rB/p + \mu_2 M/p, \tag{6.13}$$

$$S_g = T - rB/p - G[= -(\dot{M} + \dot{B})/p, \text{ see below}], \tag{6.14}$$

$$\hat{M} = \mu_0, \tag{6.15}$$

---

[4] The parameter τ has to be removed from all equations of the following model if the second alternative in equation (6.12) is chosen as the tax collection rule.

$$\dot{B} = pG + rB - pT - \dot{M}[= (\mu_2 - \mu_0)M]. \tag{6.16}$$

5 Equilibrium conditions (asset markets):

$$M = M^d = h_1 pY + h_2 pK(1 - \tau)(\bar{r} - r)[B = B^d, E = E^d], \tag{6.17}$$

$$p_e E = (1 - \tau)\rho pK/((1 - \tau)r - \pi), \tag{6.18}$$

$$\dot{M} = \dot{M}^d, \dot{B} = \dot{B}^d[\dot{E} = \dot{E}^d]. \tag{6.19}$$

6 Disequilibrium situation (goods-market adjustment):

$$S = p_e \dot{E}^d = S_p + S_g = Y - \delta K - C - G = p_e \dot{E} \neq I, \tag{6.20}$$

$$Y^d = C + I + \delta K + G, \tag{6.21}$$

$$\hat{Y} = \gamma + \beta_y(Y^d/Y - 1) = \gamma + \beta_y((I - S)/Y), \gamma = n, \tag{6.22}$$

$$\dot{N} = \delta_2 K + S - I, S = S_p + S_g = Y - \delta K - C - G,$$
$$N \text{ inventories.} \tag{6.23}$$

7 Wage–price sector (adjustment equations):

$$\hat{w} = \beta_w(V - \bar{V}) + \kappa_w \hat{p} + (1 - \kappa_w)\pi, \tag{6.24}$$

$$\hat{p} = \beta_p(U - \bar{U}) + \kappa_p \hat{w} + (1 - \kappa_p)\pi, \tag{6.25}$$

$$\dot{\pi} = \beta_{\pi_1}(\hat{p} - \pi) + \beta_{\pi_2}(\mu_0 - n - \pi). \tag{6.26}$$

This extended monetary growth model of the Keynesian type reverts to the inclusion of goods-market disequilibrium as it was present in the Keynes–Wicksell model, but not in our Keynesian reformulation of it in chapter 4. Equations (6.10) and (6.20) introduce such a disequilibrium in quantities demanded and supplied on the market for goods, which is made compatible with asset-markets equilibrium and motivated and interpreted in the same way as the corresponding equations of the Keynes–Wicksell case in chapter 3. As is generally customary in the IS–LM literature (but not in approaches of Sargent 1987, Barro 1994a, and others to Keynesian disequilibrium analysis) the present IS-disequilibrium approach is now related to quantity adjustments in the production of firms, and not, as in the Keynes–Wicksell model (and in the related models of Barro and Sargent), to price level adjustments. These latter adjustments are based here, as in the basic Keynesian prototype of chapter 4, on capacity utilization levels in their deviation from normal capacity utilization. The degree of capacity utilization U itself is changed in the light of the excesses or shortages on the output market.

In order to provide a description of the adjustment process of U in the light of observed goods-market disequilibrium, equation (6.21) first of all defines the level of aggregate demand by the sum of its various components. Note here that the following equivalent representation of excess demand holds: $Y^d - Y = S - I$ which provides a bridge to the equation (6.20) that describes the type of IS-disequilibrium that prevails in the present version of the model. The next equation (6.22) gives a description of the simple dynamic multiplier process in the context of a growing economy where the expansion or contraction of production (its growth rate) is governed by two principles. These are goods-market imbalances and an incorporation of the rate of trend growth, which provides a very simple integration of the effects of persistent growth into this quantity adjustment process. The final new equation in this model in comparison to its predecessor model in chapter 4 is given by equation (6.23), which, however, represents but a return to the simplistic (purely appended) treatment of inventories of the Keynes–Wicksell model of chapter 3. Yet, such an approach is typical for dynamic multiplier analyses, which often do not even mention the inventory changes that are implied by their quantity adjustment process.[5] Note here, finally, that we have returned to technologies with fixed proportions in this chapter.

This concludes the simple inclusion of quantity adjustment processes into our Keynesian prototype of monetary growth. The main aim of including this section in the present chapter lies in its comparison in formulation as well as implications with the much more consistently formulated Metzlerian inventory adjustment process for growing economies which we shall construct in section 6.3.[6]

In the **the general case** of an endogenous determination of taxes per unit of capital, and thus of the existence of a feedback mechanism of government debt accumulation $B(t)$ on the rest of the system, we obtain from calculations similar to those in the case of the basic Keynesian prototype (4.1)–(4.23) the following autonomous, now six-dimensional, dynamical system in the variables[7] $\omega = w/p, l = L/K, m = M/(pK), \pi, b = B/(pK)$, and $y = Y/K$:

$$\hat{\omega} = \kappa[(1 - \kappa_p)\beta_w(V - \bar{V}) + (\kappa_w - 1)\beta_p(U - \bar{U})], \tag{6.27}$$

$$\hat{l} = n - i(\cdot) = -i_1(\rho - r + \pi) - i_2(U - \bar{U}), \tag{6.28}$$

---

[5] Blanchard (1981, pp.132–133) offers two interpretations for this dynamic multiplier rule, but then observes: "A more satisfactory, and more complex formulation would allow for inventories to be rebuilt later during the adjustment process."

[6] Note here with respect to this intermediate case between goods-market equilibrium and a Metzlerian treatment of goods-market disequilibrium that this model version still assumes an income concept that is based on supply and not on (expected) demand, and that the assumption $\beta_y = \infty$ will lead us back to the Keynesian prototype model of chapter 4, thus providing a first test of whether the assumption of goods-market equilibrium of the basic Keynesian version is really justified.

[7] Note that the law of motion for the dynamic variable z, the stock of inventories, is again simply ignored in this version of IS-disequilibrium dynamics.

$$\hat{m} = \mu_0 - \pi - n - \kappa[\beta_p(U - \bar{U}) + \kappa_p\beta_w(V - \bar{V})] + \hat{l}, \qquad (6.29)$$

$$\dot{\pi} = \beta_{\pi_1}\kappa[\beta_p(U - \bar{U}) + \kappa_p\beta_w(V - \bar{V})] + \beta_{\pi_2}(\mu_0 - n - \pi), \qquad (6.30)$$

$$\dot{y} = \hat{l}y + \beta_y(y^d - y), \qquad (6.31)$$

$$\dot{b} = (\mu_2 - \mu_0)m - (\pi + n)b - [\kappa(\beta_p(U - \bar{U})$$
$$+ \kappa_p\beta w(V - \bar{V})) - \hat{l}]b, \qquad (6.32)$$

where we employ again the standard abbreviations ($\bar{r} = r_0$):

$$y^d = \omega y/x + (1 - s_c)(\rho - t^n) + i_1(\rho - r + \pi) + i_2(U - \bar{U})$$
$$+ n + \delta + g,$$
$$V = l^d/l, U = y/y^p, l^d = L^d/K = y/x \text{ (y not const.!)},$$
$$\rho = y - \delta - \omega l^d = y(1 - \omega/x) - \delta,$$
$$r = r_0 + (h_1 y - m)/(h_2(1 - \tau)),$$
$$t = T/K = \tau(\rho + rb), t^n = t - rb,$$
$$g = t^n + \mu_2 m,$$
$$s(\cdot) = s_c(\rho - t^n) - (g - t^n) \neq \hat{K} = I/K = i(\cdot) + n.$$

Let us now again assume $t^n = t - rb = $ **const.** and remove the parameter τ from the equations of the model (since taxes are now lump sum). Furthermore, we set $\bar{U} = \bar{V} = 1$ for notational simplicity. This gives a five-dimensional dynamical system in the variables $\omega = w/p, l = L/K, m = M/(pK), \pi$, and $y = Y/K$ – with an appended $\dot{b}$ dynamical system, since the influence of b on $s(\cdot)$ and g (and thus on y^d) is now suppressed (y^d and U, V, ρ, r, μ as given above):

$$\hat{\omega} = \kappa[(1 - \kappa_p)\beta_w(V - 1) + (\kappa_w - 1)\beta_p(U - 1)], \qquad (6.33)$$

$$\hat{l} = - i_1(\rho - r + \pi) - i_2(U - 1), \qquad (6.34)$$

$$\hat{m} = \mu_0 - \pi - n - \kappa[\beta_p(U - 1) + \kappa_p\beta_w(V - 1)] + \hat{l}, \qquad (6.35)$$

$$\dot{\pi} = \beta_{\pi_1}\kappa[\beta_p(U - 1) + \kappa_p\beta_w(V - 1)] + \beta_{\pi_2}(\mu_0 - n - \pi), \qquad (6.36)$$

$$\dot{y} = \hat{l}y + \beta_y(y^d - y). \qquad (6.37)$$

This is a Keynesian dynamic multiplier system which exhibits a delayed quantity adjustment besides sluggish price adjustment. We shall briefly investigate this model from the analytical point of view in the remainder of this section before we turn to the Metzlerian extension of it. From a Kaldorian perspective, one would have to investigate the isolated y, l dynamics in order to see whether the Poincaré–Bendixson theorem can again be applied to show the existence of persistent cyclical motions for this subdynamics. Tobin (1975), furthermore, investigated the m, π, y subdynamics in order to show the existence of corridor stability in particular. This leaves as complement (or as a bridge between these two prominent models of Keynesian dynamics) the ω, l subdynamics of the Rose employment cycle model. The above dynamic model can thus be subdivided in a number of ways to give rise to prominent, though always partial, models of macrodynamics of the literature on Keynesian dynamics.

The *unique steady-state solution* or point of rest of the dynamical system (6.33)–(6.37) fulfilling $\omega_0, l_0, m \neq 0$ is given by:

$$y_0 = y_0^d = y^p, l_0 = l_0^d = y/x \tag{6.38}$$

$$m_0 = h_1 y_0, \tag{6.39}$$

$$\pi_0 = \mu_0 - n, \tag{6.40}$$

$$\omega_0 = \frac{y_0 - \delta - t^n - (n + \mu_2 m_0)/s_c}{l_0^d}, \tag{6.41}$$

$$\rho_0 = y_0 - \delta - \omega_0 l_0^d, \tag{6.42}$$

$$r_0 = \rho_0 + \mu_0 - n. \tag{6.43}$$

As in the preceding chapter, we assume that the parameters of the model are chosen such that the steady state values for ω, l, and m are all positive.

Proposition 6.1: The determinant of the Jacobian J of the dynamical system (6.33)–(6.37), evaluated at the steady state, is always negative.

Proof: Since linear combinations of rows of J can be added to its rows without changing det J, the system (6.33)–(6.37) can be reduced to the following form without change in the determinant of the system:

$$\hat{\omega} = \kappa(1 - \kappa_p)\beta_w(V - 1),$$
$$\hat{l} = -i_1(\rho - r),$$
$$\hat{m} = -\kappa\beta_p(U - 1),$$
$$\dot{\pi} = \beta_{\pi_2}(\mu_0 - n - \pi),$$
$$\dot{y} = \beta_y(\tilde{y}^d - y),$$

where $\tilde{y}^d = \omega y/x + (1 - s_c)(\rho - t^n) + n + \delta + g$, and V, ρ, U, and r are as described above. Proceeding along these lines one then gets (since $\tilde{y}^d - y = -s_c\rho + g + \text{const.}$)

$$\det J = \begin{vmatrix} 0 & - & 0 & 0 & + \\ + & 0 & - & 0 & ? \\ 0 & 0 & 0 & 0 & - \\ 0 & 0 & 0 & - & 0 \\ + & 0 & + & 0 & - \end{vmatrix} = \begin{vmatrix} 0 & - & 0 & 0 & 0 \\ + & 0 & - & 0 & 0 \\ 0 & 0 & 0 & 0 & - \\ 0 & 0 & 0 & - & 0 \\ + & 0 & + & 0 & 0 \end{vmatrix}$$

$$= \begin{vmatrix} 0 & - & 0 & 0 & 0 \\ + & 0 & 0 & 0 & 0 \\ 0 & 0 & 0 & 0 & - \\ 0 & 0 & 0 & - & 0 \\ 0 & 0 & + & 0 & 0 \end{vmatrix} = \begin{vmatrix} + & 0 & 0 & 0 \\ 0 & 0 & 0 & - \\ 0 & 0 & - & 0 \\ 0 & + & 0 & 0 \end{vmatrix} = \begin{vmatrix} 0 & 0 & - \\ 0 & - & 0 \\ + & 0 & 0 \end{vmatrix} < 0. \quad \blacksquare$$

This proposition implies that the steady state of the dynamics (6.33)–6.37) will, except for a set of measure zero in the model's parameter space, only lose its stability by way of a Hopf bifurcation, since no eigenvalue can pass from the left part of the complex plane to its right part by going through the origin.

Proposition 6.2: (1) The real sector ω, l subdynamics of the dynamical system (6.33)–(6.37), with m, π, and y frozen at their steady state values, is of Goodwin (1967) growth cycle type; (2) The subdynamics m, π, y of the dynamical system (6.33)–(6.37), with ω and l frozen at their steady state values, is of what Tobin (1975) calls WPK type, if in addition $\beta_{\pi_2} = 0$, $\beta_p = 0, \kappa_p = 1(\hat{p} = \hat{w})$ is assumed.

Proof: (1) The real sector subdynamics is represented by

$$\dot{\omega} = \kappa(1 - \kappa_p)\beta_w(y_0/(xl) - 1),$$
$$\hat{l} = -i_1(y_0(1 - \omega/x) - \delta - r_0 + \pi_0),$$

which is of the same cross-dual nature as the Goodwin (1967) growth cycle dynamics.

(2) the above Tobin-type subdynamics of (6.33)–(6.37) is given by

$$\hat{m} = \mu_0 - \pi - n - \kappa\beta_w(y/(xl_0) - 1),$$
$$\dot{\pi} = \beta_{\pi_1}\kappa\beta_w(y/(xl_0) - 1),$$
$$\dot{y} = \beta_y(y^d - y),$$

where aggregate demand y^d is given by

$$y^d = \omega_0 y/x + (1 - s_c)(\rho - t^n) + i_1(\rho - r + \pi) + i_2(y/y^p - 1)$$
$$+ n + \delta + g$$

with ρ, r, and g as described above ($\omega = \omega_0$).

The Jacobian of this dynamical system evaluated at the steady state reads

$$J = \begin{pmatrix} 0 & \dot{m}_\pi & \dot{m}_y \\ 0 & 0 & \dot{\pi}_y \\ \dot{y}_m & \dot{y}_\pi & \dot{y}_y \end{pmatrix},$$

from which we obtain for the Routh–Hurwitz coefficients a_i of the Jacobian at the steady state:

$$-a_3 = \det J = \dot{\pi}_y \dot{y}_m \dot{m}_\pi < 0,$$
$$a_2 = \det J_1 + \det J_2 + \det J_3 = -(\dot{\pi}_y \dot{y}_\pi + \dot{m}_y \dot{y}_m) \gtrless 0,$$
$$-a_1 = \text{trace } J = \dot{y}_y < 0.$$

The latter inequality holds if it is assumed, as in Tobin (1975), that the dynamic multiplier considered on its own represents an asymptotically stable process. Evaluating the expression for a_2 further gives

$$a_2 = \kappa \beta_w \beta_y [m_0 y_m^d - \beta_{\pi_1} y_\pi^d]/(x l_0 y_0),$$

which provides an analog to Tobin's (1975) critical condition for local asymptotic stability concerning the speed of adjustment of adaptively formed expectations, namely,

$$\beta_{\pi_1} < m_0 y_m^d / y_\pi^d.$$

This latter condition is again based on the Keynes effect $y_m^d > 0$ and the Mundell effect $y_\pi^d > 0$, here simply with respect to aggregate demand in the place of the effective demand concept of chapter 4.

It is easy to show that the expression $a_1 a_2 - a_3$ of the Tobin-type subdynamics is a linear and strictly falling function $h(\beta_{\pi_1})$ of the parameter β_{π_1}, which takes on a negative value at $\beta_{\pi_1}^c = m_0 y_m^d / y_\pi^d$ (where $a_2 = 0$ holds). This subdynamics therefore undergoes a Hopf bifurcation (because of $a_3 > 0$) at a parameter value $\beta_{\pi_1}^H$ that is lower than the Tobin critical value $\beta_{\pi_1}^c$. Below $\beta_{\pi_1}^H$, the system is always locally asymptotically stable, while this is nowhere true above the value $\beta_{\pi_1}^H$. ∎

In light of proposition 6.2, the full dynamical system (6.33)–(6.37) therefore can be considered as representing a Goodwinian growth cycle that is interacting with a Keynesian/monetarist dynamics as investigated in Tobin (1975) with respect to its local and global stability properties.

We stress that the full five-dimensional dynamical system is not only composed of the interaction of this three-dimensional Tobin and two-dimensional Goodwin subdynamics, but is also (if $\beta_p > 0, \kappa_p < 1$) determined by influences of the Rose (1967) employment cycle type, since it then also matters whether wages or prices are more flexible with respect to labor- and goods-market disequilibrium (respectively). Furthermore, we conjecture that the full dynamical system is locally asymptotically stable for h_2, β_{π_1} sufficiently small and β_y sufficiently large, if $\dot{y}_y < 0$ holds (i.e., if a stable partial dynamic multiplier process is again assumed). If true, this assertion generalizes a result we obtained in chapter 4 for IS–LM-equilibrium to goods-market disequilibrium with its finite adjustment speed of output. A specific form of this conjecture will be stated and proved below. We also expect that the five-dimensional dynamical behavior is generally determined by two independent cycle generating mechanisms: the Goodwin–Rose (1967) growth/employment cycle and the Tobin (1975) Keynesian/monetarist inflation/unemployment one.

Another prominent cycle-generating mechanism, that of the Kaldorian trade cycle, is, however, not present in the above monetary growth dynamics. Kaldor's (1940) trade cycle model was based on the following two dynamical laws

$$\dot{Y} = \beta_y(I(Y, K) - \delta K - S), S = sY$$
$$\dot{K} = I(Y, K) - \delta K,$$

for output and capital stock adjustment, and it made critical use of an investment function $I(Y, K)$ that was *not* homogeneous of degree 0 in Y and K, but relied on a very special nonlinearity in such an investment function. Our dynamic approach is, however, based on such a homogeneity, which in the case of Kaldor's two dynamic laws would imply

$$\hat{y} = \hat{Y} - \hat{K} = (\dot{Y}/K)/y - \hat{K},$$
$$= \beta_y((I(y, 1) - \delta - sy)/y) - (I(y, 1) - \delta).$$

This is a single dynamic law in the output–capital ratio y which shows that there cannot be cyclical movements in this ratio y or its constituent parts Y and K. The Kaldorian trade cycle mechanism thus is absent from the present form of a monetary growth dynamics, despite the presence of the Kaldorian equation for goods-market adjustments.

Lemma 6.1: The three-dimensional subdynamics of the dynamical system (6.33)–(6.37) that is obtained from it by freezing the real wage and inflationary expectations at their steady-state levels exhibits a locally asymptotically stable steady state if the parameter h_2 in the money demand function is chosen sufficiently small and the parameter β_y sufficiently large.

Proof: The considered subdynamics are given by the system of differential equations

$$\hat{l} = -i_1(\rho - r + \pi_0) - i_2(y/y^p - 1), \tag{6.44}$$

$$\hat{m} = -\kappa[\beta_p(y/y^p - 1) + \kappa_p\beta_w(y/(xl) - 1)] + \hat{l}, \tag{6.45}$$

$$\dot{y} = \hat{l}y + \beta_y(y^d - y),\tag{6.46}$$

where y^d is given by

$$y^d = \omega_0 y/x + (1 - s_c)(y(1 - \omega_0/x) - \delta - t^n) + n + \delta + g$$
$$+ i_1(y(1 - \omega_0/x) - \delta - r + \pi_0) + i_2(y/y^p - 1).$$

Let us first calculate the sign of the determinant of the Jacobian J of this system at the steady state. To do this it suffices to consider the reduced dynamical system

$$\hat{l} = - i_1(\rho - r + \pi_0) - i_2(y/y^p - 1),\tag{6.47}$$

$$\hat{m} = - \kappa[\beta_p(y/y^p - 1) + \kappa_p\beta_w(y/(xl) - 1)],\tag{6.48}$$

$$\dot{y} = \omega_0 y/x + (1 - s_c)(y(1 - \omega_0/x) - \delta - t^n) + n + \delta + g - y.\tag{6.49}$$

This system can be further reduced, without change in the sign of the respective determinant, to the form

$$\hat{l} = - i_1 m/h_2,\tag{6.50}$$

$$\hat{m} = - 1/(xl),\tag{6.51}$$

$$\dot{y} = - s_c y(1 - \omega_0/x).\tag{6.52}$$

This last representation of the structure of the dynamics of the model (appropriately purified with respect to the many linear dependencies that are contained in it) immediately implies a negative sign for the determinant of its Jacobian. In addition to the establishment of this Routh–Hurwitz condition for local asymptotic stability it is also easy to show that trace J must always be negative.

The further Routh–Hurwitz condition concerns the sign of the principal minors of dimension two of the above Jacobian J. It is easy to show that one of them must be positive and one zero, while the final one will become positive if the parameter h_2 is decreased sufficiently, since the partial derivative $\hat{m}_y$ is made negative by such a choice and since $\dot{y}_m$ is positive.

The remaining Routh–Hurwitz condition $(a_1 a_2 - a_3 = (-\text{trace } J)(J_1 + J_2 + J_3) + \det J > 0)$ is then easily shown to hold true as well if the parameter β_y is chosen sufficiently large, since all three components a_i of this Routh–Hurwitz condition depend positively and linearly on this parameter value. ∎

Lemma 6.2: The four-dimensional subdynamics of the dynamical system (6.33)–(6.37) that is obtained from it by freezing the real wage at its steady-state levels exhibits a locally asymptotically stable steady state if the parameter h_2 in the money demand function and the parameter β_{π_1} are chosen sufficiently small and if the parameter β_y becomes sufficiently large.

Proof: Using the technique employed in the preceding lemma in order to calculate the sign of the determinant of the Jacobian of this dynamical system at the steady state, one can easily show that the sign of this determinant must be positive if $\beta_{\pi_1} > 0$ holds true and that it is zero if this parameter value is zero. In this latter case we have by the preceding lemma three eigenvalues with negative real parts and a fourth eigenvalue that is zero. From continuity arguments, it then follows that this fourth eigenvalue must become negative when $\beta_{\pi_1} > 0$ is made positive (and chosen sufficiently small), due to the sign of det J. ∎

Proposition 6.3: The full five-dimensional dynamical system (6.33)–(6.37) exhibits a locally asymptotically stable steady state if the parameters h_2, β_{π_1}, β_p, and β_w are all chosen sufficiently small, and the parameter β_y sufficiently large.

Proof: We have already shown in proposition 6.1 that det J must be negative for the full five-dimensional dynamics. The proof of proposition 6.3 then follows from this fact by the arguments we have already applied in the proof of the preceding lemma. ∎

Note that a more detailed proof of proposition 6.3 is given in Chiarella and Flaschel (2000). It also follows from proposition 6.1 that the full five-dimensional dynamics will undergo a variety of Hopf bifurcations if the parameters h_2, β_{π_1} and β_p or β_w are increased. This will be due to a weakening of the stabilizing Keynes effect $y_m^d > 0$ in the case of the parameter h_2, a strengthening of the destabilizing Mundell effect $y_\pi^d > 0$ in the case of the parameter β_{π_1} and is due to the Rose effect (which may be positive or negative) in the case of the final two parameters. We stress that the parameter β_y does not seem to allow for a similar proposition in an obvious way.

We shall reconsider the above dynamical system in a slightly modified form analytically and numerically in greater detail in section 6.4 after the treatment of a proper respecification of the Kaldor–Tobin model as a Keynes–Metzler monetary growth model, where besides the dynamics of sales expectations an inventory adjustment mechanism is added and replaces the above simple dynamic multiplier mechanism.

6.3   An integrated Keynes–Metzler model of monetary growth

When there is Keynesian goods-market disequilibrium as in the preceding section there are disappointed sales expectations of firms, the revision of which requires some explanation. Furthermore, there then necessarily exist unintended inventories which lead to an intended adjustment of these inventories that will generally deviate from actual inventory changes that firms will face. A consistent description of these basic ingredients of a Metzlerian inventory adjustment process will here be formulated in the context of Keynesian monetary growth dynamics in order to investigate its properties in this setup.[8] We also wish to see to what extent such a consistent formulation of quantity adjustments of firms can lead to deviations from the results obtained for the dynamic multiplier approach considered in the preceding subsection.

6.3.1   The model

The equations[9] of this Keynes–Metzler model of monetary growth are:[10]

1 Definitions (remuneration and wealth):

$$\omega = w/p, u = \omega/x, \rho^e = (Y^e - \delta K - \omega L^d)/K, \tag{6.53}$$

$$W = (M + B + p_e E)/p, p_b = 1. \tag{6.54}$$

2 Households (workers and asset holders):

$$W = (M^d + B^d + p_e E^d)/p, M^d = h_1 p Y + h_2 p K (1 - \tau)(\bar{r} - r), \tag{6.55}$$

$$C = \omega L^d + (1 - s_c)[\rho^e K + rB/p - T], s_w = 0, \tag{6.56}$$

$$S_p = \omega L^d + Y_c^D - C = Y^e - \delta K + rB/p - T - C = s_c[\rho^e K$$
$$+ rB/p - T] = s_c Y_c^D$$
$$= (\dot{M}^d + \dot{B}^d + p_e \dot{E}^d)/p, \tag{6.57}$$

$$\hat{L} = n = \text{const.} \tag{6.58}$$

3 Firms (production units and investors):

$$Y^p = y^p K, y^p = \text{const.}, U = Y/Y^p = y/y^p, (y = Y/K), \tag{6.59}$$

$$L^d = Y/x, x = \text{const.}, V = L^d/L = Y/(xL), \tag{6.60}$$

---

[8] See also Chiarella and Flaschel (1998a) for a discussion of this model type, where more stress is laid on a consideration of the government budget restraint and the occurrence of complex dynamics.

[9] The parameter τ has to be removed from all equations of the following model if the second alternative in equation (6.67) is chosen as the tax collection rule.

[10] See de la Grandville (1986), Blinder (1990), Franke and Lux (1993), and Franke (1996) for important discussions of the Metzlerian inventory mechanism in an IS–LM framework or in a Keynesian growth model. Our use of this mechanism in the following model is closely related to Franke (1996). The role and extent of nonlinearities in this cycle mechanism is further discussed in Matsumoto (1995a,b), while the interaction of the inventory cycle with the business cycle is investigated from the empirical point of view in Flood and Lowe (1995).

$$I = i_1(\rho^e - (r - \pi))K + i_2(U - \bar{U})K + \gamma K, \gamma = n, \tag{6.61}$$

$$S_f = Y_f = Y - Y^e = \mathscr{I}, \tag{6.62}$$

$$\Delta Y^e = Y^e - \delta K - C - I - G = Y^e - Y^d, \tag{6.63}$$

$$p_e \dot{E}/p = I + \Delta Y^e = I + (\dot{N} - \mathscr{I}), \tag{6.64}$$

$$I^a = I + \dot{N} = I + \Delta Y^e + \mathscr{I} = I^p + \Delta Y^e = p_e \dot{E}/p + \mathscr{I}, \tag{6.65}$$

$$\hat{K} = I/K. \tag{6.66}$$

4 Government (fiscal and monetary authority):

$$T = \tau(\rho^e K + rB/p) \ [\text{or } t^n = (T - rB/p)/K = \text{const.}], \tag{6.67}$$

$$G = T - rB/p + \mu_2 M/p, \tag{6.68}$$

$$S_g = T - rB/p - G[= -(\dot{M} + \dot{B})/p, \text{ see below}], \tag{6.69}$$

$$\hat{M} = \mu_0, \tag{6.70}$$

$$\dot{B} = pG + rB - pT - \dot{M}[= (\mu_2 - \mu_0)M]. \tag{6.71}$$

5 Equilibrium conditions (asset markets):

$$M = M^d = h_1 p Y + h_2 p K (1 - \tau)(\bar{r} - r)[B = B^d, E = E^d], \tag{6.72}$$

$$p_e E = (1 - \tau)\rho^e p K/((1 - \tau)r - \pi), \tag{6.73}$$

$$\dot{M} = \dot{M}^d, \dot{B} = \dot{B}^d[\dot{E} = \dot{E}^d]. \tag{6.74}$$

6 Disequilibrium situation (goods market adjustments):

$$S = Sp + S_g + S_f = p_e \dot{E}^d/p + \mathscr{I} = I + \dot{N} = I^a = p_e \dot{E}/p + \mathscr{I}, \tag{6.75}$$

$$Y^d = C + I + \delta K + G, \tag{6.76}$$

$$N^d = \beta_{n^d} Y^e, \mathscr{I} = \gamma N^d + \beta_n (N^d - N), \gamma = n, \tag{6.77}$$

$$Y = Y^e + \mathscr{I}, \tag{6.78}$$

$$\dot{Y} = \gamma Y^e + \beta_{y^e}(Y^d - Y^e), \gamma = n, \tag{6.79}$$

$$\dot{N} = Y - Y^d = S - I[S - I^p = Y^e - Y^d]. \tag{6.80}$$

7 Wage–price sector (adjustment equations):

$$\hat{w} = \beta_w(V - \bar{V}) + \kappa_w \hat{p} + (1 - \kappa_w)\pi, \tag{6.81}$$

$$\hat{p} = \beta_p(U - \bar{U}) + \kappa_p \hat{w} + (1 - \kappa_p)\pi, \tag{6.82}$$

$$\dot{\pi} = \beta_{\pi_1}(\hat{p} - \pi) + \beta_{\pi_2}(\mu_0 - n - \pi). \tag{6.83}$$

The first thing we have to notice with respect to this revision of the dynamic multiplier approach of the preceding section is that we now have to distinguish between production, demand, and expected demand on the one hand and between desired and actual inventory changes on the other. In the assumed disequilibrium situation on the market for goods (which we have considered already in chapter 3 in the context of the Keynes–Wicksell model) we assumed that the income expectations of asset holders (as well as those of workers) are based on actual production, though actual sales will generally differ from them. Firms were assumed to pay dividends based on the output volume they produce since they did not have any demand expectations different from it. Such an assumption may be appropriate in the supply driven Keynes–Wicksell scenario, but it is surely inadequate for the demand determined system we have considered in the preceding section. Yet, the dynamic multiplier story we have used in that section is exactly of this supply oriented type, where firms base their plans on current production and only adjust this production (later on) in view of the aggregate they then face (which is based on the income and the profits that flow from the side of production as if all output were always sold).

In a demand determined system we should, however, base income expectations on expected sales and not on actual output, which may follow expected sales with some lag due to the inventory adjustments that have to take place if expectations of sales are not fulfilled. Since workers get paid for their actual work, which is based on actual production, income expectations are only important in the case of asset-owning households. Here, the ρ^e-equation in (6.53) simply states that profit (dividend) expectations of wealth owners are now based on expected sales and are always fulfilled (for them), since firms are assumed to pay out these dividends independently of their actual sales. We thus get that only firms will suffer (or gain) from possible errors in expectations, by so-called windfall losses or gains. Of course, other assumptions on the distribution of the effects of unexpectedly high or low demand are possible, but will not be considered here.

Due to this assumption on the dividend payments of firms we get (as in the goods-market disequilibrium models of chapter 3 and as in the preceding section) the equation (6.64), again stating that the equity supply of firms must cover planned (and in fact here always realized) investments as well as dividend payments not backed up by sales, i.e., the amount $p(S - I)$. Of course, we get additional funds for these investment plans, and thus a reduction in the amount of equities needed to finance them, if sales Y^d exceed demand expectations Y^e. This procedure guarantees that equities demanded and supplied must be equal to each other if equation (6.74) is again assumed to hold (see (6.75) for the resulting presentation of the disequilibrium on the market for goods). Equation (6.76) simply gives the definition of aggregate demand – partly based on sales expectations now (see again (6.53)), and it is easily calculated from it that the difference between expected and actual demand must always be equal to total savings minus net investment in this model.

Equations (6.77) define how firms calculate their demand for new inventories. The first equation states that the desired stock of inventories is a positive fraction of current sales expectations. The second one then adds that the desired change in inventories $\mathscr{I}$ is given by the sum of a trend component (here identified with natural growth for simplicity) and a term which says that inventories are further adjusted in order to remove the observed discrepancy between desired inventories N^d and actual ones N with a time delay of $1/\beta_n$. Note here that there must be inventory investment in a growing economy even if there is always equilibrium on the market for goods, here represented through a trend term of the simplest available type.

In an economy with inventory investment, the level of production is of course determined by expected sales and this additional inventory investment, i.e., equation (6.78). Equation (6.79) in addition describes how firms form their demand expectations, here simply in the form of adaptive expectations, again augmented by a term which refers to trend growth in a straightforward way. The final new equation of this model is (6.80), which describes how the stock of inventories is actually changed, namely, by the deviation of actual production from actual aggregate demand (in this Keynesian setup always equal to planned aggregate demand) which is always equal in size to the sum of unintended and intended inventory changes.

This concludes our description of the differences of this Keynes–Metzler model from the previous dynamic multiplier version of it. In the next chapter we will augment the money-wage Phillips curve by a term representing the rate of capacity utilization of the employed workforce (as a measure of their over- or undertime work[11]). Similarly, one can augment the price Phillips curve by a term representing the influence of inventory disequilibrium on price adjustments, like $-\beta_{p_2}(N - N^d)/K$. This is a meaningful extension of the considered price dynamics which, however, will not be investigated within the scope of this book and which generally has neither yet been investigated in the applied literature on price Phillips curves (see Fair 1997a,b in particular).

In **the general case** of an endogenous determination of taxes per unit of capital and the existence of a feedback mechanism of government debt accumulation $B(t)$ on the rest of the dynamics, we get from calculations similar to those in the case of the basic Keynesian prototype (4.24)–(4.28)

---

[11] Which introduces variable work-time into the Keynes–Metzler model.

the following autonomous, now seven-dimensional, dynamical system in the variables $\omega = w/p$, $l = L/K$, $m = M/(pK)$, π, $b = B/(pK)$, $y^e = Y^e/K$, and $v = N/K$:

$$\hat{\omega} = \kappa[(1 - \kappa_p)\beta_w(V - \bar{V}) + (\kappa_w - 1)\beta_p(U - \bar{U})], \tag{6.84}$$

$$\hat{l} = n - i(\cdot) = -i_1(\rho^e - r + \pi) - i_2(U - \bar{U}), \tag{6.85}$$

$$\hat{m} = \mu_0 - \pi - n - \kappa[\beta_p(U - \bar{U}) + \kappa_p\beta_w(V - \bar{V})] + \hat{l}, \tag{6.86}$$

$$\dot{\pi} = \beta_{\pi_1}\kappa[\beta_p(U - \bar{U}) + \kappa_p\beta_w(V - \bar{V})] + \beta_{\pi_2}(\mu_0 - n - \pi), \tag{6.87}$$

$$\dot{y}^e = ny^e + \beta_{y^e}(y^d - y^e) - i(\cdot)y^e, \tag{6.88}$$

$$\dot{v} = y - y^d - i(\cdot)v, \tag{6.89}$$

$$\dot{b} = (\mu_2 - \mu_0)m - (\pi + n)b - [\kappa(\beta_p(U - \bar{U}) + \kappa_p\beta_w(V - \bar{V})) - \hat{l}]b. \tag{6.90}$$

As new relationships we now have for output $y = Y/K$, in contrast to the determination of aggregate demand $y^d = Y^d/K$, the expression

$$y = (1 + n\beta_{nd})y^e + \beta_n(\beta_{nd}y^e - v), \tag{6.91}$$

$$y^d = \omega y/x + (1 - s_c)(\rho^e - t^n) + i_1(\rho^e - r + \pi) + i_2(U - \bar{U}) + n + \delta + g, \tag{6.92}$$

and again the mostly standard abbreviations ($\bar{r} = r_0$)

$$V = l^d/l, U = y/y^p, l^d = L^d/K = y/x \ (y \text{ not const.!}),$$
$$\rho^e = y^e - \delta - \omega l^d = y - \delta - \omega y/x,$$
$$r = r_0 + (h_1 y - m)/(h_2(1 - \tau)),$$
$$t = T/K = \tau(\rho^e + rb), t^n = t - rb,$$
$$g = t^n + \mu_2 m,$$
$$s(\cdot) = s_c(\rho^e - t^n) - (g - t^n) \neq \hat{K} = I/K = i(\cdot) + n.$$

6.3.2   The dynamics of the private sector

Let us now assume for the remainder of this section's treatment of the Keynes–Metzler model type our standard rule $t^n = t - rb = $ **const.** for the collection of lump-sum taxes. We also assume the simpler rule $g = G/K = $ const. for the determination of the level of government expenditures in the place of $g = t^n + \mu_2 m$ we have used in the general description of the model. This alternative fiscal policy rule induces only very minor changes in the model's dynamic behavior. Furthermore, we set $\bar{U} = \bar{V} = 1$ for notational simplicity. This then gives an integrated six-dimensional dynamical system in ω, l, m, π, y^e and v with an appended $\dot{b}$ dynamics, since the influence of b on S_p/K (and thus on y^d) is now suppressed. The system under discussion may be written

$$\hat{\omega} = \kappa[(1 - \kappa_p)\beta_w(V - 1) + (\kappa_w - 1)\beta_p(U - 1)], \tag{6.93}$$

$$\hat{l} = -i_1(\rho^e - r + \pi) - i_2(U - 1), \tag{6.94}$$

$$\hat{m} = \mu_0 - \pi - n - \kappa[\beta_p(U - 1) + \kappa_p\beta_w(V - 1)] + \hat{l}, \tag{6.95}$$

$$\dot{\pi} = \beta_{\pi_1}\kappa[\beta_p(U - 1) + \kappa_p\beta_w(V - 1)] + \beta_{\pi_2}(\mu_0 - n - \pi), \tag{6.69}$$

$$\dot{y}^e = \beta_{y^e}(y^d - y^e) + \hat{l}y^e, \tag{6.97}$$

$$\dot{v} = y - y^d + (\hat{l} - n)v, \tag{6.98}$$

where we continue to use the abbreviations

$$y = (1 + n\beta_{nd})y^e + \beta_n(\beta_{nd}y^e - v),$$
$$y^d = \omega y/x + (1 - s_c)(\rho^e - t^n) + i_1(\rho^e - r + \pi) + i_2(U - 1)$$
$$+ n + \delta + g,$$

and

$$V = l^d/l, U = y/y^p, l^d = L^d/K = y/x,$$
$$\rho^e = y^e - \delta - \omega y/x, r = r_0 + (h_1 y - m)/h_2.$$

The system represented by equations (6.93)–(6.98) is a Keynesian goods-market disequilibrium, money-market equilibrium growth model which is based on delayed quantity adjustment as well as a sluggish wage- and price-level adjustment. This model thereby generalizes considerably a variety of its limit cases with partially infinite adjustment speeds known from the literature. We stress here again that the model's structural equations have been chosen as simply (i.e., as linearly) as possible in order to clearly separate its basic dynamical structure from additional complexities arising from more refined behavioral relationships (which may be needed subsequently in order to make the model economically viable). This in particular shows that there are always some "natural" nonlinearities involved in the construction of a model of Keynes–Metzler monetary growth because of its growth rate formulae and because of some multiplicative (and similar) expressions in the state variables of the model.

There is *a unique steady-state solution* or point of rest of the dynamical system (6.93)–(6.98) fulfilling $\omega_0, l_0, m_0 \neq 0$ which is given by the following expressions

$$y_0 = y^p, l_0 = l_0^d = y_0/x, y_0^e = y_0^d = y_0/(1 + n\beta_{nd}), \tag{6.99}$$

$$m_0 = h_1 y_0, \tag{6.100}$$

$$\pi_0 = \mu_0 - n, \tag{6.101}$$

$$\rho_0^e = \frac{g - t^n + n}{s_c} + t^n, \tag{6.102}$$

$$\omega_0 = \frac{y_0^e - \delta - \rho_0^e}{l_0^d}, \tag{6.103}$$

$$r_0 = \rho_0^e + \mu - n, \tag{6.104}$$

$$v_0 = \beta_{na} y_0^e. \tag{6.105}$$

We assume that the parameters of the model are chosen such that the steady-state values for ω, l, m, ρ^e, and r are all positive.

Proposition 6.4: Consider the Jacobian J of the dynamical system (6.93)–(6.98) at the steady state. The determinant of this $6*6$ matrix det J, is always positive. It follows that the system can only lose or gain asymptotic stability by way of a Hopf bifurcation (if its eigenvalues cross the imaginary axis with positive speed).

Proof: Since proportionality factors with positive signs do not change the sign of det J, we can replace all growth rates by time derivatives on the left hand side of dynamical system (6.93)–(6.98) without modifying the sign of det J. Moreover, parts of rows of J which are proportional to other rows of J can be suppressed without any change in det J. As far as the calculation of the sign of det J is concerned, it suffices therefore to consider the reduced system

$$\dot{\omega} \cong \text{const.} \, V - \text{const.} \, U,$$
$$\dot{l} \cong - i(\cdot) \cong i_1(\rho^e - r + \pi) - i_2 U,$$
$$\dot{m} \cong - \pi - \text{const.} \, U - \text{const.} \, V,$$
$$\dot{\pi} \cong \text{const.} \, U + \text{const.} \, V - \text{const.} \, \pi,$$
$$\dot{y}^e \cong \text{const.}(y^d - y^e),$$
$$\dot{v} \cong y - y^d,$$

where the expressions "const." always stands for positive magnitudes. Proceeding in this way, one can simplify further[12] to obtain

$$\dot{\omega} \cong \text{const.} \, V = \text{const.} \, y/l,$$
$$\dot{l} \cong - i_1(\rho^e - r + \pi),$$
$$\dot{m} \cong - \text{const.} \, U = - \text{const.} \, y,$$
$$\dot{\pi} \cong - \text{const.} \, \pi,$$
$$\dot{y}^e \cong - \text{const.} \, \rho^e,$$
$$\dot{v} \cong y - y^e.$$

[12] Since the constants in the third and fourth equation are the same and since $y^d - y^e = - t^n - s_c(\rho^e - t^n) + i(\cdot) + g$.

In this way, one can finally achieve the following reduced form of the dynamical system (6.93)–(6.98) as far as the qualitative calculation of the sign of det J is concerned (where the constants are of no importance):

$$\dot{\omega} \cong 1/l, \dot{l} \cong -m, \dot{m} \cong -y \cong +v, \dot{\pi} \cong -\pi, \dot{y}^e \cong \omega, \dot{v} \cong -y^e.$$

This last representation of our dynamical system gives rise to the following reduced sign structure in its Jacobian:

$$\begin{pmatrix}
0 & - & 0 & 0 & 0 & 0 \\
0 & 0 & - & 0 & 0 & 0 \\
0 & 0 & 0 & 0 & 0 & + \\
0 & 0 & 0 & - & 0 & 0 \\
+ & 0 & 0 & 0 & 0 & 0 \\
0 & 0 & 0 & 0 & - & 0
\end{pmatrix}$$

It is now a routine exercise to show that the sign of the determinant of this matrix is positive. ∎

Let us now investigate some numerical properties of the six-dimensional growth dynamics of Keynes–Metzler type in the neighborhood of the proven Hopf bifurcations. The parameter set for these numerical plots of the six-dimensional dynamics is given in table 6.1.

Figure 6.1 shows on its left hand side the Hopf bifurcation locus for the three parameter sets (β_p, β_w), (β_p, β_{π_1}), and (β_{y^e}, β_n), i.e., the locus where a supercritical, subcritical, or degenerate Hopf bifurcation occurs. A vertical line is used to separate sub- from supercritical Hopf bifurcations. It can also be seen from figure 6.1 that the parameter set of table 6.1 gives a point just above the Hopf loci in (β_p, β_w) space as well as (β_p, β_{π_1}) space and just below the Hopf curve in (β_{y^e}, β_n) space (in the middle of the depicted supercritical domain).

Let us consider the (β_w, β_p) space as an example. For any given β_p, increasing β_w from 0 to 1 means that the system will reach a point where it loses its stability in a cyclical fashion (at β_w^H). At a supercritical Hopf bifurcation this will happen via the birth of an attracting limit cycle which "surrounds" the now unstable steady state ($\beta_w > \beta_w^H$). At a subcritical Hopf bifurcation an unstable limit cycle (which exists for $\beta_w < \beta_w^H$, β_w sufficiently close to β_w^H) will disappear as β_w approaches β_w^H, where the corridor of local asymptotic stability that existed beforehand has vanished. At a degenerate Hopf bifurcation, this same loss of stability need not be accompanied by either the "birth" of a stable limit cycle (above β_w^H) or the "death" of an unstable limit cycle (below β_w^H), but here purely implosive behavior may

Table 6.1.

$s_c = 0.8, \delta = 0.1, y^p = 1, x = 2, n = 0.05.$
$h_1 = 0.1, h_2 = 0.2, i_1 = 0.25, i_2 = 0.5.$
$\beta_w = 0.21, \beta_p = 1, \kappa_w = \kappa_p = 0.5.$
$g = 0.32, r_0 = \rho_0 = 0.068625, \beta_{\pi_1} = 0.22, \beta_{\pi_2} = 0.5.$
$\beta_{n^d} = 0.3, \beta_n = 0.2, \beta_{y^e} = 0.75, \mu_0 = 0.05, t^n = 0.32.$

simply change into a purely explosive one. These various types of Hopf bifurcations are treated and depicted in their details in, for example, Wiggins (1990, ch. 3). The (β_p, β_w) diagram in figure 6.1 thus basically shows that there is generally – up to very small parameter values of β_p – the birth of a limit cycle as β_w crosses the depicted Hopf locus.

The same occurs in the next bifurcation diagram for β_{π_1}, the adjustment speed of inflationary expectations in the place of β_w, the adjustment speed of wages. This figure in addition shows that a choice of the parameter β_p, the adjustment speed of prices, sufficiently small will make the six-dimensional dynamical system locally unstable. The two plots considered suggest that flexible wages and inflationary expectations and very sluggish prices work against local asymptotic stability. We will return to this question when the six-dimensional dynamical system is decomposed into three two-dimensional dynamical systems in the next subsection.

The last Hopf-bifurcation diagram is for the two adjustment speeds of the Metzlerian inventory mechanism, i.e., β_{y^e} and β_n, the speed of adjustment of sales expectations and of planned inventory adjustments towards desired inventory stocks. It shows that there here exists a band of stable steady states, limited by a region of unstable steady states for low values of β_{y^e} and β_n as well as for high values of these parameters. Moreover, loss of stability via increased β_n is always "subcritical," while loss of stability via a decreased β_n may be sub- or supercritical (as shown in the diagram). Again, sufficiently low or high adjustment speeds here work against local asymptotic stability, with respect to both β_{y^e} and β_n.

Hopf bifurcations have generally been considered for two-dimensional and three-dimensional systems in the economics literature. A six-dimensional system like the one above is surely much more demanding with respect to an analysis of the complete set of the Routh–Hurwitz stability conditions and at present out of reach for this system. Yet, even for two-dimensional systems (and even more so for three-dimensional systems) it is generally a horrendous analytical task to investigate whether the Hopf bifurcation is sub- or supercritical, and a proof of this is therefore generally missing in applications in the economics literature (exceptions are Lux

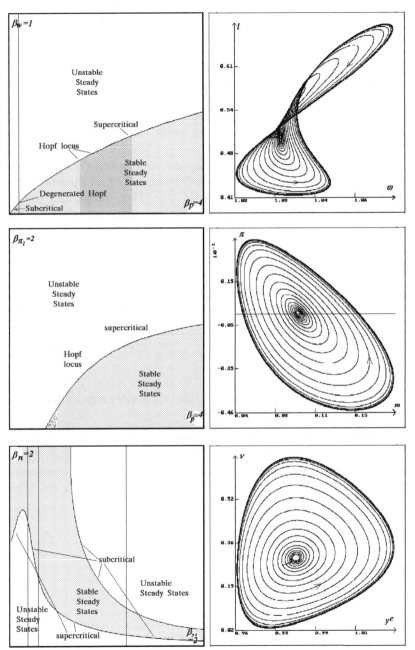

Figure 6.1   Hopf bifurcation curves, stable limit cycles (projections), or stable corridors

1993, 1995). Numerical methods therefore have to be used in all such cases in order to decide on the important part of the Hopf theorem, the existence of either *stable* limit cycles (describing persistent oscillations) or *unstable* ones (determining stability corridors).

On the right hand side of figure 6.1 we show in addition an example of a stable limit cycle, generated via a supercritical Hopf bifurcation. Note that this stable limit cycle is generated solely by the intrinsic nonlinearities of our Keynes–Metzler monetary growth model, and not by nonlinearity assumptions on the behavioral or technical relationships of this model. The figures to the right show how the limit cycle is approached when the steady state of the model is disturbed via a small l shock. We here show the (ω, l), (m, π), and (y^e, v) projections of this limit cycle. These projections will be compared with the corresponding two-dimensional decompositions of the six-dimensional dynamics in the next section.

6.3.3   The real, the monetary, and the inventory subdynamics

(a)   *The real wage and accumulation dynamics*
In order to isolate the real dynamics (ω, l) from the rest of the system, we make the following set of assumptions:

(1) $\beta_{y^e} = \beta_n = \infty, \beta_{n^d} = 0: y = y^e = y^d, v = v^d = 0$, i.e., goods market equilibrium with no inventories,

(2) $h_2 = \beta_{\pi_2} = \infty: r = r_0, \pi = \pi_0 = \mu - n$, i.e., the liquidity trap at the steady state and long-run steady-state inflationary expectations.

In particular, the second set of assumptions is of course only justified from a mathematical and methodological point of view. As before, assuming $t^n = $ const., allows us to ignore the dynamics of the GBR when studying the ω, l subsystems (the same holds for the other subsystems to be considered below). The resulting two-dimensional dynamical system turns out to be

$$\dot{\omega} = \kappa[(1 - \kappa_p)\beta_w(V - 1) + (\kappa_w - 1)\beta_p(U - 1)], \qquad (6.106)$$

$$\hat{l} = - i_1(\rho - r_0 + \pi_0) - i_2(U - 1) = n + g - t^n - s_c(\rho - t^n), \qquad (6.107)$$

with $U = y/y^p, V = (y/x)/l, \rho = y - \delta - (y/x)\omega$.

The value of $y = Y/K$ has now to be calculated from the following goods market equilibrium condition (see (6.92)):

$$y = \omega y/x + (1 - t^n) + i_1(\rho - r_0 + \pi_0) + i_2(U - 1) + n + \delta + g. \qquad (6.108)$$

At the *steady state* of the dynamical system (6.106)–(6.107), we have

$\rho_0 = t^n + (n + g - t^n)/s_c$ (via $\hat{l} = 0$) and $i_1(\cdot) = 0$ via $r_0 = \rho_0 + \pi_0$. Employing again $\hat{l} = 0$ then gives $y_0 = y^p$ and thus $l_0 = y_0/x$ due to $\hat{\omega} = 0$. The steady-state value of ω finally is given by definition of ρ as $\omega_0 = (y_0 - \delta - \rho_0)/l_0$, as in the six-dimensional case.

The goods-market equilibrium condition (6.108) thus reads in the steady state

$$y^p = \omega_0 y^p/x + (1 - s_c)(\rho_0 - t^n) + n + \delta + g.$$

Both equilibrium conditions can be brought to the form

$$[(i_1 - s_c)(1 - \omega/x) + i_2/y^p]y = t^n - s_c t^n + i_1(r_0 - \pi_0)$$
$$+ i_2 + (i_1 - s_c)\delta - g - n,$$

which gives

$$y = \frac{[(i_1 - s_c)(1 - \omega_0/x) + i_2/y^p]y^p}{(i_1 - s_c)(1 - \omega/x) + i_2/y^p}$$

$$= \frac{(i_1 - s_c)(1 - \omega_0/x)y^p + i_2}{(i_1 - s_c)(1 - \omega/x)y^p + i_2} y^p. \tag{6.109}$$

The properties of the function $y(\omega)$ have already been discussed in chapter 4, and gave rise there to three different situations for the above dynamics. One of these cases will be excluded here from consideration by way of the assumption

$$Z = (i_1 - s_c)(1 - \omega_0/x)y^p + i_2 > 0.$$

This restricts the set of admissible parameters i_1, i_2, s_c[13] such that $\rho'(\omega) < 0$ holds true, whenever the function

$$\rho(\omega) = \frac{Zy^p}{(i_1 - s_c)y^p + i_2/(1 - \omega/x)} - \delta,$$

is well defined. The dependence of the rate of profit ρ on the real wage rate ω is therefore the conventional one in our remaining cases. Nevertheless, the sign of $y'(\omega)$ will be ambiguous at and around the steady state, since there follows in this case:

$$\text{sign } y'(\omega) = \text{sign } (i_1 - s_c)$$

The real dynamics (6.106)–(6.107) therefore allows, even under the above

---

[13] $(1 - \omega_0/x)y^p = \dfrac{n + g - (1 - s_c)t^n}{s_c}.$

assumption $Z > 0$, for two very different situations of the dependence of y, U, and V on the real wage ω.

Proposition 6.5: The steady state of the dynamical system (6.106)–(6.107) is locally asymptotically stable (unstable) in case 1: $y'(\omega_0) < 0$ if β_w is chosen sufficiently high and β_p sufficiently low (β_w sufficiently low and β_p sufficiently high). The opposite statements apply to case 2: $y'(\omega_0) > 0$.

Proof: The Jacobian J of (6.106)–(6.107) at the steady state is given by

$$J = \begin{pmatrix} \kappa[(1 - \kappa_p)\beta_w V_\omega + (\kappa_w - 1)\beta_p U_\omega]\omega & \kappa(1 - \kappa_p)V_l\omega \\ -s_c\rho_\omega & 0 \end{pmatrix},$$

with $\rho_\omega < 0$ and $V_l < 0$, i.e. det $J > 0$ always.[14] The assertions then immediately follow from $V_\omega, U_\omega < 0$ (case 1) and $V_\omega, U_\omega > 0$ (case 2) via the trace of the matrix J. ■

Proposition 6.6: The Hopf bifurcation locus in (β_p, β_w) space is given by the straight line:

$$\beta_w^H = \frac{1 - \kappa_w}{1 - \kappa_p}\beta_p.$$

Proof: This locus is defined by trace $J = 0$ (det $J > 0$!), which yields the assertion, since $U_\omega = y'(\omega)/y^p$, $V_\omega = (y'(\omega)/x)/l_0$ and $l_0 = y_p/x$. ■

For $y'(\omega) < 0$ the system is locally stable above the line in proposition 6.6 and unstable below it. The opposite is true for case 2: $y'(\omega) > 0$.

As already stated, there is no easy analytical procedure by which we can determine the character of the Hopf bifurcation that is taking place along $\beta_w^H(\beta_p)$ (see Wiggins 1990, p.277, for details). Numerical investigations as in the preceding section, however, show a potential for supercritical Hopf bifurcations (as in the six-dimensional case). With respect to the basic parameter set of table 6.1 of the preceding section, we get for the two-dimensional dynamics $\beta_w^H = \beta_p$ and $y'(\omega) < 0$ ($i_1 = 0.25 < s_c = 0.8$).

We thus get the "surprising" result that wage flexibility destabilizes the six-dimensional system (the opposite holds for price flexibility), while the opposite is true for the two-dimensional limit case. In this respect, the two-dimensional case gives completely misleading information on the stability properties of the six-dimensional case.

---

[14] In the excluded case we have det $J < 0$ and thus a saddlepoint.

If unstable, the two-dimensional system can be made globally stable in a tailored domain by assuming a nonlinearity of tanh type in the investment function (as in Kaldor's 1940 trade cycle model), and a nonlinearity of tanh type in the $\beta_w(V - 1)$ Phillips curve of the model if $y'(\omega) < 0$ holds (as in Rose's 1967 employment cycle model). In this case, the model generates an employment growth cycle as in Rose (1967) via an application of the Poincaré–Bendixson theorem (see chapter 4 for details and also for the consideration of further subcases, for example, of the Goodwin 1967 growth cycle type). The real sector of our six-dimensional economy therefore exhibits features of a "Classical growth cycle" ($\rho'(\omega) < 0$, $\hat{K}(\omega) < 0$) in combination with Keynesian aggregate demand problems ($y'(\omega) \gtreqless 0$).

In sum, we may here in particular state that increased wage flexibility will be destabilizing in the case where goods-market equilibrium y responds positively to changes in income distribution (changes in the real wage), since real wage increases then increase employment, and thus the upward pressure on nominal wages (and also on real wages, for a given degree of price-flexibility). By contrast, increased price flexibility will be stabilizing in this case. If unstable, the dynamics can be made economically viable by introducing certain nonlinearities that are well known from the literature on trade and growth cycles.

(b) The monetary dynamics
To isolate the monetary dynamics from the rest of the system we make the following set of assumptions:

(1) $\beta_{y^e} = \beta_n = \infty, \beta_{n^d} = 0$: $y = y^e = y^d, v = v^d = 0$, i.e., goods market equilibrium with no inventories,

(2) $\beta_w = 0, \kappa_w = 1$: $\omega = \omega_0 (\hat{\omega} = 0)$, i.e., no real wage dynamics,

(3) $\hat{l} = 0$: $l = l_0$, i.e., no variation in relative factor proportions (medium-run analysis).

We thus in particular exclude the Goodwin–Rose growth cycle from consideration. Note, here, that investment is allowed to vary in the present case without having any capacity effects different from the growth rate n of the labor force.

The above assumptions lead to the monetary subdynamics

$$\hat{m} = \mu_0 - n - \pi - \kappa\beta_p(U - 1), \tag{6.110}$$

$$\dot{\pi} = \beta_{\pi_1}\kappa\beta_p(U - 1) + \beta_{\pi_2}(\mu_0 - n - \pi), \tag{6.111}$$

where $U = y/y^p - 1$ and where equilibrium output y is now given by

$$y = \omega_0 y/x + (1 - s_c)(\rho - t^n) + i_1(\rho - r + \pi) + i_2(y/y^p - 1) \\ + n + \delta + g, \tag{6.112}$$

with $\rho = y(1 - \omega_0/x) - \delta, r = r_0 + (h_1 y - m)/h_2$.

Making use of the steady-state values of m and π, equation (6.112) can be transformed to

$$y = y^p + \frac{(i_1/h_2)(m - m_0) + i_1(\pi - \pi_0)}{h_1 i_1/h_2 + (s_c - i_1)(1 - \omega_0/x) - i_2/y^p}$$

$$= y^p \left(1 + \frac{(i_1/h_2)(m - m_0) + i_1(\pi - \pi_0)}{h_1 i_1 y^p/h_2 + (s_c - i_1)(1 - \omega_0/x)y^p - i_2}\right)$$

$$= y^p \left(1 + \frac{(i_1/h_2)(m - m_0) + i_1(\pi - \pi_0)}{h_1 i_1 y^p/h_2 - Z}\right), \tag{6.113}$$

and we recall that Z has been defined below equation (6.109). Viewed from the perspective of the preceding subsection on the real subdynamics ($h_2 = \infty$), the related case $h_2 < \infty$ (but large) gives a negative denominator in (6.113) under the assumption we have made there, and therefore gives rise to a function $y(m, \pi)$ with $y_m < 0, y_\pi < 0$. With respect to conventional macrostatics, these two partial derivatives represent an abnormal Keynes and a negative Mundell effect on effective demand. This is so since an increase in real balances (via a decrease in the price level p) is then contractionary and an increase in π does not stimulate investment and effective demand, but rather will reduce the latter. Both effects will become positive ($y_m, y_\pi > 0$), and are regarded as normal if h_2 is decreased, s_c increased (relative to i_1) and i_2 decreased to a sufficient extent.

Solving $\dot{m} = 0, \dot{\pi} = 0$ for the unknown steady-state values $\mu_0 - n - \pi_0, U_0 - 1$ gives $\pi_0 = \mu_0 - n, U_0 = 1$, i.e., $y_0 = y^p$. Equation (6.113) then implies $r_0 = \rho_0 + \pi_0 = y^p(1 - \omega_0/x) - \delta + \mu - n$ and thus $m_0 = h_1 y^p$ for our second dynamic variable in the present situation. The *steady state* of the dynamical system (6.110)–(6.111) is therefore once again the one that is given by the six-dimensional dynamical system (6.93)–(6.98). With respect to this steady state we can now state the following.

Proposition 6.7: (1) The dynamical system (6.110)–(6.111) exhibits saddlepoint behavior around the steady state if $Q = h_1 i_1 y^p/h_2 + (s_c - i_1)(1 - \omega_0/x)y^p - i_2 < 0$ holds and exhibits a positive determinant of its Jacobian if $Q > 0$; (2) the Hopf locus in (β_p, β_{π_1}) space of the latter case is given by $\beta_{\pi_1}^H = \beta_{\pi_2}y^p/\beta_p \kappa y_\pi + m_0 y_m/y_\pi$, with $y_m = (i_1 y^p/h_2)/Q, y_\pi = i_1 y^p/Q$, i.e., $m_0 y_m/y_\pi = h_1 y^p/h_2$. This locus is therefore a decreasing function of the parameter β_p; (3) the dynamical system (6.110)–(6.111) is locally asymptotically stable below this locus and unstable above it.

Proof: (1) The Jacobian of (6.110), (6.111) at the steady state reads

$$J = \begin{pmatrix} -\kappa\beta_p U_m m & -(\kappa\beta_p U_\pi + 1)m \\ \beta_{\pi_1}\kappa\beta_p U_m & \beta_{\pi_1}\kappa\beta_p U_\pi - \beta_{\pi_2} \end{pmatrix}.$$

In the case $Q < 0$ we have $U_m, U_\pi < 0$ and the opposite signs hold for $Q > 0$. For det J we have in general

$$\det J = \begin{vmatrix} -\kappa\beta_p U_m m & -m \\ \beta_{\pi_1}\kappa\beta_p U_m & -\beta_{\pi_2} \end{vmatrix} = \kappa\beta_p U_m m(\beta_{\pi_1} + \beta_{\pi_2}).$$

Hence det J is negative in the first case and positive in the second.

(2) In the second case, the Hopf locus is characterized by trace $J = 0$ (det $J > 0$!), which gives $\beta_{\pi_1}^H \kappa\beta_p U_\pi = \beta_{\pi_2} + \kappa\beta_p U_m m$, from which the result in part (2) follows.[15]

(3) This result follows from the observation that $\beta_{\pi_1} > \beta_{\pi_1}^H$ implies trace $J > 0$ (and trace $J < 0$ in the case $\beta_{\pi_1} < {}_{\pi_1}^H$). ∎

For the basic parameter set (table 6.1) of the six-dimensional model of the preceding subsection we have

$$Q \le 0.1 \cdot 0.25 \cdot 1/0.2 + 0.55 \cdot 0.5 - 0.5 = -0.15 < 0,$$

and thus obtain a saddlepath dynamics for the two-dimensional case. Yet, det $J > 0$ in the six-dimensional case, i.e., the saddlepath behavior does not show up in the general model in an obvious way. We have exemplified in the preceding section the Hopf locus of the (β_p, β_{π_1}) space (see figure 6.1). There is no equivalent to this Hopf locus in the two-dimensional case. We have seen above that the case $Q > 0$ gives rise to a Hopf locus in (β_p, β_{π_1}) space, but now with negative slope in the place of the positive slope observed in the six-dimensional case. Fast adjustment of inflationary expectations via β_{π_1}, i.e., giving a high weight to past inflation in comparison to future steady-state inflation, leads to local instability (and in fact to the birth of stable limit cycles via supercritical Hopf bifurcations, as one can show numerically). Appropriate nonlinearities in the investment function $i(\cdot)$ should again allow for global limit cycle results via the Poincaré–Bendixson theorem.

(c)   The inventory dynamics
In this case, we combine the assumptions $h_2 = \beta_{\pi_2} = \infty$ $(r = r_0, \pi = \pi_0 = \mu_0 - n)$ with the assumptions $\beta_w = 0, \kappa_w = 1(\omega = \omega_0, \dot{\omega} = 0)$ and $\hat{K} = \hat{L} = n(l = l_0, \hat{l} = 0)$. This gives rise to the isolated sales expectations and inventory dynamics

$$\dot{y}^e = \beta_{y^e}(y^d - y^e), \tag{6.114}$$

[15] Note that $\beta_{\pi_1}^H$ is constant in the case $\beta_{\pi_2} = 0$.

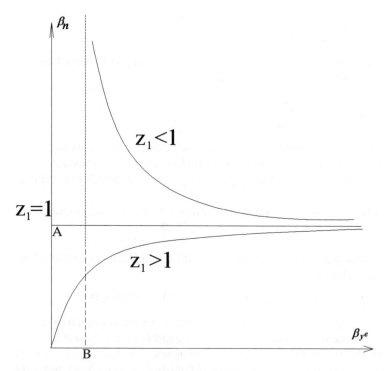

Figure 6.2   Hopf bifurcation loci of the inventory cycle for $Z < 0$

$$\dot{v} = y - y^d - nv, \tag{6.115}$$

with

$$y - y^e = n\beta_{nd}y^e + \beta_n(\beta_{nd}y^e - v), \rho^e = y^e - \delta - \omega y/x$$

and

$$
\begin{aligned}
y^d - y^e &= (i_1 - s_c)\rho^e + i_2(y/y^p - 1) - t^n(1 - s_c) - i_1(r_0 - \pi_0) \\
&\quad + n + g \\
&= [(i_1 - s_c)(1 - \omega_0/x) + i_2/y^p]y^e + [i_2/y^p \\
&\quad - (i_1 - s_c)\omega_0/x](y - y^e) + \text{const.} \\
&= Zy^e + Z_1(y - y^e) + \text{const.},
\end{aligned}
$$

where we set $Z_1 = i_2/y^p - (i_1 - s_c)\omega_0/x$.

At the *steady state* of this dynamical system we have $y_0^d = y_0^e$ and $y_0 = y_0^d + nv_0$. Moreover, $\omega = \omega_0$, $r = r_0$, and $\pi = \pi_0$ imply $y_0 = y^p$ and $y_0^e = y_0^d = y_0/(1 + n\beta_{nd})$, i.e., the steady state of (6.114)–(6.115) is again the one implied by the steady-state solution for the six-dimensional dynamics.

In order to calculate the sign of the determinant of the Jacobian of (6.114)–(6.115) at the steady state, it suffices to consider the system

$$\begin{pmatrix} y^d - y^e \\ y - y^e \end{pmatrix} \text{ or } \begin{pmatrix} Zy^e \\ y - y^e \end{pmatrix},$$

if the natural rate of growth n is chosen sufficiently close to zero. This right hand reduction of the original dynamics now immediately shows that det J is of the same sign as $-Z$. Under the assumptions of the subsection on the real dynamics, we therefore get that the inventory dynamics (we have suppressed in that subsection) is unstable and of saddlepoint type.

In the opposite case of a negative value of Z (and thus det $J > 0$), we have to investigate the trace of J in addition, i.e., the expression (for n sufficiently close to zero) trace $J = \beta_{y^e}(Z + Z_1\beta_n\beta_{nd}) + \beta_n(Z_1 - 1)$.

This expression gives rise to the following proposition.

Proposition 6.8: Assume $Z < 0$ and the rate of growth n sufficiently small. (1) The steady state of (6.114)–(6.115) is locally asymptotically stable for all β_n sufficiently small; (2) the steady state of (6.114)–(6.115) is unstable if $\beta_{y^e} > (1 - Z_1)/(Z_1\beta_n^d)$ and β_n sufficiently large; (3) the Hopf bifurcation locus is given by $\beta_n^H = -Z/(Z_1\beta_{nd} + (Z_1 - 1)/\beta_{y^e}) > 0$ if $\beta_{y^e}\beta_{nd} + 1 > 1/Z_1[Z_1 > 0!]$.

Proof: (1), (2) Obvious from the expression trace $J = \beta_{y^e}Z + \beta_n[\beta_{y^e}Z_1\beta_{nd} + (Z_1 - 1)]$.

(3) The result follows since $Z < 0 \Rightarrow i_1 < s_c$ (since $1 - \omega_0/x > 0$) $\Rightarrow Z_1 > 0(= Z + (s_c - i_1))$, i.e., $\beta_n^H > 0$ if β_{y^e} is chosen sufficiently large. ∎

Franke and Lux (1993) introduce a flexible stock adjustment principle which allows them to show global stability for a Metzlerian model of similar type by means of the Poincaré–Bendixson theorem.

Figure 6.2 shows the Hopf locus for the three cases $Z_1 > 1$, $Z_1 = 1$, and $Z_1 < 1$ to which this situation can give rise.[16]

6.3.4   Conclusions

In the preceding subsection we have considered three isolated subdynamics of the general six-dimensional dynamics by means of appropriate limit cases of the six-dimensional case. With respect to the parameter set of table 6.1 one can easily check that the real dynamics is then characterized by

---

[16] $A = -Z/y^p/(Z_1\beta_{nd}), B = (1 - Z_1)/(Z_1\beta_{nd}).$

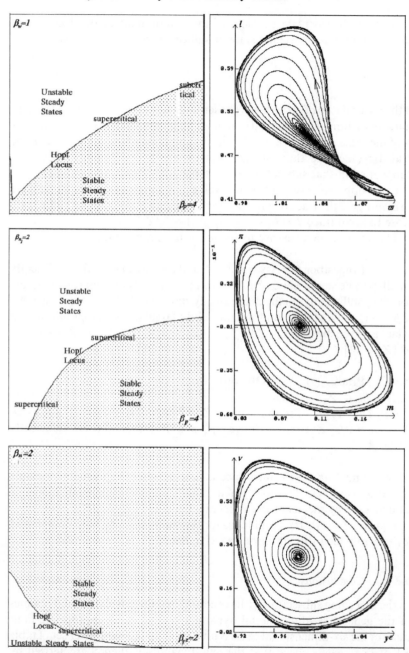

Figure 6.3   Hopf bifurcation curves, stable limit cycles, and stability corridors for $Z < 0$

$Z = 0.225 > 0(\rho'(\omega) < 0, y'(\omega) > 0)$, i.e., it falls into the range of cases considered in the subsection on the real dynamics. In particular, wage flexibility is stabilizing and price flexibility is destabilizing in this two-dimensional case. The opposite is, however, true in the general six-dimensional case with respect to the role the parameters β_w and β_p play. Furthermore, the monetary dynamics is of saddlepoint type for this parameter set, since $h_1 i_1 y^p / h_2 - Z = -0.1 < 0$ holds true ($y_m, y_\pi < 0$!). Yet, in the corresponding six-dimensional case we have found by numerical investigations that a Hopf bifurcation locus is then present and that an increasing parameter β_p will stabilize the dynamics. Finally, the two-dimensional Metzler system also exhibits a saddlepoint with respect to this basic parameter set, whereas a band of local asymptotic stability existed in the six-dimensional case, surrounded by super- or subcritical Hopf bifurcation loci. We conclude that the two-dimensional limit cases (which represent the well-established partial dynamical models of Goodwin–Rose, Tobin, and Metzler type in the literature) are not very revealing with respect to the properties of the general six-dimensional dynamics.

Hence, further possibilities for analyzing such integrated high-dimensional dynamical systems have to be found in order to gain more insight into the interaction of dynamics of the Goodwin–Rose, Tobin, and Metzler type. It is possible to decompose the six-dimensional case in still different ways, for example, into an ω, m, π subsystem and an l, y^e, v subsystem which can still be treated analytically via the Routh–Hurwitz and Hopf theorems (see chapter 4 for an example). In special cases, five-dimensional systems are also within reach, as we have seen in the case of the KT model. Yet, in general, we have to rely on numerical methods in order to get a proper feeling for the dynamic implications allowed by the general six-dimensional system of Keynes–Metzler type.

The Hopf cycle of the real dynamics can be combined with a Hopf situation for the monetary one if h_2 is decreased sufficiently (whereby interest-rate flexibility is increased). Reducing h_2 from 0.2 to 0.1 implies $h_1 i_1 y^p / h_2 - Z = 0.025$ and det $J > 0(y_m, y_\pi > 0)$ for the monetary two-dimensional dynamics whereby a positive Hopf locus can now be found in its (β_p, β_{π_1}) parameter space. Yet, due to $Z > 0$, the Metzlerian two-dimensional dynamics stays of saddlepoint type.

In the case $Z < 0$, finally, we get Hopf loci for the latter two-dimensional case (and the monetary dynamics), but saddles for the real dynamics, i.e., there is no situation where all two-dimensional dynamics allow for Hopf loci simultaneously. This is in striking contrast to the six-dimensional situation, whose typical Hopf loci are exemplified in figure 6.2. This figure shows that there can be considerable switches in stability regimes on the two-dimensional level. Yet, as the figure 6.2 demonstrates in comparison to figure 6.1, no such significant change is visible on the six-dimensional level. It seems that the six-dimensional dynamics is much more robust than its three isolated two-dimensional subcases.

6.4   A (5 + 1)-D modification of the six-dimensional Keynes–Metzler model

In this section we continue the analysis of the preceding section and investigate further the dynamic properties of a general Keynesian monetary growth model, with a conventional IS–LM block, based on Metzlerian goods-market disequilibrium adjustment processes in the place of the conventional static or dynamic multiplier approach.

Quantities on the goods market adjust through an inventory mechanism based on sales expectations and planned vs. actual inventory changes. Corresponding to this sluggish adjustment of quantities there are also sluggish price and wage adjustments, in a basically conventional way of expectations augmented wage or price Phillips curves with demand pressure and cost-push components. These real and nominal adjustment processes are supplemented by a money-market equilibrium equation as theory of the nominal rate of interest.

These are the essential building blocks of the model which is again made complete by the specification of the budget equations of households, firms, and the government, together with some additional details. The structural equations of the model introduced below will differ in some minor respects from those used in the preceding section, making the model from a mathematical point of view less intertwined and downplaying the role of the Metzlerian inventory process to some extent. Such a simplification provides an intermediate step between the Kaldorian and the Metzlerian models considered in the two preceding sections. By introducing as usual appropriate state variables in intensive form, the model can be reduced to a nonlinear autonomous differential equation system of dimension six with, however, only five state variables that are really interdependent.

Through its construction, the model again integrates three important partial (two-dimensional) views on the working of the macroeconomy which we have investigated in detail in the subsections of the preceding section. These investigations will lead to slightly different results for the present model, due to the simplifications proposed below for the Keynes–Metzler model, but will not be repeated here, since these differences can basically be neglected in what follows.

We have seen that the results obtained from these prototypic subdynamics will generally not be characteristic for the integrated system, which severely limits the value of these partial analyses. Flexibilities that work against economic stability on the two-dimensional level can work in favor of it on the six-dimensional level and vice versa, as we shall see again below. Finally, as we shall show, complex behavior can occur that is not possible on the two-dimensional level. We conclude that the use of partial models that separate growth from inflation and from inventory adjustment may be very misleading with respect to the implications they have for stability, types of fluctuations, and economic policy when compared with the results that their interaction generates.

When we come to consider high speeds of adjustment for prices or quantities in this model type, we will find again that generally the viability of such naturally nonlinear models is destroyed. It then becomes obvious that important nonlinearities due to changing economic behavior far off the steady state of the model are still lacking. After providing a list of the most basic quantity or value constraints that may come into play in situations of larger business fluctuations, we subsequently choose one (and only one) particular type of behavioral nonlinearity in order to attempt to restrict the explosive nature of the dynamics for higher adjustment speeds. This nonlinearity concerns a basic fact of the postwar period, namely, that there has been no deflation in the general level of wages even in periods of high unemployment. The wage inflation Phillips curve of the model, which generally operates in an inflationary environment, is thus modified such that no *decrease* in the nominal wage level can become possible. This simple change in the model's dynamics, the exclusion of nominal wage deflation, has dramatic consequences for its viability (and also its complexity). Thus, Keynes' (1936) judgment on workers' behavior and its stabilizing consequences finds a striking (numerical) illustration in this section in the context of a general Keynesian model of monetary growth dynamics.

6.4.1   A simplified Keynes–Metzler model of monetary growth

The following model structure represents a somewhat simplified version of the model type considered in the preceding section, more stress is now being laid on mathematical simplification in the place of full economic interaction.[17] In contrast to the six interdependent state variables of the preceding section, the last state variable of the present model will not feed back into the first five laws of motion of the model. Nevertheless, with respect to economic content the model is still very close to that of the preceding section. Its economic motivation will therefore be discussed here only briefly.

The first change concerns the household sector, and in particular its

[17] See also Chiarella and Flaschel (1996b), Chiarella et al. (1999) for related presentations of this model type and its theoretical and numerical properties.

money demand function

$$M^d = h_1 p Y^e + h_2 p K(r_0 - r). \tag{6.116}$$

Money demand M^d is now specified as a function of the nominal value of expected sales $p Y^e$ (as a proxy for expected transactions) and of interest rate r in the usual way. The form of this function has been chosen such that it allows for a simple linear formula for the rate of interest in terms of the state variables of the model.

The second and final change concerns the description of the behavior of firms, which is now based on expected sales throughout. Thus

$$Y^p = y^p K, y^p = \text{const.}, U = Y^e/Y^p = y^e/y^p, (y^e = Y^e/K), \tag{6.117}$$

$$L^d = Y^e/x, x = \text{const.}, V = L^d/L = Y^e/(xL). \tag{6.118}$$

Firms expect to sell commodities in amount Y^e and produce them in the technologically simplest way possible, namely, the fixed proportions technology characterized by the normal output capital ratio $y^p = Y^p/K$ and a fixed ratio x between expected sales Y^e and labor L^d needed to produce this output. This simple concept of technology allows for a straightforward definition of the rates of utilization U and V of capital and labor.

Note here, however, that firms may produce more or less than expected sales, depending on their inventory policy. In order to suppress some secondary economic feedback effects we have nevertheless assumed that the economic actions of firms are based on a measure of capacity utilization U as defined above, and that they pay their workforce on the basis of the employment generated by expected sales, while planned changes in inventories are accompanied by over- or undertime work of the employed (that does not show up in the wage bill).

There are thus only three changes made in the Keynes–Metzler model we have considered previously. The present model again integrates the interaction between real wages and capital accumulation, between inflation and the expected rate of inflation, and between expected sales and actual inventory levels, the latter, however, in a less complete way than in the preceding section.

The above general model of Keynesian monetary growth dynamics can be reduced to the autonomous six-dimensional dynamical system in the variables ω, l, m, π, y^e, and v,

$$\dot{\omega} = \kappa[(1 - \kappa_p)\beta_w(V - 1) + (\kappa_w - 1)\beta_p(U - 1)], \tag{6.119}$$

$$\hat{l} = -i_1(\rho^e - r + \pi) - i_2(U - 1), \tag{6.120}$$

$$\hat{m} = \mu_0 - \pi - n - \kappa[\beta_p(U - 1) + \kappa_p\beta_w(V - 1)] + \hat{l}, \tag{6.121}$$

$$\dot{\pi} = \beta_{\pi_1}\kappa[\beta_p(U - 1) + \kappa_p\beta_w(V - 1)] + \beta_{\pi_2}(\mu_0 - n - \pi), \tag{6.122}$$

$$\dot{y}^e = \beta_{y^e}(y^d - y^e) + \hat{l}y^e, \tag{6.123}$$

$$\dot{v} = y - y^d + (\hat{l} - n)v. \tag{6.124}$$

For output per unit of capital y and aggregate demand per unit of capital y^d we have the expressions

$$y = (1 + n\beta_{nd})y^e + \beta_n(\beta_{nd}y^e - v), \tag{6.125}$$

$$\begin{aligned}
y^d &= \omega y^e/x + (1 - s_c)(\rho^e - t^n) + i_1(\rho^e - r + \pi) \\
&\quad + i_2(U - 1) + n + \delta + g \\
&= y^e + (i_1 - s_c)\rho^e - i_1(r - \pi) + i_2(U - 1) + \text{const.}
\end{aligned} \tag{6.126}$$

Furthermore, we make use of the abbreviations

$$V = l^d/l = y^e/(lx), U = y^e/y^p, \tag{6.127}$$

$$\rho^e = y^e(1 - \omega/x) - \delta, \tag{6.128}$$

$$r = r_0 + (h_1 y^e - m)/h_2. \tag{6.129}$$

This reformulation of the model shows that the variable v does not appear on the right hand side of the first five laws of motion. It is thus of secondary importance in the following. Note that the variable g is here again assumed as being given exogenously.

There is *a unique steady-state solution* or point of rest of the dynamical system (6.119)–(6.124) fulfilling $\omega_0, l_0, m \neq 0$ which is given by

$$y_0^e = y_0^d = y^p, l_0 = y_0^e/x, y_0 = (1 + n\beta_{nd})y_0^e, \tag{6.130}$$

$$m_0 = h_1 y_0^e, \pi_0 = \mu_0 - n, \tag{6.131}$$

$$\rho_0^e = t^n + \frac{g - t^n + n}{s_c}, r_0 = \rho_0^e + \mu_0 - n, \tag{6.132}$$

$$\omega_0 = \frac{y_0^e - \delta - \rho_0^e}{l_0}, v_0 = \beta_{nd}y_0^e. \tag{6.133}$$

6.4.2 Dynamical properties of the integrated dynamics

Let us now immediately turn to the investigation of the full $(5 + 1)$-D system and reduce the comparison of its features with the three two-dimensional subsystems considered in the preceding section to some numerical observations in this section.

Proposition 6.9: Consider the Jacobian of the dynamical system (6.119)–(6.124) at the steady state. The determinant of this $6 * 6$-matrix, det J, is always positive. It follows that the system can only lose or gain asymptotic stability by way of a Hopf bifurcation (if its eigenvalues cross the imaginary axis with positive speed).

Proof: Similar to that of proposition 6.3. ∎

Proposition 6.10: For the entries in the trace of J there holds:

- $J_{11} = 0$, i.e., the Rose effect does not show up in the trace of J;
- $J_{22} = 0$ as in the corresponding two-dimensional case of real growth;
- $J_{33} < 0$, due to the Keynes-effect $r(p), r'(p) > 0$ in the $\hat{l}$ term of the third dynamical law;[18]
- $J_{44} < 0$, due to the forward-looking component in the fourth dynamical law;[19]
- $J_{55} = \beta_{y^e}(-Q/y^p) + y_0^e(Q/y^p - s_c(1 - \omega_0/x))$, where Q has been defined in the preceding section;[20]
- $J_{66} = y_v < 0$ and $J_{i6} = 0$ for $i = 1, \ldots, 5$. It follows from proposition 6.4 that the determinant of the Jacobian of the (independent) five-dimensional subdynamical system (6.119)–(6.123) is negative at the steady state.

Proof: Follows from straightforward calculations of the indicated elements of J. ∎

We thus have that the destabilizing (or stabilizing) role of the parameters β_w, β_p, and β_{π_1} cannot be obtained by just considering the trace of the matrix J as is true for the related two-dimensional cases. The determinant being positive and the trace of J being basically negative (if β_{y^e} is chosen appropriately), it therefore depends according to the Routh–Hurwitz conditions on the other principal minors (of dimension two to four) whether the steady state of the considered dynamics is locally asymptotically stable or not.

There are, for example, fifteen principal minors of J of dimension two, three of which are given by the three determinants considered in the two-dimensional cases in the preceding section. The calculation of the

---

[18] Note here that the state variable y^e prevents an immediate impact of the Keynes effect (and its consequences for aggregate demand) on factor utilization rates U and V, and thus on the rate of inflation and the corresponding state variable m.

[19] The above remark on the Keynes effect here applies to the Mundell effect $Y_\pi^d > 0$, i.e., there is no longer a destabilizing influence of the parameter β_{π_1} present in the trace of the Jacobian (as in the two-dimensional case).

[20] It follows that the system must be locally unstable for values of β_{y^e} sufficiently large if $Q < 0$, see proposition 6.7, since this adjustment parameter is (besides the always stabilizing parameter β_{π_2}) the only one among the adjustment speed parameters that shows up in the trace of J.

corresponding Routh–Hurwitz conditions for local asymptotic stability is thus a formidable task (and even more so for the other conditions). It is nevertheless tempting to conjecture that these Routh–Hurwitz stability conditions might be fulfilled for either generally sluggish or generally fast adjustment speeds. The following numerical investigations of the model, however, show that nothing of this sort will hold true in general.

In the presentation of the general Keynes–Metzler monetary growth model we have made use of linear relationships as much as possible. Technology, behavioral relationships and adjustment equations were all chosen in a linear fashion. Though nonlinear in extensive form, money demand was chosen such that it gave rise to a linear equation for the rate of interest when transformed to intensive form. Yet, certain relationships such as the wage dynamics must refer to rates of growth in order to make sense economically. Furthermore, and quite naturally, there are certain products of variables involved, such as total wages ωL^d or the rate of employment L^d/L. Such occurrences make the model a nonlinear one in a natural or unavoidable way. It is one of our aims in the present section to investigate the model's dynamic properties in this naturally nonlinear form in order to see to what extent the dynamical behavior so generated represents an economically, or at least mathematically, viable one despite the negative findings obtained in the preceding section from its three prototype subsystems. Of course, it is not to be expected that the dynamical behavior is viable for all meaningful parameter constellations. Further nonlinearities, in particular from the supply side, will become operative in a variety of situations. Nevertheless it is often not necessary to use nonlinearities in wage adjustment, in technology, in investment, etc., in a first step in order to get an economically bounded behavior. Where the two-dimensional cases suggest the use of such additional nonlinearities, the corresponding six-dimensional situation may nevertheless be asymptotically stable or, if not, give rise to limit-cycle behavior over certain ranges of the parameters due to the presence of the natural nonlinearities just discussed.

In the intensive form and with respect to the state variables used in equations (6.119)–(6.124), there are three types of nonlinearities induced by the structural form of the model. The first type arises because three of the state variables give rise to a growth rate law of motion (ω, l, m). The second type is due to the formulation, in per-capital terms, of two of the state variables (y^e, v) giving rise to products of the form $\hat{l}y^e, \hat{l}v$. The third type occurs because there are natural products or quotients of some of the state variables in the form $V = y^e/l$ for the rate of employment V and $\rho^e = y^e - \delta - \omega y^e/x$ for the rate of profit ρ^e.

Note here that the replacement of the state variable l by the state variable $k = 1/l$ transforms all nonlinearities into product form. Note

Table 6.2.

$s_c = 0.8, \delta = 0.1, y^p = 1, x = 2, n = 0.05.$
$h_1 = 0.1, h_2 = 0.2, i_1 = 0.5, i_2 = 0.5.$
$\beta_w = 0.16, \beta_p = 1, \kappa_w = \kappa_p = 0.5.$
$g = 0.32, r_0 = \rho_0 = 0.3875, \beta_{\pi_1} = 0.1, \beta_{\pi_2} = 0.75.$
$\beta_{n^d} = 0.2, \beta_n = 0.75, \beta_{y^e} = 1, \mu_0 = 0.05, t^n = 0.3.$

furthermore that the terms $\hat{l}z = -\hat{k}z$ with $z = m, y^e, v$ lead to trilinear expressions in their respective laws of motion.

In this representation of the dynamics we have, besides growth rates and the products just mentioned, nonlinearities present only in the $\beta_w(\cdot)$ term, in ρ^e, and consequently also in the aggregate demand term y^d. Up to growth rate formulations we have thus basically only two types of non-linearities involved in the laws of motion of the system, and they both relate to the Rose subdynamical system of the model. Though these terms re-appear in various places, it may therefore be stated that the present dynamics is in a weak sense comparable to the Rössler system (one bilinear term) and the Lorenz system (two bilinear terms), but in a less strict way, due to its higher dimension.

Let us now turn to a numerical investigation of the $(5 + 1)$-D dynamics. We shall employ the basic parameter set displayed in table 6.2 in the numerical illustrations given below (and we shall subsequently only state the changes taking place with respect to it at various places).

Corresponding to the three subdynamical systems considered in the preceding section, we here look at the stabilizing or destabilizing role of the pairs of adjustment speeds $\beta_w, \beta_p, \beta_{\pi_1}, \beta_p$, and β_{y^e}, β_n. The shaded areas in figure 6.4 show the parameter domains where the six-dimensional dynamics is locally asymptotically stable. The boundary of these domains is the Hopf-bifurcation locus where the system loses its local asymptotic stability, either by way of a supercritical Hopf-bifurcation (where a stable limit cycle is born after the boundary has been crossed) or by way of a subcritical Hopf bifurcation (where an unstable limit cycle is shrinking to "zero" when the boundary is approached). Along the bifurcation line there also exist degenerate Hopf bifurcations separating super- from subcritical bifurcations. We have found in many numerical investigations of the model that the bifurcations in the following diagrams are generally of a supercritical nature. The only important exception is the bifurcation line on the right hand side of the β_{y^e}, β_n parameter space, where the system again loses stability (at $\beta_{y^e} = 4.82$) for high adjustment speeds of the parameter β_{y^e}. Note here that figure 6.4 also shows the independence of the domain of stability from the state variable v and the parameter β_n.

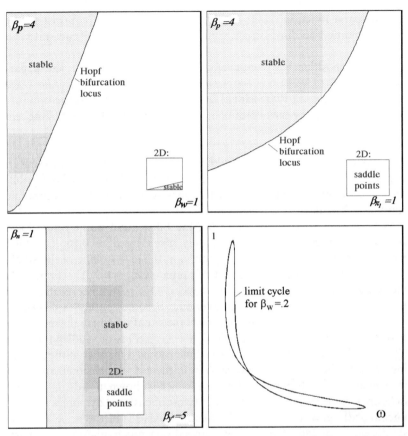

Figure 6.4   Six-dimensional bifurcation loci and a limit cycle for $h_2 = 0.2$ $(Q < 0)$

Proposition 6.5: With respect to the choice of parameter values in table 6.2, the steady state of the dynamical system (6.119)–(6.124) is locally asymptotically stable for a high adjustment speed of prices, a low adjustment speed of wages, a low adjustment speed of inflationary expectations, and all inventory adjustment speeds with respect to the given parameter set. Finally, the adjustment speed of sales expectations must be in the interval (0.98, 4.82), i.e., it should be neither too high nor too low.

The corresponding situation of the three two-dimensional subdynamical systems is shown in the small squares in the figure 6.4. We can see that the combination of an explosive real cycle with (unstable) saddlepoint situations in the monetary and the inventory subsystem gives rise to stability in the integrated six-dimensional system. Note here that there are no perverse Keynes effects $Y_p^d > 0$ or Mundell effects $Y_\pi^d < 0$ with respect to the aggregate demand function of the six-dimensional system, in contrast to the corresponding two-dimensional situation. Furthermore we can state:

Proposition 6.5 (continued): With respect to the choice of parameter values in table 6.2, the stabilizing properties of price and wage adjustment in the six-dimensional dynamical system are just the opposite of those suggested by the two-dimensional dynamical subsystem of the real cycle model.

The partial model thus provides the wrong information concerning an important policy issue, namely, that of the adequate degree of wage flexibility for economic stability. Sluggish wages work in favor of economic stability, while flexible wages do not.

With respect to the parameter β_w, the bifurcation point where local stability becomes lost is approximately given by $\beta_w^H = 0.16$. The final picture in figure 6.4 shows the projection in the $\omega - l$ plane of the stable limit cycle that is generated beyond this point at $\beta_w = 0.2$. This limit cycle increases considerably in amplitude when this parameter is increased towards $\beta_w = 0.3$. Thereafter, the dynamics becomes purely explosive.

In figure 6.4 we consider an example of the situation where the monetary two-dimensional dynamics (see the β_p vs. β_{π_1} plot) is of saddlepoint type ($Q < 0$, see the subsection on the two-dimensional dynamics in the preceding section). In the opposite case, $Q > 0$, the two-dimensional situation instead exhibits a Hopf bifurcation line (which is shown in the small square in figure 6.5; the situation for the other two-dimensional dynamics remains unchanged). Ignoring very small adjustment speeds of the price level the six-dimensional dynamics has not changed very much qualitatively by the assumption of a parameter value for h_2 that gives rise to $Q > 0$. Yet, the domain of stability is quantitatively seen to be significantly increased with respect to β_p, β_{π_1} by the possibility of stability for the monetary subdynamics. Note again that price flexibility (starting from an unstable steady state) can restore stability to the six-dimensional dynamics, but not to the two-dimensional dynamics of the monetary subsystem.

In figure 6.5 we also show some effects of parameter changes on the position of the Hopf bifurcation line. In figure 6.5(a) we can see that an increase of the parameter β_{π_1} from 0.1 to 0.4 may increase the stable domain for wage flexibility. Similarly we consider in figures 6.5(b) and 6.5(c) a decrease of β_w from 0.16 to 0.1 and a decrease of β_{π_1} from 0.4 to 0.1, respectively. The main point shown by these diagrams is, however, that two-dimensional explosive situations are combined by the integrated dynamics in such a way that local asymptotic stability can be obtained.

We have pointed above to the "naturally" nonlinear structure of our

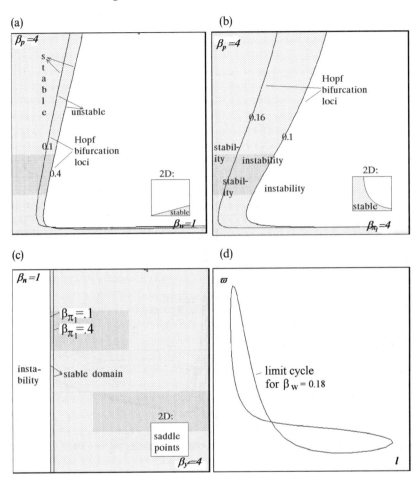

Figure 6.5   Six-dimensional bifurcation-loci and a limit cycle for $h_2 = 0.8$ ($Q > 0$)

dynamical system. The question arises whether this basically "bilinear" system allows for a period-doubling sequence towards complex dynamics as, for example, the Rössler system with its single bilinear term (see for example Strogatz 1994, p.377, for a graphical presentation in the case of this system). Figure 6.6 provides such an example for the dynamical system of this section and the basic parameter set given above (but with $h_2 = 0.08, \beta_{\pi_1} = 0.4$).

Figure 6.7 shows the kind of attractor that may be generated from such a sequence of period-doubling bifurcations of the limit cycle that is generated by the Hopf-bifurcation parameter β_w. Note that all these figures represent

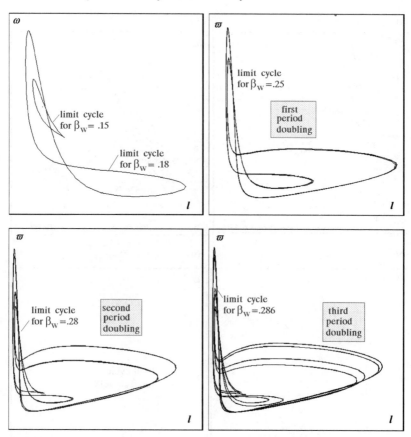

Figure 6.6   A period-doubling route to complex dynamics ($h_2 = 0.08$, $\beta_{\pi 1} = 0.4$)

projections of the dynamics that is taking place in six-dimensional phase space onto the $\omega - l$ plane.

These numerical simulations also show that the cycle generated in this way becomes larger and larger. In particular, it by no means stays in an economically meaningful subset of the phase space. Increasing the parameter β_w further than shown above will eventually also destroy mathematical boundedness. From an economic point of view, it is thus clear that additional forces must come into being when certain ceilings or floors are approached with respect to quantity or value magnitudes. This is the topic of the following subsection.

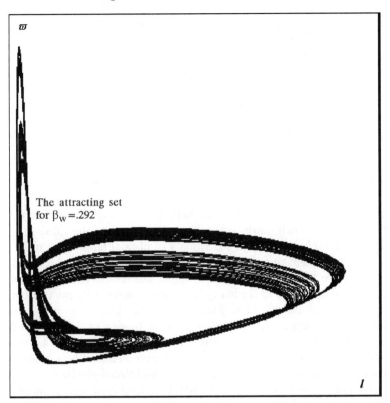

Figure 6.7 At the edge of mathematical boundedness ($h_2 = 0.08$, $\beta_{\pi 1} = 0.4$)

6.4.3   The case of no nominal wage deflation

When the fluctuations generated by the naturally nonlinear model of this section become very large, as in the situation shown in the figure 6.7, or even unbounded, they may or will leave the domain of economically admissible values. Then, or even long before such a point is reached, other economic forces may come into play which work against such occurrences.

A complete list of absolute ceilings and floors for economic fluctuations in our Keynesian monetary growth model could be the following:

- $V \leq V_{\max}$ for the rate of employment,
- $U \leq U_{\max}$ for the rate of capacity utilization,
- $\nu \geq 0$ for inventory holdings,
- $I \geq -\delta K$ for net investment (gross investment $I + \delta K \geq 0$),
- $r \geq 0$ for the nominal rate of interest,
- $\omega < x$ for real wages.

The first two items state that there are two constraints for the output of firms at each point in time t, one, $(Y^K_{max} = U_{max}y^pK)$, determined by the size of the capital stock which is in existence in t and which describes the maximum usage to which the physical means of production can be put (y^pK the normal usage), and one, $(Y^L_{max} = V_{max}xL)$, which describes the maximum of the labor effort available from a given labor force L (xL the normal usage) at each point in time. The output that is actually produced at each moment of time is thus given by

$$Y = \min\{Y^e + \mathscr{I}, Y^K_{max}, Y^L_{max}\}. \tag{6.78}'$$

This equation should be used in the place of equation (6.78) when such limits are approached.

It can, however, be expected that the behavior of the economy changes significantly before such limits are reached. Furthermore, the value V_{max} will be considerably larger than the value 1 of normal labor force utilization, since it is meant to represent absolute full employment, which may be considered to be more than twice as high as the NAIRU level 1 of normal employment, due to the many labor time reserves that exist within the firm as well as outside of it. Finally, the other limit U_{max} is not so absolute as it may appear in the present context. In view of chapter 5 and its treatment of neoclassical factor substitution this limit is given by the marginal productivity relationship which, however, need not be a binding constraint if, for example, firms decide to sell additional production at a price less than marginal wage costs in order to defend their market shares. The marginal productivity condition may thus be important for pricing and investment considerations, as we have used it in chapter 5, but not as an absolute limit to production as it is used in non-Walrasian regime switching analysis.

The third item in the above list states that inventories cannot become negative. It is also not so binding as appears at first sight since unfilled orders can be, and in fact are, treated as negative inventories in the present model. These are subsequently served on a first-come first-served basis until inventories become positive again.

The fourth item, namely, that gross investment remains non-negative, again is not as binding as appears at first sight. This is so since the depreciation rate may become endogenous in times of crisis where gross investment approaches zero.

These items are all quantity constraints, while the last two items on the above list represent price or value constraints. Negative nominal rates of interest r will not come about due to the behavior of asset markets if this floor is approached (which, however, demands the appropriate introduction of a nonlinear money demand function and the like). Finally, the mechanism that keeps real wages ω below labor productivity x is not so obvious and has been controversial throughout the history of economic theory. In the presence of smooth factor substitution, see again chapter 5, one may, however, argue that prices going below marginal wage costs will speed up the price level dynamics by so much that the occurrence of negative profits is generally prevented.

Of course, prices p and w as well as the capital stock K have to stay positive also, but this is assured by the formulation of their dynamics in terms of rates of growth. As should be obvious from the above arguments, the barriers just listed, when approached, demand the integration of various types of nonlinearities (or additional reaction patterns such as overtime work, changes in the participation rate and immigration in the case of the full employment barrier) that may often prevent the described bound from actually being reached. The Keynesian effective demand regime may therefore be considered as the generally prevailing one, though it cannot be totally excluded that the capital stock or the situation on the labor market (outside and inside of firms) may cause a departure from this regime in certain extreme situations.

Astonishingly, however, all of the above additions to our demand constrained Keynesian model of monetary growth can be bypassed in many circumstances when one simple fact of modern economies is taken into account and added to the model, namely, the nonexistence of an economy-wide wage deflation $\hat{w} < 0$. In an inflationary economy, workers may demand very small nominal wage increases in the face of high unemployment, i.e., they may not attempt to resist real wage decreases when they occur in this way. By contrast, the resistance to nominal wage decreases may be formidable due to the institutional structure of the economy. Such and further related arguments have been put forth in a forceful way by Keynes (1936)[21] in particular, and they here provide the basis for a simple modification of the money wage Phillips curve (6.81) we have employed so far, $\hat{w} = \min\{\beta_w(V - 1) + \kappa_w \hat{p} + (1 - \kappa_w)\pi, 0\}$.

This modified wage equation, which excludes the occurrence of a nominal wage deflation, has dramatic consequences for the stability and the pattern of fluctuations that are generated by the thereby revised model. This will be demonstrated here by a series of simulations of this extended

[21] Laxton, Rose, and Tambakis (1997) have recently continued the discussion on the type of nonlinearity that may characterize the Phillips curve, but then focus immediately on the conventional type of a single Phillips curve that is viewed to summarize labor and goods market nominal adjustment processes. They argue in particular that the curvature of the Phillips curve is of decisive importance for the success of stabilization policies. Periods of persistent inflation (as they reappear periodically in reality and in the model that is investigated below) and policy issues are discussed from a broad perspective in Cagan (1979).

model which will create economically meaningful trajectories for all relevant variables despite pronounced increases in adjustment parameters which formerly rapidly led to purely explosive situations.

Let us briefly describe how the model of the preceding subsections is modified by the above reformulation of the money-wage Phillips curve. The wage and price adjustment equations of those subsections can be represented in the form

$$\hat{w} - \pi = \beta_w(V - 1) + \kappa_w(\hat{p} - \pi),$$
$$\hat{p} - \pi = \beta_p(U - 1) + \kappa_p(\hat{w} - \pi),$$

which gives rise to the expressions

$$\hat{w} - \pi = \kappa[\beta_w(V - 1) + \kappa_w\beta_p(U - 1)], \tag{6.134}$$

$$\hat{p} - \pi = \kappa[\kappa_p\beta_w(V - 1) + \beta_p(U - 1)]. \tag{6.135}$$

The simultaneous determination of wage and price deflation is thereby solved and shows that both inflation rates depend on the state of excess demand in the market both for labor and for goods and on expected medium-run inflation. Subtracting the second from the first equation then gives the law of motion of the real wage we have employed so far. Yet, when the rule of downwardly rigid nominal wages applies, i.e., in the case where

$$\kappa[\beta_w(V - 1) + \kappa_w\beta_p(U - 1)] + \pi < 0 \tag{6.136}$$

holds true, we have

$$\hat{w} = 0, \hat{p} = \beta_p(U - 1) + (1 - \kappa_p)\pi,$$

and thus get for the real wage dynamics in this case

$$\hat{\omega} = -\beta_p(U - 1) - (1 - \kappa_p)\pi. \tag{6.137}$$

This is the modification to be made to (6.119) whenever the inequality (6.136) holds true. Furthermore, both (6.121) and (6.122) make use of the expression

$$\hat{p} - \pi = \kappa[\kappa_p\beta_w(V - 1) + \beta_p(U - 1)],$$

which in the case of the above inequality must be replaced by

$$\hat{p} - \pi = \beta_p(U - 1) - \kappa_p\pi. \tag{6.138}$$

This completes the set of changes induced by the assumption of downwardly rigid nominal wages.

Let us now look at the consequences of this simple modification of the model. A first example is provided by figure 6.8. This figure is based on the data of figure 6.7 ($\mu_0 = n$, i.e., no steady state inflation in particular, and

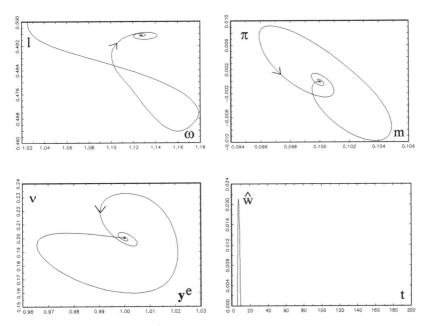

Figure 6.8 No steady state inflation ($\mu_0 = n = 0.05$, $\beta_w = 0.292$ as in figure 6.7)

also $h_2 = 0.08, \beta_{\pi_1} = 0.4$), and differs from the model of that figure only by
the above extension of the Phillips curve. In this case the revision of the
model has two basic consequences:

* The steady state of the model is now (for $\mu_0 = n$) no longer uniquely
  determined in the interior of the phase space as far as rates of employment V_0 (and l_0) are concerned. The rate V_0 may now be lower than "1"
  in the steady state, since the then implied wage deflation is prevented by
  the above change in the wage adjustment mechanism of the model (all
  other steady state values are the same as before).
* The set of steady states of the revised model is now globally asymptotically stable in a very strong way (see figure 6.8 for an example). Due to
  the changed behavior of workers the economy is rapidly trapped in an
  underemployment equilibrium that may be much higher than the
  NAIRU rate of unemployment of the former steady-state situation.

We thus have that downward wage rigidity prevents the fluctuations
shown in figure 6.7 in quite a radical way, but that this is generally
accompanied by a more depressed labor market in the steady state than
previously. These results are in our view due to the fact that there is a floor
or ratchet built into the model right at the edge of the steady state.

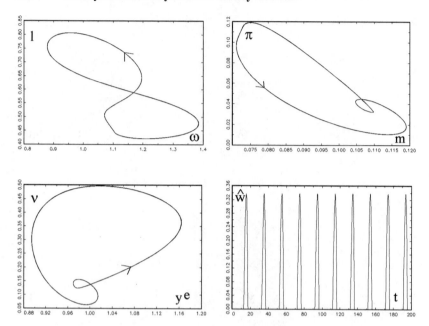

Figure 6.9 Steady-state inflation ($\mu_0 = 0.1 > n = 0.05$) and period 1 limit cycles ($\beta_w = 2$)

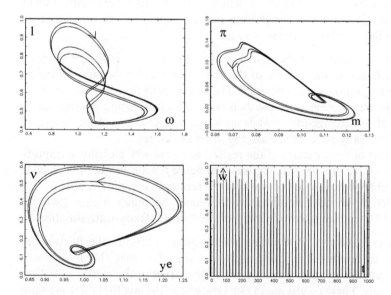

Figure 6.10 Steady-state inflation and period 4 limit cycles ($\beta_w = 10$)

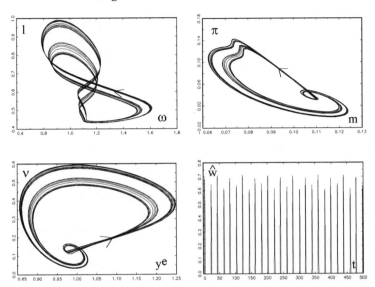

Figure 6.11 Steady-state inflation and period 16 limit cycles ($\beta_w = 11$)

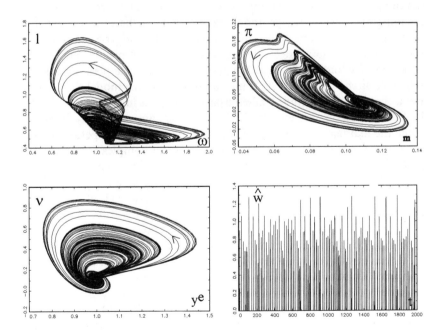

Figure 6.12 Steady-state inflation and complex dynamics ($\beta_w = 26$)

This observation suggests that there will be more fluctuations if there is steady state inflation, i.e., if $\mu_0 > n$ is assumed, since the behavior of the economy is then only modified further away from the steady state, which in this case is again uniquely determined as in the preceding model. Locally, the model is thus of the same form as that of the preceding subsection. The interesting question then is whether the dynamical behavior is again radically modified by the ratchet-effect situation that the level of nominal wages may rise, but cannot fall. Figures 6.9–6.12 illustrate the dynamical behavior for a wage adjustment speed β_w that varies from 2 to 26, i.e., over a range where the previous model would have collapsed immediately.

This series of figures indicates the existence of a period-doubling route to complex dynamics for the system with a kinked money-wage Phillips curve for extremely high adjustment speeds β_w of nominal wages w, with amplitudes of fluctuations that stay within economically meaningful bounds. Note however that wage inflation can be as high as 130 percent during this sequence, and that inventories may become slightly negative in the last figure 6.12 where the case $\beta_w = 26$ is considered.

Figures 6.9–6.12 each show the three projections of the six-dimensional dynamics onto the $\omega - l$, the $m - \pi$ and the $y^e - v$ subspaces as well as the development of wage inflation as a time series. This series of figures demonstrates several things about the behavior of the model. First, the model is now extremely viable, but, as expected, no longer asymptotically stable. Second, the model exhibits large but economically meaningful persistent fluctuations. Third, the model undergoes a period-doubling sequence as the parameter β_w is increased. Fourth, the model shows only weak changes in amplitude while the parameter β_w is increased significantly. Fifth, the economic length of the cycle stays approximately 20 years, while the mathematical period of course doubles along the period-doubling route; Sixth, the dynamics eventually becomes complex for parameter β_w between 11 and 26. The dynamics of the naturally nonlinear model is thus radically changed from a global, though not from a local,[22] perspective when we allow for a "natural" kink in the money-wage Phillips curve in conjunction with a sufficient degree of steady-state inflation.

Figure 6.13 supplements the preceding figures (for the case $\mu_0 = 0.1$) by showing a bifurcation diagram corresponding to the parameter ranges for β_w we have allowed for above. Here we seem to see period doubling and complex behavior also at low values of β_w (below 1), then a second sequence of period doubling setting in at approximately $\beta_w = 4.3$ and complex behavior emerging between $\beta_w = 11$ and $\beta_w = 14$.

However, we need to be cautious in interpreting this diagram as evidence

---

[22] Where the Hopf-bifurcation analysis of the preceding sections still applies.

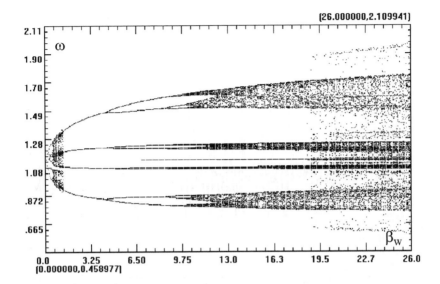

Figure 6.13   A bifurcation diagram for the dynamics considered in figures 6.9–6.12

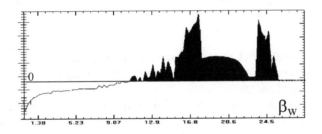

Figure 6.14   The largest Liapunov exponent of the dynamics considered in figure 6.13

of chaotic motion. This becomes apparent, for example, when the first of the above "period doubling routes to chaos" (β_w below 1) is investigated in more detail. There it is in fact found that the bifurcation diagram then solely shows the long transient behavior due to the sluggish adjustment of money wages.[23] In figure 6.14 we therefore add to the above calculations a presentation of the largest Liapunov exponent, which provides evidence for chaotic behavior in the range where it becomes positive[24] (which seems

[23] A similar observation does not hold for the second sequence of period doublings (β_w above 2), as further numerical investigations have shown.
[24] See Parker and Chua (1989) for the details on such Liapunov exponents.

334   The Dynamics of Keynesian Monetary Growth

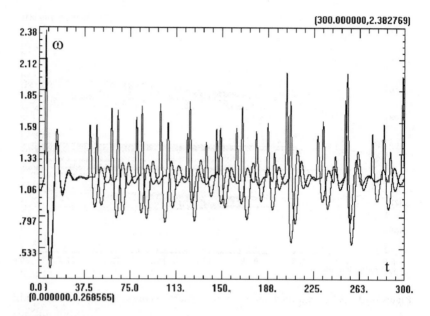

Figure 6.15 A test for sensitivity with respect to initial conditions for the above-shown attractor $(\beta_w = 20)$

to be the case for $\beta_w > 11$ already). Finally, the dynamic system then also displays sensitivity to initial conditions as shown in figure 6.15 for the parameter value $\beta_w = 20$.

All these simulations suggest from their different perspectives that flexible wages (even if they are downwardly rigid and thus guarantee economic viability) can introduce significant turbulence into the dynamics of Keynes–Metzler growth type, a turbulence that is accompanied by larger fluctuations in the state variables of the dynamics the larger the speed of adjustment of money wages becomes. Sluggish money wage adjustments are thus preferable from the point of view of the simplicity and the size of the resulting business fluctuations.

6.4.4   Concluding remarks

In Keynes (1936) it is stated:

Thus it is fortunate that workers, though unconsciously, are instinctively more reasonable economists than the classical school, inasmuch as they resist reductions of money-wages, which are seldom or never of an all-round character . . . (p.14)

The chief result of this policy (of flexible wages, CC/PF) would be to cause a great instability of prices, so violent perhaps as to make business calculations futile. (p.269)

Our working Keynesian model of monetary growth has demonstrated the validity of this view by means of numerical simulations of a system of laws of motion of considerable completeness and complexity. These simulations have shown that the assumption of downwardly rigid money wages, and the kink in the Phillips curve that is implied thereby, can alter the dynamics of the Keynes–Metzler model of monetary growth in a very radical fashion, making it not only mathematically but also economically viable even for very high (upward) adjustment speeds of money wages.[25] Of course, other sources of additional stability may also exist, but must be left for future research here.

6.5   Outlook: macroeconometric model building

We have presented in section 6.3 our working model of Keynesian monetary growth as a synthesis of the Keynes–Wicksell model type and our basic Keynesian monetary growth model of chapter 4, by way of systematic extensions of these two model types. We have furthermore shown in chapter 5 how smooth factor substitution can be introduced into this model type and in chapter 4 how the model can be extended to include Harrod neutral technological change, wage taxation, p-star expectations, and a more refined interaction of expectations and actual inflation in the form of a wage–price spiral. Taken together, we have thus arrived from the theoretical point of view at a fairly developed presentation of Keynesian monetary growth dynamics by way of a systematic extension of the early Keynes–Wicksell approach to the description of the interaction of labor- and goods-market disequilibrium in a monetary economy.

Powell and Murphy (1997) have recently published a detailed presentation of the so-called Murphy model for the Australian economy that attempts to show the theoretical foundations of their modern macroeconometric modeling of a small open economy. They use in their guide to this model the version of it which consists of 100 scalar equations including 24 behavioral equations and, of course, many accounting identities. In the course of writing the present book, however, it became more and more apparent to us that there is a close relationship between the model type considered in Powell and Murphy (1997) and the one at which we have now arrived.

Of course, Powell and Murphy have to consider an open economy right

[25] Which as we have seen introduce considerable turbulence into the considered dynamics.

from the start, whereas we have restricted our attention in our hierarchy of macrodynamic model building to closed economies throughout. There is, however, work in progress[26] where we extend our model types to include international trade in goods and financial assets along lines suggested by the seminal paper of Dornbusch (1976) on overshooting exchange rates and the many extensions of it that now exist in the literature. The Dornbusch model is also central to the Murphy model, where basically a three-goods approach is adopted (one traded and one nontraded commodity for the Australian economy and one international good) in conjunction with an asset-markets approach with rational expectations, as in many more recent presentations of the Dornbusch model. For a detailed discussion of the open economy aspects of the Murphy macroeconometric model, as well as of our theoretical working model for open economies and further extensions of it, we refer the reader to Chiarella et al. (1998) and Chiarella and Flaschel (1998c,d,e,f), and will concentrate in these brief remarks on the other structural equations of the two approaches to be compared.

With respect to the remaining equations of the Murphy model, which in number are not many more than the equations we have used to describe the Keynes–Metzler model in section 6.3, there exist in particular the following set of relationships between our theoretical approach and the applied one of Murphy. We stress here that the following list of these relationships is, however, neither complete nor very detailed, but refer the reader again to Chiarella et al. (1998) for a thorough discussion of the Murphy model and related models and their similarities to and differences from our Keynesian working model. Furthermore, we pay no attention here to the particular types of lag structure and behavioral nonlinearities that are assumed in Powell and Murphy (1997), but compare only the qualitative features of the two model types.

- The money-wage Phillips curve of the Murphy model is of the type considered in the next chapter of this book, i.e., it includes the rate of change of the rate of employment as an argument besides allowing also for the inclusion of technical change and for a purely adaptive scheme of inflationary expectations formation.
- The price dynamics for the nontraded good, though presented in a quite different format (based on marginal cost calculations), is in fact of the type we described in chapter 5 in the presence of smooth factor substitution.
- There is no forward-looking behavior in the interaction of wage and price dynamics.
- The short run in the Murphy model is always of Keynesian type, with

---

[26] See Chiarella and Flaschel (1998c,d,e,f).

output being determined by actual sales and planned inventories. There are thus no disappointed sales expectations in the Murphy model, which implies that it makes use of a combination of goods-market equilibrium and Metzlerian inventory adjustment rules, a situation that somehow lies between our Keynesian model of chapter 4 and the Keynes–Metzler model type of the present chapter.

- Asset markets are modeled in a less restrictive way using rational expectations equilibria on the basis of the perfect substitute assumption. These markets are, furthermore, as in our Keynes–Metzler model, explicitly represented only with respect to money-market equilibrium, in a way that is close to our representation of the stock equilibrium in the money market.
- Households in the Murphy model are only of one type and represented by a consumption function of Ando–Modigliani type.
- There is a much more advanced treatment of labor supply in the Murphy model, yet no endogenous determination of natural growth or natural (un)employment, which we consider in the next chapter.
- The production of firms is based on nested CES technology assumptions with three inputs and two outputs, and thus considerably more complex than our two-factor/one-output neoclassical production technology of chapter 5.
- Fixed investment behavior is basically of the same type as the one we consider in our Keynes–Metzler approach, though Powell and Murphy (1997) represent our explicit usage of the rate of capacity utilization in the form of medium-run competitive conditions (based on marginal cost relationships).
- Taxation and government expenditure, but not money supply, obey rules that differ from the still simple ones we are using and which are formulated in Powell and Murphy (1997) to some extent from the perspective of getting asymptotic stability of the steady state.
- There is a unique interior steady state in the Murphy model (as in our models).
- There is no regime switching as the economy departs from the steady state, since
  - actual prices may be lower than the competitive ones so that firms are assumed to supply what is demanded, going beyond their aggregate supply schedules when demanded in order to satisfy their customers (consumption and investment demand in particular) at each moment in time. There are, however, rising prices in such a situation, but never rationed consumers or investors;
  - there is always enough labor time available (additional labor that can be recruited if necessary or through overtime work of the employed labor force, see also our next chapter in this regard).

• As in our Keynesian approach of chapters 4, 5, and 6, the Keynesian regime of the neoKeynesian rationing approaches to short-run equilibrium (which also consider so-called Classical regimes and regimes of repressed inflation) is the only one that is relevant for the description of the temporary positions of the economy, while the other two regimes are either only present in the medium-run adjustment behavior of the economy or are of a purely hypothetical kind (since they do not come into operation in the way it is formulated in the neo-Keynesian literature).

This closes our brief comparison of models of the Murphy and the Keynes–Metzler type. We hope to have shown thereby that our theoretical working model is in fact already fairly close to an important and modern type of macroeconometric model, which therefore may be approached by extending further and further our hierarchical approach to models of monetary growth. The case of such macroeconometric models can thus be represented in the compact and consistent form of our working model (with all budget restrictions that are necessary for such consistency reasons). It can thereby be made the subject of theoretical analysis (including numerical simulations) with respect to the various dynamic effects that are consciously or unconsciously included in the interaction of its modules – the Keynes, Mundell, and Rose effects, and the like, studied extensively in this and the preceding chapters.

The *Papers and Proceedings of the American Economic Review* have recently published a discussion on "Is there a core to practical macroeconomics that we should all believe?" with contributions by Blanchard, Blinder, Eichenbaum, Solow, and Taylor (all 1997).[27] Our reading of this discussion is that the working model of Keynes–Metzler type we have developed and analyzed in this chapter (and which we extend further on the supply side in the next) provides a general prototype of an integrated macrodynamics of the short, medium, and long run of monetary economies that is in many respects closely related to this discussion, also with respect to the term "practical", and that can at the least be used as a point of departure for the further discussion of integrated macrodynamics with demand and supply side features and their relationships with structural macroeconometric model building (see also the discussion on macroeconomic modeling in a changing world in the introduction to Allen and Hall 1997). We thus believe that we have reached a stage where traditional, but integrated Keynesian macrodynamics (with long-run supply side features) we have presented and investigated in this chapter will convince many (but of course not all) readers with interest in such macrodynamics

---

[27] An alternative point of view is presented in the earlier contribution to such a discussion by Mankiw (1990).

that such modeling can be very useful for evaluating the real progress that has been made in the search for reliable structural macromodels of the short, medium, and long run in the recent past. Finally, there is work in progress (see Chiarella and Flaschel 1998f, Chiarella et al. (1998, 1999) where further attempts are made to synthesize to some extent (or at least to compare) the working model of this chapter with recent contributions to macrodynamics from various schools of economic thought, to integrate international trade in goods and financial assets into it, and to embed all these achievements into a theoretical discussion of important macro-econometric structural model building.

7 The road ahead

In this chapter we shall provide one final important example of how the "proper" Keynesian prototype model of monetary growth of this book, the working model of the preceding chapter, can be further improved and can give rise to considerably more refined adjustment processes on the macro level, here specifically with respect to the labor market (outside and inside the firm), long-run employment and long-run growth. We shall then close this chapter with a brief summary of what we have achieved in this book and what has still to be done by enumerating the weaknesses, gaps and shortcomings that remain in our modeling of a Keynesian monetary growth model. As will be obvious from this list, it is not possible to remove these shortcomings of our working model in a single book, or even in one further book.

Instead, we will concentrate in this final chapter on one important problematic characteristic which our working model still exhibits concerning the exogeneity of the full employment rate of employment $\bar{V}$ and the natural rate of growth n of the economy. Furthermore, we refine the adjustment processes on the labor market and endogenize the trend component in the investment function, thereby in sum allowing for an endogenous determination of the steady-state rate of growth as well as the steady-state rate of (un)employment.

One consequence of our choice of endogenizing these rates is that there is now hysteresis[1] in the dynamics, i.e., these endogenous rates are no longer uniquely determined, but now depend on historical conditions that remain persistent in the long-run behavior of the trajectories of the dynamics. Also, in order to allow for an adjustment of the rate of employment, we have to

---

[1] By "hysteresis" we refer to the phenomenon whereby a dynamical system may have a continuum of steady states so that the attractor to which the economy converges is dependent upon the initial conditions of the trajectories. Hence the dynamics of the system will exhibit path dependency (see Franz 1990, ch. 1, for a discussion of hysteresis in economics).

340

distinguish now between the rate of employment that, on the one hand, refers to the labor market and, on the other hand, is the one within firms (the rate of employment of the employed labor force). In this way we introduce further delays in the adjustment of the rate of employment on the labor market (by distinguishing inside from outside effects), thereby increasing the realism of our description of the employment relationships. We therefore here reduce our reliance on the use of so-called natural rates in the formulation of our Keynesian monetary growth dynamics and take account of further feedback loops in labor market adjustment processes.

However, instead of a full description of goods-market disequilibrium and its dynamic consequences, as in our Keynes–Metzler working model, we consider in this chapter again only the "naive" version of the goods-market disequilibrium adjustment process, i.e., the simple dynamic multiplier story of the KT model of section 6.2 of the preceding chapter. This version of the Keynesian model with both sluggish price and quantity adjustments is mathematically simpler to treat and, though somewhat unconvincing from the viewpoint of economic consistency, not unrelated to the mathematical structure of the monetary growth model with a full description of goods-market adjustment processes as we have seen in chapter 6. This output adjustment process will be supplemented here by a labor force adjustment process of a similar type, which in sum gives rise to a core dynamics of the model that is of dimension six, as the Keynes–Metzler model with its full description of the inventory adjustment process. In sum, this chapter thereby achieves the integration of sluggish quantity adjustments of output and employment with endogenous trend growth as well as with an endogenous determination of the long-run rate of employment of the labor force in the Keynesian monetary growth framework introduced in chapter 4 as the Keynesian extension of the Keynes–Wicksell framework of the sixties and early seventies.

7.1   Endogenous long-run growth and employment

One purpose of the monetary growth model of this chapter is to justify the assumption $\gamma = n(= \text{const.})$ which has been employed throughout the book as a description of the trend component in investment behavior and has been interpreted as a very crude expression for the "animal spirits" component of this behavior. This section now endogenizes the rate γ, still in a very simple way, by means of a certain self-reference that is here assumed to characterize the investment plans of firms on the macro level. This approach to an explanation of the generally given rate $\gamma(= n = \text{const.})$ represents the simplest way available for its endogenization. One implication of this new assumption will be that, since the model need not be locally asymptotically stable, the rate γ need not converge to the steady-state rate n of natural growth. The earlier assumption of $\gamma = n(= \text{const.})$ need therefore be fulfilled only "on average."

This average, however, will also be treated as endogenously determined in the following, since it is not very plausible that labor supply follows a given trend in reference to which the steady state can then be determined. Trend growth, including labor supply growth, must be explained by theory and not simply be assumed as given for the explanation of cycles around it. The long-run growth path cannot be determined by "closing" the system from the side of labor supply as far as the evolution of industrialized economies is concerned.

Finally, the so-called "natural" rate of (un)employment is also not a datum brought about by natural forces, but is a consequence of the process of capital accumulation and its impact on the labor market. A model of marodynamics must therefore sooner or later offer an endogenous explanation of this NAIRU-based rate of employment $\bar{V}$. Again this will be done in a particularly simple way here.[2]

For recent discussions on the NAIRU of the "Natural Rate Hypothesis," which, however, generally differ significantly from the approach that is chosen in this chapter, the reader is in particular referred to the volume edited by Cross (1995), to the papers by Phelps and Zoega (1997), Saint-Paul (1997), and Murphy and Topel (1997), to Allen and Nixon on "Two concepts of the NAIRU" in Allen and Hall (1997), to Summers (1990), to Fair (1997a,b), and to the discussion published in the *Journal of Economic Perspectives* with contributions by Blanchard and Katz, Galbraith, Gordon, Rogerson, Straiger et al., and Stiglitz (all 1997). Our point of view in the present chapter is that we use a very simple endogenization of the NAIRU, the nonaccelerating inflation rate of (labor) utilization, alongside other adjustment processes in the labor market, in order to discuss the role of this rate in a high order integrated macrodynamics and to get first results on the endogenous determination of the long-run steady and nonsteady evolution of closed economies. Of course, further work which integrates part of the approaches of the papers just mentioned is needed here to make further progress on the endogeneity of long-run growth as it derives from adjustment processes in the markets for labor, and of the trend growth rate of the capital stock.

Viewed from the perspective of what has been shown so far in this book, it would be best to choose the Keynes–Metzler model of section 6.3 and include the above-proposed modifications into it, though it may be prob-

---

[2] Our approach parallels in method, but not in substance, the approach chosen in van de Klundert and van Schaik (1990) for the evolution of inflation and the capital stock in a Keynesian environment.

lematic to do the same for its extreme equilibrium limit case considered at length in chapter 4 (as the "textbook model" of IS–LM growth). Section 6.4 has, however, shown that it may be legitimate to make use of an intermediate case, the KT model of section 6.2, in order to present and investigate the above-proposed endogenization of "natural rates," since the Keynes–Metzler growth model can be reduced to a model of KT type if some mild alterations in its structural equations are accepted. We therefore here take the KT model type of section 6.2 as starting point for our description of an endogenous determination of the trend component in investment behavior as well as in labor supply and of the NAIRU-based rate of employment. With respect to this market, we furthermore will distinguish now between the employment of the employed and the rate of employment of the labor force in order to separate the immediate impact of a fluctuating demand for goods on labor effort from its medium-run consequences for the pool, or the reserve army, of the unemployed. This adds some further inertia to the model by making the employment decisions of firms a more indirect one. This section thus offers an insider–outsider approach[3] to the labor market with endogenous solutions for the trend growth rate in this market as well as for the economy as a whole, plus a historically determined endogenous long-run level of the employment rate.

The equations of this version of the KT model of monetary growth of section 6.2 read in the case of a given tax ratio t^n (see below):[4]

1 Definitions (remuneration and wealth):

$$\omega = w/p, u = \omega/x, \rho = (Y - \delta K - \omega L^d)/K, \tag{7.1}$$

$$W = (M + B + p_e E)/p, p_b = 1. \tag{7.2}$$

2 Households (workers and asset holders):

$$W = (M^d + B^d + p_e E^d)/p, M^d = h_1 p Y + h_2 p K (1 - \tau)(\bar{r} - r), \tag{7.3}$$

$$C = \omega L^d + (1 - s_c)[\rho K + rB/p - T], s_w = 0, \tag{7.4}$$

$$\begin{aligned} S_p &= \omega L^d + Y_c^D - C = Y - \delta K + rB/p - T - C \\ &= s_c[\rho K + rB/p - T] = s_c Y_c^D \\ &= (\dot{M}^d + \dot{B}^d + p_e \dot{E}^d)/p, \end{aligned} \tag{7.5}$$

$$\hat{L} = n, \dot{n} = \beta_n(n(V, \gamma) - n), n(V, \gamma) = n_v(V - \underline{V}) + n_\gamma(\gamma - \underline{\gamma}) + \underline{n}. \tag{7.6}$$

3 Firms (production units and investors):

---

[3] See Lindbeck and Snower (1988) for a collection of articles on the insider/outsider issue.
[4] See also Chiarella and Flaschel (1998b) for a related presentation of this final model of our book and its theoretical and numerical implications.

$$Y^p = y^p K, y^p = \text{const.}, U = Y/Y^p = y/y^p, (y = Y/K), \tag{7.7}$$

$$L^d = Y/x, x = \text{const.}, V = L^w/L, V^w = L^d/L^w, \tag{7.8}$$

$$\dot{L}^w = \gamma L^w + \beta_v(L^d - L^w), \tag{7.9}$$

$$I = i_1(\rho - (r - \pi))K + i_2(U - \bar{U})K + \gamma K, \tag{7.10}$$

$$p_e \dot{E}/p = I + (S - I) = Y - \delta K - C - G = Y - Y^d + I, \tag{7.11}$$

$$\hat{K} = I/K \neq S/K, \tag{7.12}$$

$$\dot{\gamma} = \beta_\gamma(\hat{K} - \gamma). \tag{7.13}$$

4 Government (fiscal and monetary authority):

$$t^n = (T - rB/p)/K = \text{const.}, \tag{7.14}$$

$$G = T - rB/p + \mu_2 M/p, \tag{7.15}$$

$$S_g = T - rB/p - G[= -(\dot{M} + \dot{B})/p, \text{ see below}], \tag{7.16}$$

$$\hat{M} = \mu_0, \tag{7.17}$$

$$\dot{B} = pG + rB - pT - \dot{M}[= (\mu_2 - \mu_0)M]. \tag{7.18}$$

5 Equilibrium conditions (asset markets):

$$M = M^d = h_1 pY + h_2 pK(1 - \tau)(\bar{r} - r)[B = B^d, E = E^d], \tag{7.19}$$

$$p_e E = (1 - \tau)\rho pK/((1 - \tau)r - \pi), \tag{7.20}$$

$$\dot{M} = \dot{M}^d, \dot{B} = \dot{B}^d[\dot{E} = \dot{E}^d]. \tag{7.21}$$

6 Disequilibrium situation (goods market adjustment):

$$S = p_e \dot{E}^d = S_p + S_g = Y - \delta K - C - G = p_e \dot{E} \neq I, \tag{7.22}$$

$$Y^d = C + I + \delta K + G, \tag{7.23}$$

$$\hat{Y} = \gamma + \beta_y(Y^d/Y - 1) = \gamma + \beta_y((I - S)/Y), \tag{7.24}$$

$$\dot{N} = \delta_2 K + S - I, S = S_p + S_g = Y - \delta K - C - G. \tag{7.25}$$

7 The dynamics of the labor market NAIRU:

$$\dot{\bar{V}} = \beta_{\bar{v}}(V - \bar{V}). \tag{7.26}$$

8 Wage–price sector (adjustment equations):

$$\hat{w} = \beta_{w_1}(V - \bar{V}) + \beta_{w_2}(V^w - 1) + \kappa_w \hat{p} + (1 - \kappa_w)\pi, \tag{7.27}$$

$$\hat{p} = \beta_p(U - \bar{U}) + \kappa_p \hat{w} + (1 - \kappa_p)\pi, \tag{7.28}$$

$$\dot{\pi} = \beta_{\pi_1}(\hat{p} - \pi) + \beta_{\pi_2}(\mu_0 - n - \pi). \tag{7.29}$$

With this model we have returned to the $I \neq S$–LM KT model of section 6.2 (see (6.20), p. 285) in order to formulate and investigate another extension of it (besides the Keynes–Metzler model type), one that now dispenses with the exogeneity of most of its "natural" rates. In addition to that, we shall now also make use of an extended labor market Phillips curve which, as in insider–outsider approaches of the literature, distinguishes between the employment rate V of the labor force and the employment or utilization rate V^w of the employed (the insiders). This distinction is of importance since it now takes account of the fact that there is in general only a sluggish response of the rate of employment to the actual employment that exists within firms. The latter is governed by the fluctuating state of effective demand on the market for goods, which is first of all met by firms through a changing rate of employment of the employed labor force and only with a time delay through a change in the number of workers employed.

Such a delay in the response of firms to changes in effective demand with regard to their hiring or firing of workers may give additional force to our selection of the Keynesian demand constrained regime as the general one, and our neglect of the regime of so-called repressed inflation (where the labor supply has become an absolute constraint on the output of firms) and the so-called Classical regime (where the capital stock takes on the role of such an absolute constraint, a state of absolute capital shortage). The former regime will be avoided here by this increased flexibility in the employment decision of firms and by means of the reactions of wages to this insider–outsider characterization of the labor market, plus also the resulting profitability effects on the investment plans of firms. Capital shortage $U \to 1$, however, can here only be avoided through timely reactions in the investment decision of firms, possibly speeded up by a rate of profit which then significantly increases relative to the real rate of interest. As we have shown in the preceding section, the inventory policy of firms may be an additional argument for the exclusion of the Classical regime in a certain neighborhood of the steady state.

Nevertheless, regime switching may occur under certain circumstances and has therefore to be integrated in some way or another into such Keynesian demand driven systems at a later stage. At that later stage it will also become necessary to provide an endogenous explanation of the second type of NAIRU-based rate of employment we have employed in this Keynesian model, the desired or normal rate of capacity utilization $\bar{U} < 1$ of the capital stock. This, however, will also demand a more elaborate description of the decisions made within firms.

In the present context we content ourselves with an endogenous explanation of the other natural rates of the model. The main reason for this final modification of our Keynesian model is that we want to indicate to the reader that the assumption $\gamma = n$ we have employed so far can indeed be justified to some extent, but that it is not possible in a truly general growth model to state that it is "closed," and thus made a determinate model through a given growth rate of the labor force or an independent invest-ment demand function or the like.[5] In the above model these "data" of certain steady-state analyses are determined and explained simultaneously so that none of them can be given in advance in order to derive steady-state positions from it. In fact the choice of the steady state of the above model will no longer be unique here, since it turns out that there is now hysteresis in the evolution of the economy, and thus dependence of the steady state in the long run on the specific type of evolution that has taken place or will take place in response to exogenous shocks. The "natural" rates of growth of both the capital stock γ and the labor force n (which are generated by different sectors of our economy with quite different objectives in mind) will here in general converge to (or cycle around) each other and, if convergent, converge to a value which is not predetermined by the par-ameters of the model.

Since we have returned to the assumption of the KT model, we can again use actual output in the calculation of the rate of profit ρ in equation (7.1) in place of the expected demand concept we used in section 6.3. Furthermore, the explicit treatment of inventories is again no longer compelling, since inventories do not feed back into the other dynamic equations in the present formulation of the model (and will thus be suppressed here). Output adjusts again in view of the discrepancy that exists between its current level and actual aggregate demand, and also in view of the fact that the economy is assumed (by firms) to grow on an average with the rate γ.

In the household sector we now assume in (7.6) that the time rate of change of the growth rate of the labor supply depends positively on the discrepancy between a target value for it, $n(V, \gamma)$, and the current value n of the rate of natural growth. This target value $n(V, \gamma)$ in turn depends positively on the current state of the labor market as measured by the rate V and also positively on the currently existing growth climate as measured by the term γ. It is here assumed that there are segments in the economy where people are just waiting (to be called) to enter the labor market in the case of brighter prospects, which are here represented by these two vari-ables. We have assumed this particular approach to changes in the rate of natural growth mainly because of two important subcases, namely, $\beta_n = \infty$ (i.e., $n = n(V, \gamma)$), and $\beta_n < \infty, n(V, \gamma) = \gamma$ (i.e., $\dot{n} = \beta_n(\gamma - n)$).

In the first case the variable n is determined as a simple statically

---

[5] See Marglin (1984a,b) with respect to this type of approach.

endogenous variable with no need of a further dynamic law for its evolution, while in the second case we simply assume that it adjusts to the long-run rate of growth γ that firms expect to come about.

There are two alterations with respect to the assumed behavior of firms. One is that we now distinguish between the rate of employment V of the labor force (on the labor market) and the employment rate V^w of the workforce employed by the firms. This latter rate is determined by the temporary state of goods demand, which is known to firms, and by the exact basis of their output decision (which in turn determine the employment within firms). Equation (7.9) describes the adjustment of the workforce L^w that is chosen by firms in the light of their evaluation of the employment of their labor force and in the light of the trend rate of growth they expect to come about. The other change in the description of firms is the assumption (7.13), which states that the investment climate they jointly generate will feed back on their views of the trend rate of growth γ in a positive fashion.

The description of the government sector and of the asset markets is the same as before and the adjustments in the output decisions of firms in view of current aggregate demand are described as in the KT model of section 6.2.

For the NAIRU-based rate of employment $\bar{V}$, we assume in equation (7.26) that it responds to the state of the labor market. An employment rate above (below) $\bar{V}$ feeds back positively (negatively) on the rate $\bar{V}$ by enlarging or reducing that segment of the labor market where labor can be considered as "trained," i.e., sufficiently experienced in the use of the given technology and not disqualified through a longer period where it has been unemployed. We do not go into the details of such a hysteresis-creating loop between the actual and the long-run rate of employment, since we only want to employ this simplest hypothesis conceivable for describing such an effect (see Cross 1987 for a more elaborate treatment of such effects and for notes on the literature, and Heap 1980 for an early approach, and its justification, that is closely related to the one we have employed here).

Our final equation concerns the money-wage Phillips curve (7.27) which describes the outside and the inside effect of employment as we have already sketched it above. Deviations of the labor-market employment rate from the NAIRU-based rate $\bar{V}$ lead to corresponding effects on the rate of change of money wages, as do deviations of the degree of utilization of the labor force within firms from the normal utilization rate of the employed which is given by 1. Combined with equation (7.9), this general form of a money-wage Phillips curve marries in particular the views of Phillips (1958) and Kuh (1967) which therefore are complementary to each other, but not alternatives, as Kuh believed. Inserting (7.9), appropriately transformed, into (7.27) implies that the rate of employment enters the Phillips curve in proportional (V) as well as in derivative form ($\dot{V}$), leaving as empirical questions the extent to which each of these terms determines the rate of change of money wages. Note here that the derivative term must be integrated in order to give rise to the level formulation used by Kuh (1967). Neglecting the micro–macro distinction with respect to the just-considered Kuh-component of the Phillips curve, the integrated derivative control term in it can also be related to the so-called wage curve as introduced and investigated extensively in Blanchflower and Oswald (1990, 1994, 1995).

We stress once again that each building block in the model may be subject to considerable change, and that it is primarily the completeness of the presentation of macroeconomic interactions that is considered here as important. Expressions have therefore often been chosen in as simple a way as possible in order to sketch *all* basic adjustment mechanisms in a Keynesian model of monetary growth. Nevertheless, we have now obtained a very general model type for the analysis of Keynesian monetary growth with both under- and overutilization of labor and capital.

Finally, one could have called this particular extension of the KT model a Keynes–Marx model. Such a denomination is intended to express the fact that we have now laid more stress on the labor market and its structural characteristics than is generally customary in Keynesian models of the long run. It was indeed Marx (1954, ch. 25) who first pointed, in a way that is still relevant, to the crucial role played by the labor market and its structure in the shaping of the process of capital accumulation. Many of his characterizations of its structure are still relevant, although, of course, crudely formulated from today's perspective. This closes the description and the motivation of our above final model type of Keynesian monetary growth.

7.2   The dynamic structure of the model

The model of the preceding subsection is again easily reduced now to a nine-dimensional autonomous dynamical system in the state variables $u = \omega/x$, l, m, π, y, V, $\bar{V}$, γ, and n, with an appended $\dot{b}$ dynamics (not shown). These dynamics will be investigated in the remainder of this chapter with respect to the new phenomena to which they give rise.[6] The intensive form nine-dimensional dynamical system is given by

$$\hat{u} = \kappa[(1 - \kappa_p)(\beta_{w_1}(V - \bar{V}) + \beta_{w_2}(y/(xVl) - 1))$$

---

[6] Note that the derivation of the dynamic law $\hat{V} = (\gamma - n) + \beta_v(V^w - 1)$ is easily obtained from the expression $\hat{L}^w = \gamma + \beta_v(V^w - 1)$, which in turn is an obvious consequence of the law of motion we have assumed for L^w. Note also that the law for $\hat{L}^w$ is of the same type as the output adjustment rule of the KT model.

$$+ (\kappa_w - 1)\beta_p(y/y^p - 1)], \tag{7.30}$$

$$\hat{l} = n - (\gamma + i_1(\rho - r + \pi) + i_2(y/y^p - 1)), \tag{7.31}$$

$$\hat{m} = \mu_0 - n - \pi + \hat{l} - \kappa[\beta_p(y/y^p - 1) + \kappa_p(\beta_{w_1}(V - \bar{V}) + \beta_{w_2}(y/(xVl) - 1))], \tag{7.32}$$

$$\dot{\pi} = \beta_{\pi_1}\kappa[\beta_p(y/y^p - 1) + \kappa_p(\beta_{w_1}(V - \bar{V}) + \beta_{w_2}(y/(xVl) - 1))] + \beta_{\pi_2}(\mu_0 - n - \pi), \tag{7.33}$$

$$\dot{y} = -(i_1(\rho - r + \pi) + i_2(y/y^p - 1))y + \beta_y(y^d - y), \tag{7.34}$$

$$\hat{V} = (\gamma - n) + \beta_v(y/(Vxl) - 1), \tag{7.35}$$

$$\dot{\bar{V}} = \beta_{\bar{v}}(V - \bar{V}), \tag{7.36}$$

$$\dot{\gamma} = \beta_\gamma(i_1(\rho - r + \pi) + i_2(y/y^p - 1)), \tag{7.37}$$

$$\dot{n} = \beta_n(n(V, \gamma) - n), \tag{7.38}$$

where we have employed the abbreviations ($\bar{r} = r_0$):

$$\rho = y - \delta - \omega l^d = y(1 - u) - \delta, l^d = L^d/K = y/x \text{ (y not const.!)},$$
$$V^w = L^d/L^w = l^d/(Vl) = y/(xVl), U = y/y^p,$$
$$r = r_0 + (h_1 y - m)/h_2,$$
$$g = t^n + \mu_2 m,$$
$$y^d = uy + (1 - s_c)(\rho - t^n) + i_1(\rho - r + \pi) + i_2(U - \bar{U}) + n + \delta + g,$$
$$i(\cdot) = I/K = i_1(\rho - r + \pi) + i_2(y/y^p - \bar{U}) + \gamma,$$

where $u = \omega/x$ is the share of wages in gross national income.

Assume for all following considerations that the equation $n(\bar{V}, \gamma_0) = \gamma_0$ has a unique positive solution γ_0 for each meaningful level of the NAIRU rate of employment $\bar{V} \in (0, 1)$. For any choice of this NAIRU-based rate of employment $\bar{V}$ there is then a unique interior steady-state solution for the remaining state variables of the above dynamical system if one adds to it the equation $n_0 = \gamma_0$ (with γ_0 as determined above), i.e.:[7]

$$y_0 = y_0^d = y^p, l_0^d = y_0/x, \tag{7.39}$$

$$m_0 = h_1 y_0, \tag{7.40}$$

$$\pi_0 = \mu_0 - n_0, \tag{7.41}$$

$$\omega_0 = \frac{y_0 - \delta - t^n - (n_0 + \mu_2 m_0)/s_c}{l_0^d}, \tag{7.42}$$

$$\rho_0 = y_0 - \delta - \omega_0 l_0^d, \tag{7.43}$$

[7] In the special case $n(V, \gamma) = \gamma$, to be investigated numerically later on, the set of steady states is given by a surface in $\Re^9$.

$$r_0 = \rho_0 + \mu_0 - n_0 \tag{7.44}$$

$$V_0 = \bar{V}, l_0 = l_0^d / \bar{V}. \tag{7.45}$$

The set of economically meaningful steady states of the considered eight-dimensional dynamics is thus given by a curve in $\Re^9$. The model is assumed to have sufficiently large buffers $1 - \bar{V}, 1 - \bar{U}$ at its steady state so that the Keynesian demand regime we have assumed above to prevail at each point in time (in each short run of the model) can indeed be a maintained along the trajectories of the dynamics.

We stress that we have chosen all behavioral equations as linearly as possible in order to concentrate on the "natural" or intrinsic nonlinearities of the dynamics and their implications. This in particular holds for the function $n(V, \gamma)$, which implies that there is a unique solution γ_0 to the equation

$$n(\bar{V}, \gamma_0) = \gamma_0 : \gamma_0 = \frac{n_v(\bar{V} - \underline{V}) + \underline{n} - n_\gamma \underline{\gamma}}{1 - n_\gamma}, n_\gamma < 1$$

for each meaningful level of the NAIRU rate of employment $\bar{V} \in (0, 1)$.

7.3   Analysis of the employment subdynamics

In this section, we shall consider with increasing generality the special case of the model of the previous section where the rates $\gamma = n$ are still given exogenously ($\beta_\gamma = \beta_\pi = 0$), but where there is a delayed adjustment of labor according to the work-time within firms ($1/\beta_v > 0$) and where the "natural" rate of employment follows the rate of actual employment with some time delay ($\beta_{\bar{v}} > 0$). This leads us to a seven-dimensional system whose stability properties are investigated by starting from known results on the five-dimensional core situation ($\beta_v = \beta_{\bar{v}} = 0$), extending it to six-dimensional dynamics via $\beta_v > 0$, and then to the seven-dimensional dynamics via $\beta_{\bar{v}} > 0$. In this way we get some insights into the dynamic workings of the model as far as medium-run aspects of the labor market and the employment decisions of firms are concerned. We then consider in the next section the seven- and eight-dimensional subdynamics that come about when the endogeneity of the two rates n and γ is discussed in isolation from the aspects considered in the present section. In this way we obtain partial insights into the driving dynamic mechanisms of the full nine-dimensional dynamics of our general KT model.

Let us thus first consider the subcase of the above model that is described by

$$\beta_\gamma = 0, \gamma(0) = n = \text{const.},$$

$\beta_n = 0, n(0) = n = \text{const.},$

$\beta_{\bar{v}} = 0, \bar{V}(0) = \bar{V} = \text{const.} \in (0, 1).$

In the resulting six-dimensional subcase we therefore still assume that all natural rates are given exogenously, so that the only extension with respect to the KT model is the treatment of the variable V, which in the KT model was determined as a function of the state variables of the model and which has now itself become a state variable that is following the development of the variable $V^w = y/(Vxl)$ with a time delay according to the law $\dot{V} = \beta_v(y/(xl) - V)$.

Proposition 7.1: Assume $\beta_v = 0$ and V given by its steady-state value. Then the steady state of the five-dimensional dynamical system (7.30)–(7.34) is locally asymptotically stable if the parameters h_2, β_{w_1}, β_{w_2}, β_p, and β_π are chosen sufficiently small and the parameter β_y sufficiently large.

Proof: The dynamics (7.30)–(7.34) is (formally) of the type we have discussed as the KT model in section 6.2 of chapter 6. This implies the assertion, and in particular that the economically meaningful steady state of this dynamics is uniquely determined and of the type derived in section 6.2. ■

In respect of proposition 7.1, we make a number of observations. Firstly, there is also a close economic similarity between the above model (for the parameter value $\beta_v = 0$) and the KT model, since the present model then behaves as if there were no outsiders and thus only a rationing process with respect to insiders that leads to nominal wage reactions as they are postulated by the (reduced) type of Phillips curve of the KT model, now for the insiders solely. Secondly, due to the above proposition, the stability assertions of section 6.2 all apply to the present limit case of the above dynamics as well. They will therefore not be repeated here. Thirdly, the case $\beta_v \approx 0$ may be called the "Japanese" variant of the KT model, while the case $\beta_v \approx \infty$ could be considered as the "US" version of this dynamical system.

Proposition 7.2: Assume that the dynamic model considered in the preceding proposition 7.1 is locally asymptotically stable with respect to its economically meaningful steady state. Then the steady state of the full six-dimensional dynamics (7.30)–(7.35) with $\beta_v > 0$ (given as in the KT model and by $V_0 = \bar{V}$) is locally asymptotically stable for all parameter values β_v that are chosen sufficiently small.

Proof: Since the determinant is the product of the real parts of the eigenvalues of the underlying matrix, and since we already know that the first five eigenvalues have a negative real part for β_v equal to zero (and thus by continuity also for all values of this parameter that are chosen sufficiently small), it suffices to show that the determinant of the Jacobian J of the full six-dimensional dynamics (as always evaluated at the steady state) is positive. The new sixth eigenvalue, which was zero for $\beta_v = 0$, must then also have a negative real part (in fact it must be real in addition).

Exploiting again the many repetitions of the same or of linearly dependent terms in the structure of the matrix J, one can again easily show that the rows of the matrix that correspond to the various differential equations can be transformed to

$$\dot{u} = + \text{const.} \cdot V$$
$$\dot{l} = - \text{const.} \cdot m$$
$$\dot{m} = - \text{const.} \cdot y$$
$$\dot{\pi} = - \text{const.} \cdot \pi$$
$$\dot{y} = + \text{const.} \cdot u$$
$$\dot{V} = - \text{const.} \cdot l$$

without any change in the determinant to be investigated. Calculating the determinant of this latter system then gives with respect to the signs that are involved:

$$\det J = (-)(+)(-)(-)(-)(+)(-)(-) > 0$$

which proves the proposition. ∎

Choosing on the other hand $\beta_v = \infty$ reestablishes the KT model in its original form, since we then have $V = V^w$ always. The local asymptotic stability assertions for the five-dimensional KT model thus hold in the present six-dimensional version of it for small as well as for infinitely large adjustment speeds of the outside rate of employment to the employment needed within firms. They are thus independent of whether the burden of adjustment of employment to the level of intended production (following the state of aggregate demand with a time delay) falls on insiders or mainly on outsiders. It is an open question here whether the observations just made also hold for intermediate levels of the adjustment parameter β_v. Looking on the structure of the six-dimensional system, it appears not implausible that such an assertion can indeed be made, since the sixth dynamical law simply reappears as a component in the three other laws of motion of the six-dimensional case which, when it could be removed, would indeed cause the remaining dynamics to be of the KT type. Be that as it may, the considered six-dimensional dynamics can be characterized as a very natural and basic extension of the KT model. It makes use of very similar rules for delayed output as well as delayed labor demand adjustments (see the original formulations of the respective dynamical equations in the general presentation of the model).

Let us now turn to the seven-dimensional subcase of the full nine-dimensional dynamical model (7.30)–(7.36) that allows for adjustments in the "natural" rate of employment $\bar{V}$, i.e., to the situation:

$$\dot{\bar{V}} = \beta_{\bar{v}}(V - \bar{V}), \beta_\gamma = 0, \gamma(0) = n = \text{const.}, \beta_n = 0, n(0) = n = \text{const.}$$

This extension of the previous subdynamics implies the existence of hysteretic effects with respect to the long-run behavior of the model as the next proposition will show.

In general terms hysteresis is a property of dynamical systems. Hysteretic systems are path-dependent systems. The long-run solution of such a system does not only depend on the long-run values of the exogenous variables (as usually) but also on the initial conditions of each state variable. These systems have a long-lasting memory and are therefore "historical" systems. Loosely speaking: Where you get to is determined by how you get there. (Franz, 1990, p.2)

Proposition 7.3: Consider the seven-dimensional dynamical system (7.30)–(7.36) where $\beta_n = \beta_\gamma = 0$ holds with given initial rates $n = \gamma$. Then (1) for any choice of the NAIRU-based rate of employment $\bar{V}$ there is a unique steady-state solution for the remaining state variables as described in section 7.2. The set of economically meaningful steady states of the considered seven-dimensional dynamics is thus given by a ray in $\Re^7$; (2) there holds det $J = 0$ for the Jacobian J of the considered dynamical system at the steady state, i.e., at least one eigenvalue of the dynamical system is equal to zero; (3) apart from the resulting path dependency with respect to the values of $\bar{V}$ and l, the conditions for local asymptotic stability with respect to the above ray are the same as for the previously considered six-dimensional dynamical system if the parameter $\beta_{\bar{v}}$ is chosen sufficiently small.

Proof: (1) Obvious.

(2) The laws of motion for the state variables V and $\bar{V}$ allow removal of the expressions for the wage Phillips curve from the first four laws of motion as far as the calculation of determinants is concerned. It is then easy to see that both the m equation as well as the π equation can be further simplified and can then be shown to depend both on the state variable π solely. This makes these two equations proportional to each other and thus implies that the determinant of the Jacobian of the dynamics must be zero at the steady state.

(3) Obvious. ■

7.4   Analysis of the growth subdynamics

We now turn to the two natural seven-dimensional subcases of the above nine-dimensional dynamical model (7.30)–(7.38), each of which extends the six-dimensional core subdynamics by the endogenization of one of its "natural" rates of growth n and γ. These subcases of the general model can be obtained by the relationships shown below. Thereafter, the eight-dimensional case where both rates of growth adjust simultaneously will be investigated. Note that we assume throughout $n(V, \gamma) = \gamma$ in the adjustment rule for the natural rate of growth which leaves a general consideration of this adjustment process for later investigations.

Subcase 1:

$$\dot{n} = \beta_n(\gamma - n), \beta_{\bar{v}} = 0, \bar{V}(0) = \bar{V} = \text{const.}, \beta_\gamma = 0, \gamma(0) = \gamma = \text{const.},$$

Subcase 2:

$$\dot{\gamma} = \beta_\gamma(\cdot) + i_2(\cdot), \beta_n = 0, n(0) = n = \text{const.}, \beta_{\bar{v}} = 0, \bar{V}(0) = \bar{V}$$
$$= \text{const.}$$

These three extensions (i.e. the two seven-dimensional subcases and the eight-dimensional case) of the six-dimensional core dynamical system with sluggish adjustments of both output and employment will now be investigated one by one.

Proposition 7.4: Consider the seven-dimensional dynamical system (7.30)–(7.35), (7.38) as described under subcase 1. Then (1) the economically meaningful steady state of this dynamical system is uniquely determined and as described in the six-dimensional case (based on $n = \gamma$); (2) the determinant of the Jacobian of the seven-dimensional dynamical system evaluated at the steady state is always negative; (3) a locally asymptotically stable dynamical system in the six-dimensional case remains locally asymptotically stable in this seven-dimensional extension of the six-dimensional case for all parameter values β_n.

Proof: (1) Obvious.
(2) Obvious, since the new dynamical law induces only one nonzero (negative) entry in the last row of the Jacobian to be investigated and since the determinant of the Jacobian to be considered in the six-dimensional subcase has been shown to be positive always.
(3) Obvious. ∎

The dynamical system of subcase 1 just considered adds to the KT model with a delayed labor-market adjustment a very simple adjustment process for the natural rate of growth of the labor force which is simply assumed to adjust to the given trend term γ in the investment equation. Despite its extreme simplicity, this extension of the six-dimensional dynamics nevertheless portrays an important economic idea, namely, the view that investment is the independent "equation" in a capitalist economy and not the "equation" for natural growth. Or, put in another way, that labor adjusts to the conditions of capital accumulation, not capital accumulation to the conditions of natural growth (see Marx 1954, ch. 25, for such a view). In contrast to the situation considered in the preceding proposition we do not have hysteresis in the present extension of the core six-dimensional dynamics. This is due to the fact that the rate of natural growth must still converge to a predetermined value γ.

Proposition 7.5: Consider the seven-dimensional dynamical system (7.30)–(7.35), (7.37) as described under subcase 2. Then (1) the economically meaningful steady state of this dynamical system is uniquely determined and as described by the six-dimensional case (based on $\gamma_0 = n$); (2) the determinant of the Jacobian of the seven-dimensional dynamical system evaluated at the steady state is always negative; (3) a locally asymptotically stable dynamical system in the six-dimensional case remains locally asymptotically stable in this seven-dimensional extension of the six-dimensional case for all parameter values β_γ chosen sufficiently small.

Proof: (1) Obvious.
(2) Obvious, since the right hand side of the new dynamical law can be transformed to the form $\beta_\gamma(n - \gamma)$ as far as the calculation of determinants of Jacobians is concerned (by making use of the right hand side of the law of motion for the state variable l). This form then implies that the seven-dimensional Jacobian must have the opposite sign to the determinant of the Jacobian of the six-dimensional core dynamics and thus must be negative in sign.
(3) Obvious. ∎

The dynamical system just considered in proposition 7.5 adds to the KT model with a delayed labor-market adjustment a very simple self-referencing process for the determination of the trend rate of growth that is relevant for long-run investment decisions. Note that in this dynamical law for γ there is no reference made to the natural rate of growth n of the labor force. If the dynamics are locally asymptotically stable, the rate γ must nevertheless approach the given rate n, due to the fact that $\hat{l} \to 0$ implies $\hat{K} \to n$, which in turn then implies $\gamma \to n$. The process just described may be viewed as providing a (simple) neoclassical explanation of how these two independent rates of growth come together. It is useful to contrast this view with the also very simple Marxian view we sketched in our comments on the preceding proposition. Of course, both views must be developed further before they can be considered as sufficiently justified. Again we do not have hysteresis effects in the present extension of the core six-dimensional dynamics. This is due to the fact that the rate γ must still converge to a predetermined value n. Neither subcase 1 nor subcase 2 therefore allow for hysteresis effects, as was the case for the seven-dimensional dynamics in the previous section, which included the endogenous determination of the NAIRU-based rate of employment $\bar{V}$. The following proposition will, however, show that the combined adjustment processes for n and γ are capable of producing hysteresis now with respect to the growth rate of the economy. We thereby turn to the investigation of an important eight-dimensional subcase of the full nine-dimensional dynamical model.

Proposition 7.6: Consider the eight-dimensional dynamical system (7.30)–(7.35), (7.37), (7.38) with $\beta_{\bar{V}} = 0$. Then (1) for any choice of the trend growth rate γ in the investment function there is a unique steady-state solution for the remaining state variables of the type described in section 7.2. The set of economically meaningful steady states of the considered eight-dimensional dynamical system is thus given by a ray in $\Re^8$; (2) corresponding to the situation just described, there holds det $J = 0$ for the Jacobian J of the considered dynamical system at the steady state, and thus one eigenvalue is always zero; (3) apart from path dependency, the conditions for local asymptotic stability with respect to the above described ray are the same as for the previously considered seven-dimensional dynamics if the parameter β_γ is chosen sufficiently small.

Proof: (1) Obvious.
(2) It is sufficient to note here that the equation governing the law of motion of l can be expressed in the present case as a simple linear combination of the two laws for n and γ.
(3) Obvious. ∎

7.5   Analysis of the complete dynamical system

Finally, we come to an investigation of the full dynamical structure of the KT-model with endogenous growth and labor force participation. We here proceed in two steps: (1) the full integration of the seven-dimensional cases we have considered above, and (2) the investigation of the model with a general type of function $n(V, \gamma)$ as far as the dynamics of the natural rate of growth is concerned.

Proposition 7.7: Consider the steady state of the full nine-dimensional dynamical system (7.30)–(7.38). Then (1) for any choice of the NAIRU-based rate $\bar{V}$ and the trend growth rate γ in the investment function there is a unique steady-state solution for the remaining state variables of the type described in section 7.2. The set of economically meaningful steady states of the considered nine-dimensional dynamical system is thus given by a surface in $\mathfrak{R}^9$; (2) corresponding to the situation just described, rank $(J) = 7$ for the Jacobian J of the considered dynamics at the steady state, and thus two eigenvalues are always zero.

Proof: (1) Obvious.

(2) It is sufficient to note here again that the equation governing the law of motion of l can be expressed in the present case as a simple linear combination of the two laws for n and γ, and that in addition the further linear dependency we considered in proposition 7.3 can be shown to hold true in this case. ∎

Proposition 7.7 implies that hysteresis is now present in the model in two dimensions, concerning "natural" employment and "natural" growth. Furthermore, this dependence on historically given conditions of the long-run behavior of these magnitudes does not only apply to steady states, but also to all other attractors that may exist for this nine-dimensional nonlinear dynamical system. Since our analytical discussion has been confined to local stability analysis, however, it is unknown what these attractors may look like. Clearly this would depend on the numerous parameter constellations this high-dimensional system allows for. At present, the attractor behavior can only be further investigated by turning to some numerical simulations of the model, which are performed in the next section.

The above twofold hysteretic situation can again be reduced to a (single) hysteretic evolution of the NAIRU by way of proposition 7.8.

Proposition 7.8: Consider the full nine-dimensional dynamical system (7.30)–(7.38), but now given a function $n(V, \gamma)$ that differs from the special choice $n(V, \gamma) = \gamma$ we have considered so far. Assume, furthermore, that the equation $n(\bar{V}, \gamma_0) = \gamma_0$ has a unique positive solution γ_0 for (all meaningful) $\bar{V} \in (0, 1)$. Then (1) for any choice of the NAIRU-based rate $\bar{V}$ there is a unique steady-state solution for the remaining state variables of the type described in section 7.2. The set of economically meaningful steady states of the considered eight-dimensional dynamical system is thus given by a ray in $\mathfrak{R}^9$; (2) corresponding to the situation just described rank $(J) = 8$ for the Jacobian J of the considered dynamical system at the steady state, and thus one eigenvalue is always zero.

With this proposition we terminate the theoretical discussion of the nine-dimensional dynamical system with endogenous growth and endogenous NAIRU (and its various subdynamics). It is obvious that we have formulated with these propositions only very basic results for this extension of the KT dynamics and its various subcases. This must suffice here as an outlook on Keynesian monetary growth theory which attempts to endogenize important "natural" rates of economic theory.

7.6   Some numerical simulations

Before closing, we provide some numerical illustrations of the various dynamical systems we have considered in this chapter. We here stress once again that the full dynamical system is characterized by a number of adjustment lags of employment and of endogenous growth which together may be briefly summarized as follows:[8]

$$V \to V^w, \gamma \to \hat{K}, n \to \gamma \text{ (or } n(V, \gamma)), \bar{V} \to V.$$

In the following simulation studies these various routes of adjustment will be switched on one-by-one in the order that we have discussed them above. We will thereby be provided with quantitative impressions of the working of these various feedback mechanisms in isolation as well as in their interaction.

Simulating our model of endogenous long-run growth and employment on its various levels of generality (six-, seven-, eight-, and nine-dimensional) provides us with various scenarios of fluctuating growth, yet generally ones with an increasing amplitude of the cycle. We are here back in the situation, frequently observed throughout this book, that the intrinsically determined nonlinearities of our dynamic models are in general too weak to generate overall viability of the dynamics in the case of their local instability. Once again, we therefore have to add extrinsic nonlinearities to the structure of our models of monetary growth, and shall do this by again making use of the kinked money-wage Phillips curve of section 6.4.3 in order to show some basic numerical features of the endogenous growth models (and their limit cases) in the presence of this extrinsic nonlinearity.

Let us start with the six-dimensional core dynamical system of, in fact, no endogenous growth, but only delayed output and employment adjustments. We make use in the following of the basic parameter set provided in table 7.1, where a number of adjustment coefficients are chosen as zero in order to reflect this six-dimensional case properly.

---

[8] Note that we assume $n(V, \gamma) = \gamma$ for the adjustment rule of natural growth in the following simulations. This leaves a general consideration of this adjustment process for later investigations.

Table 7.1.

$s_c = 0.8, \delta = 0.1, y^p = 1, x = 2, \underline{n} = \underline{\gamma} = 0.05, n_0 = \gamma_0 = 0.05.$
$h_1 = 0.1, h_2 = 0.05, i_1 = 0.25, i_2 = 0.5.$
$\beta_{w_1} = 2.5, \beta_{w_2} = 2.5, \beta_p = 1, \kappa_w = 0.5, \kappa_p = 0.5.$
$\beta_{\pi_1} = 0.6, \beta_{\pi_2} = 1, \beta_n = \beta_y = \beta_{\bar{v}} = 0, \beta_y = 2, \beta_v = 2.$
$n_v = 0, n_\gamma = 1, \underline{V} = 1.$
$\mu_0 = 0.08, \mu_2 = 0.08, t^n = 0.08, \beta_m = \beta_g = 0.$

We note that the initial values of the rates $\bar{V}$, n, and γ are set equal to 1, 0.05 and 0.05, respectively, and that they do not change their value in the presently considered situation. Also, in order to avoid the system getting stuck in a depressed situation, we generally assume that there is steady-state inflation (of the kind $\hat{p}_0 = \mu_0 - n_0 > 0$), so that the kink in the Phillips curve does not apply to the steady state itself (only becoming operative at a level "somewhat below" it). Such a situation is represented, for example, through the simulation run of the model over a time horizon of 200 years displayed in figure 7.1.

We can see in this figure that the three rates $\bar{V}$, γ, and n are still kept constant. The figures also show irregular and asymmetric fluctuations (of the variable V in particular) of considerable phase length and a large amplitude, the latter being due to the high adjustment speeds that we have assumed here for the level of money wages, prices, and expectations, while the asymmetry in amplitude and time duration of depressions vs. booms is due to the kink in the Phillips curve.[9] The question arises as to how this irregular behavior will change if longer time horizons are allowed for. An example of this is shown in figure 7.2.

Extending the time horizon to 1,000 years (and beyond) thus shows that the irregularity of the fluctuations does not disappear from the dynamics. Some sort of complex dynamics seems to be generated in the present situation. This impression is confirmed by the bifurcation diagram shown in figure 7.3, which corresponds to the plots shown so far. We here see that the situation found to hold for the particular parameter value $\beta_v = 2$ holds true for all values of this parameter in the range $[0.5, 20]$. Furthermore, the attractor that is indicated by each vertical slice in this bifurcation diagram is of a fairly fixed shape with regard to the considered parameter and its range.

Before we leave the six-dimensional core dynamics of no endogenous growth, let us briefly contrast the results obtained above with the situation

[9] Note that price level deflation is not excluded from the dynamics by a corresponding kink in the price Phillips curve, so the kink in the figure top right is solely due to the kink in money-wage behavior.

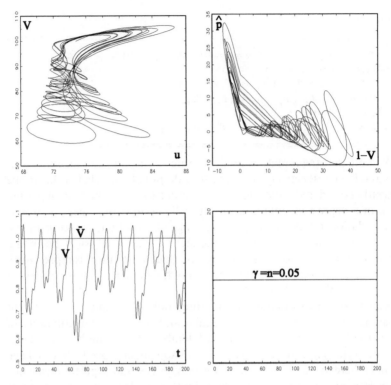

Figure 7.1   Phase plots and times series representations over a time horizon of 200 years (6D case) (see table 7.1)

where there is no inflation in the steady state. We thus now assume $\mu_0 = \mu_2 = 0.05$ in the place of $\mu_0 = \mu_2 = 0.08$. The consequence of this simple alteration in our parameter set is that there is now a continuum of steady states below the initial one, onto which the economy can settle. This is due to the fact that money wages cannot fall at each of these lower steady-state values. Though the system may thus be very far away from the NAIRU-based level $\bar{V} = 1$, it can no longer recover back to and beyond this level, because money wages cannot fall at the new steady states of the model. The economy (see figure 7.4) therefore gets stuck in a depressed state, and this in a way that no longer allows for the irregular and persistent fluctuations we observed beforehand.

The simulations we have thus far shown indicate that there is an important choice for monetary policy to be made between a situation where the economy is very stable, but maybe also (very) depressed, as in figure 7.4, and one, as in figure 7.2, where the economy in fact recovers (slowly) from each depression, but this at the cost of large and persistent fluctuations

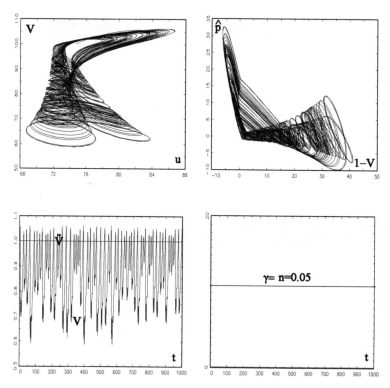

Figure 7.2 Phase plots and times series representations over a time horizon of 1,000 years (6D case) (see table 7.1)

around the original steady state (of "full" employment), depending on the degree of steady-state inflation allowed for. There is thus an important role for inflation in the steady state (due to $\mu_0 > n_0$), since it avoids the implementation of an institutional constraint in the wage–price module at this steady state which would, if operative at the steady state, alter the behavior of the model in the radical fashion shown in figure 7.4.

Let us now, however, come to the inclusion of endogenous growth into the situations of fluctuations and exogenous trend growth just considered. To do this step by step, we first consider the case of a positive adjustment parameter $\beta_\gamma = 0.2$ in an otherwise unchanged environment (and again with steady-state inflation: $\mu_0 = \mu_2 = 0.06$ now). The trend growth rate used by investors in their investment function thus now follows the actual rate of growth of the capital stock with a time delay in the way we have introduced it in section 7.2. As figures 7.5 and 7.6 suggest, these modifications of the dynamics alter its dynamical features significantly, in particular with respect to the amplitudes of the cycle.

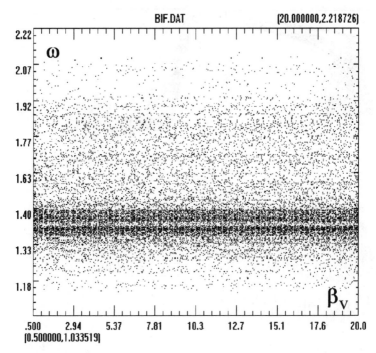

Figure 7.3   Bifurcation diagram of the 6D case for $\beta_v \in [0.5, 20]$ (see table 7.1)

Figure 7.5 shows this extended seven-dimensional dynamics over a time horizon of 220 years, and shows a transient part of it after the steady-state values have been shocked at time $t = 1$ by a 10 percent increase in the money supply. The most important thing in these figures is the movement (shown bottom right) of the "animal spirits" rate γ, and the corresponding movement in the employment rate V.

Figure 7.6 extends the time horizon shown to 1,000 years, and shows that the irregularity observed in the first 220 years is not removed from the dynamics through this large time horizon. We stress once again that assuming high adjustment speeds for all prices and quantities (as well as the kink in the Phillips curve) is responsible for the amplitudes we observe in the cycles shown (see figure 7.6). From an empirical point of view, one may therefore be inclined to reduce the corresponding parameters in size. However, the fact that in theory there are often situations where these adjustment parameters are set equal even to infinity makes it worthwhile to consider what in fact comes about in situations of flexible price and quantity adjustment.

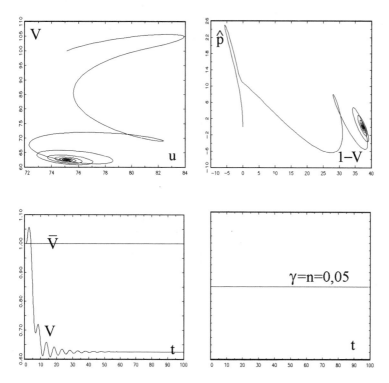

Figure 7.4 Downwardly rigid money wages at the inflationless steady state (table 7.1 with $\mu_0 = \mu_2 = 0.05\ (\ = n))$

The next step now is to allow also the rate of natural growth to adjust to the medium-run growth dynamics of the model by making it respond with a delay to the rate γ that prevails at each moment in time. The data relevant to figures 7.7 and 7.8 are summarized in table 7.2.

Figure 7.7 shows (bottom right) that the natural rate of growth n is now also moving in time, following the movement of the rate γ in an adaptive fashion. Observe also that the NAIRU-based rate $\bar{V}$ is still assumed as constant in this simulation of endogenous growth. Note finally that the amplitude of the fluctuations shown are somewhat larger than before.

Figure 7.8 considers the behavior of this dynamical system after the removal of its transient part after 1,000 years and for a period of 300 years. It shows that the presently considered situation in fact eventually gives rise solely to a somewhat complicated limit cycle behavior (with an indication of period-doubling processes). Note also that there is now hysteresis visible in the evolution of the rate n which stays below its initial steady state value of 0.05 in the time series shown.

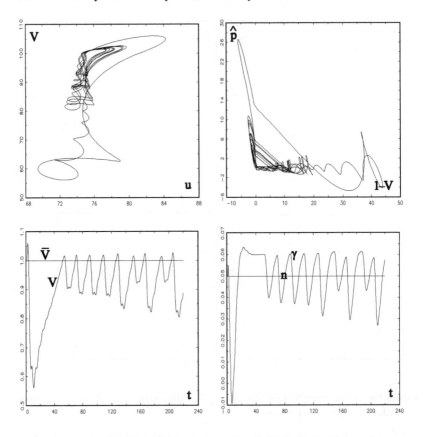

Figure 7.5   Phase plots and times series representations of endogenous "animal spirits" over a time horizon of 220 years (7D case) (see table 7.1)

The above type of limit-cycle behavior is confirmed by the bifurcation diagram in figure 7.9, drawn with respect to the parameter $\beta_v \in [0.5, 5]$. This diagram again suggests that the attracting set is (for each β_v) little more than a somewhat complicated limit cycle (at least for most values of the parameter β_v). Therefore, a similar sort of "complex" dynamics over the first 500 years may possess very different attracting sets when the transient behavior of the dynamics is removed.

Increasing the speeds of adjustment β_{w_1} and β_{w_2} of wages from 2.5 to 6, however, leads us back to complex dynamics (via period doublings) in the considered situation ($\beta_n = 0.1$ in addition) as the plots in figure 7.10 show. These are based on a transient period of 300 years (not shown), and a simulation run thereafter for 2,000 years. Fluctuations in employment, the

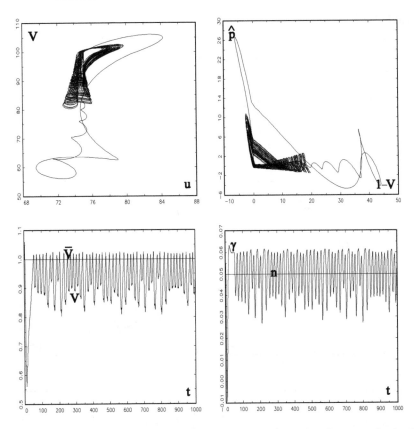

Figure 7.6 Phase plots and times series representations of endogenous "animal spirits" over a time horizon of 1,000 years (7D case)

wage share, and rates of growth are now considerably larger than before, but still within an economically viable domain. They again exhibit the irregular and now extremely asymmetric pattern in employment (and now also growth) we have already observed in figures 7.1 and 7.2, and they also again show that there is hysteresis present in evolution of the rates of growth γ and n. Note finally that the rate of price inflation can be minus 20 percent during the course of the large fluctuations shown, and that the trend growth rate of the capital stock is sometimes slightly negative.

Let us now turn to an endogenous determination of the NAIRU-based rate $\bar{V}$, and consider this situation first for growth rates γ and n that are given exogenously. We thus assume now as (modified) parameter values $\beta_{\bar{v}} = 0.1$ and $\beta_{\gamma} = \beta_n = 0$ and as adjustment speeds of wages β_{w_1} and β_{w_2} equal to 1.5 (the relevant parameter set is displayed in table 7.3). In this case

Table 7.2.

$s_c = 0.8, \delta = 0.1, y^p = 1, x = 2, \underline{n} = \gamma = 0.05, n_0 = \gamma_0 = 0.05.$
$h_1 = 0.1, h_2 = 0.05, i_1 = 0.25, i_2 = 0.5.$
$\beta_{w_1} = 2.5, \beta_{w_2} = 2.5, \beta_p = 1, \kappa_w = 0.5, \kappa_p = 0.5.$
$\beta_{\pi_1} = 0.6, \beta_{\pi_2} = 1, n_v = 0, n_y = 1, \underline{V} = 1.$
$\beta_n = 0.1, \beta_\gamma = 0.2, \beta_{\bar{v}} = 0, \beta_y = 2, \beta_v = 2.$
$\mu_0 = 0.06, \mu_2 = 0.06, t^n = 0.08, \beta_m = \beta_g = 0.$

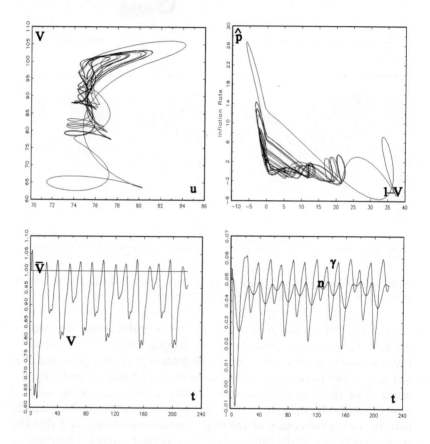

Figure 7.7   Phase plots and times series representations of endogenous "natural growth" over a time horizon of 220 years (8D case) (see table 7.2)

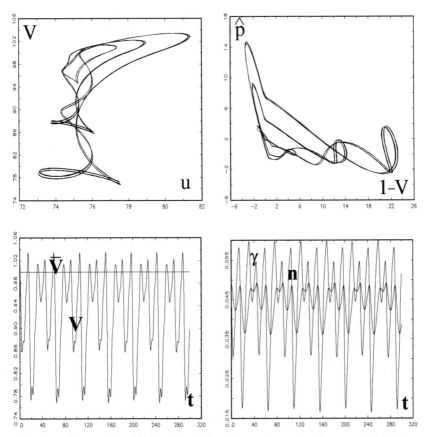

Figure 7.8   Phase plots and times series representations of endogenous "natural growth" after a transient period of 1,000 years (8D case) (see table 7.2)

we find, despite an inflationary steady-state situation, that the economy becomes more and more depressed. This is so since low employment rates deskill unemployed workers, thereby reducing the "natural" rate $\bar{V}$, which in turn permits lower and lower actual rates of employment V with respect to the working of the labor market. As figure 7.11 suggests, there is no real end to this process above the level of zero employment. In this case we thus get the result that each succeeding depression is more severe than the preceding one, with no sign that this process will ever come to a standstill.

Decreasing the adjustment speed of wages further, however, can alter this situation and remove the downturn trend in the model at some later point in time. This is shown in figure 7.12, where the adjustment speeds β_{w_1} of money wages have both been reduced to the value 1. Here, the model

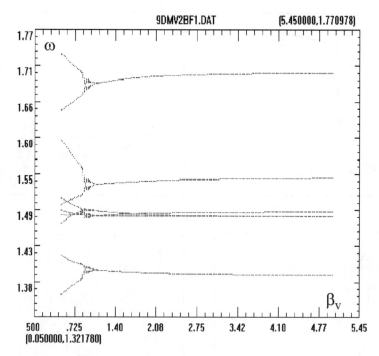

Figure 7.9 Bifurcation diagram for $\beta_v \in [0.5, 5]$ in the case of endogenous growth (8D case)

converges to a very low level of the actual as well as the NAIRU-based rate of employment, V, $\bar{V} = 0.63$ approximately, with persistent cyclical movements on the way down to this level and damped fluctuations thereafter. As other simulations have shown, there is considerable dependence on initial conditions (the size and direction of the monetary shock) in the present situation.

Finally, we consider the situation where all three rates $\bar{V}$, γ, and n are determined endogenously (figure 7.13[10]). Here, too, we get a long period of cyclical downturns now with respect to employment and growth which, however, as in the previous figure, comes to a halt after approximately 350 years, again with fluctuations that die out when the floor in the movement of the rate $\bar{V}$ has been reached. We stress here that the long-run features of the dynamics are not close to empirically observed figures. Nevertheless, the figures drastically exemplify how downturns that are longer than upturns, due to the asymmetry in the money-wage Phillips curve that is

[10] The parameters that are set to new values in this simulation run are $\beta_{w_1} = \beta_{w_2} = 2$, $\beta_v = 5$, $\beta_n = \beta_{\bar{v}} = 0.1$, $\beta_\gamma = 0.05$, $\mu_0 = 0.66$.

Table 7.3.

$s_c = 0.8, \delta = 0.1, y^p = 1, x = 2, \underline{n} = \underline{\gamma} = 0.05, n_0 = \gamma_0 = 0.05.$
$h_1 = 0.1, h_2 = 0.05, i_1 = 0.25, i_2 = 0.5.$
$\beta_{w_1} = 1.5, \beta_{w_2} = 1.5, \beta_p = 1, \kappa_w = 0.5, \kappa_p = 0.5.$
$\beta_{\pi_1} = 0.6, \beta_{\pi_2} = 1, \beta_n = \beta_\gamma = 0, \beta_{\bar{v}} = 0.1, \beta_y = 2, \beta_v = 2.$
$n_v = 0, n_\gamma = 0, \underline{V} = 1, \mu_0 = 0.1, \mu_2 = 0.1, t^n = 0.08, \beta_m = \beta_g = 0.$

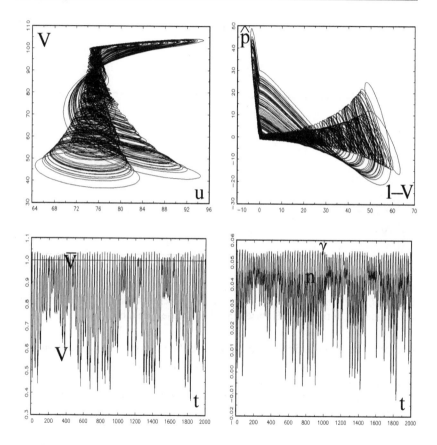

Figure 7.10 High adjustment speeds of wages and the occurrence of "complex" dynamics (8D case)

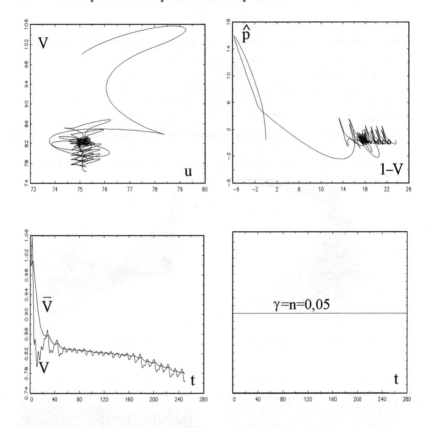

Figure 7.11 Phase plots and times series representations of an endogenous determination of the NAIRU-based rate $\bar{V}$ (7D case) (see table 7.3)

operative here in the downturns, can drag the rates of employment and the rates of growth down to levels that must be considered as highly problematic if not catastrophic. Such situations of self-enforcing depressions may have characterized to some extent the period of growth slowdown that followed the sixties and early seventies.

Let us contrast this result with a situation where the economy fluctuates in such a mild way around its inflationary steady state that the kink in the money-wage Phillips curve does not become operative. As figure 7.14 then shows, there are then no longer self-enforcing downturns, but there is here in fact a slight increase in the steady-state rate of employment, due to the path dependency of the natural rate of growth and employment. Such a situation may be (loosely) compared with the development in the sixties and seventies where in fact the growth rate of money wages did not

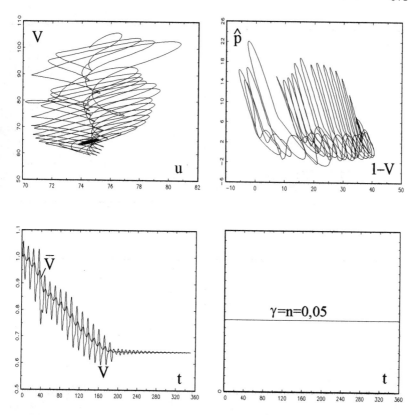

Figure 7.12 Phase plots and times series representations of an endogenous determination of the NAIRU-based rate of employment $\bar{V}$ (7D case) (table 7.3 with $\beta_{w1} = \beta_{w2} = 1$)

approach the value zero, where the kink in the Phillips curve would have become operative.

Finally, it is of interest to see what would have happened in the situation considered in figure 7.13 if the money-wage Phillips curve were not kinked, so that money wages would as easily fall in situations of underemployment as they rise in the opposite case. As figure 7.15 shows, the economy then becomes very explosive and would already be nonviable after a period of about twelve years. Again, the floor in the development of money wages is of decisive importance for the viability of the economy (though it is certainly not the only means by which such viability is achieved). The cost of this viability-generating mechanism is, however, obvious from what has been said in this section. Nevertheless, advocating downward flexibility for

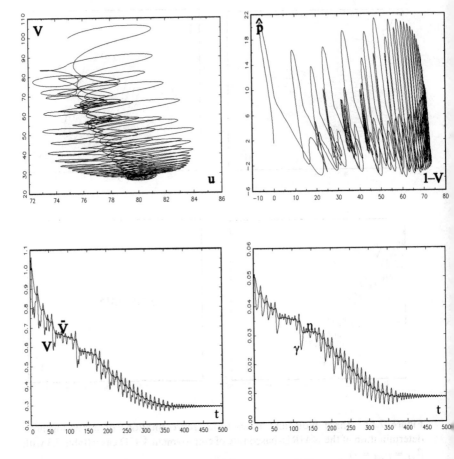

Figure 7.13 Phase plots and times series representations of an endogenous determination of "natural" rates of employment and of growth (9D case)

the behavior of money wages to be the better alternative and sound advice for economic income policies appears to be the opposite of the truth in the dynamic model considered in this chapter. This example of a dramatic lack of economic viability ends our numerical investigation of the KT model with endogenous long-run employment and growth.

7.7   Summary and directions for future research

In this book, we have provided a systematic theory of endogenous business fluctuations and growth with a hierarchical structure of integrated macro-dynamical models where each subsequent model type removed one or

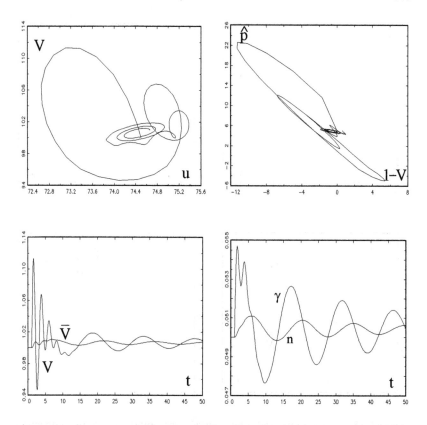

Figure 7.14   Phase plots and times series representations of small fluctuations in the level of economic activity (9D case) $(\beta_{w1} = \beta_{w2} = 0.3)$

more important limitations of the model preceding it. We have also shown that our analysis of the long run of monetary growth requires neither a given "natural" rate of growth, nor a given income distribution, nor a closure from the side of the market for goods via independent savings and investment behavior. The discussion of such closures of theories of capital accumulation provided in particular by Marglin (1984b) and Dutt (1990) is therefore no longer applicable to the general type of monetary growth theory of this book. Nevertheless, the growth models developed by Dutt and Marglin, see Dutt (1984, 1990, 1992), Marglin (1984a,b) and Marglin and Bhaduri (1991), are an important reference point for the working model of this book, and are investigated from this perspective in Flaschel (1998d).

Dore (1993), in his book on the macrodynamics of business cycles,

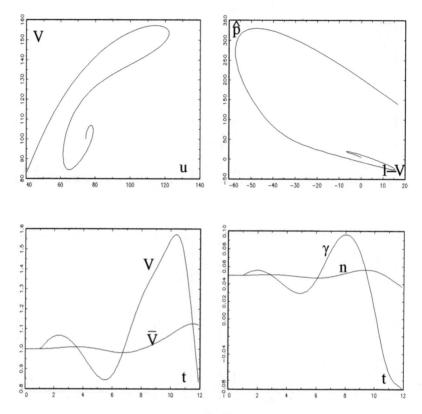

Figure 7.15 Phase plots and times series representations of an endogenous determination of "natural" rates of employment and of growth (9D case) without extrinsic nonlinearities $(\beta_{w_1} = \beta_{w_2} = 1.5, \quad \beta_v = 10, \quad \beta_n = \beta_{\bar{v}} = 0.1, \quad \beta_y = 0.2, \mu_0 = \mu_2 = 0.05)$

distinguishes basically three different approaches: The new Classical one, the new Keynesian one, and the endogenous cycle approach, where it is maintained that business cycles are inherent to a free-enterprise economy. In this respect, our approach is definitely of the third type, though the modules we have employed on the various stages toward the derivation of our working Keynesian model of monetary growth can surely be reformulated, modified, or refined from the new Keynesian perspective and others. Our approach furthermore exhibits the components discussed by Dore (1993, part III) as essential aspects for the endogenous business-cycle approach: The Kaldor (1940) trade cycle mechanism, the Benassy (1986a) IS–LM approach to labor market dynamics and the Goodwinian (1967) growth cycle model.

In this respect we have, on the one hand, refined Kaldor's dynamic multiplier process toward a Metzlerian (1941) treatment of goods-market disequilibrium and output (plus inventory) adjustments, Benassy's sluggish wage adjustment toward a sluggish adjustment of both wages and prices, as in Rose (1990), and Goodwin's growth dynamics toward a monetary growth dynamics that generalizes the Keynes–Wicksell approach of Rose (1967). On the other hand, we have only occasionally made use of the extrinsic nonlinearities employed by Kaldor (1940), Benassy (1986a), or Rose (1967) (and others), since we wanted to concentrate on the intrinsic nonlinearities at first and their implications for the generation of endogenous damped, explosive, or persistent business fluctuations. At the end of the book we have, however, stressed a crucial and very basic extrinsic nonlinearity (not unrelated to the labor-market assumptions made by Benassy, Goodwin, and Rose), namely, the kinked Phillips curve which removes the possibility of wage deflation from the business cycle in the simplest way possible. We saw there that the exclusion of nominal wage deflation had dramatic consequences for the viability of the considered monetary growth dynamics.[11]

In line with Benassy's (1986a) treatment of the dominance of the Keynesian regime in the theory of business fluctuations, we have used the Keynesian effective demand regime as determining the short-run position of the economy in each moment of time, and this for the basic Keynesian prototype model of chapter 4 and all models following it. There are a variety of mechanisms in a free-enterprise economy that, taken together, guarantee this outcome.[12] The discussion of regimes other than the Keynesian one – see Benassy (1996b), Dore (1993, ch. 10), and also Snowdon, Vane, and Wynarczyk (1994, 3.5) – thus does not apply to the Keynesian monetary growth theory here developed. In view of chapter 3 in Snowdon, Vane, and Wynarczyk (1994) we would, however, accept that our approach to monetary growth dynamics belongs to the traditional Keynesian one[13] of such growth dynamics, as, for example, that of Turnovsky (1977a), but now on the basis of a full scenario of price, wage, output, and employment adjustment processes and more.

As is obvious from Dore (1993), Snowdon, Vane, and Wynarczyk (1994), Orphanides and Solow (1990), and many other surveys on macrodynamic theory, the approach we are offering in this book has been very much neglected in the literature. There are few formalized contributions to

[11] Nonlinearities in investment behavior not unrelated to those in Kaldor (1940) have been discussed in chapters 3 and 4 in their role of generating persistent real or even monetary growth cycles (see Skott 1991, however, on the difficulties of incorporating Kaldor's trade cycle theory into the context of a growing economy).

[12] These have been or could be incorporated into our monetary growth framework.

[13] These have rarely been considered in the literature.

a Keynesian theory of monetary growth in general, whether of neo-Keynesian, new Keynesian or post-Keynesian type.[14] We hope in this book to have laid the foundations of such a theory, on the basis of which the contributions of these various schools of thought can be evaluated and, when considered as important, be integrated into the present general framework of the dynamics of Keynesian monetary growth, based on work by Kaldor (1940, 1956), Metzler (1941), Goodwin (1967), Rose (1967, 1990), Tobin (1975), Turnovsky (1977a), Malinvaud (1980), Sargent (1987, part I), and their discussion in the literature. To integrate these partial views on economic dynamics into a consistent whole was one of the main aims of this book, and will continue to be our aim with respect to further extensions of the framework presented here.[15]

Let us therefore review in more detail what has been done in this book and what is required of future work in this framework. We have considered in this final chapter a more refined treatment of the labor market, outside and inside the firm, and have endogenized trend growth in the context of the KT model of the preceding chapter, i.e., in the presence of a simple, sluggish adjustment process of quantities besides the sluggish adjustment of wages and prices. We have seen that quite new dynamic patterns are established through these extensions of the KT model of monetary growth. In this way, the final step of our hierarchy of Keynesian models of monetary growth was reached, though so far not in such a way that the various extensions, presented in chapters 4–6 and this chapter, have all been combined into one single large model. These extensions have concerned factor substitution and technological change, wage taxation and forward-looking expectations of p-star type, averages of wage and price inflation, Metzlerian inventory adjustment processes, and, in this chapter, endogenous long-run rates of growth and employment and further labor-market adjustment processes. The obtained structural form of our Keynesian model of monetary growth, when everything is put together, is therefore already of a fairly advanced type, since it allows for

- various types of delayed adjustment processes in prices, wages, quantities, inventories, and employment;
- delayed adjustments of inflationary expectations of households and firms (with forward- and backward-looking components) and in sales expectations of firms;
- under- or overutilization of the workforce as well as the capital stock, with demand pressure effects on wage inflation and price inflation, respectively;

---

[14] See again Dore (1993), Snowdon, Vane, and Wynarczyk (1994) for details on these schools of thought.   [15] See Chiarella et al. (1998, 1999), Chiarella and Flaschel (1998f).

- smooth factor substitution, again coupled with under- or overemployment of the capital stock, where one interprets the marginal wage cost barrier of output expansions as a principle that (when approached and passed) speeds up investment and prices, but does not limit production in the strict sense of non-Walrasian temporary equilibrium theory;
- aggregate investment depending on both relative profitability and the rate of capacity utilization;
- Harrod-neutral technical change coupled with an endogenous determination of the trend term of investment and of labor force growth;
- taxation of labor and capital income categories (but not yet taxation of firms or of wealth, or value added taxes, payroll taxes, and the like);[16]
- endogenous determination of the long-run rate of employment (but not yet of the long-run rate of capacity utilization).

Of course, all these aspects or extensions of the basic Keynesian prototype model of monetary growth have to be integrated with each other into a consistent whole (to be done in a fairly obvious way as chapters 4–7 should have made clear) when one wants to provide a truly general (integrated) model of Keynesian dynamics of a growing monetary economy. Furthermore, such a general theoretical framework and model should now be ready for macroeconometric model building and its application to actual economies which, in addition, demands that it must be reformulated as an open economy. Providing such a model type for open economies surely indicates one strand for future progress in the modeling of Keynesian monetary growth with both underutilized labor and capital, and its application to the study of actual economies. Here in fact work in progress already exists, see Chiarella et al. (1998, 1999), which when finished will provide exactly this type of modeling for small open, large open, and interacting open economies, including detailed comparisons with macroeconometric models of this type as the one of Powell and Murphy (1997) for the Australian economy.

Yet, there are further aspects of our general Keynesian theory of monetary growth that may require a significant overhaul of the modules we have employed so far for describing this approach to growth theory, in particular in view of the numerous contributions to macrodynamic theory of the recent past.[17]

There is for example the approach to the theory of unemployment by Layard, Nickell, and Jackman (1991) and also by Carlin and Soskice (1990) (to some extent related to earlier, but nevertheless significantly different,

---

[16] See Chiarella et al. (1998) for the extensive treatment of government taxation and transfers with respect to workers, asset holders, and firms.

[17] A to some extent incomplete survey on this literature is provided by Snowdon, Vane, and Wynarczyk (1994).

work by Rowthorn 1980) with, on the one hand, their thorough micro foundations of wage- and price-setting behavior, but, on the other hand, their restricted modeling of the macroeconomic feedback structure (which allows for the operation of the stabilizing Keynes effect solely). Nevertheless, these authors have surely provided an important alternative of the dynamic interaction of wages and prices as we have formulated it so far.[18] We add that Rowthorn's (1980, ch. 6) original model of the distributional conflict and inflation in a monetary framework is reformulated and contrasted with the fundamental monetarist model of inflation and unemployment in Flaschel (1993, ch. 5) and Flaschel and Groh (1996a, ch. 4).

There is, furthermore, extensive work by Skott (1989a,b, 1991) which treats effective demand and the conflict over income distribution from a perspective not unrelated to the Keynes–Wicksell monetary growth model of this book, yet integrates this perspective with post-Keynesian and neo-Marxian approaches of the literature.[19] We thus see that the Keynes–Wicksell approach to a supply-side determined Keynesian theory of effective demand and growth and its implications for the theory of inflation is far from being a subject of the past, but in fact is further refined through the introduction of a micro-founded output expansion function into the historically first formulation of Keynesian monetary growth dynamics.

There is, as another example, the work by Lance Taylor (see for example Taylor 1983, 1984, 1991), with the stress it lays on financial markets as well as on the distributional conflict and its impacts on output and inflation (see also Dutt 1984, 1990, 1992 for a treatment of this latter topic in the context of growing economies). A fairly general formulation of the role of financial markets along Tobinian lines is furthermore provided in Franke and Semmler (1999), extending earlier approaches of Franke and Semmler on financial markets, an approach that in our view can be integrated with the analysis presented in this book in a fairly direct way. Aspects of the structural approach to macrodynamics of Taylor, Dutt, and others, which has also been applied to less developed countries, are brought together in the volume edited by Epstein and Gintis (1995), where various theories of sustainable economic growth are discussed and evaluated, also from the empirical perspective.

There is the literature on endogenous growth which has revitalized the various approaches on the production of human knowledge and quality improvements, see Barro and Sala-i-Martin (1995) and Aghion and Howitt (1998), for example. This type of endogenous growth theory is reconsidered

---

[18] See also Dixon and Rankin (1995).
[19] See also Flaschel, Franke, and Semmler (1997) on this approach and its relationships to models of AD–AS growth and Flaschel (1998c) for a treatment of his work from the perspective of the general Keynes–Wicksell model we have developed and investigated in chapter 3 of this book.

from a Keynesian perspective in Flaschel and Groh (1996a).

There is, furthermore, the vast literature on real business cycle models, for closed as well as open economies, on their theoretical relevance and their empirical validity, and their extension to include nominal or real rigidities and monopolistic competition (see Hénin 1995 for example).

This varied set of approaches, as well as further ones, to modern macro-dynamic model building are explored, extended, to some extent integrated, and put into perspective in Chiarella et al. (1999). This work in particular shows how various supply bottlenecks can be integrated into the working Keynesian model of the present book, thereby adding a complete and coherent treatment of large business swings which can run into such supply bottlenecks. The Keynesian dynamical system (still of traditional type) so obtained thus then allows for regime switching in particular circumstances. Its strengths and weaknesses are compared with the competing approaches of the new Classical and the new Keynesian variety. Furthermore, recent contributions of Keynes–Wicksell type are also treated extensively, generalized, and compared with the Keynes–Metzler approach to monetary growth, as well as post-Keynesian ones and their particular treatments of the conflict about income distribution, financial markets, and more. Flaschel (1998f), therefore, puts into perspective what has been achieved in the present volume by its systematic reconstruction and hierarchical development of integrated Keynesian models of monetary growth.

There is, finally, the literature on macroeconometric model building (see Bodkin, Klein, and Marwah 1991 and Whitley 1994 for recent surveys on this literature). We have already stressed in this regard the Murphy model for the Australian economy as it is presented in Powell and Murphy (1997). This model of a small open economy is fairly close in its theoretical structure to the (closed economy) working model, and its various extensions, that we have introduced and analyzed in this book and which will be analyzed in our future work in the way we have indicated above (see Chiarella et al. 1998). There are, of course, many other important macro-econometric models of (larger) open economies, such as the Fair-model for the US economy (see Fair 1994 for a detailed presentation and review of his work on macroeconometric model building [also in the multi-country context], and Godley and Anyadike-Danes 1987, Godley 1998; see also Godley and Cripps 1983 for a textbook presentation of such an approach, and the Westphal model for the German economy in Dieckmann and Westphal 1995). These models are, however, generally much larger than the Murphy model for the Australian economy, as presented in a very detailed way in Powell and Murphy (1997), and therefore also less close to the theoretical working model developed in this book and to be developed in our future work.

In view of the foregoing discussion, further extensions of the working

Keynesian monetary growth model of this book thus could and will involve the following aspects which would lead to a further improvement of its various sectors and the modules:

1   *The household sector, and there in particular:*
(a) The distinction between short-term and long-term bonds by which cash-management processes and the treatment of long-term credit relationships can be distinguished from each other, implying the existence of a term structure of interest rates for the model.
(b) A more advanced and less "tranquil" asset structure on the asset markets and an explicit treatment of expected capital gains for equities as well as long-term bonds.
(c) The existence of chartist and fundamentalist groups of asset owners, and thus of heterogeneous expectation formation processes.
(d) Imperfect substitutability between all assets and the inclusion of a dynamic portfolio balance approach as in Turnovsky (1995).
(e) A more advanced theory of money demand and of processes of cash management.
(f) More advanced concepts of perceived disposable income (as these were, for example, considered in chapter 2).
(g) Positive savings out of wages ($s_w > 0$) and further differentiated saving habits and their implications for the accumulation of financial assets.
(h) Intertemporal aspects and micro foundations of household behavior.

2   *The sector of firms, and there in particular:*
(a) More complex technological relationships in production.
(b) A more elaborate theory of investment and of its financing by retained earnings or the issuing of new equities or by bank loans.
(c) Debt financing and money holdings of firms.
(d) Further intertemporal aspects and micro foundations of the behavior of firms.
(e) An endogenous treatment of the "normal" rate of capacity utilization introduced in chapter 4.
(f) Micro foundations and modifications of the price-level Phillips curve with its demand-pull and cost-push components.
(g) Micro foundations of quantity adjustments, and in particular the inventory adjustment behavior of firms.

3   *The government sector, and there in particular:*
(a) The introduction of more elaborate fiscal and monetary (and interest rate) policy rules.

(b) An active debt policy of the government (and marketing difficulties in the sale of new bonds $\dot{B}$).

(c) Further intertemporal aspects in the behavior of the government and the central bank.

(d) Problems for policy coordination.

4   *The wage–price module of the models*:

(a) Further improvements in the price and wage adjustment rules to be based on micro-founded target levels for prices as well as nominal wages.

(b) More advanced expectations formation mechanism and forecasting rules of backward- and/or forward-looking type (chartist time series methods and fundamentalist theory based types of behavior).

5   *Discrete time analysis*:

(a) Discrete time formulations of the considered models with an exact dating of all activities and the expectations to which they give rise.

(b) A more thorough discussion and formulation of the various budget restraints in discrete time as well as in the continuous time limit.

(c) The role of lags in economic dynamics.

(d) The integration of stochastic elements into certain behavioral equations, and thus the inclusion of stochastic shocks into the endogenous and so far deterministic theories of monetary growth, inflation, and business fluctuations.

6   *Open economies*:

(a) The treatment of open economies (small, large, and interacting ones) with trade in goods as well as in financial assets which integrates the achievements in points 1 to 5 above.

(b) A detailed comparison with, and theoretical reflection of, prominent econometric models of such economies.

(c) Monetary and fiscal policy issues and feedback policy rules in open economies.

(d) The comparison of theoretical feedback analysis and the implied dynamic patterns with those generated from macroeconometric simulation studies.

We have already referred to work in progress, which extends the presently achieved level of generality of the dynamics of Keynesian monetary growth, inflation and endogenous fluctuations to isolated or interacting open economies, in Chiarella and Flaschel (1998c–f), with respect to macroeconometric model building in Chiarella et al. (1998) and Flaschel,

Gong, and Semmler (1998), and with respect to alternative approaches to Keynesian and related macrodynamics in Flaschel (1998a–d), Chiarella et al. (1999), Flaschel (1998a–d), approaches which are there investigated from the integrated perspective we have developed in this book.[20]

These extensions include consideration of less tranquil financial markets (which distinguish short- from long-term bonds, equities, and bank loans to firms), further supply side problems, a more advanced treatment of heterogeneous households and their income distribution, modern government policy feedback rules,[21] and a more detailed description of the employment, pricing and investment decisions of firms. In this way we ultimately hope to provide a Keynesian theory of business fluctuations, inflation, and growth which, on the one hand, is consistent in its use of economic dimensions, budget restraints, and behavioral relationships and which, on the other hand, is general and transparent enough to provide a sound basis for the understanding of structural macroeconometric model building and applied economic theory. At the same time we hope to provide a specific answer to the views that are expressed in Blanchard (1997), Blinder (1997), Eichenbaum (1997), Solow (1997), and Taylor (1997) concerning the question "Is there a core to practical macroeconomics that we should all believe?"

[20] The numerical analysis of all these model types is in particular grounded on Chiarella, Flaschel, and Khomin (1998).
[21] See here also Flaschel and Groh (1996b).

References

Aghion, P. and P. Howitt (1998) *Endogenous Growth Theory.* Cambridge, MA: MIT Press

Akerlof, G.A. and J.E. Stiglitz (1969) Capital, wages and structural unemployment. *Economic Journal, 79, 269–281*

Allen, C. and S. Hall (1997) *Macroeconomic Modelling in a Changing World.* New York John Wiley & Sons

Allen, H. and M.P. Taylor (1990) Chart analysis and the foreign exchange market. *Review of Futures Markets, 9, 288–319*

Andronov, A.A., A.A. Vitt and S.E. Chaikin (1966) *Theory of Oscillators.* Oxford Pergamon Press

Arrowsmith, D.K. and C.M. Place (1990), *Ordinary Differential Equations.* London Chapman and Hall

Asada, T. (1991) On a mixed competitive-monopolistic macrodynamic model in a monetary economy. *Journal of Economics, 54, 33–53*

Barro, R. (1974) Are government bonds net wealth? *Journal of Political Economy,* 82, 1095–1117

(1994a) *Macroeconomics.* New York John Wiley

(1994b) The aggregate-supply aggregate-demand model. *Eastern Economic Journal, 20, 1–6*

Barro, R. and X. Sala-i-Martin (1995) *Economic Growth.* New York: McGraw-Hill

Benassy, J.-P. (1986a) A non-Walrasian model of the business cycle. In R. Day and G. Eliasson (eds.), *The Dynamics of Market Economies.* Amsterdam: North-Holland.

(1986b) *Macroeconomics. An Introduction to the Non-Walrasian Approach.* New York Academic Press

Benhabib, J. and T. Miyao (1981) Some new results on the dynamics of the generalized Tobin model. *International Economic Review, 22, 589–596*

Blanchard, O.J. (1981) Output, the stock market, and interest rates. *American Economic Review, 71, 132–143*

(1997) Is there a core of usable macroeconomics? *American Economic Review, Papers and Proceedings, 87, 244–246*

Blanchard, O.J. and S. Fischer (1989) *Lectures on Macroeconomics.* Cambridge, MA: MIT Press

Blanchard, O.J. and C.M. Kahn (1980) The solution of linear difference models under rational expectations. *Econometrica,* 48, 1305–1311

Blanchard, O. and L.F. Katz (1997) What we know and do not know about the natural rate of unemployment. *Journal of Economic Perspectives,* 11, 51–72

Blanchflower, D.G. and A.J. Oswald (1990) The wage curve. *Scandinavian Journal of Economics, 92, 215–235*

(1994) The Wage Curve. Cambridge, MA: MIT Press

(1995) An introduction to the wage curve. *Journal of Economic Perspectives,* 9, 153–167

Blinder, A.S. (1990) *Inventory Theory and Consumer Behavior.* Hemel Hempstead: Harvester Wheatsheaf

(1997) Is there a core of practical macroeconomics that we should all believe? *American Economic Review, Papers and Proceedings,* 87, 240–243

Bodkin, R., L. Klein and K. Marwah (1991) *A History of Macroeconometric Model-Building.* Aldershot: Edward Elgar

Brems, H. (1980) *Inflation, Interest, and Growth.* Lexington, MA D.C. Heath

Brock, W.A. and C.H. Hommes (1997) A rational route to randomness. *Econometrica,* 65, 1059–1095

Brock, W.A. and A.G. Malliaris (1989) *Differential Equations, Stability and Chaos in Dynamic Economics.* Amsterdam North Holland

Buiter, W. (1984) Saddlepoint problems in continuous time rational expectations models: a general method and some macrodynamic examples. *Econometrica,* 52, 665–680

Burmeister, E. (1980) On some conceptual issues in rational expectations modelling. *Journal of Money, Credit and Banking,* 12, 217–228

Burmeister, E. and R. Dobell (1970) *Mathematical Theories of Economic Growth.* New York: Macmillan

Cagan, P. (1967) The monetary dynamics of hyperinflation. In Milton Friedman (ed.), *Studies in the Quantity Theory of Money.* Chicago: University of Chicago Press

(1979) *Persistent Inflation. Historical and Policy Essays.* New York: Columbia University Press

(1991) Expectations in the German hyperinflation reconsidered. *Journal of International Money and Finance,* 10, 552–560

Carlin, W. and D. Soskice (1990) *Macroeconomics and the Wage Bargain.* Oxford: Oxford University Press

Chiarella, C. (1986) Perfect foresight models and the dynamic instability problem from a higher viewpoint. *Economic Modelling,* 3, 283–292

(1990) *The Elements of a Nonlinear Theory of Economic Dynamics.* Berlin: Springer Verlag

Chiarella, C. and P. Flaschel (1995) Keynesian monetary growth dynamics: the missing prototype. In J. Flemmig (ed.), *Moderne Makroökonomik. Eine kritische Bestandsaufnahme.* Marburg: Metropolis-Verlag, 345–411

(1996a) Real and monetary cycles in models of Keynes–Wicksell type. *Journal of Economic Behavior and Organisation,* 30, 327–351

(1996b) An integrative approach to prototype 2D-macromodels of growth, price and inventory dynamics. *Chaos, Solitons & Fractals*, 7, 2105–2133

(1998a) Some policy experiments in a complete Keynesian model of monetary growth with sluggish price and quantity adjustments. To appear in W.A. Barnett, C. Chiarella, S. Keen, R. Marks, and H. Schnabl (eds.), *Commerce, Complexity and Evolution*. Cambridge: Cambridge University Press

(1998b) Dynamics of "natural" rates of growth and employment. *Macroeconomic Dynamics*, 2, 345–368

(1998c) An integrative approach to disequilibrium growth dynamics in open economies. Discussion paper, University of Bielefeld

(1998d) Keynesian monetary growth dynamics in open economies. *Annals of Operations Research*, 89, 35–59

(1998e) "High order" disequilibrium growth dynamics: theoretical aspects and numerical features. *Journal of Economic Dynamics and Control* (special issue)

(1998f) *Disequilibrium Growth Dynamics in Open Economies*. Heidelberg: Springer Verlag

(2000) Stability properties of high-dimensional AS–AD disequilibrium growth dynamics. Working paper, School of Finance and Economics, University of Technology, Sydney

Chiarella, C., P. Flaschel, G. Groh, C. Köper and W. Semmler (1998) *Modern Macroeconometric Model Building: Theory, Numerical Analysis and Applications*. Bielefeld/Sydney: Book Manuscript

Chiarella, C., P. Flaschel, G. Groh and W. Semmler (1999) *Disequilibrium, Growth and Labor Market Dynamics: Macroperspectives*. Heidelberg: Springer Verlag

Chiarella, C., P. Flaschel and A. Khomin (1998) *Numerical Simulation of High Order Macrodynamic Systems: Tools and Results*. University of Technology, Sydney: Book Manuscript

Chiarella, C. and Khomin (1999) Adaptively evolving expectations in models of monetary dynamics: the fundamentalists forward looking. *Annals of Operations Research*, 89, 21–34

Chiarella, C. and H.-W. Lorenz (1996) The nonlinear generalized Tobin model. University of Technology, Sydney, mimeo; revised as The dynamics of the nonlinear generalised Tobin model. Working paper, School of Finance and Economics, University of Technology, Sydney, 2000

Cross, R.B. (1987) Hysteresis and instability in the natural rate of unemployment. *Scandinavian Journal of Economics*, 89, 71–89

(1995) (ed.) *The Natural Rate of Unemployment*. Cambridge: Cambridge University Press.

Dieckmann, O. and U. Westphal (1995) *Sysifo: Ein ökonmetrisches Modell der deutschen Volkswirtschaft*. Hamburg Dr. Siegel & Partner

Dixon, H.D. and N. Rankin (1995) (eds.) *The New Macroeconomics: Imperfect Markets and Policy Effectiveness*. Cambridge: Cambridge University Press

Dore, M. (1993) *The Macrodynamics of Business Cycles: A Comparative Evaluation*. Oxford: Blackwell

Dornbusch, R. (1976) Expectations and exchange rate dynamics. *Journal of Political Economy*, 84, 1161–1176

386   References

Dutt, A. (1984) Stagnation, income distribution, and monopoly power. *Cambridge Journal of Economics,* 8, 25–40
(1990) *Growth, Distribution, and Uneven Development.* Cambridge: Cambridge University Press
(1992) On the long-run stability of capitalist economies: implications of a model of growth and distribution. University of Notre Dame, mimeo
Eichenbaum, M. (1997) Some thoughts on practical stabilization policy. *American Economic Review, Papers and Proceedings,* 87, 236–239
Epstein, G. and H. Gintis (1995) *Macroeconomic Policy after the Conservative Era: Studies in Investment, Saving and Finance.* Cambridge: Cambridge University Press
Fair, R. (1994) *Testing Macroeconometric Models.* Cambridge, MA: Harvard University Press
(1997a) Testing the NAIRU model for the United States. Yale University, mimeo
(1997b) Testing the NAIRU model for 27 countries. Yale University, mimeo
Ferri, P. and E. Greenberg (1989) *The Labor Market and Business Cycle Theories.* Heidelberg: Springer Verlag
Fischer, S. (1972) Keynes–Wicksell and neoclassical models of money and growth. *American Economic Review,* 62, 880–890
Flaschel, P. (1984) Some stability properties of Goodwin's growth cycle model. *Zeitschrift für Nationalökonomie,* 44, 63–69
(1993) *Macrodynamics: Income Distribution, Effective Demand and Cyclical Growth.* Bern: Verlag Peter Lang
(1998a) On the dominance of the Keynesian regime in disequilibrium growth theory: a note. To appear in *Journal of Economics*
(1998b) Disequilibrium growth theory with insider/outsider effects: a note. To appear in *Structural Change and Economic Dynamics*
(1998c) Corridor stability and viability in economic growth. Discussion paper, University of Bielefeld
(1998d) Keynes–Marx and Keynes–Wicksell models of monetary growth: a framework for future analysis. To appear in *Review of Political Economy*
Flaschel, P., Franke, R. and W. Semmler (1997) *Dynamic Macroeconomics Instability, Fluctuations and Growth in Monetary Economies.* Cambridge, MA: MIT Press
Flaschel, P., Gong, G. and W. Semmler (1998) A Keynesian based econometric framework for studying monetary policy rules. University of Bielefeld, mimeo
Flaschel, P. and G. Groh (1995) The Classical growth cycle: reformulation, simulation and some facts. *Economic Notes,* 24, 293–326
(1996a) *Keynesianische Makroökonomik: Unterbeschäftigung, Inflation und Wachstum.* Heidelberg: Springer Verlag
(1996b) The stabilizing potential of policy rules in Keynesian monetary growth dynamics. *Systems Analysis – Modelling – Simulation,* 23, 39–72
Flaschel, P. and R. Sethi (1996) Classical dynamics in a general model of Keynes–Wicksell type. *Structural Change and Economic Dynamics,* 7, 401–428
(1999) The stability of models of monetary growth: implications of nonlinearity.

Economic Modelling, 16, 221–233

Flood, D. and P. Lowe (1995) Inventories and the business cycle. *Economic Record,* 71, 27–39

Franke, R. (1992a) Stable, unstable, and cyclical behaviour in a Keynes–Wicksell monetary growth model. *Oxford Economic Papers,* 44, 242–256

(1992b) Inflation and distribution in a Keynes–Wicksell model of the business cycle. *European Journal of Political Economy,* 8, 599–624

(1996) A Metzlerian model of inventory growth cycles. *Structural Change and Economic Dynamics,* 7, 243–262

Franke, R. and T. Asada (1993) A Keynes–Goodwin model of the business cycle. *Journal of Economic Behavior and Organization,* 24, 273–295

Franke, R. and T. Lux (1993) Adaptive expectations and perfect foresight in a nonlinear Metzler model of the inventory cycle. *Scandinavian Journal of Economics,* 95, 355–363

Franke, R. and W. Semmler (1999) Bond rate, loan rate and Tobin's q in a temporary equilibrium model of the financial sector. To appear in *Metroeconomica*

Frankel, J.A. and K. Froot (1987) Using survey data to test standard propositions regarding exchange rate expectations. *American Economic Review,* 77, 133–153

(1990) Chartists, fundamentalists and trading in the foreign exchange market. *American Economic Review,* 80, 181–185

Franz, W. (1990) *Hysteresis Effects in Economic Models.* Heidelberg: Physica Verlag

Friedman, B. and F. Hahn (1990) (eds.) *Handbook of Monetary Economics.* Amsterdam: North-Holland

Fujino, S. (1974) *A Neokeynesian Theory of Inflation and Economic Growth.* Heidelberg: Springer Verlag

Galbraith, J.K. (1997) Time to ditch the NAIRU. *Journal of Economic Perspectives,* 11, 93–108.

Gale, D. (1983) *Money in Disequilibrium.* Cambridge: Cambridge University Press

Gandolfo, G. (1997) *Economic Dynamics.* Heidelberg: Springer Verlag

Gantmacher, F.R. (1959), *Applications of the Theory of Matrices.* New York: Interscience Publishers

George, D.A.R. and L.T. Oxley (1985) Structural stability and model design. *Economic Modelling,* 2, 307–316

Godley, W. (1998) Money and credit in a Keynesian model of income determination. Jerome Levy Economics Institute, New York: mimeo

Godley, W. and M. Anyadike-Danes (1987) A stock-adjustment model of income determination with inside money and private debt with some preliminary empirical results for the United States. In M. deCecco and J.-P. Fitoussi (eds.), *Monetary Theory and Economic Institutions.* New York: St. Martin's Press

Godley, W. and F. Cripps (1983) *Macroeconomics.* Oxford: Oxford University Press

Goldman, S.M. (1972) Hyper inflation and the rate of growth in the money supply. *Journal of Economic Theory,* 5, 250–257

Goodwin, R.M. (1967) A growth cycle. In C.H. Feinstein (ed.), *Socialism, Capitalism and Economic Growth.* Cambridge: Cambridge University Press, 54–58

Gordon, R. (1997) The time-varying NAIRU and its implications for economic policy. *Journal of Economic Perspectives,* 11, 11–32

Grandville, O. de la (1986) Dynamics and stability in IS–LM model: a reexamination. *Journal of Macroeconomics,* 8, 31–41

Groth, C. (1988) IS–LM dynamics and the hypothesis of combined adaptive forward-looking expectations. In P. Flaschel and M. Krüger (eds.), *Recent Approaches to Economic Dynamics.* Bern: Verlag Peter Lang, 251–265

(1992) Keynesian-monetarist dynamics and the corridor: a note. University of Copenhagen, mimeo

(1993) Some unfamiliar dynamics of a familiar macro model. *Journal of Economics,* 58, 293–305

Guckenheimer, J. and P. Holmes (1983) *Nonlinear Oscillations, Dynamical Systems and Bifurcations of Vector Fields.* Heidelberg: Springer Verlag

Hadjimichalakis, M.G. (1971a) Money, expectations and dynamics: an alternative view. *International Economic Review,* 12, 381–402

(1971b) Equilibrium and disequilibrium growth with money: the Tobin models. *Review of Economic Studies,* 38, 457–479

(1973) On the effectiveness of monetary policy as a stabilization device. *Review of Economic Studies,* 40, 561–570

(1981a) The Rose–Wicksell model: inside money, stability and stabilization policies. *Journal of Macroeconomics,* 3, 369–390

(1981b) Expectations of the "myopic perfect foresight" variety in monetary dynamics. *Journal of Economic Dynamics and Control,* 3, 157–176

Hadjimichalakis, M.G. and K. Okuguchi (1979) The stability of a generalized Tobin model. *Review of Economic Studies,* 46, 175–178

Hahn, F. and R. Solow (1995) *A Critical Essay on Modern Macroeconomic Theory.* Cambridge, MA: MIT Press

Hairer E., S.P. Nørsett and G. Wanner (1987) *Solving Ordinary Differential Equations I: Nonstiff Problems.* Heidelberg: Springer Verlag

Hayakawa, H. (1979) Real purchasing power in the neoclassical growth model. *Journal of Macroeconomics,* 1, 19–31

(1983) Rationality of liquidity preferences and the neoclassical growth model. *Journal of Macroeconomics,* 5, 495–501

(1984) A dynamic generalization of the Tobin model. *Journal of Economic Dynamics and Control,* 7, 209–231

Heap, H.S. (1980) Choosing the wrong natural rate: accelerating inflation or decelerating employment and growth. *Economic Journal,* 90, 611–620

Hénin, P.-Y. (1995) (ed.) *Advances in Business Cycle Research.* Heidelberg: Springer Verlag

Hénin, P.-Y. and P. Michel (1982) *Croissance et accumulation en déséquilibre.* Paris: Economica

Hicks, J. (1974) Real and monetary factors in economic fluctuations. *Scottish Journal of Political Economy,* 21, 205–214

Hirsch, M.W. and S. Smale (1974) *Differential Equations, Dynamical Systems, and Linear Algebra.* New York: Academic Press

Ito, T. (1980) Disequilibrium growth theory. *Journal of Economic Theory*, 23, 380–409

Iwai, K. (1981) *Disequilibrium Dynamics*. New Haven: Yale University Press

Johnson, H.G. (1966) The neoclassical one-sector growth model: a geometrical exposition and extension to a monetary economy. *Economica*, 33, 265–287

(1967a) Money in a neoclassical one sector growth model. In H.G. Johnson, *Essays in Monetary Economics*. Cambridge, MA: Harvard University Press

(1967b) The neutrality of money in growth models: a reply. *Economica*, 34, 73–74

Jones, H.G. (1975) *An Introduction to Modern Theories of Economic Growth*. London: Thomas Nelson & Sons

Kaldor, N. (1940) A model of the trade cycle. *Economic Journal*, 50, 78–92

(1956) Alternative theories of distribution. *Review of Economic Studies*, 23, 83–100

Karakitsos, E. (1992) *Macrosystems: The Dynamics of Economic Policy*. Oxford: Basil Blackwell

Kearney, C. and R. MacDonald (1985) Asset markets and the exchange rate: a structural model of the sterling–dollar rate, 1972–1982. *Journal of Economic Studies*, 12, 3–20

Keynes, J.M. (1936) *The General Theory of Employment, Interest and Money*. New York: Macmillan

Khibnik, A., Y. Kuznetsov, V. Levitin and E. Nikolaev (1993) Continuation techniques and interactive software for bifurcation analysis of ODEs and iterated maps. *Physica D*, 62, 360–371

Klundert, T. van de and A. van Schaik (1990) Unemployment persistence and the loss of productive capacity: a Keynesian approach. *Journal of Macroeconomics*, 12, 363–380.

Kuh, E. (1967) A productivity theory of the wage levels – an alternative to the Phillips curve. *Review of Economic Studies*, 31, 333–360

Kuznetsov, Y.A. (1995) *Elements of Applied Bifurcation Theory*. Heidelberg: Springer Verlag

Laxton, D., D. Rose and D. Tambakis (1997) The US Phillips curve: the case for asymmetry. Mimeo

Layard, R., S. Nickell and R. Jackman (1991) *Unemployment: Macroeconomic Performance and the Labor Market*. Oxford: Oxford University Press

Leslie, D. (1993) *Advanced Macroeconomics: Beyond IS/LM*. London: McGraw-Hill

Lindbeck, A. and D. Snower (1988) *The Insider–Outsider Theory of Employment and Unemployment*. Cambridge, MA: MIT Press

Lorenz, H.-W. (1997) *Nonlinear Dynamical Economic and Chaotic Motion*. Heidelberg: Springer Verlag

Lux, T. (1993) A note on the stability of endogenous cycles in Diamond's model of search and barter. *Journal of Economics*, 56, 185–196

(1995) Corridor stability in the Dendrinos model of regional factor movements. *Geographical Analysis*, 27, 360–368

Malinvaud, E. (1980) *Profitability and Unemployment*. Cambridge: Cambridge University Press

Mankiw, G. (1990) A quick refresher course in macroeconomics. *Journal of Economic Literature*, 28, 1645–1660

Marglin, S. (1984a) Growth, distribution, and inflation: a centennial synthesis. *Cambridge Journal of Economics*, 8, 115–144

(1984b) *Growth, Distribution, and Prices*. Cambridge, MA: Harvard University Press

Marglin, S. and A. Bhaduri (1991) Profit squeeze and Keynesian theory. In E. Nell and W. Semmler (eds.), *Nicholas Kaldor and Mainstream Economics: Confrontation or Convergence?* London: Macmillan, 123–163

Marx, K. (1954) *Capital*, vol. I. London: Lawrence and Wishart

Matsumoto, A. (1995a) Non-linear structure of a Metzlerian inventory cycle model. Niigata University, Japan, mimeo

(1995b) A non-linear macro model of endogenous inventory oscillations. Niigata University, Japan, mimeo

McCallum, B.T. (1983) On non-uniqueness in rational expectations models. *Journal of Monetary Economics*, 11, 139–168

(1989) *Monetary Economics Theory and Policy*. New York: Macmillan

Medio, A. (1991) Continuous-time models of chaos in economics. *Journal of Economic Behavior and Organization*, 16, 133–151

(1992) *Chaotic Dynamics: Theory and Applications to Economics*. Cambridge: Cambridge University Press

Metzler, L.A. (1941) The nature and stability of inventory cycles. *Review of Economic Statistics*, 23, 113–129

Murphy, K.M. and R. Topel (1997) Unemployment and nonemployment. *American Economic Review, Papers and Proceedings*, 87, 295–300

Nagatani, K. (1970) A note on Professor Tobin's money and economic growth. *Econometrica*, 38, 171–175

(1978) *Monetary Theory*. Amsterdam: North-Holland

Orphanides, A. and R. Solow (1990) Money, inflation and growth. In B. Friedman and F. Hahn (eds.), *Handbook of Monetary Economics*. Amsterdam: North-Holland, 223–261

Oxley, L. and D.A.R. George (1994) Linear saddlepoint dynamics "on their head": the scientific content of the new orthodoxy in macrodynamics. *European Journal of Political Economy*, 10, 389–400

Papell, D. (1992) Exchange rate and price dynamics under adaptive and rational expectations: an empirical analysis. *Journal of International Money and Finance*, 11, 382–396

Parker, T.S. and L.O. Chua (1989) *Practical Numerical Algorithms for Chaotic Systems*. Berlin: Springer Verlag

Patinkin, D. (1965) *Money, Interest and Prices*. New York: Harper and Row

Perko, M.L. (1993) *Differential Equations and Dynamical Systems*. Heidelberg: Springer Verlag

Phelps, E. and G. Zoega (1997) The rise and downward trend of the natural rate. *American Economic Review, Papers and Proceedings*, 87, 283–289

Phillips, A.W. (1958) The relation between unemployment and the rate of change of money wage rates in the United Kingdom, 1861–1957. *Economica*, 25, 283–299

Pohjola, M. (1981) Stable, cyclic and chaotic growth: the dynamics of a discrete-time version of Goodwin's growth cycle model. *Zeitschrift für Nationalökonomie*, 41, 27–38

Powell, A. and C. Murphy (1997) *Inside a Modern Macroeconometric Model: A Guide to the Murphy Model*. Heidelberg: Springer Verlag

Puu, T. (1997) *Nonlinear Economic Dynamics*. Heidelberg: Springer Verlag

Rogerson, R. (1997) Theory ahead of language in the economics of unemployment. *Journal of Economic Perspectives*, 11, 73–92

Romer, D. (1996) *Advanced Macroeconomics*. London: McGraw-Hill

Rose, H. (1966) Unemployment in a theory of growth. *International Economic Review*, 7, 260–282

(1967) On the non-linear theory of the employment cycle. *Review of Economic Studies*, 34, 153–173

(1969) Real and monetary factors in the business cycle. *Journal of Money, Credit and Banking*, 1, 138–152

(1990) *Macroeconomic Dynamics: A Marshallian Synthesis*. Cambridge, MA: Basil Blackwell

Rowthorn, B. (1980) *Capitalism, Conflict and Inflation*. London: Lawrence and Wishart

Saint-Paul, G. (1997) The rise and persistence of rigidities. *American Economic Review, Papers and Proceedings*, 87, 290–294

Samuelson, P. and R. Solow (1960) The problem of achieving and maintaining a stable price level: analytical aspects of of anti-inflation policy. *American Economic Review*, 50, 177–194

Sargent, T. (1987) *Macroeconomic Theory*. New York: Academic Press

Sargent, T. and N. Wallace (1973) The stability of models of money and growth with perfect foresight. *Econometrica*, 41, 1043–1048

Sethi, R. (1996) Endogenous regime switching in speculative markets. *Structural Change and Economic Dynamics*, 7, 99–118

Sidrauski, M. (1967a) Inflation and economic growth. *Journal of Political Economy*, 75, 796–810

(1967b) Rational choice and patterns of growth in a monetary economy. *American Economic Review*, 57, 534–544

Sijben, J. (1977) *Money and Economic Growth*. Leiden: Martinus Nijhoff

Skott, P. (1989a) *Conflict and Effective Demand in Economic Growth*. Cambridge: Cambridge University Press

(1989b) Effective demand, class struggle and cyclical growth. *International Economic Review*, 30, 231–247

(1991) *Cyclical Growth in a Kaldorian model*. In E.J. Nell and W. Semmler (eds.), *Nicholas Kaldor and Mainstream Economics: Confrontation or Convergence?* London: Macmillan, 379–394

Snowdon, B., H. Vane and P. Wynarczyk (1994) *A Modern Guide to Macroeconomics: An Introduction to Competing Schools of Thought*. Aldershot: Edward Elgar

Solow, R. (1956) A contribution to the theory of economic growth. *Quarterly Journal of Economics*, 70, 65–94

(1990) Goodwin's growth cycle: reminiscence and rumination. In K. Velupillai (ed.), *Nonlinear and Multisectoral Macrodynamics*. London: Macmillan, 31–41

(1997) Is there a core of usable macroeconomics we should all believe in? *American Economic Review, Papers and Proceedings*, 87, 230–232

Solow, R. and J. Stiglitz (1968) Output, employment and wages in the short-run. *Quarterly Journal of Economics*, 82, 537–560

Staiger, D., J.H. Stock and M.W. Watson (1997) The NAIRU, unemployment and monetary policy. *Journal of Economic Perspectives*, 11, 33–50

Stein, J. (1966) Money and capacity growth. *Journal of Political Economy*, 74, 451–465

(1968) Rational choice and the patterns of economic growth in a monetary economy: comment. *American Economic Review*, 58, 944–950

(1969) Neoclassical and Keynes–Wicksell monetary growth models. *Journal of Money, Credit and Banking*, 1, 153–171

(1970) Monetary growth theory in perspective. *American Economic Review*, 60, 85–106

(1971) *Money and Capacity Growth*. New York: Columbia University Press

(1982) *Monetarist, Keynesian and New Classical Economics*. London: Basil Blackwell

Stiglitz, J. (1997) Reflections on the natural rate hypothesis. *Journal of Economic Perspectives*, 11, 3–10

Strogatz, S.H. (1994) *Nonlinear Dynamics and Chaos*. New York: Addison-Wesley

Summers, L. (1990) *Understanding Unemployment*. Cambridge, MA: MIT Press

Taylor, J.B. (1997) A core of practical macroeconomics. *American Economic Review, Papers and Proceedings*, 87, 233–235

Taylor, L. (1983) *Structuralist Macroeconomics*. New York: Basic Books

(1984) A stagnationist model of economic growth. *Cambridge Journal of Economics*, 9, 383–503

(1991) *Income Distribution, Inflation, and Growth*. Cambridge, MA: MIT Press

Tobin, J. (1955) A dynamic aggregative model. *Journal of Political Economy*, 63, 103–115

(1961) Money, capital, and other stores of value. *American Economic Review*, 51, 26–37

(1965) Money and economic growth. *Econometrica*, 33, 671–684

(1975) Keynesian models of recession and depression. *American Economic Review*, 65, 195–202

(1992) An old Keynesian counterattacks. *Eastern Economic Journal*, 18, 387–400

(1993) Price flexibility and output stability. *Journal of Economic Perspectives*, 18, 387–400

Tsiang, S.C. (1982) Stock or portfolio approach to monetary theory and the neo-Keynesian school of James Tobin. *IHS Journal*, 6, 149–171

Tu, P. (1994) *Dynamical Systems*. Heidelberg: Springer Verlag

Turnovsky, S.J. (1977a) *Macroeconomic Analysis and Stabilization Policies.* Cambridge: Cambridge University Press
(1977b) On the formulation of continuous time macroeconomic models with asset accumulation. *International Economic Review* 18, 1–27
(1995) *Methods of Macroeconomic Dynamics.* Cambridge, MA: MIT Press
Whitley, J. (1994) *A Course in Macroeconomic Modelling and Forecasting.* New York: Harvester Wheatsheaf
Wiggins, S. (1990) *Introduction to Applied Nonlinear Dynamical Systems and Chaos.* Heidelberg: Springer Verlag
Wolfstetter, E. (1982) Fiscal policy and the classical growth cycle. *Journal of Economics,* 42, 375–393

Author index

Subject index

accelerator, 36, 38, 234
accumulation
  asset, 26
  capital, 15, 16, 18, 27, 28, 75, 133, 144,
    146, 171, 342, 355
  government debt, 182, 286
AD–AS growth model(s)
  the bastard limit case, 268–275
  classical, 39
  Keynesian, 16
  Keynes–Wicksell variant, 230
adaptive expectations, 16–20, 39–46, 48–53,
  237, 290, 297
  backward looking, *see* backward looking
  and Benassy business cycle model, 232
  and Cagan model, 58
  forward looking, *see* forward looking
  and myopic perfect foresight, 47, 49, 50,
    55, 109, 159
  and pure monetary cycle, 159–160, 162,
    215
  and Sargent model, 31, 45
  and Tobin model, 28–31, 81, 109,
    243–245, 253
adjustment mechanism
  macroeconomic, 348
  Metzlerian inventory, 22, 63, 181
  Phillips-type, 161, 216
  price, *see* price adjustment
  rate of employment, 229, 341, 353, 358
  wage, *see* wage adjustment
agents
  under adaptive expectations, 48
  with complete knowledge, 54
  with optimizing behavior, 13, 30
aggregate demand
  and bastard limit case: AD–AS growth,
    269, 271
  and Benassy business cycle model, 235

and IS equilibria, 196–197
and Kaldor–Tobin model, 285, 290,
  346–347, 352
and Keynes–Metzler model, 296–298,
  317, 322
and Keynes–Wicksell model, 133, 171
and Keynesian cyclical growth model
  with infinite speed of price adjustment,
  217
and Keynesian monetary growth model,
  179, 181, 307
animal spirits, 341, 362
asset market equilibrium, 21, 239
  and Kaldor–Tobin model, 285
  and Keynes–Metzler model, 295, 299
  and Keynes–Wicksell model, 129, 131
  and Keynesian cyclical growth model
    with infinite speed of price adjustment,
    217
  and Keynesian monetary growth model,
    178, 180, 263, 270
  and Tobin model, 72, 83, 93, 104, 113

backward looking
  components of delayed adjustments of
    inflationary expectations, 376
  expectations, 43, 159, 162, 216
  inflationary expectations, 76, 80
  mechanism, 48
  see also expectations
bifurcation
  degenerate, 87, 301, 320
  and Keynes–Wicksell prototype model,
    157–158, 160–161
  and steady-state inflation and complex
    dynamics, 332–333
  subcritical, 87, 301, 309, 320
  supercritical, 87, 301–304, 306, 309, 320
  see also Hopf bifurcation